LUPANO ❖ ANDRÉAE

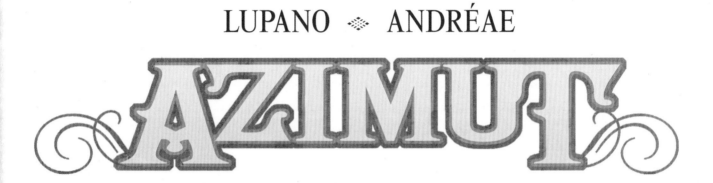

Titan
COMICS

Group Editor
JAKE DEVINE

Designer
DONNA ASKEM

TITAN COMICS

Editorial Assistant
CALUM COLLINS

Editor
PHOEBE HEDGES

Production Controllers
CATERINA FALQUI & KELLY FENLON

Production Manager
JACKIE FLOOK

Art Director
OZ BROWNE

Sales & Circulation Manager
STEVE TOTHILL

Marketing Coordinator
LAUREN NODING

Digital & Marketing Manager
JO TEATHER

Publicist
PHOEBE TRILLO

Head Of Rights
JENNY BOYCE

Acquisitions Editor
DUNCAN BAIZLEY

Publishing Directors
RICKY CLAYDON & JOHN DZIEWIATKOWSKI

Operations Director
LEIGH BAULCH

Publishers
VIVIAN CHEUNG & NICK LANDAU

AZIMUT
Published by Titan Comics, a division of Titan Publishing Group, Ltd. 144 Southwark Street, London SE1 0UP. Titan Comics is a registered trademark of Titan Publishing Group, Ltd. All rights reserved.

First published in French as Azimut by W. Lupano & J-B Andreae © 2012-2019, Editions Glénat – ALL RIGHTS RESERVED

ISBN 9781787735880
A CIP catalogue for this title is available from the British Library.

First published in March 2022
10 9 8 7 6 5 4 3 2 1
Printed in China

www.titan-comics.com
Follow us on twitter@ComicsTitan | Visit us at facebook.com/comicstitan

AZIMUT

WRITER
WILFRID LUPANO

ARTIST
JEAN-BAPTISTE ANDRÉAE

TRANSLATOR
MARC BOURBON-CROOK

LETTERER
LAUREN BOWES

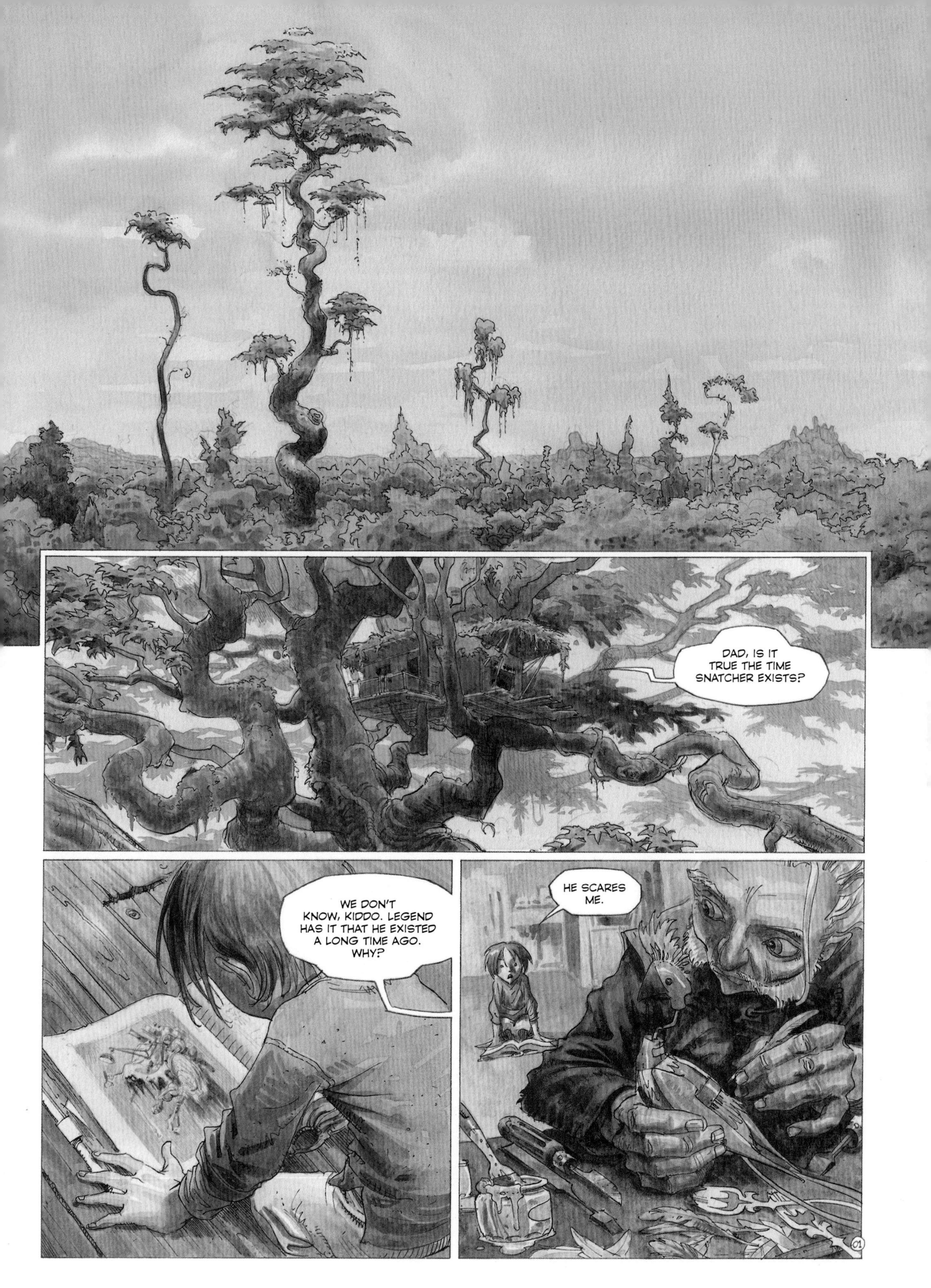
DAD, IS IT TRUE THE TIME SNATCHER EXISTS?
WE DON'T KNOW, KIDDO. LEGEND HAS IT THAT HE EXISTED A LONG TIME AGO. WHY?
HE SCARES ME.

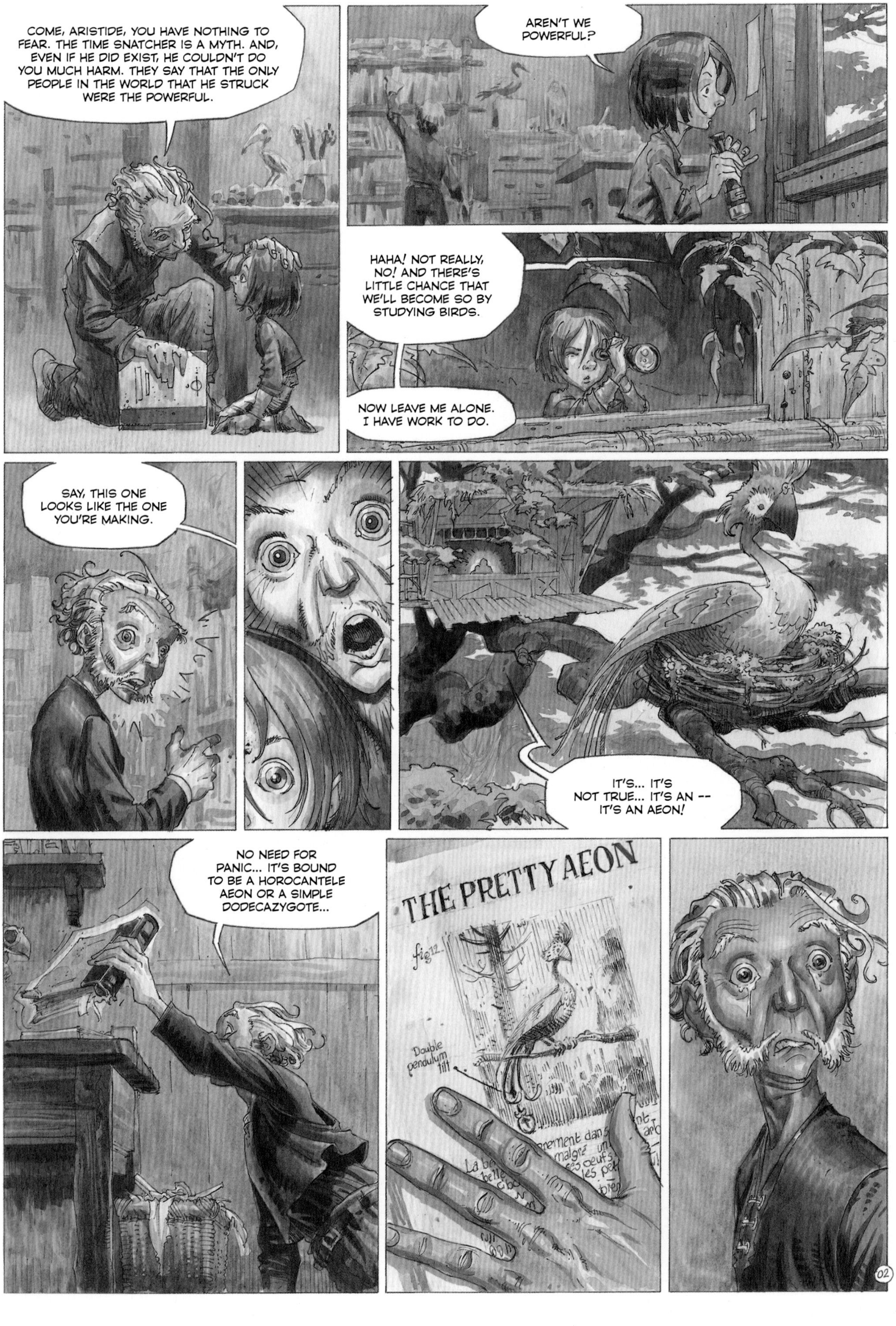

COME, ARISTIDE, YOU HAVE NOTHING TO FEAR. THE TIME SNATCHER IS A MYTH. AND, EVEN IF HE DID EXIST, HE COULDN'T DO YOU MUCH HARM. THEY SAY THAT THE ONLY PEOPLE IN THE WORLD THAT HE STRUCK WERE THE POWERFUL.
AREN'T WE POWERFUL?
HAHA! NOT REALLY, NO! AND THERE'S LITTLE CHANCE THAT WE'LL BECOME SO BY STUDYING BIRDS.
NOW LEAVE ME ALONE. I HAVE WORK TO DO.
SAY, THIS ONE LOOKS LIKE THE ONE YOU'RE MAKING.
IT'S... IT'S NOT TRUE... IT'S AN -- IT'S AN AEON!
NO NEED FOR PANIC... IT'S BOUND TO BE A HOROCANTELE AEON OR A SIMPLE DODECAZYGOTE...
THE PRETTY AEON
fig 12.
Double pendulum tilt

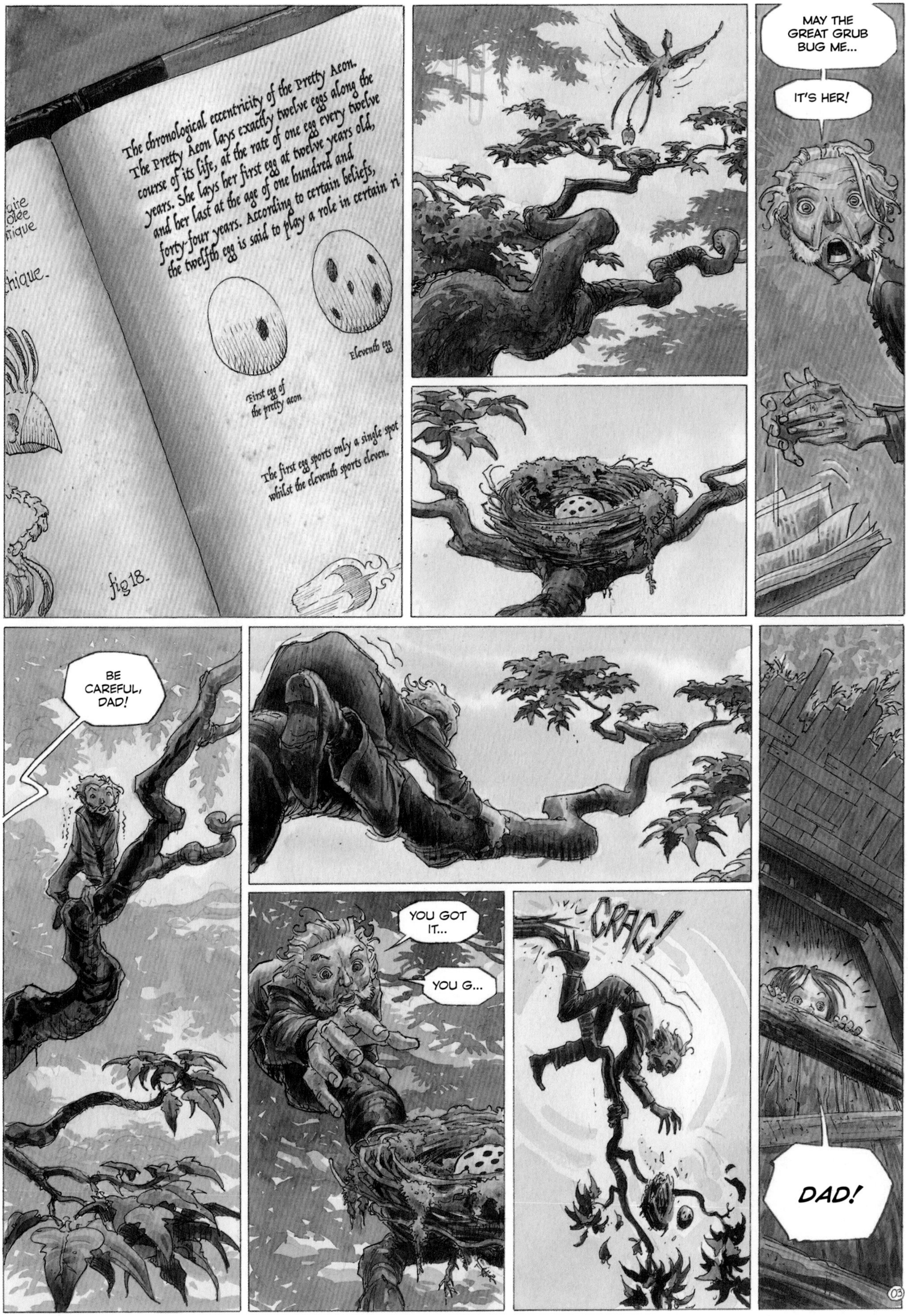
The chronological eccentricity of the Pretty Aeon.
The Pretty Aeon lays exactly twelve eggs along the course of its life, at the rate of one egg every twelve years. She lays her first egg at twelve years old, and her last at the age of one hundred and forty-four years. According to certain beliefs, the twelfth egg is said to play a role in certain ri
First egg of the pretty aeon
Eleventh egg
The first egg sports only a single spot whilst the eleventh sports eleven.
fig 18.
MAY THE GREAT GRUB BUG ME...
IT'S HER!
BE CAREFUL, DAD!
YOU GOT IT...
YOU G...
CRAC!
DAD!
03

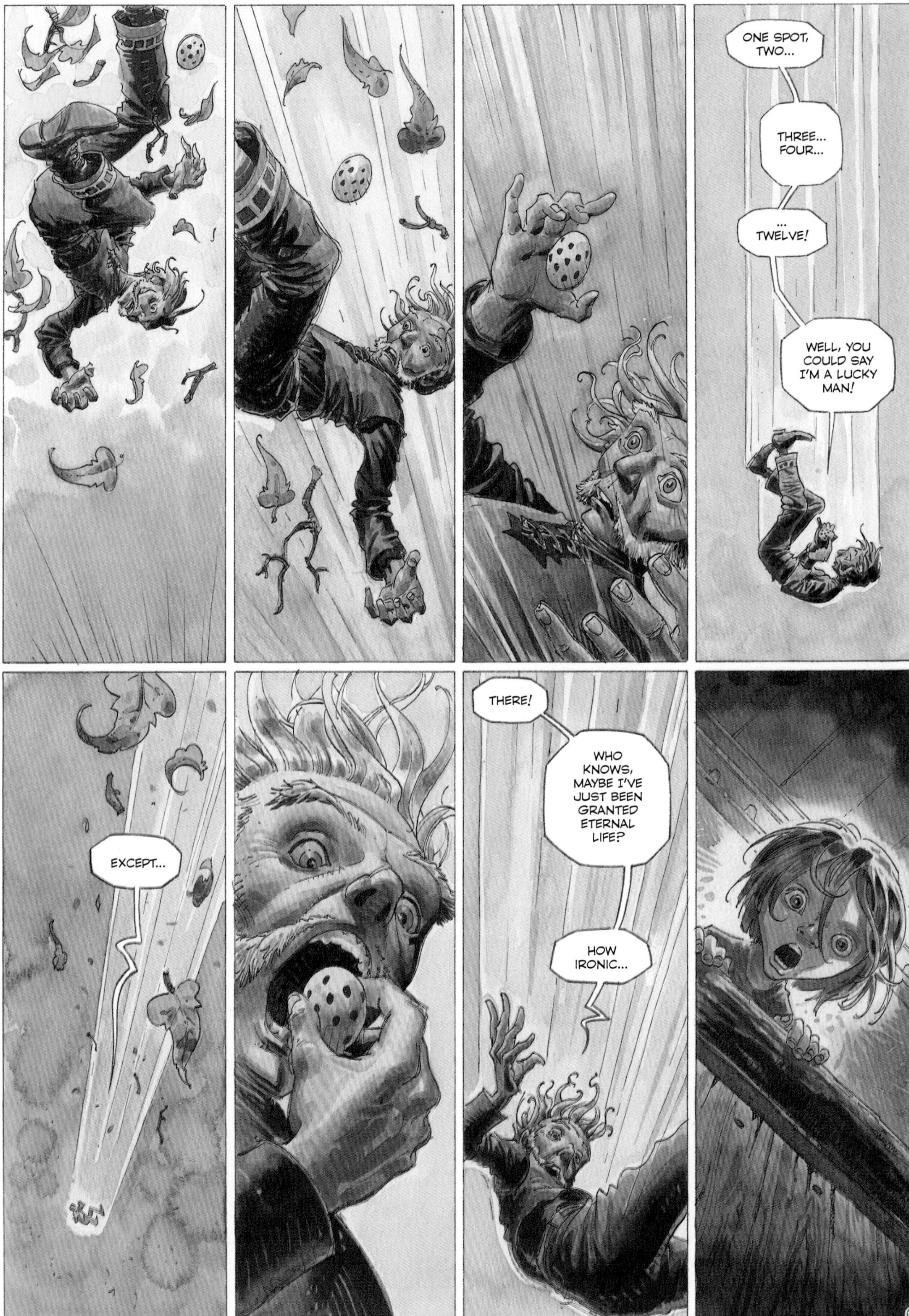
ONE SPOT, TWO...
THREE... FOUR...
... TWELVE!
WELL, YOU COULD SAY I'M A LUCKY MAN!
EXCEPT...
THERE!
WHO KNOWS, MAYBE I'VE JUST BEEN GRANTED ETERNAL LIFE?
HOW IRONIC...

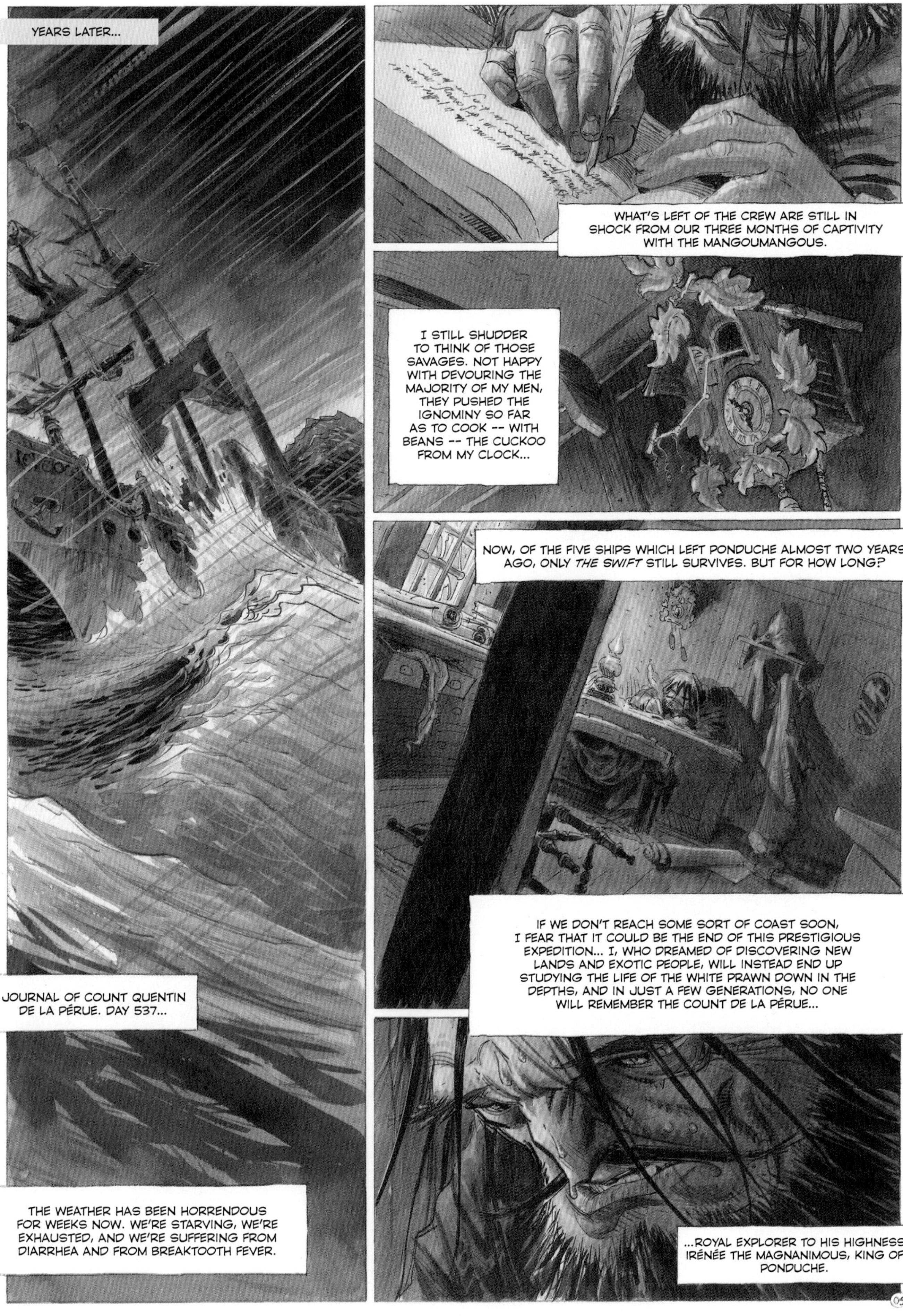
YEARS LATER...
JOURNAL OF COUNT QUENTIN DE LA PÉRUE. DAY 537...
THE WEATHER HAS BEEN HORRENDOUS FOR WEEKS NOW. WE'RE STARVING, WE'RE EXHAUSTED, AND WE'RE SUFFERING FROM DIARRHEA AND FROM BREAKTOOTH FEVER.
WHAT'S LEFT OF THE CREW ARE STILL IN SHOCK FROM OUR THREE MONTHS OF CAPTIVITY WITH THE MANGOUMANGOUS.
I STILL SHUDDER TO THINK OF THOSE SAVAGES. NOT HAPPY WITH DEVOURING THE MAJORITY OF MY MEN, THEY PUSHED THE IGNOMINY SO FAR AS TO COOK -- WITH BEANS -- THE CUCKOO FROM MY CLOCK...
NOW, OF THE FIVE SHIPS WHICH LEFT PONDUCHE ALMOST TWO YEARS AGO, ONLY *THE SWIFT* STILL SURVIVES. BUT FOR HOW LONG?
IF WE DON'T REACH SOME SORT OF COAST SOON, I FEAR THAT IT COULD BE THE END OF THIS PRESTIGIOUS EXPEDITION... I, WHO DREAMED OF DISCOVERING NEW LANDS AND EXOTIC PEOPLE, WILL INSTEAD END UP STUDYING THE LIFE OF THE WHITE PRAWN DOWN IN THE DEPTHS, AND IN JUST A FEW GENERATIONS, NO ONE WILL REMEMBER THE COUNT DE LA PÉRUE...
...ROYAL EXPLORER TO HIS HIGHNESS IRÉNÉE THE MAGNANIMOUS, KING OF PONDUCHE.

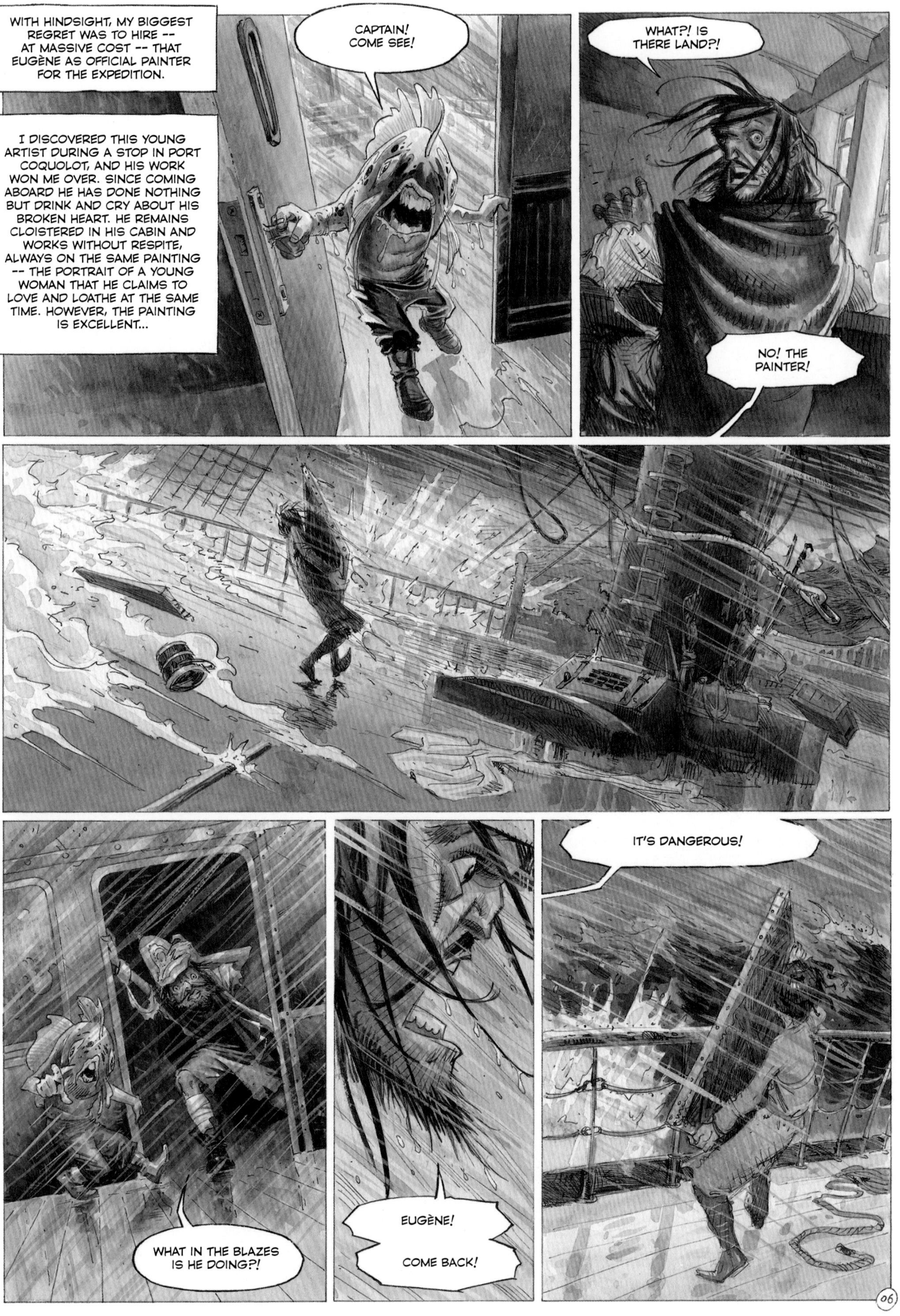
WITH HINDSIGHT, MY BIGGEST REGRET WAS TO HIRE -- AT MASSIVE COST -- THAT EUGÈNE AS OFFICIAL PAINTER FOR THE EXPEDITION.
I DISCOVERED THIS YOUNG ARTIST DURING A STOP IN PORT COQUOLOT, AND HIS WORK WON ME OVER. SINCE COMING ABOARD HE HAS DONE NOTHING BUT DRINK AND CRY ABOUT HIS BROKEN HEART. HE REMAINS CLOISTERED IN HIS CABIN AND WORKS WITHOUT RESPITE, ALWAYS ON THE SAME PAINTING -- THE PORTRAIT OF A YOUNG WOMAN THAT HE CLAIMS TO LOVE AND LOATHE AT THE SAME TIME. HOWEVER, THE PAINTING IS EXCELLENT...
CAPTAIN! COME SEE!
WHAT?! IS THERE LAND?!
NO! THE PAINTER!
WHAT IN THE BLAZES IS HE DOING?!
EUGÈNE!
COME BACK!
IT'S DANGEROUS!

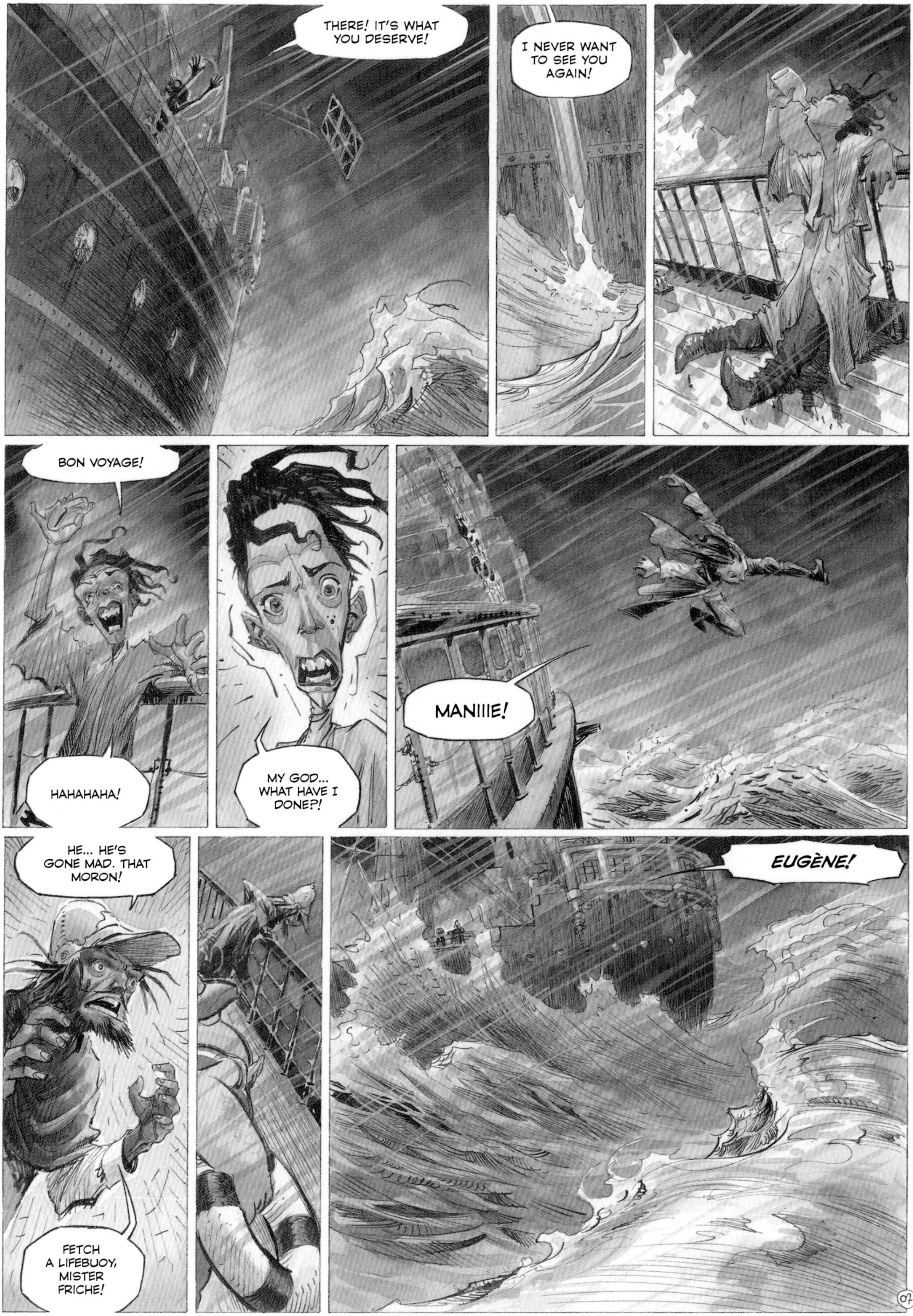

THERE! IT'S WHAT YOU DESERVE!
I NEVER WANT TO SEE YOU AGAIN!
BON VOYAGE!
HAHAHAHA!
MY GOD... WHAT HAVE I DONE?!
MANIIIE!
HE... HE'S GONE MAD. THAT MORON!
FETCH A LIFEBUOY, MISTER FRICHE!
EUGÈNE!

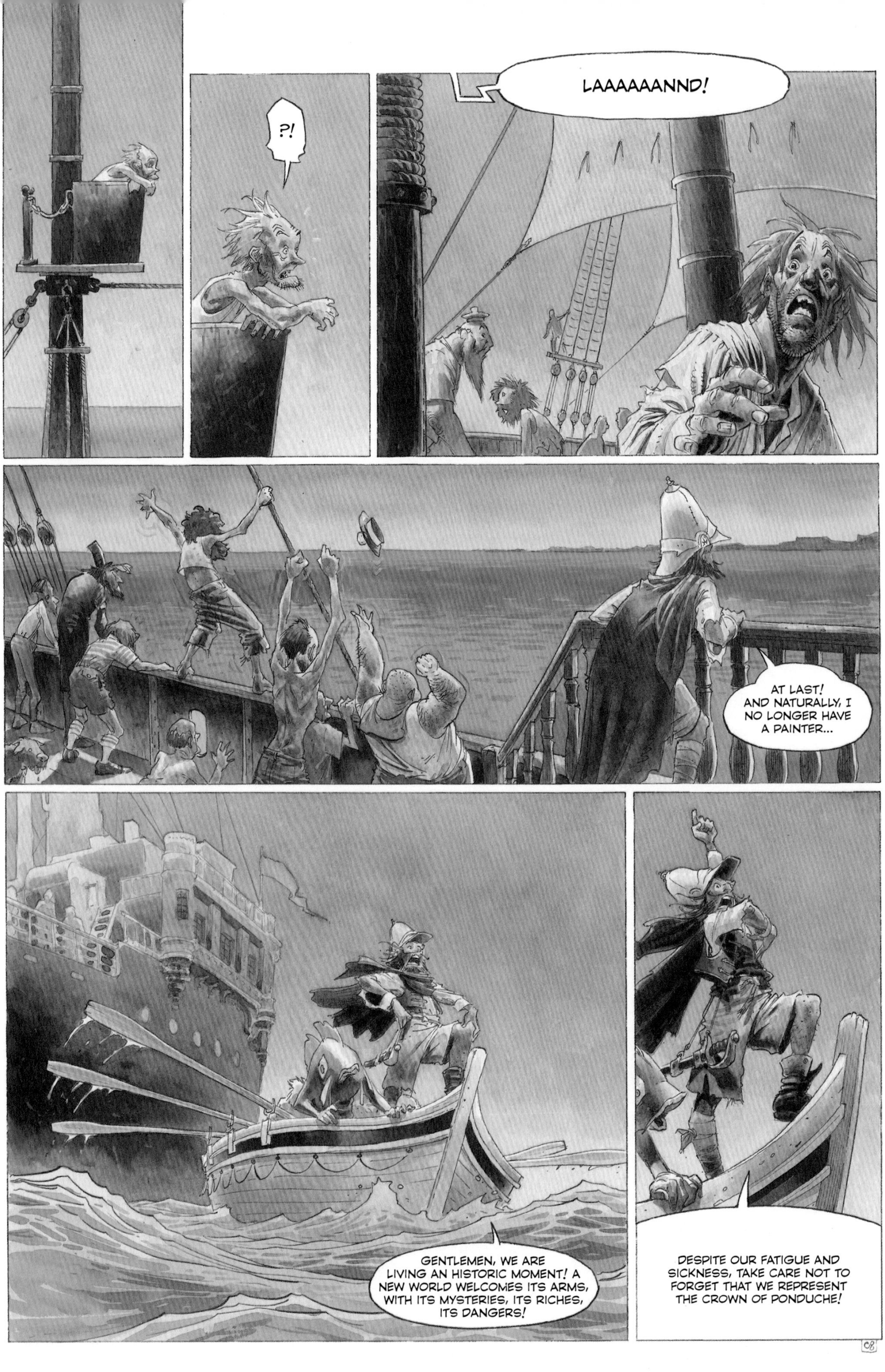
?!
LAAAAAAANND!
AT LAST! AND NATURALLY, I NO LONGER HAVE A PAINTER...
GENTLEMEN, WE ARE LIVING AN HISTORIC MOMENT! A NEW WORLD WELCOMES ITS ARMS, WITH ITS MYSTERIES, ITS RICHES, ITS DANGERS!
DESPITE OUR FATIGUE AND SICKNESS, TAKE CARE NOT TO FORGET THAT WE REPRESENT THE CROWN OF PONDUCHE!

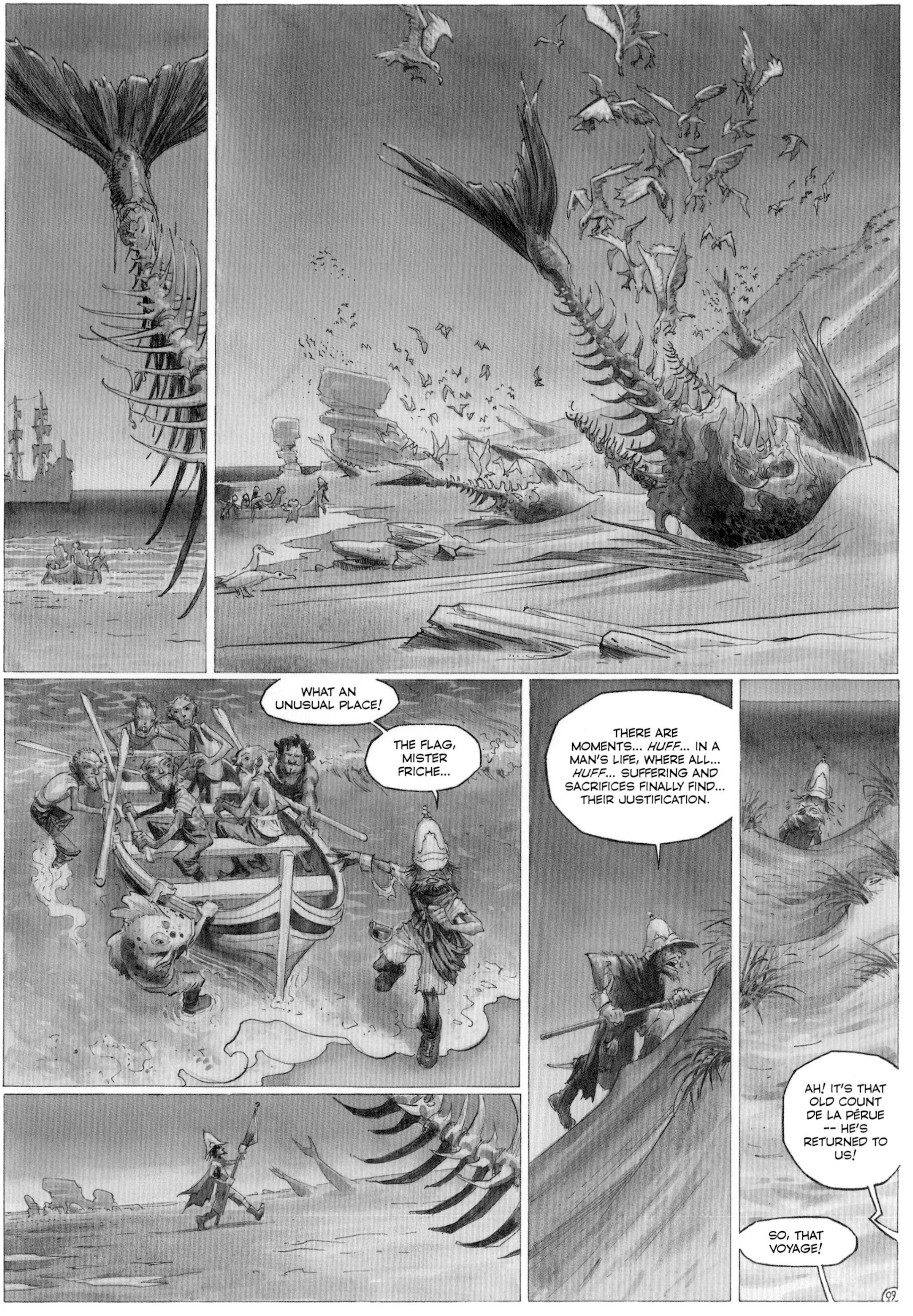
WHAT AN UNUSUAL PLACE!
THE FLAG, MISTER FRICHE...
THERE ARE MOMENTS... HUFF... IN A MAN'S LIFE, WHERE ALL... HUFF... SUFFERING AND SACRIFICES FINALLY FIND... THEIR JUSTIFICATION.
AH! IT'S THAT OLD COUNT DE LA PÉRUE -- HE'S RETURNED TO US!
SO, THAT VOYAGE!

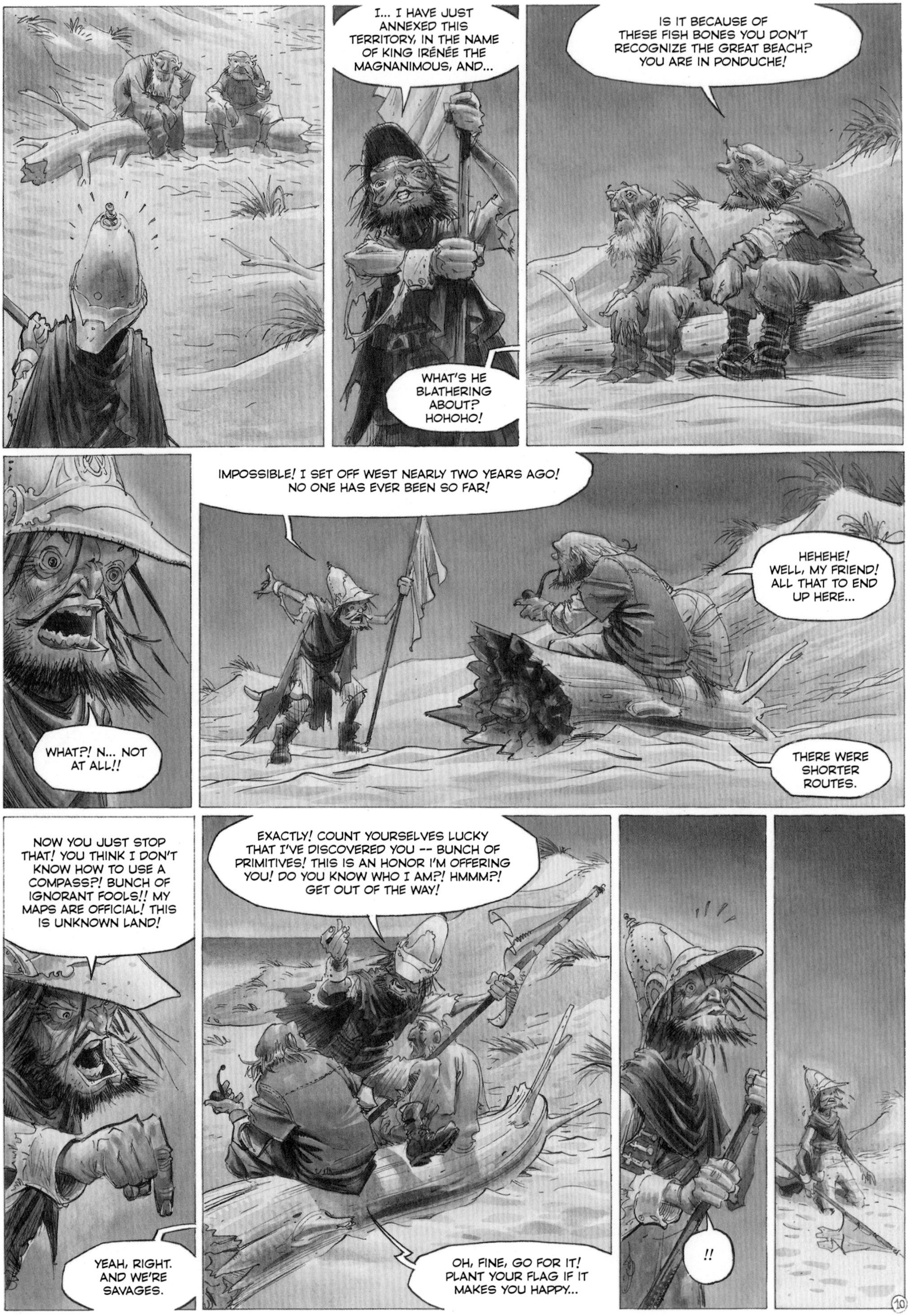
I... I HAVE JUST ANNEXED THIS TERRITORY, IN THE NAME OF KING IRÉNÉE THE MAGNANIMOUS, AND...
WHAT'S HE BLATHERING ABOUT? HOHOHO!
IS IT BECAUSE OF THESE FISH BONES YOU DON'T RECOGNIZE THE GREAT BEACH? YOU ARE IN PONDUCHE!
WHAT?! N... NOT AT ALL!!
IMPOSSIBLE! I SET OFF WEST NEARLY TWO YEARS AGO! NO ONE HAS EVER BEEN SO FAR!
HEHEHE! WELL, MY FRIEND! ALL THAT TO END UP HERE...
THERE WERE SHORTER ROUTES.
NOW YOU JUST STOP THAT! YOU THINK I DON'T KNOW HOW TO USE A COMPASS?! BUNCH OF IGNORANT FOOLS!! MY MAPS ARE OFFICIAL! THIS IS UNKNOWN LAND!
YEAH, RIGHT. AND WE'RE SAVAGES.
EXACTLY! COUNT YOURSELVES LUCKY THAT I'VE DISCOVERED YOU -- BUNCH OF PRIMITIVES! THIS IS AN HONOR I'M OFFERING YOU! DO YOU KNOW WHO I AM?! HMMM?! GET OUT OF THE WAY!
OH, FINE, GO FOR IT! PLANT YOUR FLAG IF IT MAKES YOU HAPPY...
!!

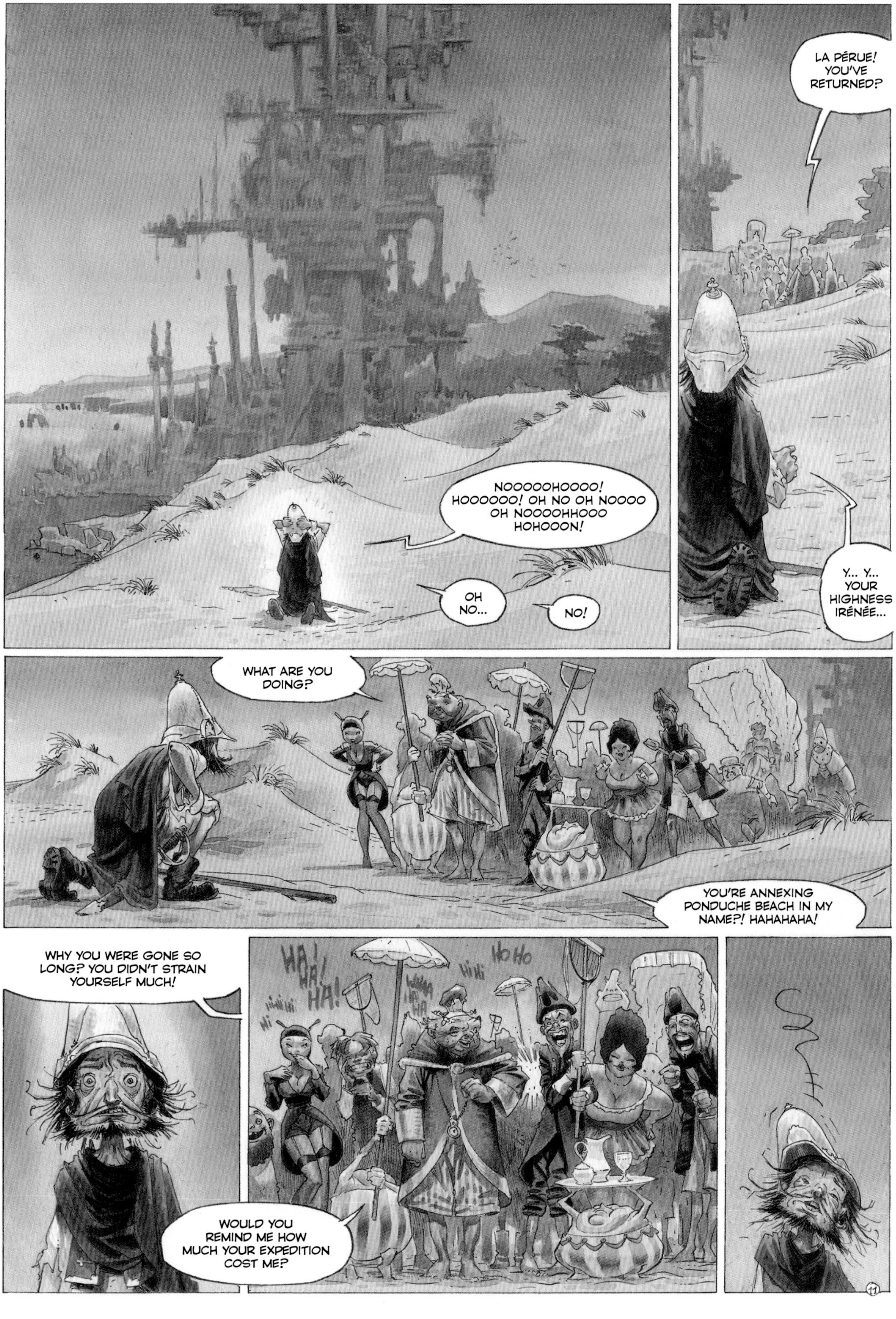
NOOOOOHOOOO! HOOOOOO! OH NO OH NOOOO OH NOOOOHHOOO HOHOOON!
OH NO...
NO!
LA PÉRUE! YOU'VE RETURNED?
Y... Y... YOUR HIGHNESS IRÉNÉE...
WHAT ARE YOU DOING?
YOU'RE ANNEXING PONDUCHE BEACH IN MY NAME?! HAHAHAHA!
WHY YOU WERE GONE SO LONG? YOU DIDN'T STRAIN YOURSELF MUCH!
HO HO
WOULD YOU REMIND ME HOW MUCH YOUR EXPEDITION COST ME?

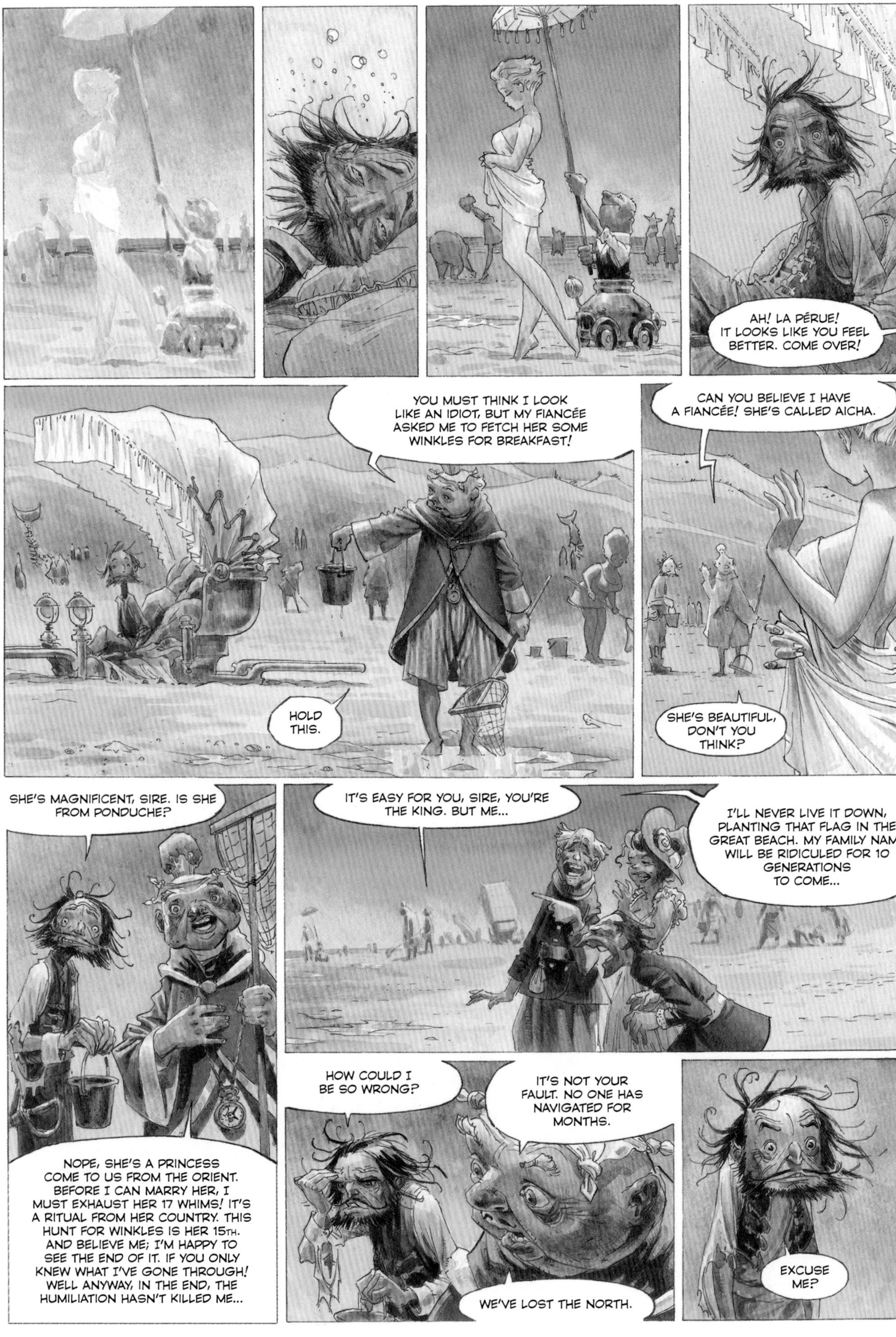
AH! LA PÉRUE! IT LOOKS LIKE YOU FEEL BETTER. COME OVER!
YOU MUST THINK I LOOK LIKE AN IDIOT, BUT MY FIANCÉE ASKED ME TO FETCH HER SOME WINKLES FOR BREAKFAST!
HOLD THIS.
CAN YOU BELIEVE I HAVE A FIANCÉE! SHE'S CALLED AICHA.
SHE'S BEAUTIFUL, DON'T YOU THINK?
SHE'S MAGNIFICENT, SIRE. IS SHE FROM PONDUCHE?
NOPE, SHE'S A PRINCESS COME TO US FROM THE ORIENT. BEFORE I CAN MARRY HER, I MUST EXHAUST HER 17 WHIMS! IT'S A RITUAL FROM HER COUNTRY. THIS HUNT FOR WINKLES IS HER 15TH. AND BELIEVE ME; I'M HAPPY TO SEE THE END OF IT. IF YOU ONLY KNEW WHAT I'VE GONE THROUGH! WELL ANYWAY, IN THE END, THE HUMILIATION HASN'T KILLED ME...
IT'S EASY FOR YOU, SIRE, YOU'RE THE KING. BUT ME...
I'LL NEVER LIVE IT DOWN, PLANTING THAT FLAG IN THE GREAT BEACH. MY FAMILY NAME WILL BE RIDICULED FOR 10 GENERATIONS TO COME...
HOW COULD I BE SO WRONG?
IT'S NOT YOUR FAULT. NO ONE HAS NAVIGATED FOR MONTHS.
WE'VE LOST THE NORTH.
EXCUSE ME?
12

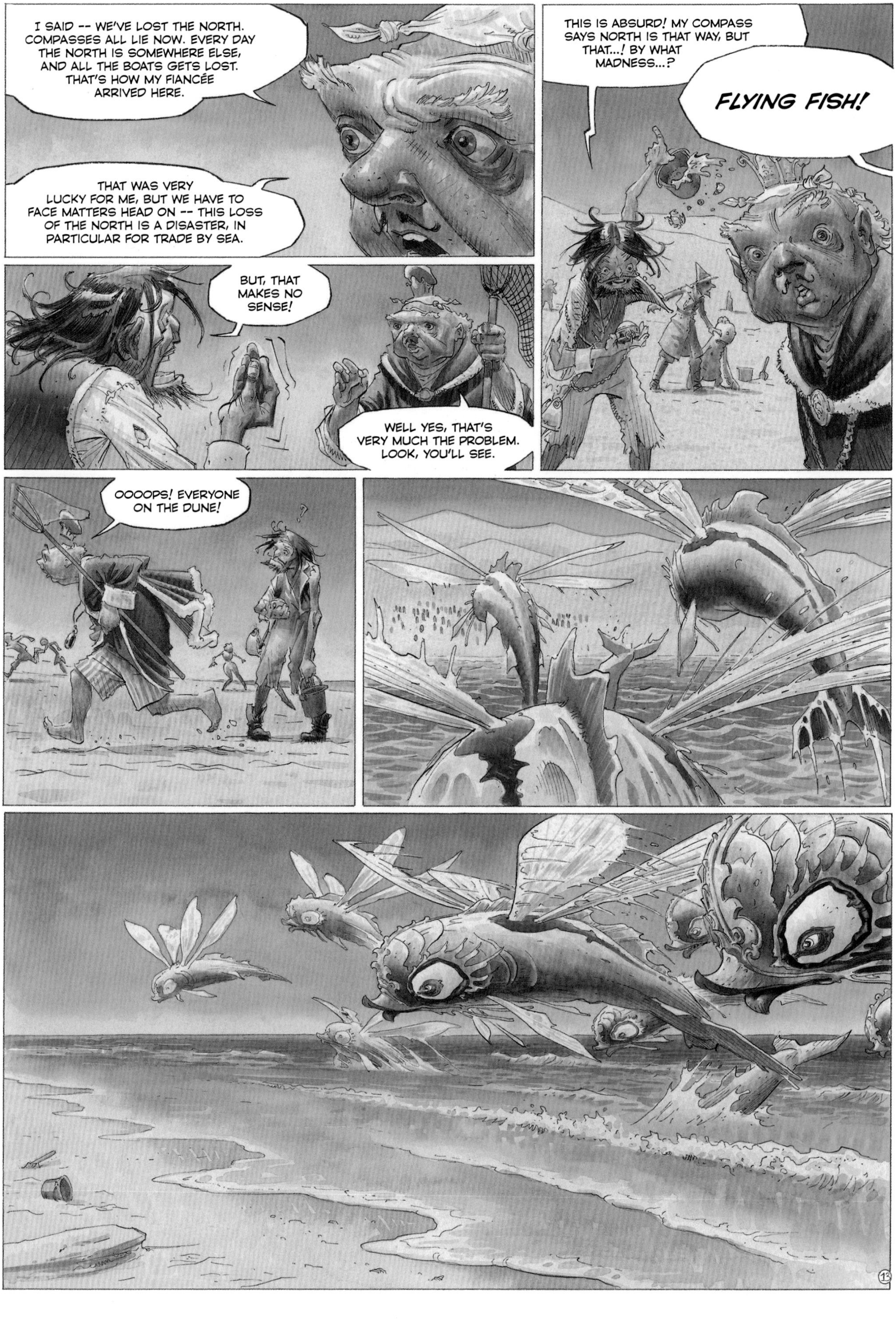
I SAID -- WE'VE LOST THE NORTH. COMPASSES ALL LIE NOW. EVERY DAY THE NORTH IS SOMEWHERE ELSE, AND ALL THE BOATS GETS LOST. THAT'S HOW MY FIANCÉE ARRIVED HERE.
THAT WAS VERY LUCKY FOR ME, BUT WE HAVE TO FACE MATTERS HEAD ON -- THIS LOSS OF THE NORTH IS A DISASTER, IN PARTICULAR FOR TRADE BY SEA.
BUT, THAT MAKES NO SENSE!
WELL YES, THAT'S VERY MUCH THE PROBLEM. LOOK, YOU'LL SEE.
THIS IS ABSURD! MY COMPASS SAYS NORTH IS THAT WAY, BUT THAT...! BY WHAT MADNESS...?
FLYING FISH!
OOOOPS! EVERYONE ON THE DUNE!
?

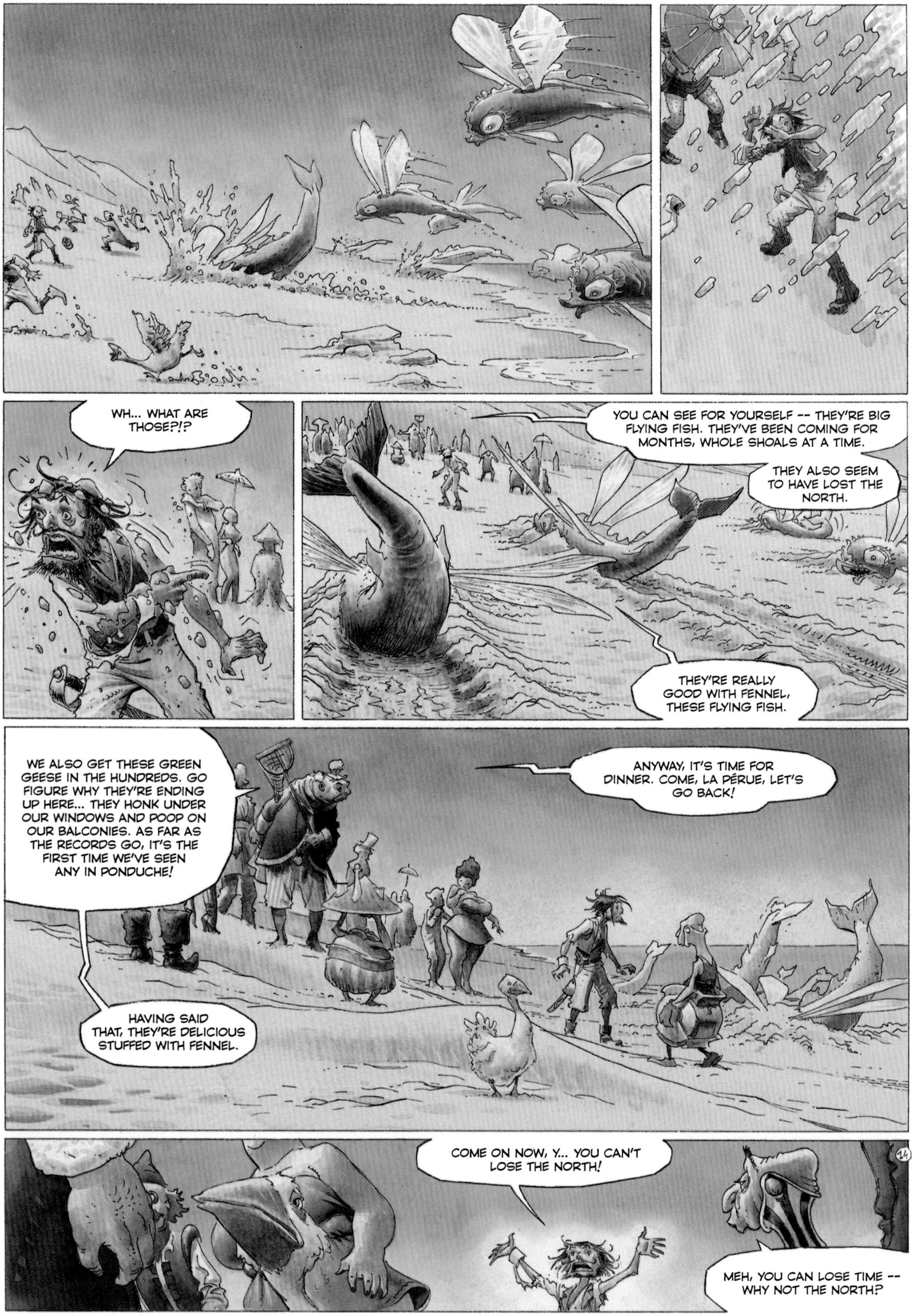
WH... WHAT ARE THOSE?!?
YOU CAN SEE FOR YOURSELF -- THEY'RE BIG FLYING FISH. THEY'VE BEEN COMING FOR MONTHS, WHOLE SHOALS AT A TIME.
THEY ALSO SEEM TO HAVE LOST THE NORTH.
THEY'RE REALLY GOOD WITH FENNEL, THESE FLYING FISH.
WE ALSO GET THESE GREEN GEESE IN THE HUNDREDS. GO FIGURE WHY THEY'RE ENDING UP HERE... THEY HONK UNDER OUR WINDOWS AND POOP ON OUR BALCONIES. AS FAR AS THE RECORDS GO, IT'S THE FIRST TIME WE'VE SEEN ANY IN PONDUCHE!
ANYWAY, IT'S TIME FOR DINNER. COME, LA PÉRUE, LET'S GO BACK!
HAVING SAID THAT, THEY'RE DELICIOUS STUFFED WITH FENNEL.
COME ON NOW, Y... YOU CAN'T LOSE THE NORTH!
MEH, YOU CAN LOSE TIME -- WHY NOT THE NORTH?

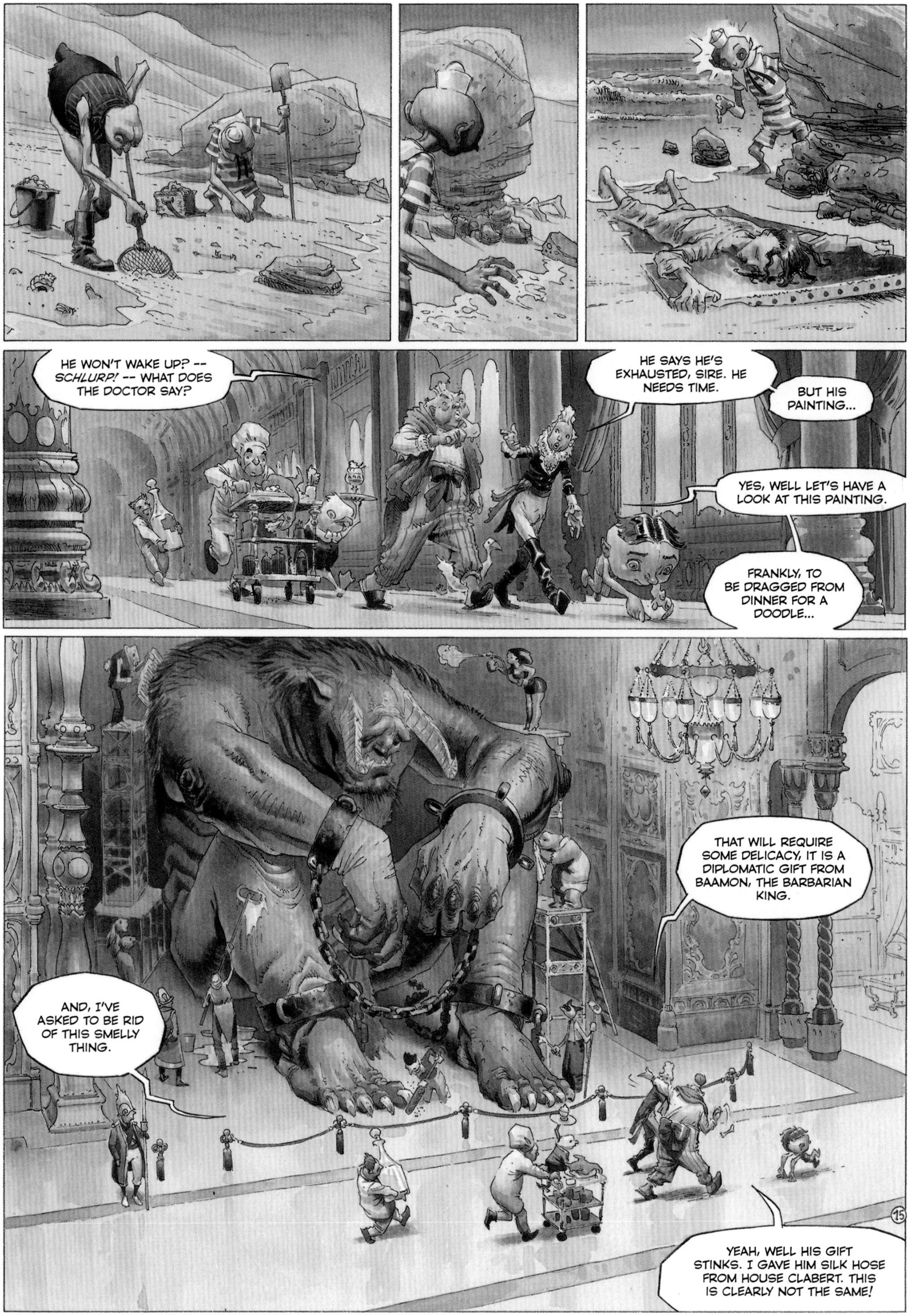
HE WON'T WAKE UP? -- *SCHLURP!* -- WHAT DOES THE DOCTOR SAY?
HE SAYS HE'S EXHAUSTED, SIRE. HE NEEDS TIME.
BUT HIS PAINTING...
YES, WELL LET'S HAVE A LOOK AT THIS PAINTING.
FRANKLY, TO BE DRAGGED FROM DINNER FOR A DOODLE...
THAT WILL REQUIRE SOME DELICACY, IT IS A DIPLOMATIC GIFT FROM BAAMON, THE BARBARIAN KING.
AND, I'VE ASKED TO BE RID OF THIS SMELLY THING.
YEAH, WELL HIS GIFT STINKS. I GAVE HIM SILK HOSE FROM HOUSE CLABERT. THIS IS CLEARLY NOT THE SAME!

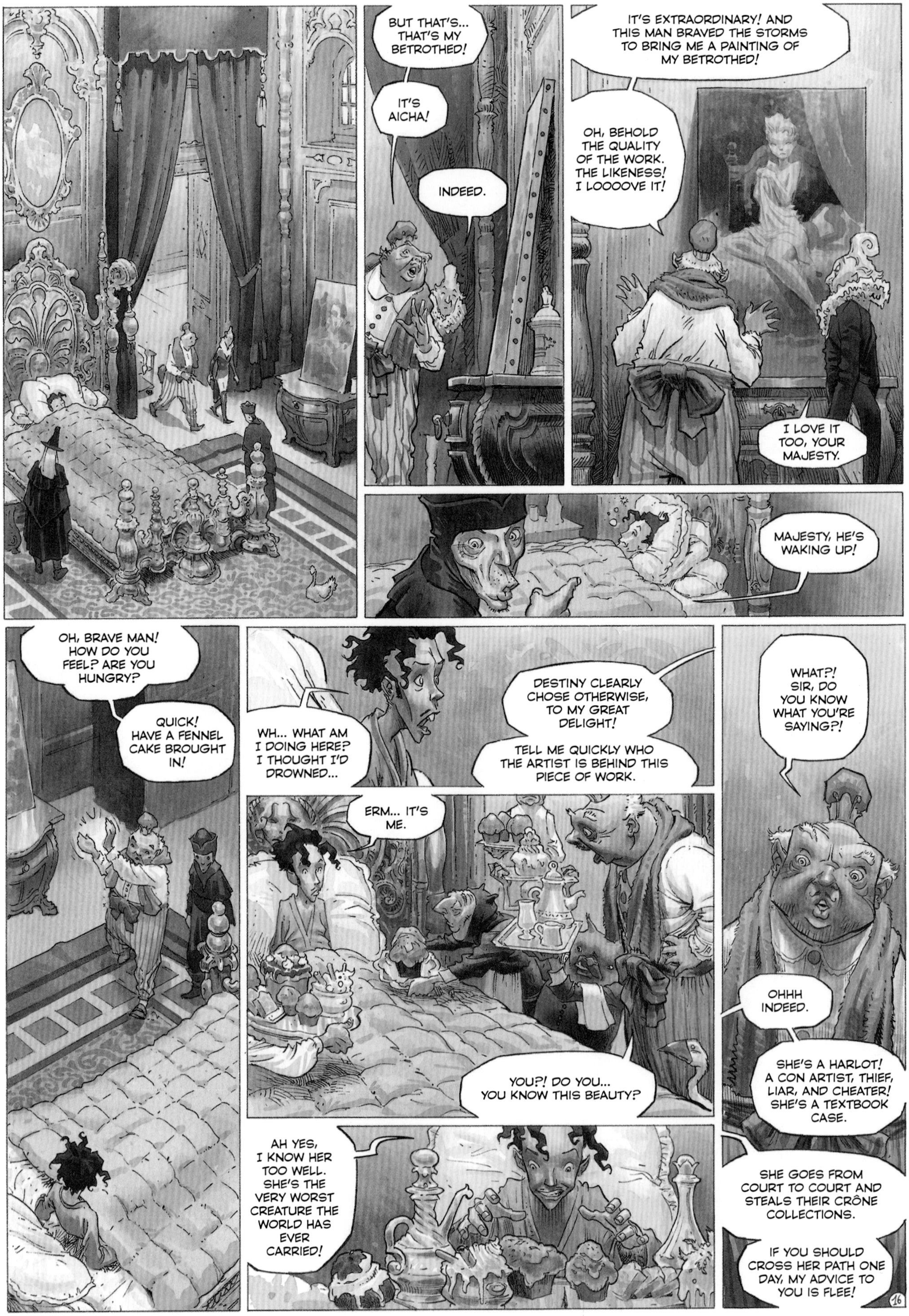
BUT THAT'S... THAT'S MY BETROTHED!
IT'S AICHA!
INDEED.
IT'S EXTRAORDINARY! AND THIS MAN BRAVED THE STORMS TO BRING ME A PAINTING OF MY BETROTHED!
OH, BEHOLD THE QUALITY OF THE WORK. THE LIKENESS! I LOOOOVE IT!
I LOVE IT TOO, YOUR MAJESTY.
MAJESTY, HE'S WAKING UP!
OH, BRAVE MAN! HOW DO YOU FEEL? ARE YOU HUNGRY?
QUICK! HAVE A FENNEL CAKE BROUGHT IN!
WH... WHAT AM I DOING HERE? I THOUGHT I'D DROWNED...
DESTINY CLEARLY CHOSE OTHERWISE, TO MY GREAT DELIGHT!
TELL ME QUICKLY WHO THE ARTIST IS BEHIND THIS PIECE OF WORK.
ERM... IT'S ME.
YOU?! DO YOU... YOU KNOW THIS BEAUTY?
AH YES, I KNOW HER TOO WELL. SHE'S THE VERY WORST CREATURE THE WORLD HAS EVER CARRIED!
WHAT?! SIR, DO YOU KNOW WHAT YOU'RE SAYING?!
OHHH INDEED.
SHE'S A HARLOT! A CON ARTIST, THIEF, LIAR, AND CHEATER! SHE'S A TEXTBOOK CASE.
SHE GOES FROM COURT TO COURT AND STEALS THEIR CRÔNE COLLECTIONS.
IF YOU SHOULD CROSS HER PATH ONE DAY, MY ADVICE TO YOU IS FLEE!
16

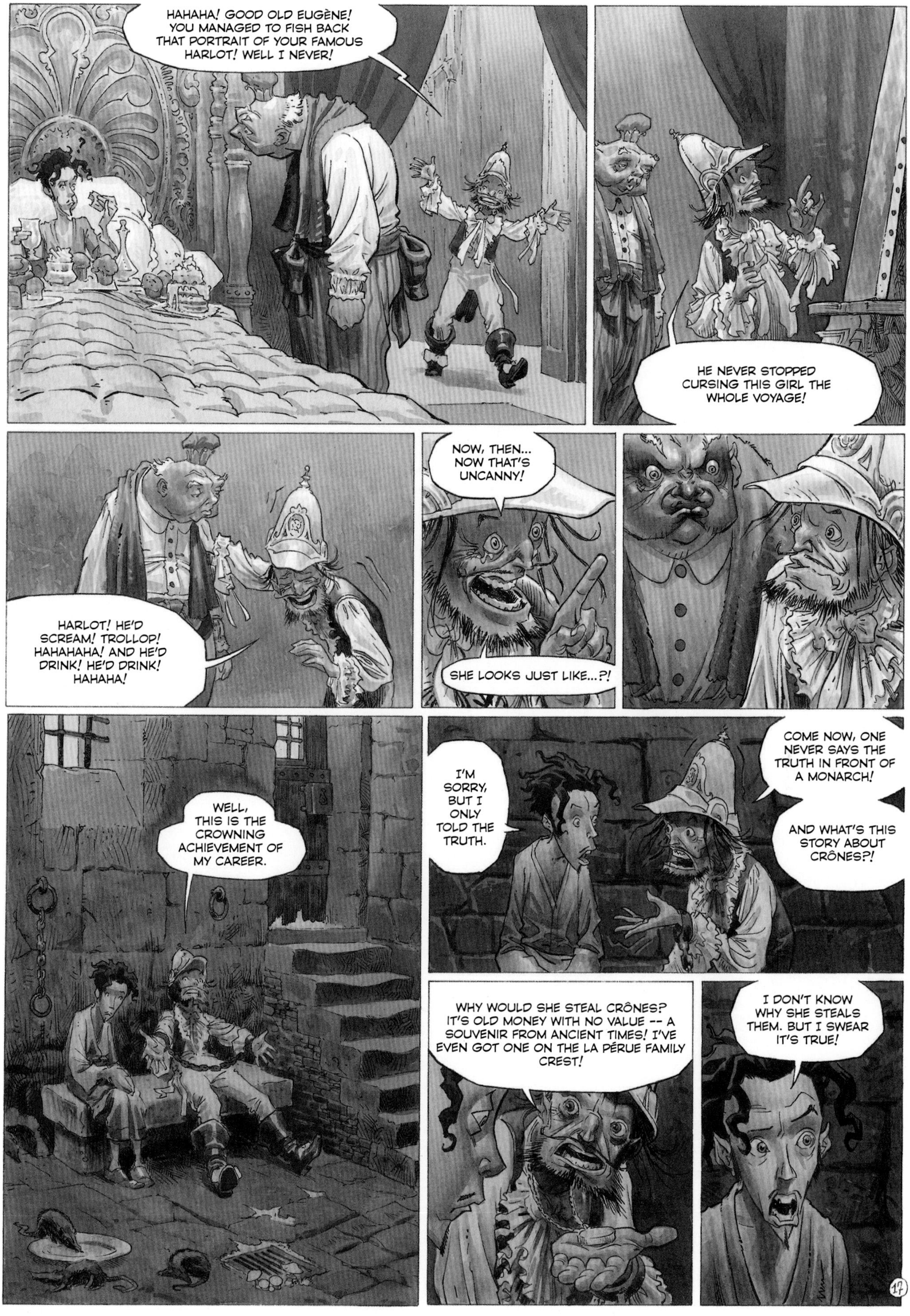
HAHAHA! GOOD OLD EUGÈNE! YOU MANAGED TO FISH BACK THAT PORTRAIT OF YOUR FAMOUS HARLOT! WELL I NEVER!
HE NEVER STOPPED CURSING THIS GIRL THE WHOLE VOYAGE!
HARLOT! HE'D SCREAM! TROLLOP! HAHAHAHA! AND HE'D DRINK! HE'D DRINK! HAHAHA!
NOW, THEN... NOW THAT'S UNCANNY!
SHE LOOKS JUST LIKE...?!
WELL, THIS IS THE CROWNING ACHIEVEMENT OF MY CAREER.
I'M SORRY, BUT I ONLY TOLD THE TRUTH.
COME NOW, ONE NEVER SAYS THE TRUTH IN FRONT OF A MONARCH!
AND WHAT'S THIS STORY ABOUT CRÔNES?!
WHY WOULD SHE STEAL CRÔNES? IT'S OLD MONEY WITH NO VALUE -- A SOUVENIR FROM ANCIENT TIMES! I'VE EVEN GOT ONE ON THE LA PÉRUE FAMILY CREST!
I DON'T KNOW WHY SHE STEALS THEM. BUT I SWEAR IT'S TRUE!

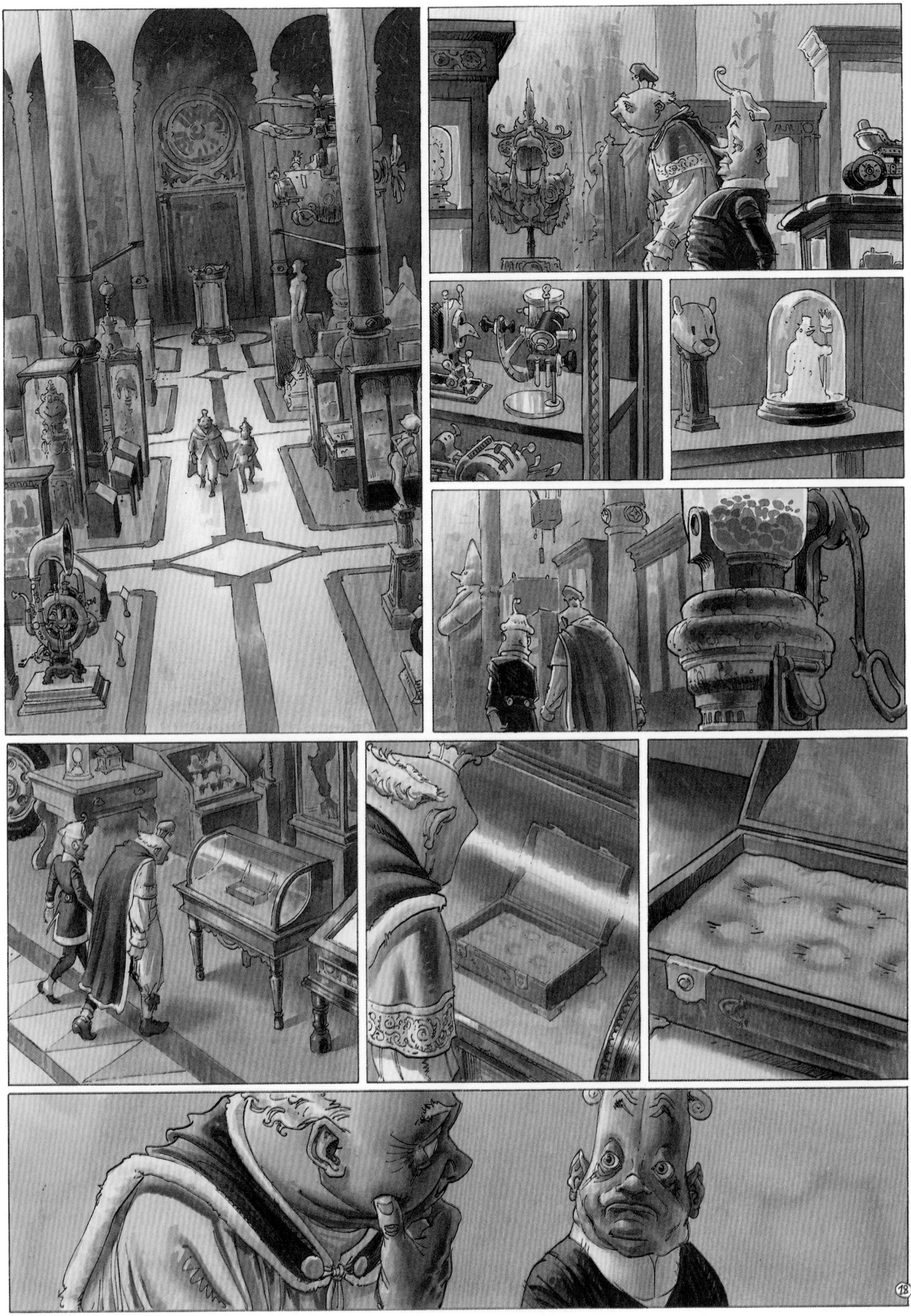

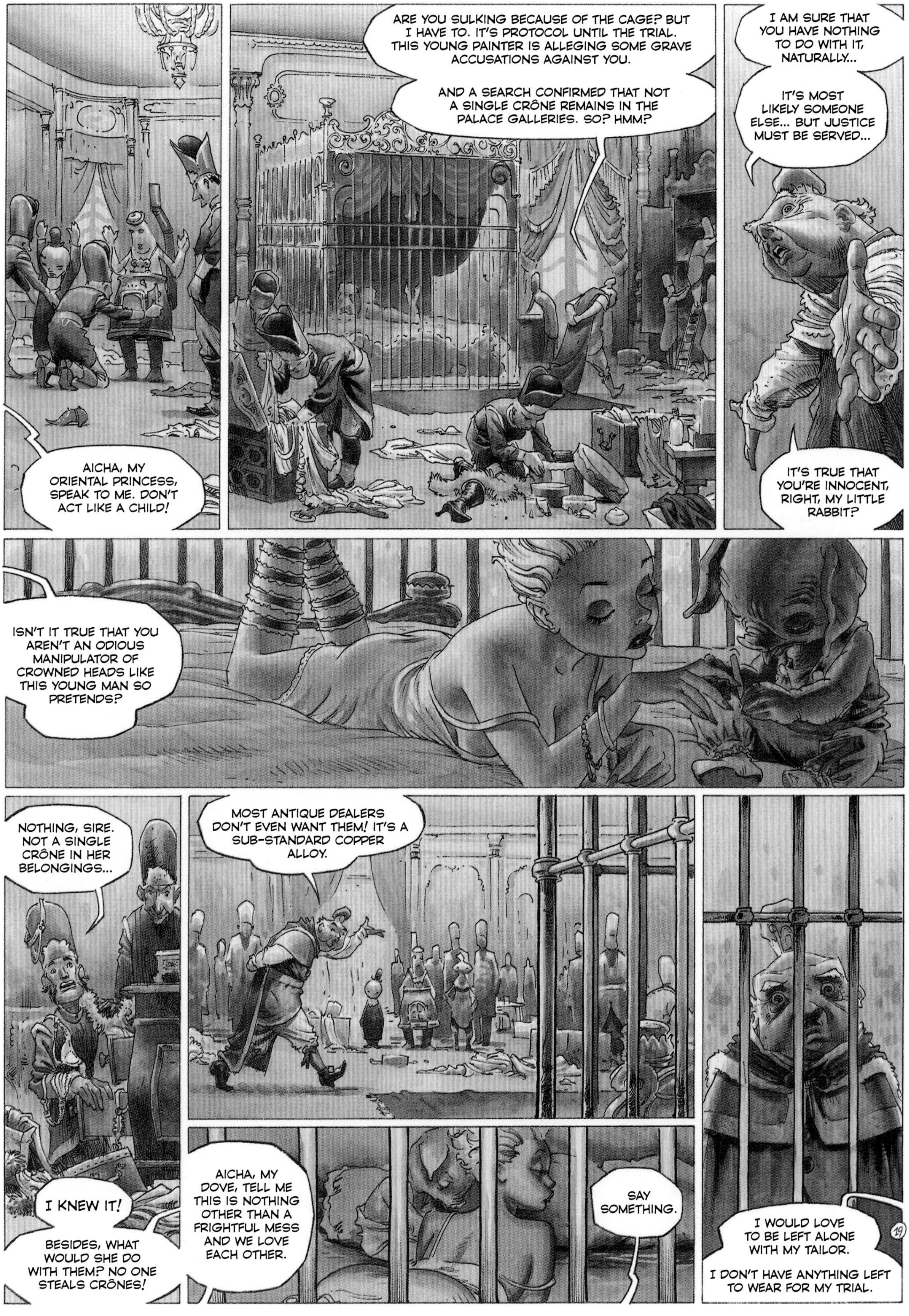

ARE YOU SULKING BECAUSE OF THE CAGE? BUT I HAVE TO. IT'S PROTOCOL UNTIL THE TRIAL. THIS YOUNG PAINTER IS ALLEGING SOME GRAVE ACCUSATIONS AGAINST YOU.
AND A SEARCH CONFIRMED THAT NOT A SINGLE CRÔNE REMAINS IN THE PALACE GALLERIES. SO? HMM?
AICHA, MY ORIENTAL PRINCESS, SPEAK TO ME. DON'T ACT LIKE A CHILD!
I AM SURE THAT YOU HAVE NOTHING TO DO WITH IT, NATURALLY...
IT'S MOST LIKELY SOMEONE ELSE... BUT JUSTICE MUST BE SERVED...
IT'S TRUE THAT YOU'RE INNOCENT, RIGHT, MY LITTLE RABBIT?
ISN'T IT TRUE THAT YOU AREN'T AN ODIOUS MANIPULATOR OF CROWNED HEADS LIKE THIS YOUNG MAN SO PRETENDS?
NOTHING, SIRE. NOT A SINGLE CRÔNE IN HER BELONGINGS...
I KNEW IT!
BESIDES, WHAT WOULD SHE DO WITH THEM? NO ONE STEALS CRÔNES!
MOST ANTIQUE DEALERS DON'T EVEN WANT THEM! IT'S A SUB-STANDARD COPPER ALLOY.
AICHA, MY DOVE, TELL ME THIS IS NOTHING OTHER THAN A FRIGHTFUL MESS AND WE LOVE EACH OTHER.
SAY SOMETHING.
I WOULD LOVE TO BE LEFT ALONE WITH MY TAILOR.
I DON'T HAVE ANYTHING LEFT TO WEAR FOR MY TRIAL.

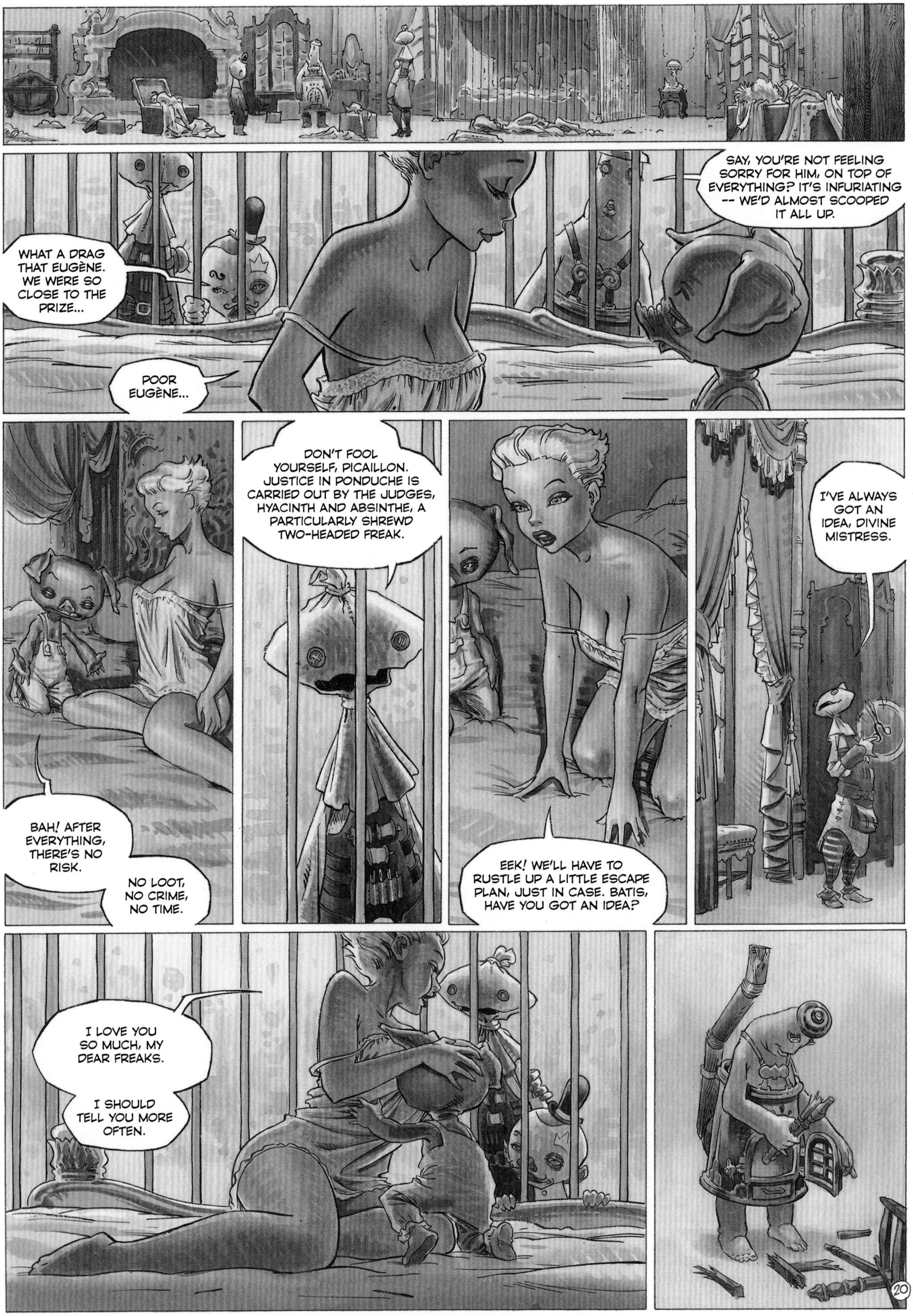

WHAT A DRAG THAT EUGÈNE. WE WERE SO CLOSE TO THE PRIZE...
SAY, YOU'RE NOT FEELING SORRY FOR HIM, ON TOP OF EVERYTHING? IT'S INFURIATING -- WE'D ALMOST SCOOPED IT ALL UP.
POOR EUGÈNE...
BAH! AFTER EVERYTHING, THERE'S NO RISK.
NO LOOT, NO CRIME, NO TIME.
DON'T FOOL YOURSELF, PICAILLON. JUSTICE IN PONDUCHE IS CARRIED OUT BY THE JUDGES, HYACINTH AND ABSINTHE, A PARTICULARLY SHREWD TWO-HEADED FREAK.
EEK! WE'LL HAVE TO RUSTLE UP A LITTLE ESCAPE PLAN, JUST IN CASE. BATIS, HAVE YOU GOT AN IDEA?
I'VE ALWAYS GOT AN IDEA, DIVINE MISTRESS.
I LOVE YOU SO MUCH, MY DEAR FREAKS.
I SHOULD TELL YOU MORE OFTEN.

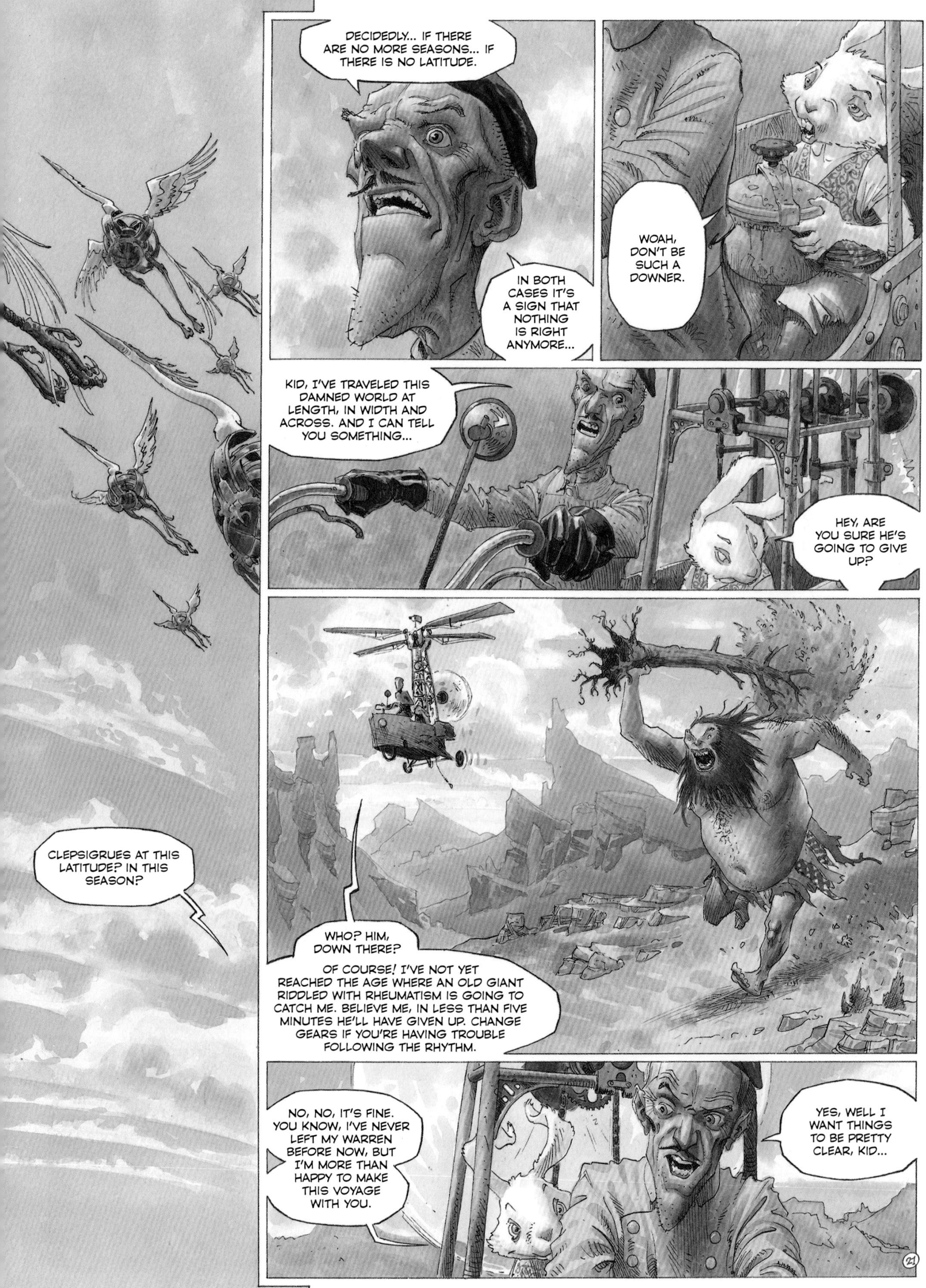
CLEPSIGRUES AT THIS LATITUDE? IN THIS SEASON?
DECIDEDLY... IF THERE ARE NO MORE SEASONS... IF THERE IS NO LATITUDE.
IN BOTH CASES IT'S A SIGN THAT NOTHING IS RIGHT ANYMORE...
WOAH, DON'T BE SUCH A DOWNER.
KID, I'VE TRAVELED THIS DAMNED WORLD AT LENGTH, IN WIDTH AND ACROSS. AND I CAN TELL YOU SOMETHING...
HEY, ARE YOU SURE HE'S GOING TO GIVE UP?
WHO? HIM, DOWN THERE?
OF COURSE! I'VE NOT YET REACHED THE AGE WHERE AN OLD GIANT RIDDLED WITH RHEUMATISM IS GOING TO CATCH ME. BELIEVE ME, IN LESS THAN FIVE MINUTES HE'LL HAVE GIVEN UP. CHANGE GEARS IF YOU'RE HAVING TROUBLE FOLLOWING THE RHYTHM.
NO, NO, IT'S FINE. YOU KNOW, I'VE NEVER LEFT MY WARREN BEFORE NOW, BUT I'M MORE THAN HAPPY TO MAKE THIS VOYAGE WITH YOU.
YES, WELL I WANT THINGS TO BE PRETTY CLEAR, KID...

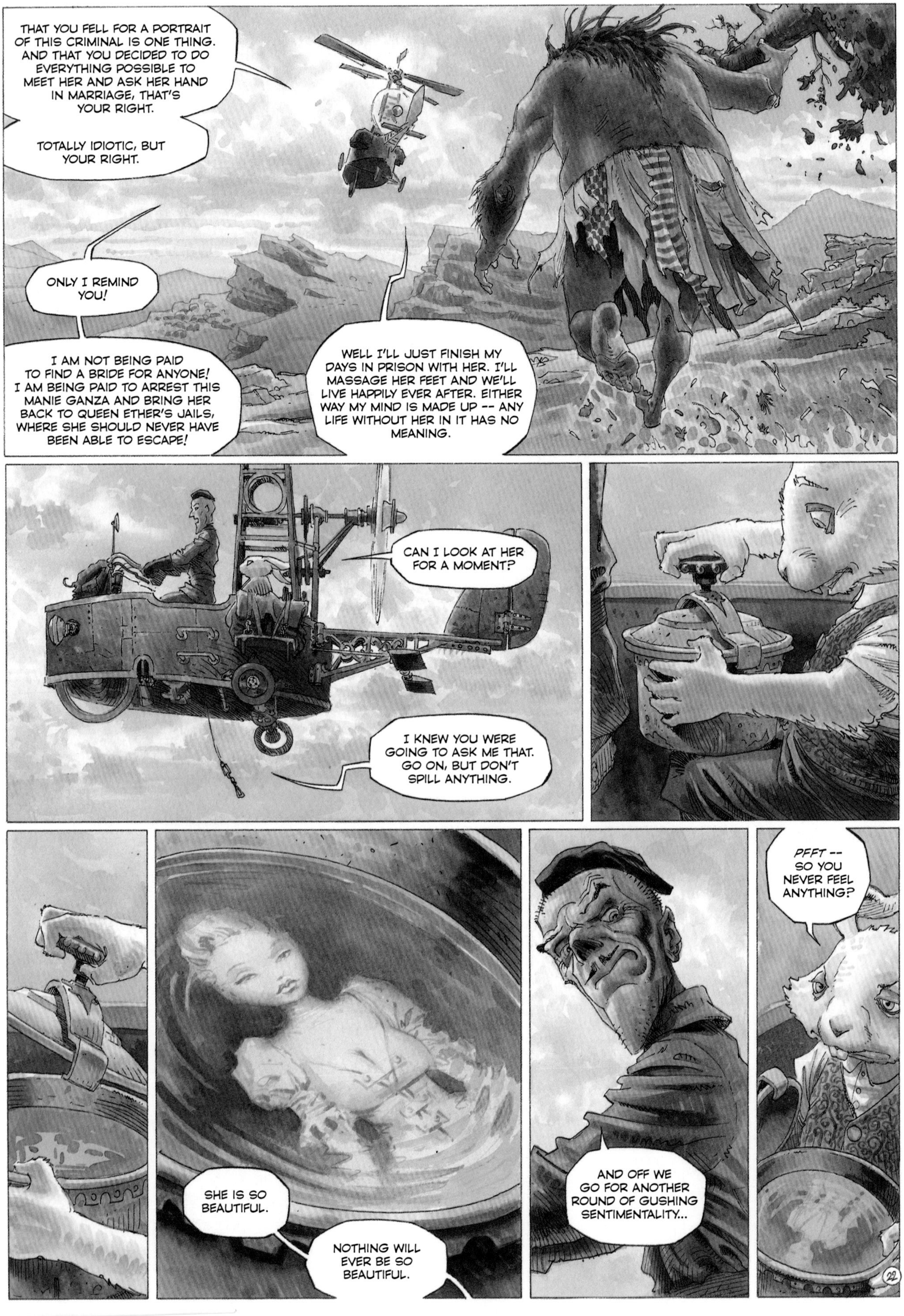

THAT YOU FELL FOR A PORTRAIT OF THIS CRIMINAL IS ONE THING. AND THAT YOU DECIDED TO DO EVERYTHING POSSIBLE TO MEET HER AND ASK HER HAND IN MARRIAGE, THAT'S YOUR RIGHT.
TOTALLY IDIOTIC, BUT YOUR RIGHT.
ONLY I REMIND YOU!
I AM NOT BEING PAID TO FIND A BRIDE FOR ANYONE! I AM BEING PAID TO ARREST THIS MANIE GANZA AND BRING HER BACK TO QUEEN ETHER'S JAILS, WHERE SHE SHOULD NEVER HAVE BEEN ABLE TO ESCAPE!
WELL I'LL JUST FINISH MY DAYS IN PRISON WITH HER. I'LL MASSAGE HER FEET AND WE'LL LIVE HAPPILY EVER AFTER. EITHER WAY MY MIND IS MADE UP -- ANY LIFE WITHOUT HER IN IT HAS NO MEANING.
CAN I LOOK AT HER FOR A MOMENT?
I KNEW YOU WERE GOING TO ASK ME THAT. GO ON, BUT DON'T SPILL ANYTHING.
SHE IS SO BEAUTIFUL.
NOTHING WILL EVER BE SO BEAUTIFUL.
AND OFF WE GO FOR ANOTHER ROUND OF GUSHING SENTIMENTALITY...
PFFT -- SO YOU NEVER FEEL ANYTHING?

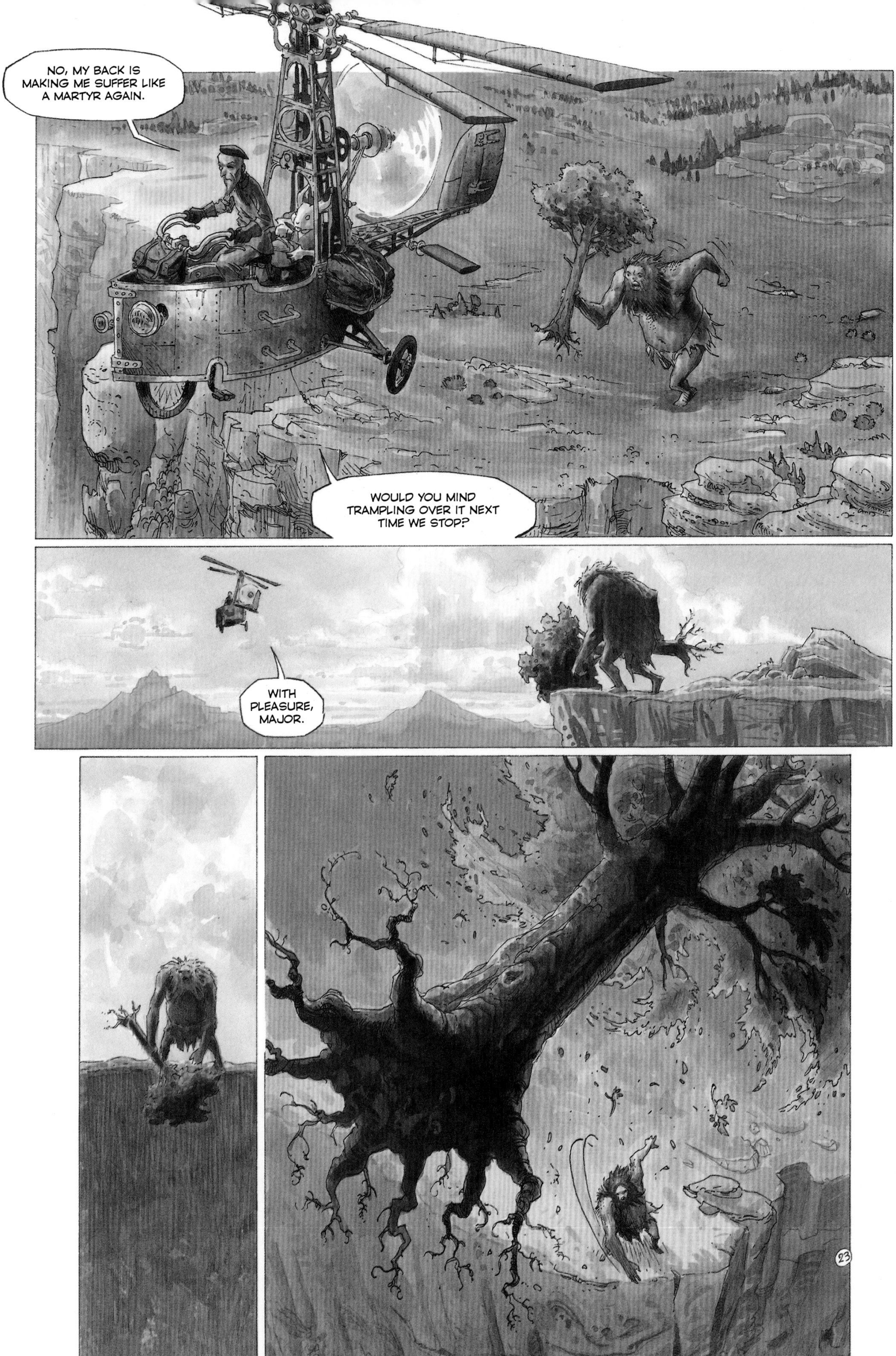
NO, MY BACK IS MAKING ME SUFFER LIKE A MARTYR AGAIN.
WOULD YOU MIND TRAMPLING OVER IT NEXT TIME WE STOP?
WITH PLEASURE, MAJOR.

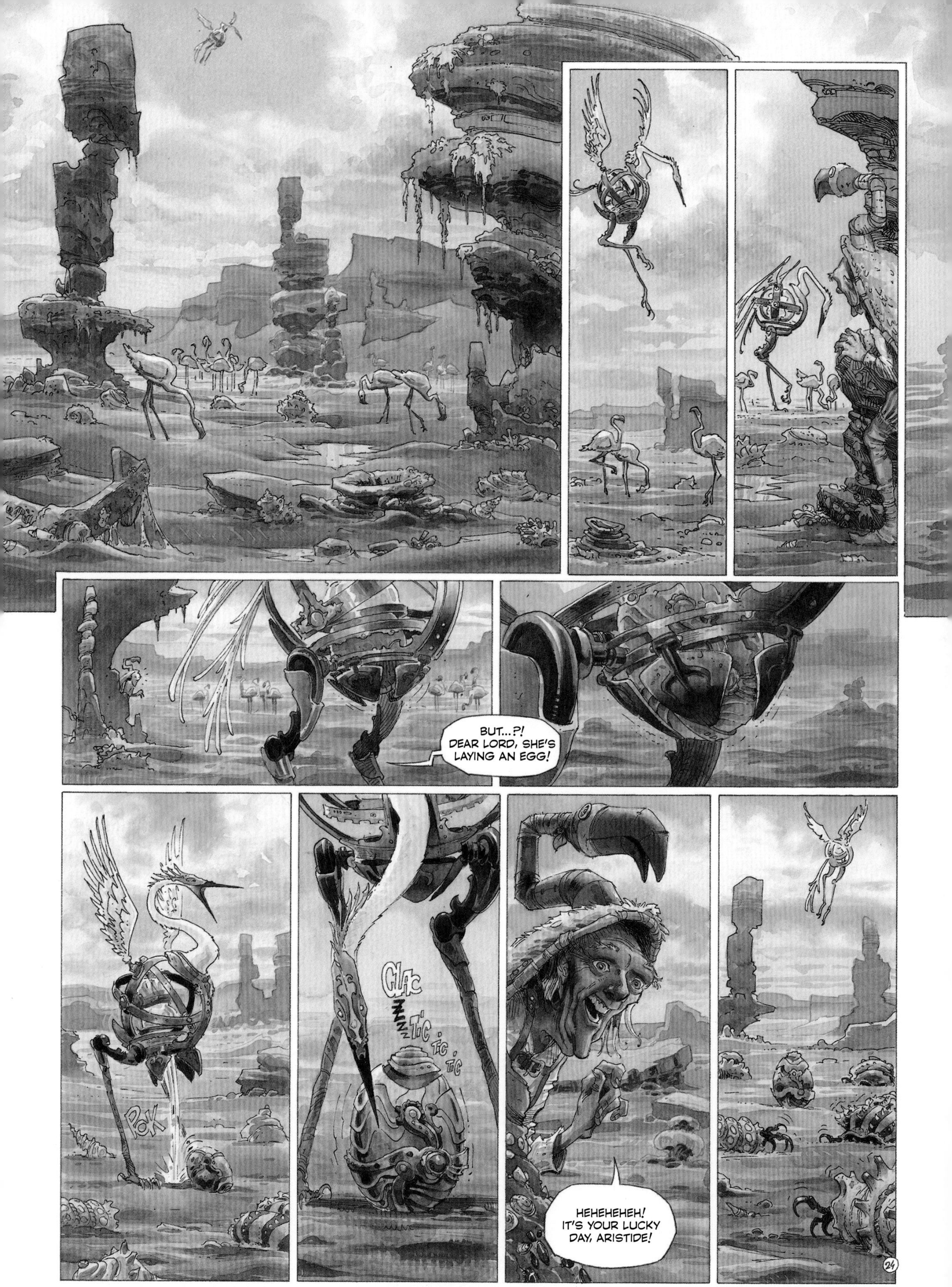
BUT...?!
DEAR LORD, SHE'S LAYING AN EGG!
POK
CLAC
ZZZZ
TIC
TIC
TIC
HEHEHEHEH! IT'S YOUR LUCKY DAY, ARISTIDE!
24

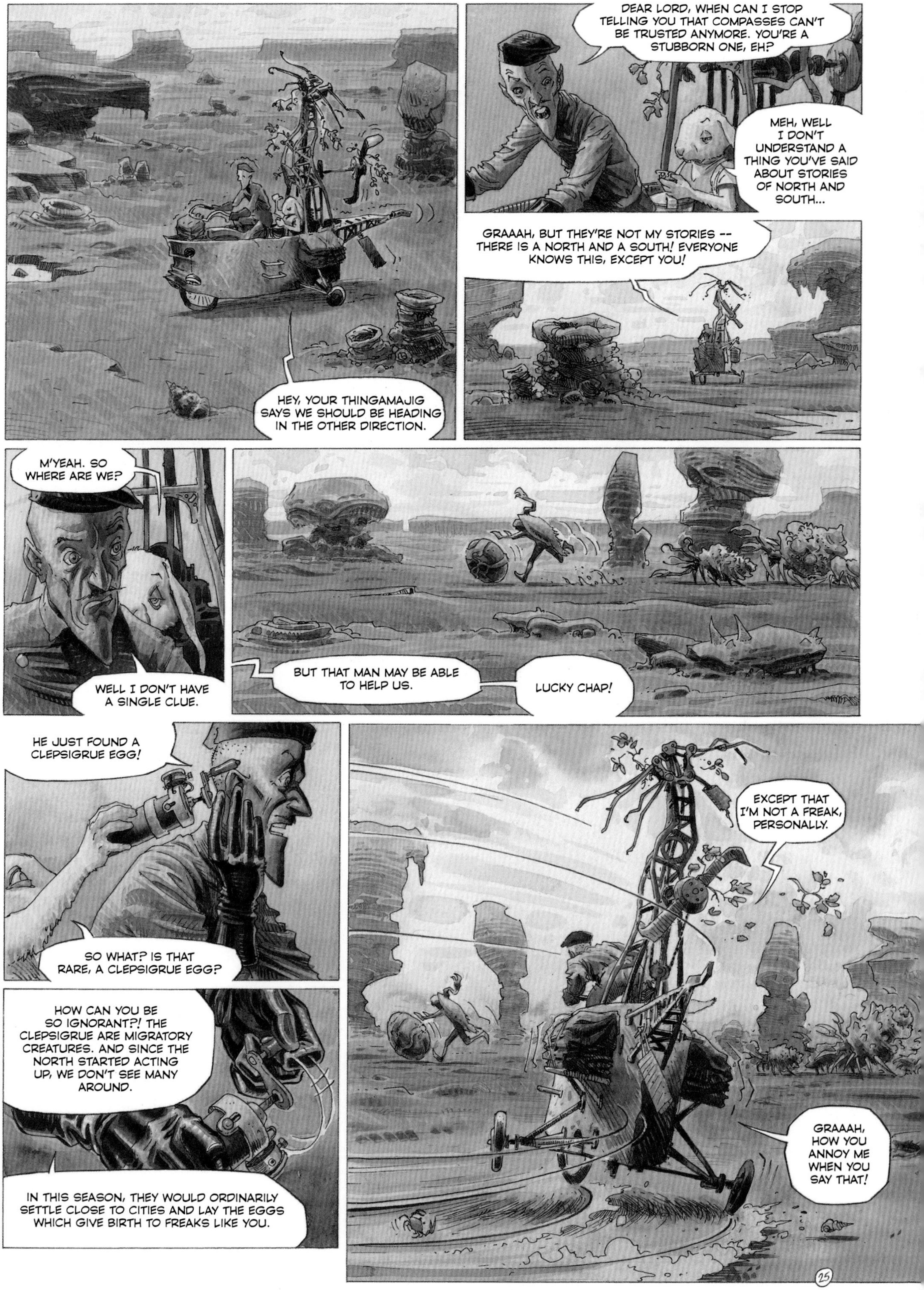
HEY, YOUR THINGAMAJIG SAYS WE SHOULD BE HEADING IN THE OTHER DIRECTION.
DEAR LORD, WHEN CAN I STOP TELLING YOU THAT COMPASSES CAN'T BE TRUSTED ANYMORE. YOU'RE A STUBBORN ONE, EH?
MEH, WELL I DON'T UNDERSTAND A THING YOU'VE SAID ABOUT STORIES OF NORTH AND SOUTH...
GRAAAH, BUT THEY'RE NOT MY STORIES -- THERE IS A NORTH AND A SOUTH! EVERYONE KNOWS THIS, EXCEPT YOU!
M'YEAH. SO WHERE ARE WE?
WELL I DON'T HAVE A SINGLE CLUE.
BUT THAT MAN MAY BE ABLE TO HELP US.
LUCKY CHAP!
HE JUST FOUND A CLEPSIGRUE EGG!
SO WHAT? IS THAT RARE, A CLEPSIGRUE EGG?
HOW CAN YOU BE SO IGNORANT?! THE CLEPSIGRUE ARE MIGRATORY CREATURES. AND SINCE THE NORTH STARTED ACTING UP, WE DON'T SEE MANY AROUND.
IN THIS SEASON, THEY WOULD ORDINARILY SETTLE CLOSE TO CITIES AND LAY THE EGGS WHICH GIVE BIRTH TO FREAKS LIKE YOU.
EXCEPT THAT I'M NOT A FREAK, PERSONALLY.
GRAAAH, HOW YOU ANNOY ME WHEN YOU SAY THAT!

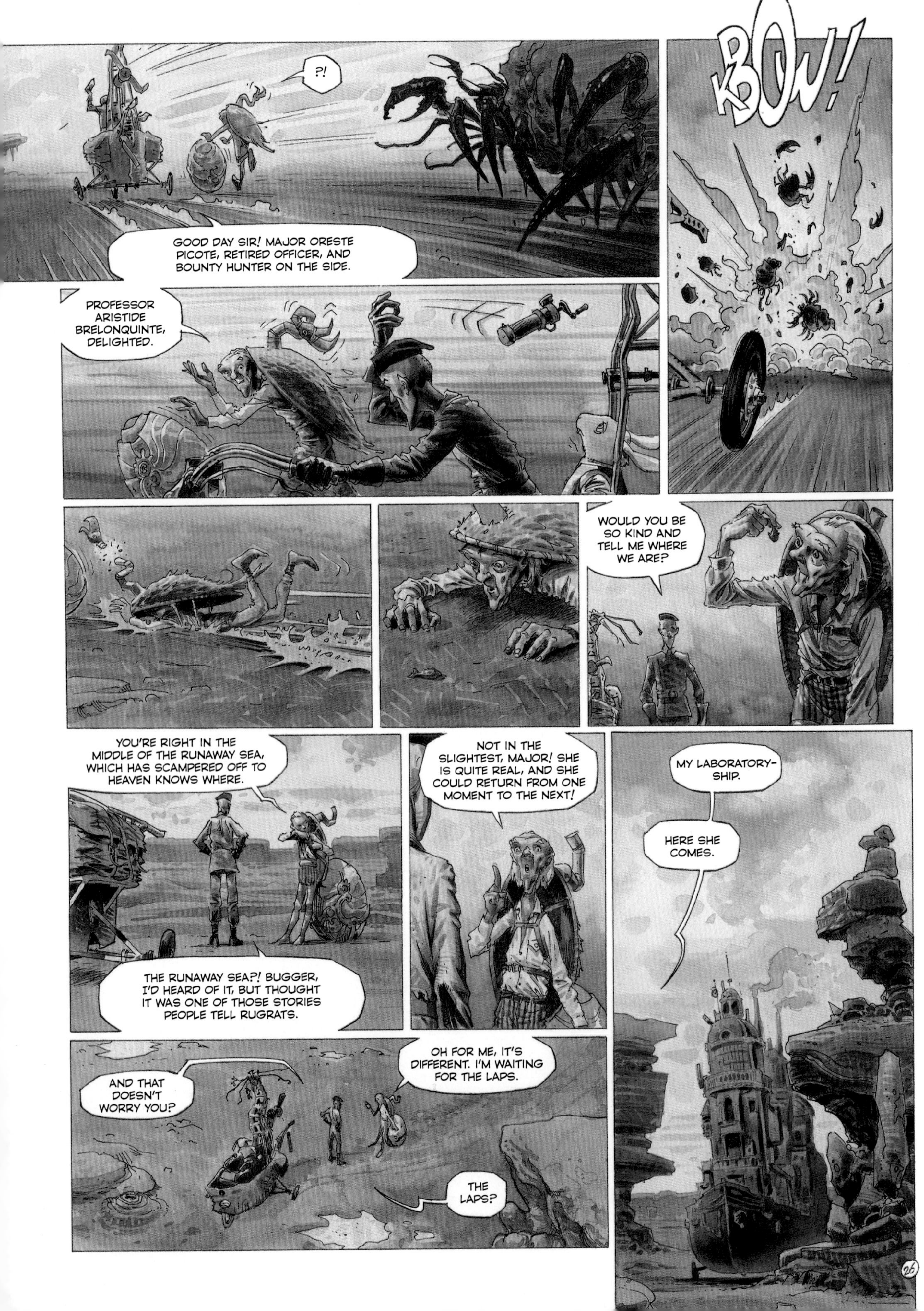
?!
GOOD DAY SIR! MAJOR ORESTE PICOTE, RETIRED OFFICER, AND BOUNTY HUNTER ON THE SIDE.
KBOOM!
PROFESSOR ARISTIDE BRELONQUINTE, DELIGHTED.
WOULD YOU BE SO KIND AND TELL ME WHERE WE ARE?
YOU'RE RIGHT IN THE MIDDLE OF THE RUNAWAY SEA, WHICH HAS SCAMPERED OFF TO HEAVEN KNOWS WHERE.
THE RUNAWAY SEA?! BUGGER, I'D HEARD OF IT, BUT THOUGHT IT WAS ONE OF THOSE STORIES PEOPLE TELL RUGRATS.
NOT IN THE SLIGHTEST, MAJOR! SHE IS QUITE REAL, AND SHE COULD RETURN FROM ONE MOMENT TO THE NEXT!
AND THAT DOESN'T WORRY YOU?
OH FOR ME, IT'S DIFFERENT. I'M WAITING FOR THE LAPS.
THE LAPS?
MY LABORATORY-SHIP.
HERE SHE COMES.
26

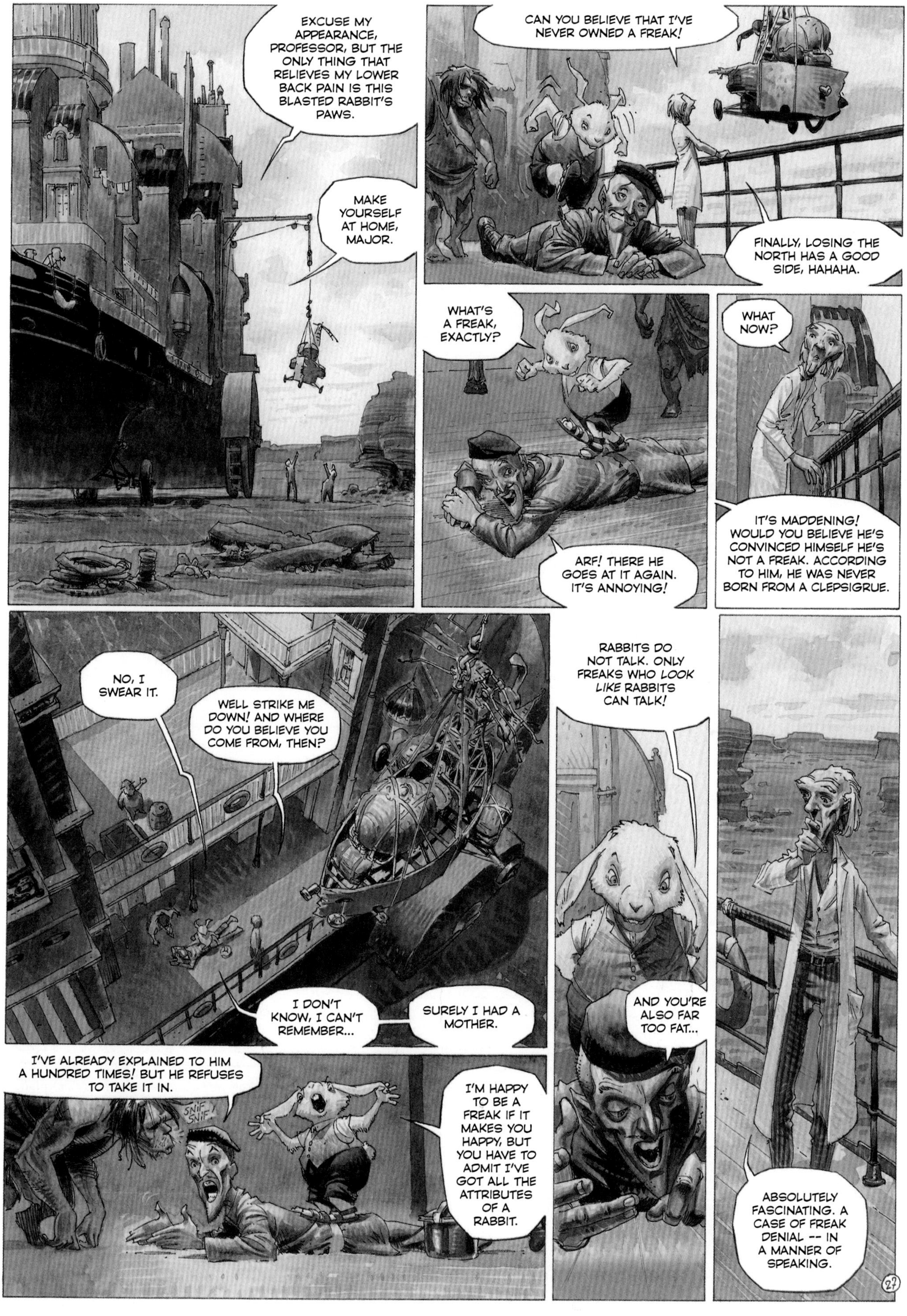
EXCUSE MY APPEARANCE, PROFESSOR, BUT THE ONLY THING THAT RELIEVES MY LOWER BACK PAIN IS THIS BLASTED RABBIT'S PAWS.
MAKE YOURSELF AT HOME, MAJOR.
CAN YOU BELIEVE THAT I'VE NEVER OWNED A FREAK!
FINALLY, LOSING THE NORTH HAS A GOOD SIDE, HAHAHA.
WHAT'S A FREAK, EXACTLY?
ARF! THERE HE GOES AT IT AGAIN. IT'S ANNOYING!
WHAT NOW?
IT'S MADDENING! WOULD YOU BELIEVE HE'S CONVINCED HIMSELF HE'S NOT A FREAK. ACCORDING TO HIM, HE WAS NEVER BORN FROM A CLEPSIGRUE.
NO, I SWEAR IT.
WELL STRIKE ME DOWN! AND WHERE DO YOU BELIEVE YOU COME FROM, THEN?
I DON'T KNOW, I CAN'T REMEMBER...
SURELY I HAD A MOTHER.
RABBITS DO NOT TALK. ONLY FREAKS WHO *LOOK LIKE* RABBITS CAN TALK!
AND YOU'RE ALSO FAR TOO FAT...
I'VE ALREADY EXPLAINED TO HIM A HUNDRED TIMES! BUT HE REFUSES TO TAKE IT IN.
SNIF SNIF
I'M HAPPY TO BE A FREAK IF IT MAKES YOU HAPPY, BUT YOU HAVE TO ADMIT I'VE GOT ALL THE ATTRIBUTES OF A RABBIT.
ABSOLUTELY FASCINATING. A CASE OF FREAK DENIAL -- IN A MANNER OF SPEAKING.

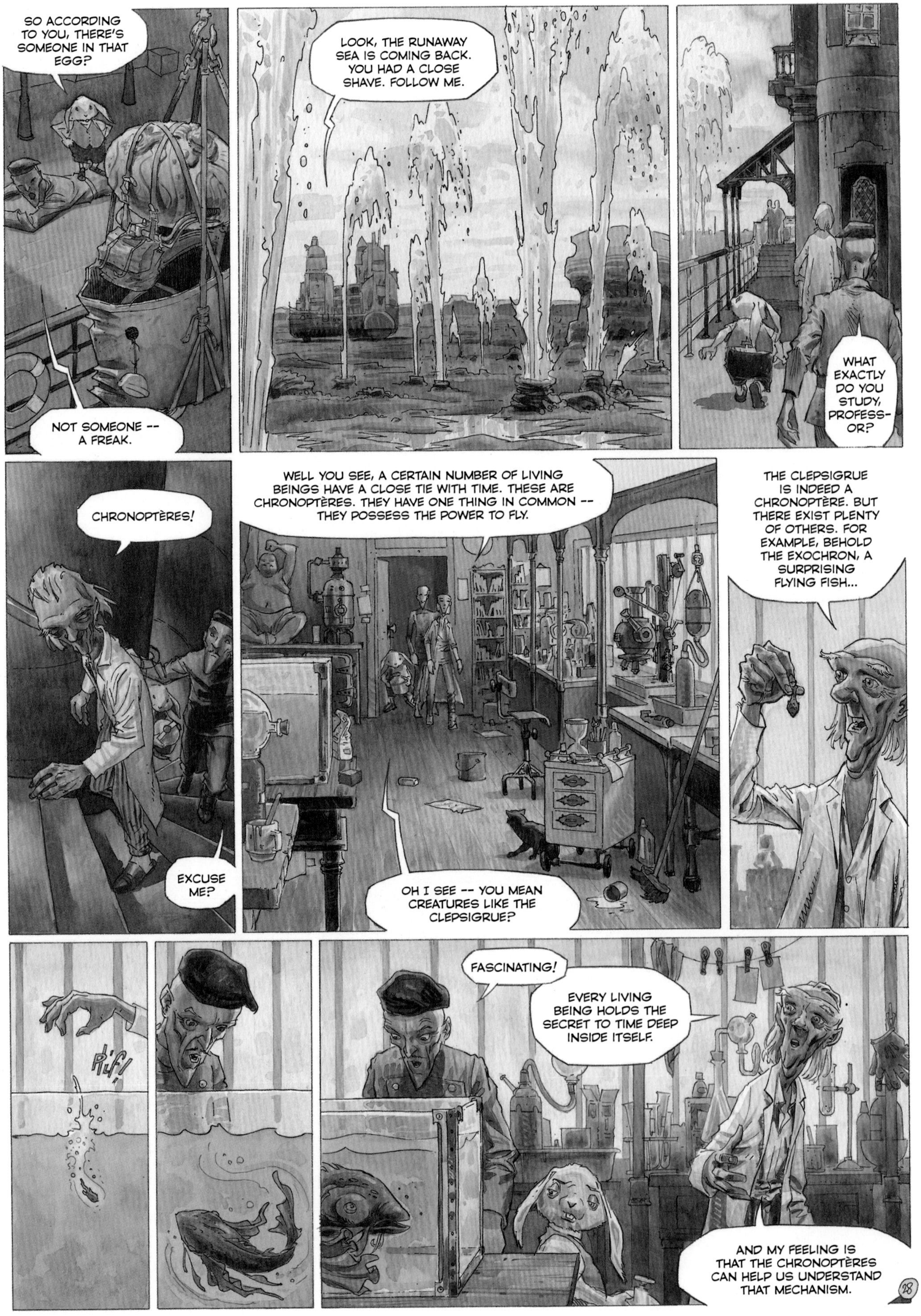
SO ACCORDING TO YOU, THERE'S SOMEONE IN THAT EGG?
NOT SOMEONE -- A FREAK.
LOOK, THE RUNAWAY SEA IS COMING BACK. YOU HAD A CLOSE SHAVE. FOLLOW ME.
WHAT EXACTLY DO YOU STUDY, PROFESS-OR?
CHRONOPTÈRES!
EXCUSE ME?
WELL YOU SEE, A CERTAIN NUMBER OF LIVING BEINGS HAVE A CLOSE TIE WITH TIME. THESE ARE CHRONOPTÈRES. THEY HAVE ONE THING IN COMMON -- THEY POSSESS THE POWER TO FLY.
OH I SEE -- YOU MEAN CREATURES LIKE THE CLEPSIGRUE?
THE CLEPSIGRUE IS INDEED A CHRONOPTÈRE. BUT THERE EXIST PLENTY OF OTHERS. FOR EXAMPLE, BEHOLD THE EXOCHRON, A SURPRISING FLYING FISH...
PLIF!
FASCINATING!
EVERY LIVING BEING HOLDS THE SECRET TO TIME DEEP INSIDE ITSELF.
AND MY FEELING IS THAT THE CHRONOPTÈRES CAN HELP US UNDERSTAND THAT MECHANISM.

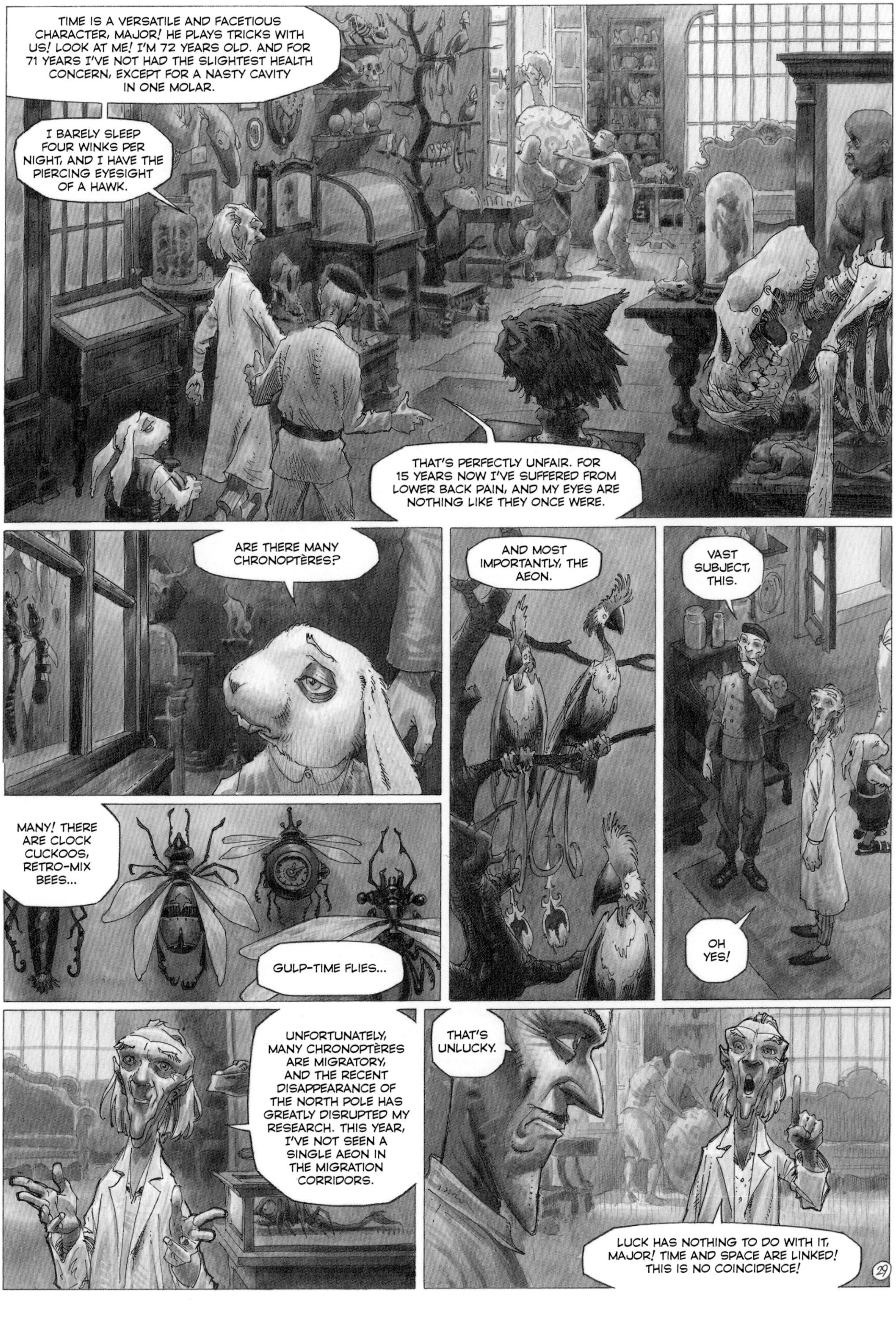

TIME IS A VERSATILE AND FACETIOUS CHARACTER, MAJOR! HE PLAYS TRICKS WITH US! LOOK AT ME! I'M 72 YEARS OLD. AND FOR 71 YEARS I'VE NOT HAD THE SLIGHTEST HEALTH CONCERN, EXCEPT FOR A NASTY CAVITY IN ONE MOLAR.
I BARELY SLEEP FOUR WINKS PER NIGHT, AND I HAVE THE PIERCING EYESIGHT OF A HAWK.
THAT'S PERFECTLY UNFAIR. FOR 15 YEARS NOW I'VE SUFFERED FROM LOWER BACK PAIN, AND MY EYES ARE NOTHING LIKE THEY ONCE WERE.
ARE THERE MANY CHRONOPTÈRES?
MANY! THERE ARE CLOCK CUCKOOS, RETRO-MIX BEES...
GULP-TIME FLIES...
AND MOST IMPORTANTLY, THE AEON.
VAST SUBJECT, THIS.
OH YES!
UNFORTUNATELY, MANY CHRONOPTÈRES ARE MIGRATORY, AND THE RECENT DISAPPEARANCE OF THE NORTH POLE HAS GREATLY DISRUPTED MY RESEARCH. THIS YEAR, I'VE NOT SEEN A SINGLE AEON IN THE MIGRATION CORRIDORS.
THAT'S UNLUCKY.
LUCK HAS NOTHING TO DO WITH IT, MAJOR! TIME AND SPACE ARE LINKED! THIS IS NO COINCIDENCE!

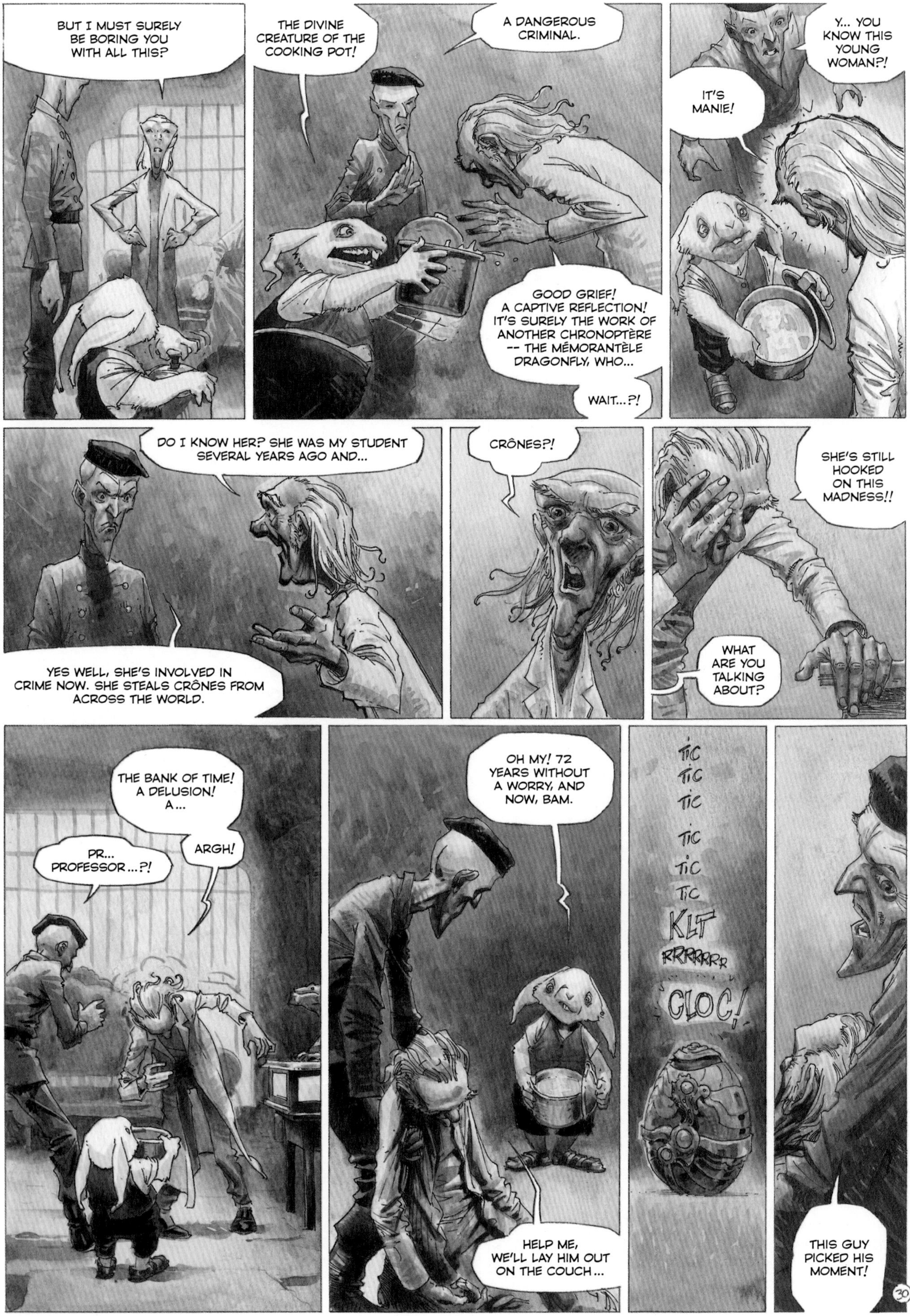

BUT I MUST SURELY BE BORING YOU WITH ALL THIS?
THE DIVINE CREATURE OF THE COOKING POT!
A DANGEROUS CRIMINAL.
GOOD GRIEF! A CAPTIVE REFLECTION! IT'S SURELY THE WORK OF ANOTHER CHRONOPTÈRE -- THE MÉMORANTÈLE DRAGONFLY, WHO...
WAIT...?!
Y... YOU KNOW THIS YOUNG WOMAN?!
IT'S MANIE!
DO I KNOW HER? SHE WAS MY STUDENT SEVERAL YEARS AGO AND...
YES WELL, SHE'S INVOLVED IN CRIME NOW. SHE STEALS CRÔNES FROM ACROSS THE WORLD.
CRÔNES?!
SHE'S STILL HOOKED ON THIS MADNESS!!
WHAT ARE YOU TALKING ABOUT?
THE BANK OF TIME! A DELUSION! A...
PR... PROFESSOR...?!
ARGH!
OH MY! 72 YEARS WITHOUT A WORRY, AND NOW, BAM.
HELP ME, WE'LL LAY HIM OUT ON THE COUCH...
TIC
TIC
TIC
TIC
TIC
TIC
KLT
RRRRRRR
CLOC!
THIS GUY PICKED HIS MOMENT!

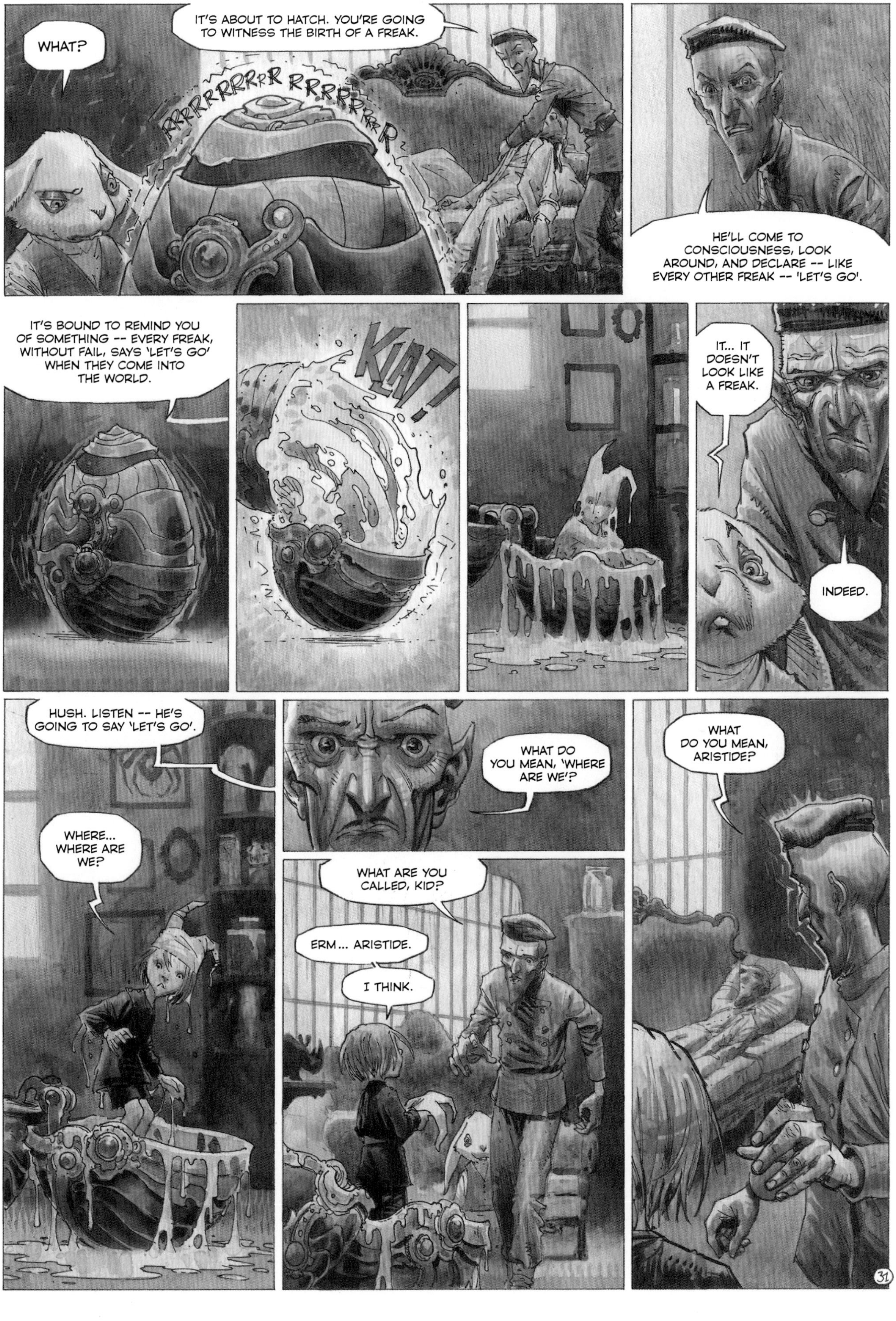

WHAT?
IT'S ABOUT TO HATCH. YOU'RE GOING TO WITNESS THE BIRTH OF A FREAK.
RRRRRRRRRRR RRRRRRRRRR
HE'LL COME TO CONSCIOUSNESS, LOOK AROUND, AND DECLARE -- LIKE EVERY OTHER FREAK -- 'LET'S GO'.
IT'S BOUND TO REMIND YOU OF SOMETHING -- EVERY FREAK, WITHOUT FAIL, SAYS 'LET'S GO' WHEN THEY COME INTO THE WORLD.
KLAT!
IT... IT DOESN'T LOOK LIKE A FREAK.
INDEED.
HUSH. LISTEN -- HE'S GOING TO SAY 'LET'S GO'.
WHERE... WHERE ARE WE?
WHAT DO YOU MEAN, 'WHERE ARE WE'?
WHAT ARE YOU CALLED, KID?
ERM... ARISTIDE.
I THINK.
WHAT DO YOU MEAN, ARISTIDE?

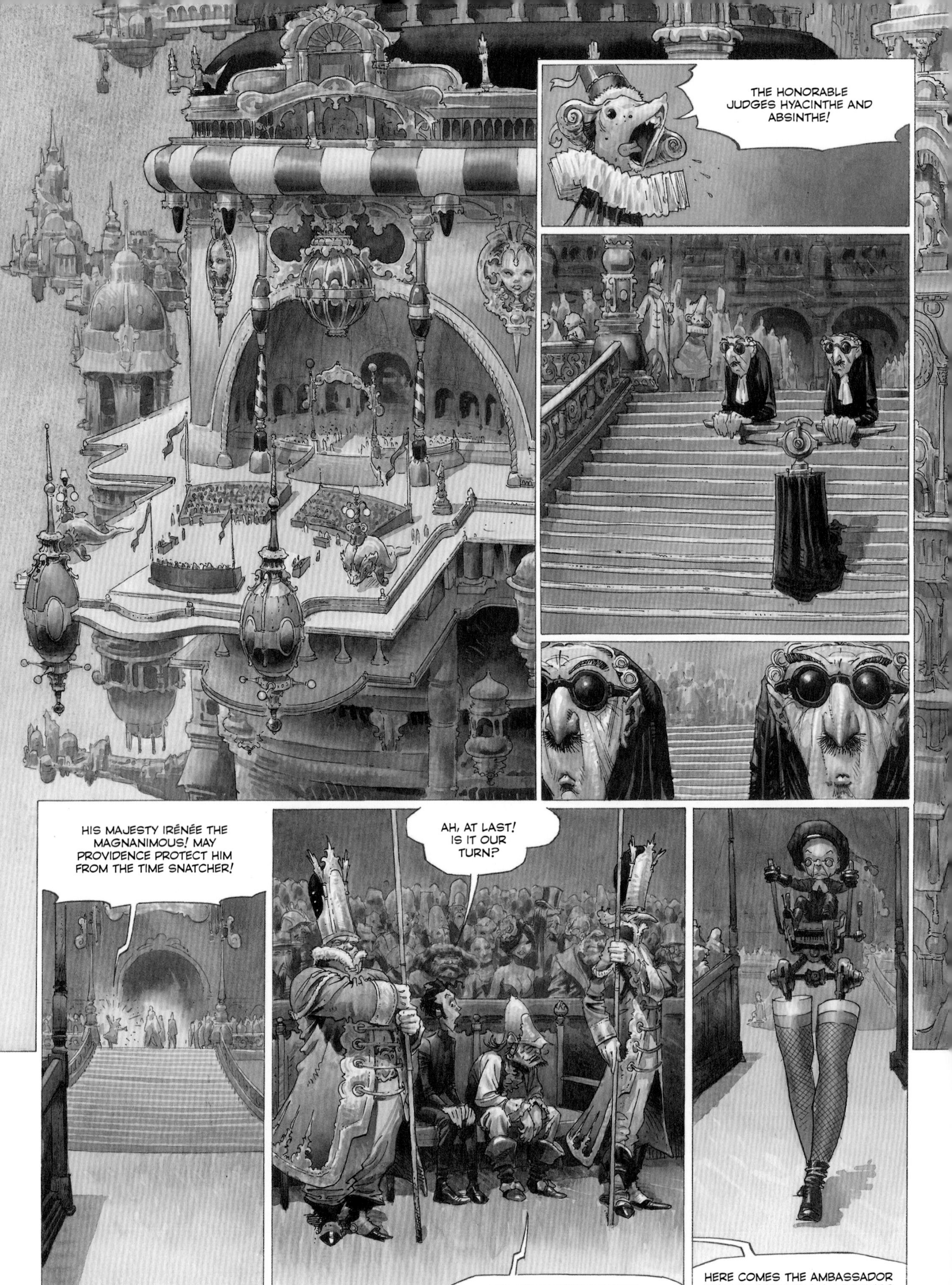
THE HONORABLE JUDGES HYACINTHE AND ABSINTHE!
HIS MAJESTY IRÉNÉE THE MAGNANIMOUS! MAY PROVIDENCE PROTECT HIM FROM THE TIME SNATCHER!
AH, AT LAST! IS IT OUR TURN?
NO. FIRST THEY RESOLVE ANY DIPLOMATIC CONFLICTS.
HERE COMES THE AMBASSADOR OF LITTLEGHISTAN, A PROVINCE CONTROLLED BY PONDUCHE.

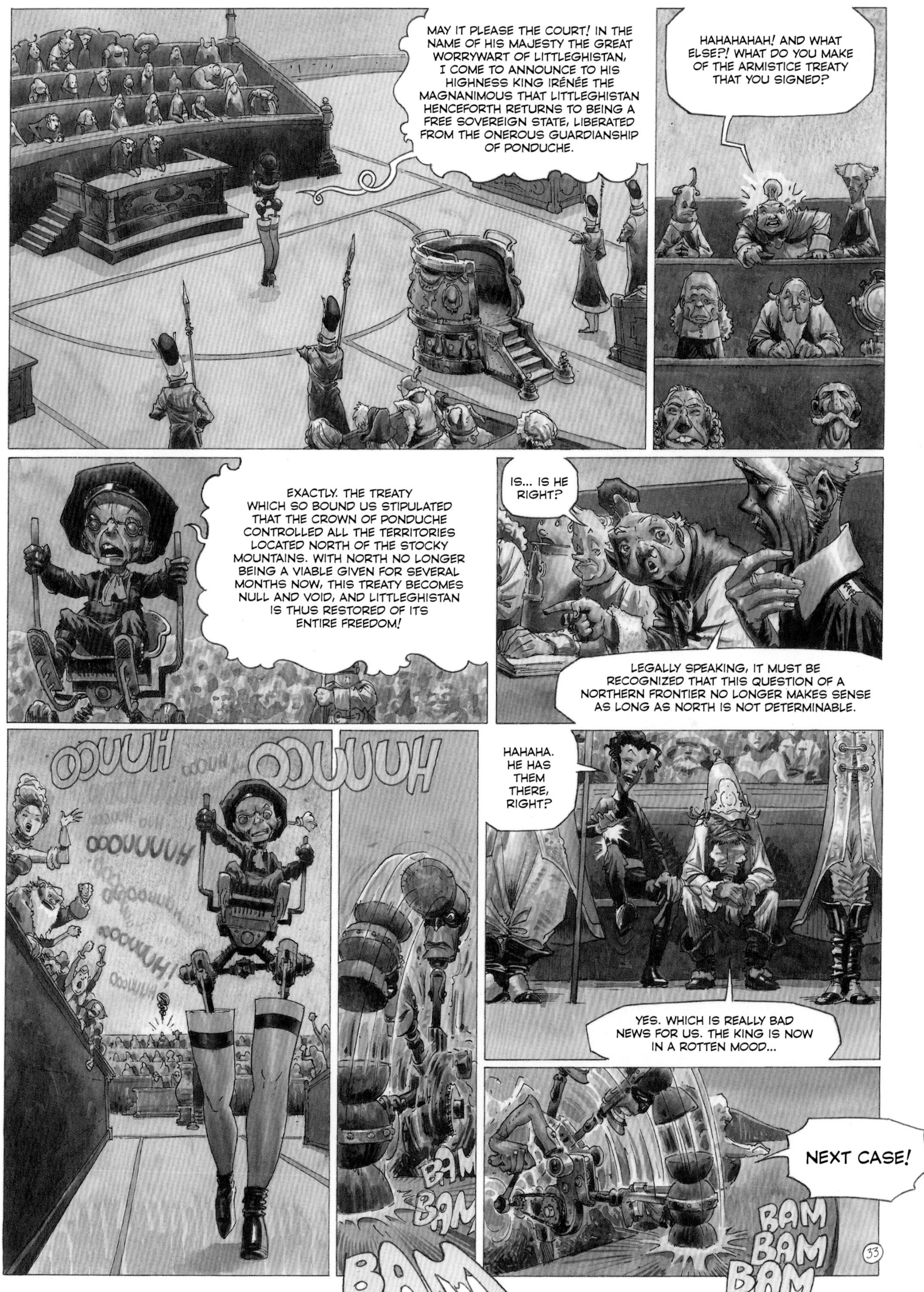
MAY IT PLEASE THE COURT! IN THE NAME OF HIS MAJESTY THE GREAT WORRYWART OF LITTLEGHISTAN, I COME TO ANNOUNCE TO HIS HIGHNESS KING IRÉNÉE THE MAGNANIMOUS THAT LITTLEGHISTAN HENCEFORTH RETURNS TO BEING A FREE SOVEREIGN STATE, LIBERATED FROM THE ONEROUS GUARDIANSHIP OF PONDUCHE.
HAHAHAHAH! AND WHAT ELSE?! WHAT DO YOU MAKE OF THE ARMISTICE TREATY THAT YOU SIGNED?
EXACTLY. THE TREATY WHICH SO BOUND US STIPULATED THAT THE CROWN OF PONDUCHE CONTROLLED ALL THE TERRITORIES LOCATED NORTH OF THE STOCKY MOUNTAINS. WITH NORTH NO LONGER BEING A VIABLE GIVEN FOR SEVERAL MONTHS NOW, THIS TREATY BECOMES NULL AND VOID, AND LITTLEGHISTAN IS THUS RESTORED OF ITS ENTIRE FREEDOM!
IS... IS HE RIGHT?
LEGALLY SPEAKING, IT MUST BE RECOGNIZED THAT THIS QUESTION OF A NORTHERN FRONTIER NO LONGER MAKES SENSE AS LONG AS NORTH IS NOT DETERMINABLE.
OOUUUH
OOUUUH
HAHAHA. HE HAS THEM THERE, RIGHT?
YES. WHICH IS REALLY BAD NEWS FOR US. THE KING IS NOW IN A ROTTEN MOOD...
BAM
BAM
BAM
NEXT CASE!
BAM BAM BAM BAM

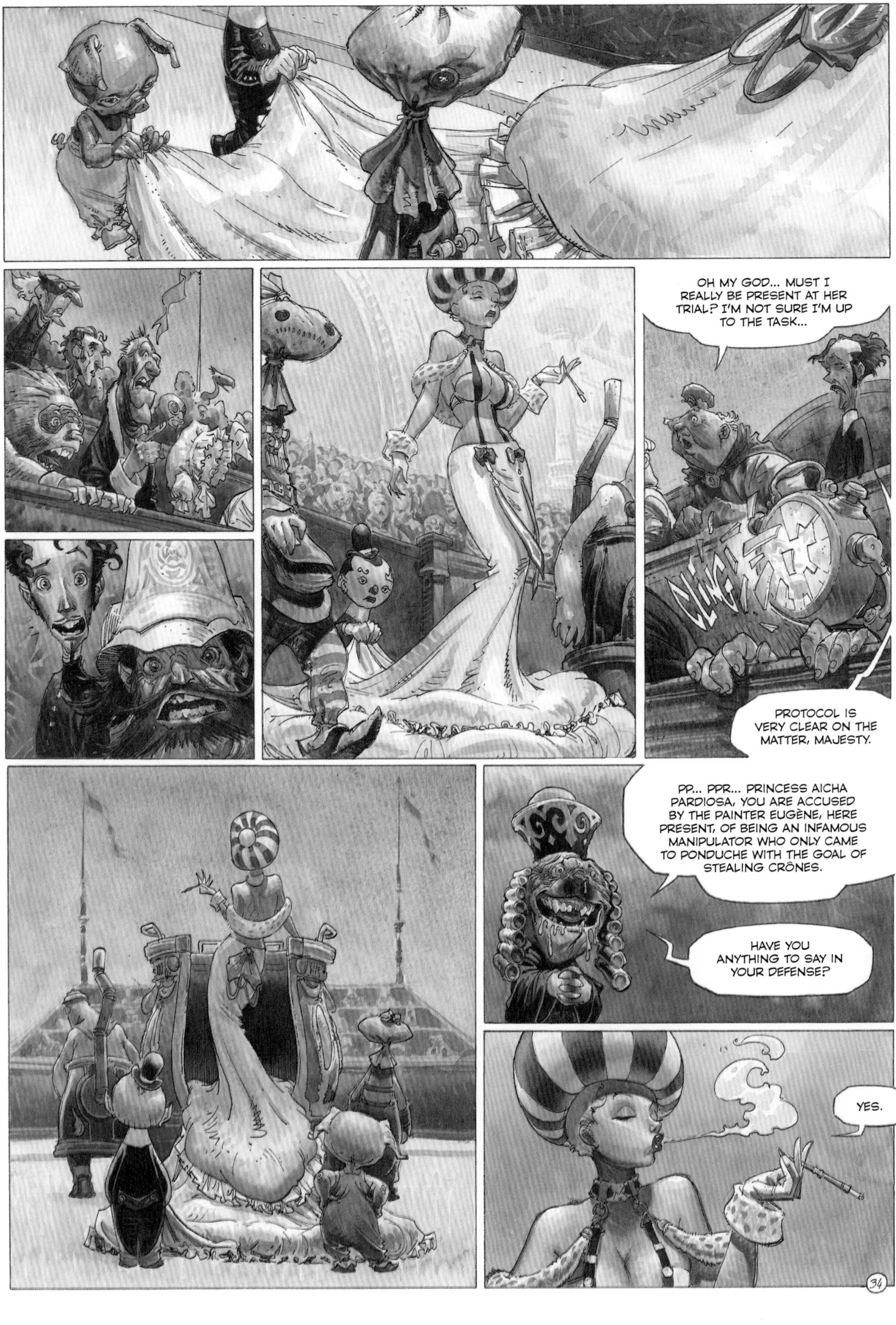
OH MY GOD... MUST I REALLY BE PRESENT AT HER TRIAL? I'M NOT SURE I'M UP TO THE TASK...
CLING
PROTOCOL IS VERY CLEAR ON THE MATTER, MAJESTY.
PP... PPR... PRINCESS AICHA PARDIOSA, YOU ARE ACCUSED BY THE PAINTER EUGÈNE, HERE PRESENT, OF BEING AN INFAMOUS MANIPULATOR WHO ONLY CAME TO PONDUCHE WITH THE GOAL OF STEALING CRÔNES.
HAVE YOU ANYTHING TO SAY IN YOUR DEFENSE?
YES.

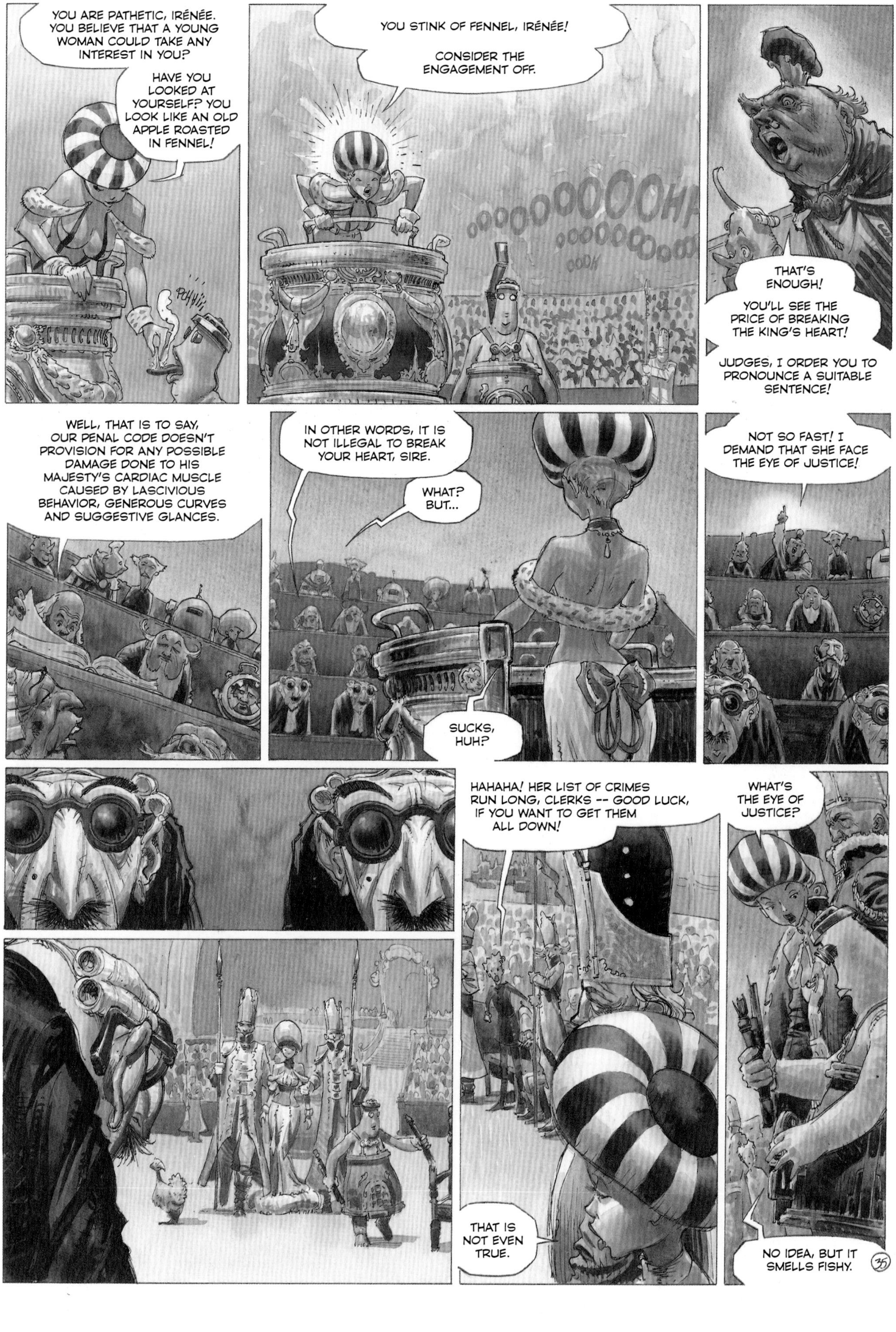
YOU ARE PATHETIC, IRÉNÉE. YOU BELIEVE THAT A YOUNG WOMAN COULD TAKE ANY INTEREST IN YOU?
HAVE YOU LOOKED AT YOURSELF? YOU LOOK LIKE AN OLD APPLE ROASTED IN FENNEL!
PCHHH
YOU STINK OF FENNEL, IRÉNÉE!
CONSIDER THE ENGAGEMENT OFF.
OOOOOOOOOOHH
THAT'S ENOUGH!
YOU'LL SEE THE PRICE OF BREAKING THE KING'S HEART!
JUDGES, I ORDER YOU TO PRONOUNCE A SUITABLE SENTENCE!
WELL, THAT IS TO SAY, OUR PENAL CODE DOESN'T PROVISION FOR ANY POSSIBLE DAMAGE DONE TO HIS MAJESTY'S CARDIAC MUSCLE CAUSED BY LASCIVIOUS BEHAVIOR, GENEROUS CURVES AND SUGGESTIVE GLANCES.
IN OTHER WORDS, IT IS NOT ILLEGAL TO BREAK YOUR HEART, SIRE.
WHAT? BUT...
SUCKS, HUH?
NOT SO FAST! I DEMAND THAT SHE FACE THE EYE OF JUSTICE!
HAHAHA! HER LIST OF CRIMES RUN LONG, CLERKS -- GOOD LUCK, IF YOU WANT TO GET THEM ALL DOWN!
THAT IS NOT EVEN TRUE.
WHAT'S THE EYE OF JUSTICE?
NO IDEA, BUT IT SMELLS FISHY.
35

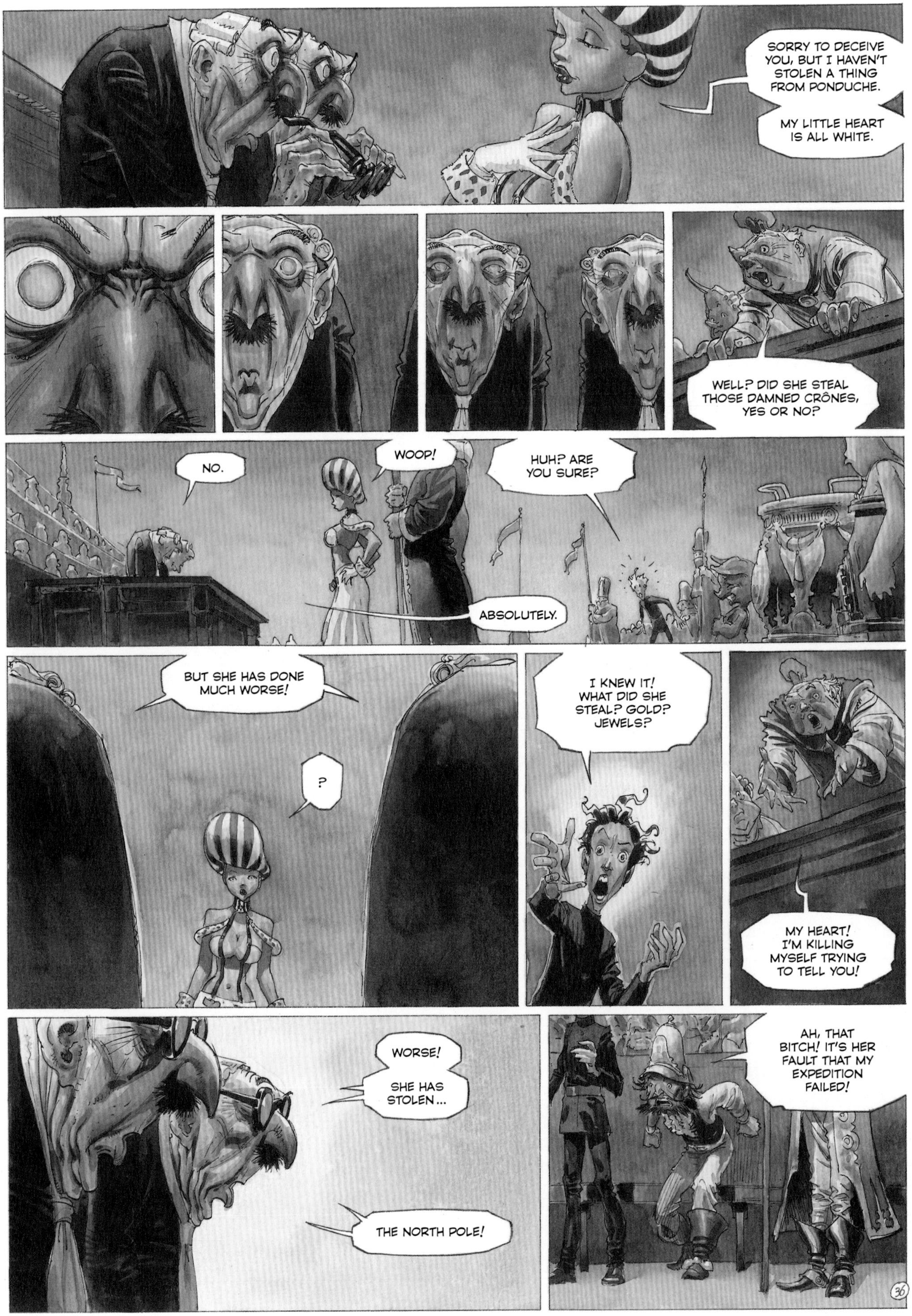
SORRY TO DECEIVE YOU, BUT I HAVEN'T STOLEN A THING FROM PONDUCHE.
MY LITTLE HEART IS ALL WHITE.
WELL? DID SHE STEAL THOSE DAMNED CRÔNES, YES OR NO?
NO.
WOOP!
HUH? ARE YOU SURE?
ABSOLUTELY.
BUT SHE HAS DONE MUCH WORSE!
?
I KNEW IT! WHAT DID SHE STEAL? GOLD? JEWELS?
MY HEART! I'M KILLING MYSELF TRYING TO TELL YOU!
WORSE!
SHE HAS STOLEN...
THE NORTH POLE!
AH, THAT BITCH! IT'S HER FAULT THAT MY EXPEDITION FAILED!
36

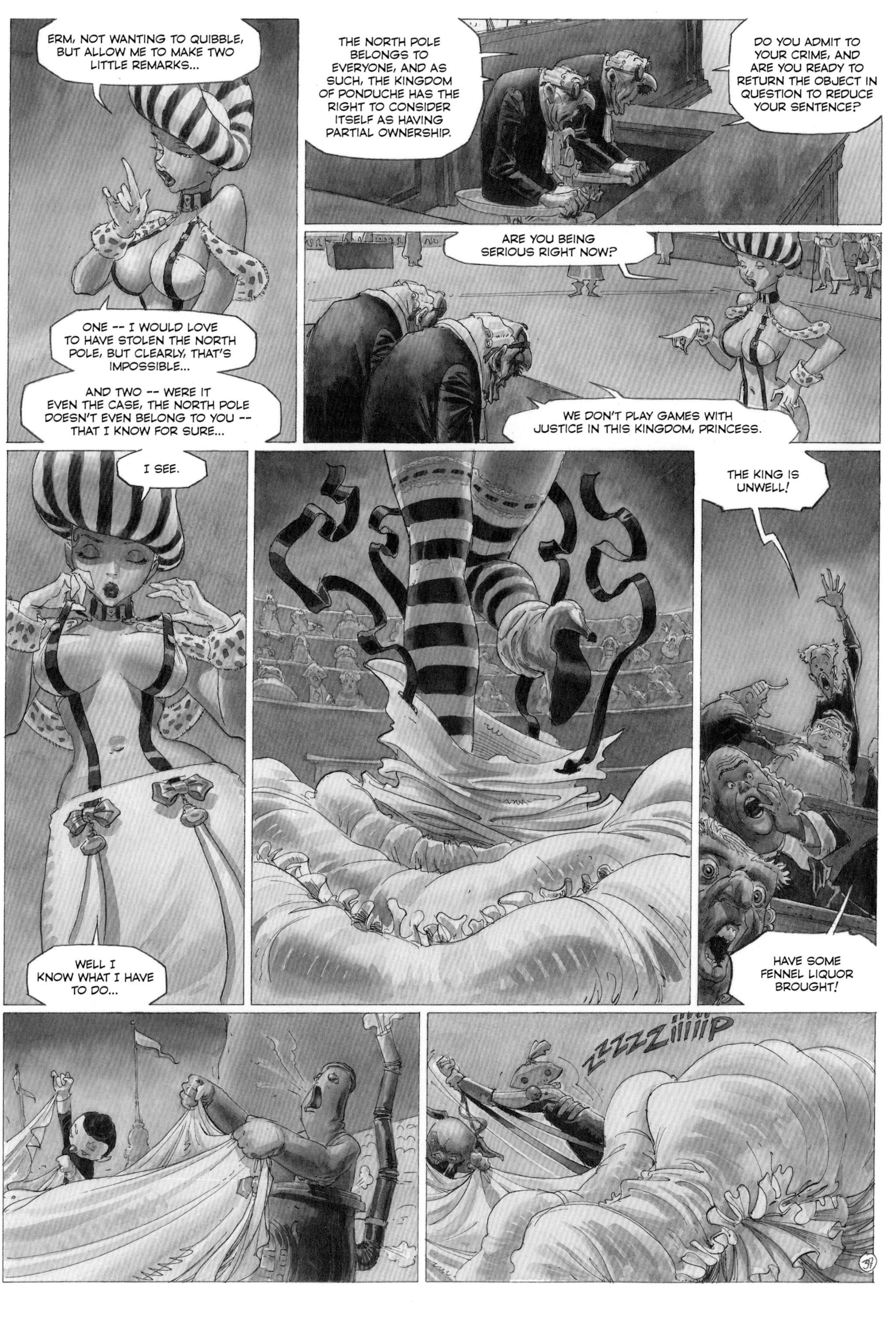

ERM, NOT WANTING TO QUIBBLE, BUT ALLOW ME TO MAKE TWO LITTLE REMARKS...
ONE -- I WOULD LOVE TO HAVE STOLEN THE NORTH POLE, BUT CLEARLY, THAT'S IMPOSSIBLE...
AND TWO -- WERE IT EVEN THE CASE, THE NORTH POLE DOESN'T EVEN BELONG TO YOU -- THAT I KNOW FOR SURE...
THE NORTH POLE BELONGS TO EVERYONE, AND AS SUCH, THE KINGDOM OF PONDUCHE HAS THE RIGHT TO CONSIDER ITSELF AS HAVING PARTIAL OWNERSHIP.
DO YOU ADMIT TO YOUR CRIME, AND ARE YOU READY TO RETURN THE OBJECT IN QUESTION TO REDUCE YOUR SENTENCE?
ARE YOU BEING SERIOUS RIGHT NOW?
WE DON'T PLAY GAMES WITH JUSTICE IN THIS KINGDOM, PRINCESS.
I SEE.
WELL I KNOW WHAT I HAVE TO DO...
THE KING IS UNWELL!
HAVE SOME FENNEL LIQUOR BROUGHT!
ZZZZZIIIIIP

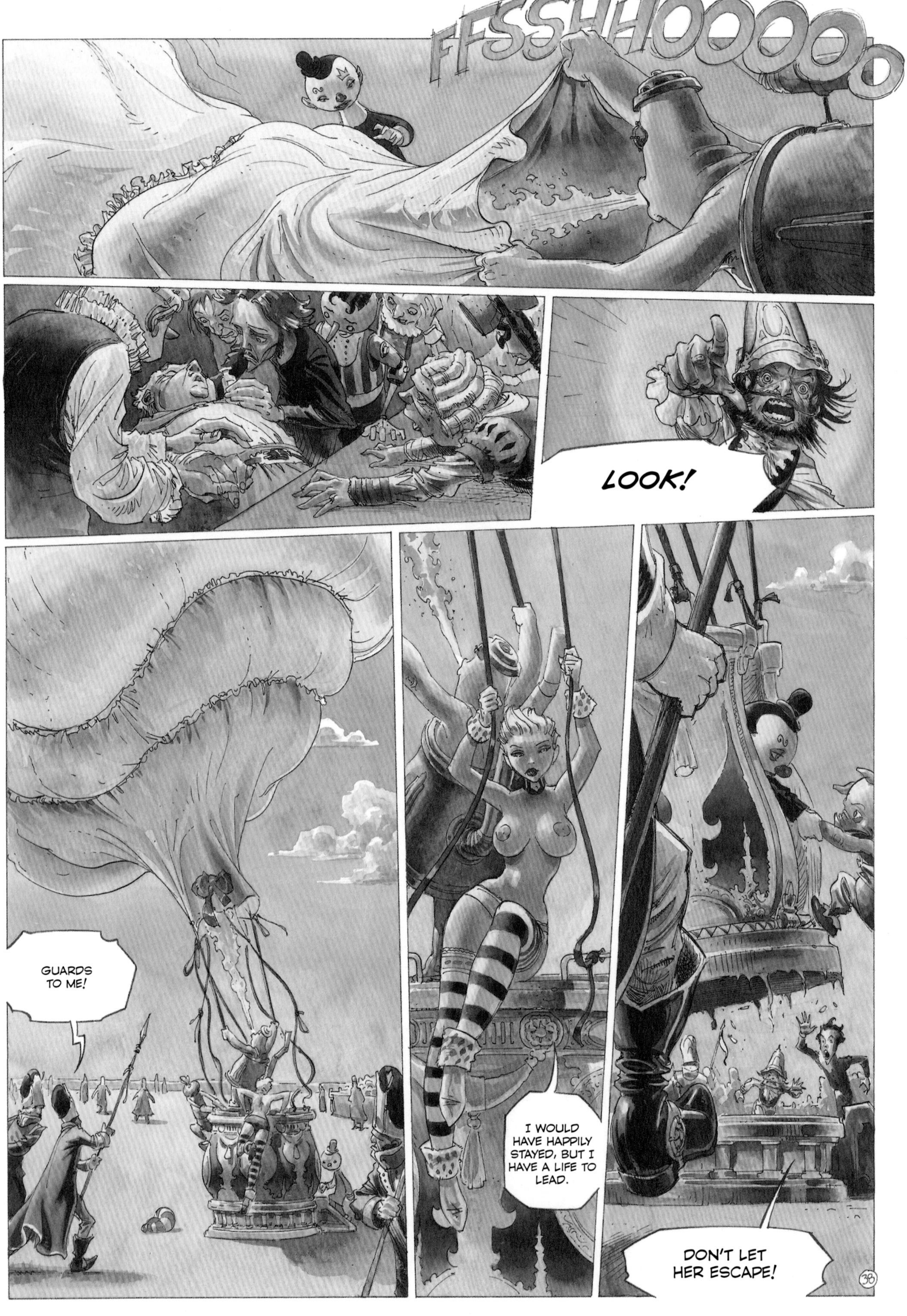
FFSSHHOOOOOO
LOOK!
GUARDS TO ME!
I WOULD HAVE HAPPILY STAYED, BUT I HAVE A LIFE TO LEAD.
DON'T LET HER ESCAPE!
38

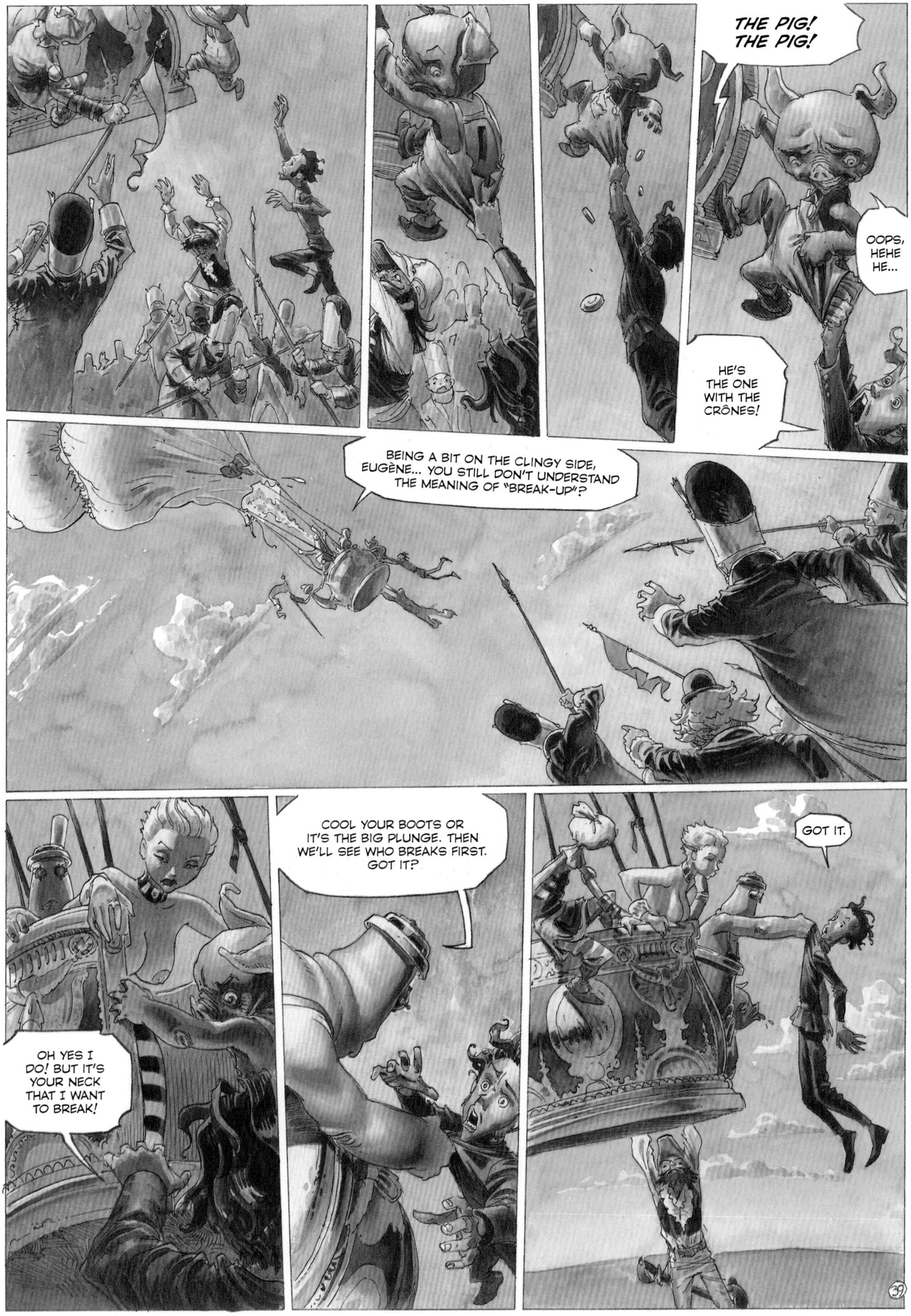
THE PIG!
THE PIG!
OOPS, HEHE HE...
HE'S THE ONE WITH THE CRÔNES!
BEING A BIT ON THE CLINGY SIDE, EUGÈNE... YOU STILL DON'T UNDERSTAND THE MEANING OF "BREAK-UP"?
OH YES I DO! BUT IT'S YOUR NECK THAT I WANT TO BREAK!
COOL YOUR BOOTS OR IT'S THE BIG PLUNGE. THEN WE'LL SEE WHO BREAKS FIRST. GOT IT?
GOT IT.
39

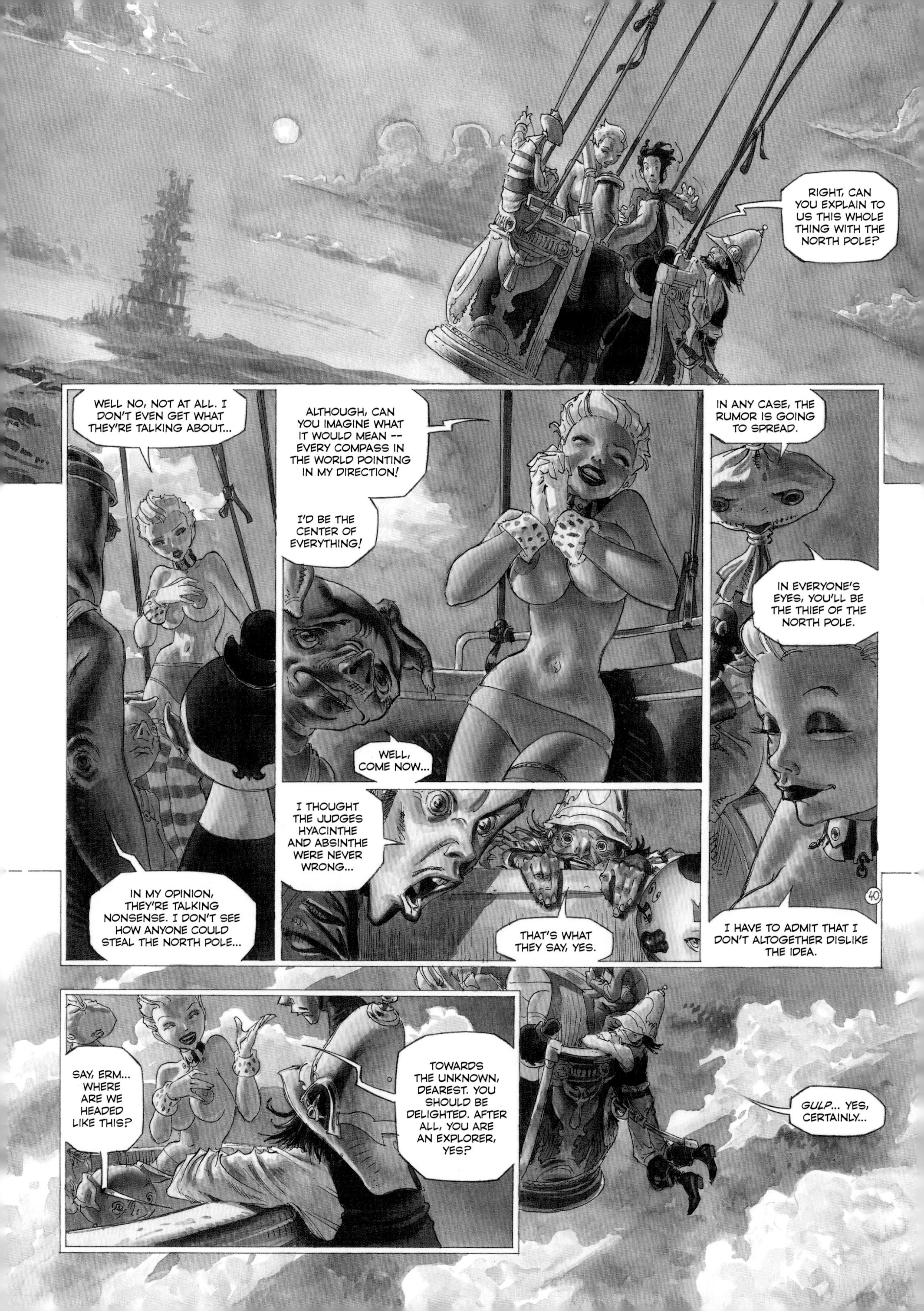
RIGHT, CAN YOU EXPLAIN TO US THIS WHOLE THING WITH THE NORTH POLE?
WELL NO, NOT AT ALL. I DON'T EVEN GET WHAT THEY'RE TALKING ABOUT...
IN MY OPINION, THEY'RE TALKING NONSENSE. I DON'T SEE HOW ANYONE COULD STEAL THE NORTH POLE...
ALTHOUGH, CAN YOU IMAGINE WHAT IT WOULD MEAN -- EVERY COMPASS IN THE WORLD POINTING IN MY DIRECTION!
I'D BE THE CENTER OF EVERYTHING!
WELL, COME NOW...
I THOUGHT THE JUDGES HYACINTHE AND ABSINTHE WERE NEVER WRONG...
THAT'S WHAT THEY SAY, YES.
IN ANY CASE, THE RUMOR IS GOING TO SPREAD.
IN EVERYONE'S EYES, YOU'LL BE THE THIEF OF THE NORTH POLE.
I HAVE TO ADMIT THAT I DON'T ALTOGETHER DISLIKE THE IDEA.
SAY, ERM... WHERE ARE WE HEADED LIKE THIS?
TOWARDS THE UNKNOWN, DEAREST. YOU SHOULD BE DELIGHTED. AFTER ALL, YOU ARE AN EXPLORER, YES?
GULP... YES, CERTAINLY...
40

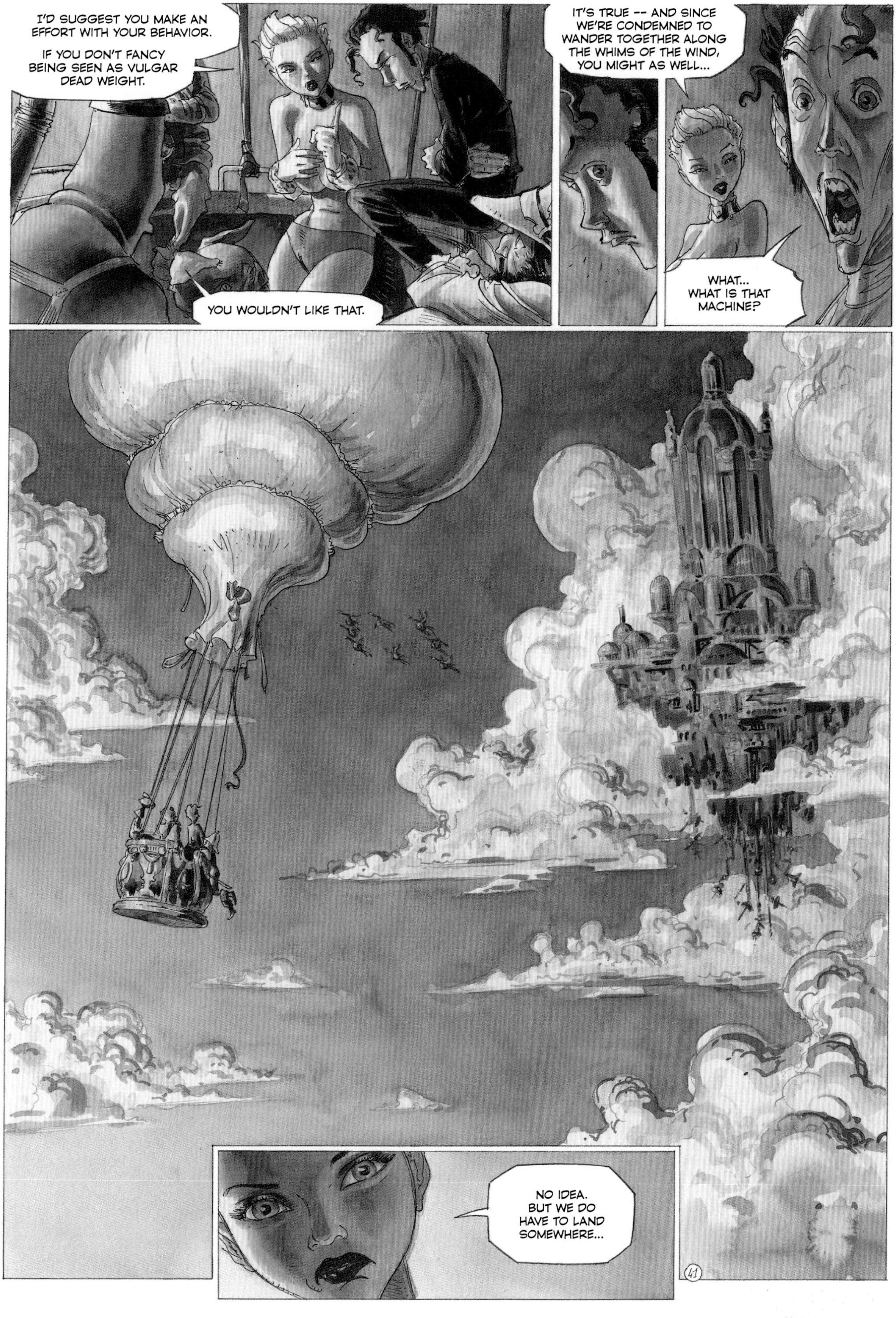
I'D SUGGEST YOU MAKE AN EFFORT WITH YOUR BEHAVIOR.
IF YOU DON'T FANCY BEING SEEN AS VULGAR DEAD WEIGHT.
YOU WOULDN'T LIKE THAT.
IT'S TRUE -- AND SINCE WE'RE CONDEMNED TO WANDER TOGETHER ALONG THE WHIMS OF THE WIND, YOU MIGHT AS WELL...
WHAT... WHAT IS THAT MACHINE?
NO IDEA. BUT WE DO HAVE TO LAND SOMEWHERE...
41

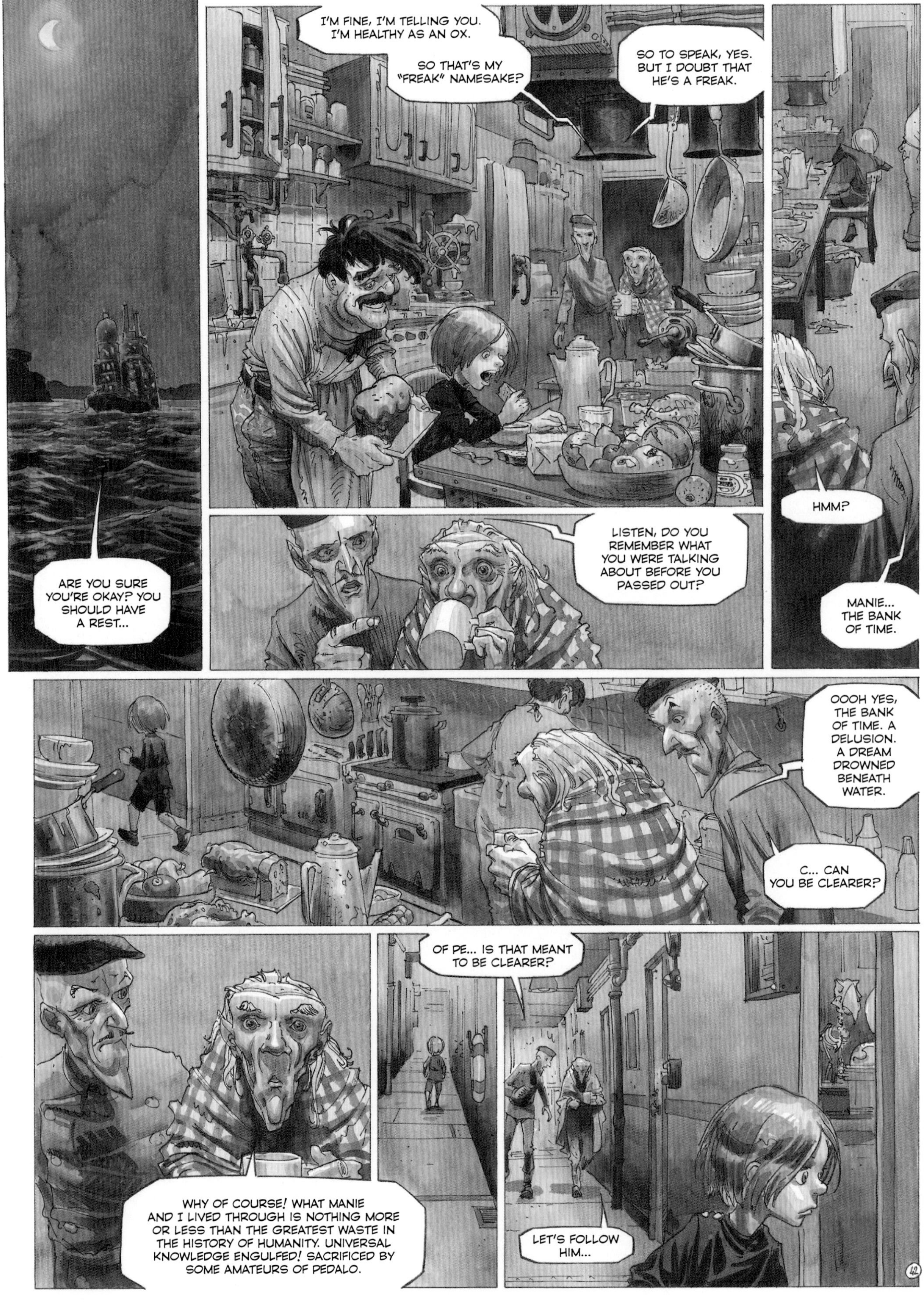
ARE YOU SURE YOU'RE OKAY? YOU SHOULD HAVE A REST...
I'M FINE, I'M TELLING YOU. I'M HEALTHY AS AN OX.
SO THAT'S MY "FREAK" NAMESAKE?
SO TO SPEAK, YES. BUT I DOUBT THAT HE'S A FREAK.
HMM?
LISTEN, DO YOU REMEMBER WHAT YOU WERE TALKING ABOUT BEFORE YOU PASSED OUT?
MANIE... THE BANK OF TIME.
OOOH YES, THE BANK OF TIME. A DELUSION. A DREAM DROWNED BENEATH WATER.
C... CAN YOU BE CLEARER?
WHY OF COURSE! WHAT MANIE AND I LIVED THROUGH IS NOTHING MORE OR LESS THAN THE GREATEST WASTE IN THE HISTORY OF HUMANITY. UNIVERSAL KNOWLEDGE ENGULFED! SACRIFICED BY SOME AMATEURS OF PEDALO.
OF PE... IS THAT MEANT TO BE CLEARER?
LET'S FOLLOW HIM...
42

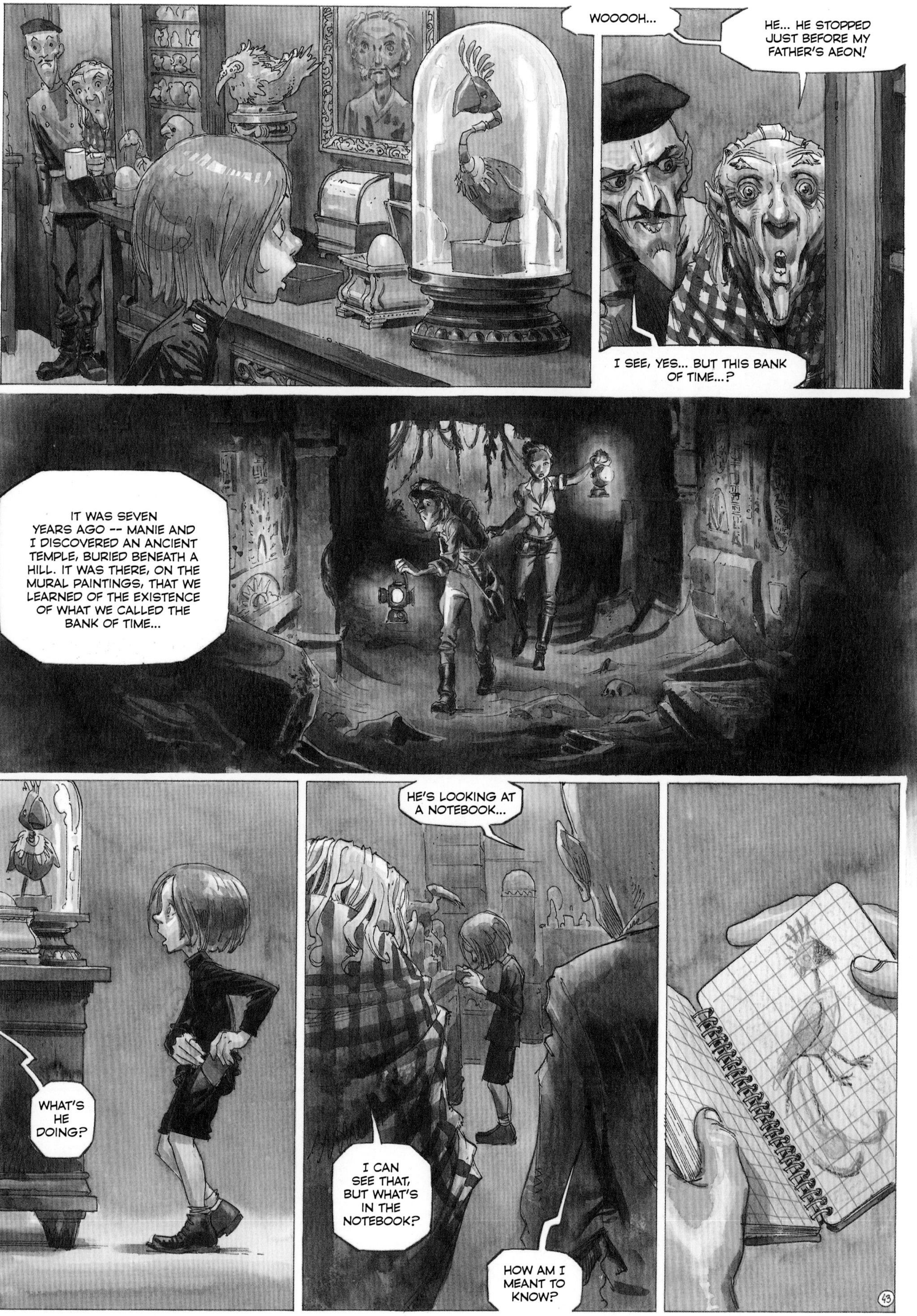
WOOOOH...
HE... HE STOPPED JUST BEFORE MY FATHER'S AEON!
I SEE, YES... BUT THIS BANK OF TIME...?
IT WAS SEVEN YEARS AGO -- MANIE AND I DISCOVERED AN ANCIENT TEMPLE, BURIED BENEATH A HILL. IT WAS THERE, ON THE MURAL PAINTINGS, THAT WE LEARNED OF THE EXISTENCE OF WHAT WE CALLED THE BANK OF TIME...
WHAT'S HE DOING?
HE'S LOOKING AT A NOTEBOOK...
I CAN SEE THAT, BUT WHAT'S IN THE NOTEBOOK?
HOW AM I MEANT TO KNOW?

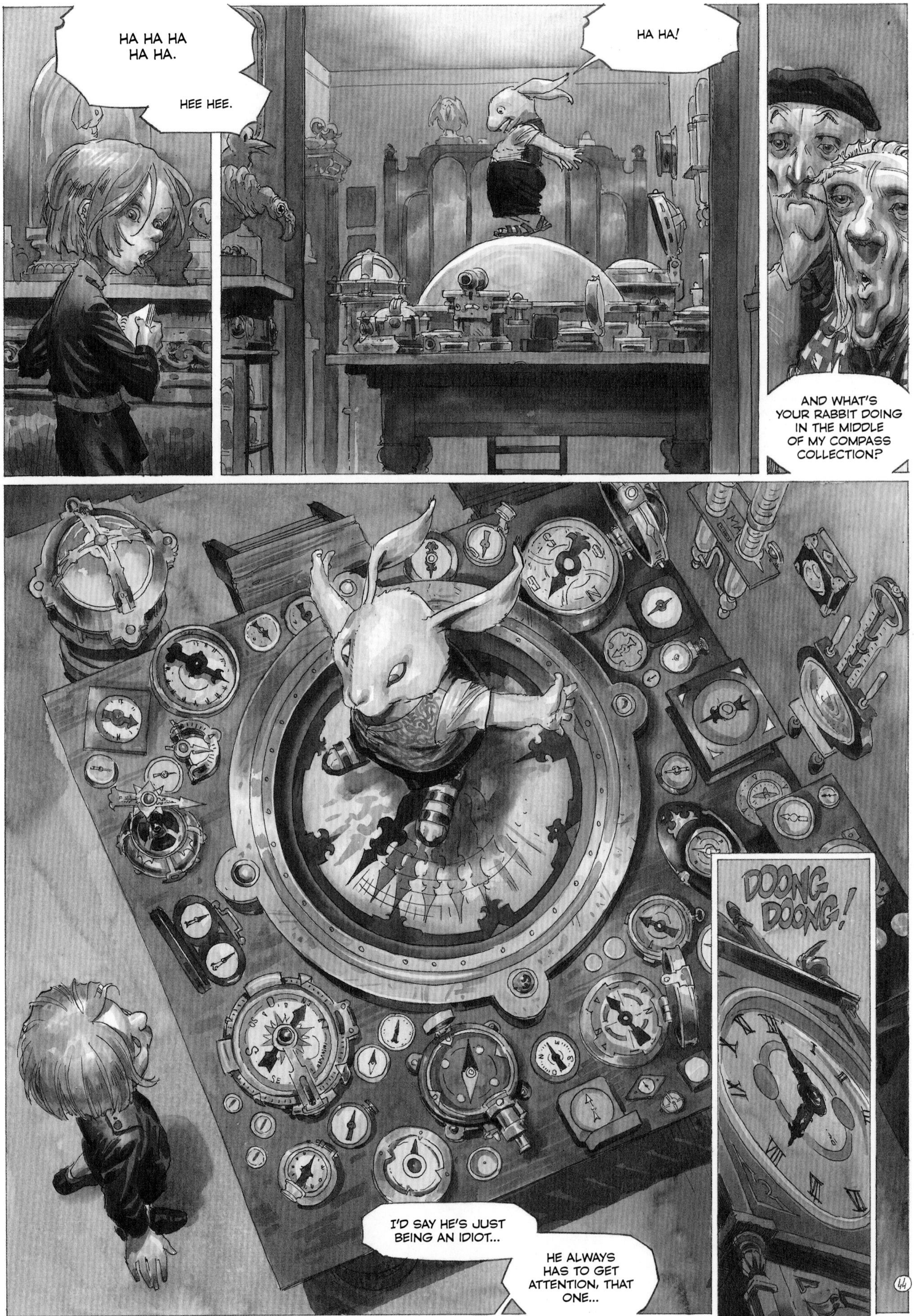

HA HA HA
HA HA.
HEE HEE.
HA HA!
AND WHAT'S YOUR RABBIT DOING IN THE MIDDLE OF MY COMPASS COLLECTION?
DOONG DOONG!
I'D SAY HE'S JUST BEING AN IDIOT...
HE ALWAYS HAS TO GET ATTENTION, THAT ONE...
44

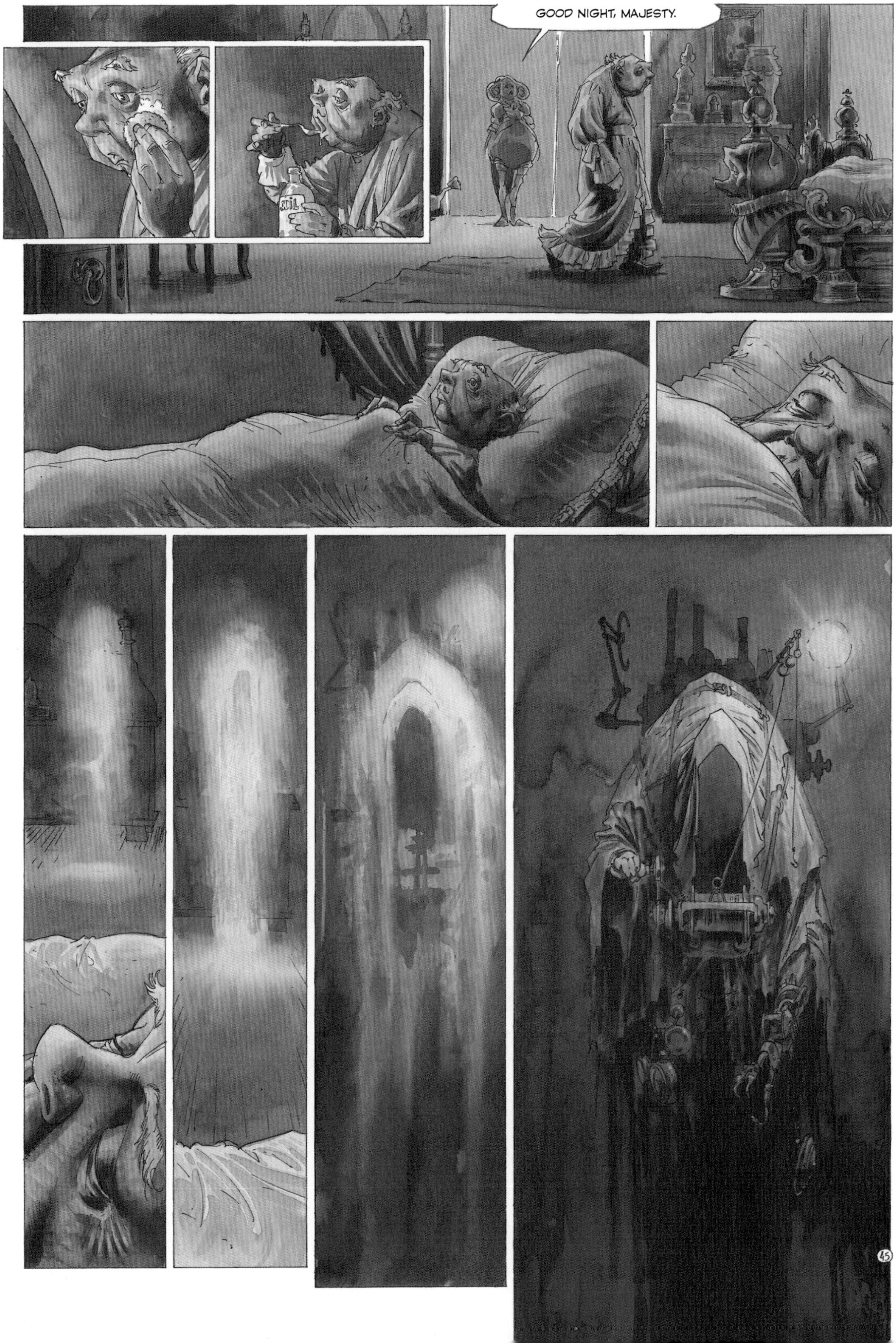
GOOD NIGHT, MAJESTY.
OIL

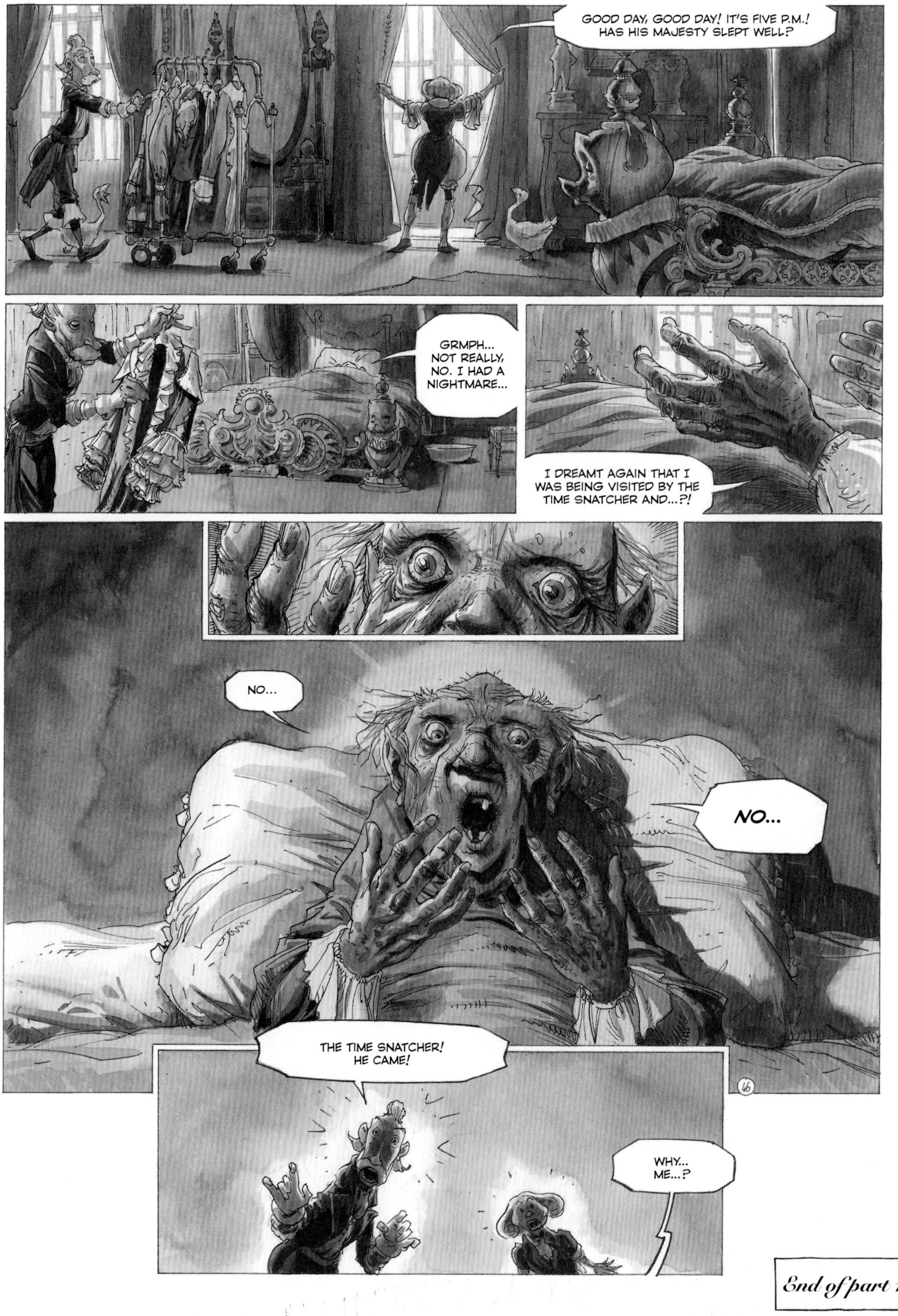
GOOD DAY, GOOD DAY! IT'S FIVE P.M.! HAS HIS MAJESTY SLEPT WELL?
GRMPH... NOT REALLY, NO. I HAD A NIGHTMARE...
I DREAMT AGAIN THAT I WAS BEING VISITED BY THE TIME SNATCHER AND...?!
NO...
NO...
THE TIME SNATCHER! HE CAME!
WHY... ME...?

End of part 1

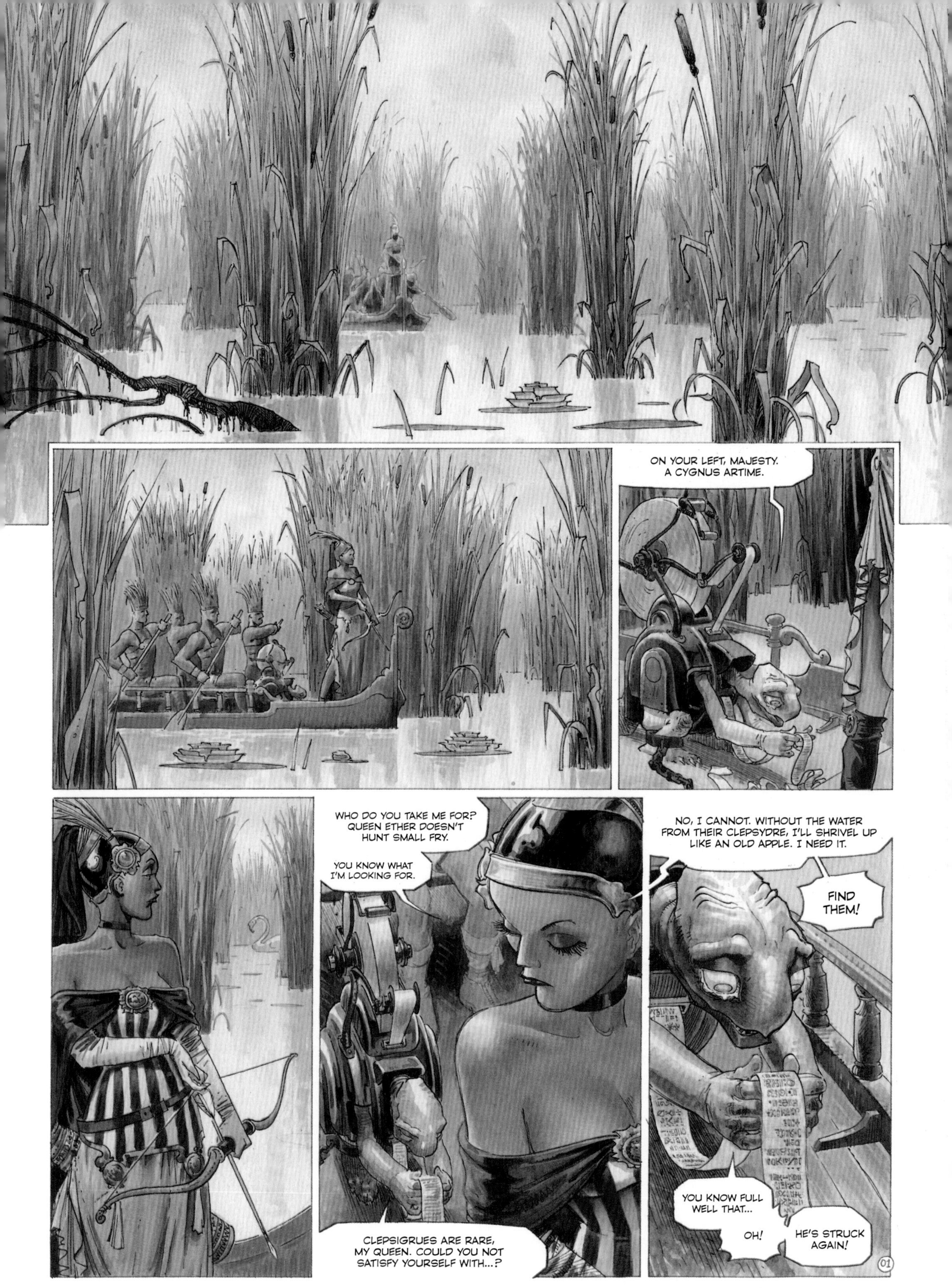
ON YOUR LEFT, MAJESTY.
A CYGNUS ARTIME.
WHO DO YOU TAKE ME FOR? QUEEN ETHER DOESN'T HUNT SMALL FRY.
YOU KNOW WHAT I'M LOOKING FOR.
CLEPSIGRUES ARE RARE, MY QUEEN. COULD YOU NOT SATISFY YOURSELF WITH...?
NO, I CANNOT. WITHOUT THE WATER FROM THEIR CLEPSYDRE, I'LL SHRIVEL UP LIKE AN OLD APPLE. I NEED IT.
FIND THEM!
YOU KNOW FULL WELL THAT...
OH!
HE'S STRUCK AGAIN!
01

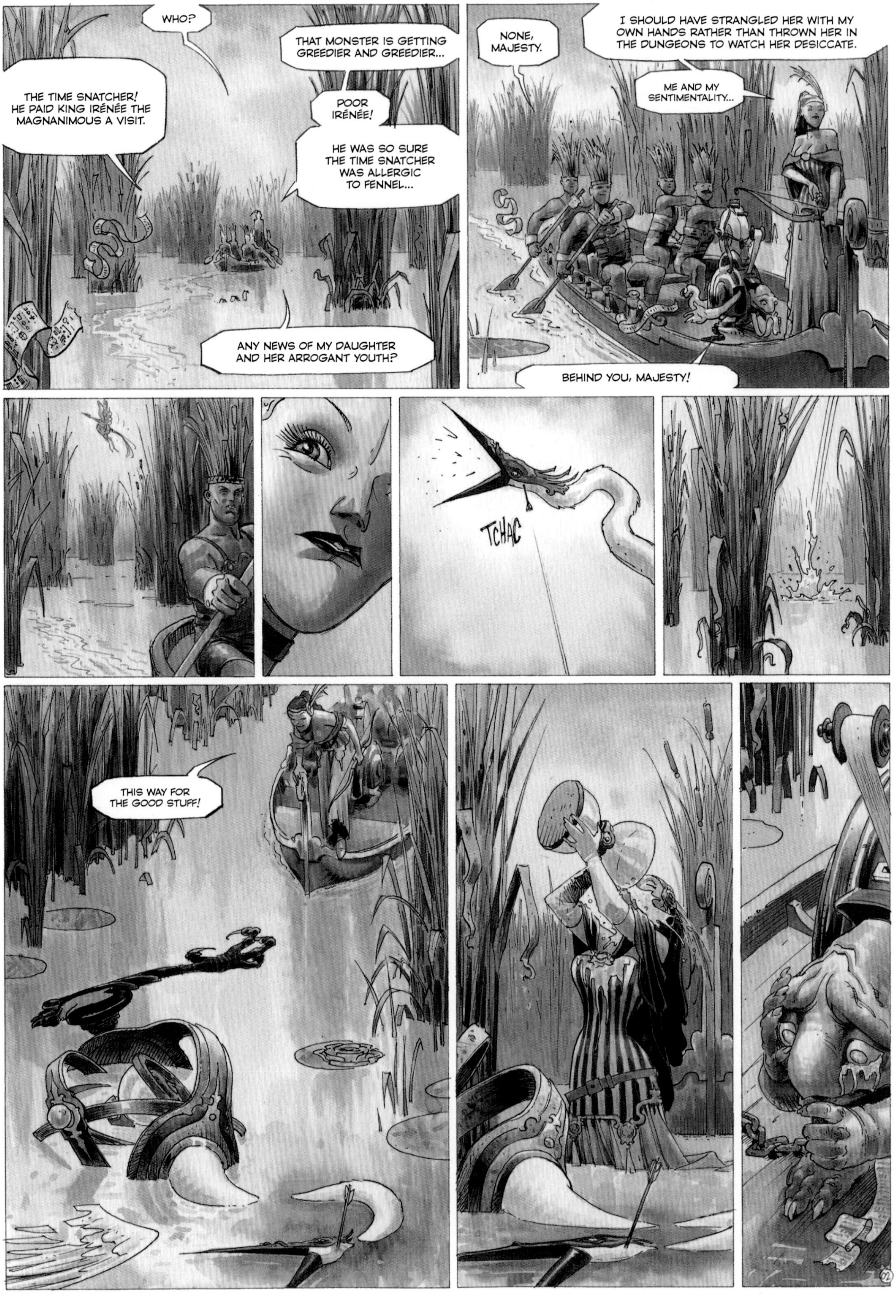
WHO?
THE TIME SNATCHER! HE PAID KING IRÉNÉE THE MAGNANIMOUS A VISIT.
THAT MONSTER IS GETTING GREEDIER AND GREEDIER...
POOR IRÉNÉE!
HE WAS SO SURE THE TIME SNATCHER WAS ALLERGIC TO FENNEL...
ANY NEWS OF MY DAUGHTER AND HER ARROGANT YOUTH?
NONE, MAJESTY.
I SHOULD HAVE STRANGLED HER WITH MY OWN HANDS RATHER THAN THROWN HER IN THE DUNGEONS TO WATCH HER DESICCATE.
ME AND MY SENTIMENTALITY...
BEHIND YOU, MAJESTY!
TCHAC
THIS WAY FOR THE GOOD STUFF!
52

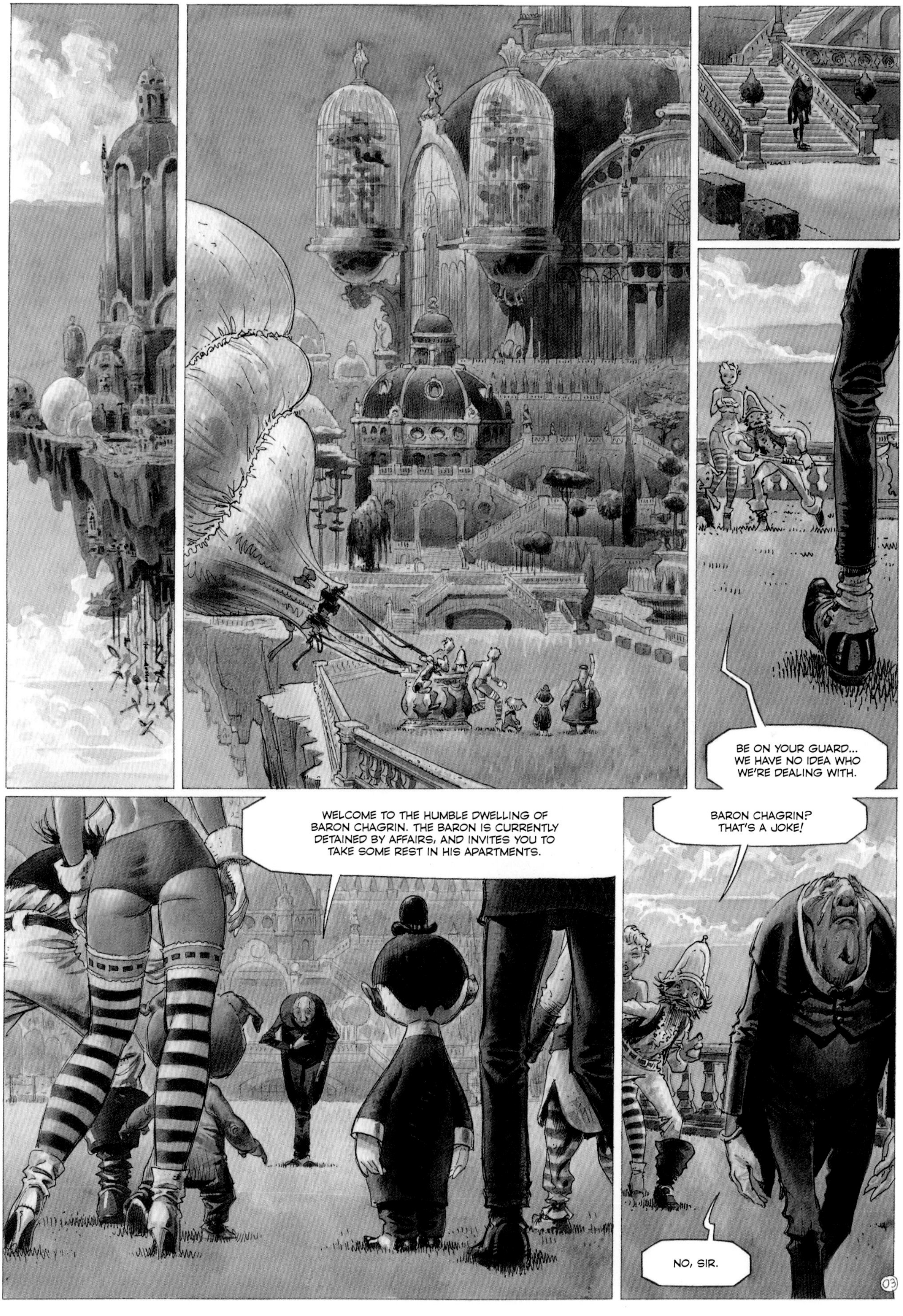
BE ON YOUR GUARD... WE HAVE NO IDEA WHO WE'RE DEALING WITH.
WELCOME TO THE HUMBLE DWELLING OF BARON CHAGRIN. THE BARON IS CURRENTLY DETAINED BY AFFAIRS, AND INVITES YOU TO TAKE SOME REST IN HIS APARTMENTS.
BARON CHAGRIN? THAT'S A JOKE!
NO, SIR.

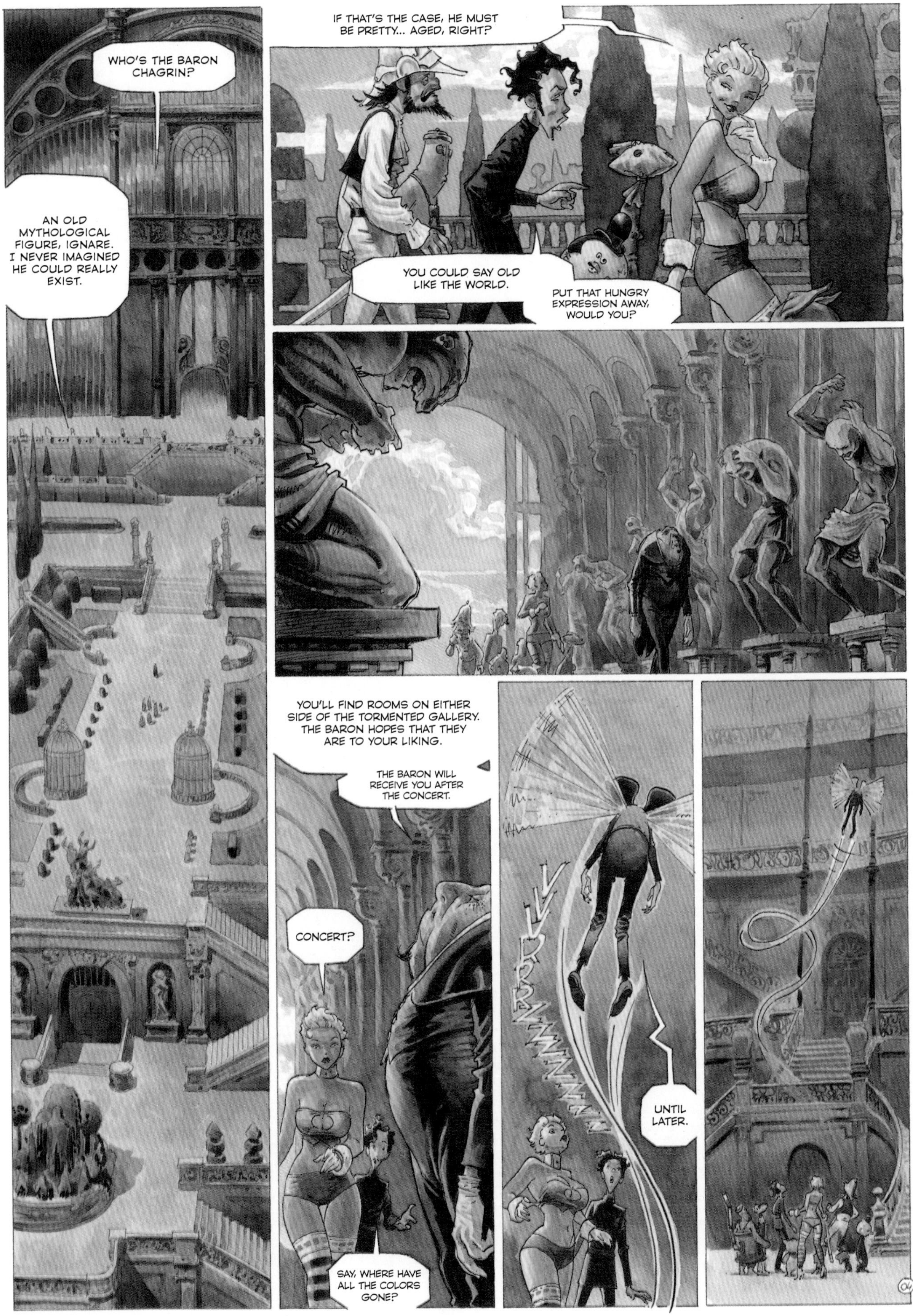
WHO'S THE BARON CHAGRIN?
AN OLD MYTHOLOGICAL FIGURE, IGNARE. I NEVER IMAGINED HE COULD REALLY EXIST.
IF THAT'S THE CASE, HE MUST BE PRETTY... AGED, RIGHT?
YOU COULD SAY OLD LIKE THE WORLD.
PUT THAT HUNGRY EXPRESSION AWAY, WOULD YOU?
YOU'LL FIND ROOMS ON EITHER SIDE OF THE TORMENTED GALLERY. THE BARON HOPES THAT THEY ARE TO YOUR LIKING.
THE BARON WILL RECEIVE YOU AFTER THE CONCERT.
CONCERT?
SAY, WHERE HAVE ALL THE COLORS GONE?
VVVRRRZZZZZZZZZZ
UNTIL LATER.
04

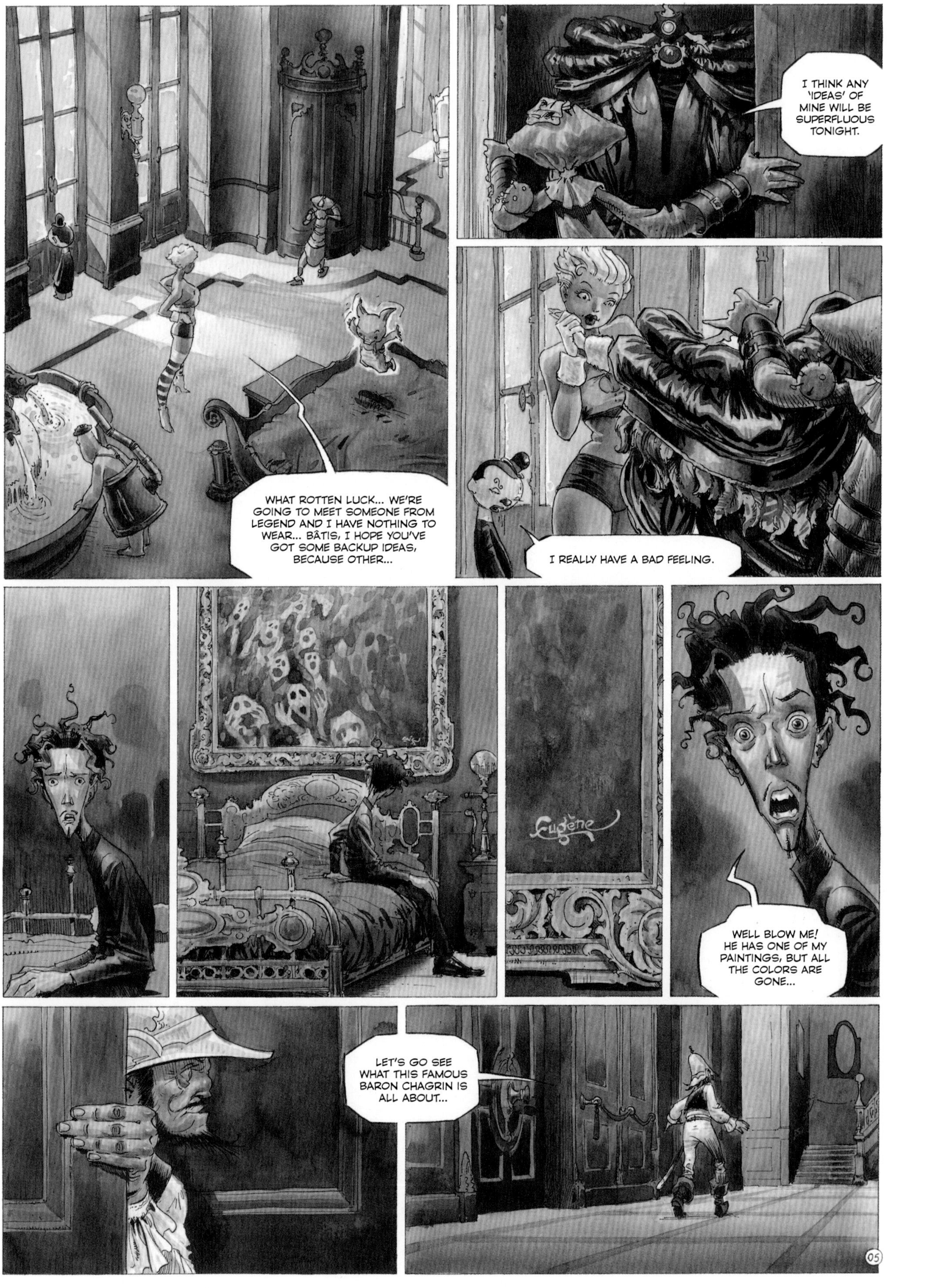
WHAT ROTTEN LUCK... WE'RE GOING TO MEET SOMEONE FROM LEGEND AND I HAVE NOTHING TO WEAR... BÂTIS, I HOPE YOU'VE GOT SOME BACKUP IDEAS, BECAUSE OTHER...
I THINK ANY 'IDEAS' OF MINE WILL BE SUPERFLUOUS TONIGHT.
I REALLY HAVE A BAD FEELING.
Eugène
WELL BLOW ME! HE HAS ONE OF MY PAINTINGS, BUT ALL THE COLORS ARE GONE...
LET'S GO SEE WHAT THIS FAMOUS BARON CHAGRIN IS ALL ABOUT...

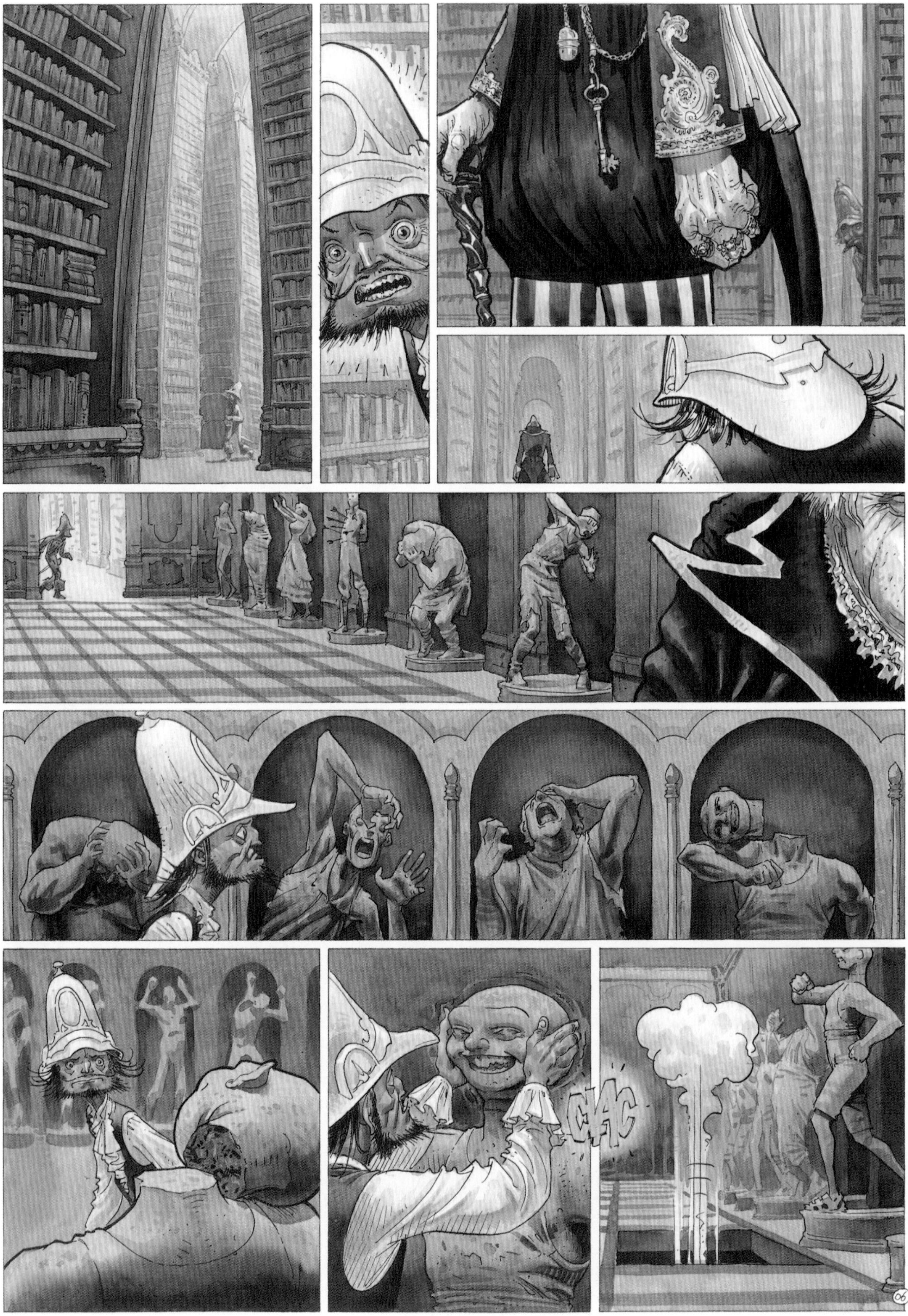
CLAC

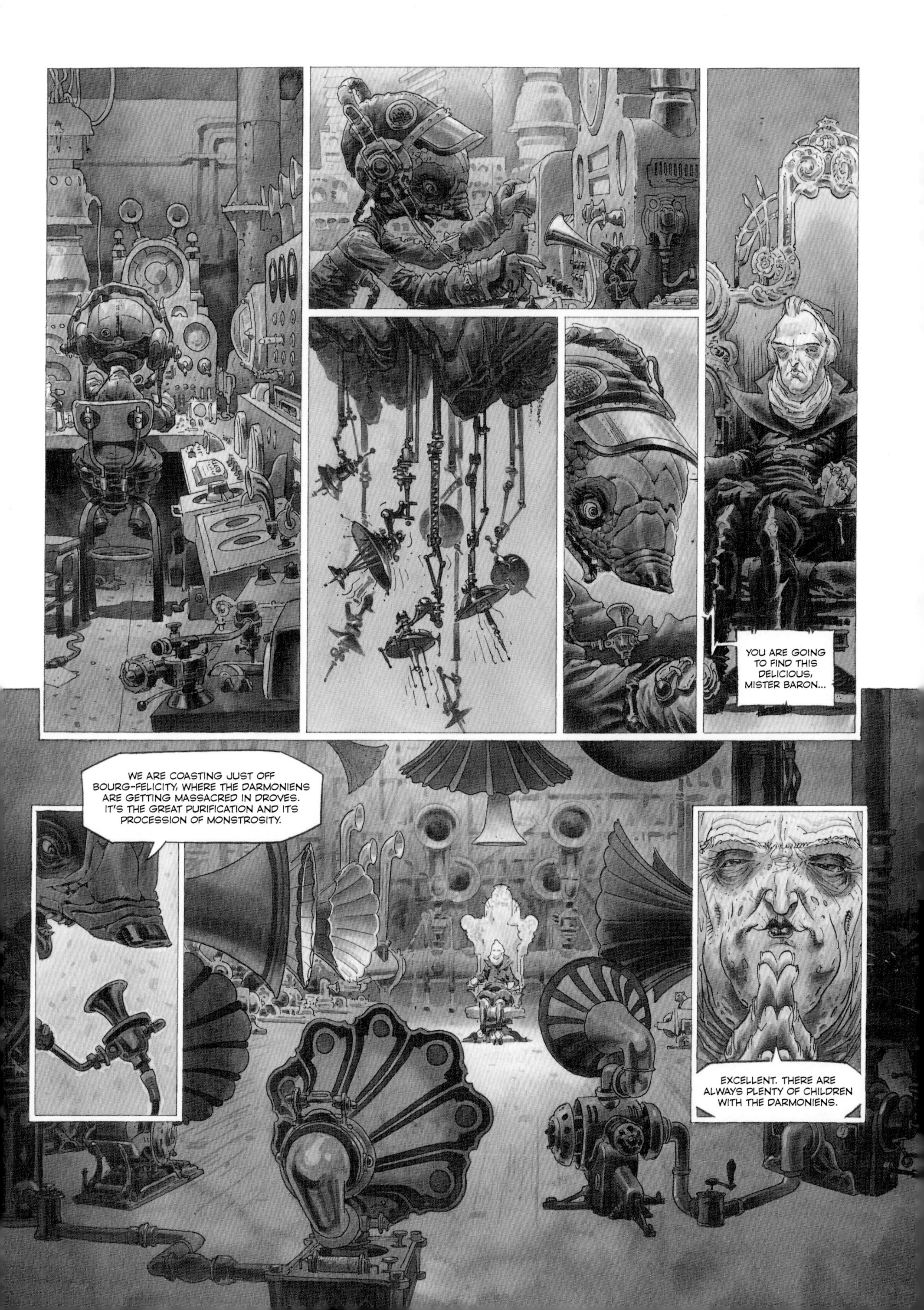
YOU ARE GOING TO FIND THIS DELICIOUS, MISTER BARON...
WE ARE COASTING JUST OFF BOURG-FELICITY, WHERE THE DARMONIENS ARE GETTING MASSACRED IN DROVES. IT'S THE GREAT PURIFICATION AND ITS PROCESSION OF MONSTROSITY.
EXCELLENT. THERE ARE ALWAYS PLENTY OF CHILDREN WITH THE DARMONIENS.

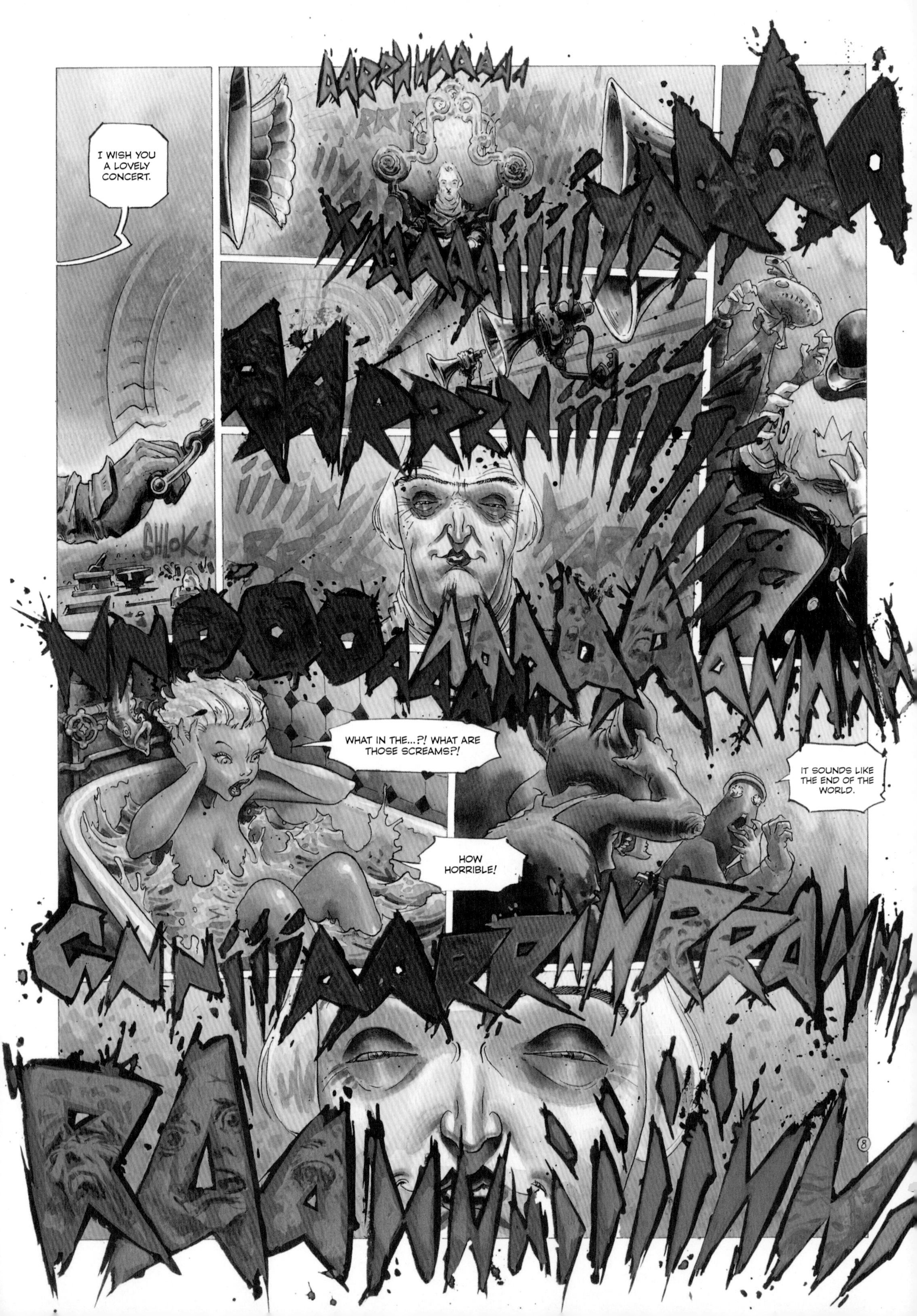
I WISH YOU A LOVELY CONCERT.
AARRHAAAA
SHLOK!
WHAT IN THE...?! WHAT ARE THOSE SCREAMS?!
HOW HORRIBLE!
IT SOUNDS LIKE THE END OF THE WORLD.

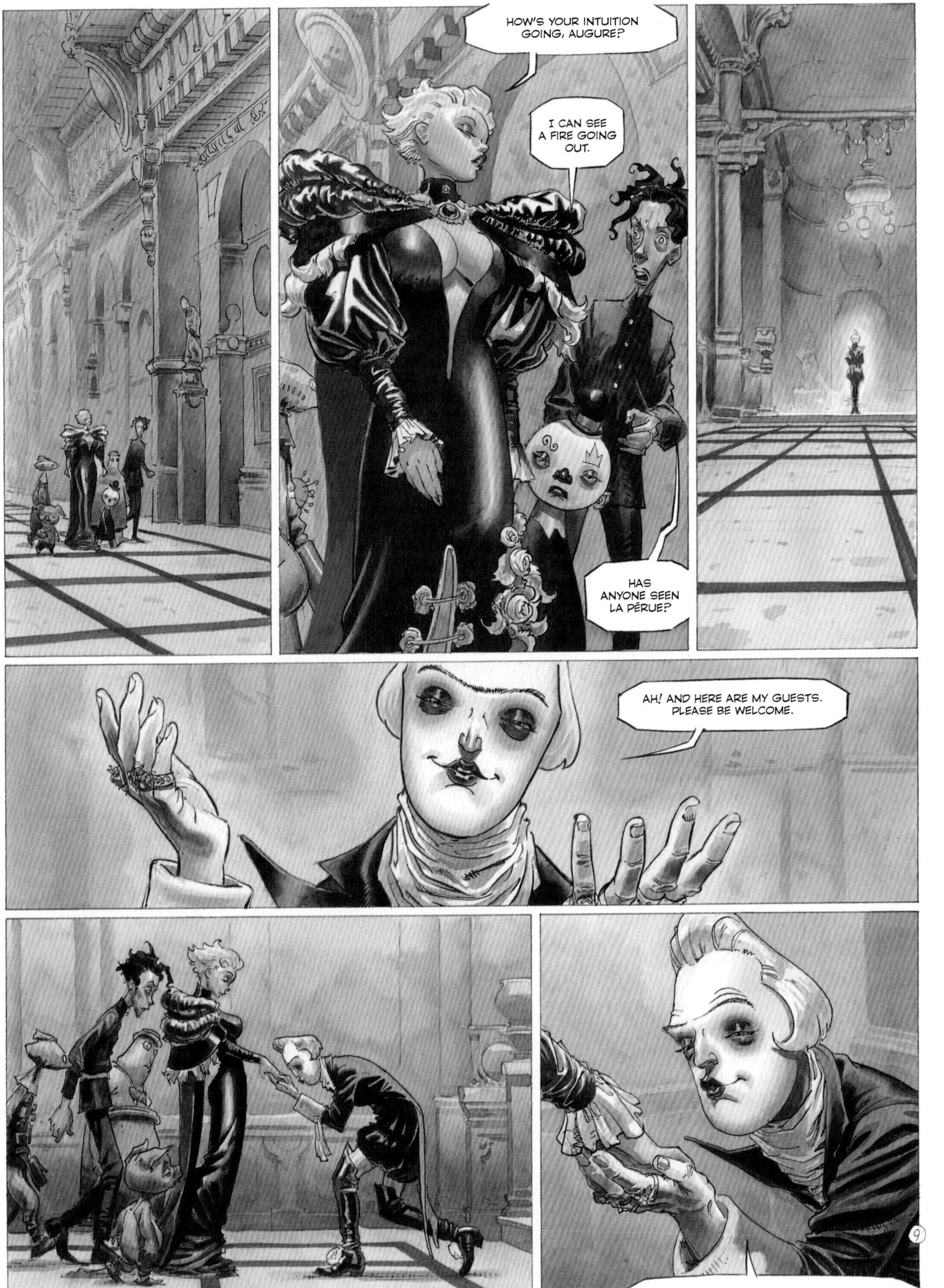
HOW'S YOUR INTUITION GOING, AUGURE?
I CAN SEE A FIRE GOING OUT.
HAS ANYONE SEEN LA PÉRUE?
AH! AND HERE ARE MY GUESTS. PLEASE BE WELCOME.
I AM DELIGHTED TO MEET THE YOUNG AND BEAUTIFUL MANIE GANZA.
9

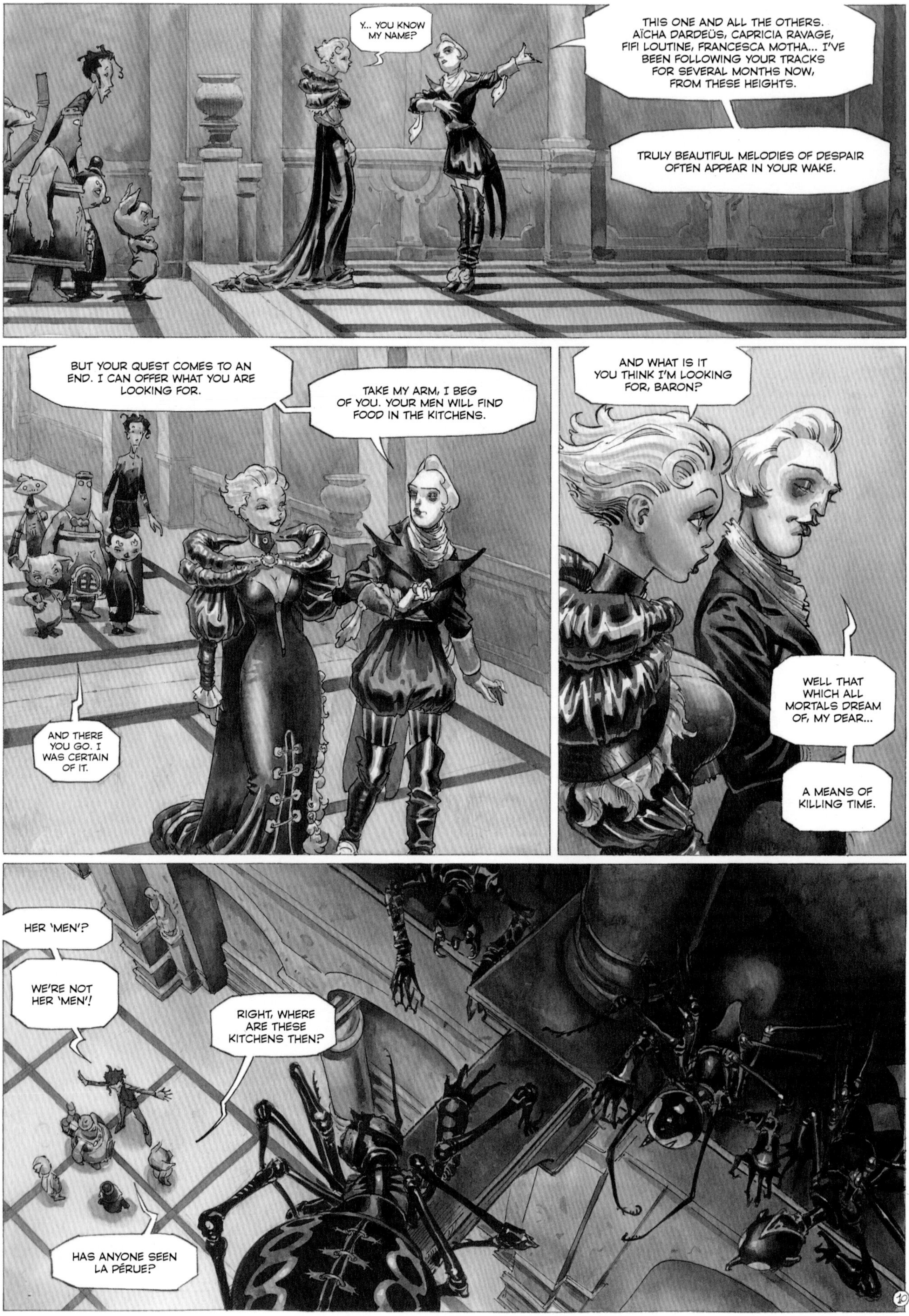

Y... YOU KNOW MY NAME?
THIS ONE AND ALL THE OTHERS. AÏCHA DARDEÜS, CAPRICIA RAVAGE, FIFI LOUTINE, FRANCESCA MOTHA... I'VE BEEN FOLLOWING YOUR TRACKS FOR SEVERAL MONTHS NOW, FROM THESE HEIGHTS.
TRULY BEAUTIFUL MELODIES OF DESPAIR OFTEN APPEAR IN YOUR WAKE.
BUT YOUR QUEST COMES TO AN END. I CAN OFFER WHAT YOU ARE LOOKING FOR.
TAKE MY ARM, I BEG OF YOU. YOUR MEN WILL FIND FOOD IN THE KITCHENS.
AND THERE YOU GO. I WAS CERTAIN OF IT.
AND WHAT IS IT YOU THINK I'M LOOKING FOR, BARON?
WELL THAT WHICH ALL MORTALS DREAM OF, MY DEAR...
A MEANS OF KILLING TIME.
HER 'MEN'?
WE'RE NOT HER 'MEN'!
RIGHT, WHERE ARE THESE KITCHENS THEN?
HAS ANYONE SEEN LA PÉRUE?

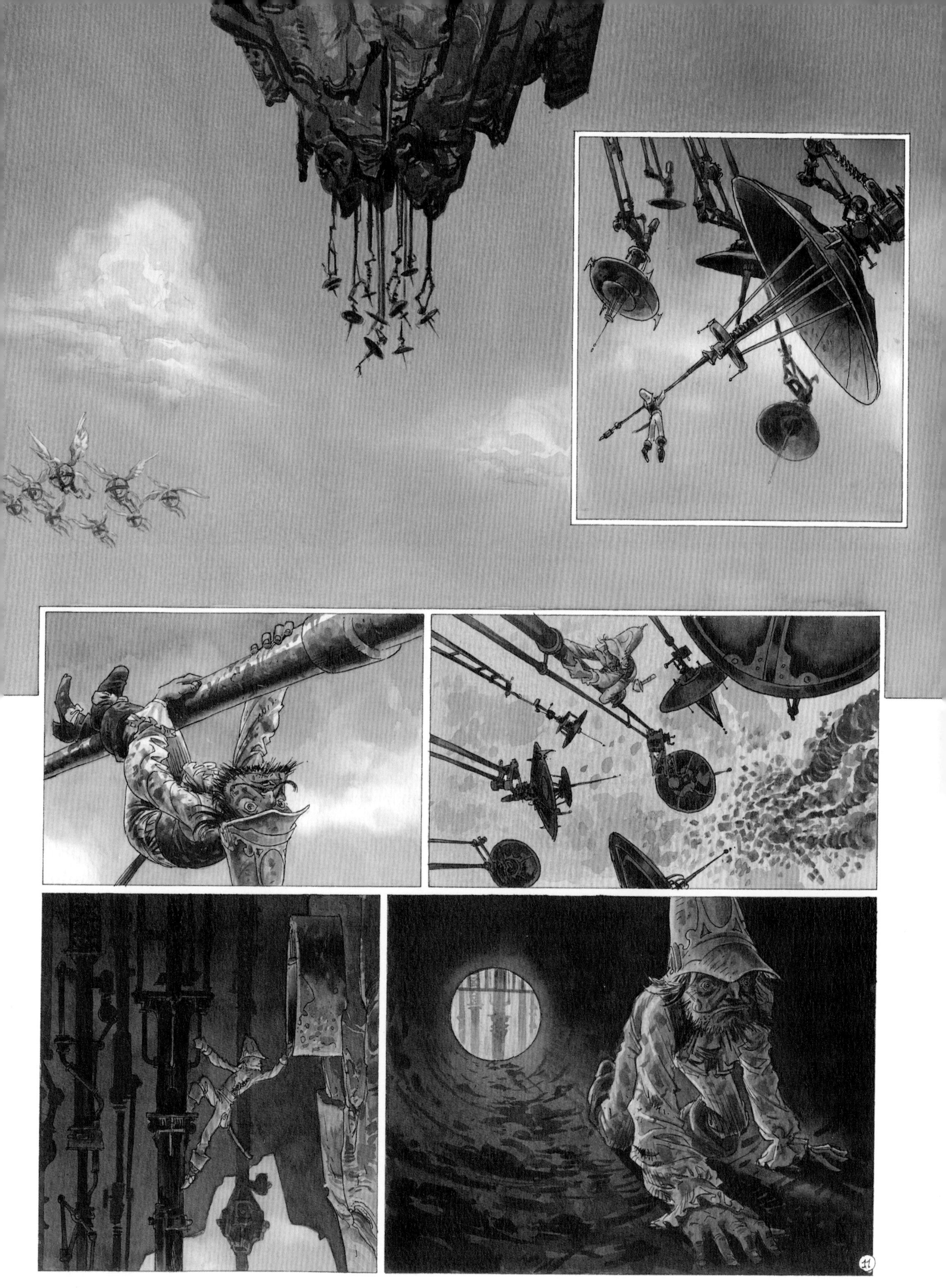

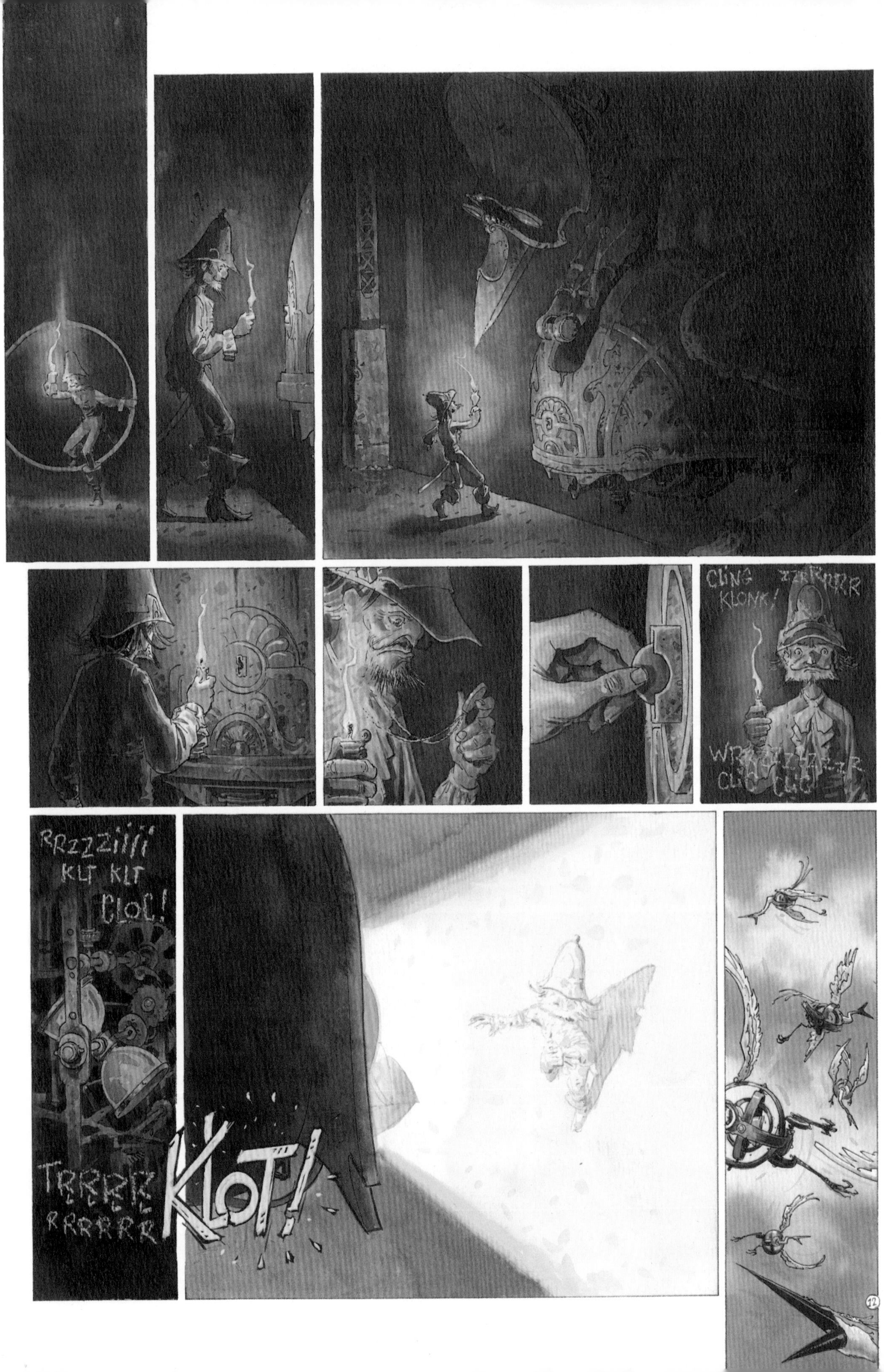
CLING
KLONK!
ZZRRRRR
WRRRZZZRRRR
CLOC CLOC
RRZZZiiii
KLT KLT
CLOC!
TRRRR
RRRRRR
KLOT!

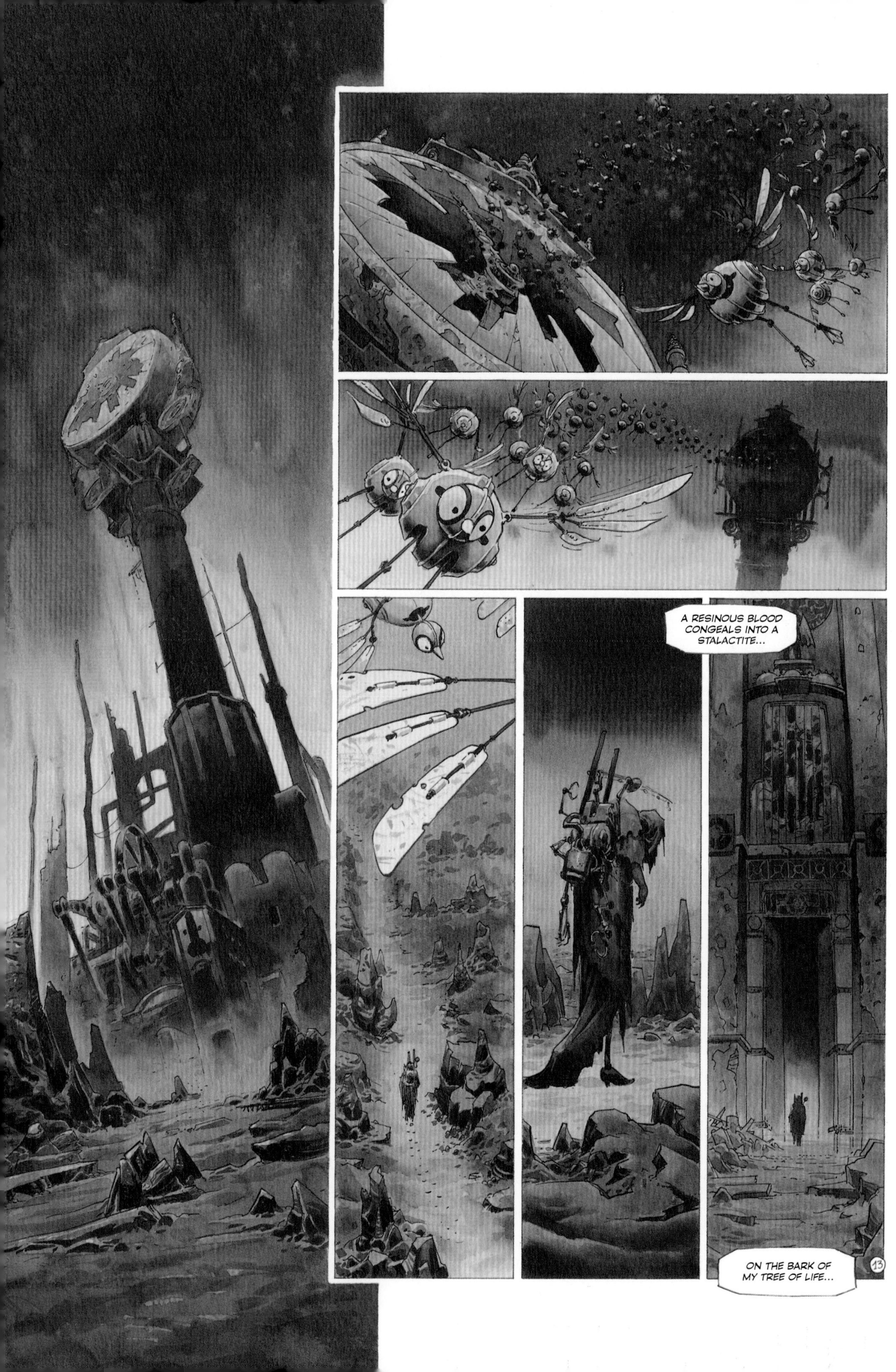
A RESINOUS BLOOD
CONGEALS INTO A
STALACTITE...
ON THE BARK OF
MY TREE OF LIFE...

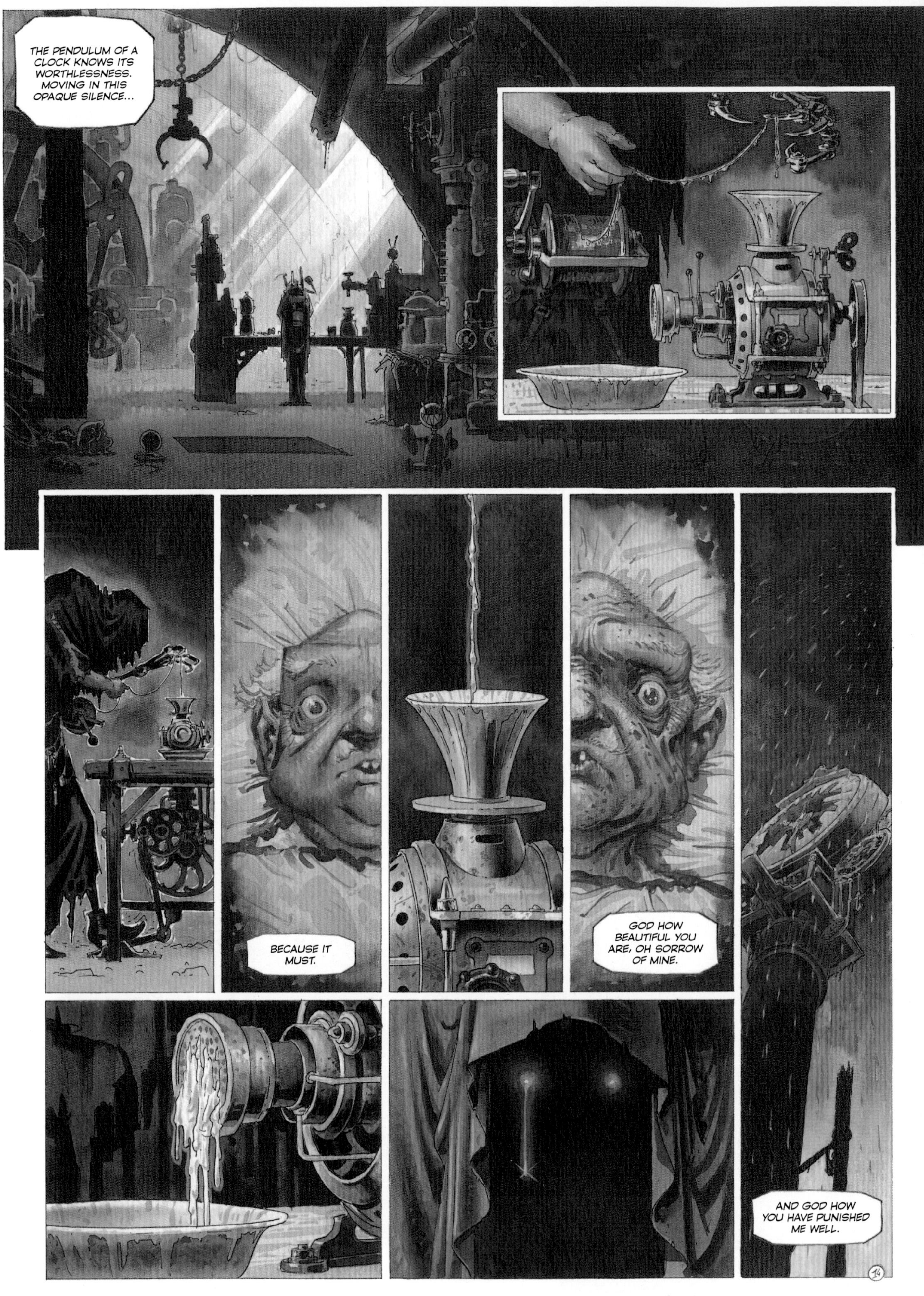

THE PENDULUM OF A CLOCK KNOWS ITS WORTHLESSNESS. MOVING IN THIS OPAQUE SILENCE...
BECAUSE IT MUST.
GOD HOW BEAUTIFUL YOU ARE, OH SORROW OF MINE.
AND GOD HOW YOU HAVE PUNISHED ME WELL.

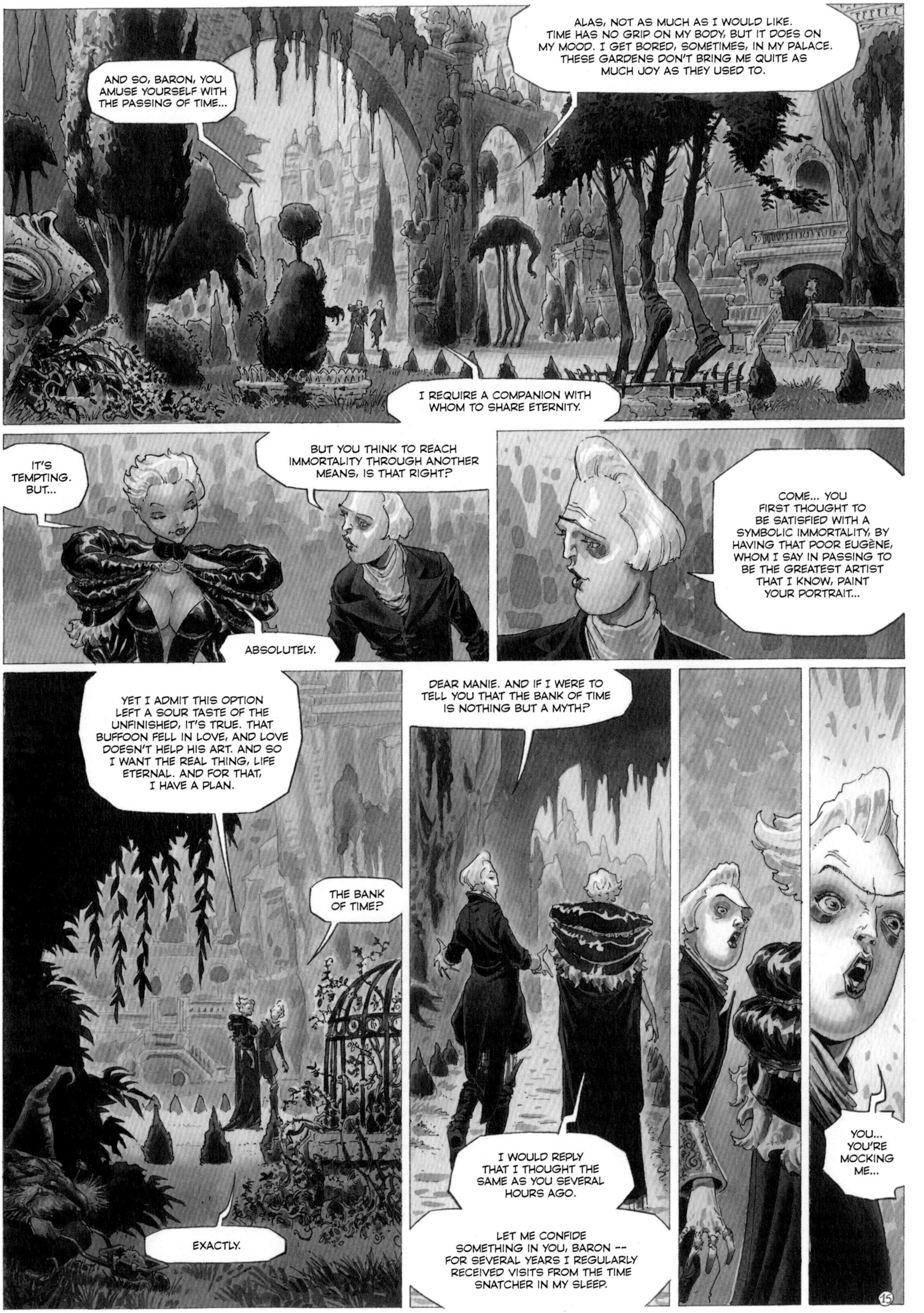
AND SO, BARON, YOU AMUSE YOURSELF WITH THE PASSING OF TIME...
ALAS, NOT AS MUCH AS I WOULD LIKE. TIME HAS NO GRIP ON MY BODY, BUT IT DOES ON MY MOOD. I GET BORED, SOMETIMES, IN MY PALACE. THESE GARDENS DON'T BRING ME QUITE AS MUCH JOY AS THEY USED TO.
I REQUIRE A COMPANION WITH WHOM TO SHARE ETERNITY.
IT'S TEMPTING. BUT...
BUT YOU THINK TO REACH IMMORTALITY THROUGH ANOTHER MEANS, IS THAT RIGHT?
ABSOLUTELY.
COME... YOU FIRST THOUGHT TO BE SATISFIED WITH A SYMBOLIC IMMORTALITY, BY HAVING THAT POOR EUGÈNE, WHOM I SAY IN PASSING TO BE THE GREATEST ARTIST THAT I KNOW, PAINT YOUR PORTRAIT...
YET I ADMIT THIS OPTION LEFT A SOUR TASTE OF THE UNFINISHED, IT'S TRUE. THAT BUFFOON FELL IN LOVE, AND LOVE DOESN'T HELP HIS ART. AND SO I WANT THE REAL THING, LIFE ETERNAL. AND FOR THAT, I HAVE A PLAN.
THE BANK OF TIME?
EXACTLY.
DEAR MANIE. AND IF I WERE TO TELL YOU THAT THE BANK OF TIME IS NOTHING BUT A MYTH?
I WOULD REPLY THAT I THOUGHT THE SAME AS YOU SEVERAL HOURS AGO.
LET ME CONFIDE SOMETHING IN YOU, BARON -- FOR SEVERAL YEARS I REGULARLY RECEIVED VISITS FROM THE TIME SNATCHER IN MY SLEEP.
YOU... YOU'RE MOCKING ME...

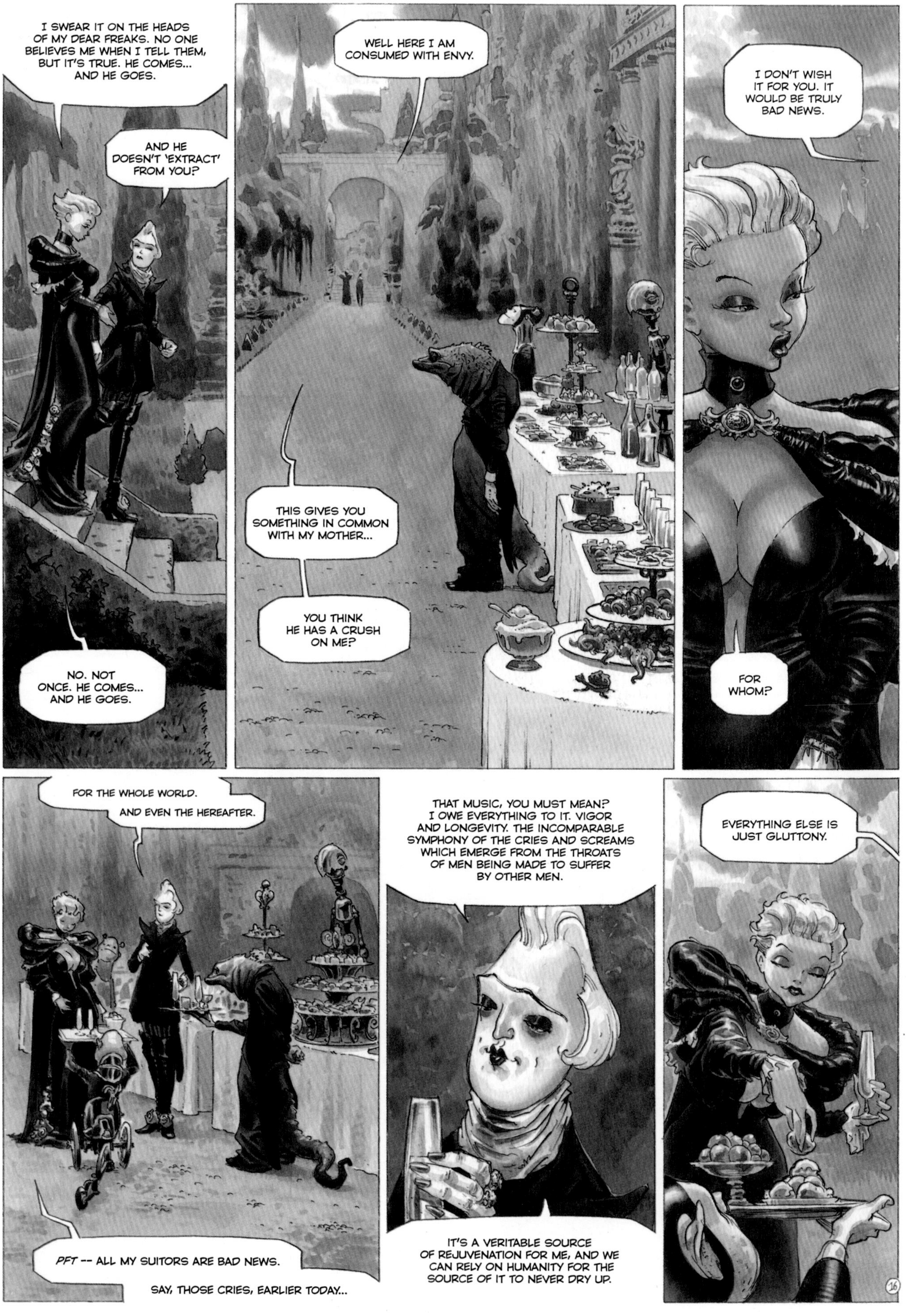

I SWEAR IT ON THE HEADS OF MY DEAR FREAKS. NO ONE BELIEVES ME WHEN I TELL THEM, BUT IT'S TRUE. HE COMES... AND HE GOES.
AND HE DOESN'T 'EXTRACT' FROM YOU?
NO. NOT ONCE. HE COMES... AND HE GOES.
WELL HERE I AM CONSUMED WITH ENVY.
THIS GIVES YOU SOMETHING IN COMMON WITH MY MOTHER...
YOU THINK HE HAS A CRUSH ON ME?
I DON'T WISH IT FOR YOU. IT WOULD BE TRULY BAD NEWS.
FOR WHOM?
FOR THE WHOLE WORLD.
AND EVEN THE HEREAFTER.
PFT -- ALL MY SUITORS ARE BAD NEWS.
SAY, THOSE CRIES, EARLIER TODAY...
THAT MUSIC, YOU MUST MEAN? I OWE EVERYTHING TO IT. VIGOR AND LONGEVITY. THE INCOMPARABLE SYMPHONY OF THE CRIES AND SCREAMS WHICH EMERGE FROM THE THROATS OF MEN BEING MADE TO SUFFER BY OTHER MEN.
IT'S A VERITABLE SOURCE OF REJUVENATION FOR ME, AND WE CAN RELY ON HUMANITY FOR THE SOURCE OF IT TO NEVER DRY UP.
EVERYTHING ELSE IS JUST GLUTTONY.

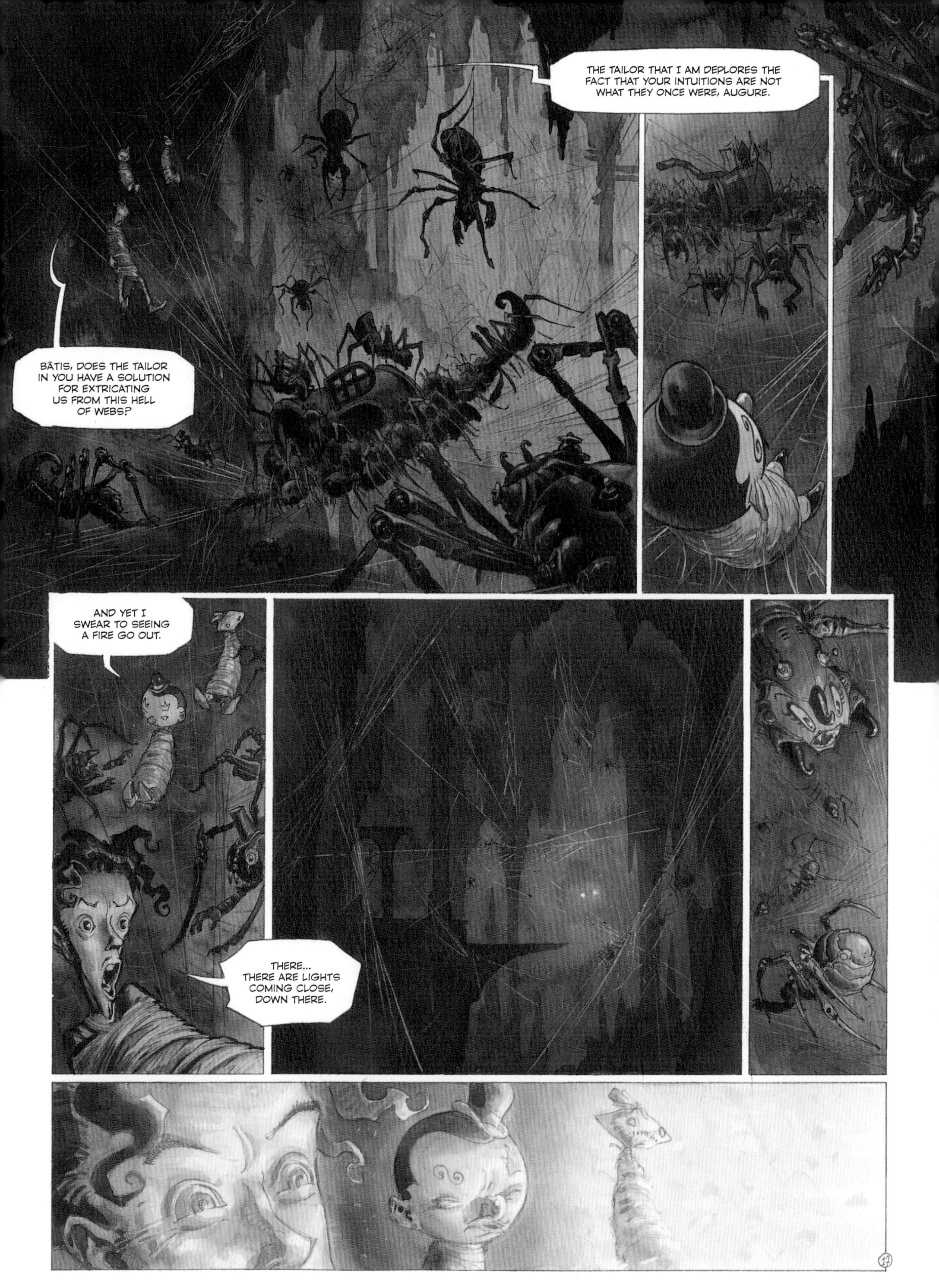
BÂTIS, DOES THE TAILOR IN YOU HAVE A SOLUTION FOR EXTRICATING US FROM THIS HELL OF WEBS?
THE TAILOR THAT I AM DEPLORES THE FACT THAT YOUR INTUITIONS ARE NOT WHAT THEY ONCE WERE, AUGURE.
AND YET I SWEAR TO SEEING A FIRE GO OUT.
THERE... THERE ARE LIGHTS COMING CLOSE, DOWN THERE.

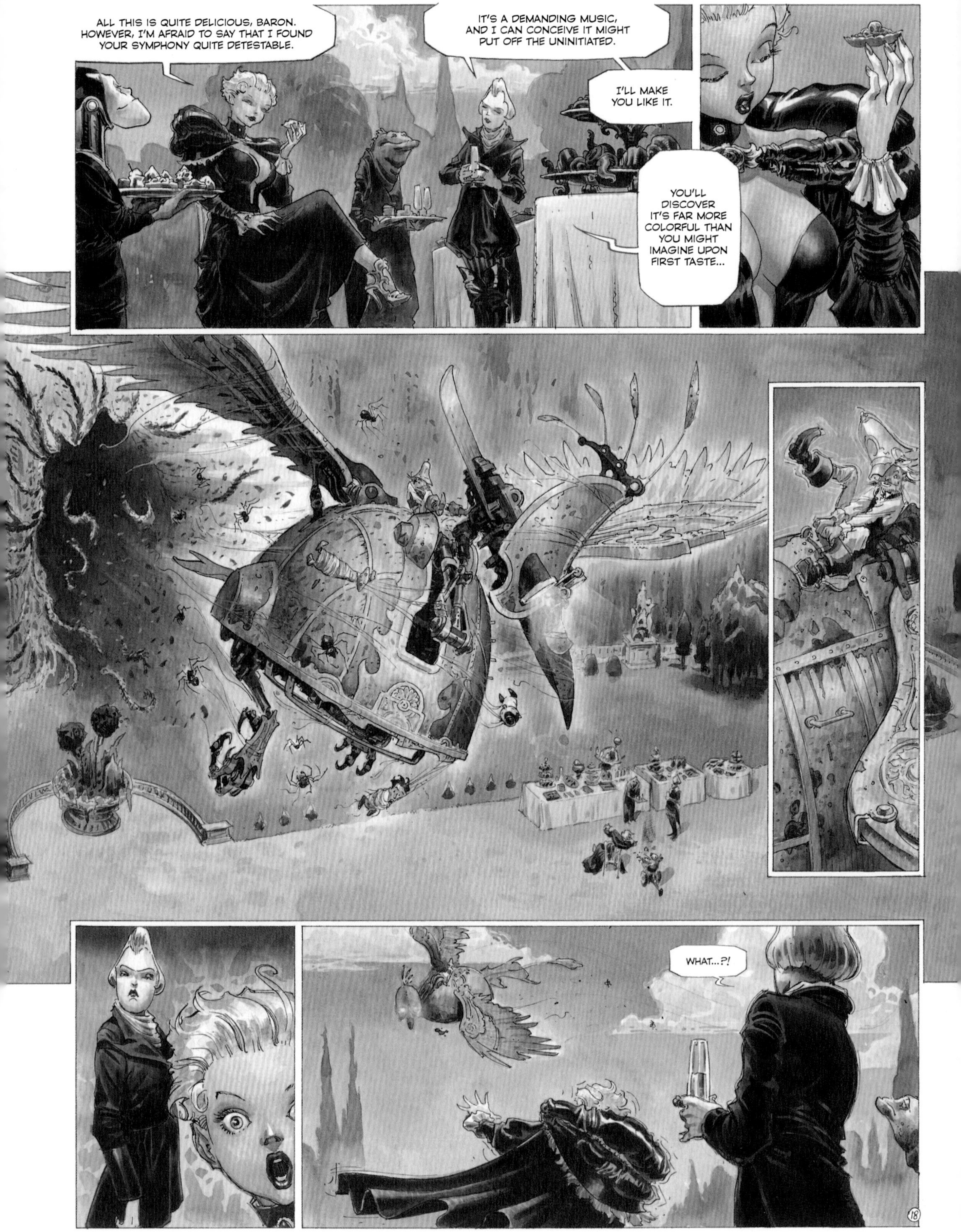
ALL THIS IS QUITE DELICIOUS, BARON. HOWEVER, I'M AFRAID TO SAY THAT I FOUND YOUR SYMPHONY QUITE DETESTABLE.
IT'S A DEMANDING MUSIC, AND I CAN CONCEIVE IT MIGHT PUT OFF THE UNINITIATED.
I'LL MAKE YOU LIKE IT.
YOU'LL DISCOVER IT'S FAR MORE COLORFUL THAN YOU MIGHT IMAGINE UPON FIRST TASTE...
WHAT...?!
18

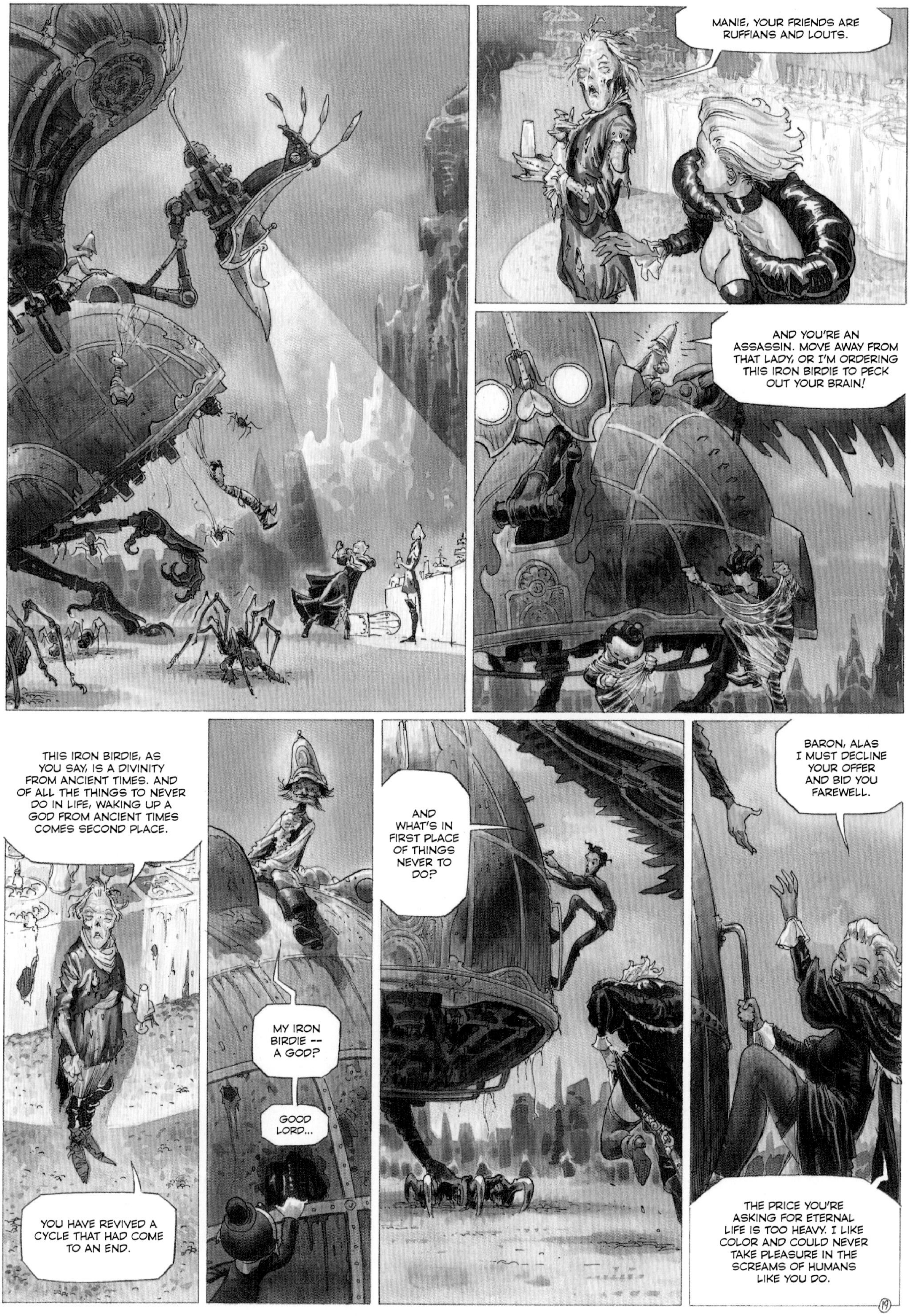

MANIE, YOUR FRIENDS ARE RUFFIANS AND LOUTS.
AND YOU'RE AN ASSASSIN. MOVE AWAY FROM THAT LADY, OR I'M ORDERING THIS IRON BIRDIE TO PECK OUT YOUR BRAIN!
THIS IRON BIRDIE, AS YOU SAY, IS A DIVINITY FROM ANCIENT TIMES. AND OF ALL THE THINGS TO NEVER DO IN LIFE, WAKING UP A GOD FROM ANCIENT TIMES COMES SECOND PLACE.
YOU HAVE REVIVED A CYCLE THAT HAD COME TO AN END.
MY IRON BIRDIE -- A GOD?
GOOD LORD...
AND WHAT'S IN FIRST PLACE OF THINGS NEVER TO DO?
BARON, ALAS I MUST DECLINE YOUR OFFER AND BID YOU FAREWELL.
THE PRICE YOU'RE ASKING FOR ETERNAL LIFE IS TOO HEAVY. I LIKE COLOR AND COULD NEVER TAKE PLEASURE IN THE SCREAMS OF HUMANS LIKE YOU DO.

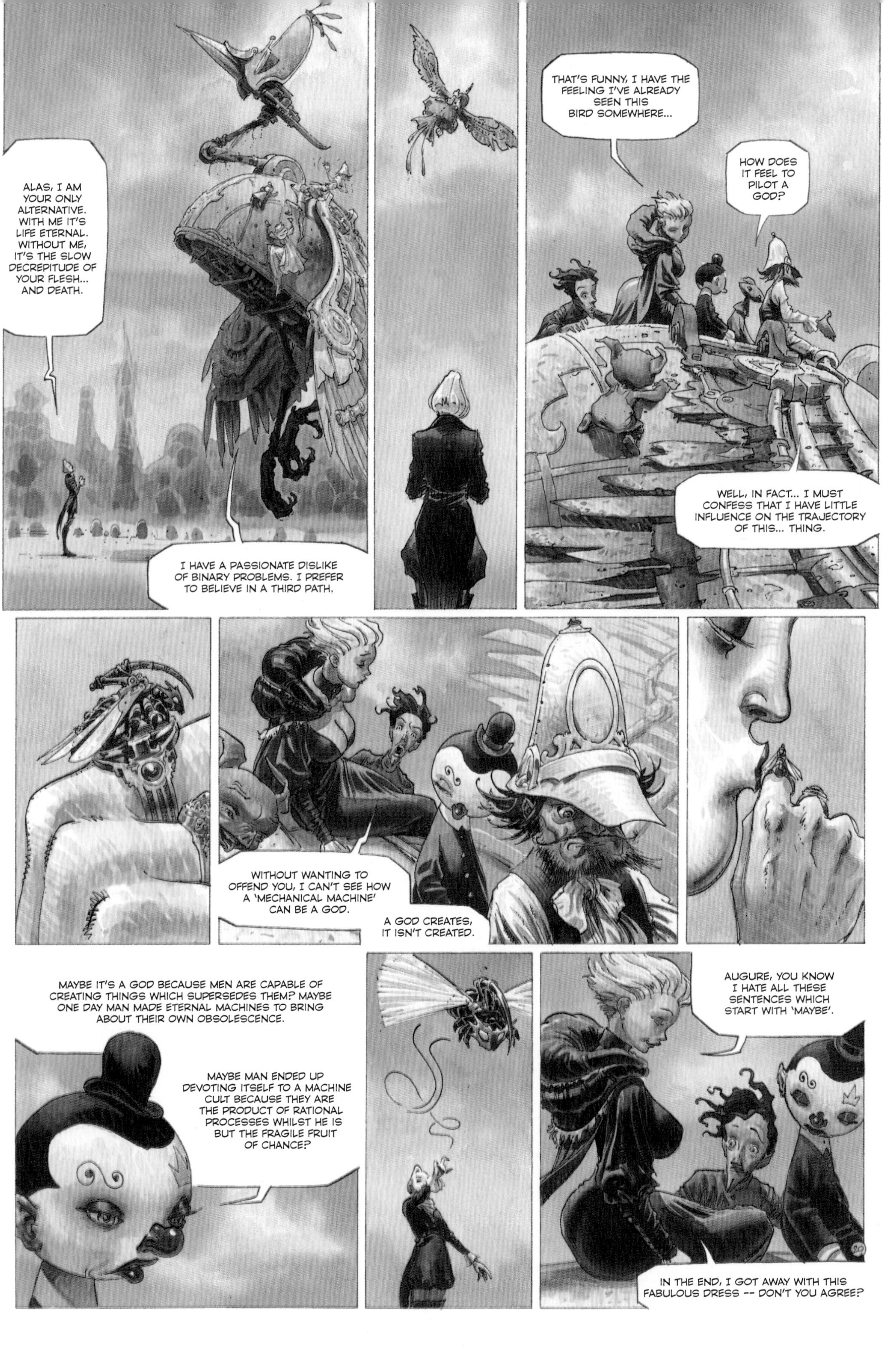

ALAS, I AM YOUR ONLY ALTERNATIVE. WITH ME IT'S LIFE ETERNAL. WITHOUT ME, IT'S THE SLOW DECREPITUDE OF YOUR FLESH... AND DEATH.
I HAVE A PASSIONATE DISLIKE OF BINARY PROBLEMS. I PREFER TO BELIEVE IN A THIRD PATH.
THAT'S FUNNY, I HAVE THE FEELING I'VE ALREADY SEEN THIS BIRD SOMEWHERE...
HOW DOES IT FEEL TO PILOT A GOD?
WELL, IN FACT... I MUST CONFESS THAT I HAVE LITTLE INFLUENCE ON THE TRAJECTORY OF THIS... THING.
WITHOUT WANTING TO OFFEND YOU, I CAN'T SEE HOW A 'MECHANICAL MACHINE' CAN BE A GOD.
A GOD CREATES, IT ISN'T CREATED.
MAYBE IT'S A GOD BECAUSE MEN ARE CAPABLE OF CREATING THINGS WHICH SUPERSEDES THEM? MAYBE ONE DAY MAN MADE ETERNAL MACHINES TO BRING ABOUT THEIR OWN OBSOLESCENCE.
MAYBE MAN ENDED UP DEVOTING ITSELF TO A MACHINE CULT BECAUSE THEY ARE THE PRODUCT OF RATIONAL PROCESSES WHILST HE IS BUT THE FRAGILE FRUIT OF CHANCE?
AUGURE, YOU KNOW I HATE ALL THESE SENTENCES WHICH START WITH 'MAYBE'.
IN THE END, I GOT AWAY WITH THIS FABULOUS DRESS -- DON'T YOU AGREE?

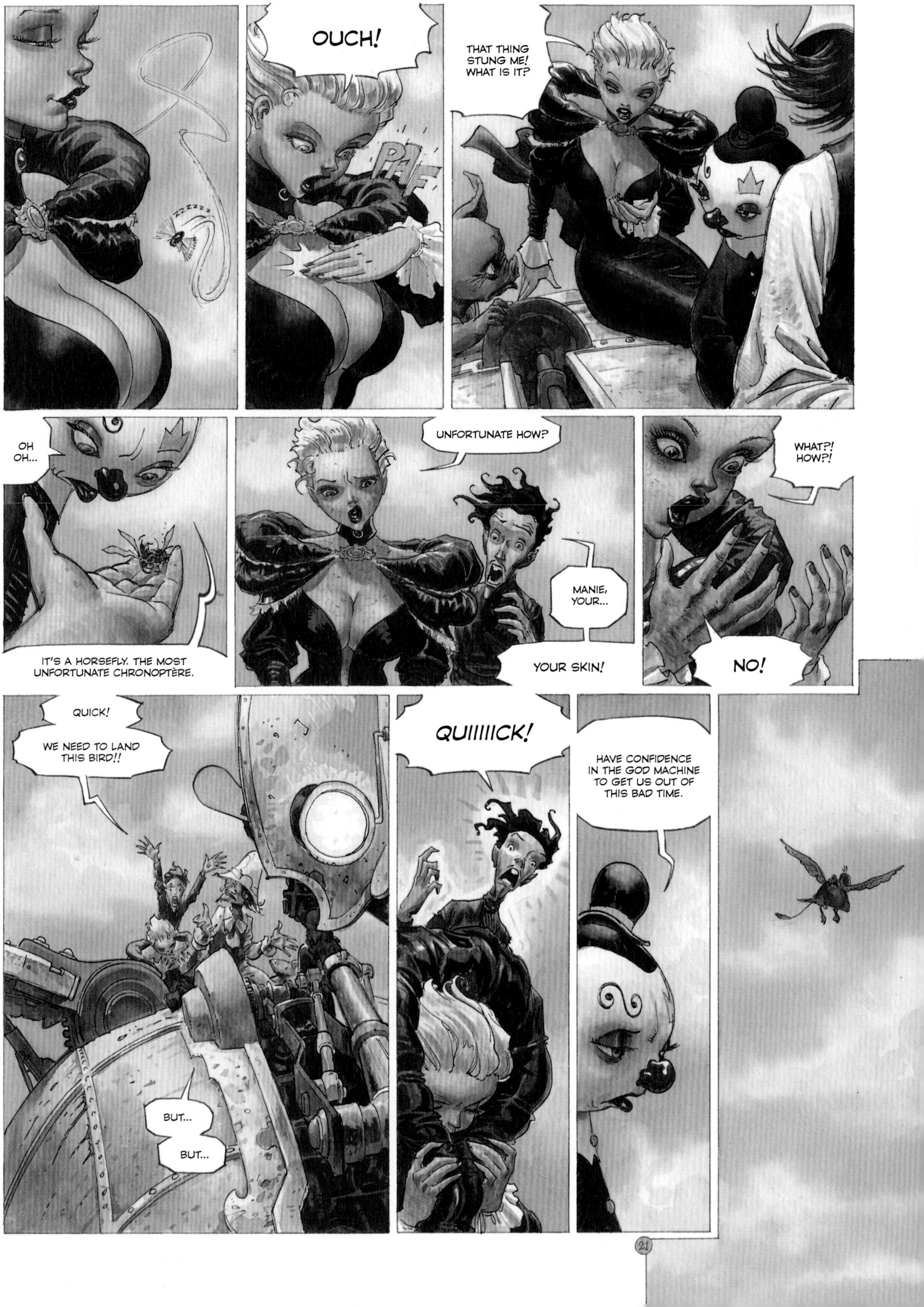
OUCH!
PAF
THAT THING STUNG ME! WHAT IS IT?
OH OH...
IT'S A HORSEFLY. THE MOST UNFORTUNATE CHRONOPTÈRE.
UNFORTUNATE HOW?
MANIE, YOUR...
YOUR SKIN!
WHAT?! HOW?!
NO!
QUICK!
WE NEED TO LAND THIS BIRD!!
BUT...
BUT...
QUIIIIICK!
HAVE CONFIDENCE IN THE GOD MACHINE TO GET US OUT OF THIS BAD TIME.

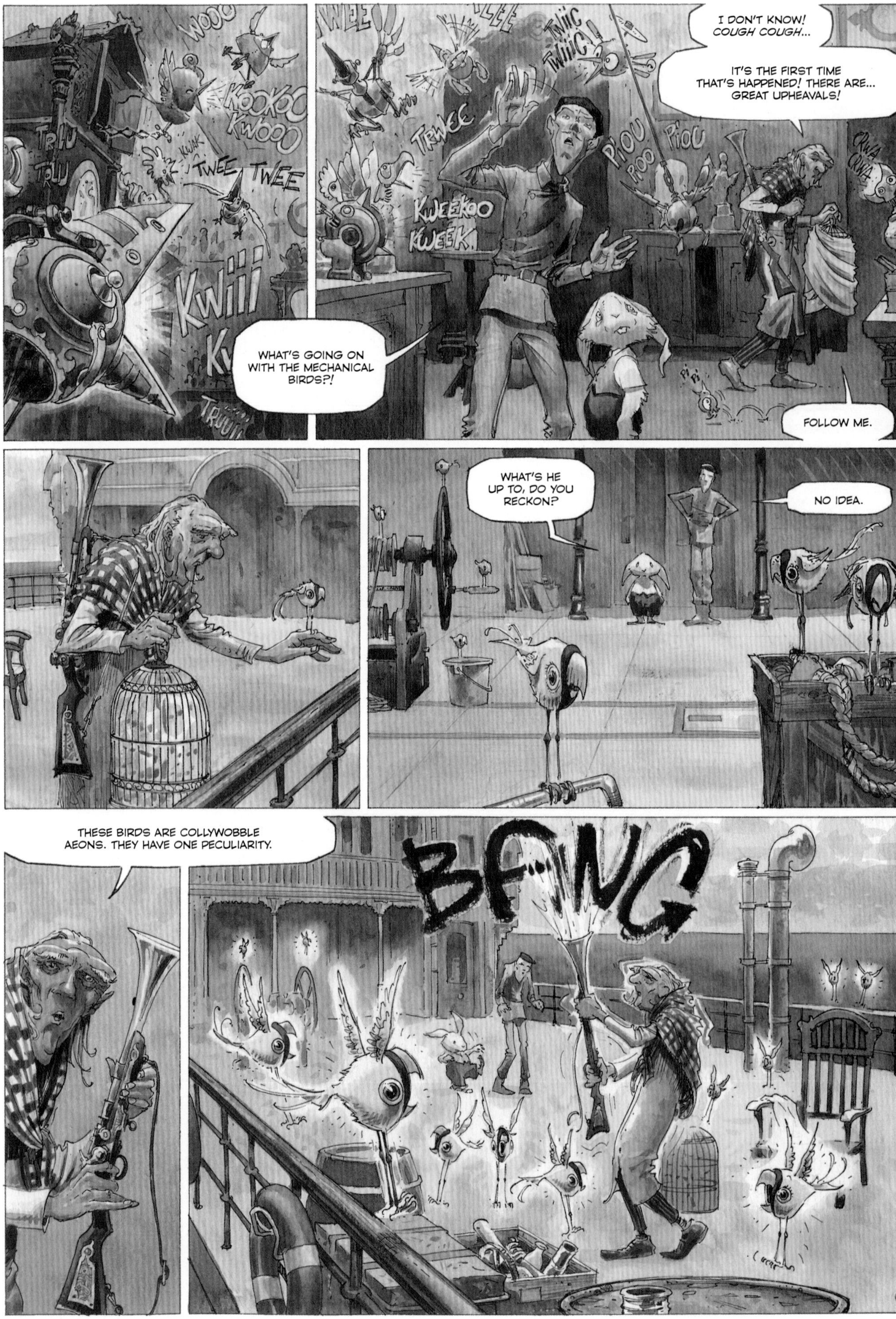
WOOO
KOOKOO
KWOOO
TWEE TWEE
KWIII
TWIIC
TWIIIC
TRWEE
PIOU
ROO
PIOU
KWEEKOO
KWEEK
CRWA
CRWA
WHAT'S GOING ON WITH THE MECHANICAL BIRDS?!
I DON'T KNOW! COUGH COUGH...
IT'S THE FIRST TIME THAT'S HAPPENED! THERE ARE... GREAT UPHEAVALS!
FOLLOW ME.
WHAT'S HE UP TO, DO YOU RECKON?
NO IDEA.
THESE BIRDS ARE COLLYWOBBLE AEONS. THEY HAVE ONE PECULIARITY.
BANG

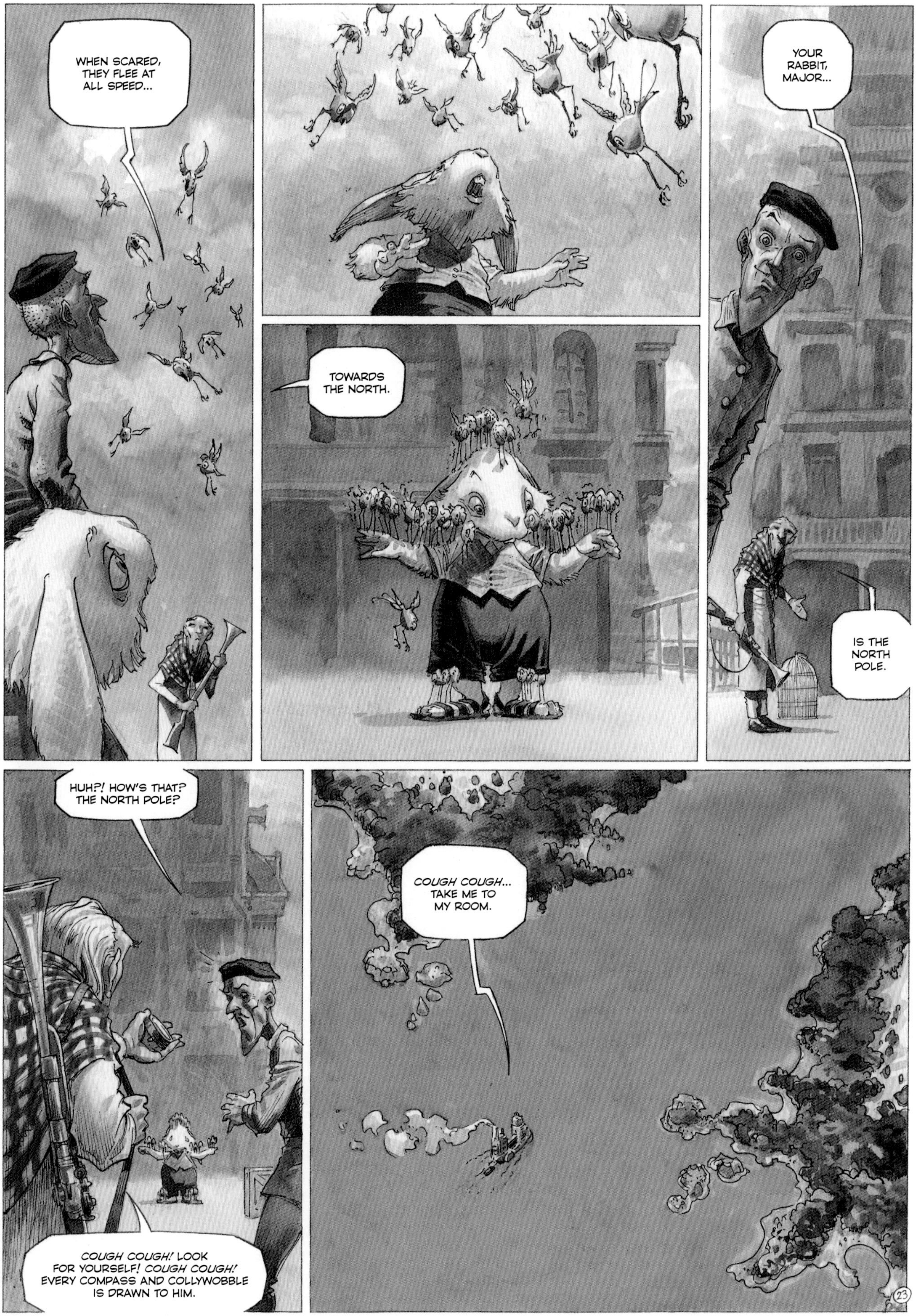
WHEN SCARED, THEY FLEE AT ALL SPEED...
YOUR RABBIT, MAJOR...
TOWARDS THE NORTH.
IS THE NORTH POLE.
HUH?! HOW'S THAT? THE NORTH POLE?
COUGH COUGH! LOOK FOR YOURSELF! COUGH COUGH! EVERY COMPASS AND COLLYWOBBLE IS DRAWN TO HIM.
COUGH COUGH... TAKE ME TO MY ROOM.
23

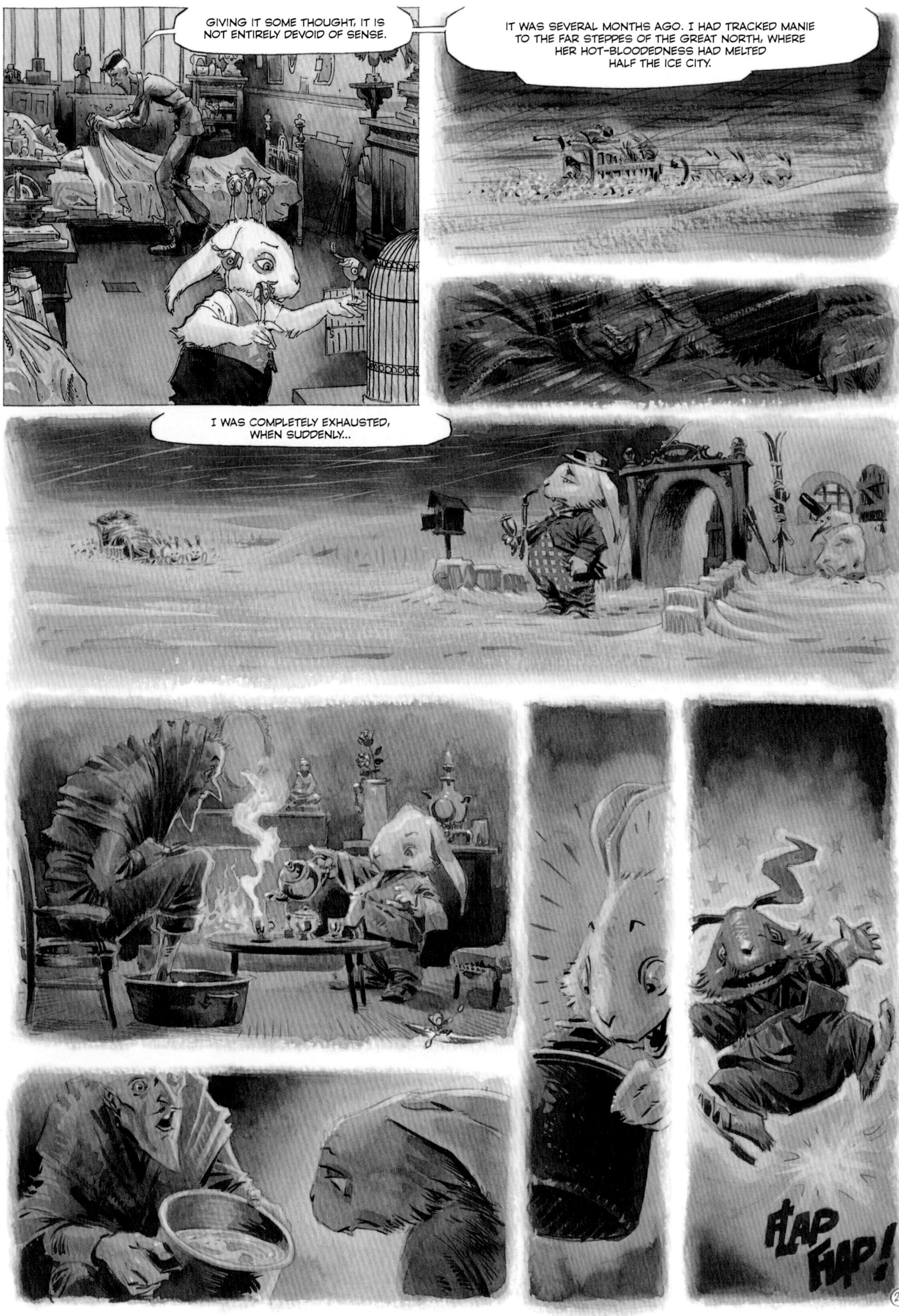
GIVING IT SOME THOUGHT, IT IS NOT ENTIRELY DEVOID OF SENSE.
IT WAS SEVERAL MONTHS AGO. I HAD TRACKED MANIE TO THE FAR STEPPES OF THE GREAT NORTH, WHERE HER HOT-BLOODEDNESS HAD MELTED HALF THE ICE CITY.
I WAS COMPLETELY EXHAUSTED, WHEN SUDDENLY...
FLAP FLAP!

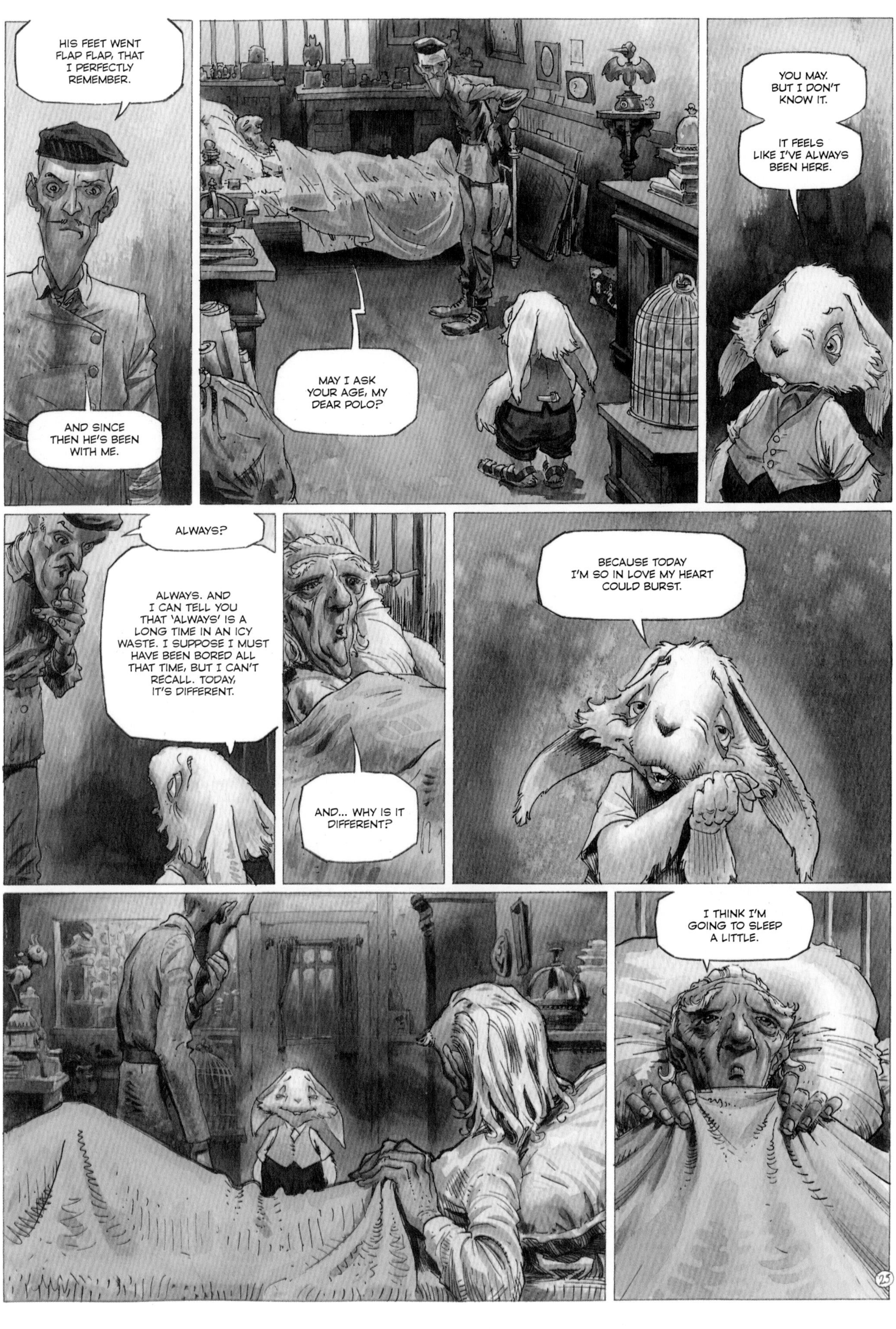

HIS FEET WENT FLAP FLAP, THAT I PERFECTLY REMEMBER.
AND SINCE THEN HE'S BEEN WITH ME.
MAY I ASK YOUR AGE, MY DEAR POLO?
YOU MAY. BUT I DON'T KNOW IT.
IT FEELS LIKE I'VE ALWAYS BEEN HERE.
ALWAYS?
ALWAYS. AND I CAN TELL YOU THAT 'ALWAYS' IS A LONG TIME IN AN ICY WASTE. I SUPPOSE I MUST HAVE BEEN BORED ALL THAT TIME, BUT I CAN'T RECALL. TODAY, IT'S DIFFERENT.
AND... WHY IS IT DIFFERENT?
BECAUSE TODAY I'M SO IN LOVE MY HEART COULD BURST.
I THINK I'M GOING TO SLEEP A LITTLE.

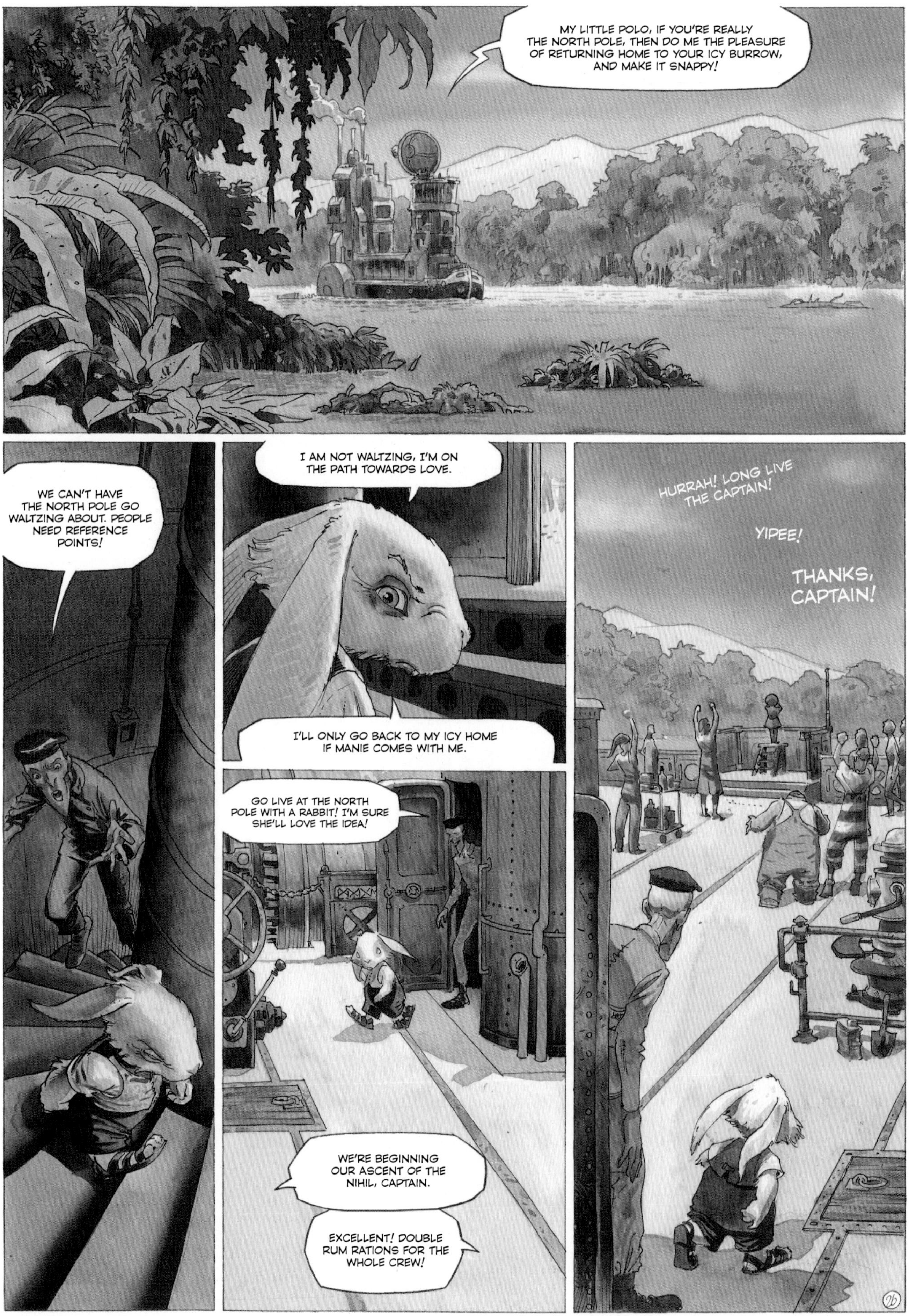
MY LITTLE POLO, IF YOU'RE REALLY THE NORTH POLE, THEN DO ME THE PLEASURE OF RETURNING HOME TO YOUR ICY BURROW, AND MAKE IT SNAPPY!
WE CAN'T HAVE THE NORTH POLE GO WALTZING ABOUT. PEOPLE NEED REFERENCE POINTS!
I AM NOT WALTZING, I'M ON THE PATH TOWARDS LOVE.
I'LL ONLY GO BACK TO MY ICY HOME IF MANIE COMES WITH ME.
GO LIVE AT THE NORTH POLE WITH A RABBIT! I'M SURE SHE'LL LOVE THE IDEA!
WE'RE BEGINNING OUR ASCENT OF THE NIHIL, CAPTAIN.
EXCELLENT! DOUBLE RUM RATIONS FOR THE WHOLE CREW!
HURRAH! LONG LIVE THE CAPTAIN!
YIPEE!
THANKS, CAPTAIN!

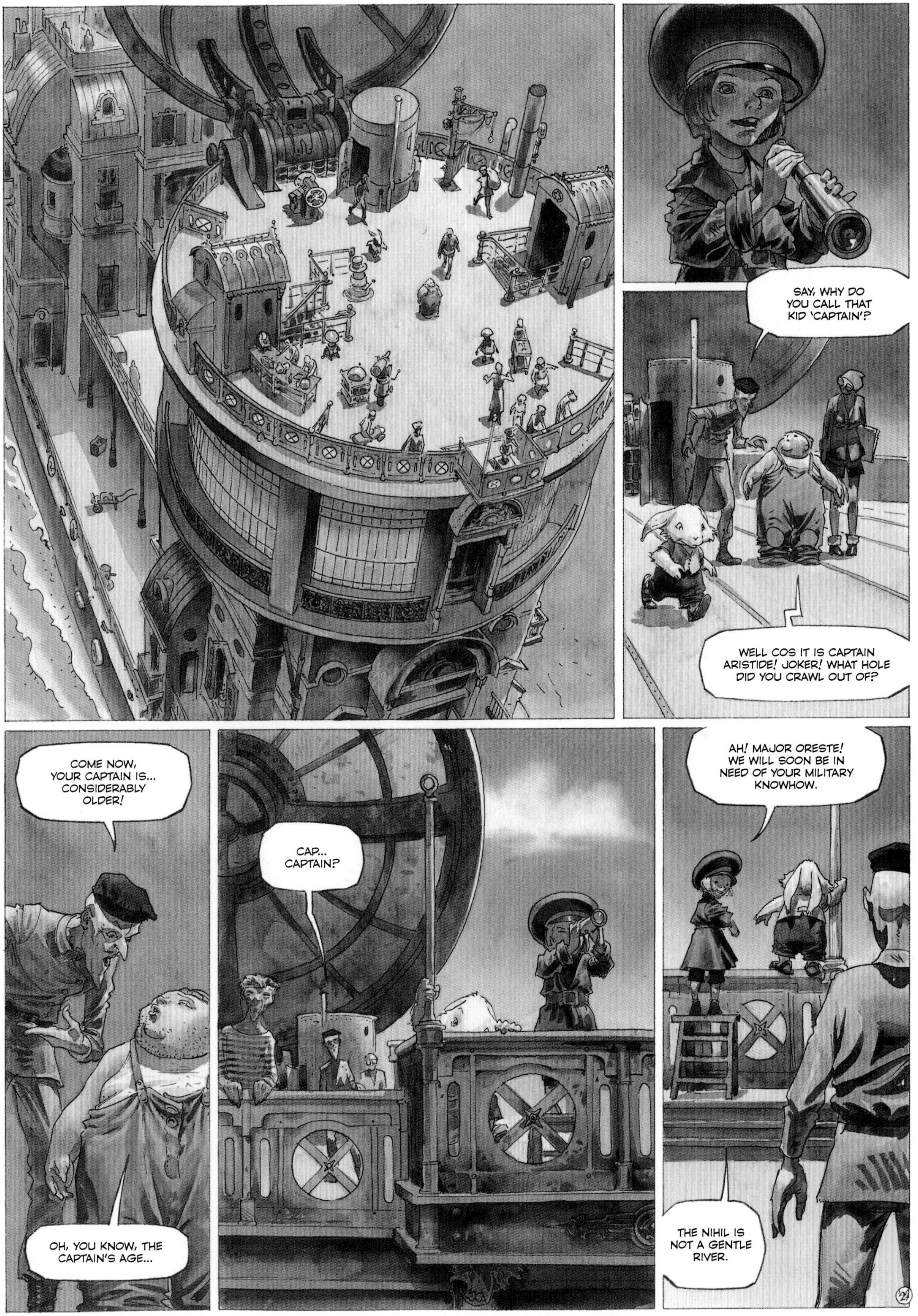
SAY, WHY DO YOU CALL THAT KID 'CAPTAIN'?
WELL COS IT IS CAPTAIN ARISTIDE! JOKER! WHAT HOLE DID YOU CRAWL OUT OF?
COME NOW, YOUR CAPTAIN IS... CONSIDERABLY OLDER!
OH, YOU KNOW, THE CAPTAIN'S AGE...
CAP... CAPTAIN?
AH! MAJOR ORESTE! WE WILL SOON BE IN NEED OF YOUR MILITARY KNOWHOW.
THE NIHIL IS NOT A GENTLE RIVER.
24

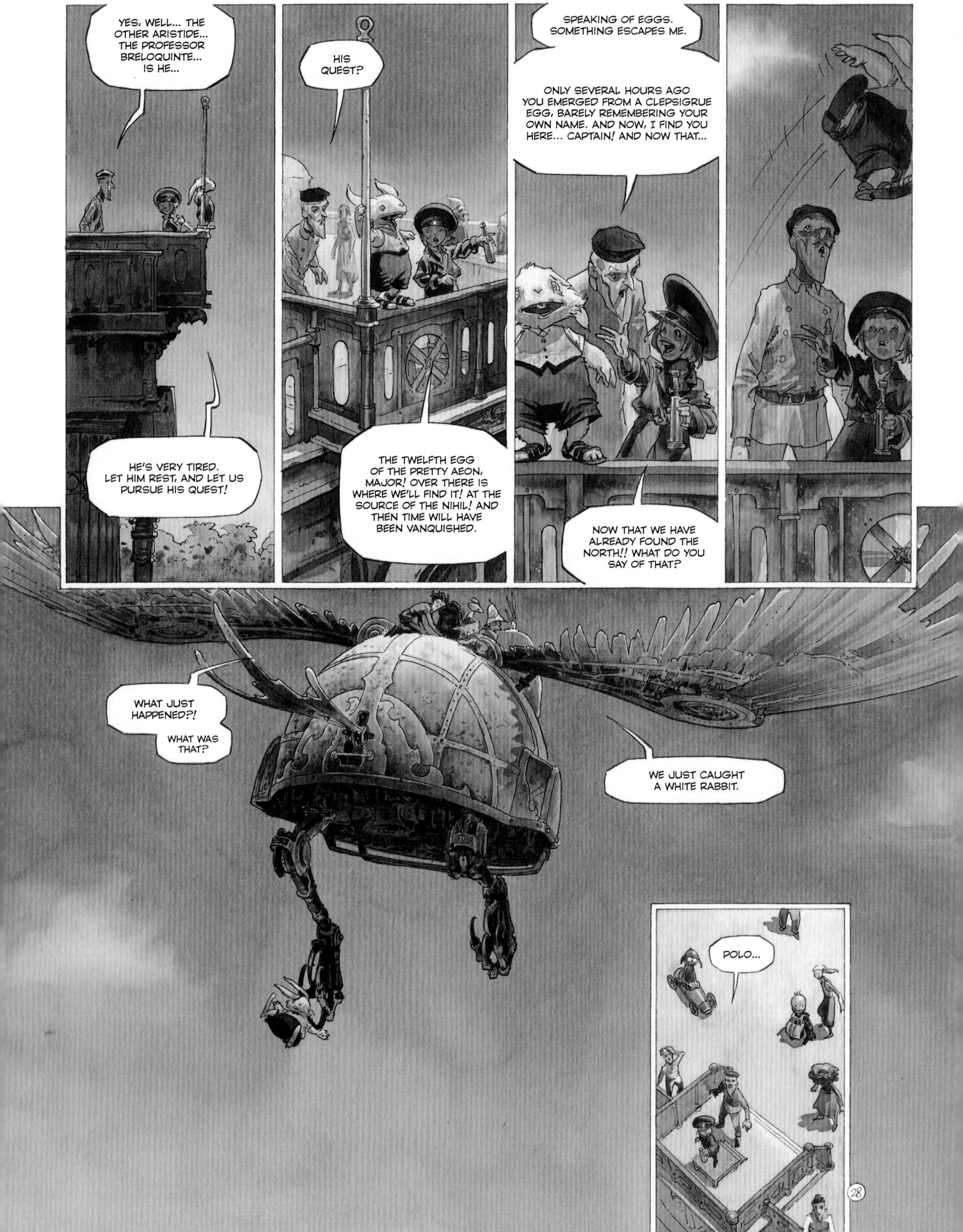
YES, WELL... THE OTHER ARISTIDE... THE PROFESSOR BRELOQUINTE... IS HE...
HE'S VERY TIRED. LET HIM REST, AND LET US PURSUE HIS QUEST!
HIS QUEST?
THE TWELFTH EGG OF THE PRETTY AEON, MAJOR! OVER THERE IS WHERE WE'LL FIND IT! AT THE SOURCE OF THE NIHIL! AND THEN TIME WILL HAVE BEEN VANQUISHED.
SPEAKING OF EGGS. SOMETHING ESCAPES ME.
ONLY SEVERAL HOURS AGO YOU EMERGED FROM A CLEPSIGRUE EGG, BARELY REMEMBERING YOUR OWN NAME. AND NOW, I FIND YOU HERE... CAPTAIN! AND NOW THAT...
NOW THAT WE HAVE ALREADY FOUND THE NORTH!! WHAT DO YOU SAY OF THAT?
WHAT JUST HAPPENED?!
WHAT WAS THAT?
WE JUST CAUGHT A WHITE RABBIT.
POLO...

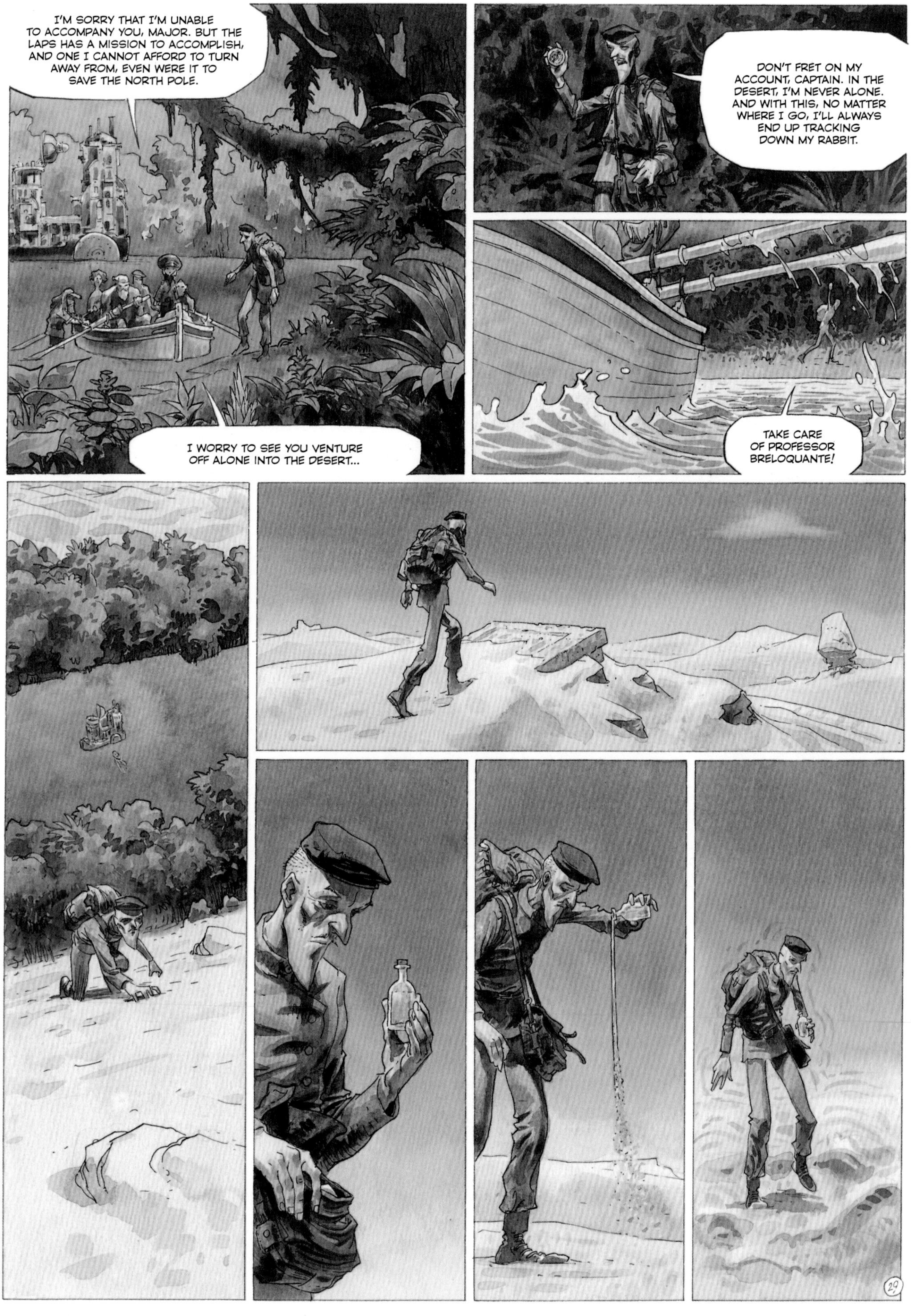
I'M SORRY THAT I'M UNABLE TO ACCOMPANY YOU, MAJOR. BUT THE LAPS HAS A MISSION TO ACCOMPLISH, AND ONE I CANNOT AFFORD TO TURN AWAY FROM, EVEN WERE IT TO SAVE THE NORTH POLE.
I WORRY TO SEE YOU VENTURE OFF ALONE INTO THE DESERT...
DON'T FRET ON MY ACCOUNT, CAPTAIN. IN THE DESERT, I'M NEVER ALONE. AND WITH THIS, NO MATTER WHERE I GO, I'LL ALWAYS END UP TRACKING DOWN MY RABBIT.
TAKE CARE OF PROFESSOR BRELOQUANTE!

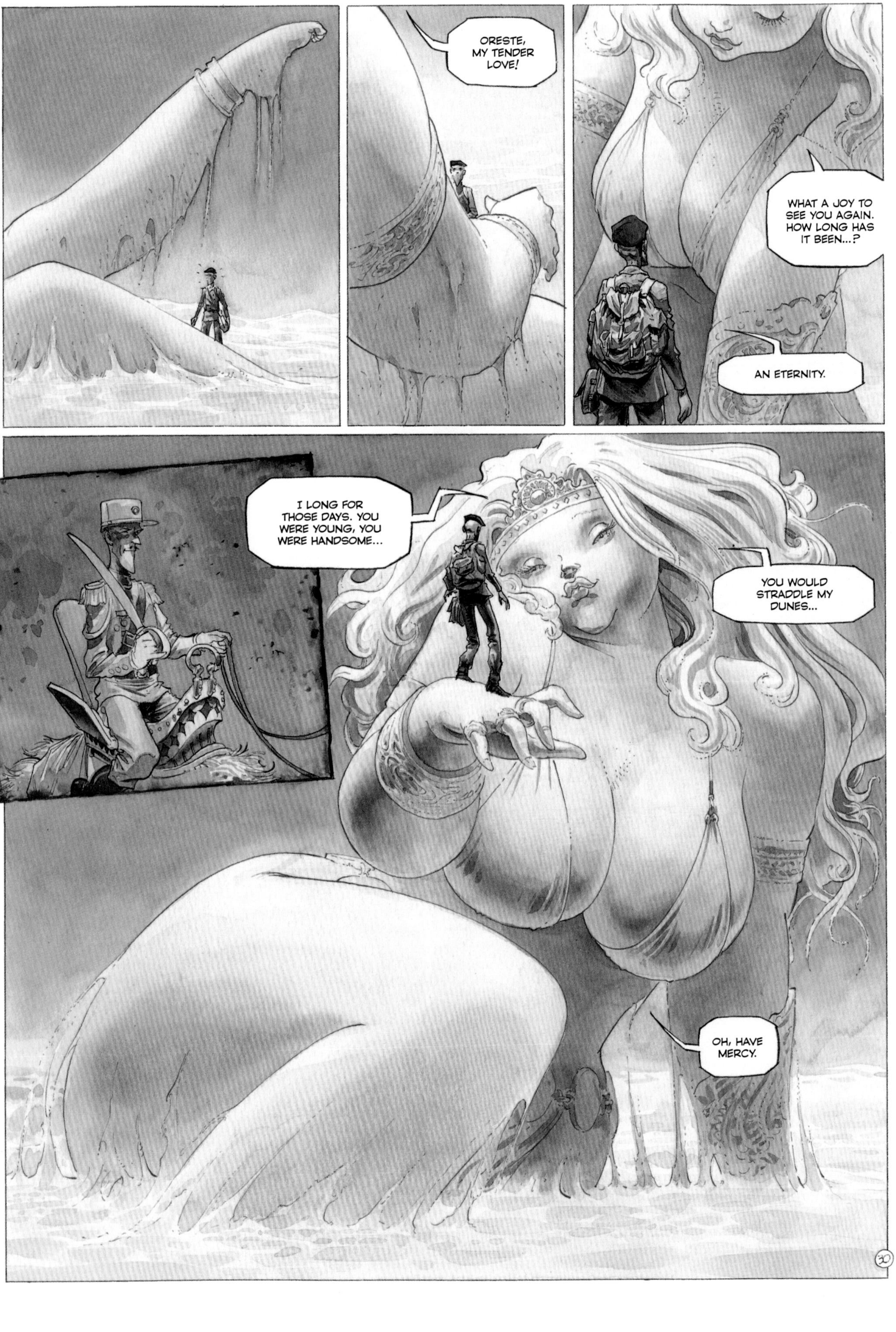
ORESTE, MY TENDER LOVE!
WHAT A JOY TO SEE YOU AGAIN. HOW LONG HAS IT BEEN...?
AN ETERNITY.
I LONG FOR THOSE DAYS. YOU WERE YOUNG, YOU WERE HANDSOME...
YOU WOULD STRADDLE MY DUNES...
OH, HAVE MERCY.

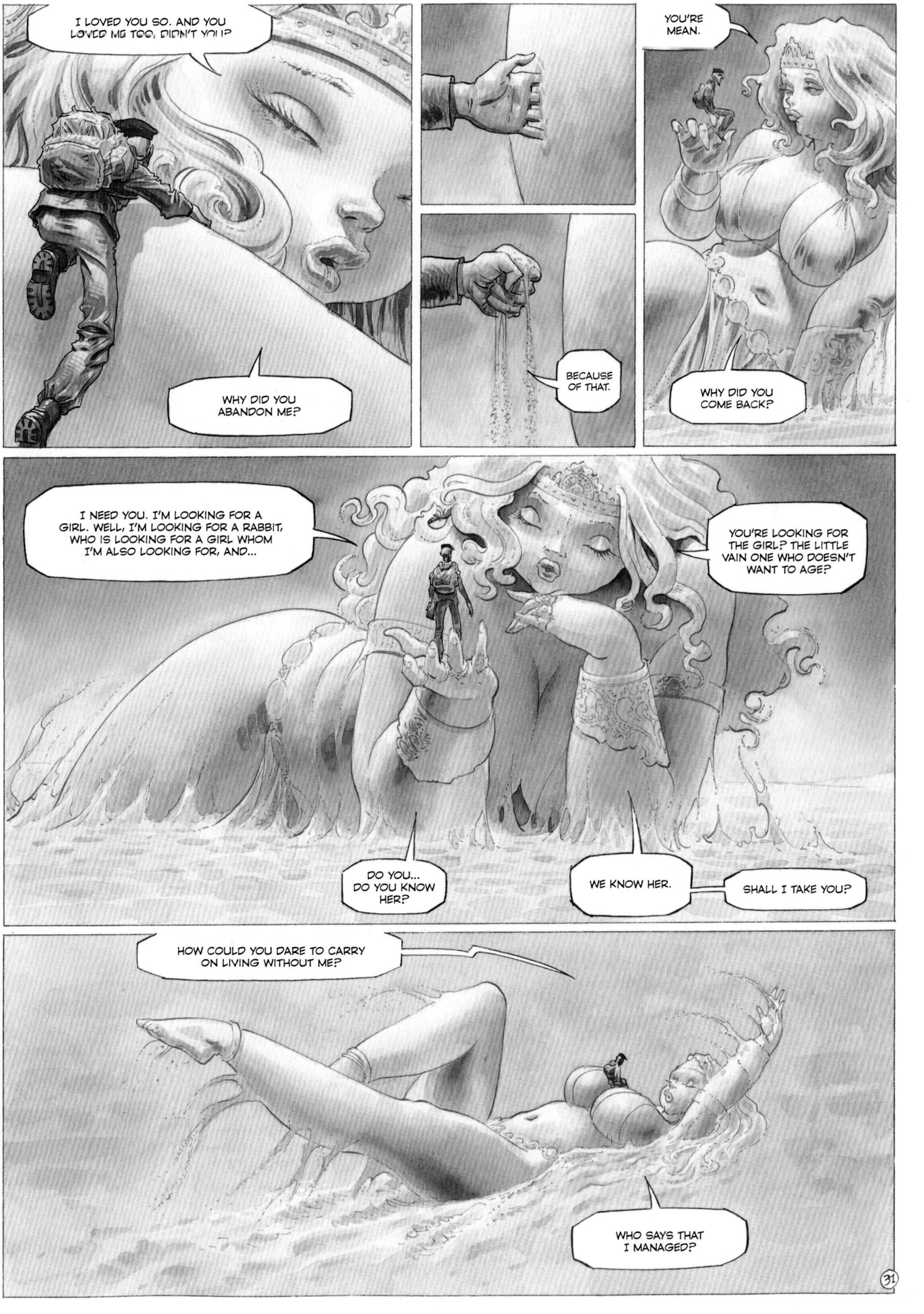
I LOVED YOU SO. AND YOU LOVED ME TOO, DIDN'T YOU?
WHY DID YOU ABANDON ME?
BECAUSE OF THAT.
YOU'RE MEAN.
WHY DID YOU COME BACK?
I NEED YOU. I'M LOOKING FOR A GIRL. WELL, I'M LOOKING FOR A RABBIT, WHO IS LOOKING FOR A GIRL WHOM I'M ALSO LOOKING FOR, AND...
YOU'RE LOOKING FOR THE GIRL? THE LITTLE VAIN ONE WHO DOESN'T WANT TO AGE?
DO YOU... DO YOU KNOW HER?
WE KNOW HER.
SHALL I TAKE YOU?
HOW COULD YOU DARE TO CARRY ON LIVING WITHOUT ME?
WHO SAYS THAT I MANAGED?
31

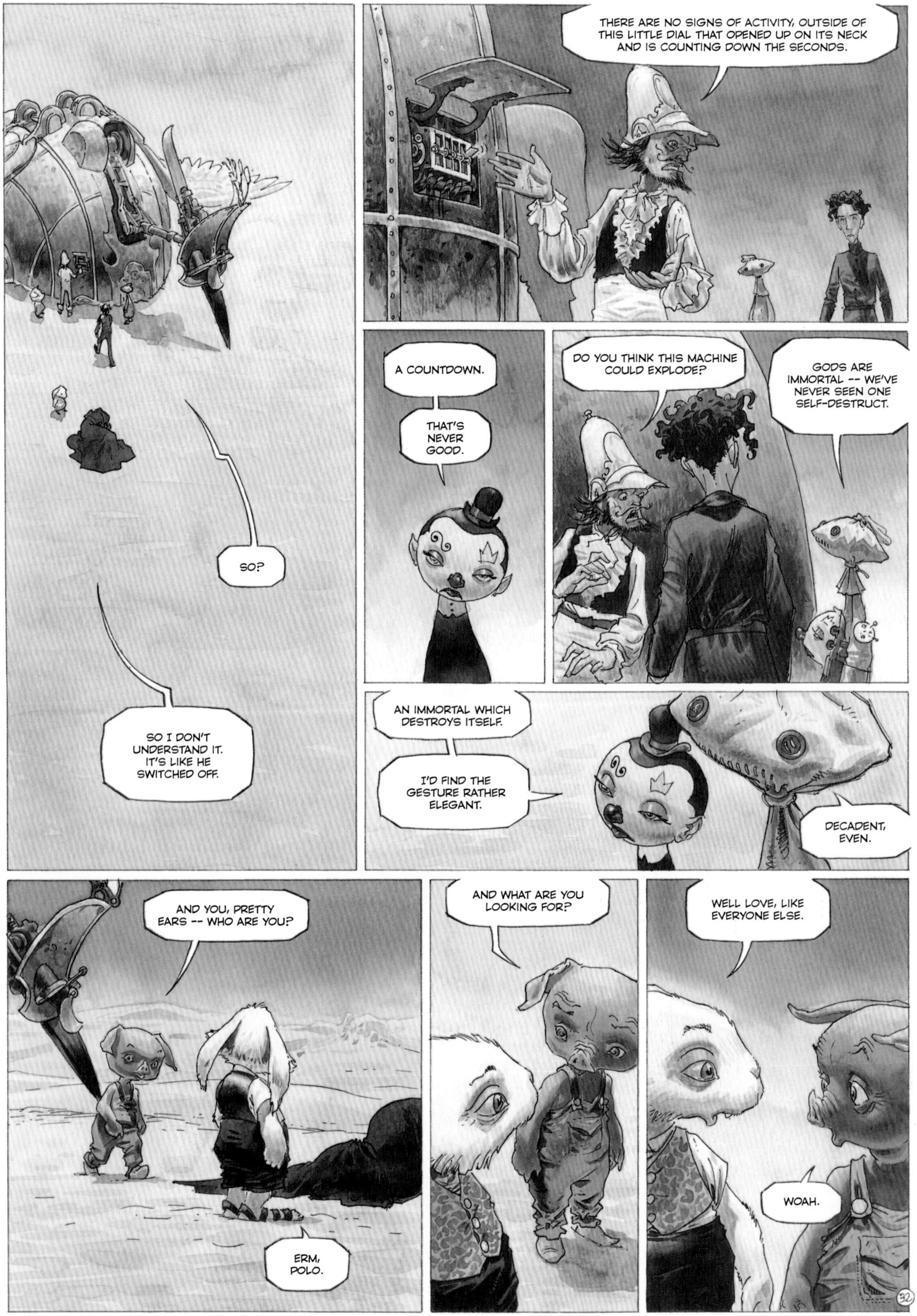
THERE ARE NO SIGNS OF ACTIVITY, OUTSIDE OF THIS LITTLE DIAL THAT OPENED UP ON ITS NECK AND IS COUNTING DOWN THE SECONDS.
A COUNTDOWN.
THAT'S NEVER GOOD.
DO YOU THINK THIS MACHINE COULD EXPLODE?
GODS ARE IMMORTAL -- WE'VE NEVER SEEN ONE SELF-DESTRUCT.
SO?
SO I DON'T UNDERSTAND IT. IT'S LIKE HE SWITCHED OFF.
AN IMMORTAL WHICH DESTROYS ITSELF.
I'D FIND THE GESTURE RATHER ELEGANT.
DECADENT, EVEN.
AND YOU, PRETTY EARS -- WHO ARE YOU?
ERM, POLO.
AND WHAT ARE YOU LOOKING FOR?
WELL LOVE, LIKE EVERYONE ELSE.
WOAH.
32

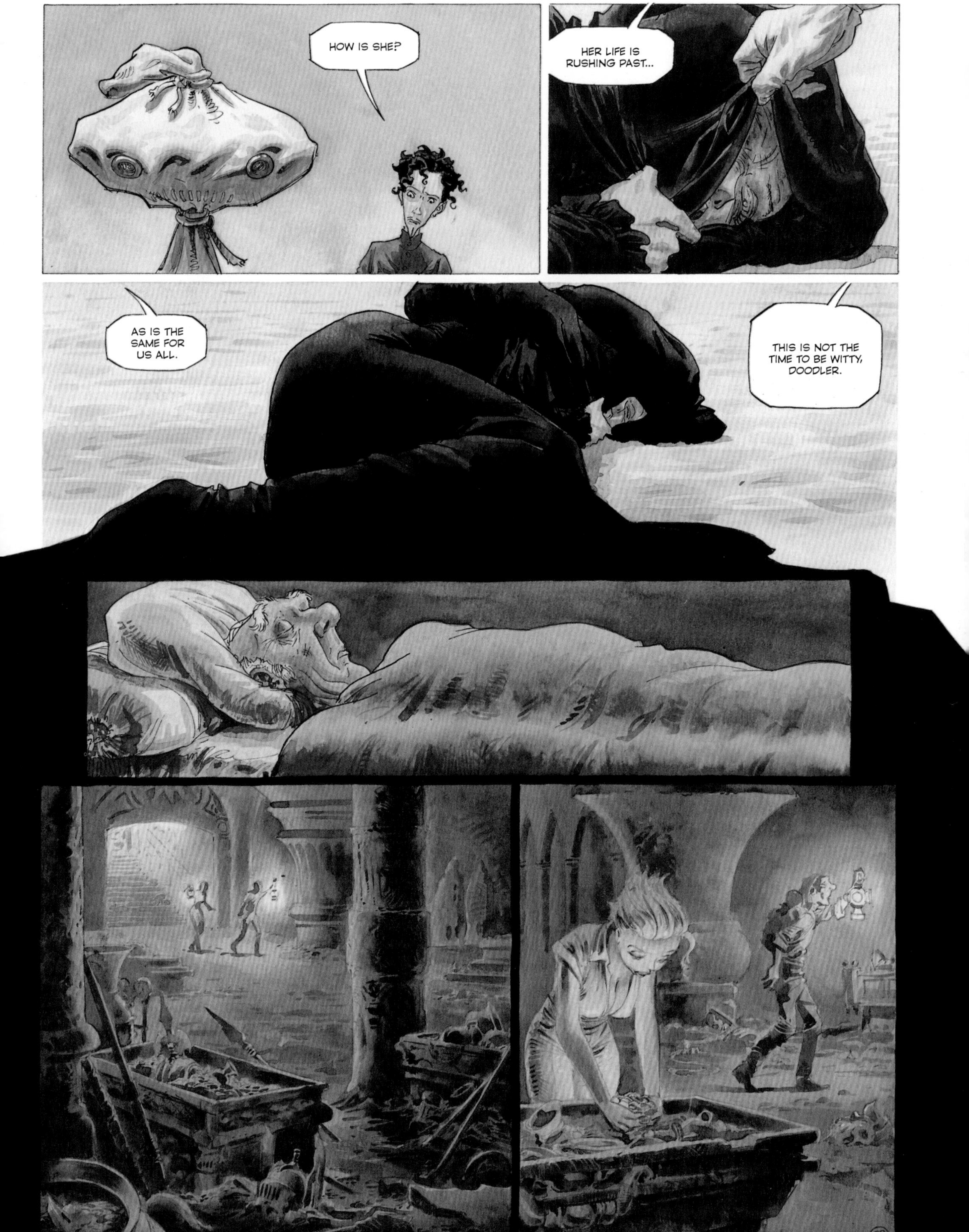

HOW IS SHE?
HER LIFE IS RUSHING PAST...
AS IS THE SAME FOR US ALL.
THIS IS NOT THE TIME TO BE WITTY, DOODLER.

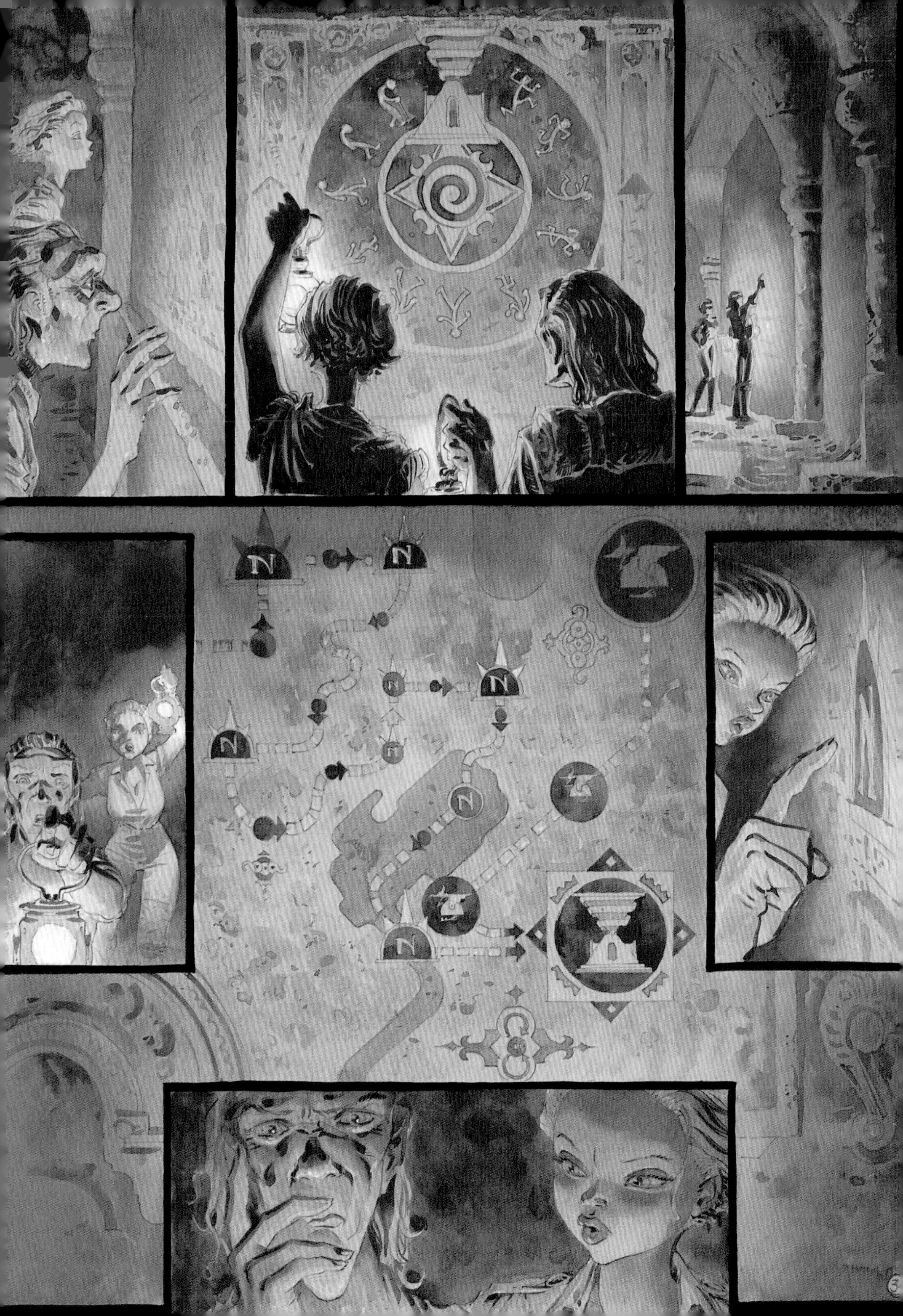

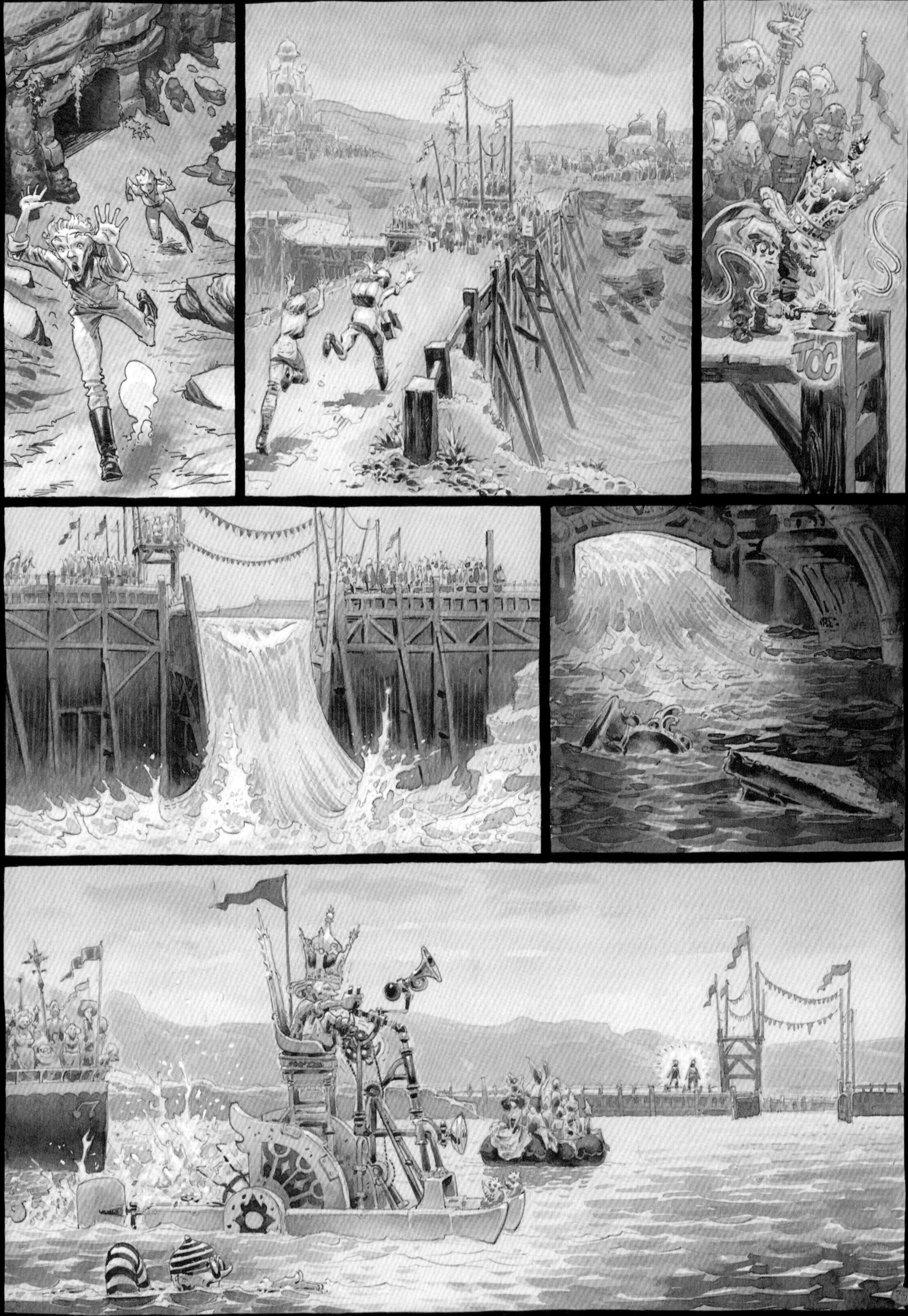
TOC

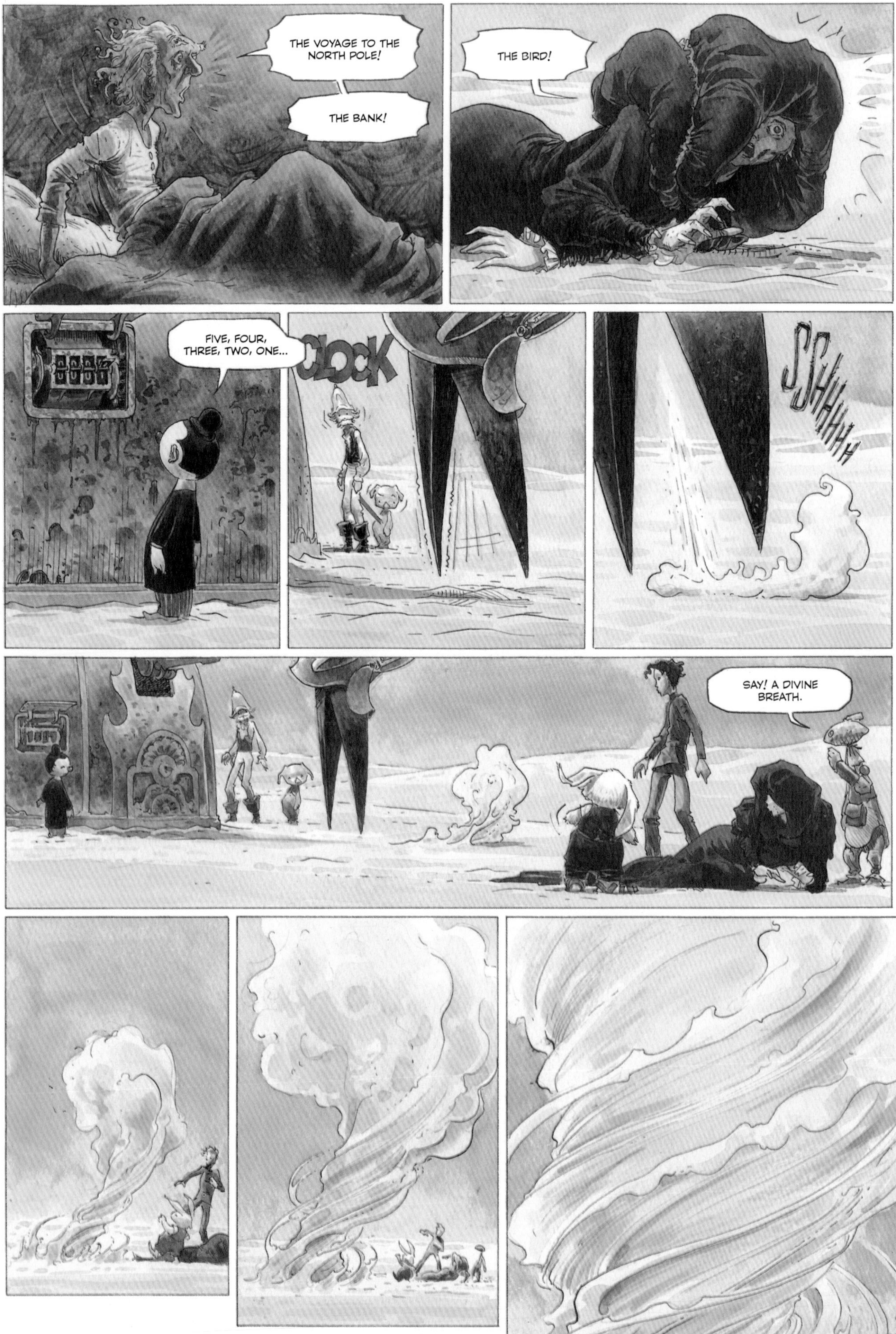
THE VOYAGE TO THE NORTH POLE!
THE BANK!
THE BIRD!
FIVE, FOUR, THREE, TWO, ONE...
CLOCK
SSHHHH
SAY! A DIVINE BREATH.

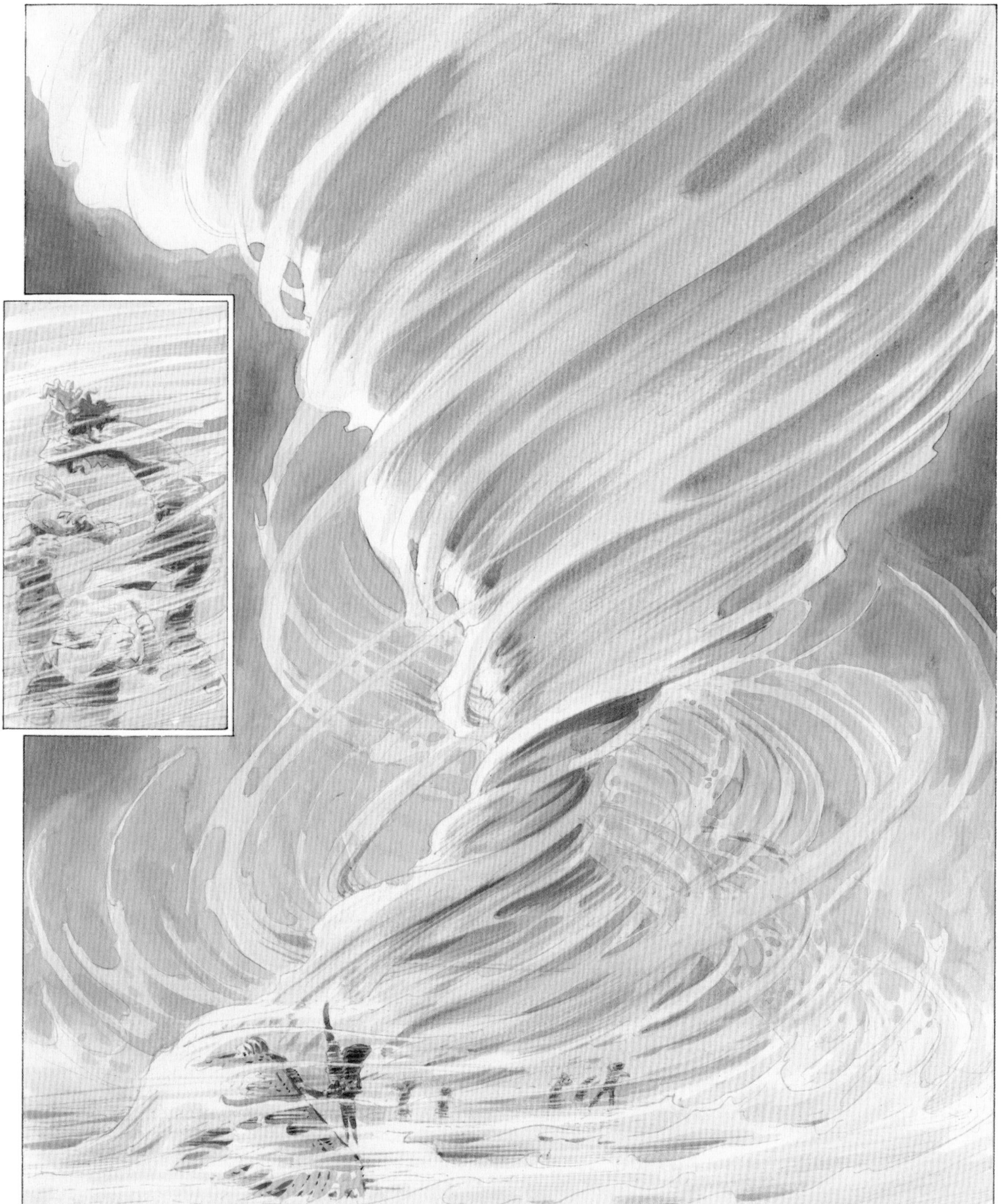

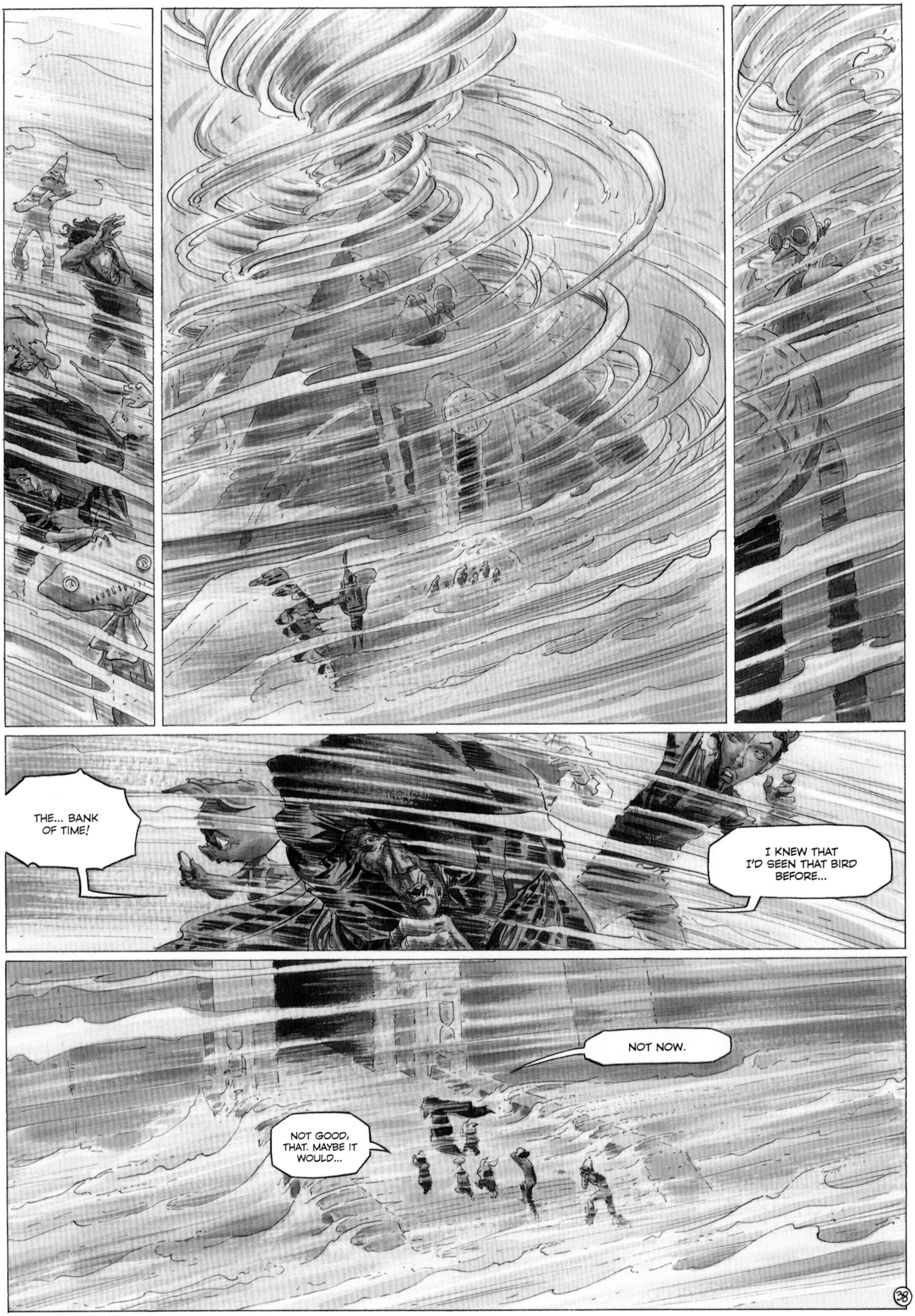
THE... BANK OF TIME!
I KNEW THAT I'D SEEN THAT BIRD BEFORE...
NOT NOW.
NOT GOOD, THAT. MAYBE IT WOULD...
38

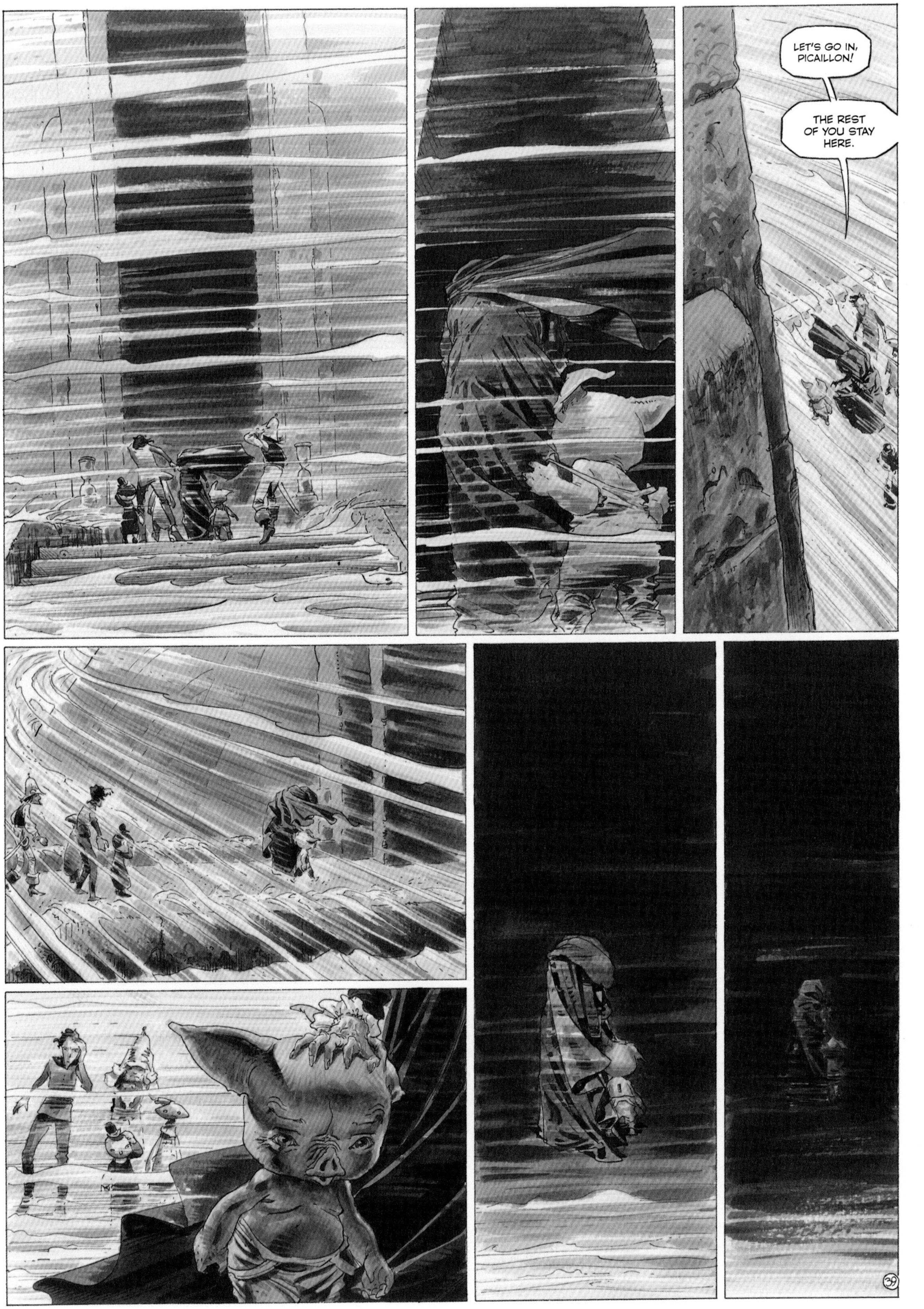
LET'S GO IN, PICAILLON!
THE REST OF YOU STAY HERE.
39

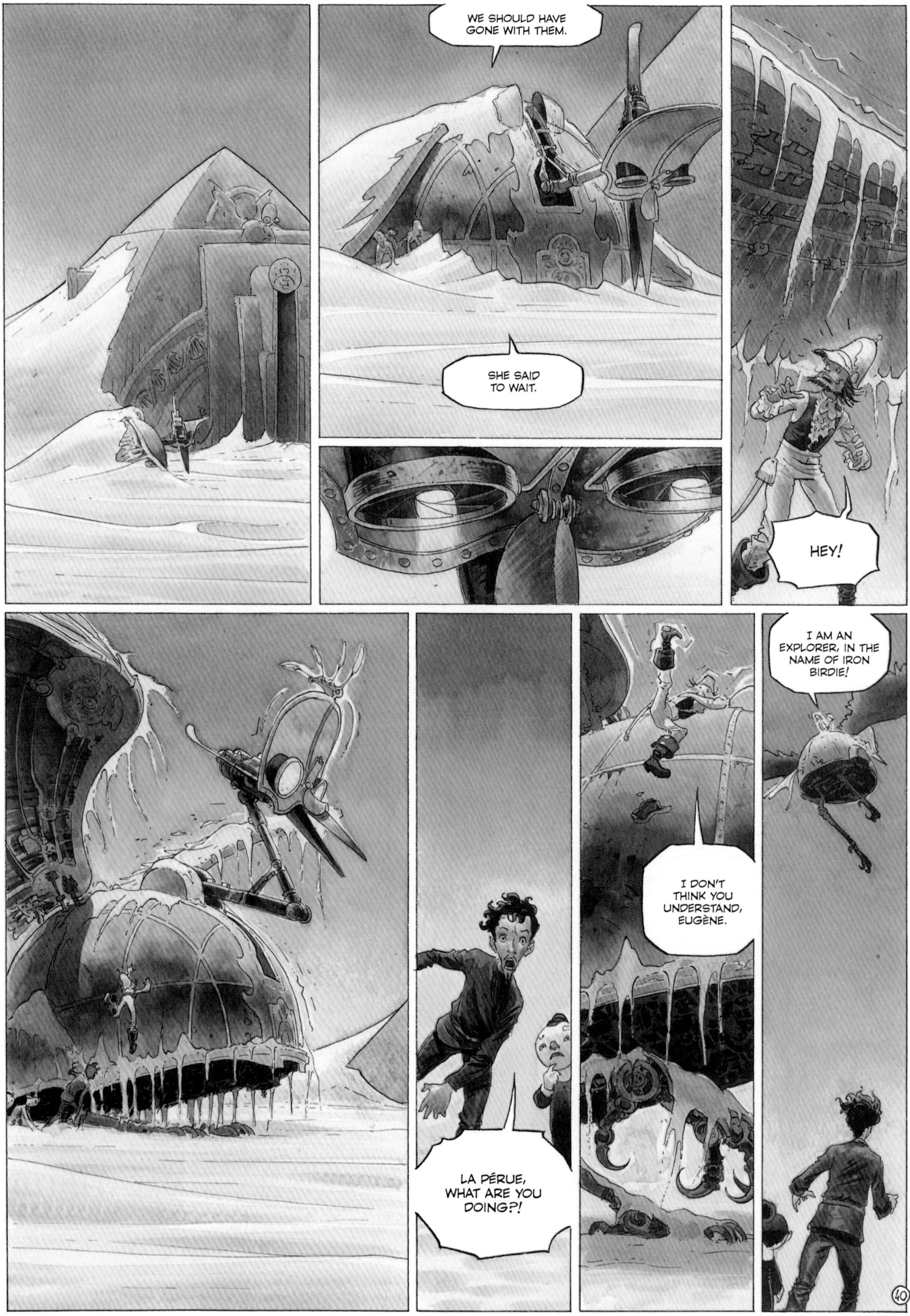
WE SHOULD HAVE GONE WITH THEM.
SHE SAID TO WAIT.
HEY!
LA PÉRUE, WHAT ARE YOU DOING?!
I DON'T THINK YOU UNDERSTAND, EUGÈNE.
I AM AN EXPLORER, IN THE NAME OF IRON BIRDIE!

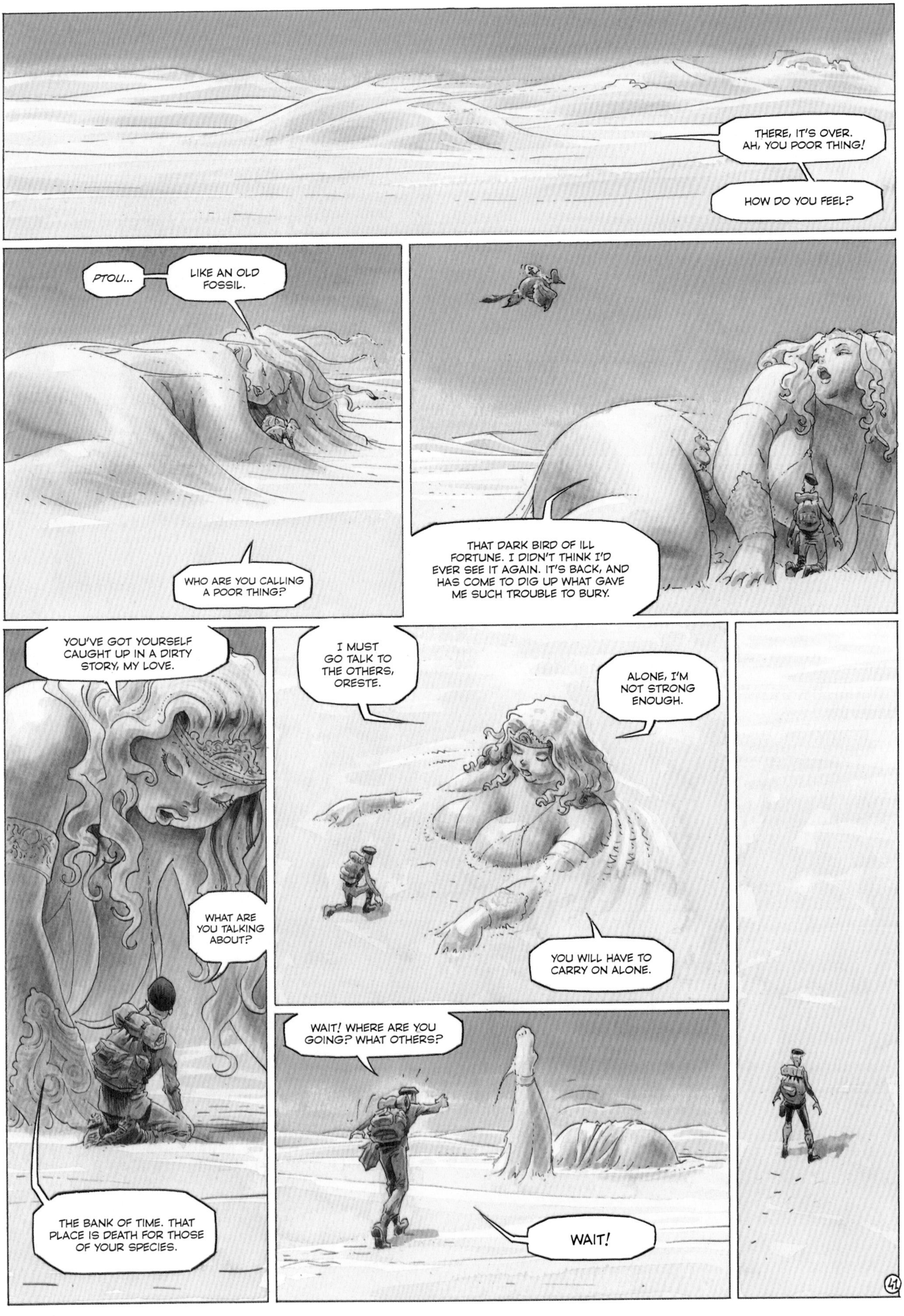
THERE, IT'S OVER. AH, YOU POOR THING!
HOW DO YOU FEEL?
PTOU...
LIKE AN OLD FOSSIL.
WHO ARE YOU CALLING A POOR THING?
THAT DARK BIRD OF ILL FORTUNE. I DIDN'T THINK I'D EVER SEE IT AGAIN. IT'S BACK, AND HAS COME TO DIG UP WHAT GAVE ME SUCH TROUBLE TO BURY.
YOU'VE GOT YOURSELF CAUGHT UP IN A DIRTY STORY, MY LOVE.
WHAT ARE YOU TALKING ABOUT?
THE BANK OF TIME. THAT PLACE IS DEATH FOR THOSE OF YOUR SPECIES.
I MUST GO TALK TO THE OTHERS, ORESTE.
ALONE, I'M NOT STRONG ENOUGH.
YOU WILL HAVE TO CARRY ON ALONE.
WAIT! WHERE ARE YOU GOING? WHAT OTHERS?
WAIT!

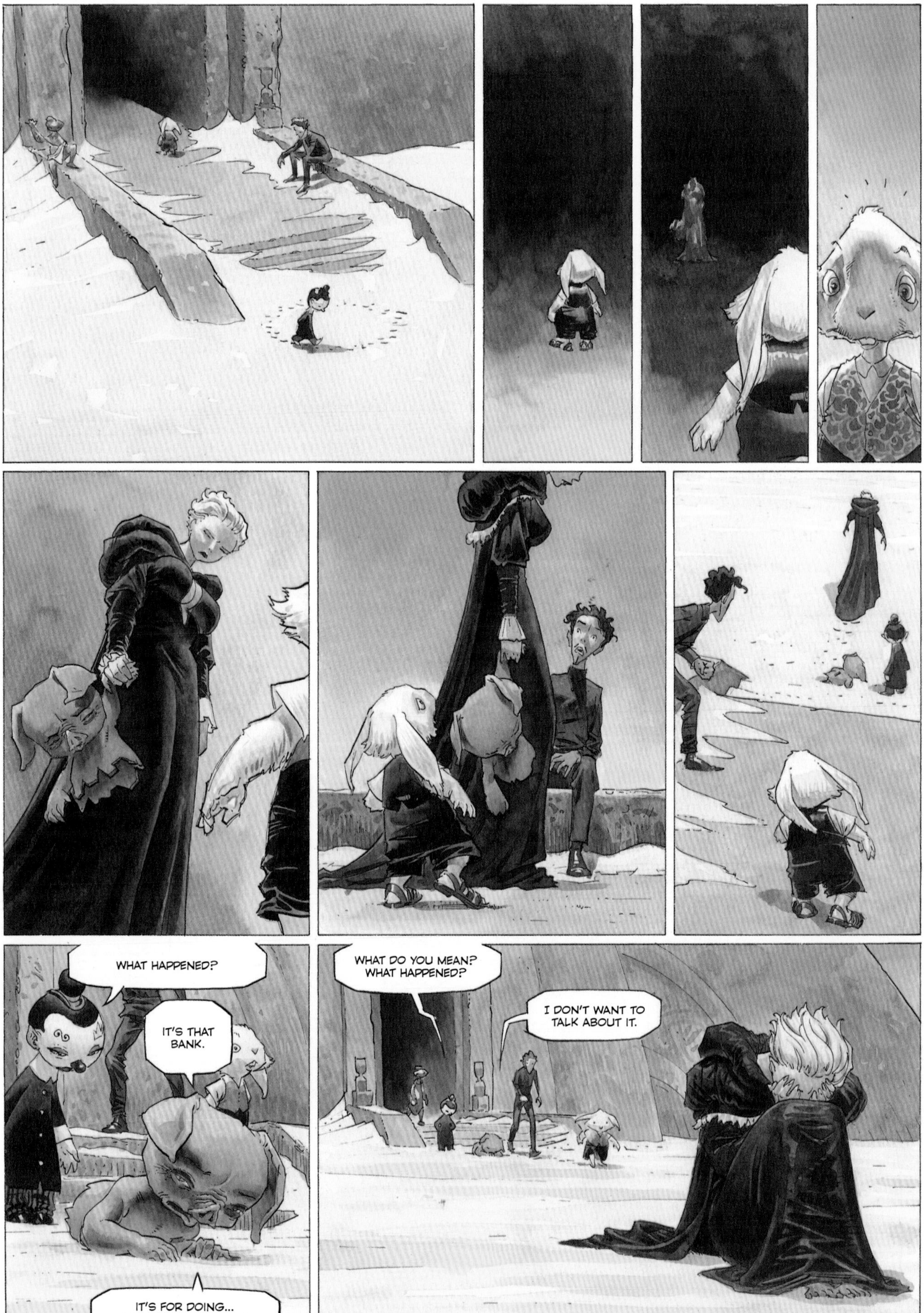
WHAT HAPPENED?
IT'S THAT BANK.
IT'S FOR DOING... REAL NASTY BUSINESS.
WHAT DO YOU MEAN? WHAT HAPPENED?
I DON'T WANT TO TALK ABOUT IT.

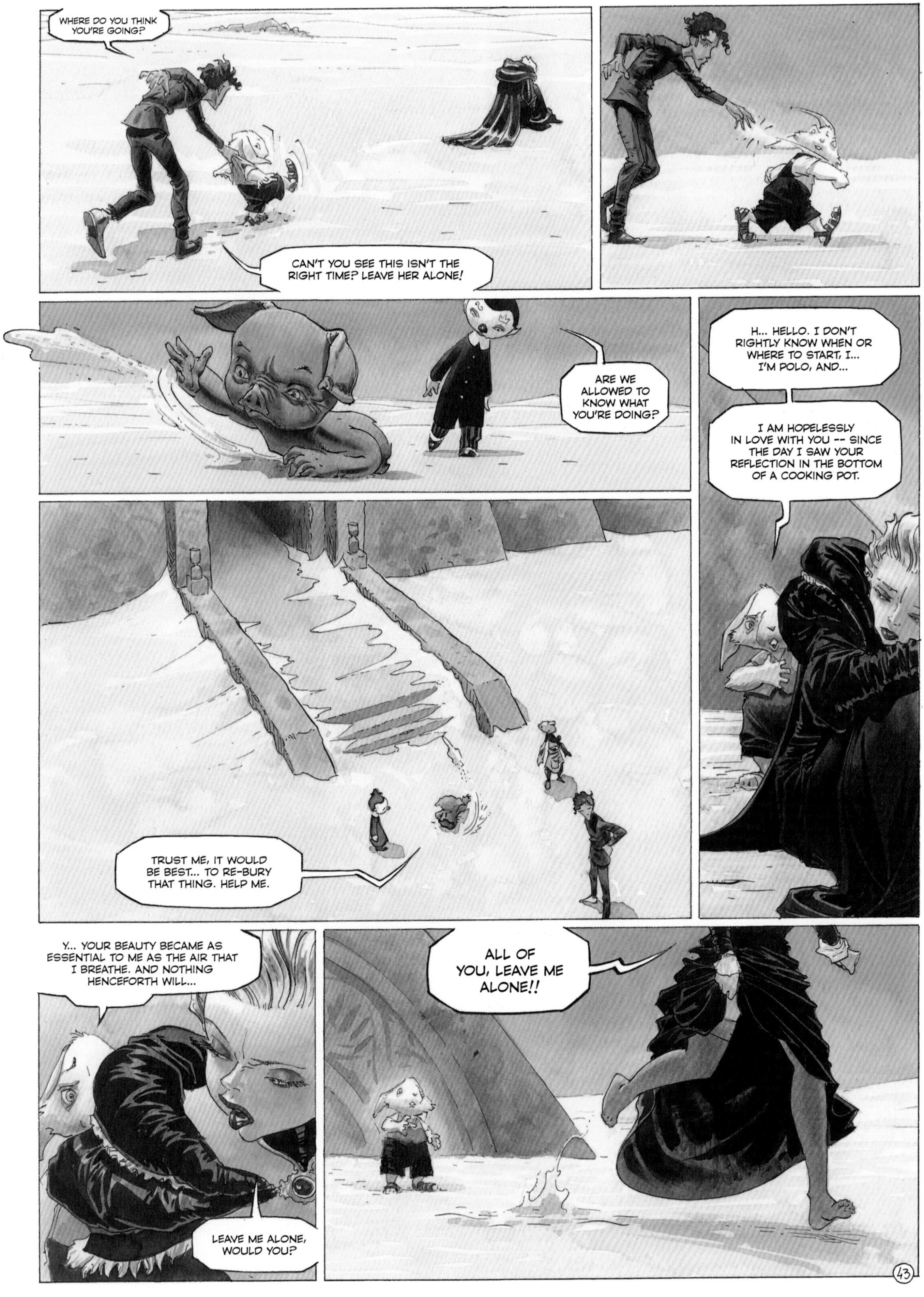
WHERE DO YOU THINK YOU'RE GOING?
CAN'T YOU SEE THIS ISN'T THE RIGHT TIME? LEAVE HER ALONE!
ARE WE ALLOWED TO KNOW WHAT YOU'RE DOING?
H... HELLO. I DON'T RIGHTLY KNOW WHEN OR WHERE TO START, I... I'M POLO, AND...
I AM HOPELESSLY IN LOVE WITH YOU -- SINCE THE DAY I SAW YOUR REFLECTION IN THE BOTTOM OF A COOKING POT.
TRUST ME, IT WOULD BE BEST... TO RE-BURY THAT THING. HELP ME.
Y... YOUR BEAUTY BECAME AS ESSENTIAL TO ME AS THE AIR THAT I BREATHE. AND NOTHING HENCEFORTH WILL...
LEAVE ME ALONE, WOULD YOU?
ALL OF YOU, LEAVE ME ALONE!!

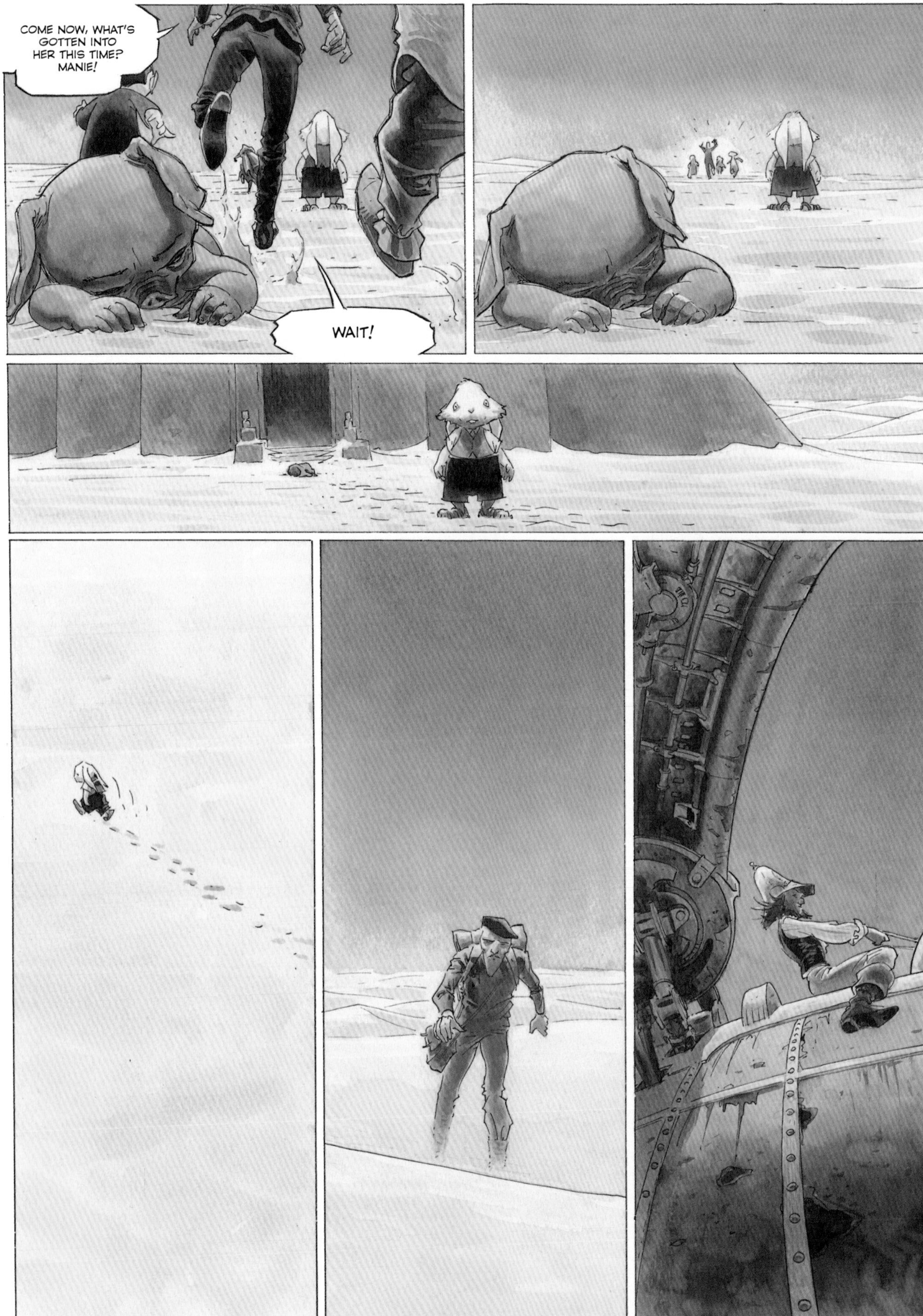
COME NOW, WHAT'S GOTTEN INTO HER THIS TIME? MANIE!
WAIT!

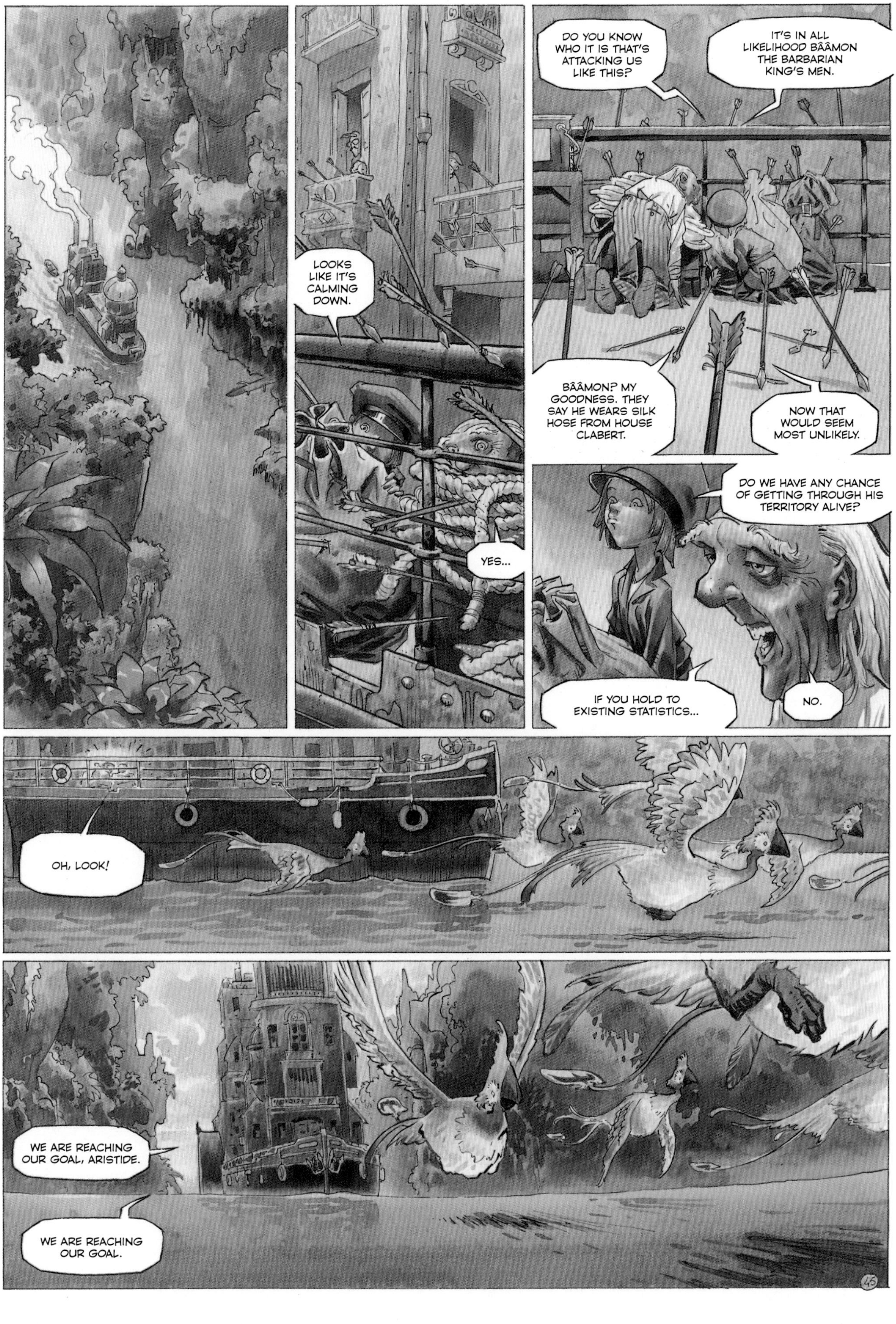

LOOKS LIKE IT'S CALMING DOWN.
YES...
DO YOU KNOW WHO IT IS THAT'S ATTACKING US LIKE THIS?
IT'S IN ALL LIKELIHOOD BÂÂMON THE BARBARIAN KING'S MEN.
BÂÂMON? MY GOODNESS. THEY SAY HE WEARS SILK HOSE FROM HOUSE CLABERT.
NOW THAT WOULD SEEM MOST UNLIKELY.
DO WE HAVE ANY CHANCE OF GETTING THROUGH HIS TERRITORY ALIVE?
IF YOU HOLD TO EXISTING STATISTICS...
NO.
OH, LOOK!
WE ARE REACHING OUR GOAL, ARISTIDE.
WE ARE REACHING OUR GOAL.

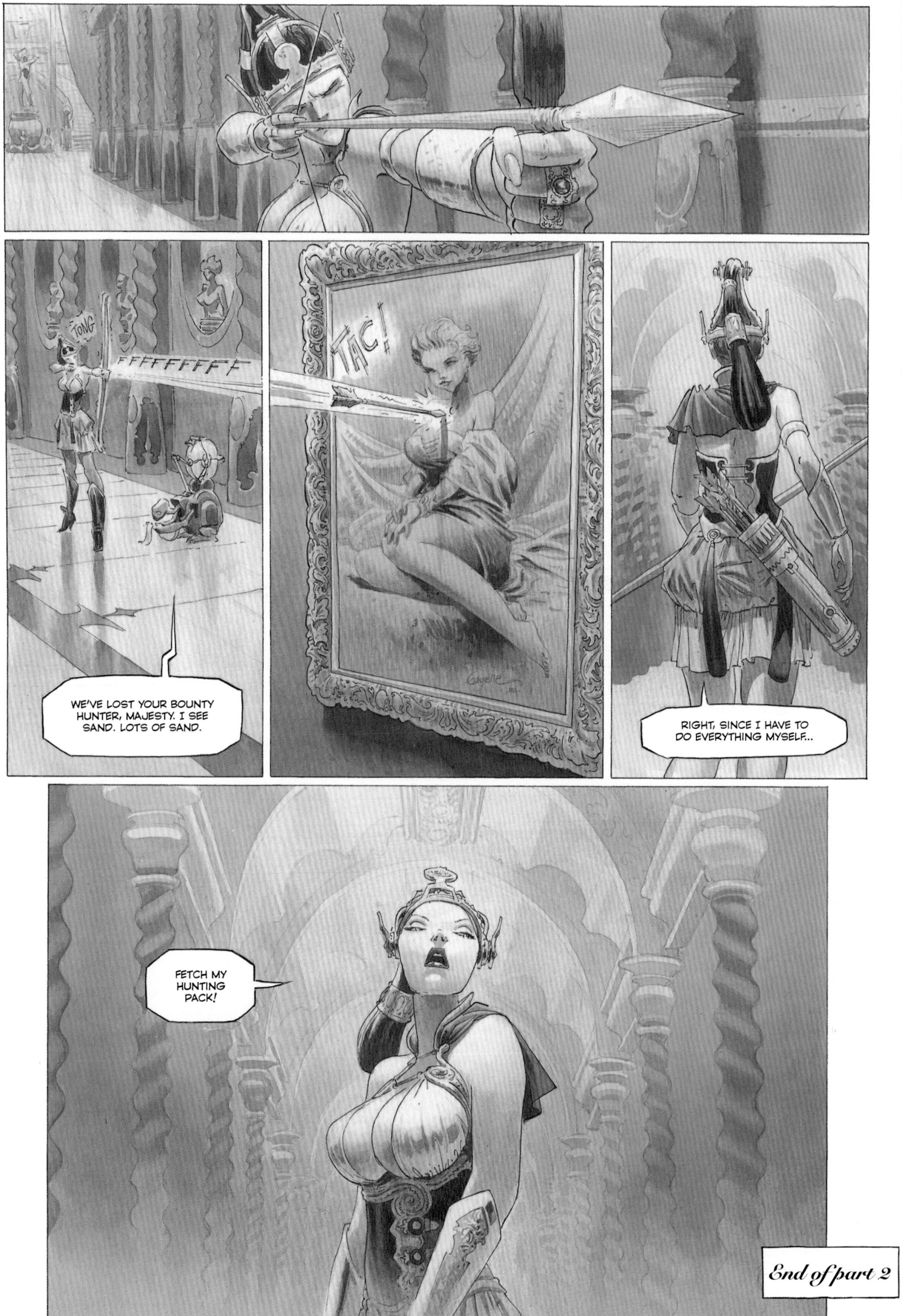
TONG
FFFFFFFFF
WE'VE LOST YOUR BOUNTY HUNTER, MAJESTY. I SEE SAND. LOTS OF SAND.
TAC!
RIGHT, SINCE I HAVE TO DO EVERYTHING MYSELF...
FETCH MY HUNTING PACK!
End of part 2

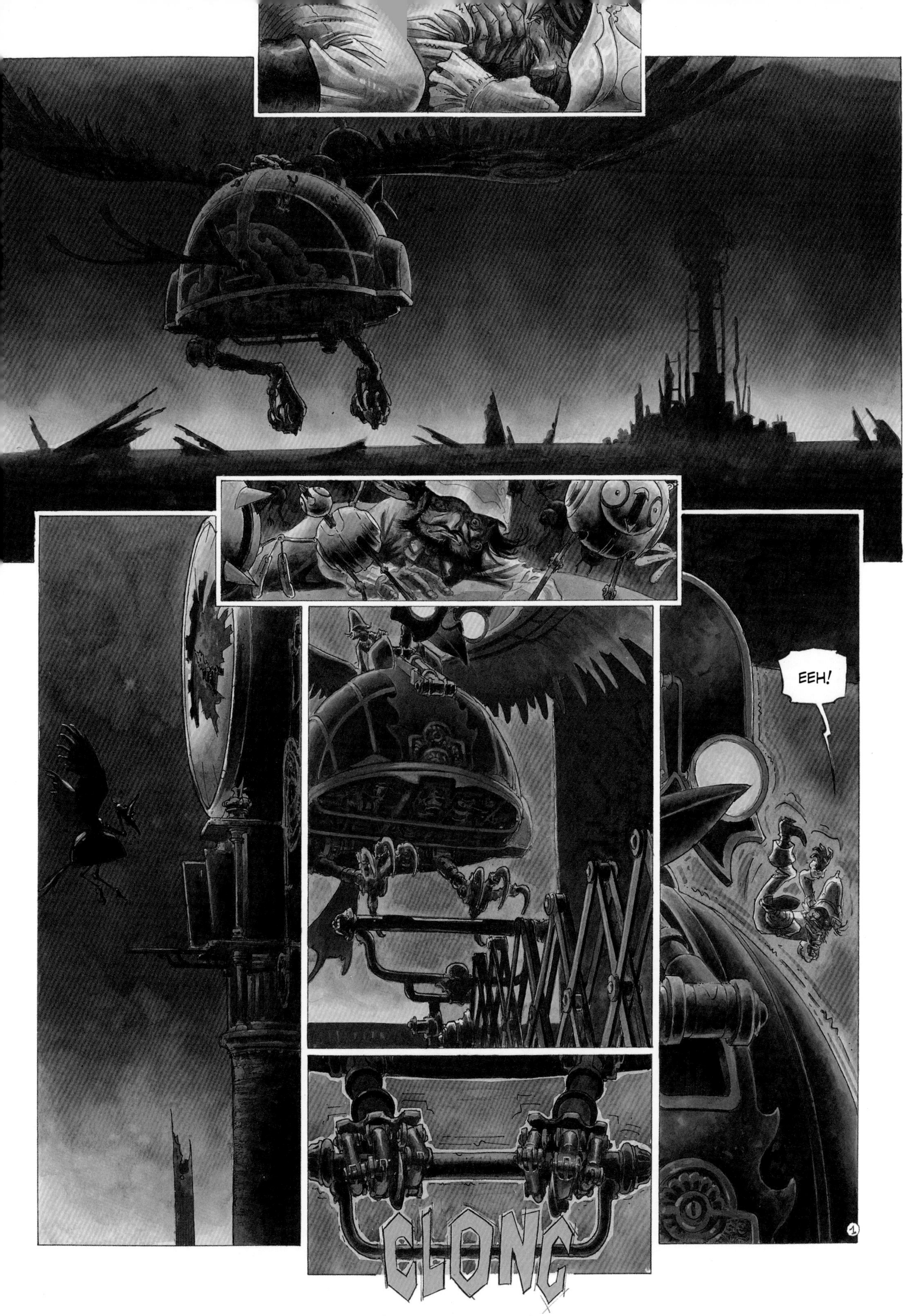
EEH!
CLONG

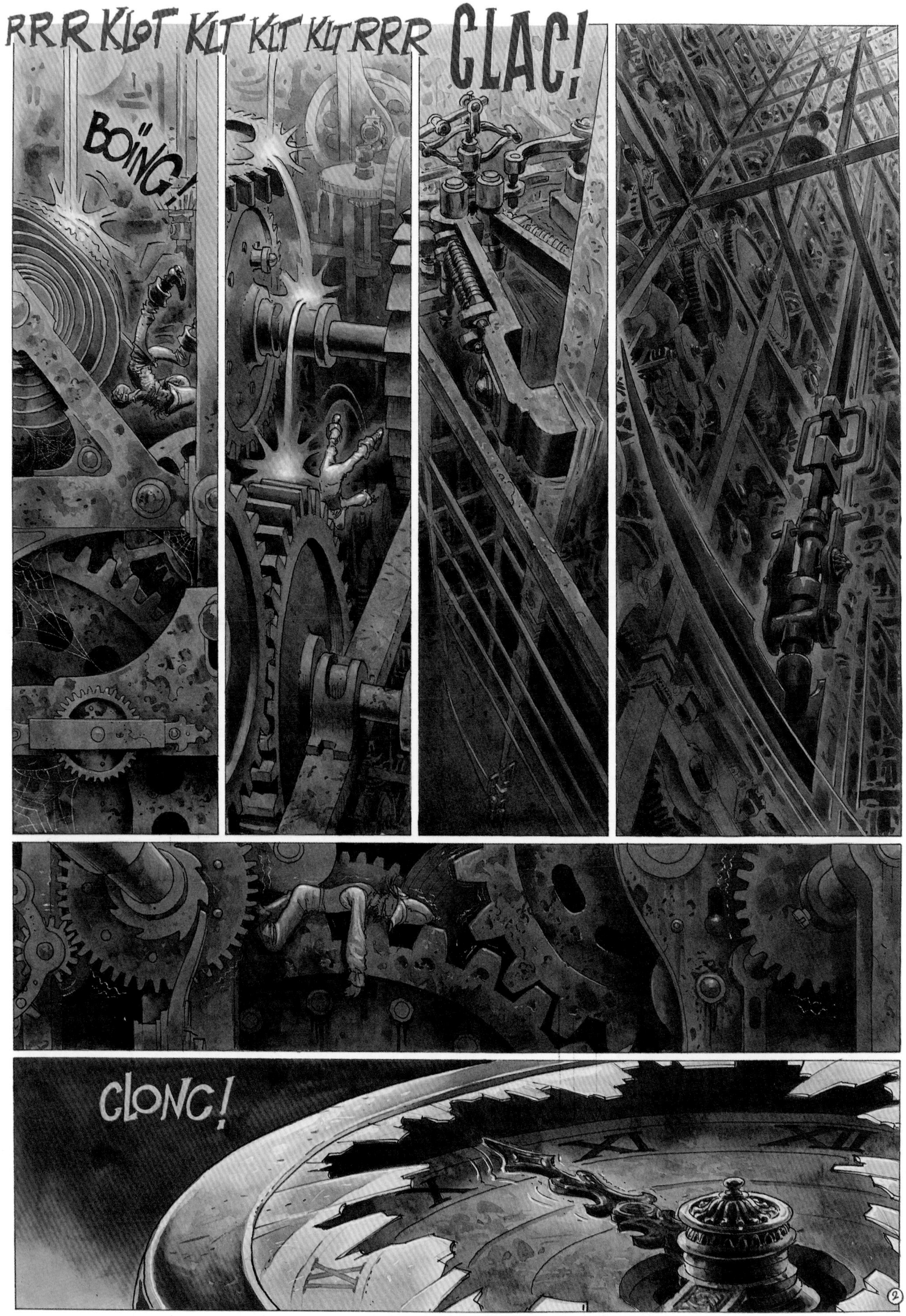
RRR KLOT KLT KLT KLT RRR
BOÏNG!
GLAC!
CLONC!

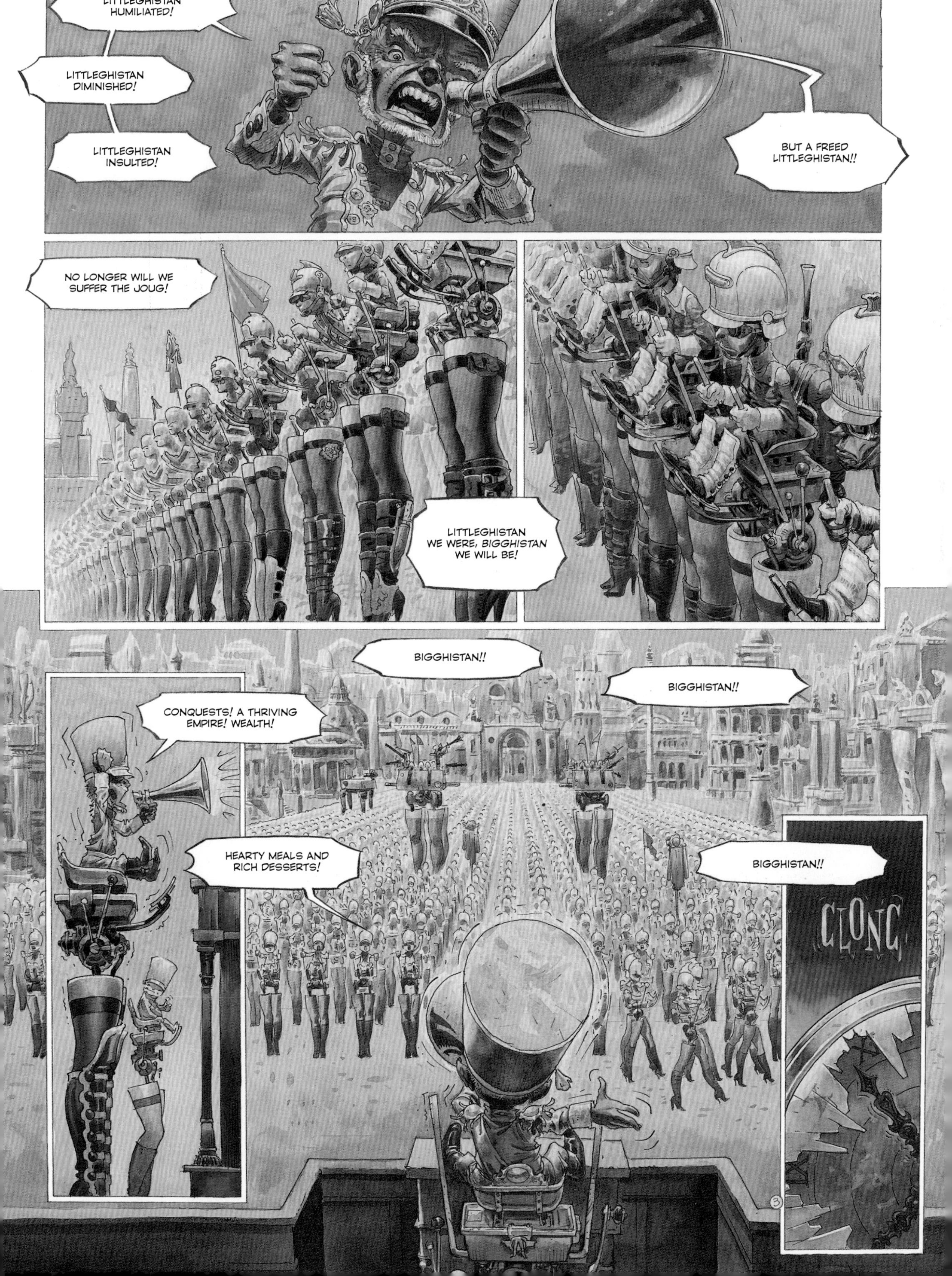
LITTLEGHISTAN HUMILIATED!
LITTLEGHISTAN DIMINISHED!
LITTLEGHISTAN INSULTED!
BUT A FREED LITTLEGHISTAN!!
NO LONGER WILL WE SUFFER THE JOUG!
LITTLEGHISTAN WE WERE, BIGGHISTAN WE WILL BE!
CONQUESTS! A THRIVING EMPIRE! WEALTH!
HEARTY MEALS AND RICH DESSERTS!
BIGGHISTAN!!
BIGGHISTAN!!
BIGGHISTAN!!
CLONG

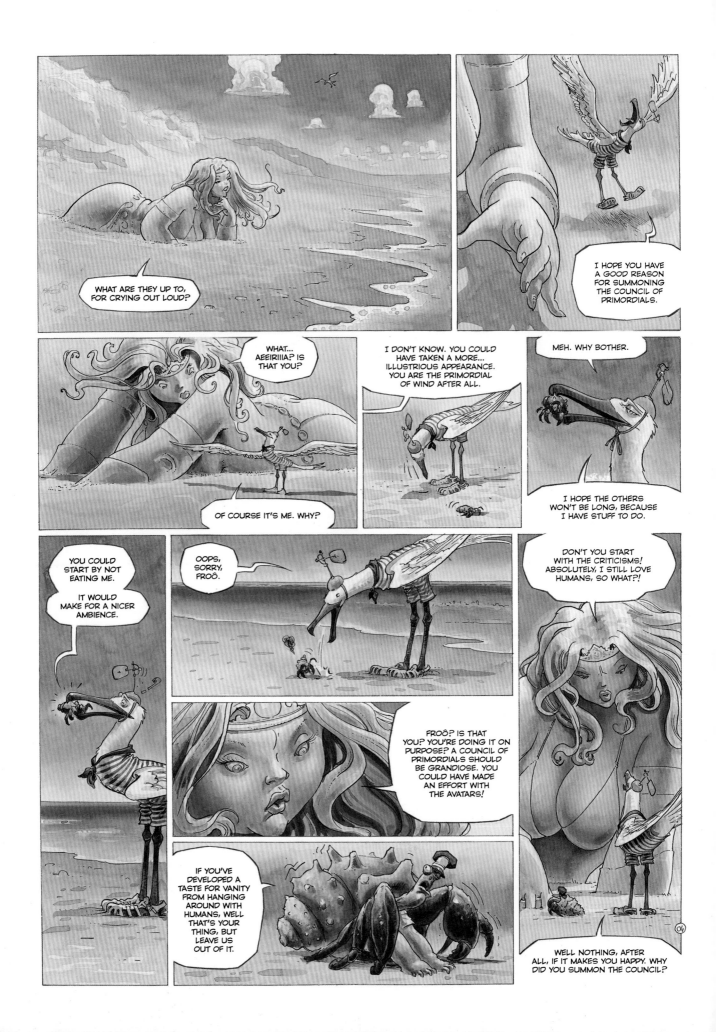

WHAT ARE THEY UP TO, FOR CRYING OUT LOUD?

I HOPE YOU HAVE A GOOD REASON FOR SUMMONING THE COUNCIL OF PRIMORDIALS.

WHAT... AEEIRIIIA? IS THAT YOU?

OF COURSE IT'S ME. WHY?

I DON'T KNOW. YOU COULD HAVE TAKEN A MORE... ILLUSTRIOUS APPEARANCE. YOU ARE THE PRIMORDIAL OF WIND AFTER ALL.

MEH. WHY BOTHER.

I HOPE THE OTHERS WON'T BE LONG, BECAUSE I HAVE STUFF TO DO.

YOU COULD START BY NOT EATING ME.

IT WOULD MAKE FOR A NICER AMBIENCE.

OOPS, SORRY, FROÔ.

FROÔ? IS THAT YOU? YOU'RE DOING IT ON PURPOSE? A COUNCIL OF PRIMORDIALS SHOULD BE GRANDIOSE. YOU COULD HAVE MADE AN EFFORT WITH THE AVATARS!

DON'T YOU START WITH THE CRITICISMS! ABSOLUTELY, I STILL LOVE HUMANS, SO WHAT?!

IF YOU'VE DEVELOPED A TASTE FOR VANITY FROM HANGING AROUND WITH HUMANS, WELL THAT'S YOUR THING, BUT LEAVE US OUT OF IT.

WELL NOTHING, AFTER ALL, IF IT MAKES YOU HAPPY. WHY DID YOU SUMMON THE COUNCIL?

04

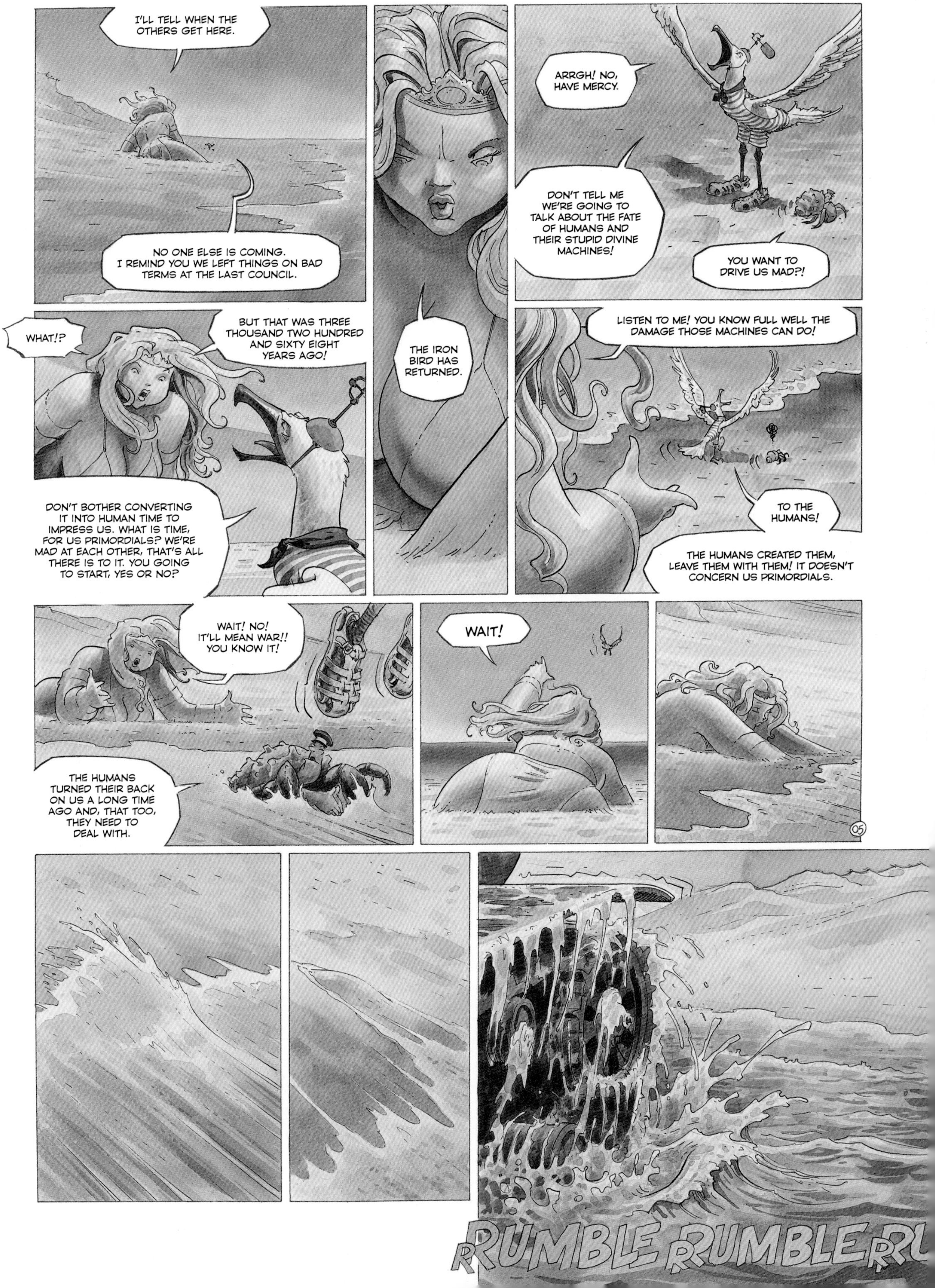
I'LL TELL WHEN THE OTHERS GET HERE.
NO ONE ELSE IS COMING. I REMIND YOU WE LEFT THINGS ON BAD TERMS AT THE LAST COUNCIL.
THE IRON BIRD HAS RETURNED.
ARRGH! NO, HAVE MERCY.
DON'T TELL ME WE'RE GOING TO TALK ABOUT THE FATE OF HUMANS AND THEIR STUPID DIVINE MACHINES!
YOU WANT TO DRIVE US MAD?!
WHAT!?
BUT THAT WAS THREE THOUSAND TWO HUNDRED AND SIXTY EIGHT YEARS AGO!
DON'T BOTHER CONVERTING IT INTO HUMAN TIME TO IMPRESS US. WHAT IS TIME, FOR US PRIMORDIALS? WE'RE MAD AT EACH OTHER, THAT'S ALL THERE IS TO IT. YOU GOING TO START, YES OR NO?
LISTEN TO ME! YOU KNOW FULL WELL THE DAMAGE THOSE MACHINES CAN DO!
TO THE HUMANS!
THE HUMANS CREATED THEM, LEAVE THEM WITH THEM! IT DOESN'T CONCERN US PRIMORDIALS.
WAIT! NO! IT'LL MEAN WAR!! YOU KNOW IT!
THE HUMANS TURNED THEIR BACK ON US A LONG TIME AGO AND, THAT TOO, THEY NEED TO DEAL WITH.
WAIT!
05
RUMBLE RUMBLE RU

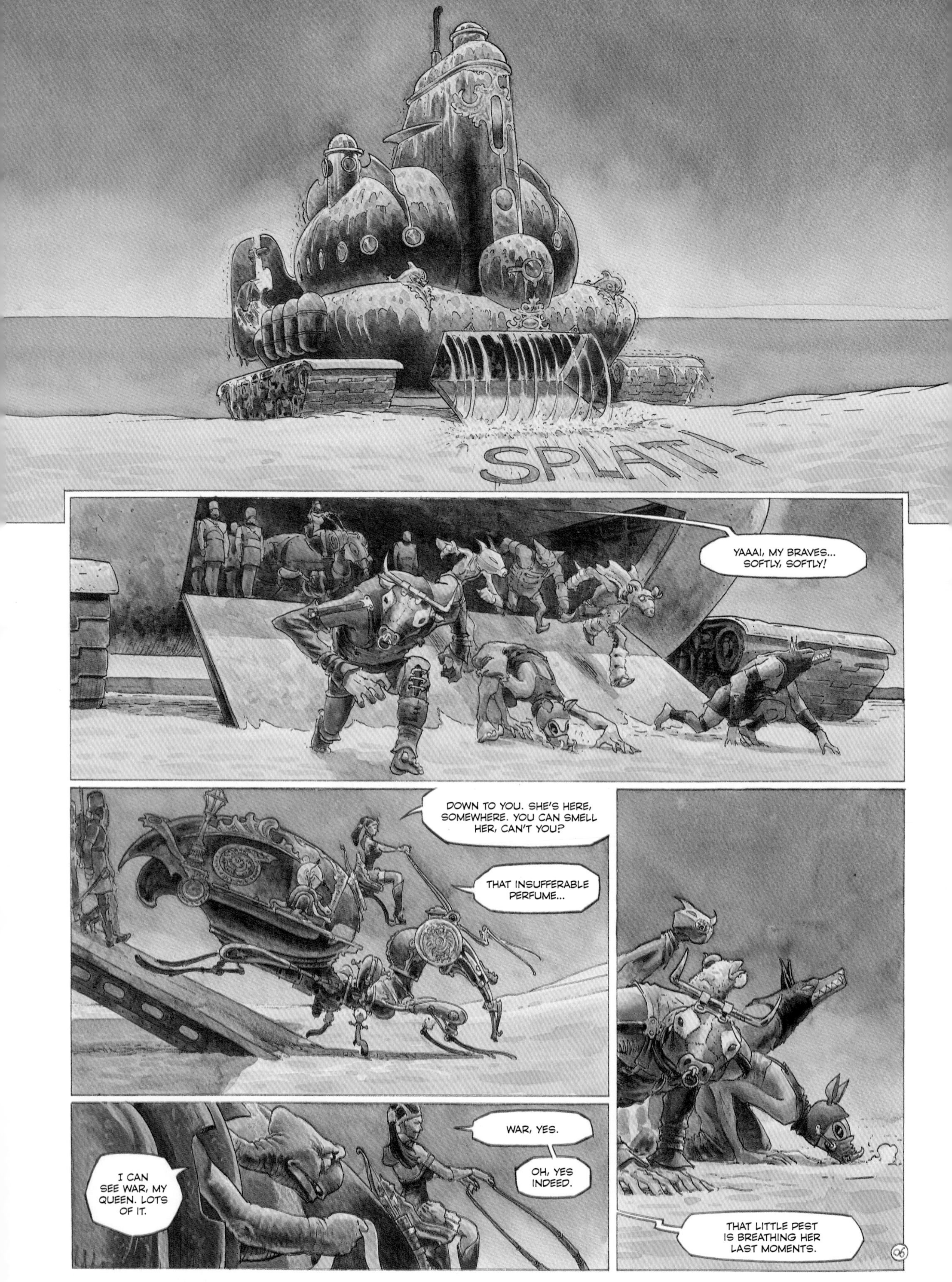
SPLAT!
YAAAI, MY BRAVES... SOFTLY, SOFTLY!
DOWN TO YOU. SHE'S HERE, SOMEWHERE. YOU CAN SMELL HER, CAN'T YOU?
THAT INSUFFERABLE PERFUME...
I CAN SEE WAR, MY QUEEN. LOTS OF IT.
WAR, YES.
OH, YES INDEED.
THAT LITTLE PEST IS BREATHING HER LAST MOMENTS.
06

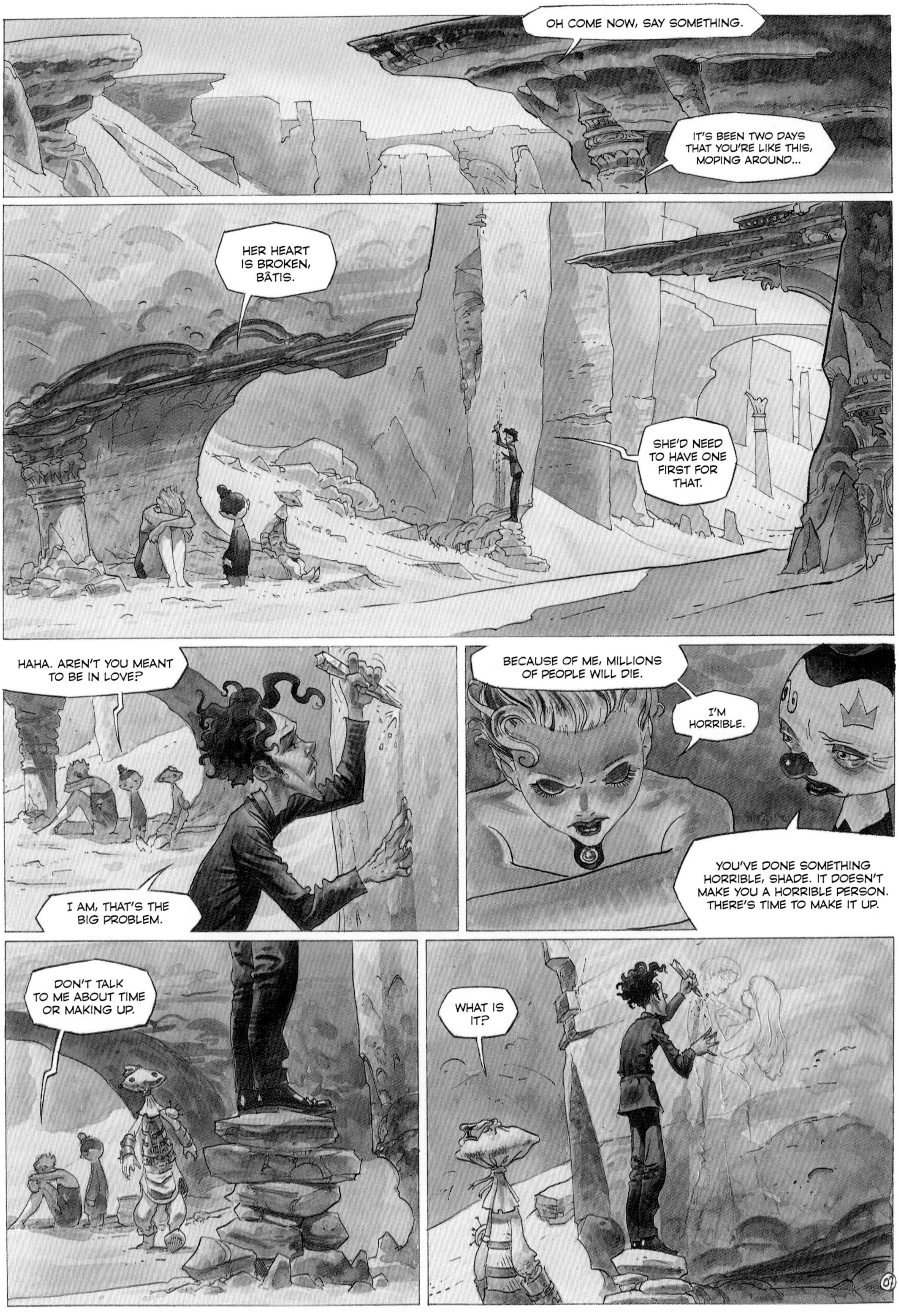

OH COME NOW, SAY SOMETHING.
IT'S BEEN TWO DAYS THAT YOU'RE LIKE THIS, MOPING AROUND...
HER HEART IS BROKEN, BÂTIS.
SHE'D NEED TO HAVE ONE FIRST FOR THAT.
HAHA. AREN'T YOU MEANT TO BE IN LOVE?
I AM, THAT'S THE BIG PROBLEM.
BECAUSE OF ME, MILLIONS OF PEOPLE WILL DIE.
I'M HORRIBLE.
YOU'VE DONE SOMETHING HORRIBLE, SHADE. IT DOESN'T MAKE YOU A HORRIBLE PERSON. THERE'S TIME TO MAKE IT UP.
DON'T TALK TO ME ABOUT TIME OR MAKING UP.
WHAT IS IT?

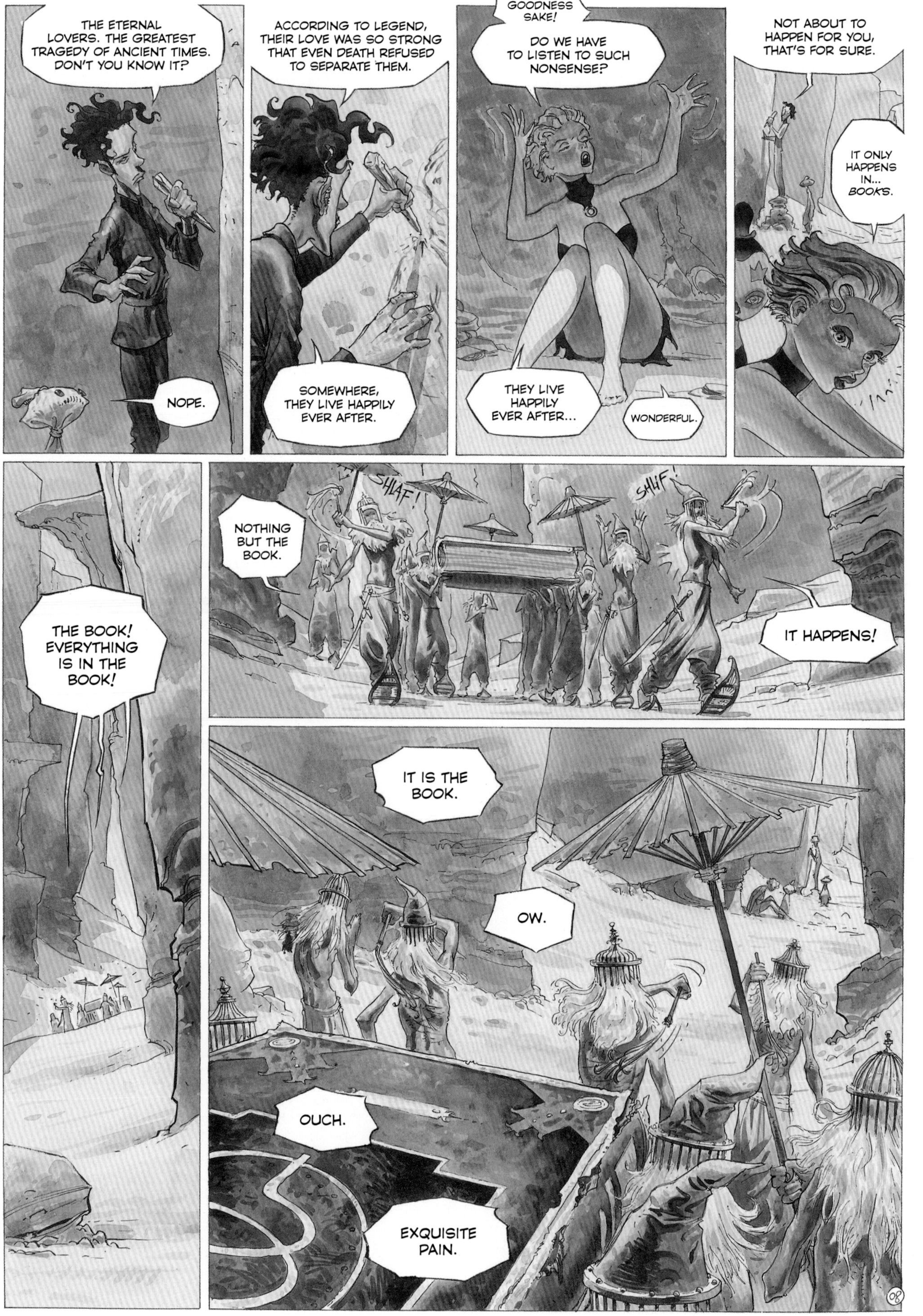
THE ETERNAL LOVERS. THE GREATEST TRAGEDY OF ANCIENT TIMES. DON'T YOU KNOW IT?
NOPE.
ACCORDING TO LEGEND, THEIR LOVE WAS SO STRONG THAT EVEN DEATH REFUSED TO SEPARATE THEM.
SOMEWHERE, THEY LIVE HAPPILY EVER AFTER.
GOODNESS SAKE!
DO WE HAVE TO LISTEN TO SUCH NONSENSE?
THEY LIVE HAPPILY EVER AFTER...
WONDERFUL.
NOT ABOUT TO HAPPEN FOR YOU, THAT'S FOR SURE.
IT ONLY HAPPENS IN... BOOKS.
THE BOOK! EVERYTHING IS IN THE BOOK!
SHLAF!
SHLIF!
NOTHING BUT THE BOOK.
IT HAPPENS!
IT IS THE BOOK.
OW.
OUCH.
EXQUISITE PAIN.

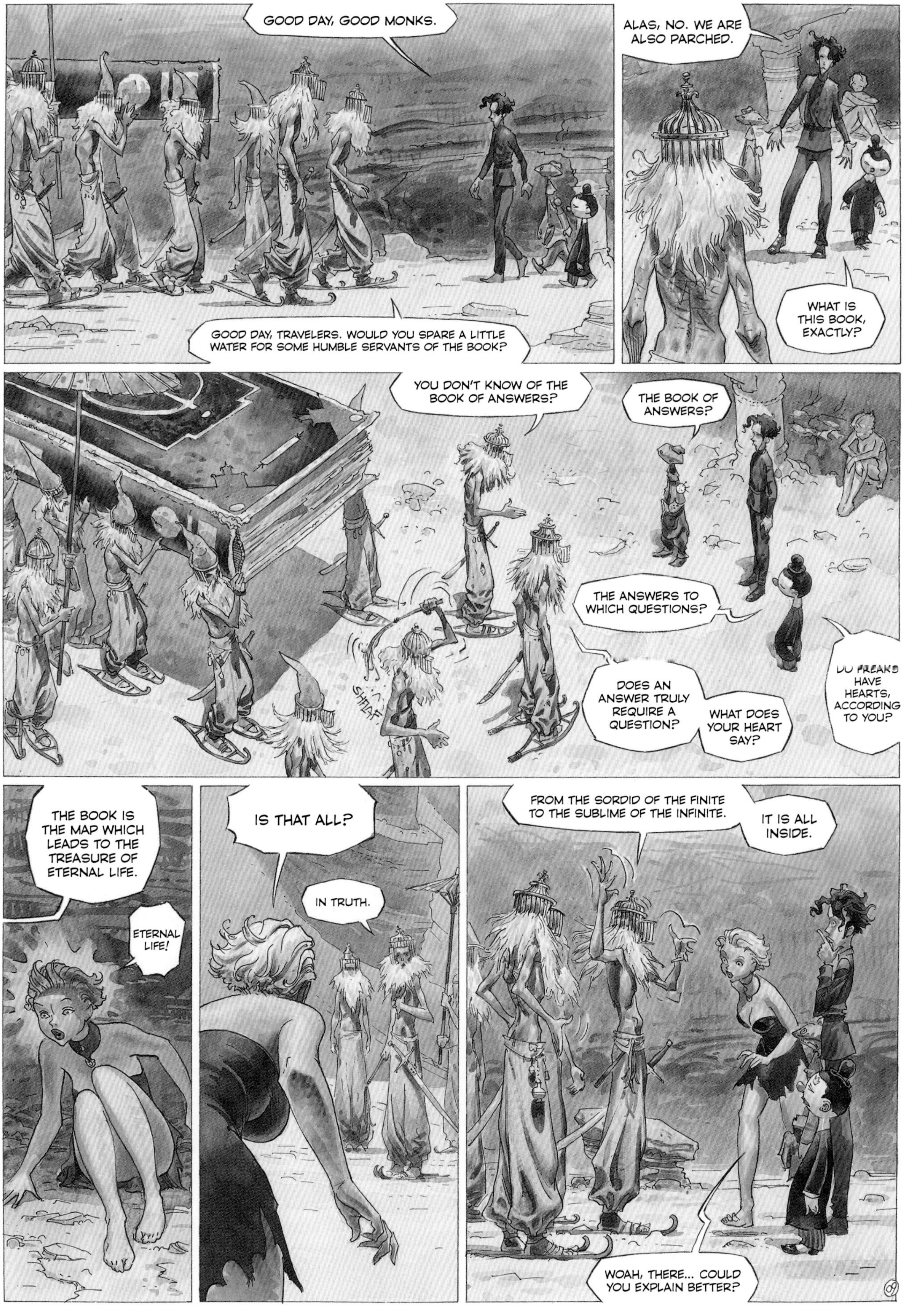
GOOD DAY, GOOD MONKS.
GOOD DAY, TRAVELERS. WOULD YOU SPARE A LITTLE WATER FOR SOME HUMBLE SERVANTS OF THE BOOK?
ALAS, NO. WE ARE ALSO PARCHED.
WHAT IS THIS BOOK, EXACTLY?
YOU DON'T KNOW OF THE BOOK OF ANSWERS?
THE BOOK OF ANSWERS?
THE ANSWERS TO WHICH QUESTIONS?
SHLAF
DOES AN ANSWER TRULY REQUIRE A QUESTION?
WHAT DOES YOUR HEART SAY?
DO FREAKS HAVE HEARTS, ACCORDING TO YOU?
THE BOOK IS THE MAP WHICH LEADS TO THE TREASURE OF ETERNAL LIFE.
ETERNAL LIFE!
IS THAT ALL?
IN TRUTH.
FROM THE SORDID OF THE FINITE TO THE SUBLIME OF THE INFINITE.
IT IS ALL INSIDE.
WOAH, THERE... COULD YOU EXPLAIN BETTER?

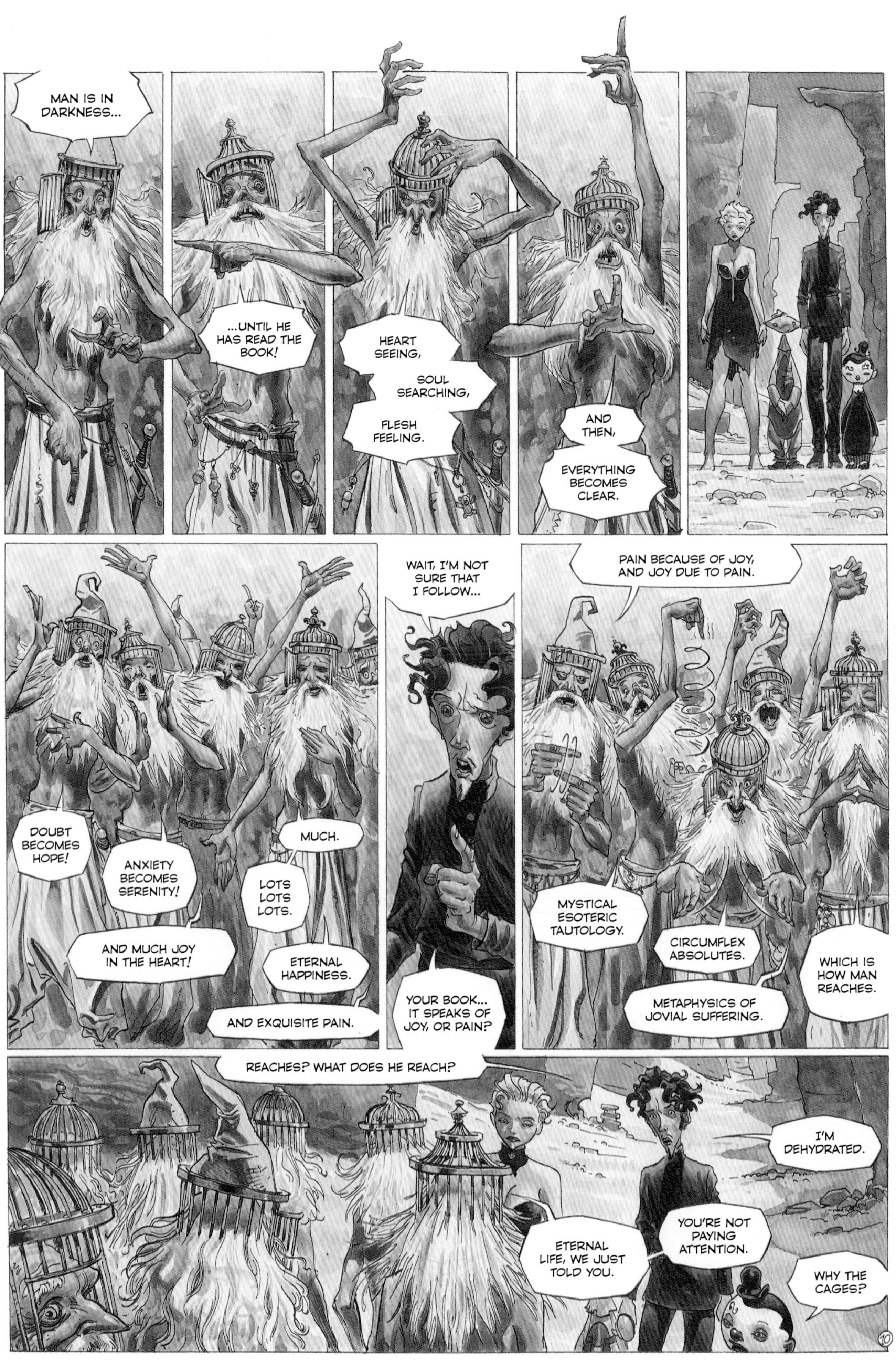

MAN IS IN DARKNESS...
...UNTIL HE HAS READ THE BOOK!
HEART SEEING,
SOUL SEARCHING,
FLESH FEELING.
AND THEN,
EVERYTHING BECOMES CLEAR.
DOUBT BECOMES HOPE!
ANXIETY BECOMES SERENITY!
MUCH.
LOTS LOTS LOTS.
AND MUCH JOY IN THE HEART!
ETERNAL HAPPINESS.
AND EXQUISITE PAIN.
WAIT, I'M NOT SURE THAT I FOLLOW...
YOUR BOOK... IT SPEAKS OF JOY, OR PAIN?
PAIN BECAUSE OF JOY, AND JOY DUE TO PAIN.
MYSTICAL ESOTERIC TAUTOLOGY.
CIRCUMFLEX ABSOLUTES.
METAPHYSICS OF JOVIAL SUFFERING.
WHICH IS HOW MAN REACHES.
REACHES? WHAT DOES HE REACH?
I'M DEHYDRATED.
YOU'RE NOT PAYING ATTENTION.
ETERNAL LIFE, WE JUST TOLD YOU.
WHY THE CAGES?

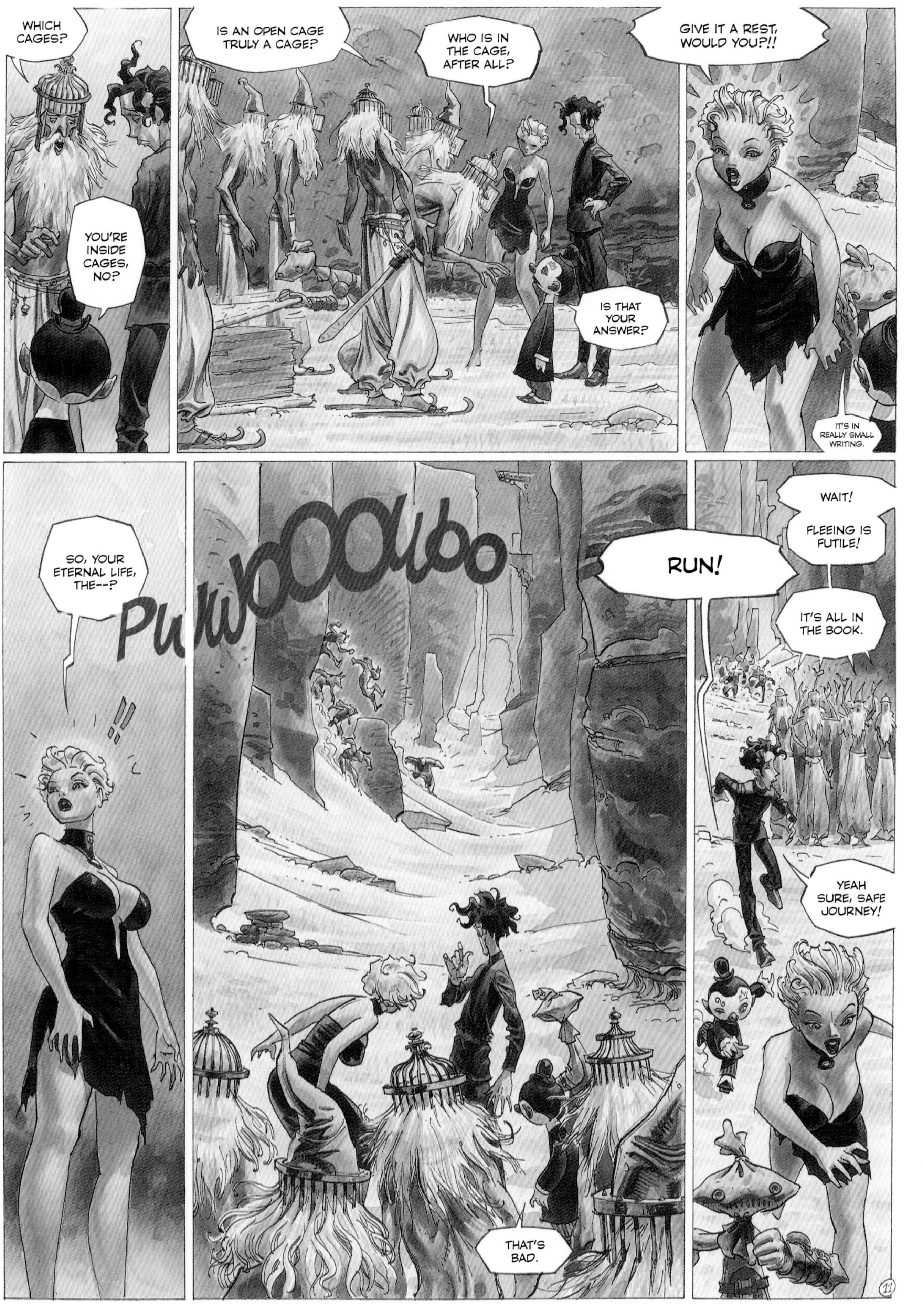
WHICH CAGES?
YOU'RE INSIDE CAGES, NO?
IS AN OPEN CAGE TRULY A CAGE?
WHO IS IN THE CAGE, AFTER ALL?
IS THAT YOUR ANSWER?
GIVE IT A REST, WOULD YOU?!!
IT'S IN REALLY SMALL WRITING.
SO, YOUR ETERNAL LIFE, THE--?
!!
PUWOOOUBO
THAT'S BAD.
RUN!
WAIT!
FLEEING IS FUTILE!
IT'S ALL IN THE BOOK.
YEAH SURE, SAFE JOURNEY!

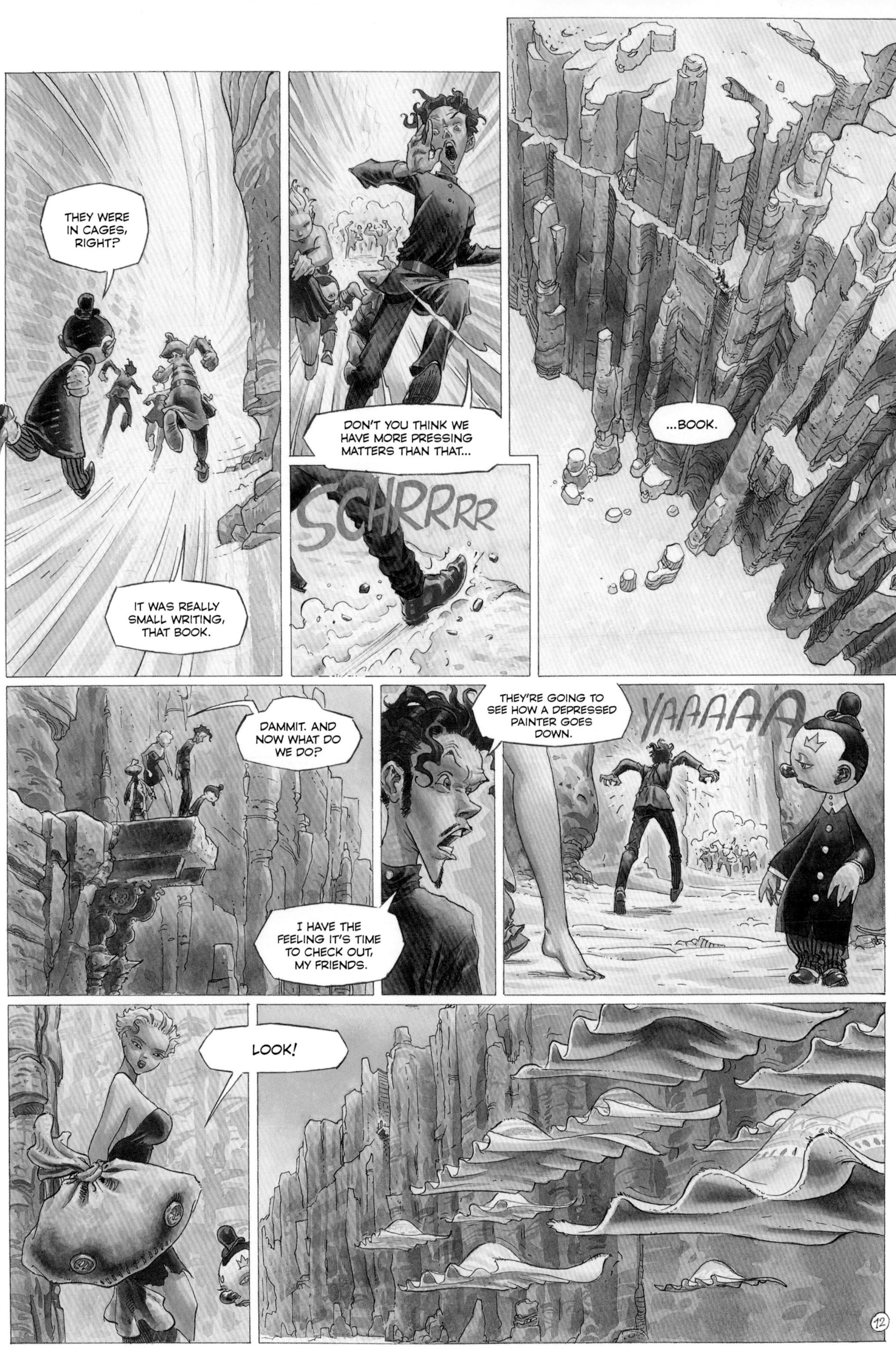
THEY WERE IN CAGES, RIGHT?
IT WAS REALLY SMALL WRITING, THAT BOOK.
DON'T YOU THINK WE HAVE MORE PRESSING MATTERS THAN THAT...
SCHRRRR
...BOOK.
DAMMIT. AND NOW WHAT DO WE DO?
I HAVE THE FEELING IT'S TIME TO CHECK OUT, MY FRIENDS.
THEY'RE GOING TO SEE HOW A DEPRESSED PAINTER GOES DOWN.
YAAAAA
LOOK!

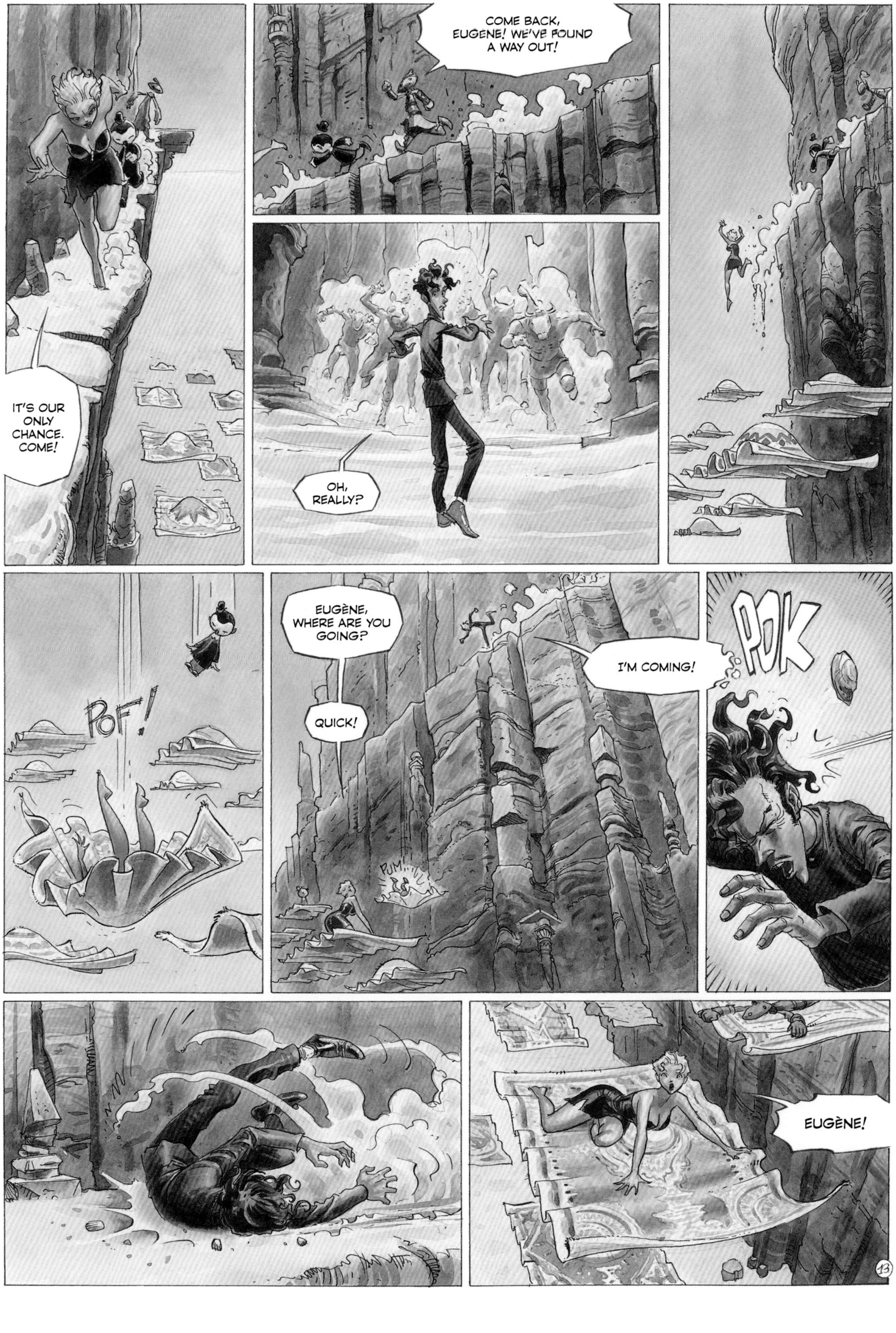

COME BACK, EUGENE! WE'VE FOUND A WAY OUT!
IT'S OUR ONLY CHANCE. COME!
OH, REALLY?
POF!
EUGÈNE, WHERE ARE YOU GOING?
QUICK!
I'M COMING!
POK
EUGÈNE!

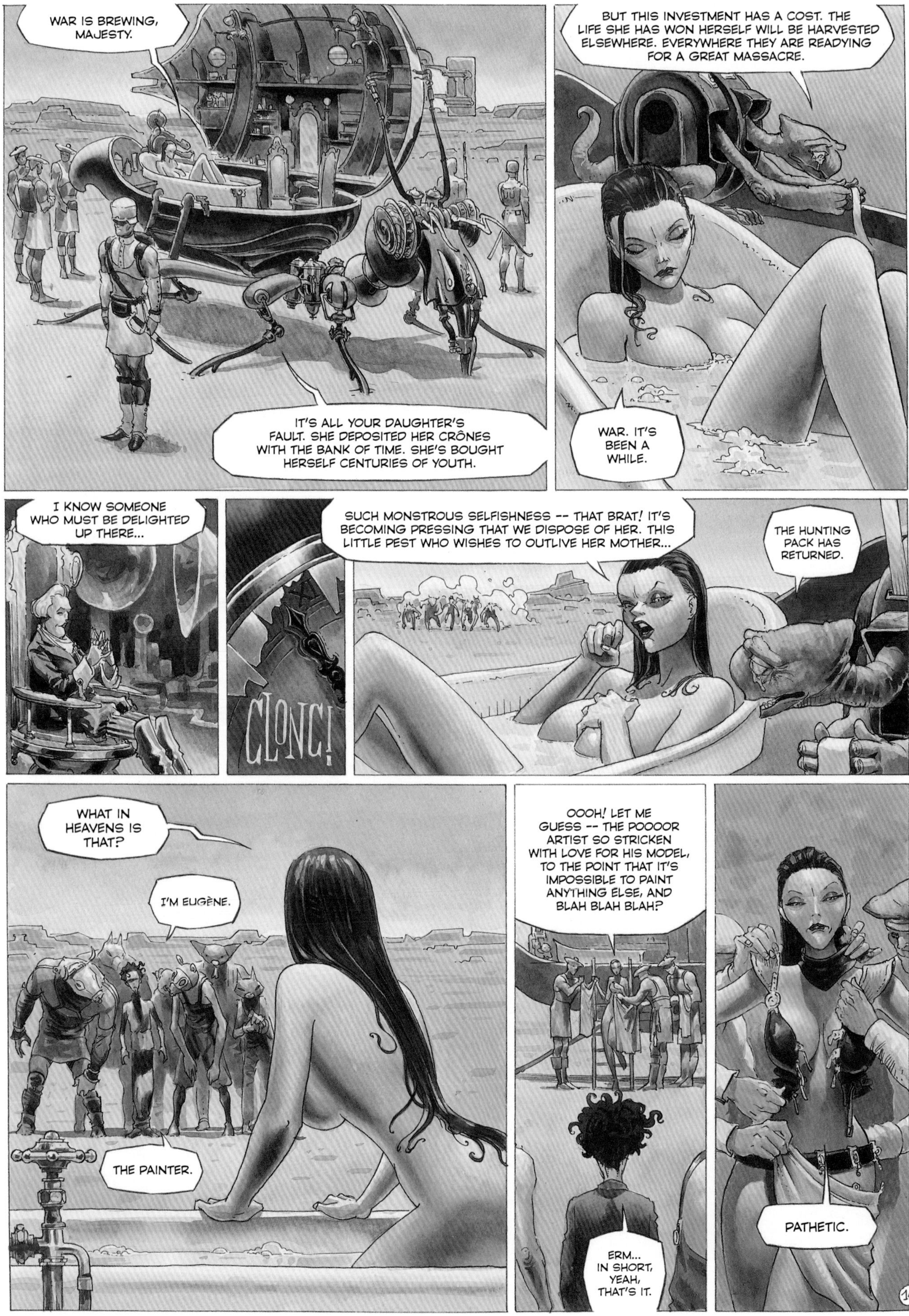
WAR IS BREWING, MAJESTY.
IT'S ALL YOUR DAUGHTER'S FAULT. SHE DEPOSITED HER CRÔNES WITH THE BANK OF TIME. SHE'S BOUGHT HERSELF CENTURIES OF YOUTH.
BUT THIS INVESTMENT HAS A COST. THE LIFE SHE HAS WON HERSELF WILL BE HARVESTED ELSEWHERE. EVERYWHERE THEY ARE READYING FOR A GREAT MASSACRE.
WAR. IT'S BEEN A WHILE.
I KNOW SOMEONE WHO MUST BE DELIGHTED UP THERE...
CLONC!
SUCH MONSTROUS SELFISHNESS -- THAT BRAT! IT'S BECOMING PRESSING THAT WE DISPOSE OF HER. THIS LITTLE PEST WHO WISHES TO OUTLIVE HER MOTHER...
THE HUNTING PACK HAS RETURNED.
WHAT IN HEAVENS IS THAT?
I'M EUGÈNE.
THE PAINTER.
OOOH! LET ME GUESS -- THE POOOOR ARTIST SO STRICKEN WITH LOVE FOR HIS MODEL, TO THE POINT THAT IT'S IMPOSSIBLE TO PAINT ANYTHING ELSE, AND BLAH BLAH BLAH?
ERM... IN SHORT, YEAH, THAT'S IT.
PATHETIC.

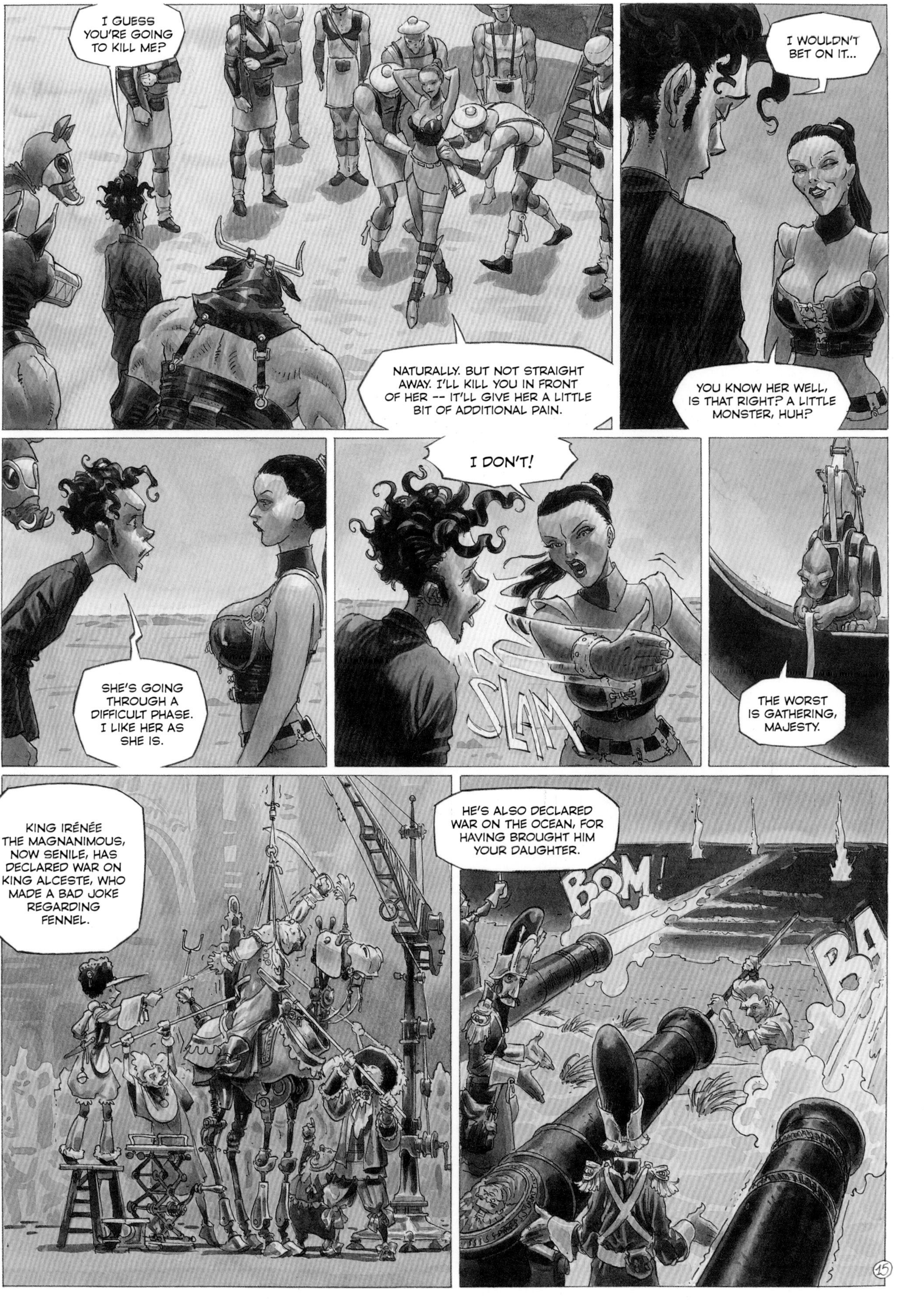
I GUESS YOU'RE GOING TO KILL ME?
NATURALLY. BUT NOT STRAIGHT AWAY. I'LL KILL YOU IN FRONT OF HER -- IT'LL GIVE HER A LITTLE BIT OF ADDITIONAL PAIN.
I WOULDN'T BET ON IT...
YOU KNOW HER WELL, IS THAT RIGHT? A LITTLE MONSTER, HUH?
SHE'S GOING THROUGH A DIFFICULT PHASE. I LIKE HER AS SHE IS.
I DON'T!
SLAM
THE WORST IS GATHERING, MAJESTY.
KING IRÉNÉE THE MAGNANIMOUS, NOW SENILE, HAS DECLARED WAR ON KING ALCESTE, WHO MADE A BAD JOKE REGARDING FENNEL.
HE'S ALSO DECLARED WAR ON THE OCEAN, FOR HAVING BROUGHT HIM YOUR DAUGHTER.
BÔM!

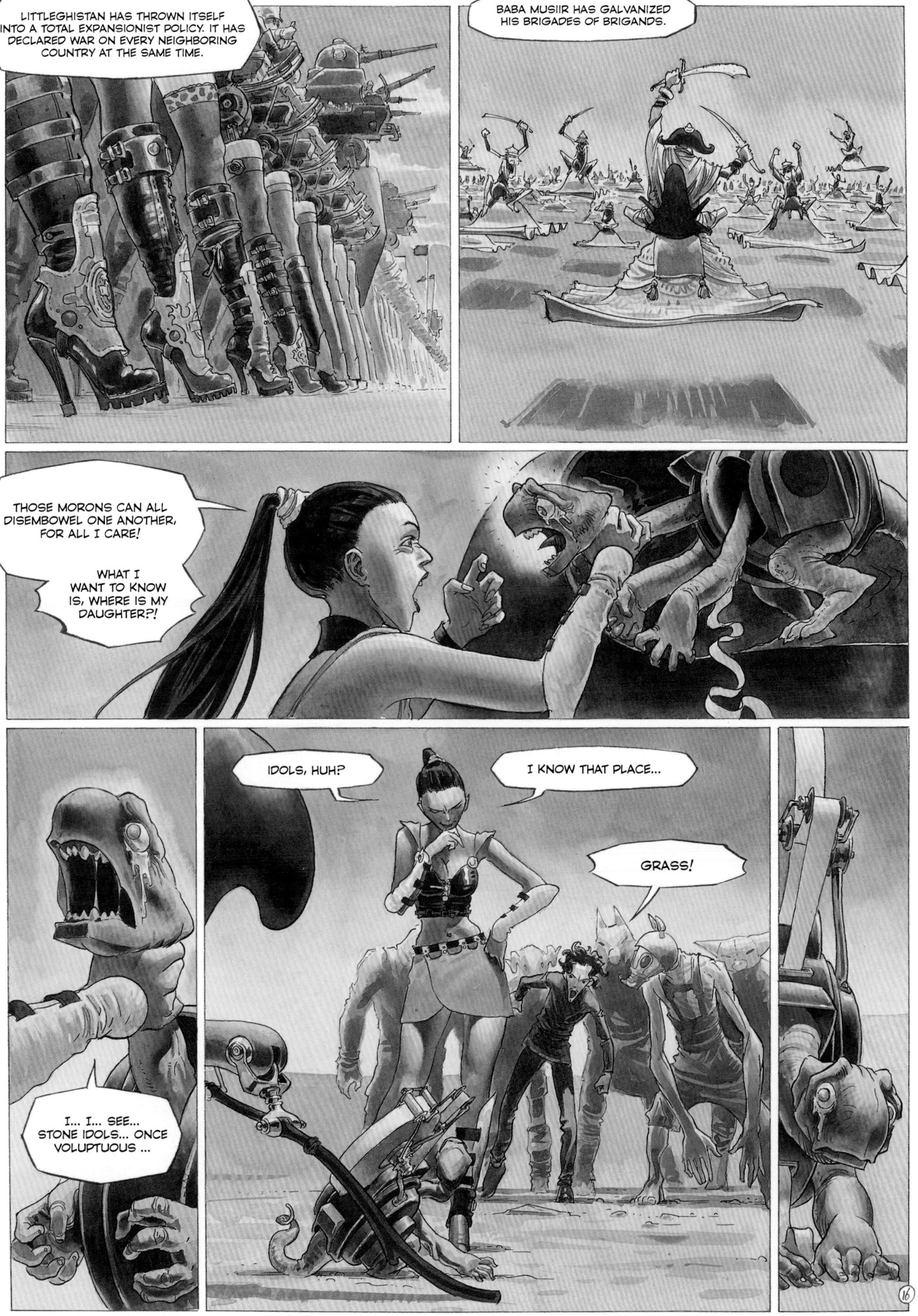
LITTLEGHISTAN HAS THROWN ITSELF INTO A TOTAL EXPANSIONIST POLICY. IT HAS DECLARED WAR ON EVERY NEIGHBORING COUNTRY AT THE SAME TIME.
BABA MUSIIR HAS GALVANIZED HIS BRIGADES OF BRIGANDS.
THOSE MORONS CAN ALL DISEMBOWEL ONE ANOTHER, FOR ALL I CARE!
WHAT I WANT TO KNOW IS, WHERE IS MY DAUGHTER?!
I... I... SEE... STONE IDOLS... ONCE VOLUPTUOUS ...
IDOLS, HUH?
I KNOW THAT PLACE...
GRASS!

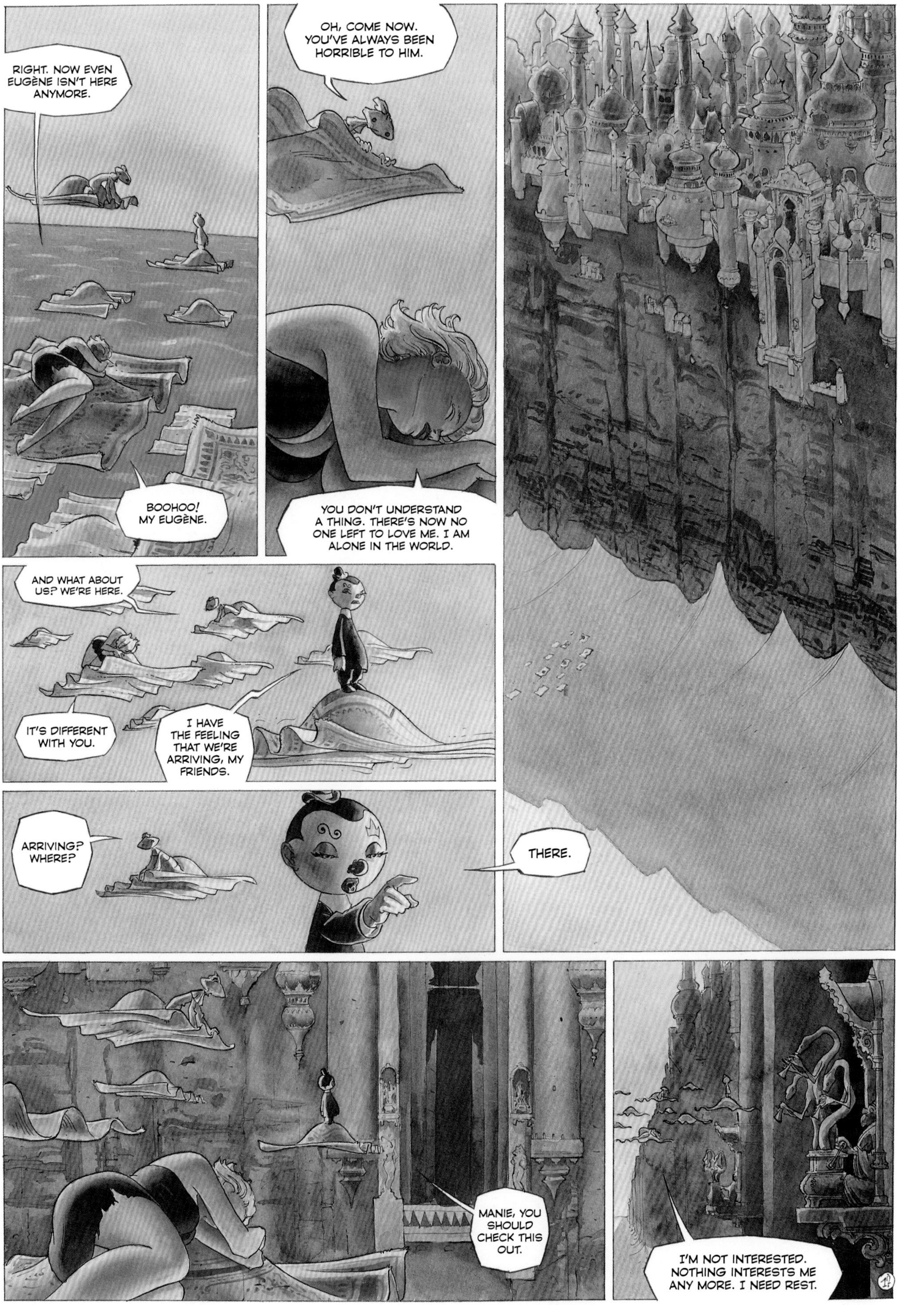
RIGHT. NOW EVEN EUGÈNE ISN'T HERE ANYMORE.
BOOHOO! MY EUGÈNE.
OH, COME NOW. YOU'VE ALWAYS BEEN HORRIBLE TO HIM.
YOU DON'T UNDERSTAND A THING. THERE'S NOW NO ONE LEFT TO LOVE ME. I AM ALONE IN THE WORLD.
AND WHAT ABOUT US? WE'RE HERE.
IT'S DIFFERENT WITH YOU.
I HAVE THE FEELING THAT WE'RE ARRIVING, MY FRIENDS.
ARRIVING? WHERE?
THERE.
MANIE, YOU SHOULD CHECK THIS OUT.
I'M NOT INTERESTED. NOTHING INTERESTS ME ANY MORE. I NEED REST.

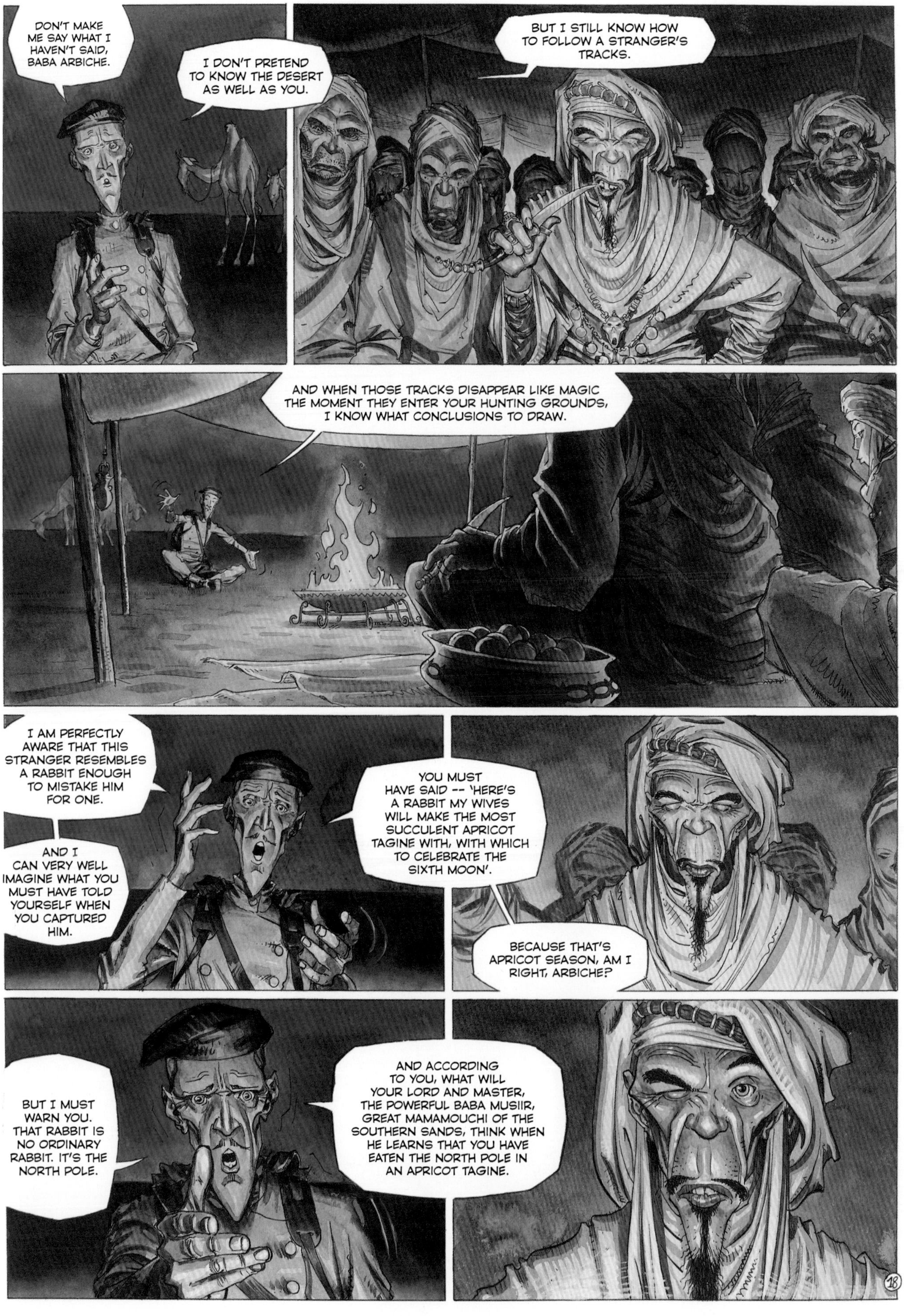
DON'T MAKE ME SAY WHAT I HAVEN'T SAID, BABA ARBICHE.
I DON'T PRETEND TO KNOW THE DESERT AS WELL AS YOU.
BUT I STILL KNOW HOW TO FOLLOW A STRANGER'S TRACKS.
AND WHEN THOSE TRACKS DISAPPEAR LIKE MAGIC THE MOMENT THEY ENTER YOUR HUNTING GROUNDS, I KNOW WHAT CONCLUSIONS TO DRAW.
I AM PERFECTLY AWARE THAT THIS STRANGER RESEMBLES A RABBIT ENOUGH TO MISTAKE HIM FOR ONE.
AND I CAN VERY WELL IMAGINE WHAT YOU MUST HAVE TOLD YOURSELF WHEN YOU CAPTURED HIM.
YOU MUST HAVE SAID -- 'HERE'S A RABBIT MY WIVES WILL MAKE THE MOST SUCCULENT APRICOT TAGINE WITH, WITH WHICH TO CELEBRATE THE SIXTH MOON'.
BECAUSE THAT'S APRICOT SEASON, AM I RIGHT, ARBICHE?
BUT I MUST WARN YOU. THAT RABBIT IS NO ORDINARY RABBIT. IT'S THE NORTH POLE.
AND ACCORDING TO YOU, WHAT WILL YOUR LORD AND MASTER, THE POWERFUL BABA MUSIIR, GREAT MAMAMOUCHI OF THE SOUTHERN SANDS, THINK WHEN HE LEARNS THAT YOU HAVE EATEN THE NORTH POLE IN AN APRICOT TAGINE.
18

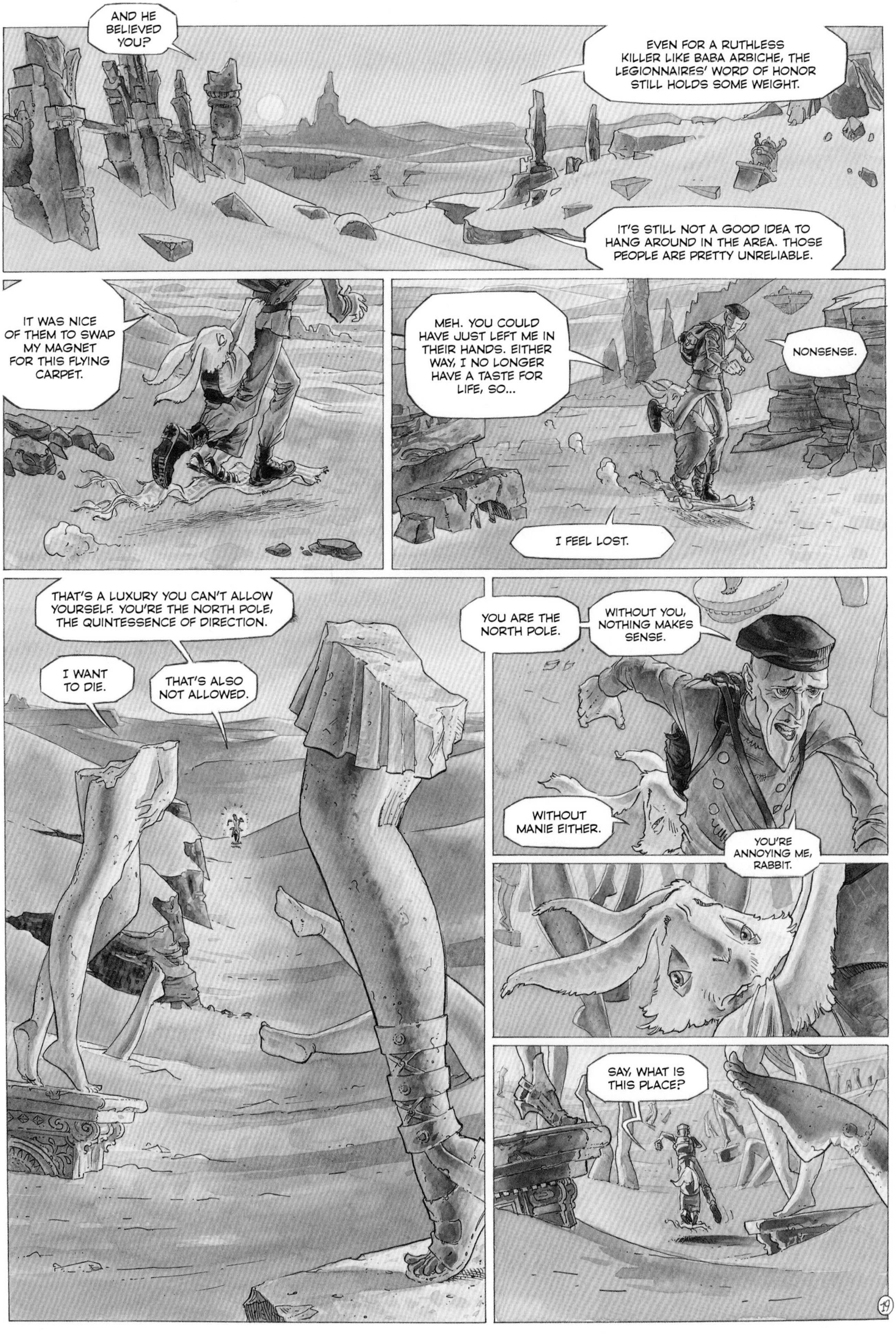
AND HE BELIEVED YOU?
EVEN FOR A RUTHLESS KILLER LIKE BABA ARBICHE, THE LEGIONNAIRES' WORD OF HONOR STILL HOLDS SOME WEIGHT.
IT'S STILL NOT A GOOD IDEA TO HANG AROUND IN THE AREA. THOSE PEOPLE ARE PRETTY UNRELIABLE.
IT WAS NICE OF THEM TO SWAP MY MAGNET FOR THIS FLYING CARPET.
MEH. YOU COULD HAVE JUST LEFT ME IN THEIR HANDS. EITHER WAY, I NO LONGER HAVE A TASTE FOR LIFE, SO...
NONSENSE.
I FEEL LOST.
THAT'S A LUXURY YOU CAN'T ALLOW YOURSELF. YOU'RE THE NORTH POLE, THE QUINTESSENCE OF DIRECTION.
I WANT TO DIE.
THAT'S ALSO NOT ALLOWED.
YOU ARE THE NORTH POLE.
WITHOUT YOU, NOTHING MAKES SENSE.
WITHOUT MANIE EITHER.
YOU'RE ANNOYING ME, RABBIT.
SAY, WHAT IS THIS PLACE?

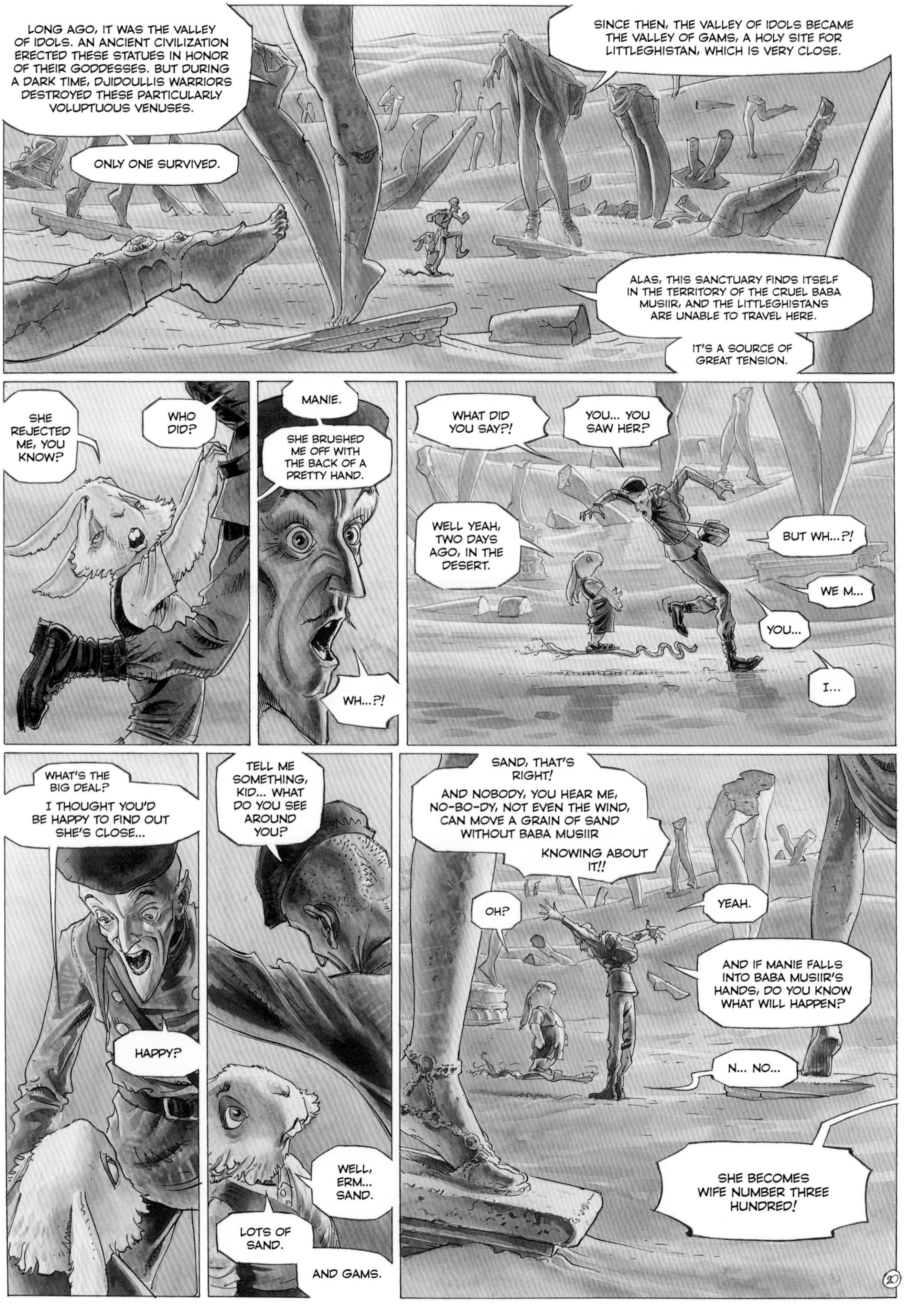

LONG AGO, IT WAS THE VALLEY OF IDOLS. AN ANCIENT CIVILIZATION ERECTED THESE STATUES IN HONOR OF THEIR GODDESSES. BUT DURING A DARK TIME, DJIDOULLIS WARRIORS DESTROYED THESE PARTICULARLY VOLUPTUOUS VENUSES.
ONLY ONE SURVIVED.
SINCE THEN, THE VALLEY OF IDOLS BECAME THE VALLEY OF GAMS, A HOLY SITE FOR LITTLEGHISTAN, WHICH IS VERY CLOSE.
ALAS, THIS SANCTUARY FINDS ITSELF IN THE TERRITORY OF THE CRUEL BABA MUSIIR, AND THE LITTLEGHISTANS ARE UNABLE TO TRAVEL HERE.
IT'S A SOURCE OF GREAT TENSION.
SHE REJECTED ME, YOU KNOW?
WHO DID?
MANIE.
SHE BRUSHED ME OFF WITH THE BACK OF A PRETTY HAND.
WH...?!
WHAT DID YOU SAY?!
YOU... YOU SAW HER?
WELL YEAH, TWO DAYS AGO, IN THE DESERT.
BUT WH...?!
WE M...
YOU...
I...
WHAT'S THE BIG DEAL?
I THOUGHT YOU'D BE HAPPY TO FIND OUT SHE'S CLOSE...
HAPPY?
TELL ME SOMETHING, KID... WHAT DO YOU SEE AROUND YOU?
WELL, ERM... SAND.
LOTS OF SAND.
AND GAMS.
SAND, THAT'S RIGHT!
AND NOBODY, YOU HEAR ME, NO-BO-DY, NOT EVEN THE WIND, CAN MOVE A GRAIN OF SAND WITHOUT BABA MUSIIR
KNOWING ABOUT IT!!
OH?
YEAH.
AND IF MANIE FALLS INTO BABA MUSIIR'S HANDS, DO YOU KNOW WHAT WILL HAPPEN?
N... NO...
SHE BECOMES WIFE NUMBER THREE HUNDRED!

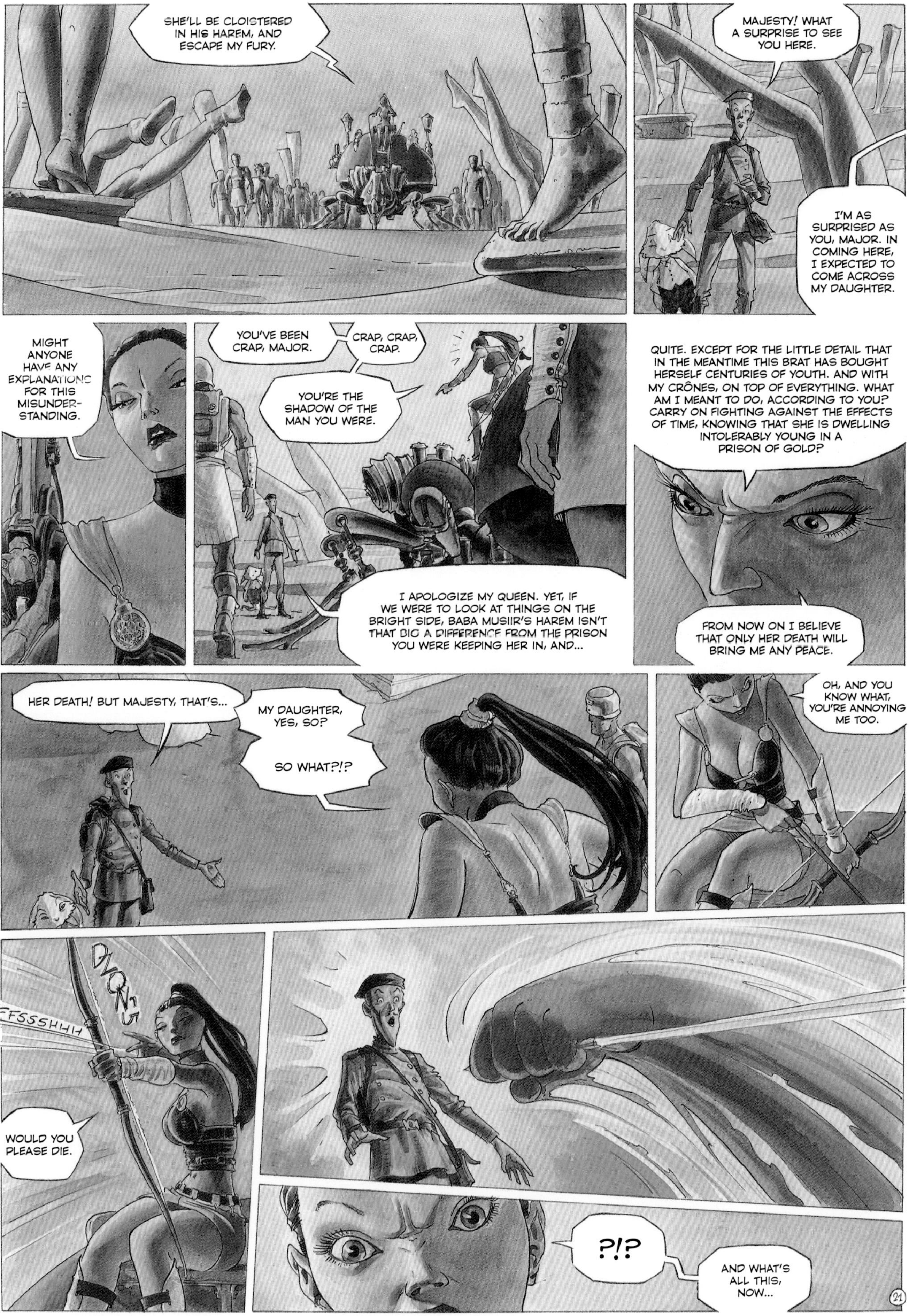
SHE'LL BE CLOISTERED IN HIS HAREM, AND ESCAPE MY FURY.
MAJESTY! WHAT A SURPRISE TO SEE YOU HERE.
I'M AS SURPRISED AS YOU, MAJOR. IN COMING HERE, I EXPECTED TO COME ACROSS MY DAUGHTER.
MIGHT ANYONE HAVE ANY EXPLANATIONS FOR THIS MISUNDER-STANDING.
YOU'VE BEEN CRAP, MAJOR.
CRAP, CRAP, CRAP.
YOU'RE THE SHADOW OF THE MAN YOU WERE.
I APOLOGIZE MY QUEEN. YET, IF WE WERE TO LOOK AT THINGS ON THE BRIGHT SIDE, BABA MUSIIR'S HAREM ISN'T THAT BIG A DIFFERENCE FROM THE PRISON YOU WERE KEEPING HER IN, AND...
QUITE. EXCEPT FOR THE LITTLE DETAIL THAT IN THE MEANTIME THIS BRAT HAS BOUGHT HERSELF CENTURIES OF YOUTH. AND WITH MY CRÔNES, ON TOP OF EVERYTHING. WHAT AM I MEANT TO DO, ACCORDING TO YOU? CARRY ON FIGHTING AGAINST THE EFFECTS OF TIME, KNOWING THAT SHE IS DWELLING INTOLERABLY YOUNG IN A PRISON OF GOLD?
FROM NOW ON I BELIEVE THAT ONLY HER DEATH WILL BRING ME ANY PEACE.
HER DEATH! BUT MAJESTY, THAT'S...
MY DAUGHTER, YES, SO?
SO WHAT?!?
OH, AND YOU KNOW WHAT, YOU'RE ANNOYING ME TOO.
DVONG
FFFSSSHHH
WOULD YOU PLEASE DIE.
?!?
AND WHAT'S ALL THIS, NOW...

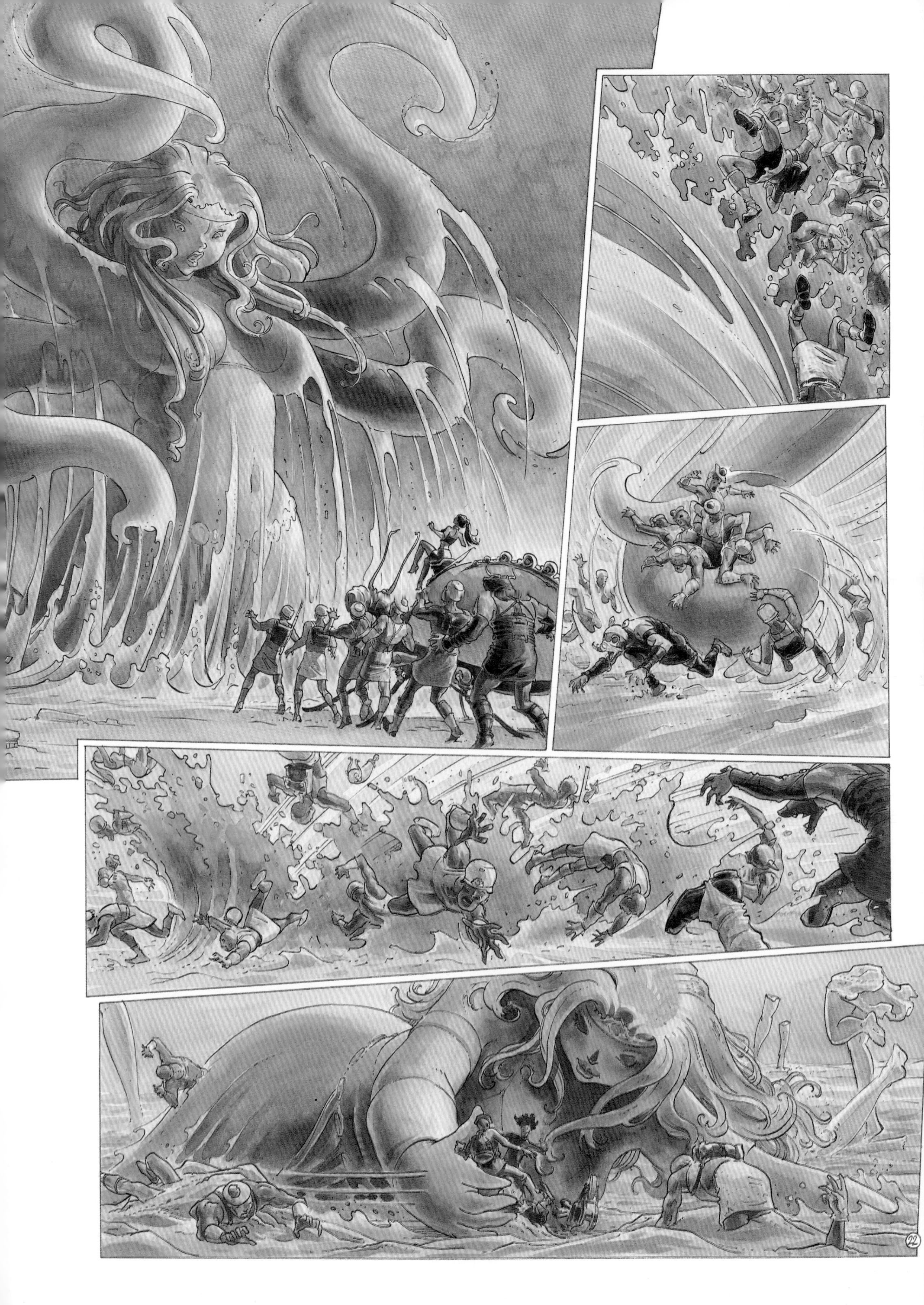

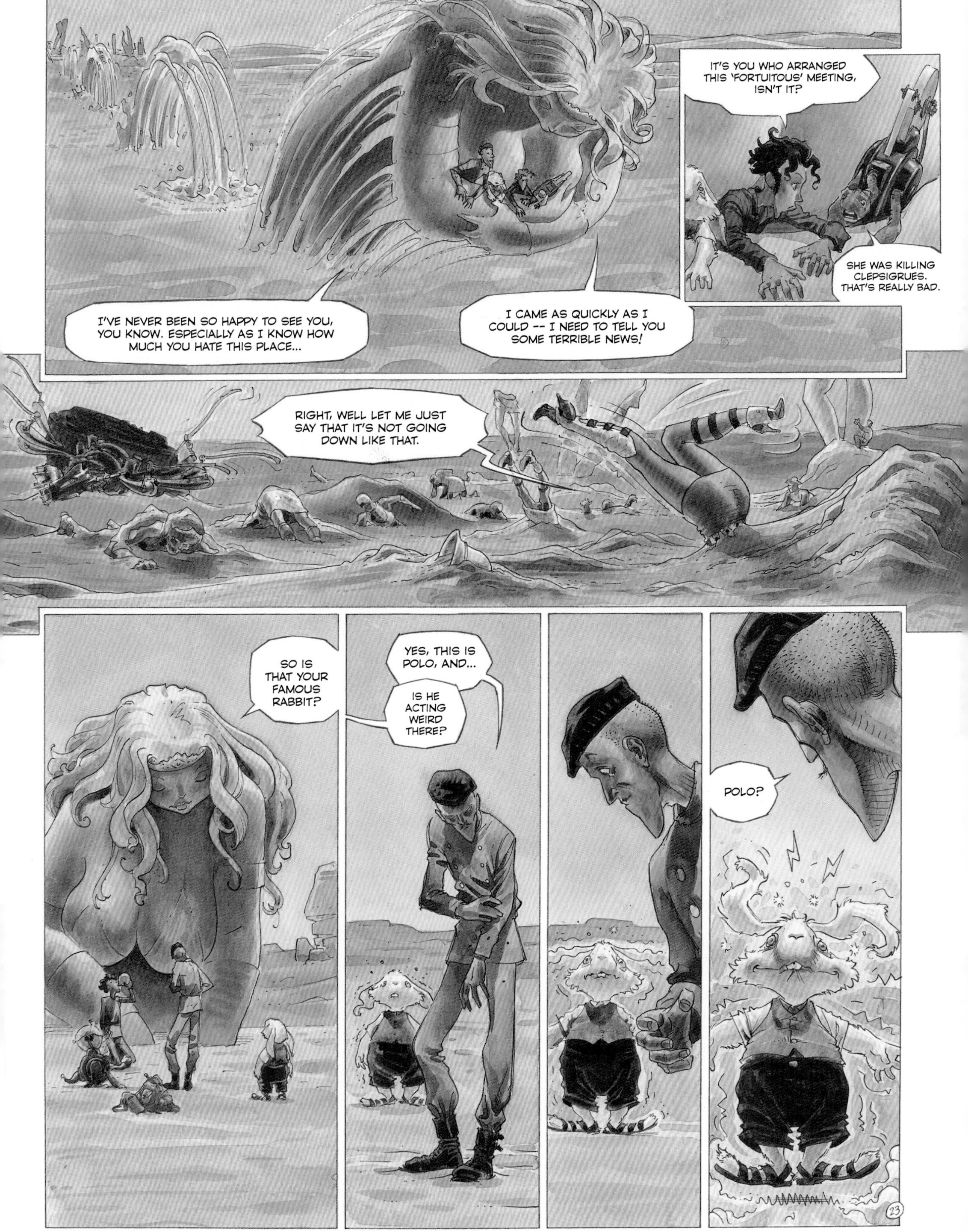
IT'S YOU WHO ARRANGED THIS 'FORTUITOUS' MEETING, ISN'T IT?
SHE WAS KILLING CLEPSIGRUES. THAT'S REALLY BAD.
I'VE NEVER BEEN SO HAPPY TO SEE YOU, YOU KNOW. ESPECIALLY AS I KNOW HOW MUCH YOU HATE THIS PLACE...
I CAME AS QUICKLY AS I COULD -- I NEED TO TELL YOU SOME TERRIBLE NEWS!
RIGHT, WELL LET ME JUST SAY THAT IT'S NOT GOING DOWN LIKE THAT.
SO IS THAT YOUR FAMOUS RABBIT?
YES, THIS IS POLO, AND...
IS HE ACTING WEIRD THERE?
POLO?

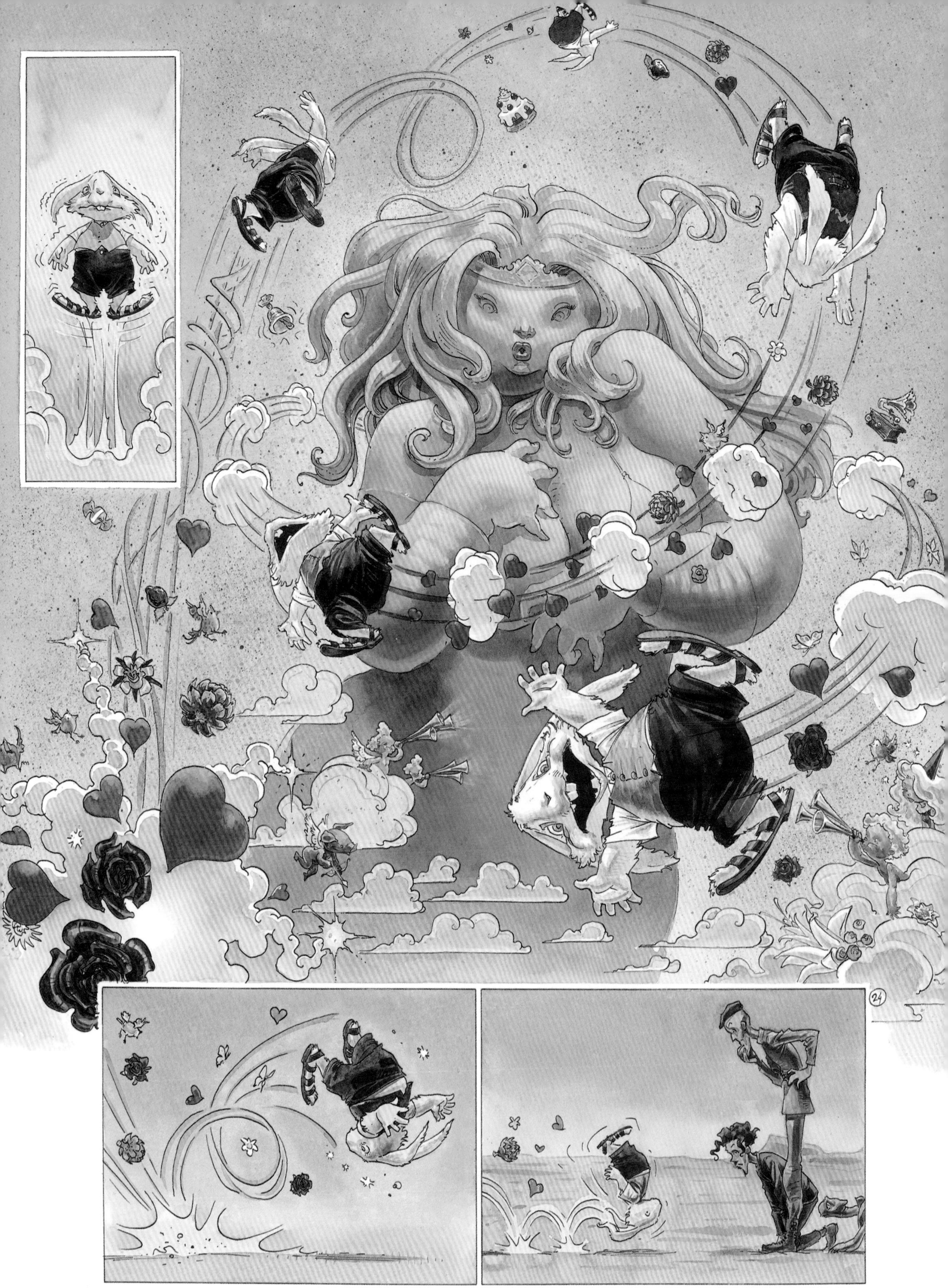

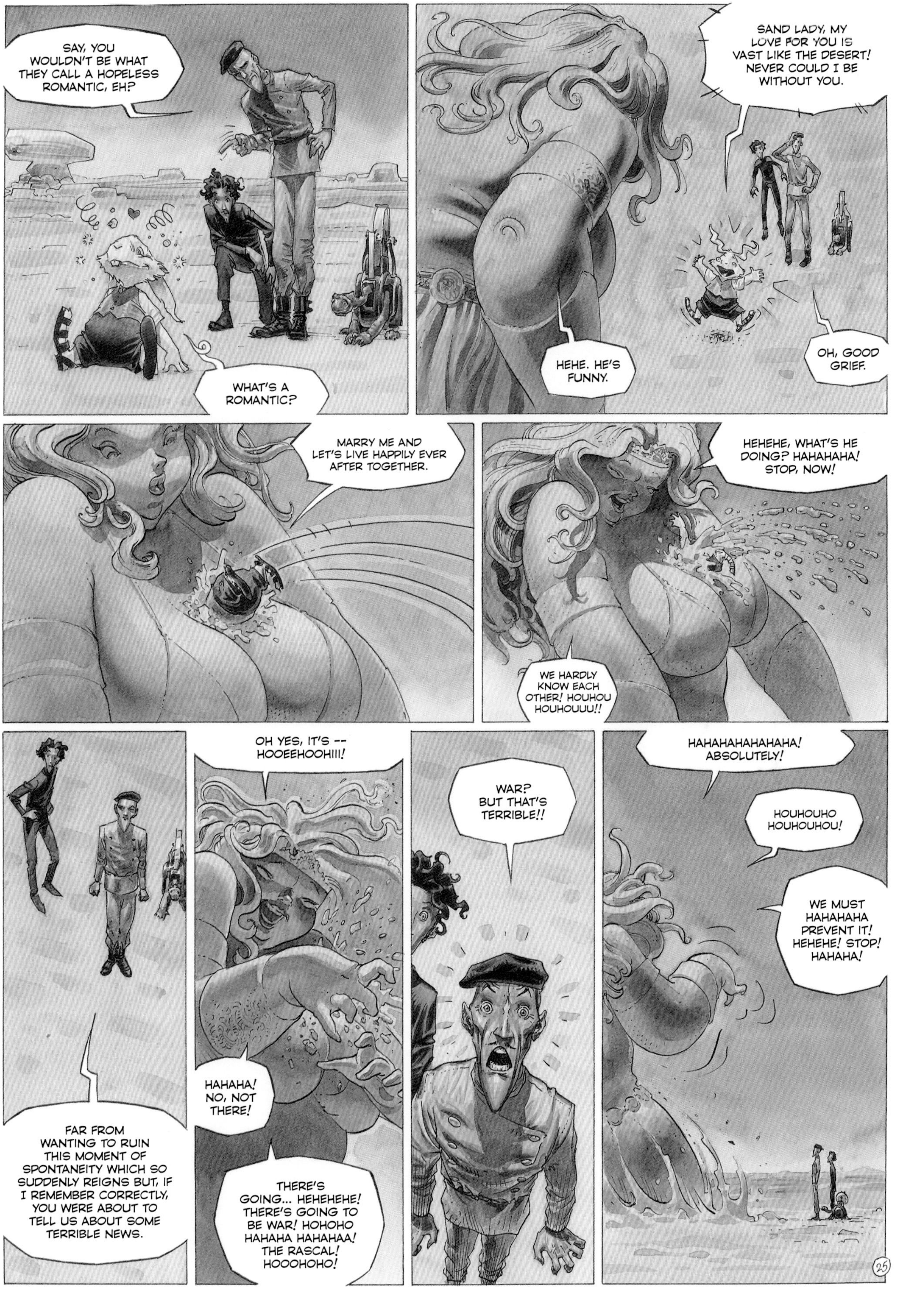

SAY, YOU WOULDN'T BE WHAT THEY CALL A HOPELESS ROMANTIC, EH?
WHAT'S A ROMANTIC?
SAND LADY, MY LOVE FOR YOU IS VAST LIKE THE DESERT! NEVER COULD I BE WITHOUT YOU.
HEHE. HE'S FUNNY.
OH, GOOD GRIEF.
MARRY ME AND LET'S LIVE HAPPILY EVER AFTER TOGETHER.
HEHEHE, WHAT'S HE DOING? HAHAHAHA! STOP, NOW!
WE HARDLY KNOW EACH OTHER! HOUHOU HOUHOUUU!!
FAR FROM WANTING TO RUIN THIS MOMENT OF SPONTANEITY WHICH SO SUDDENLY REIGNS BUT, IF I REMEMBER CORRECTLY, YOU WERE ABOUT TO TELL US ABOUT SOME TERRIBLE NEWS.
OH YES, IT'S -- HOOEEHOOHIII!
HAHAHA! NO, NOT THERE!
THERE'S GOING... HEHEHEHE! THERE'S GOING TO BE WAR! HOHOHO HAHAHA HAHAHAA! THE RASCAL! HOOOHOHO!
WAR? BUT THAT'S TERRIBLE!!
HAHAHAHAHAHAHA! ABSOLUTELY!
HOUHOUHO HOUHOUHOU!
WE MUST HAHAHAHA PREVENT IT! HEHEHE! STOP! HAHAHA!

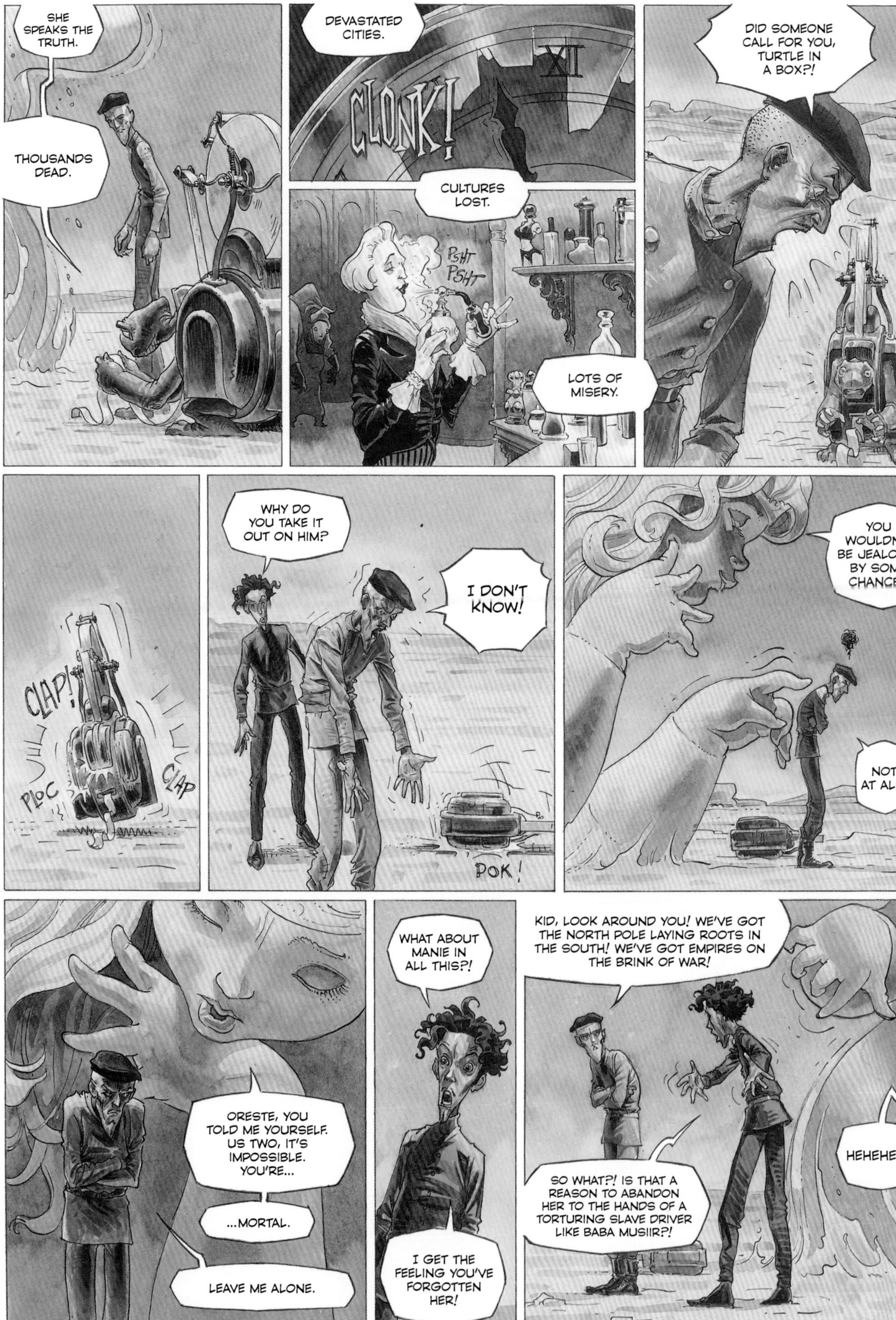
SHE SPEAKS THE TRUTH.
THOUSANDS DEAD.
DEVASTATED CITIES.
CLONK!
CULTURES LOST.
PSHT PSHT
LOTS OF MISERY.
DID SOMEONE CALL FOR YOU, TURTLE IN A BOX?!
CLAP! CLAP PLOC
WHY DO YOU TAKE IT OUT ON HIM?
I DON'T KNOW!
POK!
YOU WOULDN'T BE JEALOUS, BY SOME CHANCE?
NOT AT ALL!
ORESTE, YOU TOLD ME YOURSELF. US TWO, IT'S IMPOSSIBLE. YOU'RE...
...MORTAL.
LEAVE ME ALONE.
WHAT ABOUT MANIE IN ALL THIS?!
I GET THE FEELING YOU'VE FORGOTTEN HER!
KID, LOOK AROUND YOU! WE'VE GOT THE NORTH POLE LAYING ROOTS IN THE SOUTH! WE'VE GOT EMPIRES ON THE BRINK OF WAR!
SO WHAT?! IS THAT A REASON TO ABANDON HER TO THE HANDS OF A TORTURING SLAVE DRIVER LIKE BABA MUSIIR?!
HEHEHEHE!

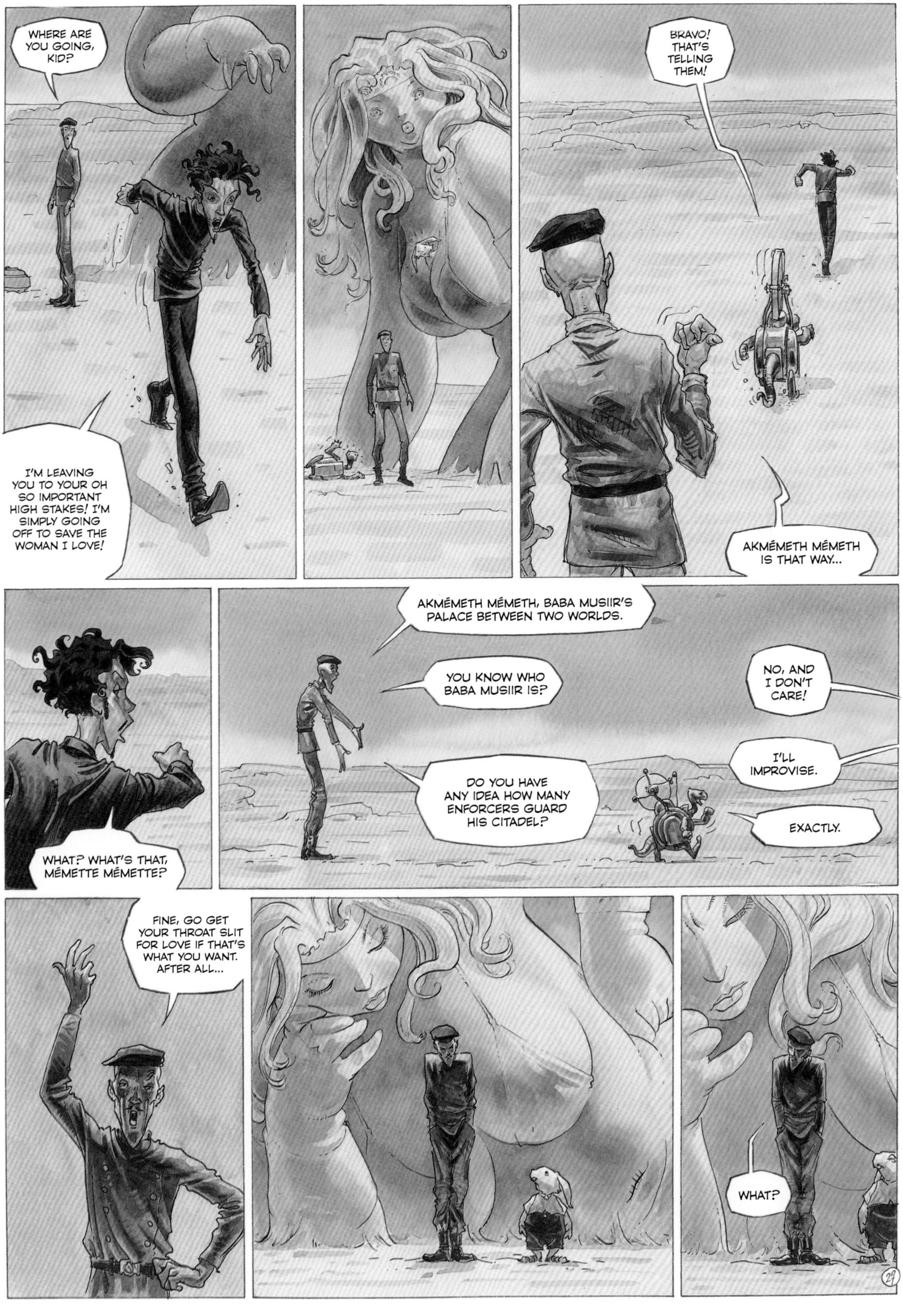
WHERE ARE YOU GOING, KID?
I'M LEAVING YOU TO YOUR OH SO IMPORTANT HIGH STAKES! I'M SIMPLY GOING OFF TO SAVE THE WOMAN I LOVE!
BRAVO! THAT'S TELLING THEM!
AKMÉMETH MÉMETH IS THAT WAY...
WHAT? WHAT'S THAT, MÉMETTE MÉMETTE?
AKMÉMETH MÉMETH, BABA MUSIIR'S PALACE BETWEEN TWO WORLDS.
YOU KNOW WHO BABA MUSIIR IS?
NO, AND I DON'T CARE!
DO YOU HAVE ANY IDEA HOW MANY ENFORCERS GUARD HIS CITADEL?
I'LL IMPROVISE.
EXACTLY.
FINE, GO GET YOUR THROAT SLIT FOR LOVE IF THAT'S WHAT YOU WANT. AFTER ALL...
WHAT?

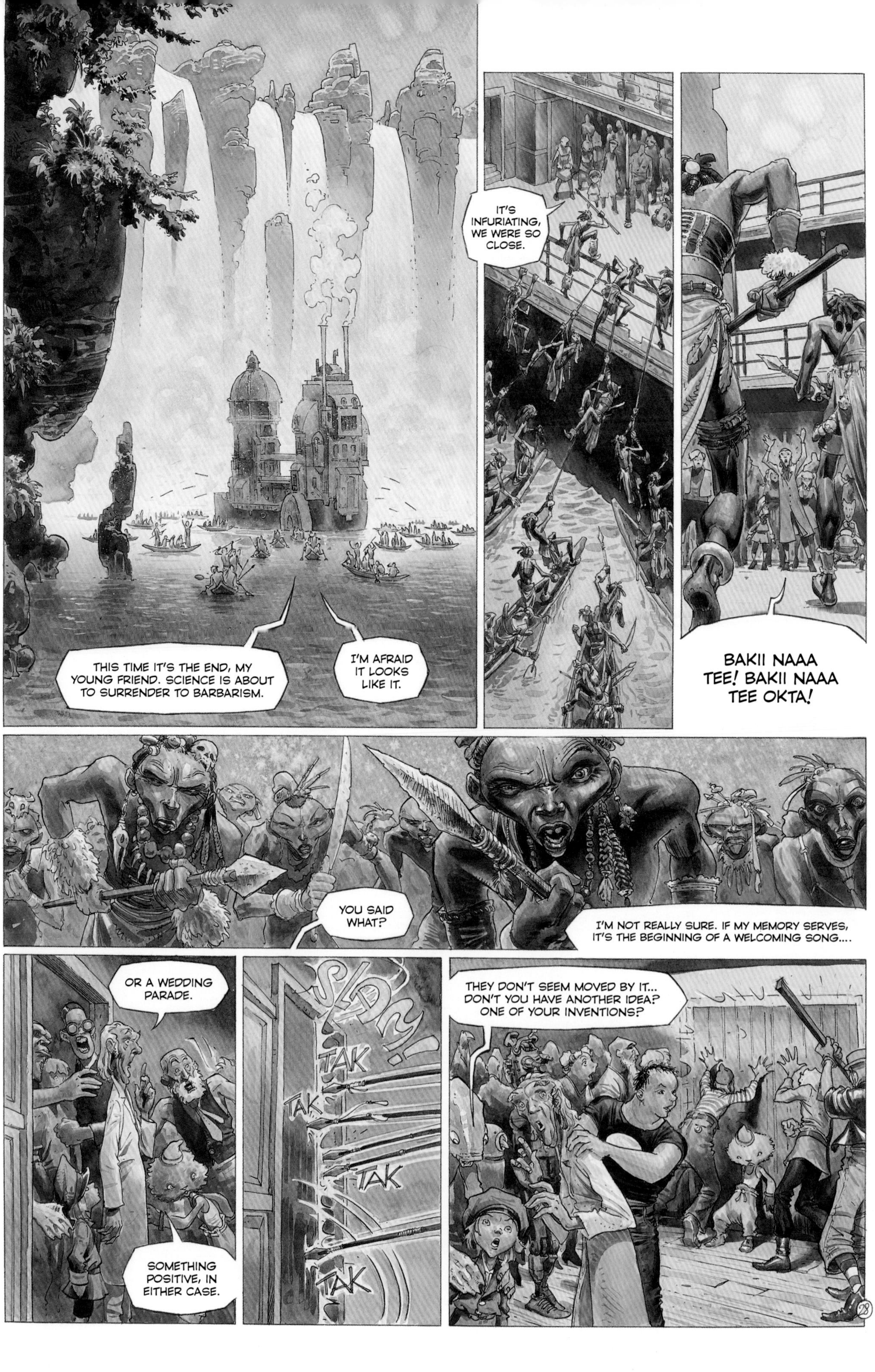
THIS TIME IT'S THE END, MY YOUNG FRIEND. SCIENCE IS ABOUT TO SURRENDER TO BARBARISM.
I'M AFRAID IT LOOKS LIKE IT.
IT'S INFURIATING, WE WERE SO CLOSE.
BAKII NAAA TEE! BAKII NAAA TEE OKTA!
YOU SAID WHAT?
I'M NOT REALLY SURE. IF MY MEMORY SERVES, IT'S THE BEGINNING OF A WELCOMING SONG....
OR A WEDDING PARADE.
SOMETHING POSITIVE, IN EITHER CASE.
SLOY!
TAK
TAK
TAK
TAK
THEY DON'T SEEM MOVED BY IT... DON'T YOU HAVE ANOTHER IDEA? ONE OF YOUR INVENTIONS?

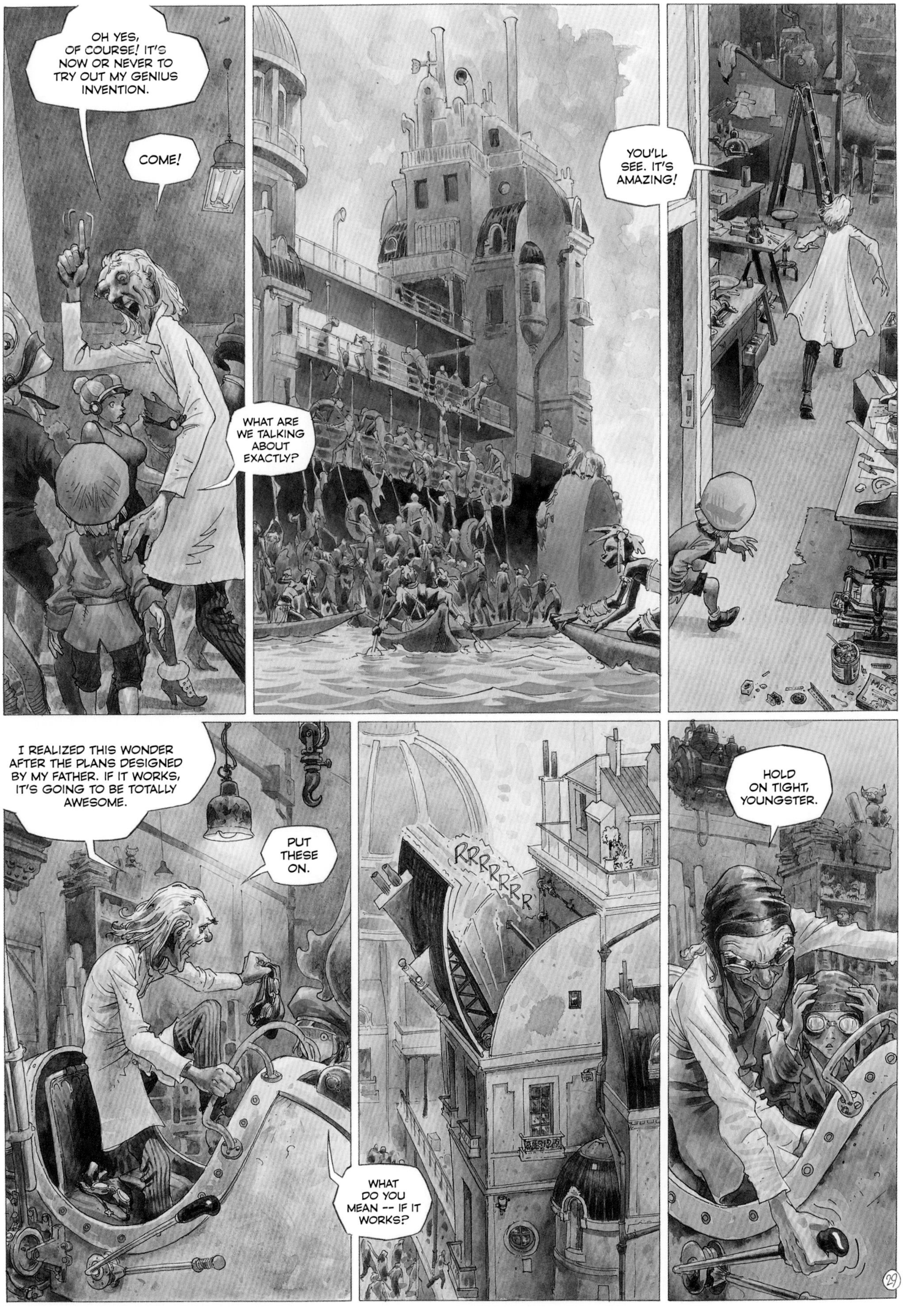
OH YES, OF COURSE! IT'S NOW OR NEVER TO TRY OUT MY GENIUS INVENTION.
COME!
WHAT ARE WE TALKING ABOUT EXACTLY?
YOU'LL SEE. IT'S AMAZING!
I REALIZED THIS WONDER AFTER THE PLANS DESIGNED BY MY FATHER. IF IT WORKS, IT'S GOING TO BE TOTALLY AWESOME.
PUT THESE ON.
RRRRRRRR
WHAT DO YOU MEAN -- IF IT WORKS?
HOLD ON TIGHT, YOUNGSTER.

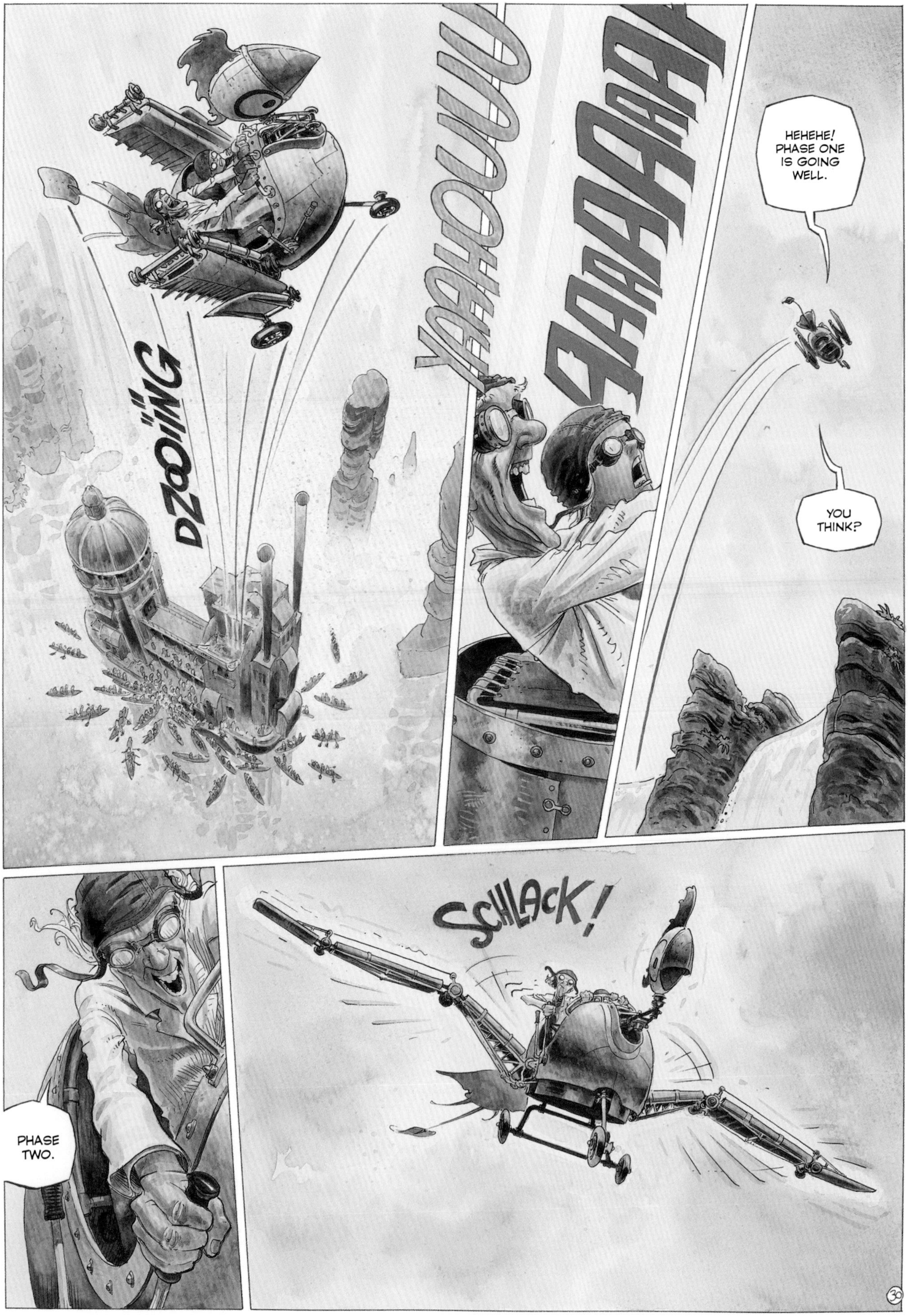
DZOOIING
HEHEHE! PHASE ONE IS GOING WELL.
YOU THINK?
PHASE TWO.
SCHLACK!

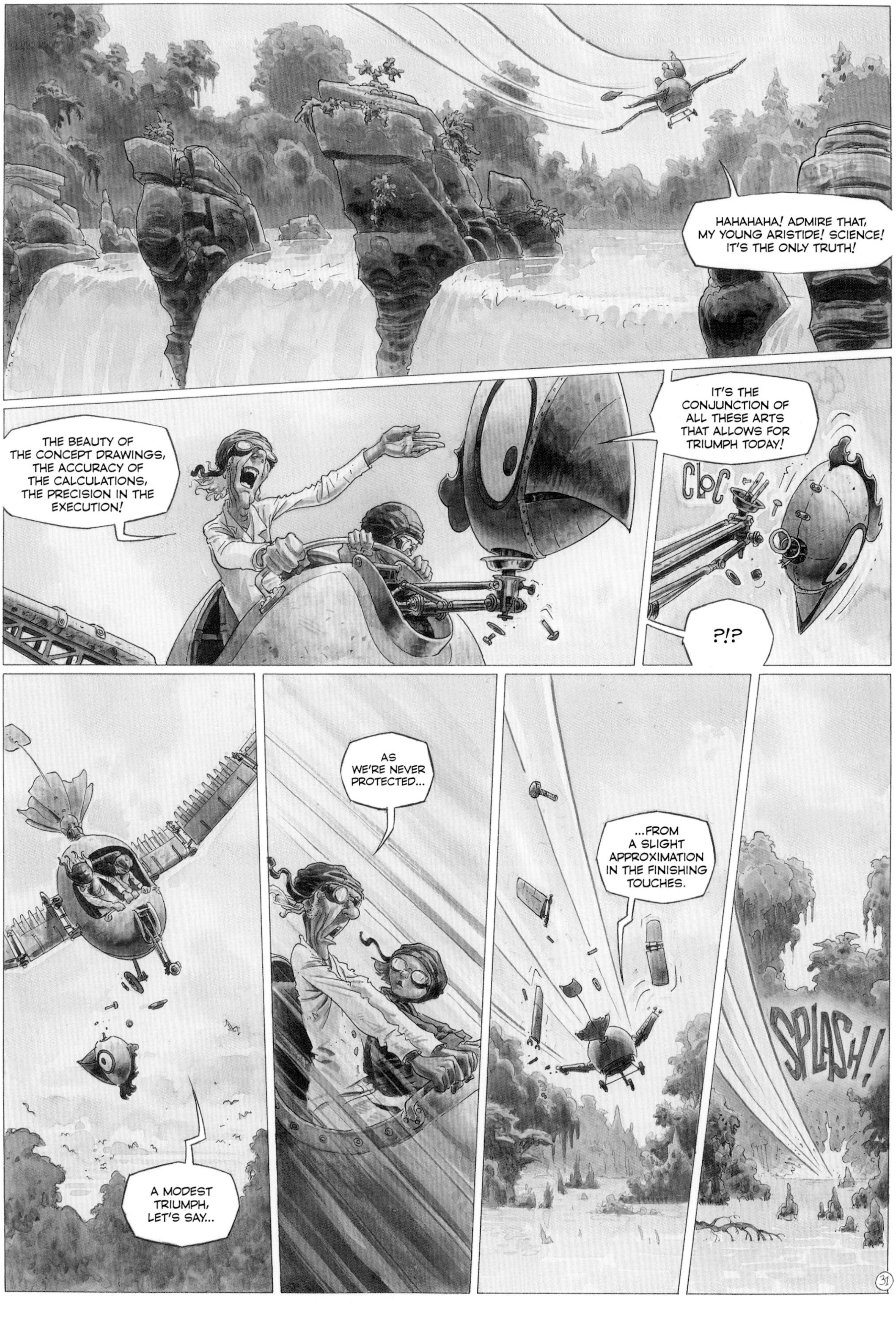

HAHAHAHA! ADMIRE THAT, MY YOUNG ARISTIDE! SCIENCE! IT'S THE ONLY TRUTH!
THE BEAUTY OF THE CONCEPT DRAWINGS, THE ACCURACY OF THE CALCULATIONS, THE PRECISION IN THE EXECUTION!
IT'S THE CONJUNCTION OF ALL THESE ARTS THAT ALLOWS FOR TRIUMPH TODAY!
CLOC
?!?
A MODEST TRIUMPH, LET'S SAY...
AS WE'RE NEVER PROTECTED...
...FROM A SLIGHT APPROXIMATION IN THE FINISHING TOUCHES.
SPLASH!

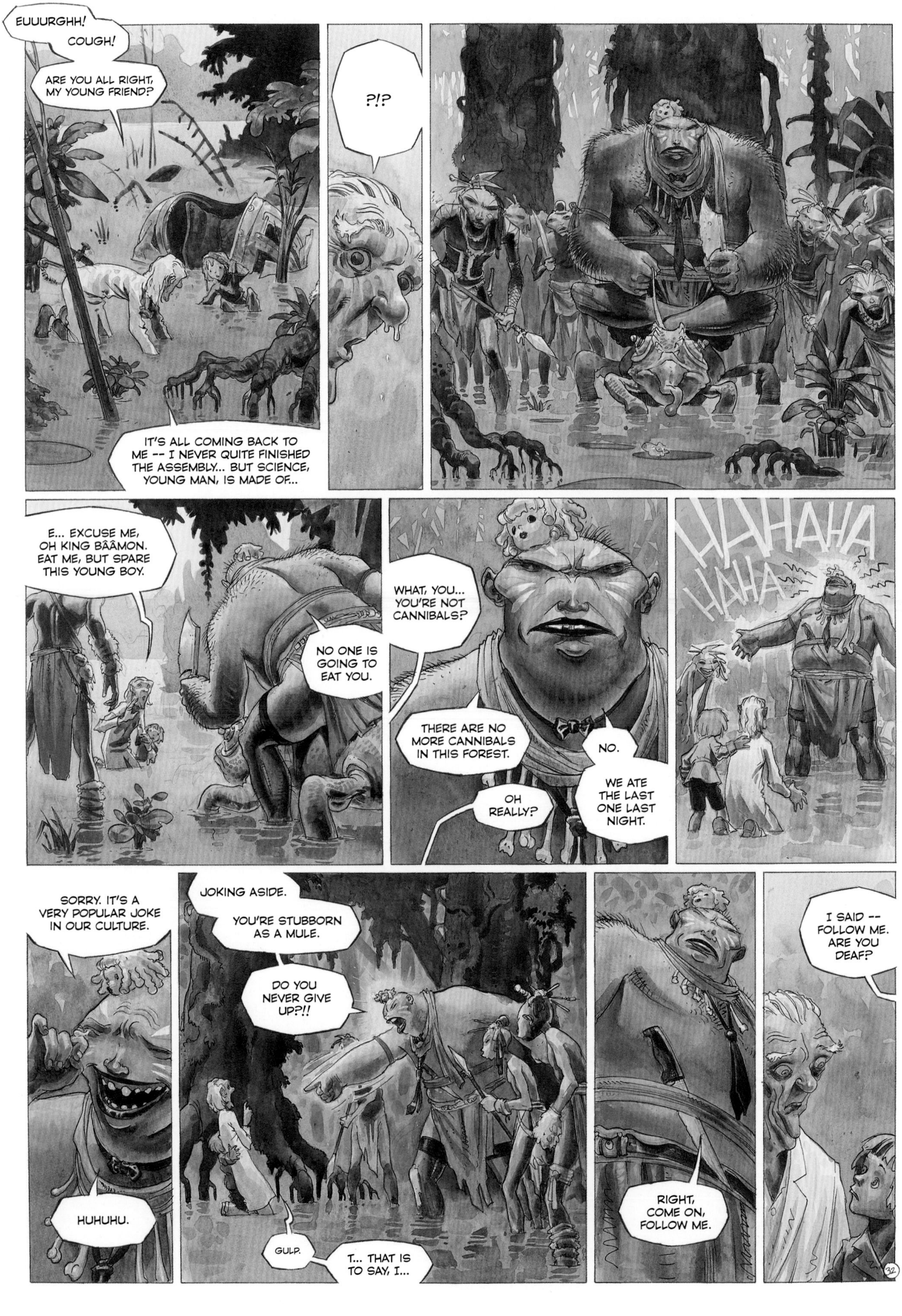
EUUURGHH!
COUGH!
ARE YOU ALL RIGHT, MY YOUNG FRIEND?
IT'S ALL COMING BACK TO ME -- I NEVER QUITE FINISHED THE ASSEMBLY... BUT SCIENCE, YOUNG MAN, IS MADE OF...
?!?
E... EXCUSE ME, OH KING BÂÂMON. EAT ME, BUT SPARE THIS YOUNG BOY.
NO ONE IS GOING TO EAT YOU.
WHAT, YOU... YOU'RE NOT CANNIBALS?
THERE ARE NO MORE CANNIBALS IN THIS FOREST.
OH REALLY?
NO.
WE ATE THE LAST ONE LAST NIGHT.
HAHAHA
HAHA
SORRY. IT'S A VERY POPULAR JOKE IN OUR CULTURE.
HUHUHU.
JOKING ASIDE.
YOU'RE STUBBORN AS A MULE.
DO YOU NEVER GIVE UP?!!
GULP.
T... THAT IS TO SAY, I...
RIGHT, COME ON, FOLLOW ME.
I SAID -- FOLLOW ME. ARE YOU DEAF?

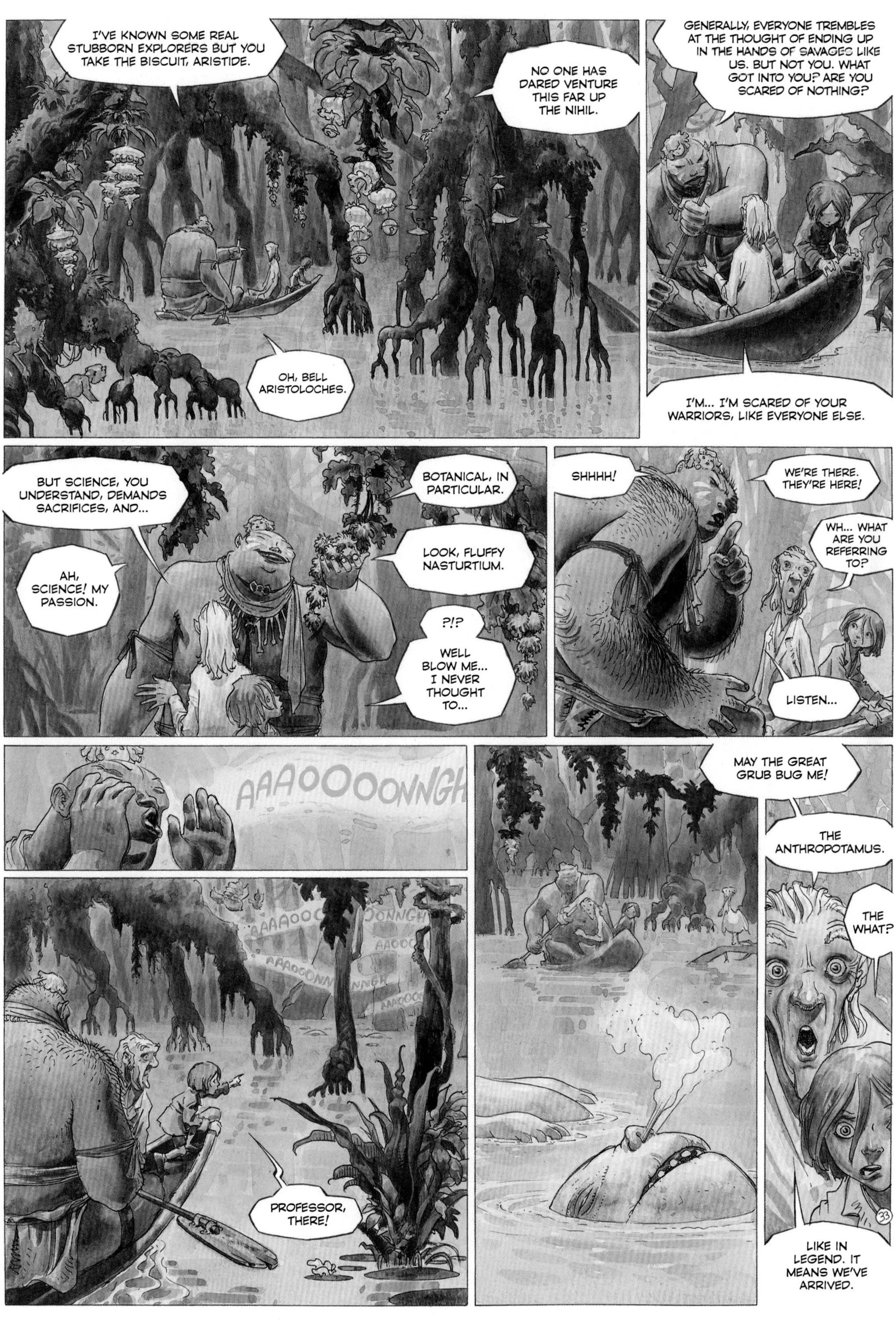
I'VE KNOWN SOME REAL STUBBORN EXPLORERS BUT YOU TAKE THE BISCUIT, ARISTIDE.
NO ONE HAS DARED VENTURE THIS FAR UP THE NIHIL.
OH, BELL ARISTOLOCHES.
GENERALLY, EVERYONE TREMBLES AT THE THOUGHT OF ENDING UP IN THE HANDS OF SAVAGES LIKE US. BUT NOT YOU. WHAT GOT INTO YOU? ARE YOU SCARED OF NOTHING?
I'M... I'M SCARED OF YOUR WARRIORS, LIKE EVERYONE ELSE.
BUT SCIENCE, YOU UNDERSTAND, DEMANDS SACRIFICES, AND...
AH, SCIENCE! MY PASSION.
BOTANICAL, IN PARTICULAR.
LOOK, FLUFFY NASTURTIUM.
?!?
WELL BLOW ME... I NEVER THOUGHT TO...
SHHHH!
WE'RE THERE. THEY'RE HERE!
WH... WHAT ARE YOU REFERRING TO?
LISTEN...
AAAOOOONNGH
AAAAOOO
OONNGH
AAAOOO
AAAOOONN
NNGH
AAAOOO
PROFESSOR, THERE!
MAY THE GREAT GRUB BUG ME!
THE ANTHROPOTAMUS.
THE WHAT?
LIKE IN LEGEND. IT MEANS WE'VE ARRIVED.
33

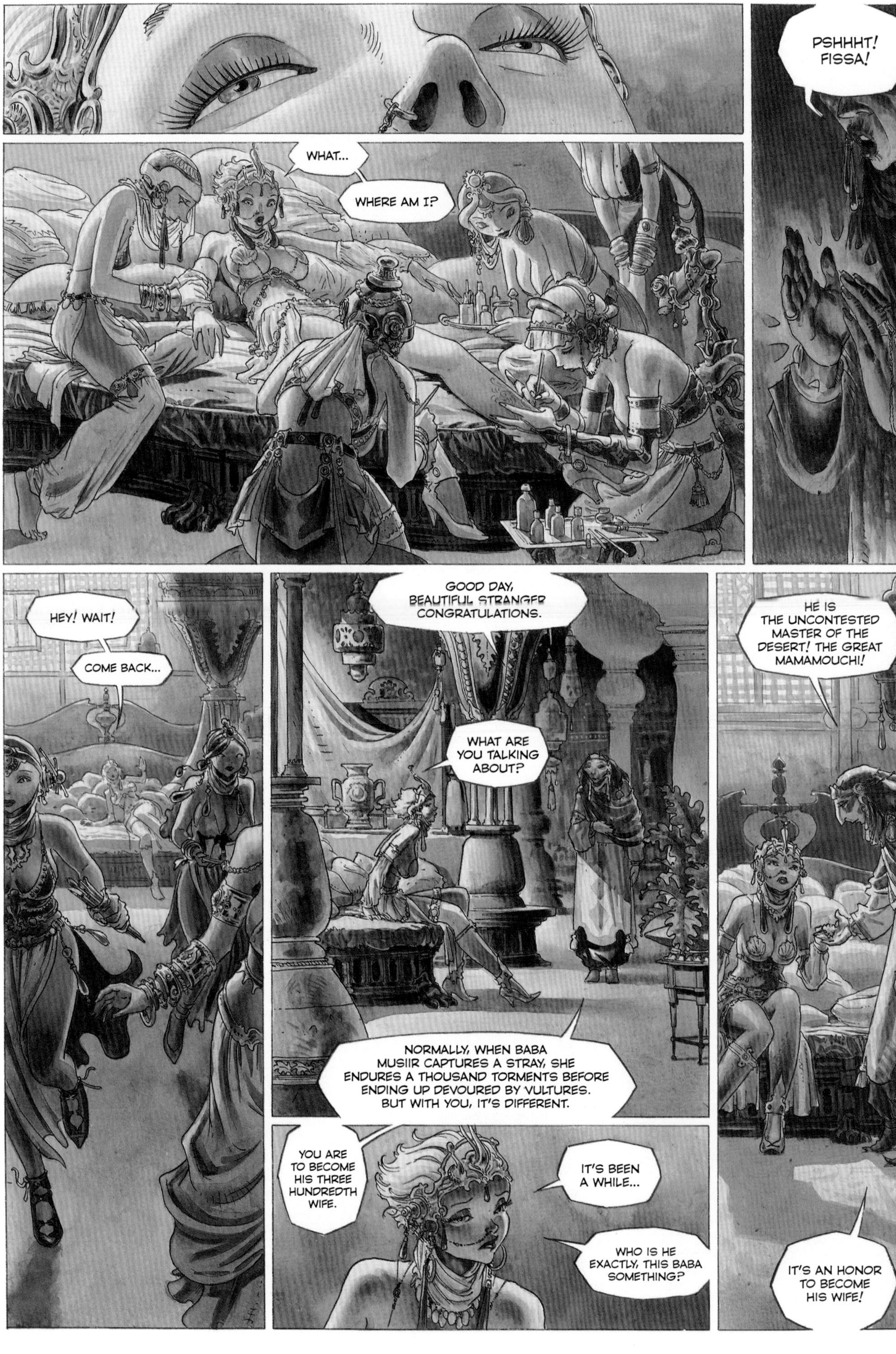
WHAT...
WHERE AM I?
PSHHHT! FISSA!
HEY! WAIT!
COME BACK...
GOOD DAY, BEAUTIFUL STRANGER CONGRATULATIONS.
WHAT ARE YOU TALKING ABOUT?
NORMALLY, WHEN BABA MUSIIR CAPTURES A STRAY, SHE ENDURES A THOUSAND TORMENTS BEFORE ENDING UP DEVOURED BY VULTURES. BUT WITH YOU, IT'S DIFFERENT.
YOU ARE TO BECOME HIS THREE HUNDREDTH WIFE.
IT'S BEEN A WHILE...
WHO IS HE EXACTLY, THIS BABA SOMETHING?
HE IS THE UNCONTESTED MASTER OF THE DESERT! THE GREAT MAMAMOUCHI!
IT'S AN HONOR TO BECOME HIS WIFE!
34

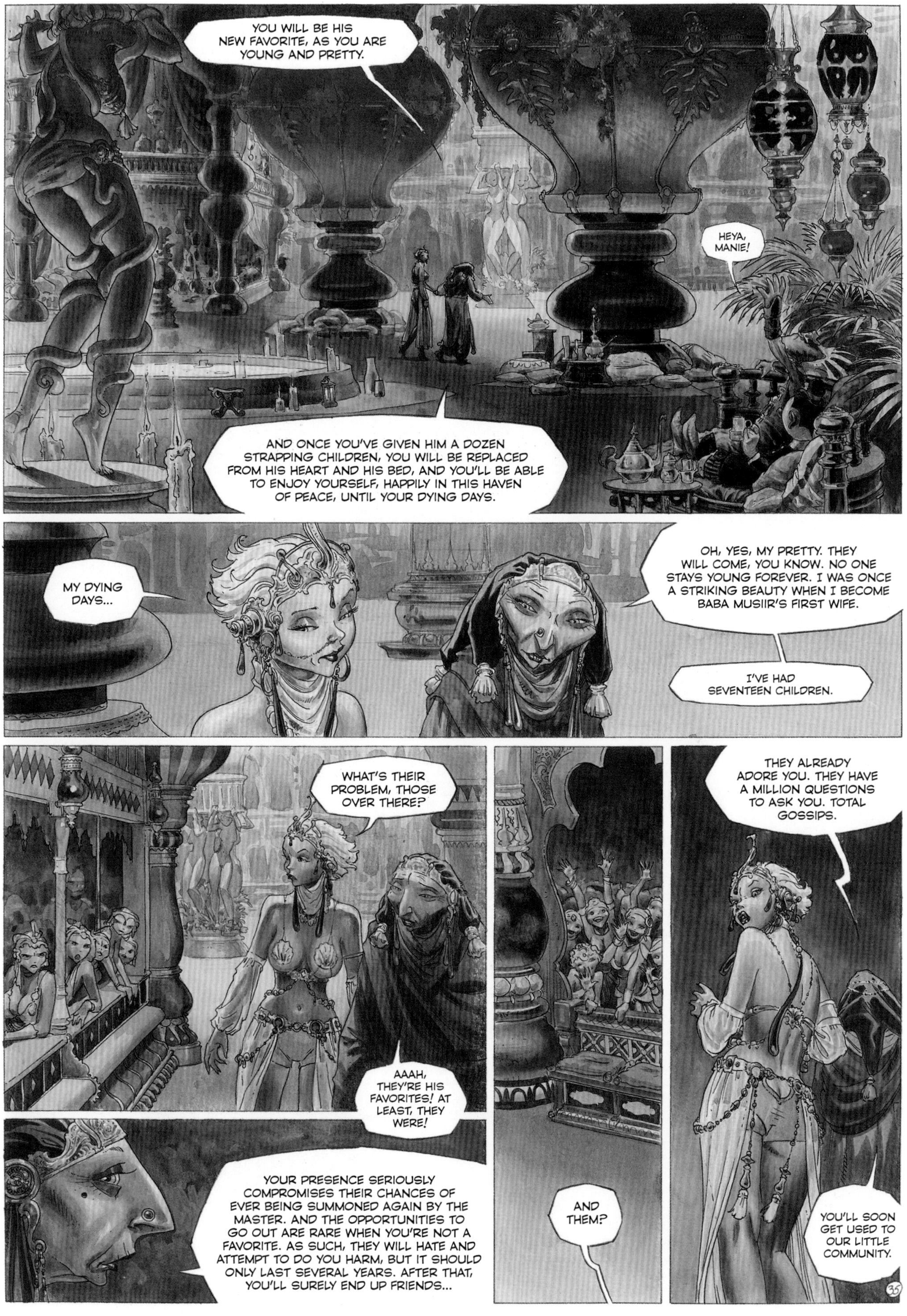
YOU WILL BE HIS NEW FAVORITE, AS YOU ARE YOUNG AND PRETTY.
HEYA, MANIE!
AND ONCE YOU'VE GIVEN HIM A DOZEN STRAPPING CHILDREN, YOU WILL BE REPLACED FROM HIS HEART AND HIS BED, AND YOU'LL BE ABLE TO ENJOY YOURSELF, HAPPILY IN THIS HAVEN OF PEACE, UNTIL YOUR DYING DAYS.
MY DYING DAYS...
OH, YES, MY PRETTY. THEY WILL COME, YOU KNOW. NO ONE STAYS YOUNG FOREVER. I WAS ONCE A STRIKING BEAUTY WHEN I BECOME BABA MUSIIR'S FIRST WIFE.
I'VE HAD SEVENTEEN CHILDREN.
WHAT'S THEIR PROBLEM, THOSE OVER THERE?
AAAH, THEY'RE HIS FAVORITES! AT LEAST, THEY WERE!
YOUR PRESENCE SERIOUSLY COMPROMISES THEIR CHANCES OF EVER BEING SUMMONED AGAIN BY THE MASTER. AND THE OPPORTUNITIES TO GO OUT ARE RARE WHEN YOU'RE NOT A FAVORITE. AS SUCH, THEY WILL HATE AND ATTEMPT TO DO YOU HARM, BUT IT SHOULD ONLY LAST SEVERAL YEARS. AFTER THAT, YOU'LL SURELY END UP FRIENDS...
AND THEM?
THEY ALREADY ADORE YOU. THEY HAVE A MILLION QUESTIONS TO ASK YOU. TOTAL GOSSIPS.
YOU'LL SOON GET USED TO OUR LITTLE COMMUNITY.
35

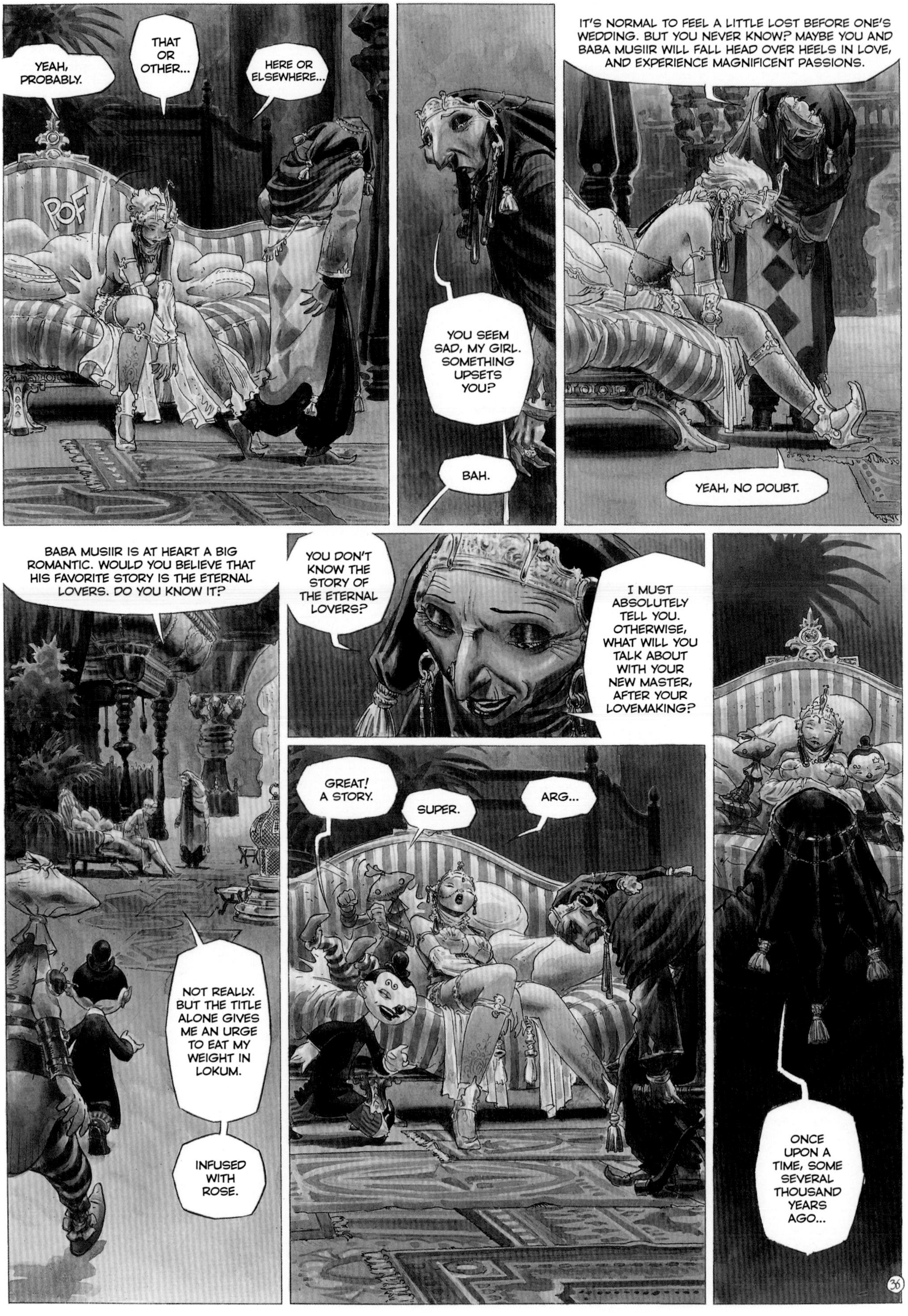
YEAH, PROBABLY.
THAT OR OTHER...
HERE OR ELSEWHERE...
POF
YOU SEEM SAD, MY GIRL. SOMETHING UPSETS YOU?
BAH.
IT'S NORMAL TO FEEL A LITTLE LOST BEFORE ONE'S WEDDING. BUT YOU NEVER KNOW? MAYBE YOU AND BABA MUSIIR WILL FALL HEAD OVER HEELS IN LOVE, AND EXPERIENCE MAGNIFICENT PASSIONS.
YEAH, NO DOUBT.
BABA MUSIIR IS AT HEART A BIG ROMANTIC. WOULD YOU BELIEVE THAT HIS FAVORITE STORY IS THE ETERNAL LOVERS. DO YOU KNOW IT?
NOT REALLY. BUT THE TITLE ALONE GIVES ME AN URGE TO EAT MY WEIGHT IN LOKUM.
INFUSED WITH ROSE.
YOU DON'T KNOW THE STORY OF THE ETERNAL LOVERS?
I MUST ABSOLUTELY TELL YOU. OTHERWISE, WHAT WILL YOU TALK ABOUT WITH YOUR NEW MASTER, AFTER YOUR LOVEMAKING?
GREAT! A STORY.
SUPER.
ARG...
ONCE UPON A TIME, SOME SEVERAL THOUSAND YEARS AGO...

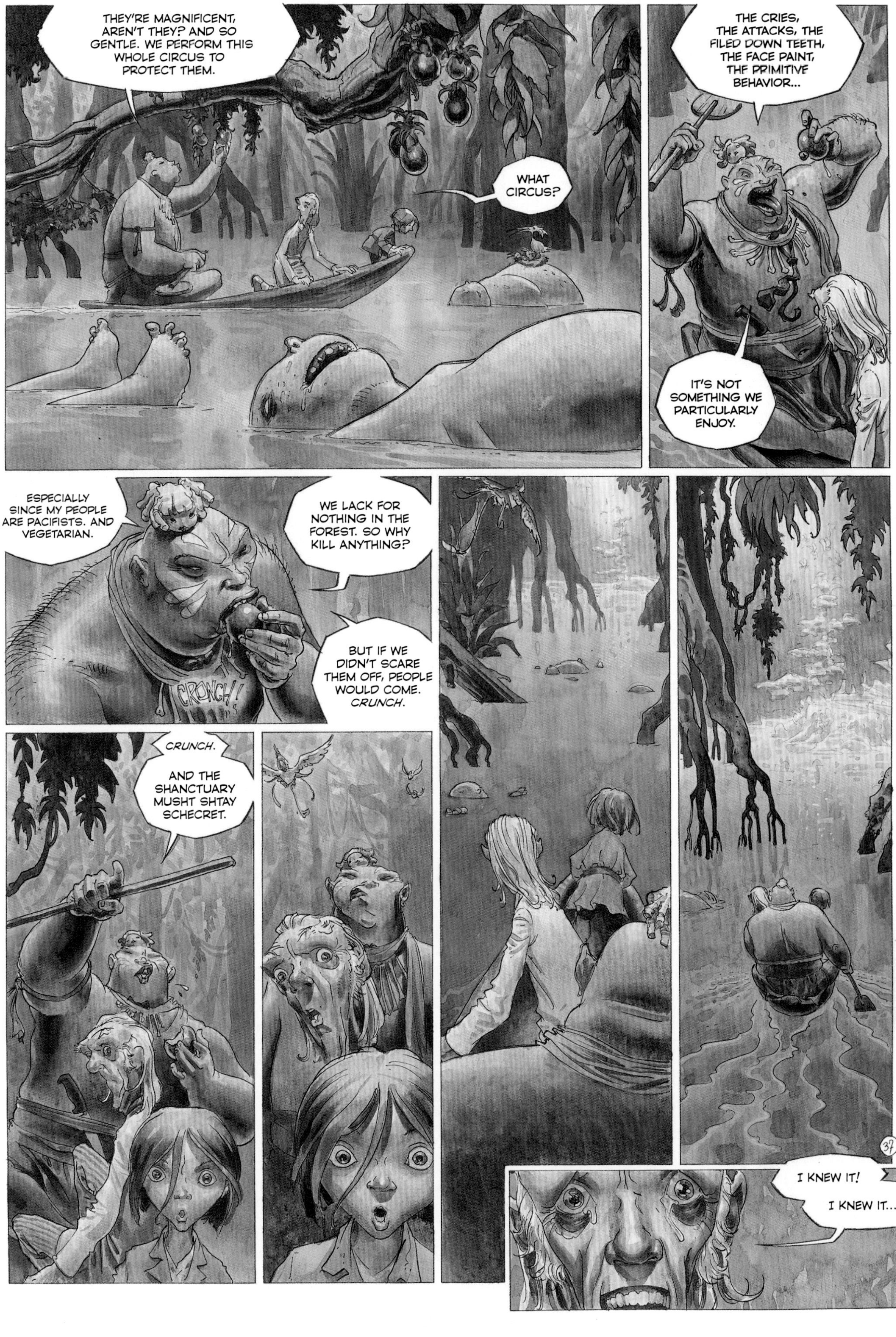
THEY'RE MAGNIFICENT, AREN'T THEY? AND SO GENTLE. WE PERFORM THIS WHOLE CIRCUS TO PROTECT THEM.
WHAT CIRCUS?
THE CRIES, THE ATTACKS, THE FILED DOWN TEETH, THE FACE PAINT, THE PRIMITIVE BEHAVIOR...
IT'S NOT SOMETHING WE PARTICULARLY ENJOY.
ESPECIALLY SINCE MY PEOPLE ARE PACIFISTS. AND VEGETARIAN.
WE LACK FOR NOTHING IN THE FOREST. SO WHY KILL ANYTHING?
BUT IF WE DIDN'T SCARE THEM OFF, PEOPLE WOULD COME. *CRUNCH*.
CRONCH!
CRUNCH.
AND THE SHANCTUARY MUSHT SHTAY SCHECRET.
I KNEW IT!
I KNEW IT...
37

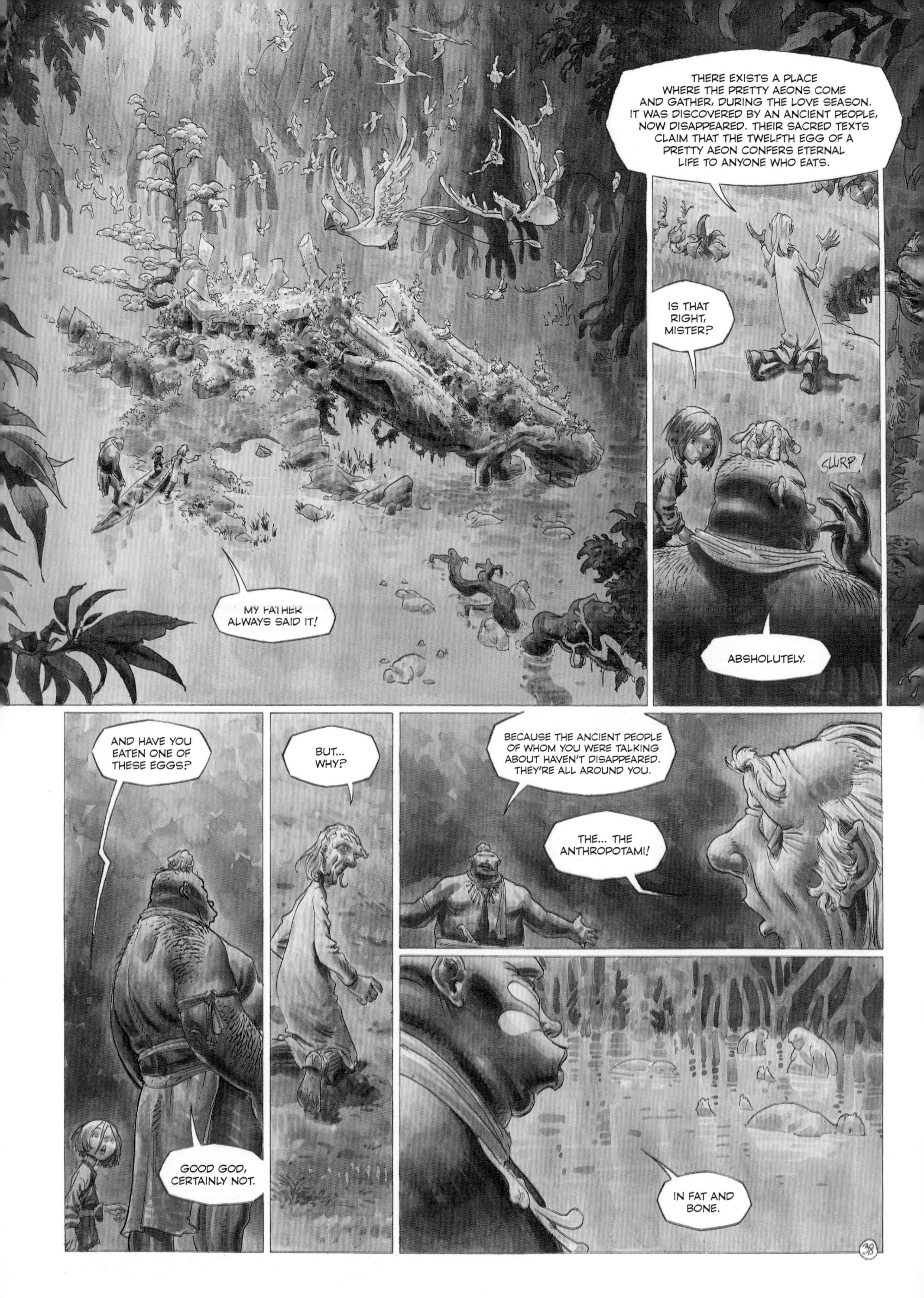
MY FATHER ALWAYS SAID IT!
THERE EXISTS A PLACE WHERE THE PRETTY AEONS COME AND GATHER, DURING THE LOVE SEASON. IT WAS DISCOVERED BY AN ANCIENT PEOPLE, NOW DISAPPEARED. THEIR SACRED TEXTS CLAIM THAT THE TWELFTH EGG OF A PRETTY AEON CONFERS ETERNAL LIFE TO ANYONE WHO EATS.
IS THAT RIGHT, MISTER?
SLURP!
ABSHOLUTELY.
AND HAVE YOU EATEN ONE OF THESE EGGS?
GOOD GOD, CERTAINLY NOT.
BUT... WHY?
BECAUSE THE ANCIENT PEOPLE OF WHOM YOU WERE TALKING ABOUT HAVEN'T DISAPPEARED. THEY'RE ALL AROUND YOU.
THE... THE ANTHROPOTAMI!
IN FAT AND BONE.

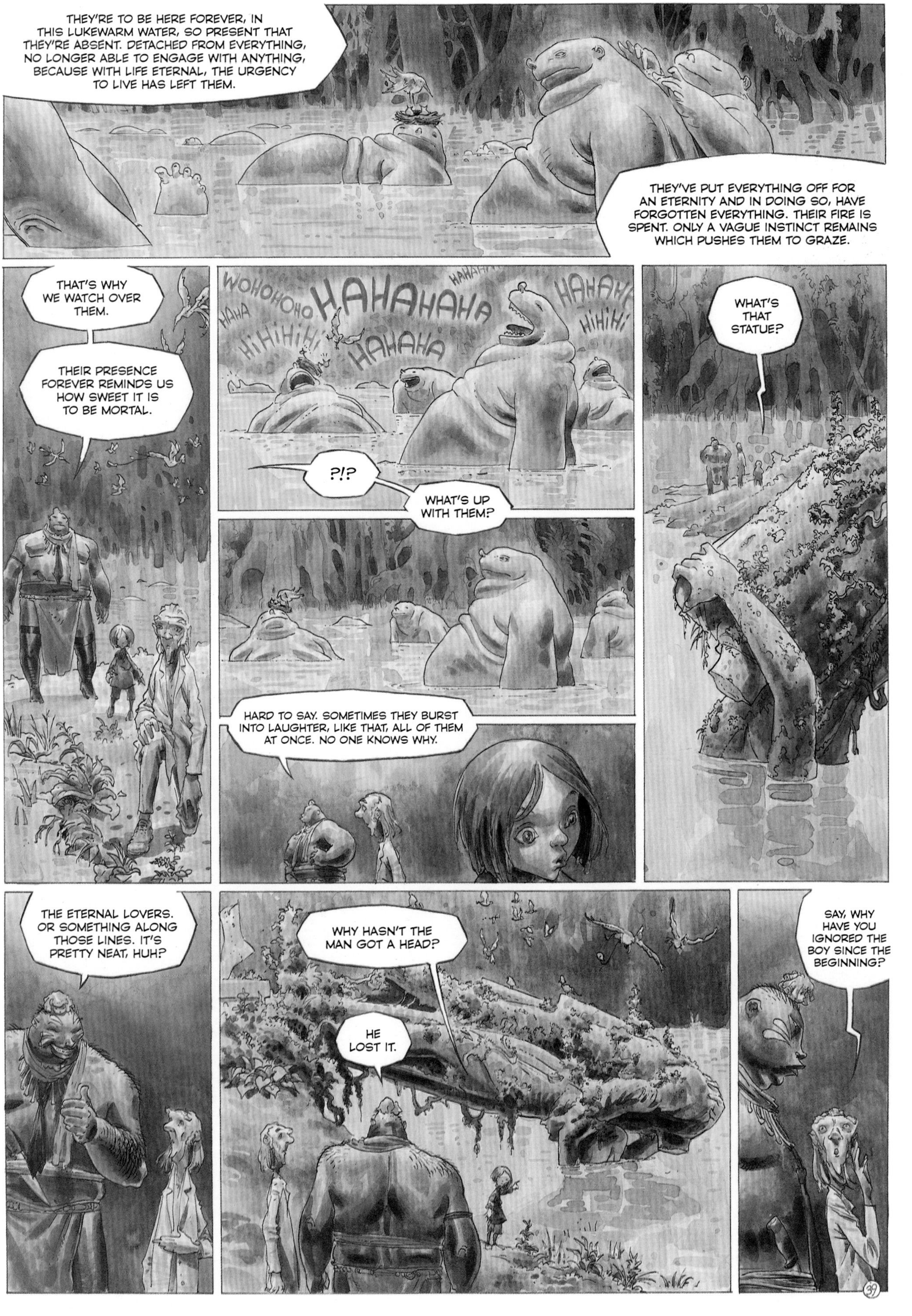
THEY'RE TO BE HERE FOREVER, IN THIS LUKEWARM WATER, SO PRESENT THAT THEY'RE ABSENT. DETACHED FROM EVERYTHING, NO LONGER ABLE TO ENGAGE WITH ANYTHING, BECAUSE WITH LIFE ETERNAL, THE URGENCY TO LIVE HAS LEFT THEM.
THEY'VE PUT EVERYTHING OFF FOR AN ETERNITY AND IN DOING SO, HAVE FORGOTTEN EVERYTHING. THEIR FIRE IS SPENT. ONLY A VAGUE INSTINCT REMAINS WHICH PUSHES THEM TO GRAZE.
THAT'S WHY WE WATCH OVER THEM.
THEIR PRESENCE FOREVER REMINDS US HOW SWEET IT IS TO BE MORTAL.
WOHOHOHO HAHAHAHA HAHAHA HIHIHI HAHA HAHAHA HIHIHI
?!?
WHAT'S UP WITH THEM?
HARD TO SAY. SOMETIMES THEY BURST INTO LAUGHTER, LIKE THAT, ALL OF THEM AT ONCE. NO ONE KNOWS WHY.
WHAT'S THAT STATUE?
THE ETERNAL LOVERS. OR SOMETHING ALONG THOSE LINES. IT'S PRETTY NEAT, HUH?
WHY HASN'T THE MAN GOT A HEAD?
HE LOST IT.
SAY, WHY HAVE YOU IGNORED THE BOY SINCE THE BEGINNING?

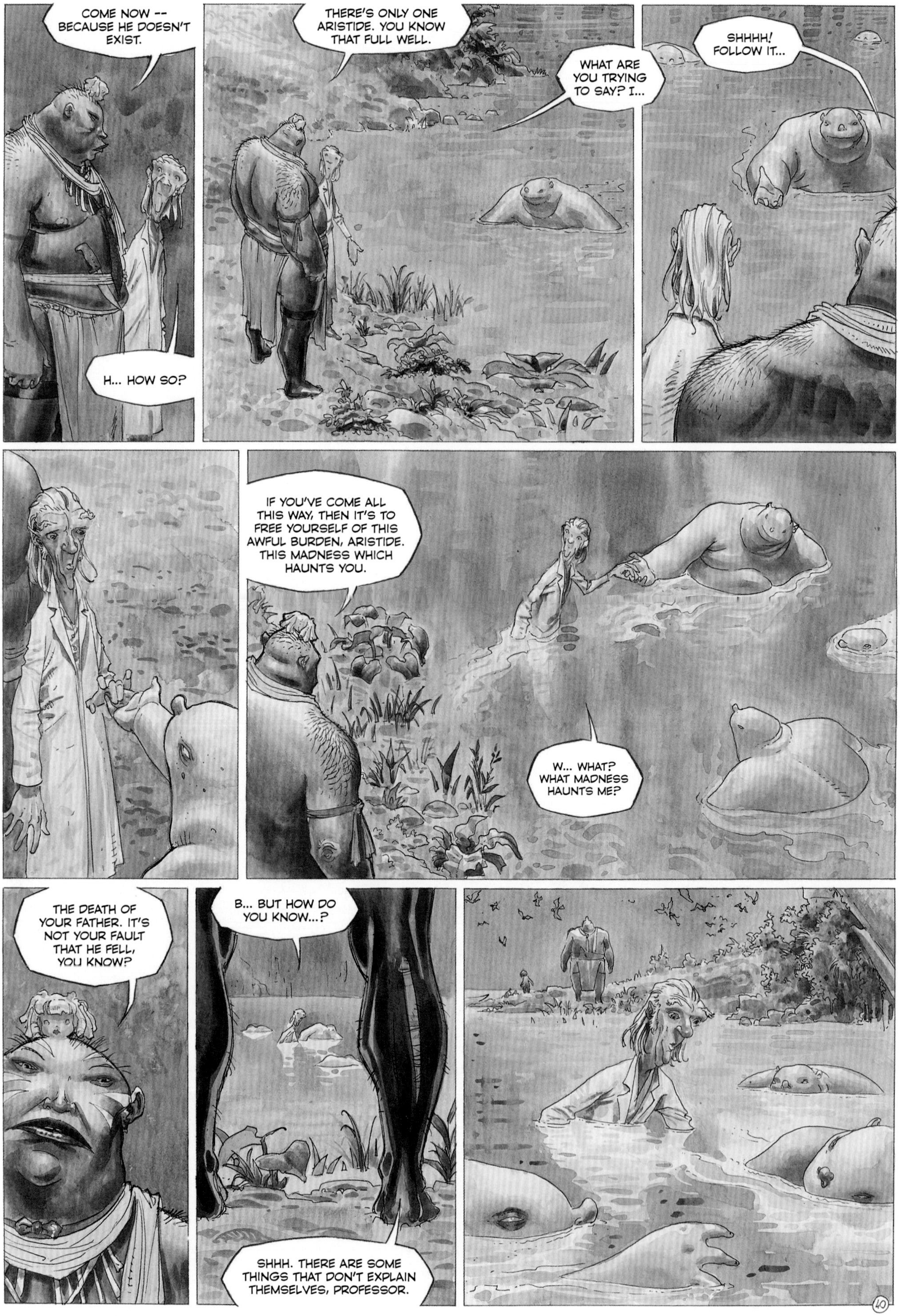
COME NOW -- BECAUSE HE DOESN'T EXIST.
H... HOW SO?
THERE'S ONLY ONE ARISTIDE. YOU KNOW THAT FULL WELL.
WHAT ARE YOU TRYING TO SAY? I...
SHHHH! FOLLOW IT...
IF YOU'VE COME ALL THIS WAY, THEN IT'S TO FREE YOURSELF OF THIS AWFUL BURDEN, ARISTIDE. THIS MADNESS WHICH HAUNTS YOU.
W... WHAT? WHAT MADNESS HAUNTS ME?
THE DEATH OF YOUR FATHER. IT'S NOT YOUR FAULT THAT HE FELL, YOU KNOW?
B... BUT HOW DO YOU KNOW...?
SHHH. THERE ARE SOME THINGS THAT DON'T EXPLAIN THEMSELVES, PROFESSOR.

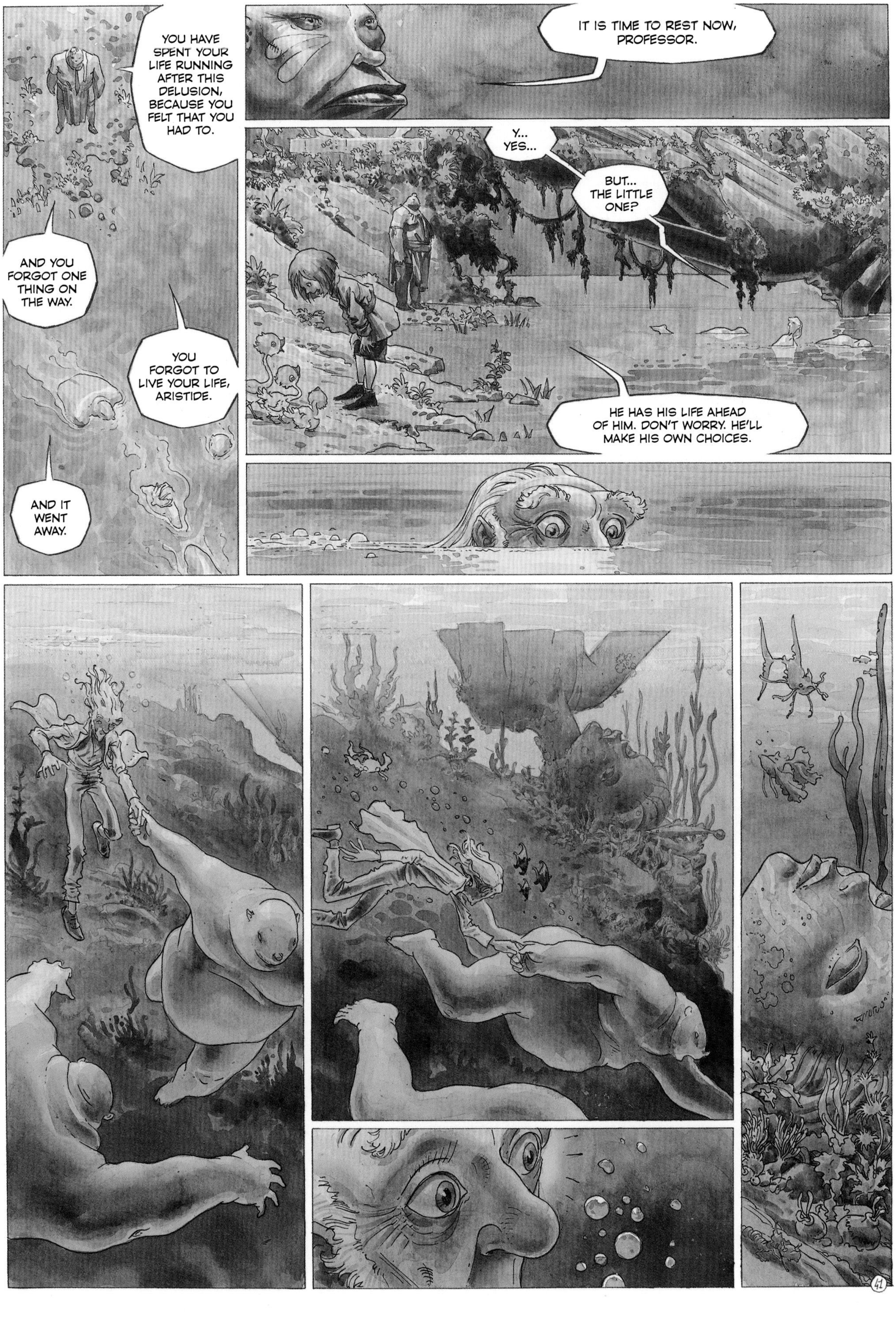
YOU HAVE SPENT YOUR LIFE RUNNING AFTER THIS DELUSION, BECAUSE YOU FELT THAT YOU HAD TO.
AND YOU FORGOT ONE THING ON THE WAY.
YOU FORGOT TO LIVE YOUR LIFE, ARISTIDE.
AND IT WENT AWAY.
IT IS TIME TO REST NOW, PROFESSOR.
Y... YES...
BUT... THE LITTLE ONE?
HE HAS HIS LIFE AHEAD OF HIM. DON'T WORRY. HE'LL MAKE HIS OWN CHOICES.

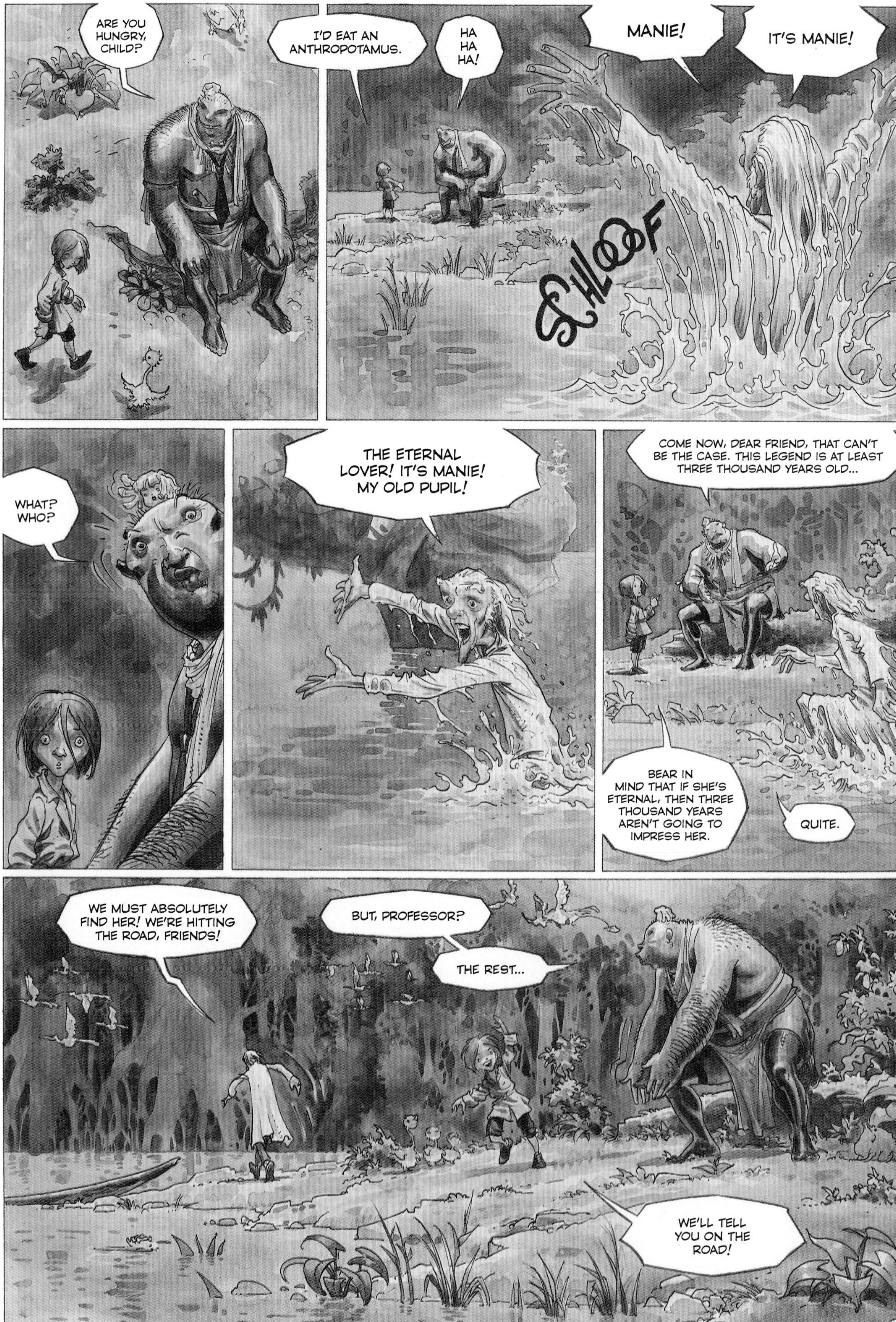

ARE YOU HUNGRY, CHILD?
I'D EAT AN ANTHROPOTAMUS.
HA HA HA!
MANIE!
IT'S MANIE!
SHLOOF
WHAT? WHO?
THE ETERNAL LOVER! IT'S MANIE! MY OLD PUPIL!
COME NOW, DEAR FRIEND, THAT CAN'T BE THE CASE. THIS LEGEND IS AT LEAST THREE THOUSAND YEARS OLD...
BEAR IN MIND THAT IF SHE'S ETERNAL, THEN THREE THOUSAND YEARS AREN'T GOING TO IMPRESS HER.
QUITE.
WE MUST ABSOLUTELY FIND HER! WE'RE HITTING THE ROAD, FRIENDS!
BUT, PROFESSOR?
THE REST...
WE'LL TELL YOU ON THE ROAD!

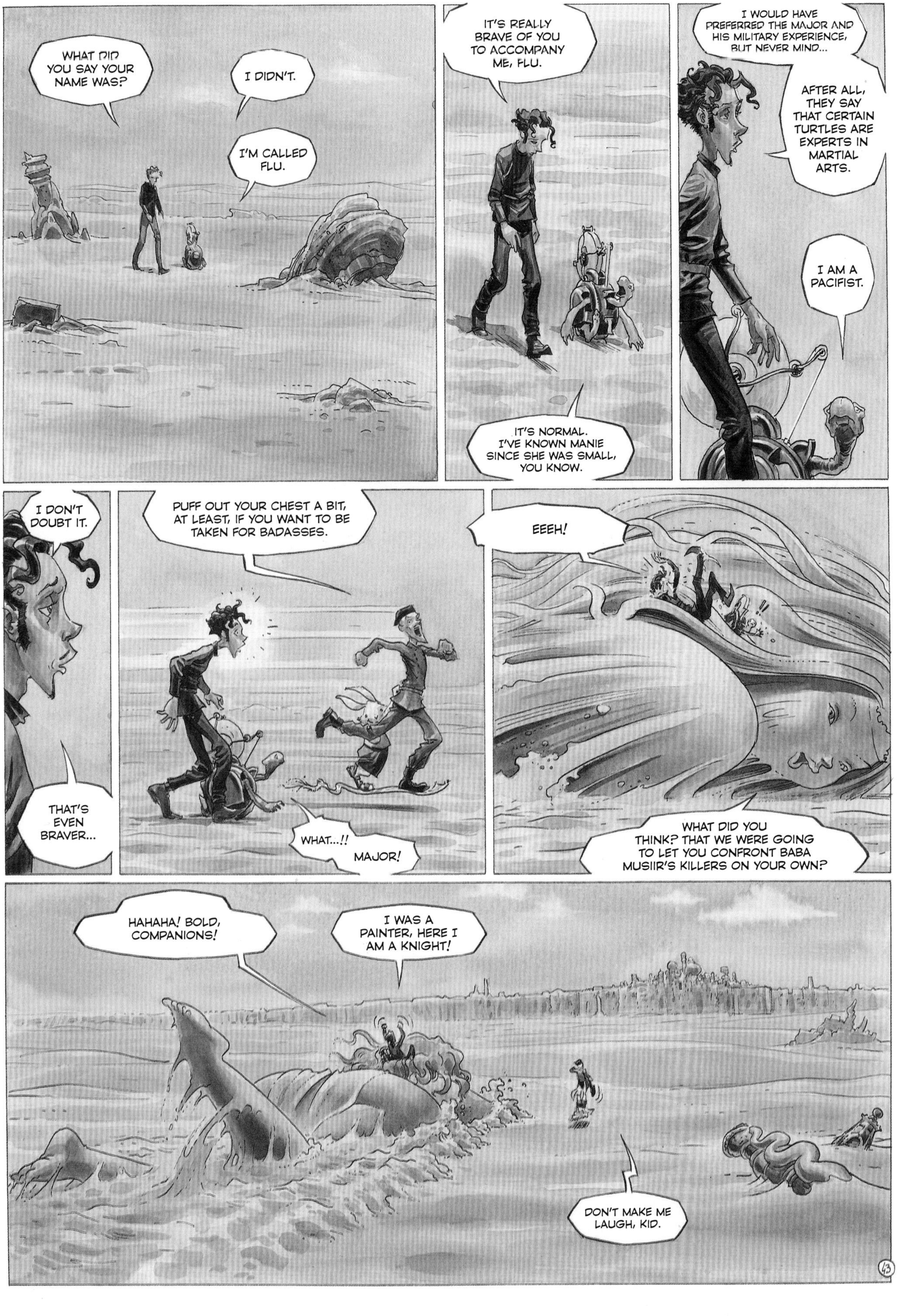

WHAT DID YOU SAY YOUR NAME WAS?
I DIDN'T.
I'M CALLED FLU.
IT'S REALLY BRAVE OF YOU TO ACCOMPANY ME, FLU.
IT'S NORMAL. I'VE KNOWN MANIE SINCE SHE WAS SMALL, YOU KNOW.
I WOULD HAVE PREFERRED THE MAJOR AND HIS MILITARY EXPERIENCE, BUT NEVER MIND...
AFTER ALL, THEY SAY THAT CERTAIN TURTLES ARE EXPERTS IN MARTIAL ARTS.
I AM A PACIFIST.
I DON'T DOUBT IT.
THAT'S EVEN BRAVER...
PUFF OUT YOUR CHEST A BIT, AT LEAST, IF YOU WANT TO BE TAKEN FOR BADASSES.
WHAT...!!
MAJOR!
EEEH!
WHAT DID YOU THINK? THAT WE WERE GOING TO LET YOU CONFRONT BABA MUSIIR'S KILLERS ON YOUR OWN?
HAHAHA! BOLD, COMPANIONS!
I WAS A PAINTER, HERE I AM A KNIGHT!
DON'T MAKE ME LAUGH, KID.
43

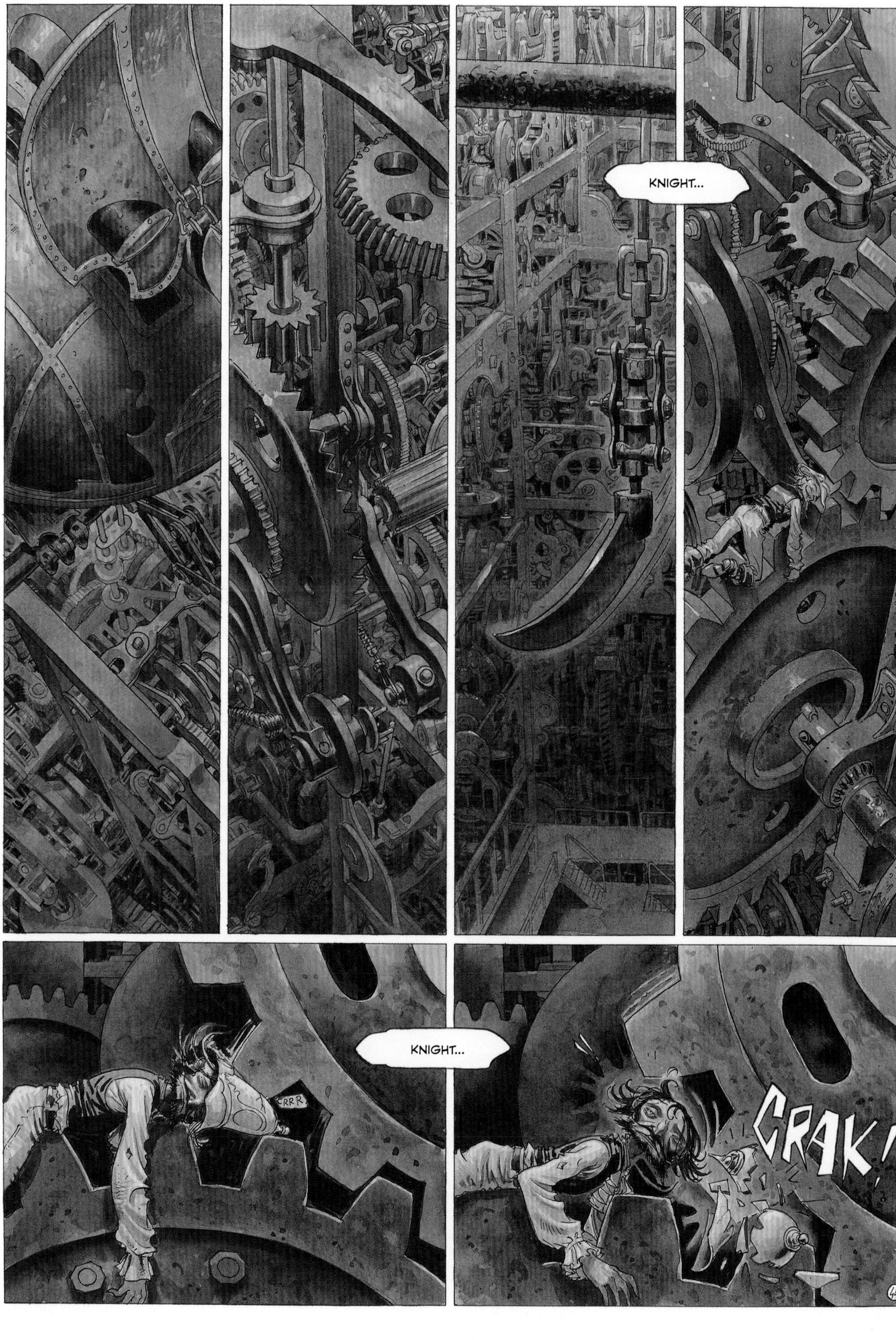
KNIGHT...
KNIGHT...
CRRR
CRAK!

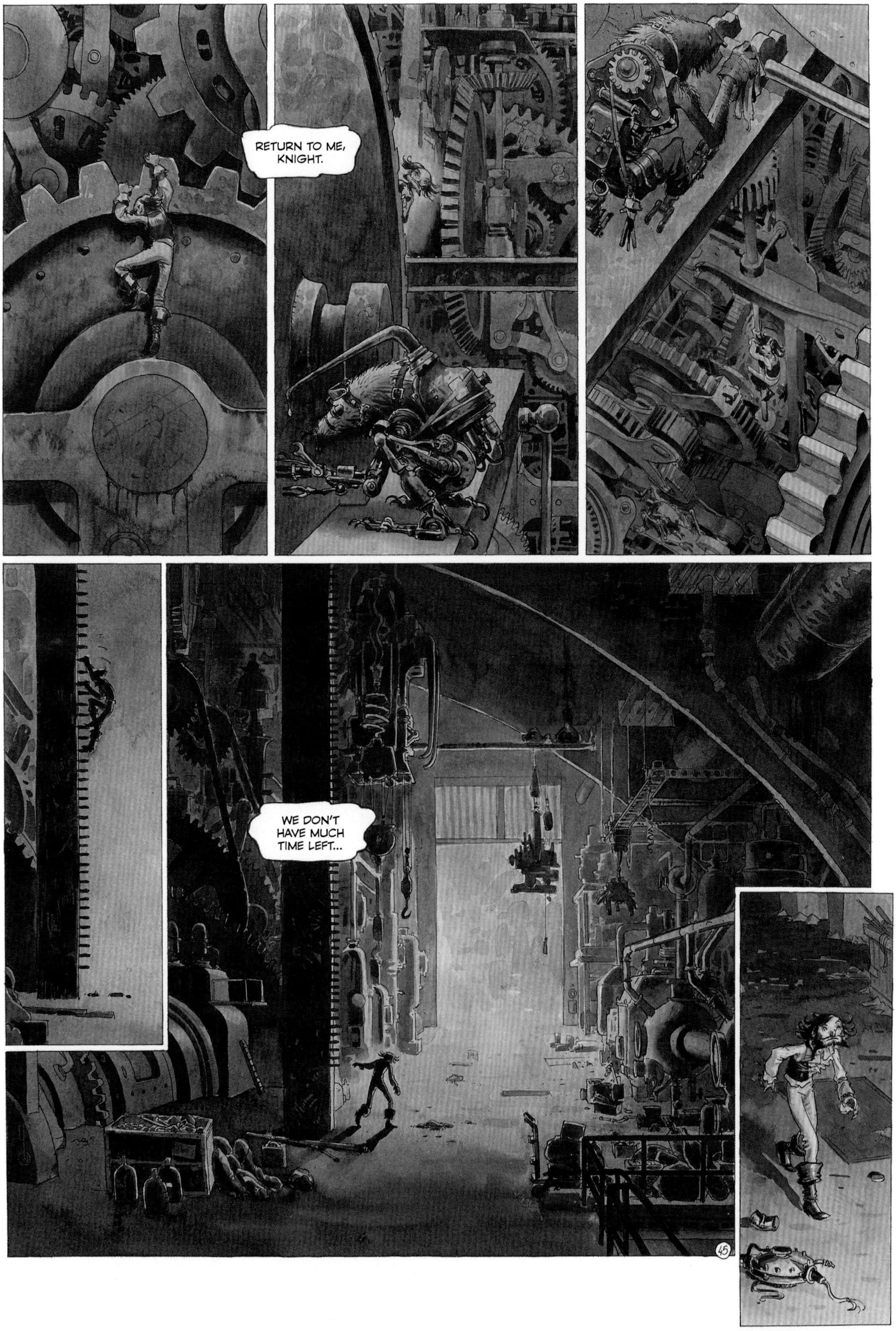
RETURN TO ME, KNIGHT.
WE DON'T HAVE MUCH TIME LEFT...
45

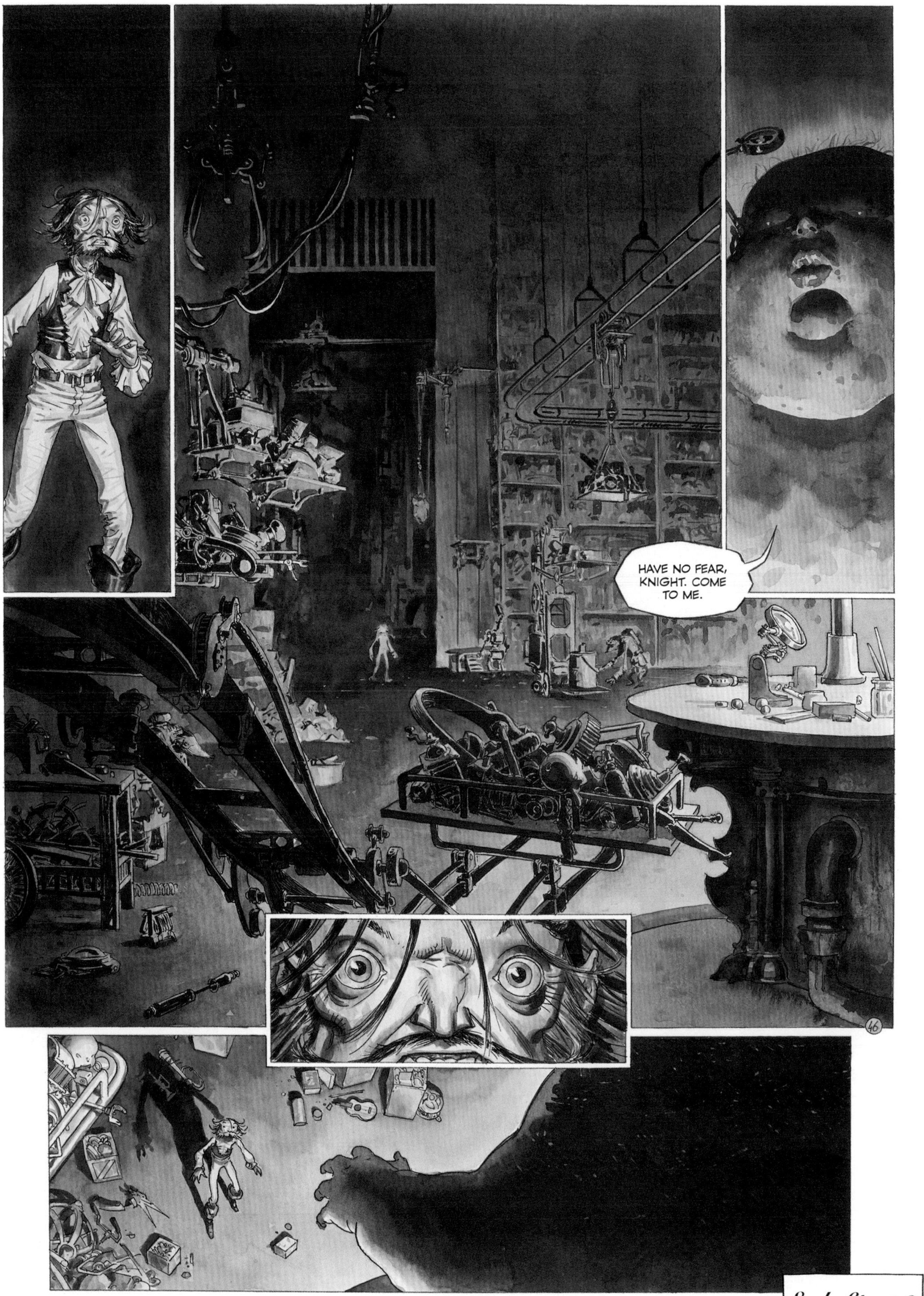
HAVE NO FEAR, KNIGHT. COME TO ME.
46
End of part 3

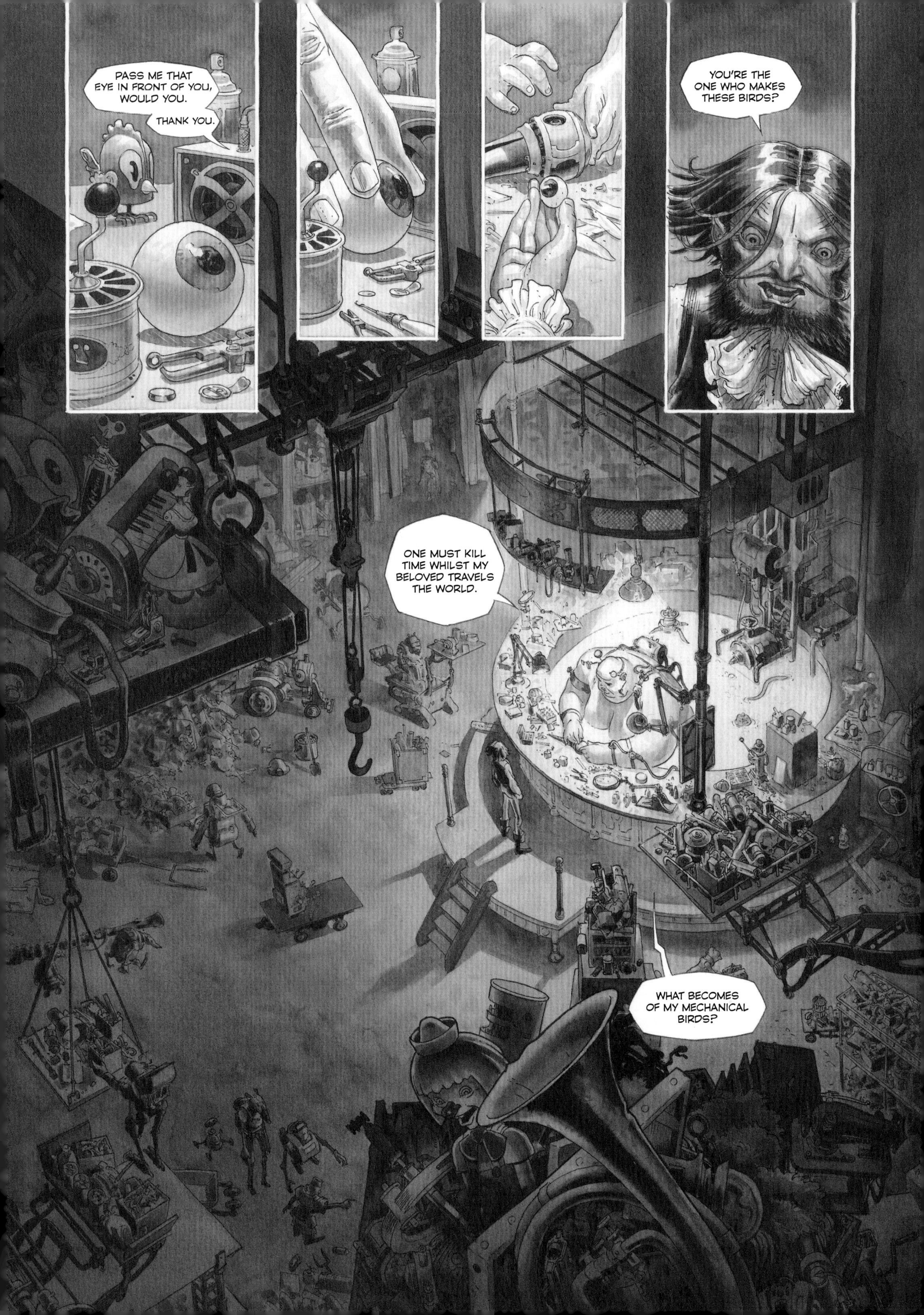
PASS ME THAT EYE IN FRONT OF YOU, WOULD YOU.
THANK YOU.
YOU'RE THE ONE WHO MAKES THESE BIRDS?
ONE MUST KILL TIME WHILST MY BELOVED TRAVELS THE WORLD.
WHAT BECOMES OF MY MECHANICAL BIRDS?

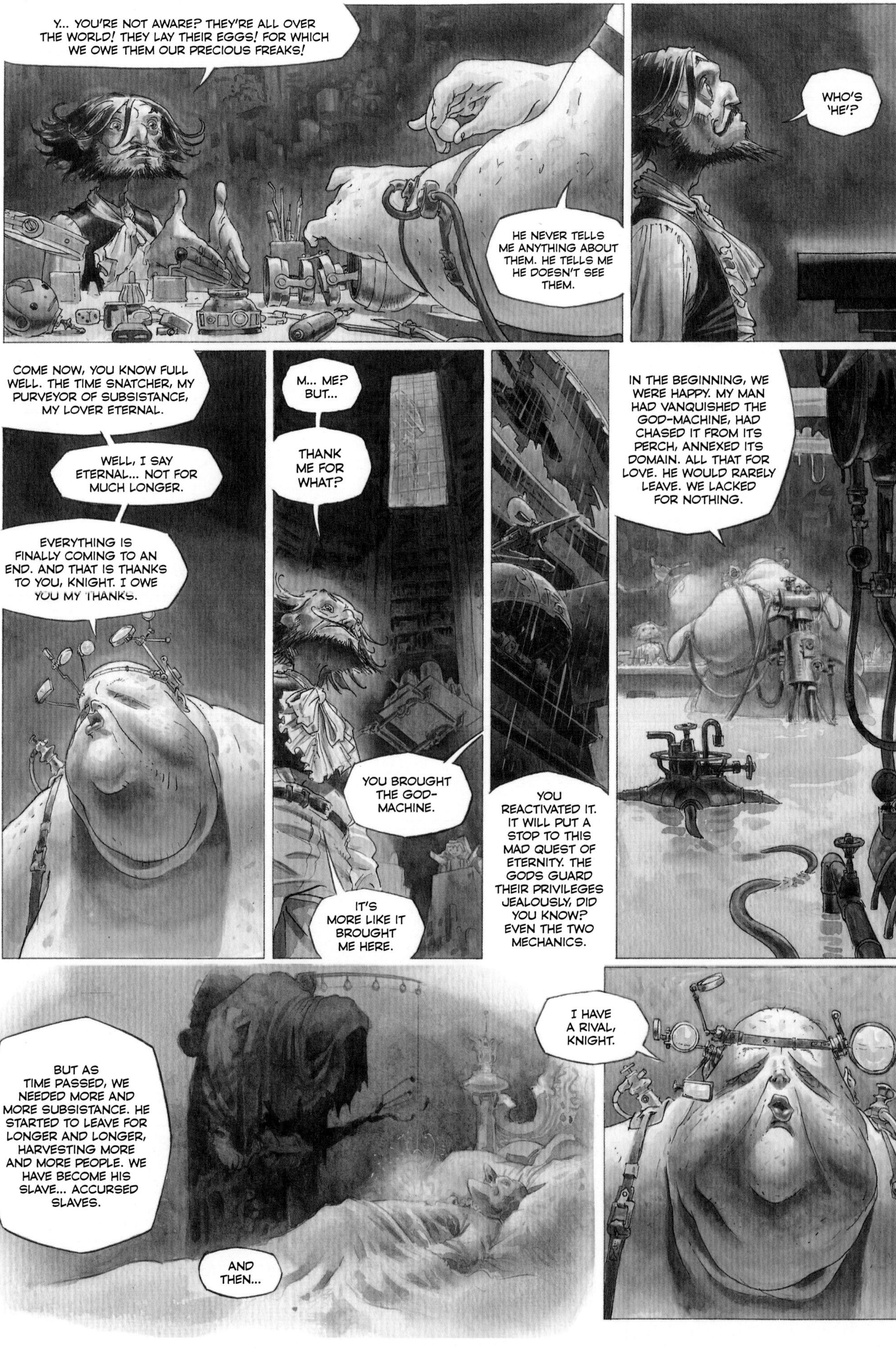
Y... YOU'RE NOT AWARE? THEY'RE ALL OVER THE WORLD! THEY LAY THEIR EGGS! FOR WHICH WE OWE THEM OUR PRECIOUS FREAKS!
HE NEVER TELLS ME ANYTHING ABOUT THEM. HE TELLS ME HE DOESN'T SEE THEM.
WHO'S 'HE'?
COME NOW, YOU KNOW FULL WELL. THE TIME SNATCHER, MY PURVEYOR OF SUBSISTANCE, MY LOVER ETERNAL.
WELL, I SAY ETERNAL... NOT FOR MUCH LONGER.
EVERYTHING IS FINALLY COMING TO AN END. AND THAT IS THANKS TO YOU, KNIGHT. I OWE YOU MY THANKS.
M... ME? BUT...
THANK ME FOR WHAT?
YOU BROUGHT THE GOD-MACHINE.
IT'S MORE LIKE IT BROUGHT ME HERE.
YOU REACTIVATED IT. IT WILL PUT A STOP TO THIS MAD QUEST OF ETERNITY. THE GODS GUARD THEIR PRIVILEGES JEALOUSLY, DID YOU KNOW? EVEN THE TWO MECHANICS.
IN THE BEGINNING, WE WERE HAPPY. MY MAN HAD VANQUISHED THE GOD-MACHINE, HAD CHASED IT FROM ITS PERCH, ANNEXED ITS DOMAIN. ALL THAT FOR LOVE. HE WOULD RARELY LEAVE. WE LACKED FOR NOTHING.
BUT AS TIME PASSED, WE NEEDED MORE AND MORE SUBSISTANCE. HE STARTED TO LEAVE FOR LONGER AND LONGER, HARVESTING MORE AND MORE PEOPLE. WE HAVE BECOME HIS SLAVE... ACCURSED SLAVES.
AND THEN...
I HAVE A RIVAL, KNIGHT.

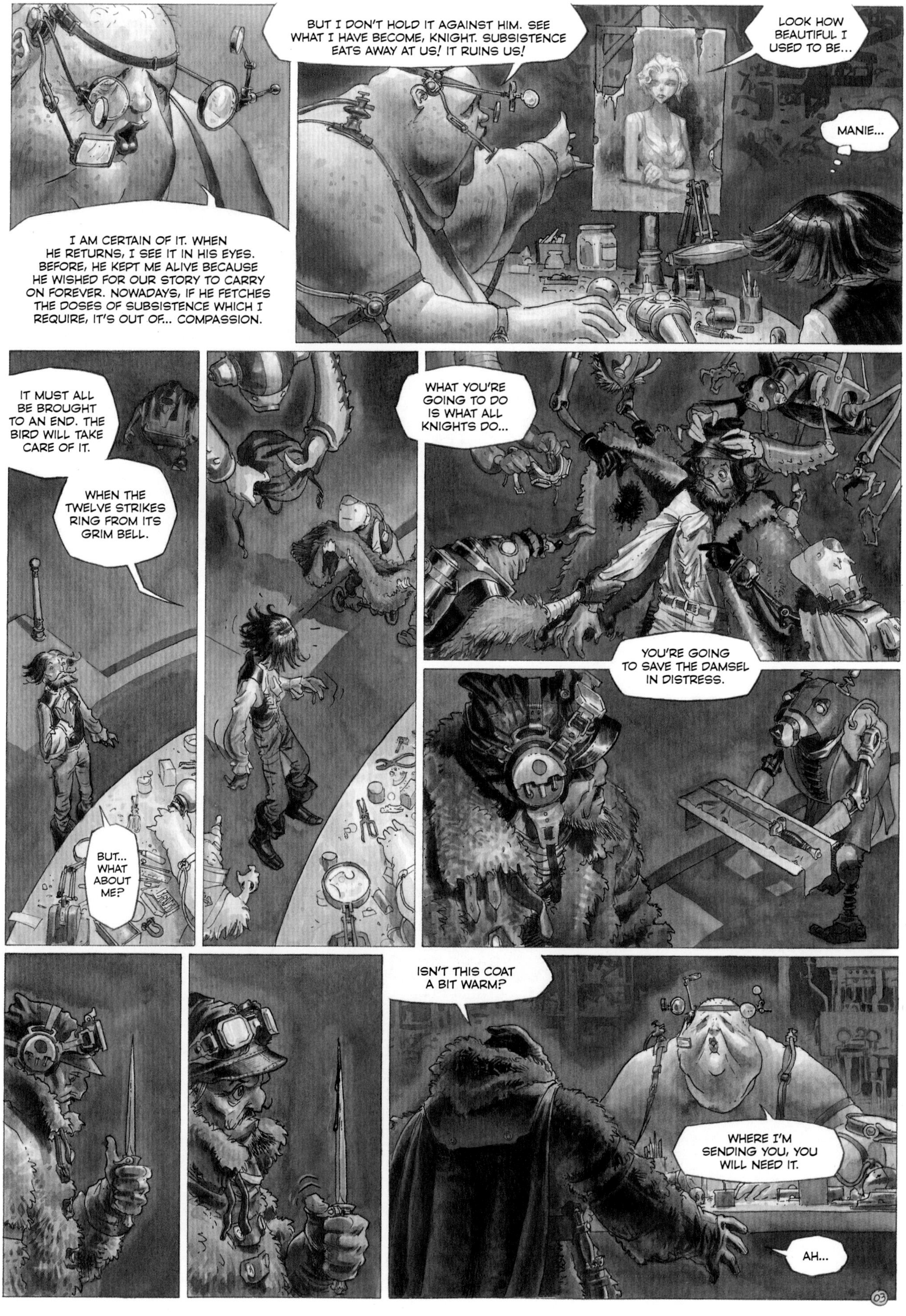
I AM CERTAIN OF IT. WHEN HE RETURNS, I SEE IT IN HIS EYES. BEFORE, HE KEPT ME ALIVE BECAUSE HE WISHED FOR OUR STORY TO CARRY ON FOREVER. NOWADAYS, IF HE FETCHES THE DOSES OF SUBSISTENCE WHICH I REQUIRE, IT'S OUT OF... COMPASSION.
BUT I DON'T HOLD IT AGAINST HIM. SEE WHAT I HAVE BECOME, KNIGHT. SUBSISTENCE EATS AWAY AT US! IT RUINS US!
LOOK HOW BEAUTIFUL I USED TO BE...
MANIE...
IT MUST ALL BE BROUGHT TO AN END. THE BIRD WILL TAKE CARE OF IT.
WHEN THE TWELVE STRIKES RING FROM ITS GRIM BELL.
BUT... WHAT ABOUT ME?
WHAT YOU'RE GOING TO DO IS WHAT ALL KNIGHTS DO...
YOU'RE GOING TO SAVE THE DAMSEL IN DISTRESS.
ISN'T THIS COAT A BIT WARM?
WHERE I'M SENDING YOU, YOU WILL NEED IT.
AH...

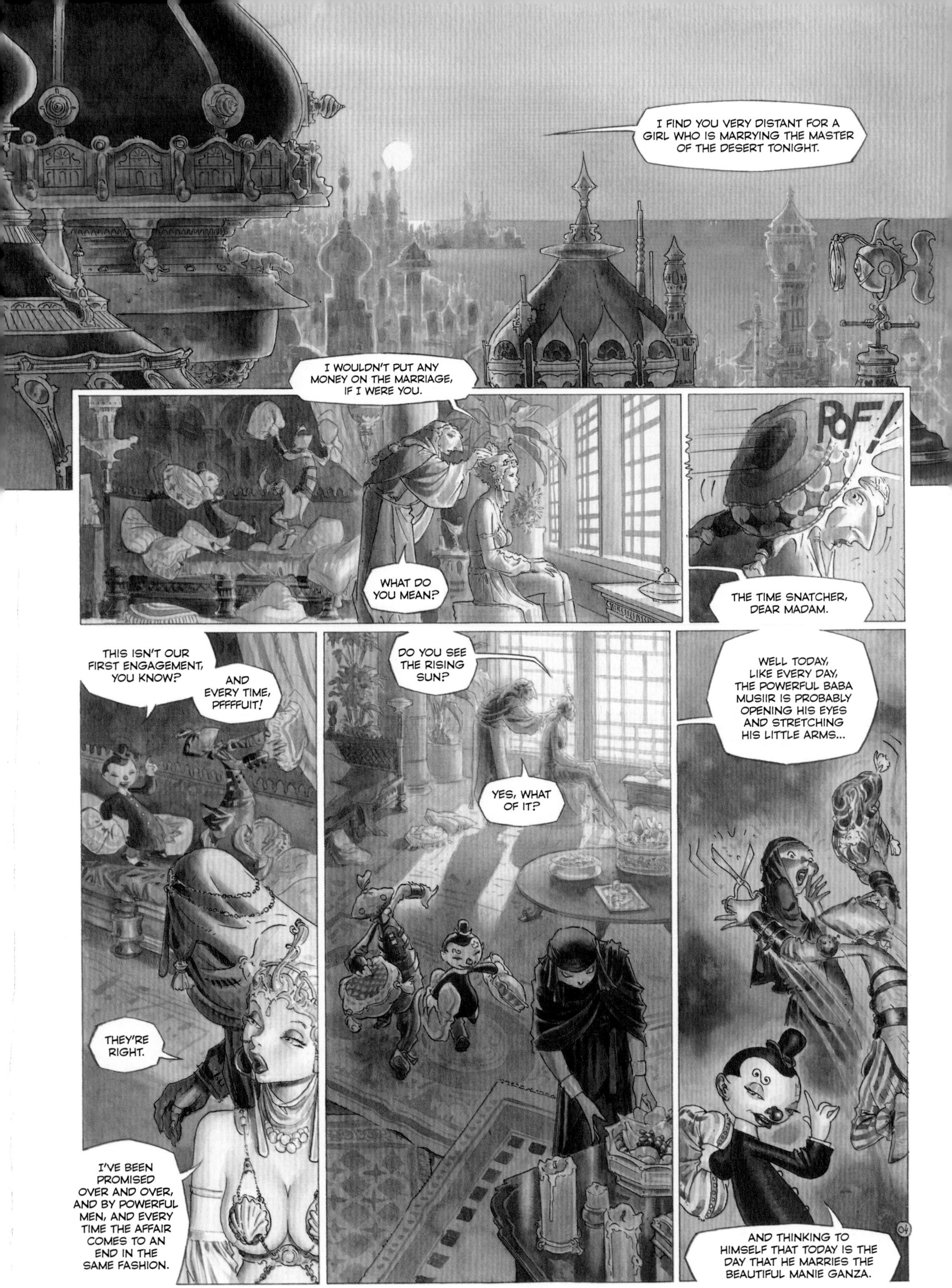

I FIND YOU VERY DISTANT FOR A GIRL WHO IS MARRYING THE MASTER OF THE DESERT TONIGHT.
I WOULDN'T PUT ANY MONEY ON THE MARRIAGE, IF I WERE YOU.
WHAT DO YOU MEAN?
ROF!
THE TIME SNATCHER, DEAR MADAM.
THIS ISN'T OUR FIRST ENGAGEMENT, YOU KNOW?
AND EVERY TIME, PFFFFUIT!
THEY'RE RIGHT.
I'VE BEEN PROMISED OVER AND OVER, AND BY POWERFUL MEN, AND EVERY TIME THE AFFAIR COMES TO AN END IN THE SAME FASHION.
DO YOU SEE THE RISING SUN?
YES, WHAT OF IT?
WELL TODAY, LIKE EVERY DAY, THE POWERFUL BABA MUSIIR IS PROBABLY OPENING HIS EYES AND STRETCHING HIS LITTLE ARMS...
AND THINKING TO HIMSELF THAT TODAY IS THE DAY THAT HE MARRIES THE BEAUTIFUL MANIE GANZA.

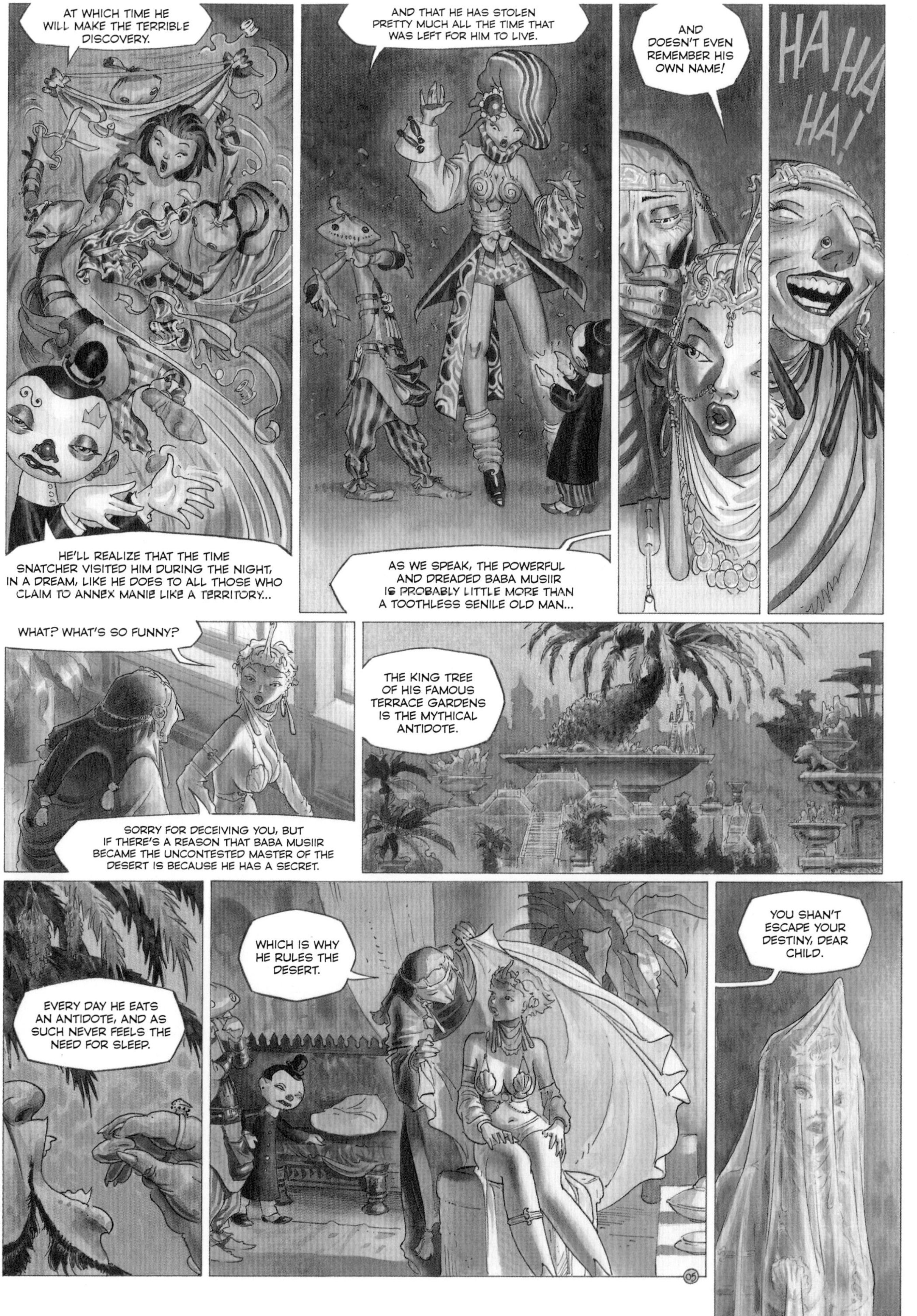
AT WHICH TIME HE WILL MAKE THE TERRIBLE DISCOVERY.
HE'LL REALIZE THAT THE TIME SNATCHER VISITED HIM DURING THE NIGHT, IN A DREAM, LIKE HE DOES TO ALL THOSE WHO CLAIM TO ANNEX MANIE LIKE A TERRITORY...
AND THAT HE HAS STOLEN PRETTY MUCH ALL THE TIME THAT WAS LEFT FOR HIM TO LIVE.
AS WE SPEAK, THE POWERFUL AND DREADED BABA MUSIIR IS PROBABLY LITTLE MORE THAN A TOOTHLESS SENILE OLD MAN...
AND DOESN'T EVEN REMEMBER HIS OWN NAME!
HA HA HA!
WHAT? WHAT'S SO FUNNY?
SORRY FOR DECEIVING YOU, BUT IF THERE'S A REASON THAT BABA MUSIIR BECAME THE UNCONTESTED MASTER OF THE DESERT IS BECAUSE HE HAS A SECRET.
THE KING TREE OF HIS FAMOUS TERRACE GARDENS IS THE MYTHICAL ANTIDOTE.
EVERY DAY HE EATS AN ANTIDOTE, AND AS SUCH NEVER FEELS THE NEED FOR SLEEP.
WHICH IS WHY HE RULES THE DESERT.
YOU SHAN'T ESCAPE YOUR DESTINY, DEAR CHILD.

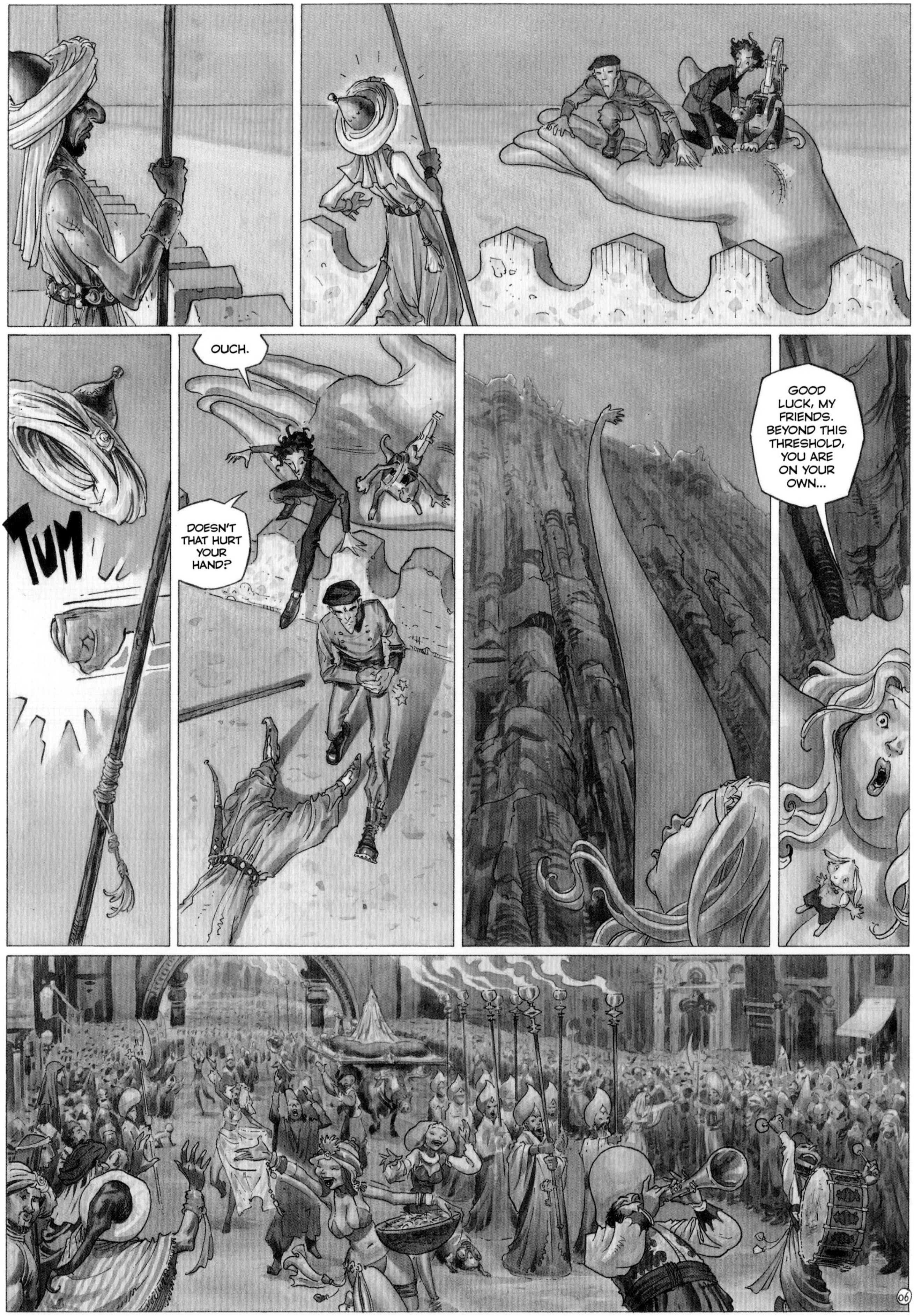

TUM
OUCH.
DOESN'T THAT HURT YOUR HAND?
GOOD LUCK, MY FRIENDS. BEYOND THIS THRESHOLD, YOU ARE ON YOUR OWN...

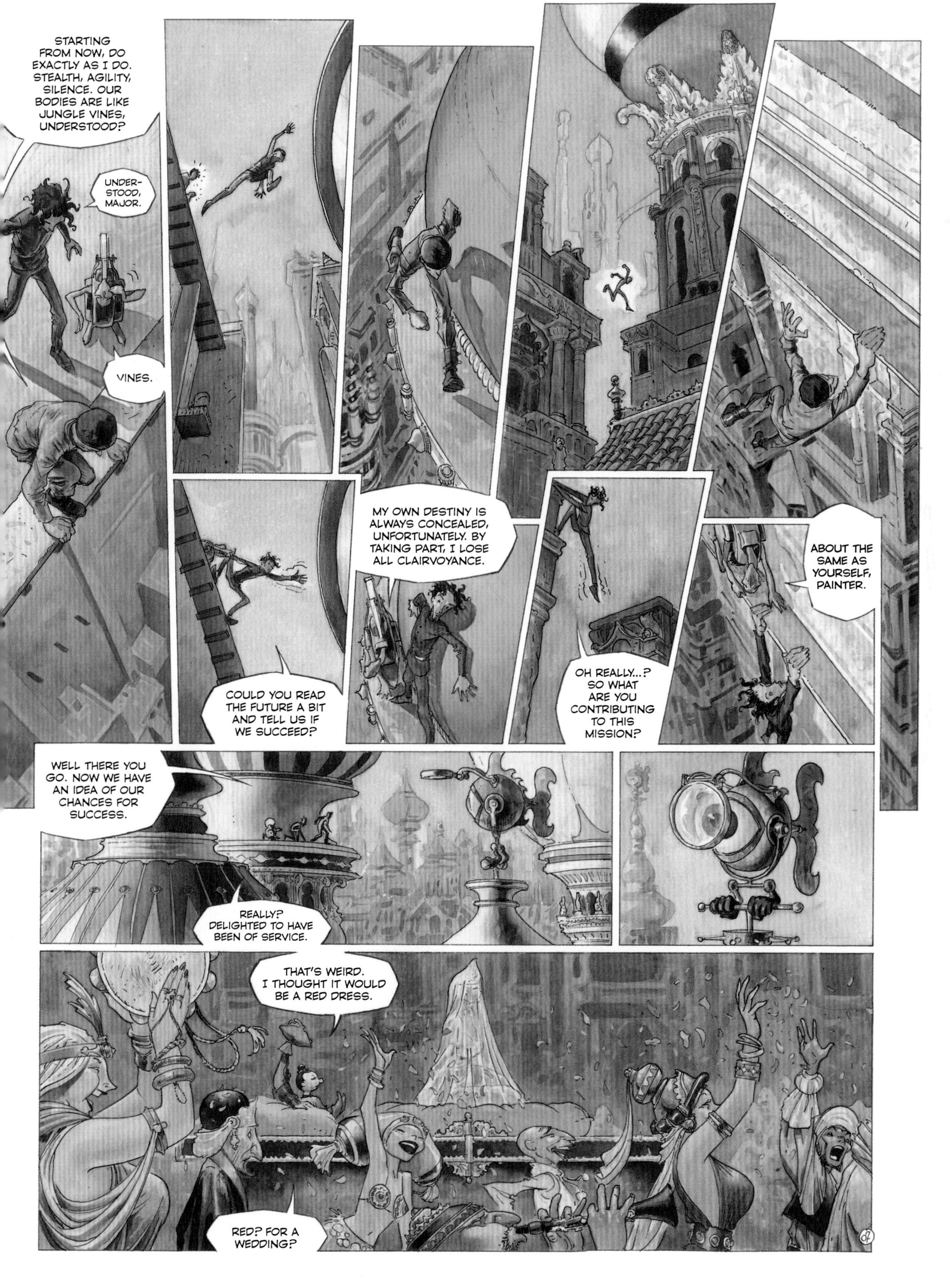
STARTING FROM NOW, DO EXACTLY AS I DO. STEALTH, AGILITY, SILENCE. OUR BODIES ARE LIKE JUNGLE VINES, UNDERSTOOD?
UNDER-STOOD, MAJOR.
VINES.
COULD YOU READ THE FUTURE A BIT AND TELL US IF WE SUCCEED?
MY OWN DESTINY IS ALWAYS CONCEALED, UNFORTUNATELY. BY TAKING PART, I LOSE ALL CLAIRVOYANCE.
OH REALLY...? SO WHAT ARE YOU CONTRIBUTING TO THIS MISSION?
ABOUT THE SAME AS YOURSELF, PAINTER.
WELL THERE YOU GO. NOW WE HAVE AN IDEA OF OUR CHANCES FOR SUCCESS.
REALLY? DELIGHTED TO HAVE BEEN OF SERVICE.
THAT'S WEIRD. I THOUGHT IT WOULD BE A RED DRESS.
RED? FOR A WEDDING?
07

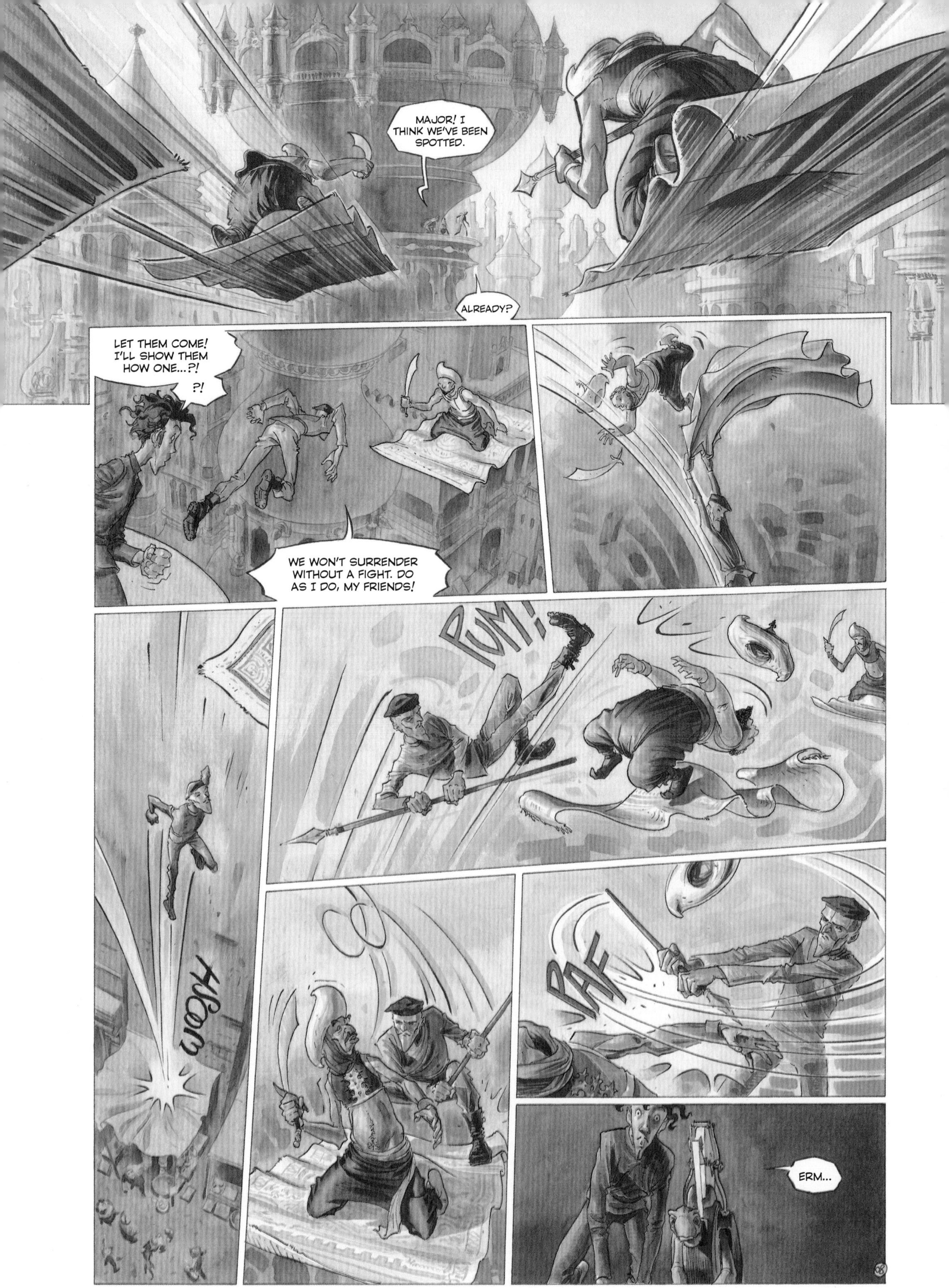
MAJOR! I THINK WE'VE BEEN SPOTTED.
ALREADY?
LET THEM COME! I'LL SHOW THEM HOW ONE...?!
?!
WE WON'T SURRENDER WITHOUT A FIGHT. DO AS I DO, MY FRIENDS!
PUM!
WOOSH
PAF
ERM...

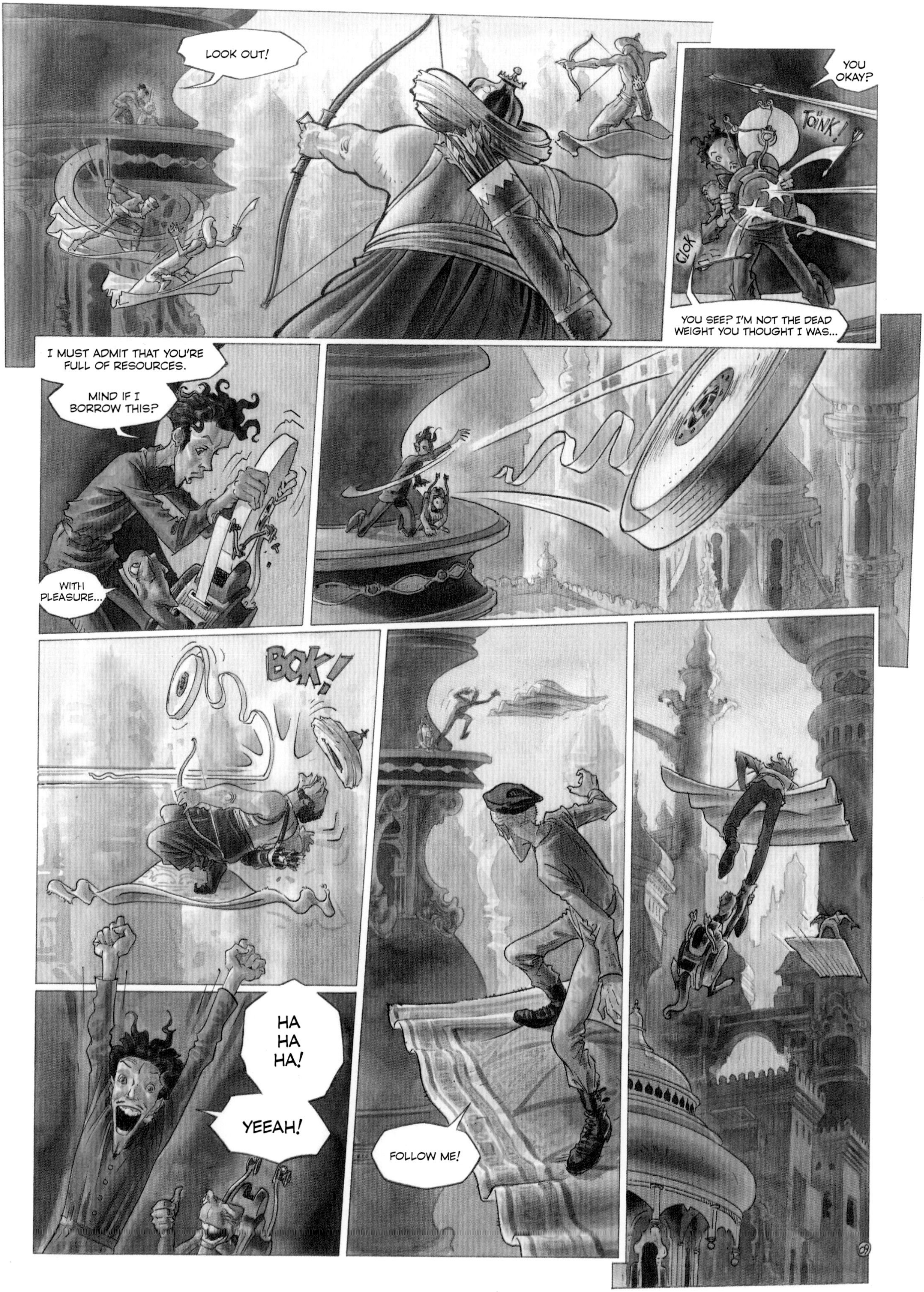
LOOK OUT!
YOU OKAY?
TOÏNK!
CLOK
YOU SEE? I'M NOT THE DEAD WEIGHT YOU THOUGHT I WAS...
I MUST ADMIT THAT YOU'RE FULL OF RESOURCES.
MIND IF I BORROW THIS?
WITH PLEASURE...
BOK!
HA HA HA!
YEEAH!
FOLLOW ME!

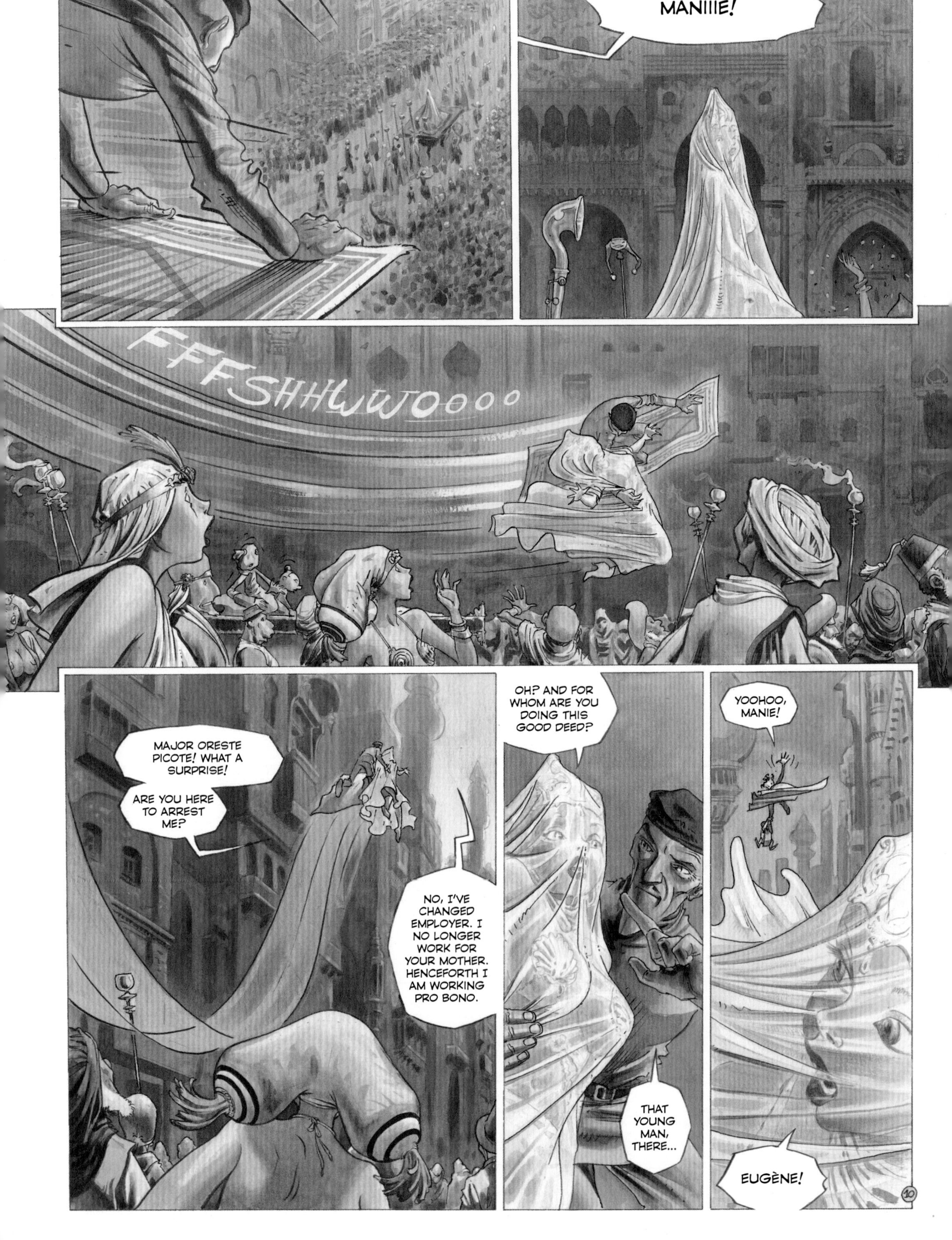
MANIIIE!
FFFSHHWWOooo
MAJOR ORESTE PICOTE! WHAT A SURPRISE!
ARE YOU HERE TO ARREST ME?
NO, I'VE CHANGED EMPLOYER. I NO LONGER WORK FOR YOUR MOTHER. HENCEFORTH I AM WORKING PRO BONO.
OH? AND FOR WHOM ARE YOU DOING THIS GOOD DEED?
THAT YOUNG MAN, THERE...
YOOHOO, MANIE!
EUGÈNE!

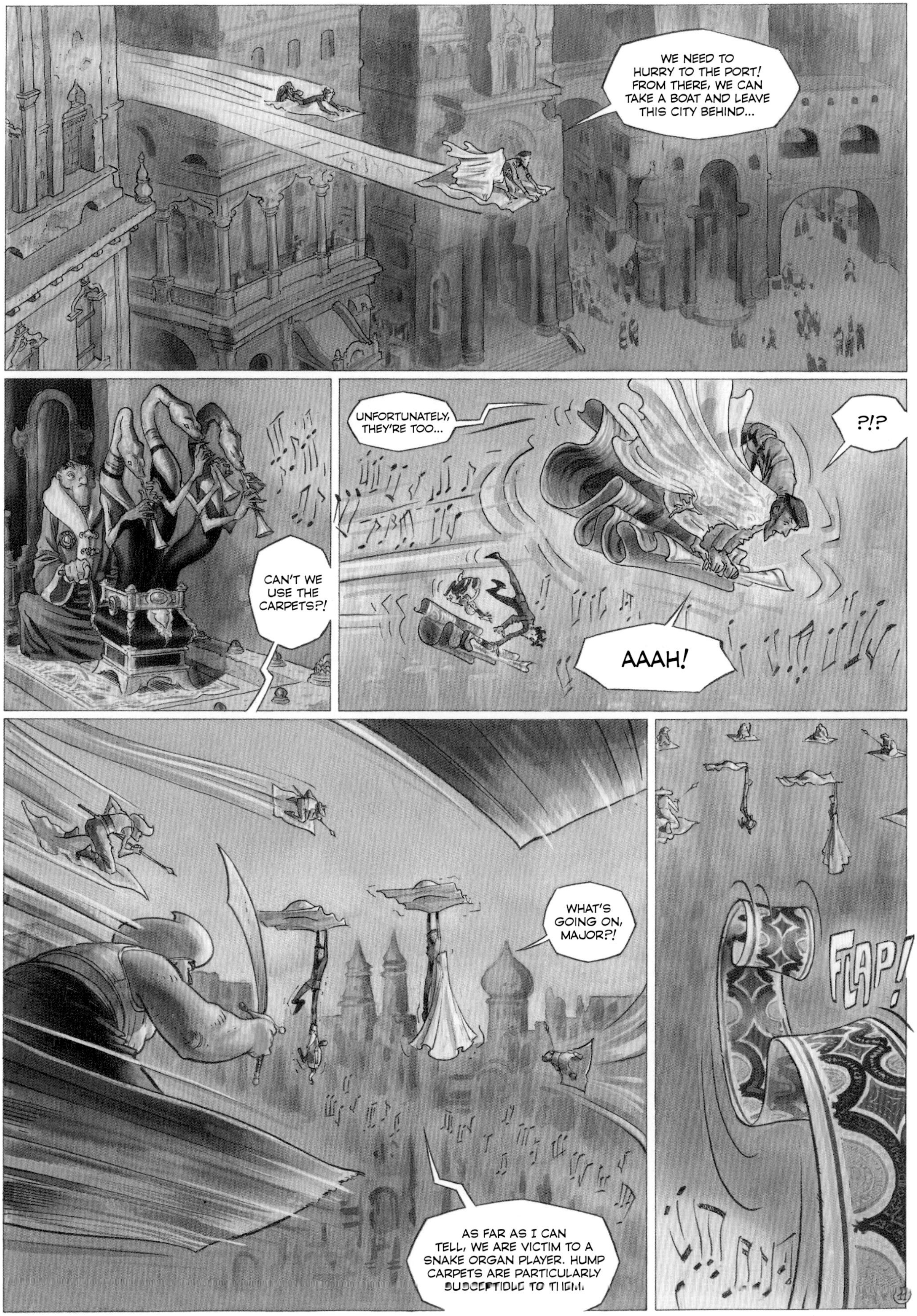
WE NEED TO HURRY TO THE PORT! FROM THERE, WE CAN TAKE A BOAT AND LEAVE THIS CITY BEHIND...
CAN'T WE USE THE CARPETS?!
UNFORTUNATELY, THEY'RE TOO...
?!?
AAAH!
WHAT'S GOING ON, MAJOR?!
AS FAR AS I CAN TELL, WE ARE VICTIM TO A SNAKE ORGAN PLAYER. HUMP CARPETS ARE PARTICULARLY SUSCEPTIBLE TO THEM.
FLAP!

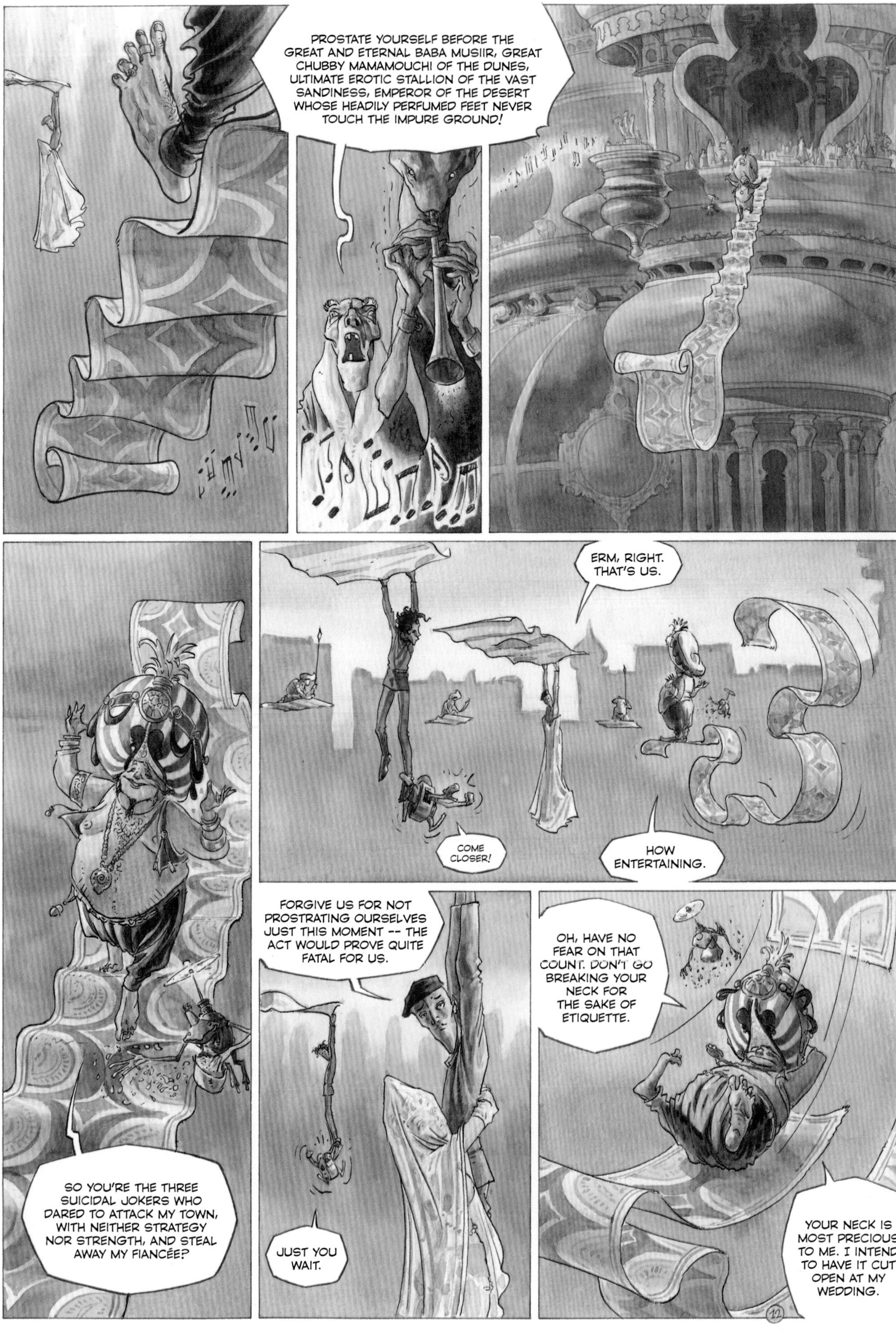
PROSTATE YOURSELF BEFORE THE GREAT AND ETERNAL BABA MUSIIR, GREAT CHUBBY MAMAMOUCHI OF THE DUNES, ULTIMATE EROTIC STALLION OF THE VAST SANDINESS, EMPEROR OF THE DESERT WHOSE HEADILY PERFUMED FEET NEVER TOUCH THE IMPURE GROUND!
ERM, RIGHT. THAT'S US.
COME CLOSER!
HOW ENTERTAINING.
SO YOU'RE THE THREE SUICIDAL JOKERS WHO DARED TO ATTACK MY TOWN, WITH NEITHER STRATEGY NOR STRENGTH, AND STEAL AWAY MY FIANCÉE?
FORGIVE US FOR NOT PROSTRATING OURSELVES JUST THIS MOMENT -- THE ACT WOULD PROVE QUITE FATAL FOR US.
JUST YOU WAIT.
OH, HAVE NO FEAR ON THAT COUNT. DON'T GO BREAKING YOUR NECK FOR THE SAKE OF ETIQUETTE.
YOUR NECK IS MOST PRECIOUS TO ME. I INTEND TO HAVE IT CUT OPEN AT MY WEDDING.

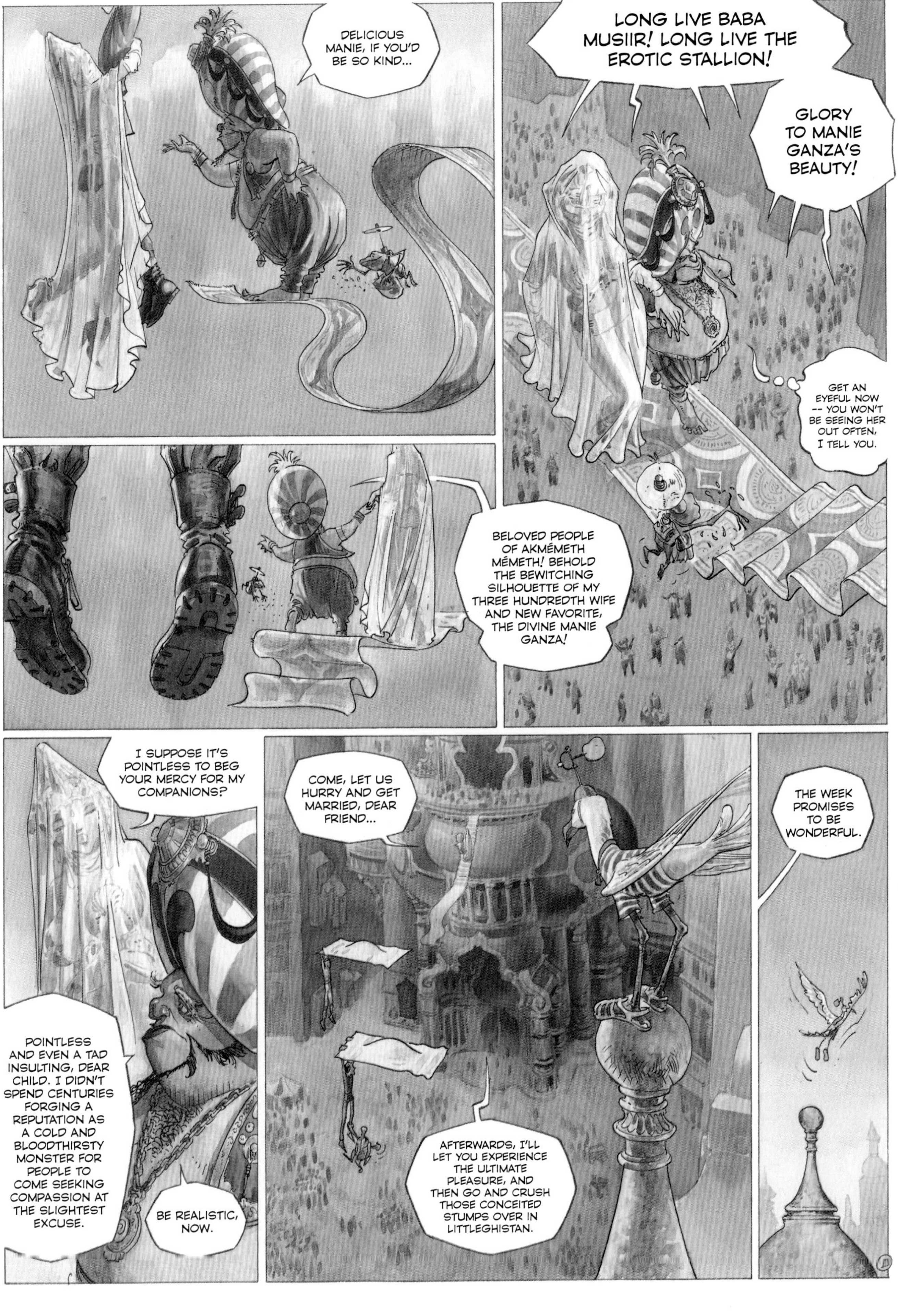
DELICIOUS MANIE, IF YOU'D BE SO KIND...
LONG LIVE BABA MUSIIR! LONG LIVE THE EROTIC STALLION!
GLORY TO MANIE GANZA'S BEAUTY!
GET AN EYEFUL NOW -- YOU WON'T BE SEEING HER OUT OFTEN, I TELL YOU.
BELOVED PEOPLE OF AKMÉMETH MÉMETH! BEHOLD THE BEWITCHING SILHOUETTE OF MY THREE HUNDREDTH WIFE AND NEW FAVORITE, THE DIVINE MANIE GANZA!
I SUPPOSE IT'S POINTLESS TO BEG YOUR MERCY FOR MY COMPANIONS?
POINTLESS AND EVEN A TAD INSULTING, DEAR CHILD. I DIDN'T SPEND CENTURIES FORGING A REPUTATION AS A COLD AND BLOODTHIRSTY MONSTER FOR PEOPLE TO COME SEEKING COMPASSION AT THE SLIGHTEST EXCUSE.
BE REALISTIC, NOW.
COME, LET US HURRY AND GET MARRIED, DEAR FRIEND...
AFTERWARDS, I'LL LET YOU EXPERIENCE THE ULTIMATE PLEASURE, AND THEN GO AND CRUSH THOSE CONCEITED STUMPS OVER IN LITTLEGHISTAN.
THE WEEK PROMISES TO BE WONDERFUL.

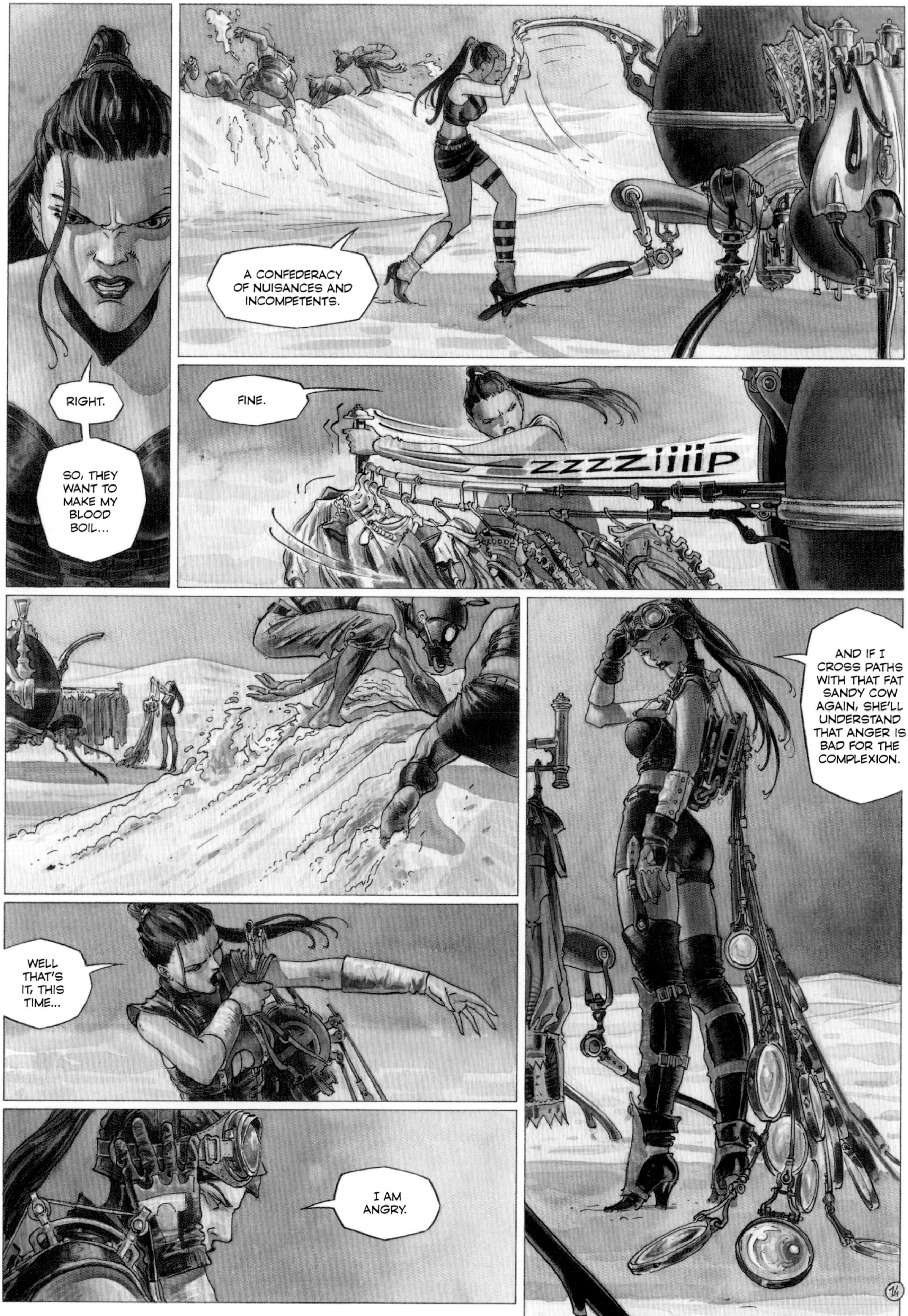
A CONFEDERACY OF NUISANCES AND INCOMPETENTS.
RIGHT.
SO, THEY WANT TO MAKE MY BLOOD BOIL...
FINE.
ZZZZIIIIP
WELL THAT'S IT, THIS TIME...
I AM ANGRY.
AND IF I CROSS PATHS WITH THAT FAT SANDY COW AGAIN, SHE'LL UNDERSTAND THAT ANGER IS BAD FOR THE COMPLEXION.
14

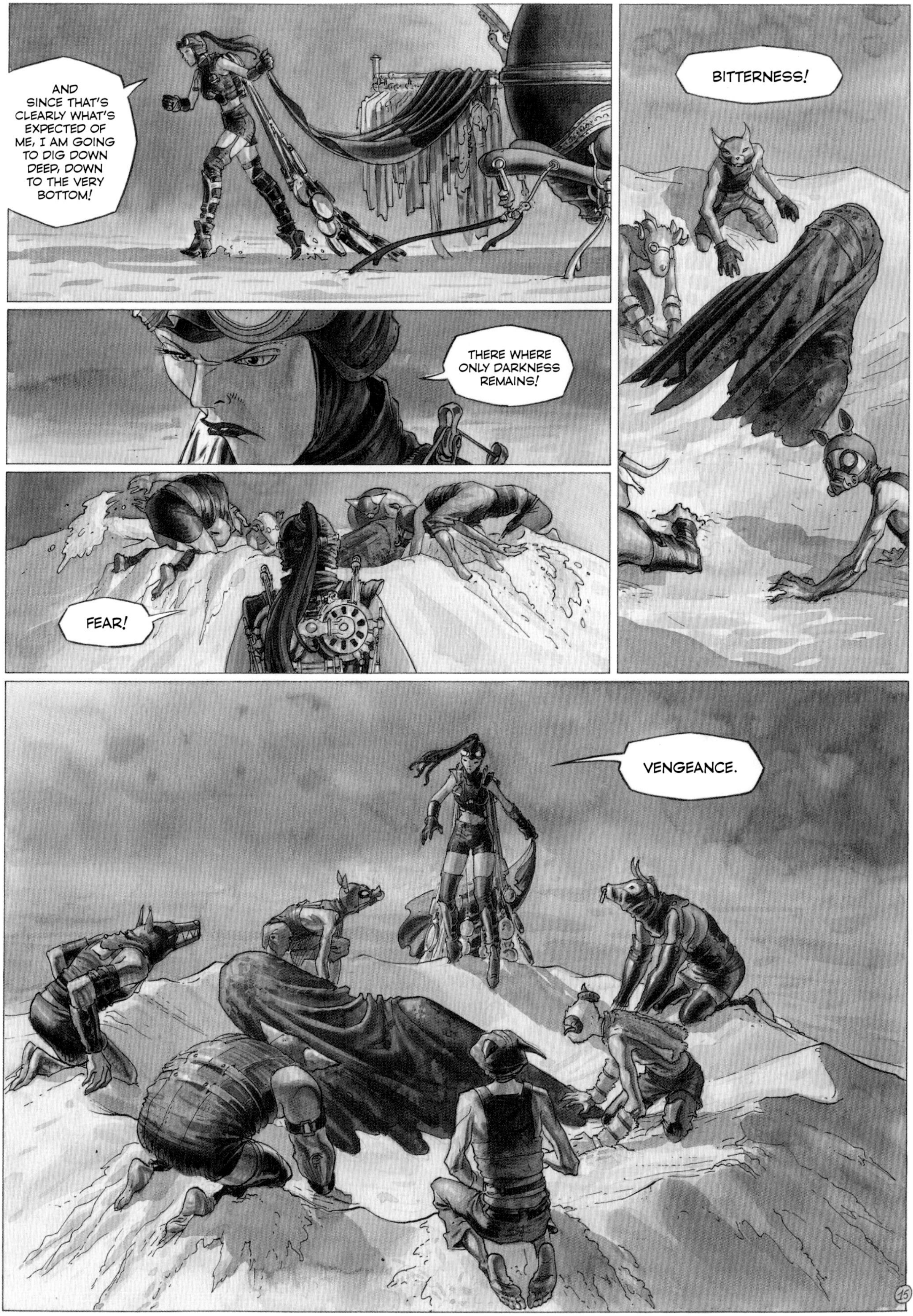
AND SINCE THAT'S CLEARLY WHAT'S EXPECTED OF ME, I AM GOING TO DIG DOWN DEEP, DOWN TO THE VERY BOTTOM!
THERE WHERE ONLY DARKNESS REMAINS!
FEAR!
BITTERNESS!
VENGEANCE.

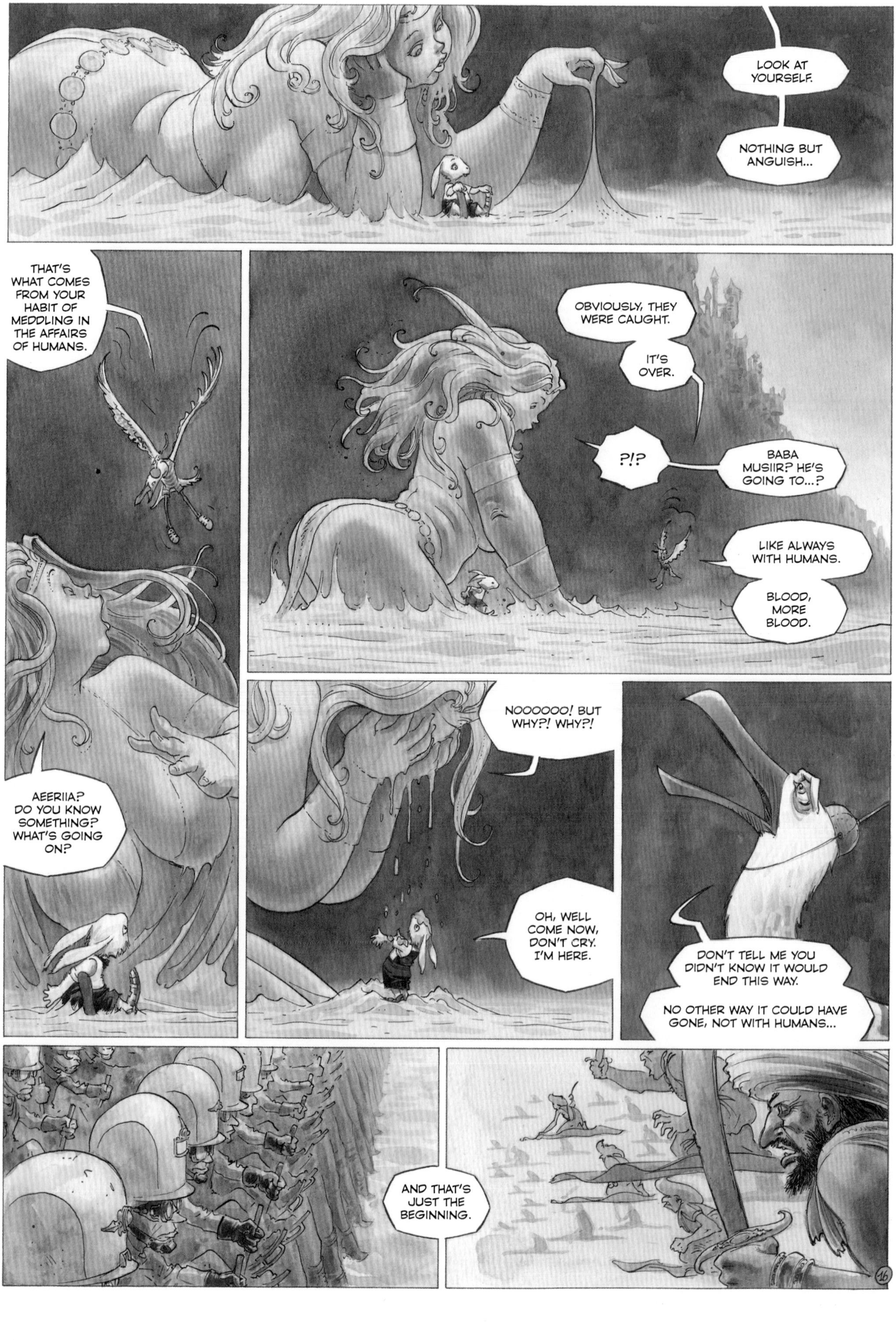
LOOK AT YOURSELF.
NOTHING BUT ANGUISH...
THAT'S WHAT COMES FROM YOUR HABIT OF MEDDLING IN THE AFFAIRS OF HUMANS.
OBVIOUSLY, THEY WERE CAUGHT.
IT'S OVER.
?!?
BABA MUSIIR? HE'S GOING TO...?
LIKE ALWAYS WITH HUMANS.
BLOOD, MORE BLOOD.
AEERIIA? DO YOU KNOW SOMETHING? WHAT'S GOING ON?
NOOOOOO! BUT WHY?! WHY?!
OH, WELL COME NOW, DON'T CRY. I'M HERE.
DON'T TELL ME YOU DIDN'T KNOW IT WOULD END THIS WAY.
NO OTHER WAY IT COULD HAVE GONE, NOT WITH HUMANS...
AND THAT'S JUST THE BEGINNING.
16

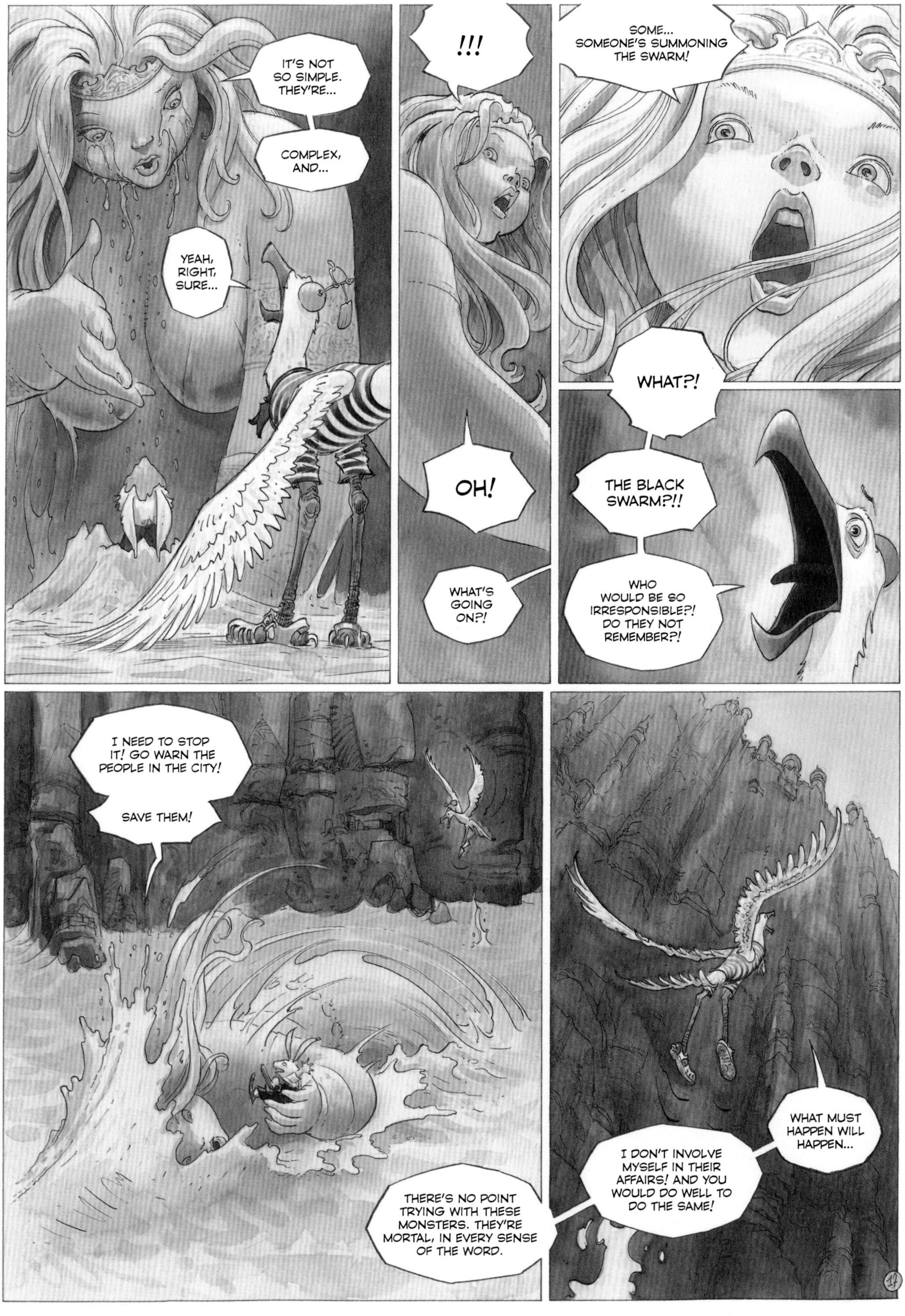

IT'S NOT SO SIMPLE. THEY'RE...
COMPLEX, AND...
YEAH, RIGHT, SURE...
!!!
SOME... SOMEONE'S SUMMONING THE SWARM!
WHAT?!
OH!
THE BLACK SWARM?!!
WHAT'S GOING ON?!
WHO WOULD BE SO IRRESPONSIBLE?! DO THEY NOT REMEMBER?!
I NEED TO STOP IT! GO WARN THE PEOPLE IN THE CITY!
SAVE THEM!
WHAT MUST HAPPEN WILL HAPPEN...
I DON'T INVOLVE MYSELF IN THEIR AFFAIRS! AND YOU WOULD DO WELL TO DO THE SAME!
THERE'S NO POINT TRYING WITH THESE MONSTERS. THEY'RE MORTAL, IN EVERY SENSE OF THE WORD.

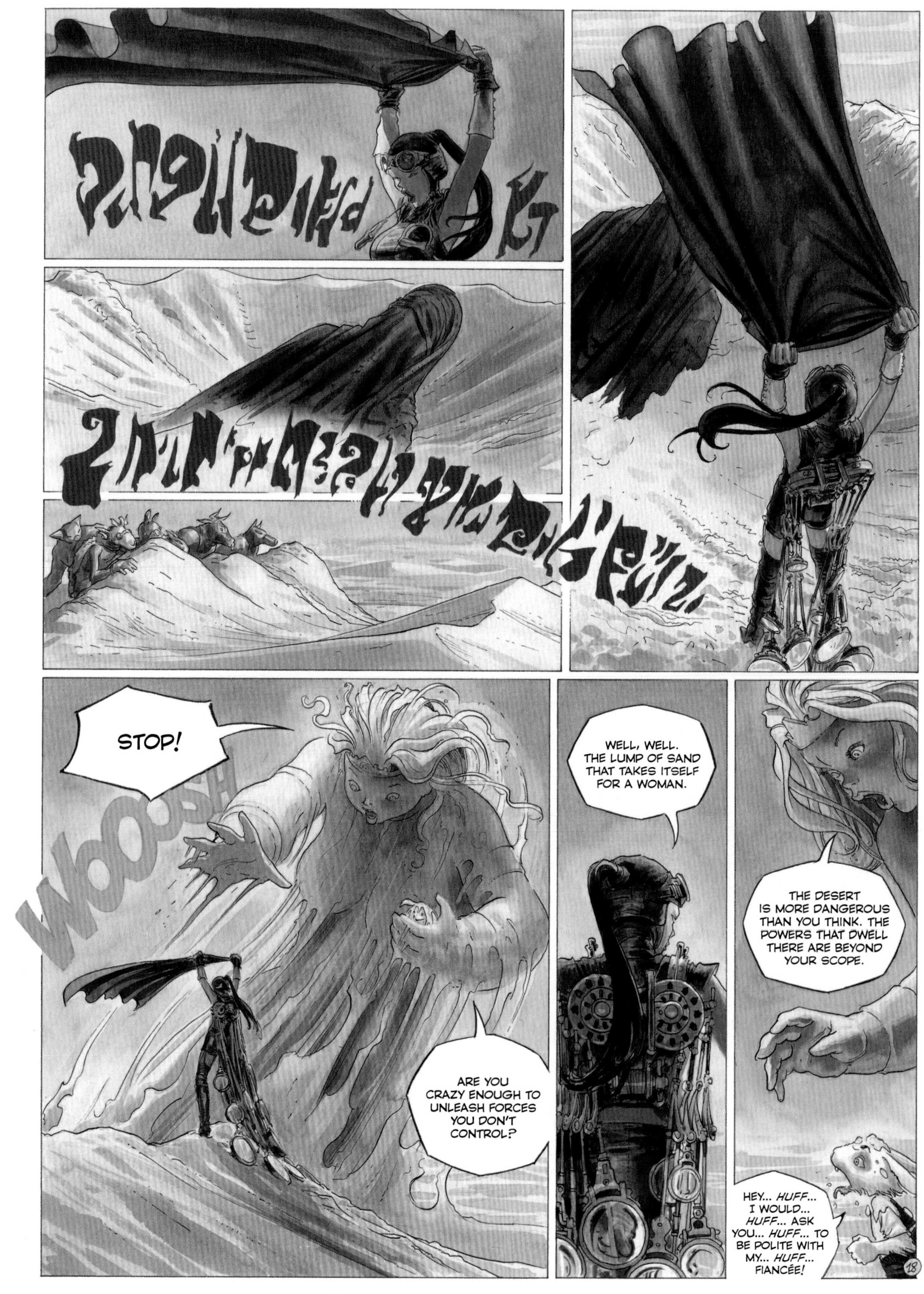
STOP!
WOOOSH
ARE YOU CRAZY ENOUGH TO UNLEASH FORCES YOU DON'T CONTROL?
WELL, WELL. THE LUMP OF SAND THAT TAKES ITSELF FOR A WOMAN.
THE DESERT IS MORE DANGEROUS THAN YOU THINK. THE POWERS THAT DWELL THERE ARE BEYOND YOUR SCOPE.
HEY... *HUFF*... I WOULD... *HUFF*... ASK YOU... *HUFF*... TO BE POLITE WITH MY... *HUFF*... FIANCÉE!

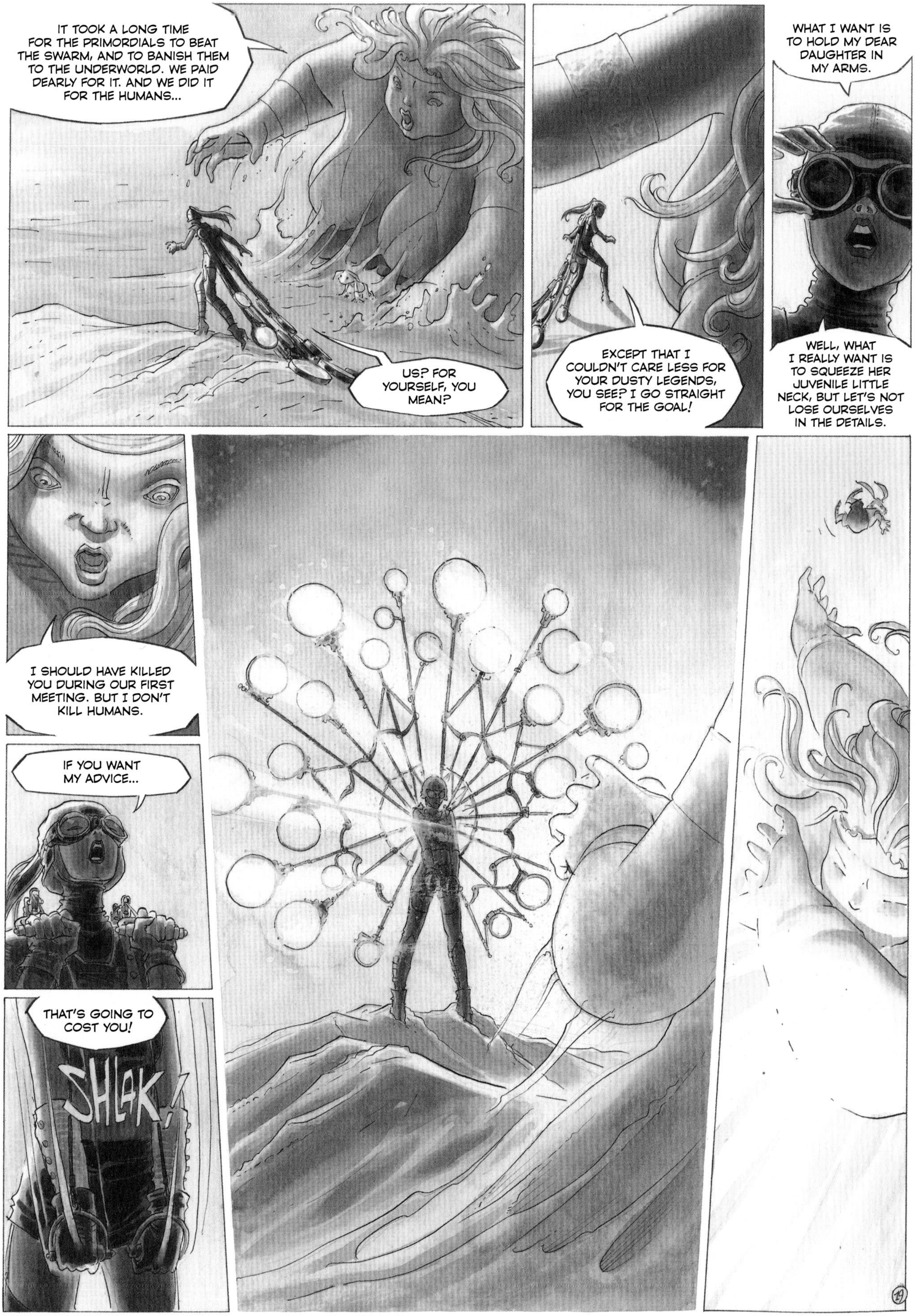
IT TOOK A LONG TIME FOR THE PRIMORDIALS TO BEAT THE SWARM, AND TO BANISH THEM TO THE UNDERWORLD. WE PAID DEARLY FOR IT. AND WE DID IT FOR THE HUMANS...
US? FOR YOURSELF, YOU MEAN?
EXCEPT THAT I COULDN'T CARE LESS FOR YOUR DUSTY LEGENDS, YOU SEE? I GO STRAIGHT FOR THE GOAL!
WHAT I WANT IS TO HOLD MY DEAR DAUGHTER IN MY ARMS.
WELL, WHAT I REALLY WANT IS TO SQUEEZE HER JUVENILE LITTLE NECK, BUT LET'S NOT LOSE OURSELVES IN THE DETAILS.
I SHOULD HAVE KILLED YOU DURING OUR FIRST MEETING. BUT I DON'T KILL HUMANS.
IF YOU WANT MY ADVICE...
THAT'S GOING TO COST YOU!
SHLAK!

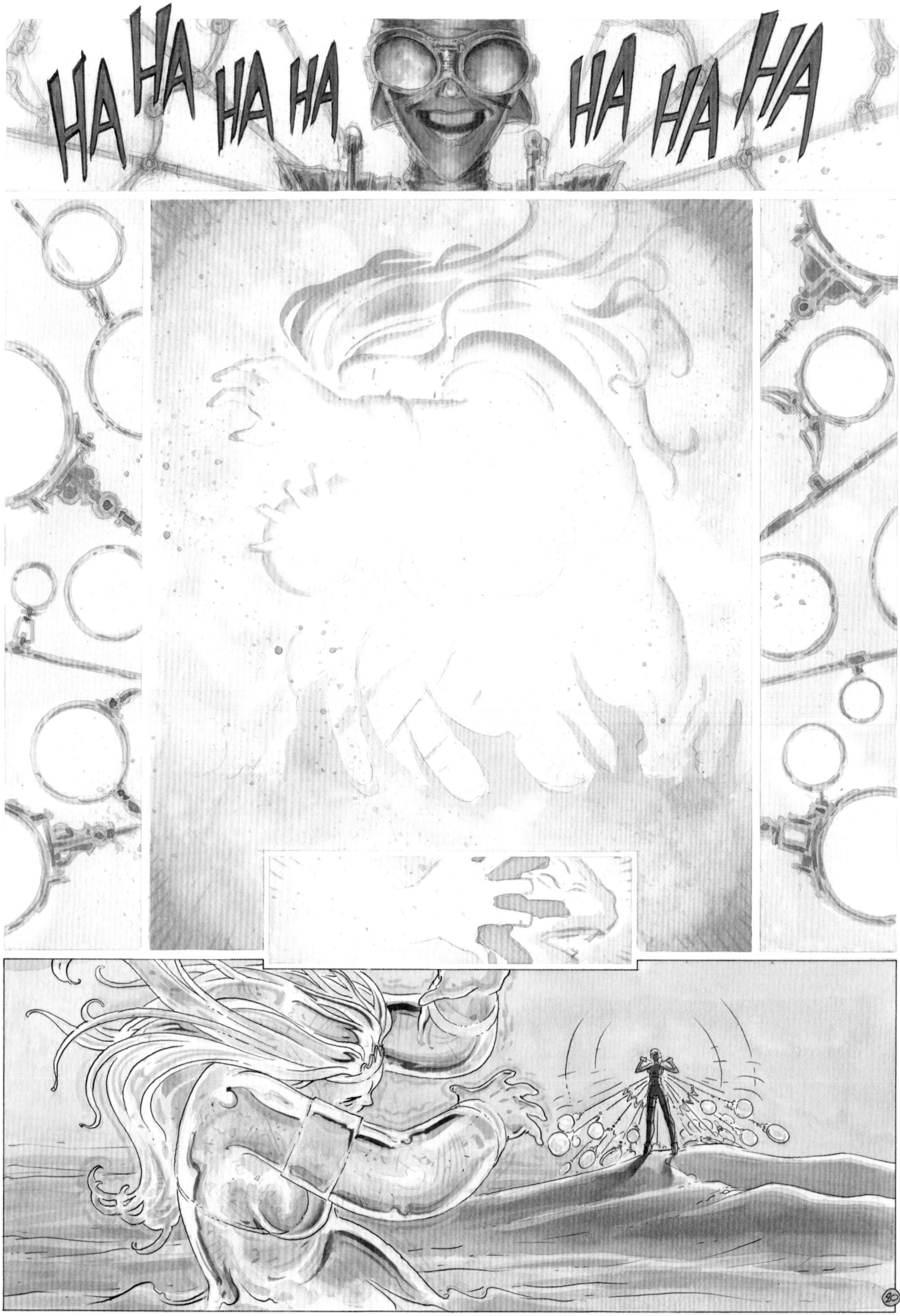
HA HA HA HA HA HA HA HA

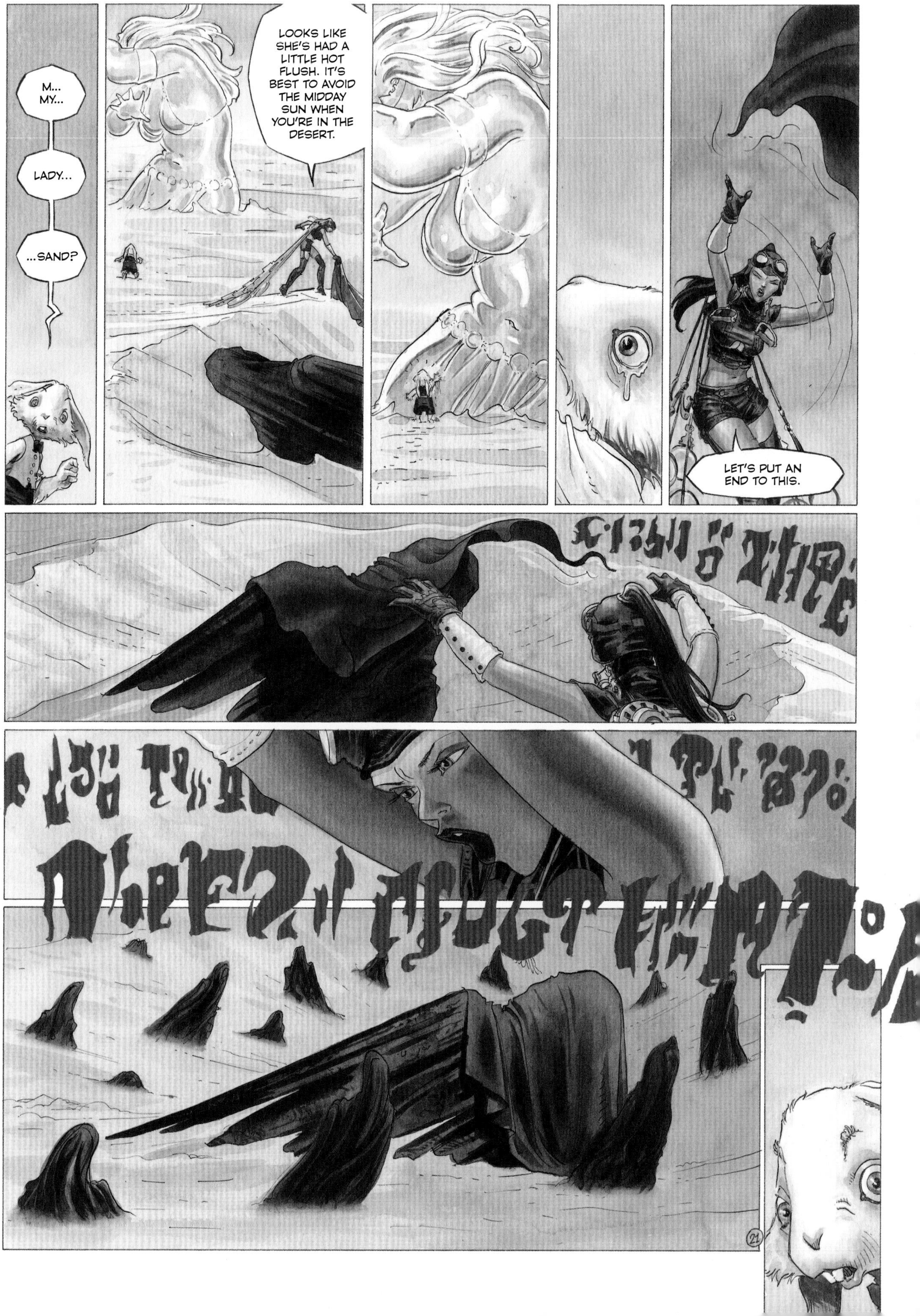
M... MY...
LADY...
...SAND?
LOOKS LIKE SHE'S HAD A LITTLE HOT FLUSH. IT'S BEST TO AVOID THE MIDDAY SUN WHEN YOU'RE IN THE DESERT.
LET'S PUT AN END TO THIS.

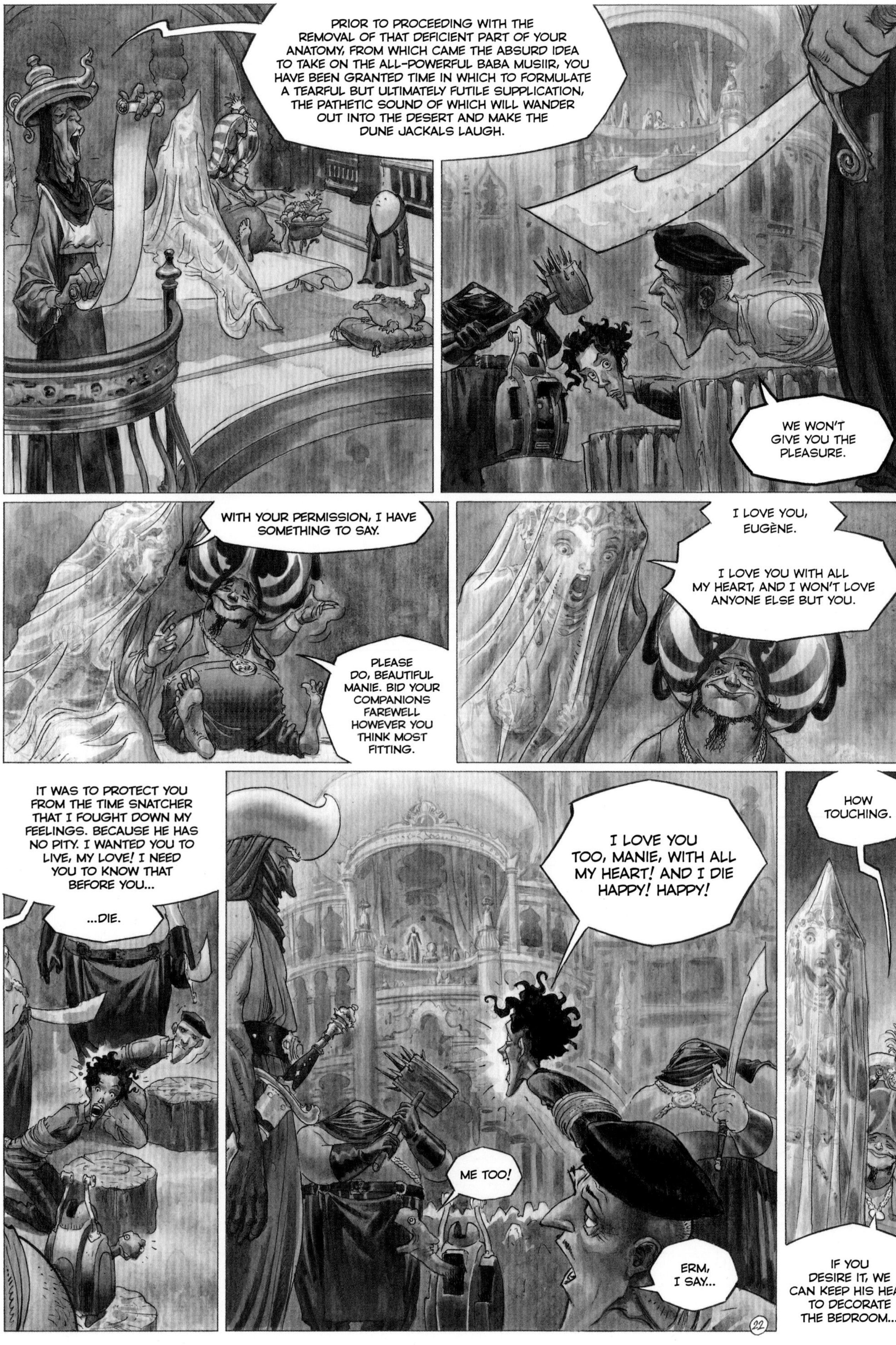
PRIOR TO PROCEEDING WITH THE REMOVAL OF THAT DEFICIENT PART OF YOUR ANATOMY, FROM WHICH CAME THE ABSURD IDEA TO TAKE ON THE ALL-POWERFUL BABA MUSIIR, YOU HAVE BEEN GRANTED TIME IN WHICH TO FORMULATE A TEARFUL BUT ULTIMATELY FUTILE SUPPLICATION, THE PATHETIC SOUND OF WHICH WILL WANDER OUT INTO THE DESERT AND MAKE THE DUNE JACKALS LAUGH.
WE WON'T GIVE YOU THE PLEASURE.
WITH YOUR PERMISSION, I HAVE SOMETHING TO SAY.
PLEASE DO, BEAUTIFUL MANIE. BID YOUR COMPANIONS FAREWELL HOWEVER YOU THINK MOST FITTING.
I LOVE YOU, EUGÈNE.
I LOVE YOU WITH ALL MY HEART, AND I WON'T LOVE ANYONE ELSE BUT YOU.
IT WAS TO PROTECT YOU FROM THE TIME SNATCHER THAT I FOUGHT DOWN MY FEELINGS. BECAUSE HE HAS NO PITY. I WANTED YOU TO LIVE, MY LOVE! I NEED YOU TO KNOW THAT BEFORE YOU...
...DIE.
I LOVE YOU TOO, MANIE, WITH ALL MY HEART! AND I DIE HAPPY! HAPPY!
ME TOO!
ERM, I SAY...
HOW TOUCHING.
IF YOU DESIRE IT, WE CAN KEEP HIS HEAD TO DECORATE THE BEDROOM...

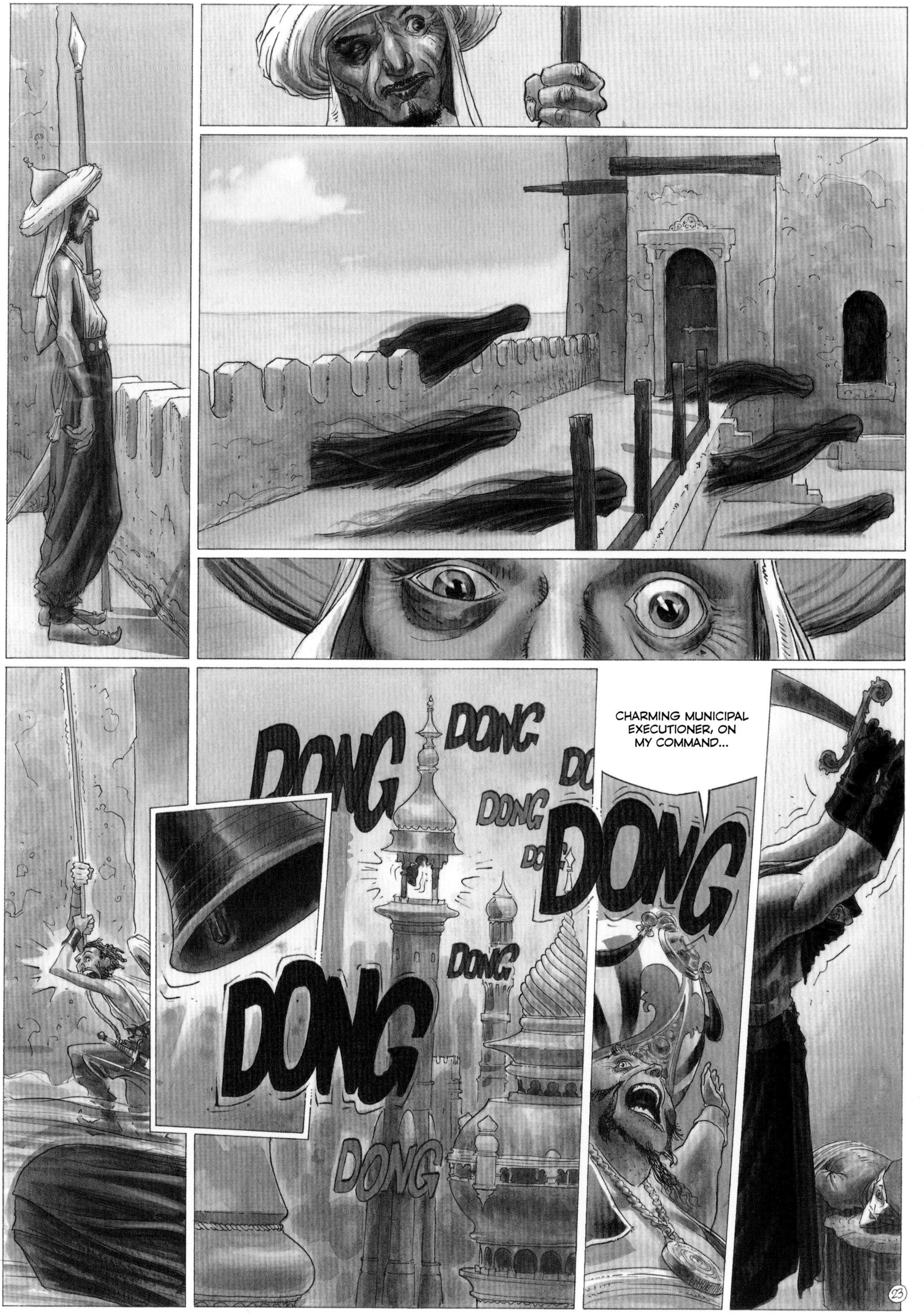
DONG
DONG
DONG
DONG
DONG
DONG
DONG
DONG
DONG
CHARMING MUNICIPAL EXECUTIONER, ON MY COMMAND...

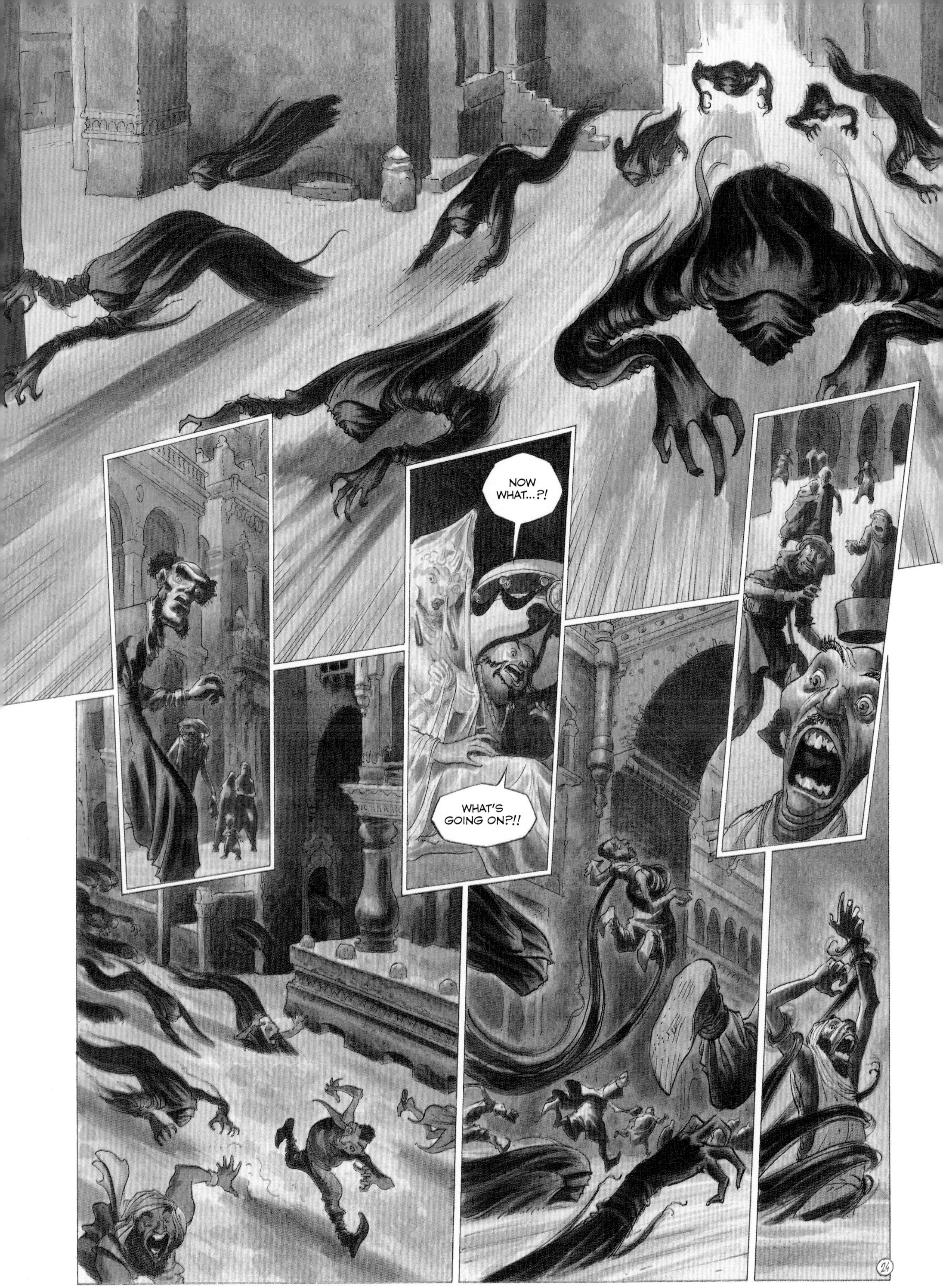
NOW WHAT...?!
WHAT'S GOING ON?!!

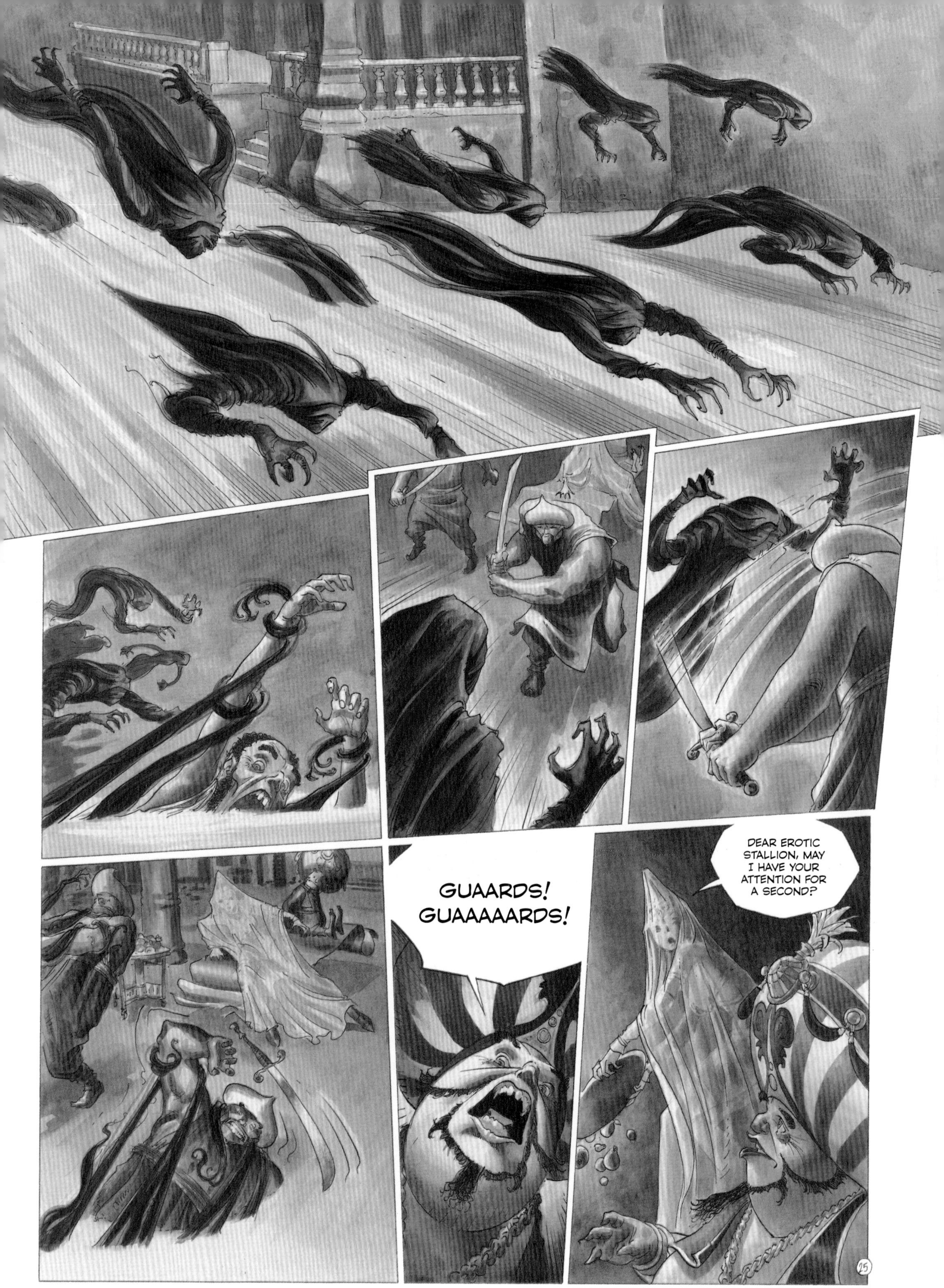
GUAARDS! GUAAAAARDS!
DEAR EROTIC STALLION, MAY I HAVE YOUR ATTENTION FOR A SECOND?

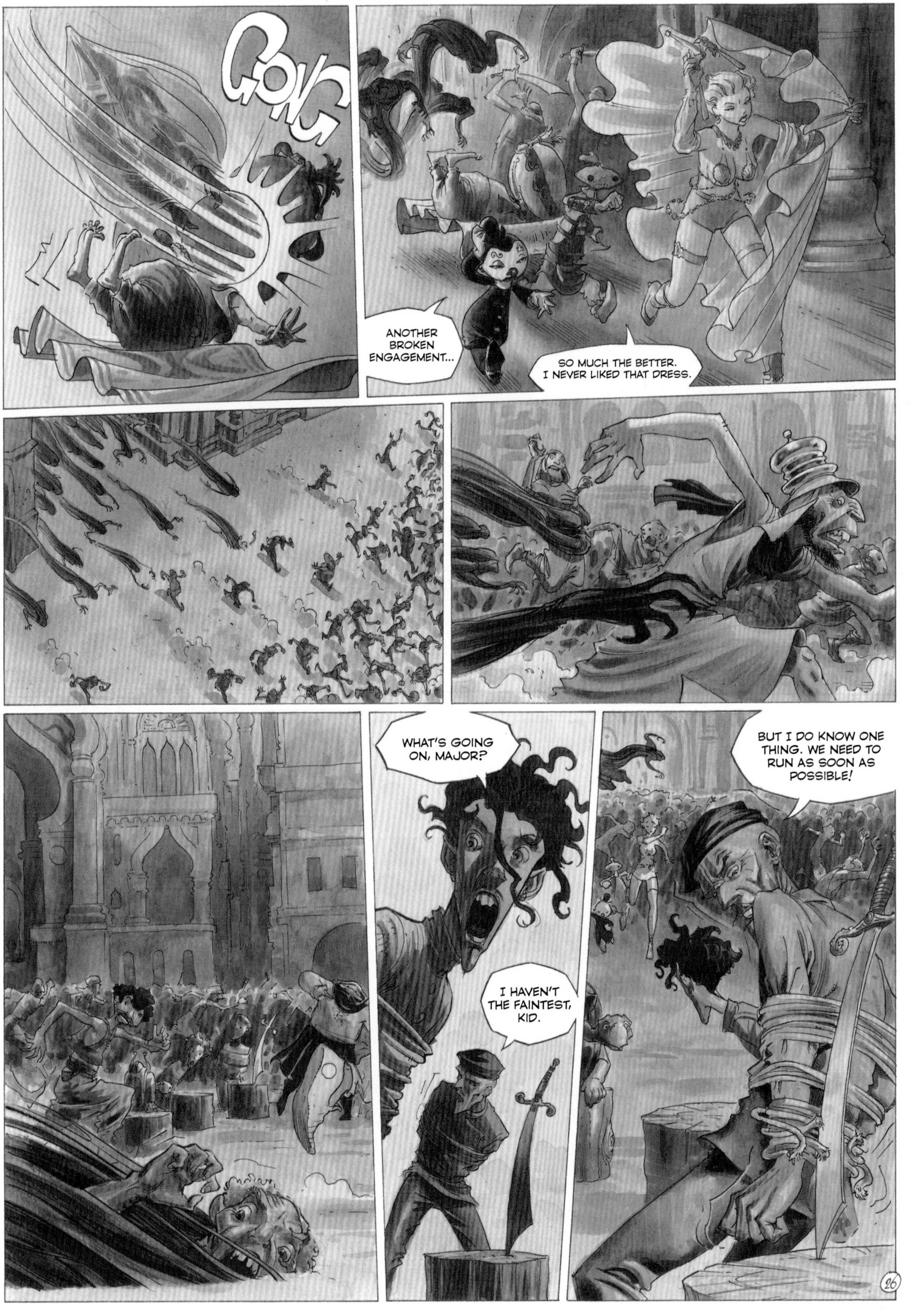
GONG
ANOTHER BROKEN ENGAGEMENT...
SO MUCH THE BETTER. I NEVER LIKED THAT DRESS.
WHAT'S GOING ON, MAJOR?
I HAVEN'T THE FAINTEST, KID.
BUT I DO KNOW ONE THING. WE NEED TO RUN AS SOON AS POSSIBLE!
26

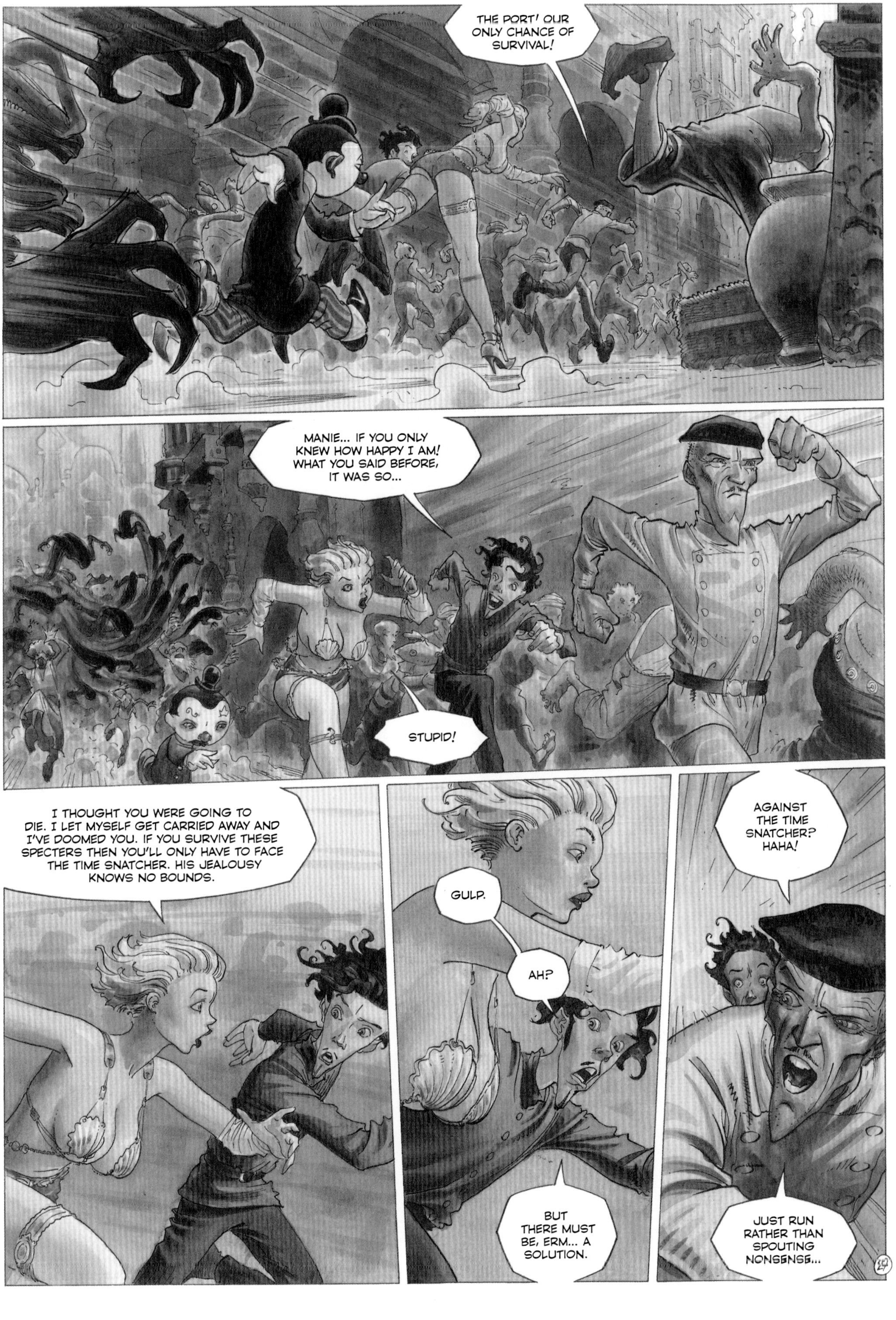
THE PORT! OUR ONLY CHANCE OF SURVIVAL!
MANIE... IF YOU ONLY KNEW HOW HAPPY I AM! WHAT YOU SAID BEFORE, IT WAS SO...
STUPID!
I THOUGHT YOU WERE GOING TO DIE. I LET MYSELF GET CARRIED AWAY AND I'VE DOOMED YOU. IF YOU SURVIVE THESE SPECTERS THEN YOU'LL ONLY HAVE TO FACE THE TIME SNATCHER. HIS JEALOUSY KNOWS NO BOUNDS.
GULP.
AH?
BUT THERE MUST BE, ERM... A SOLUTION.
AGAINST THE TIME SNATCHER? HAHA!
JUST RUN RATHER THAN SPOUTING NONSENSE...

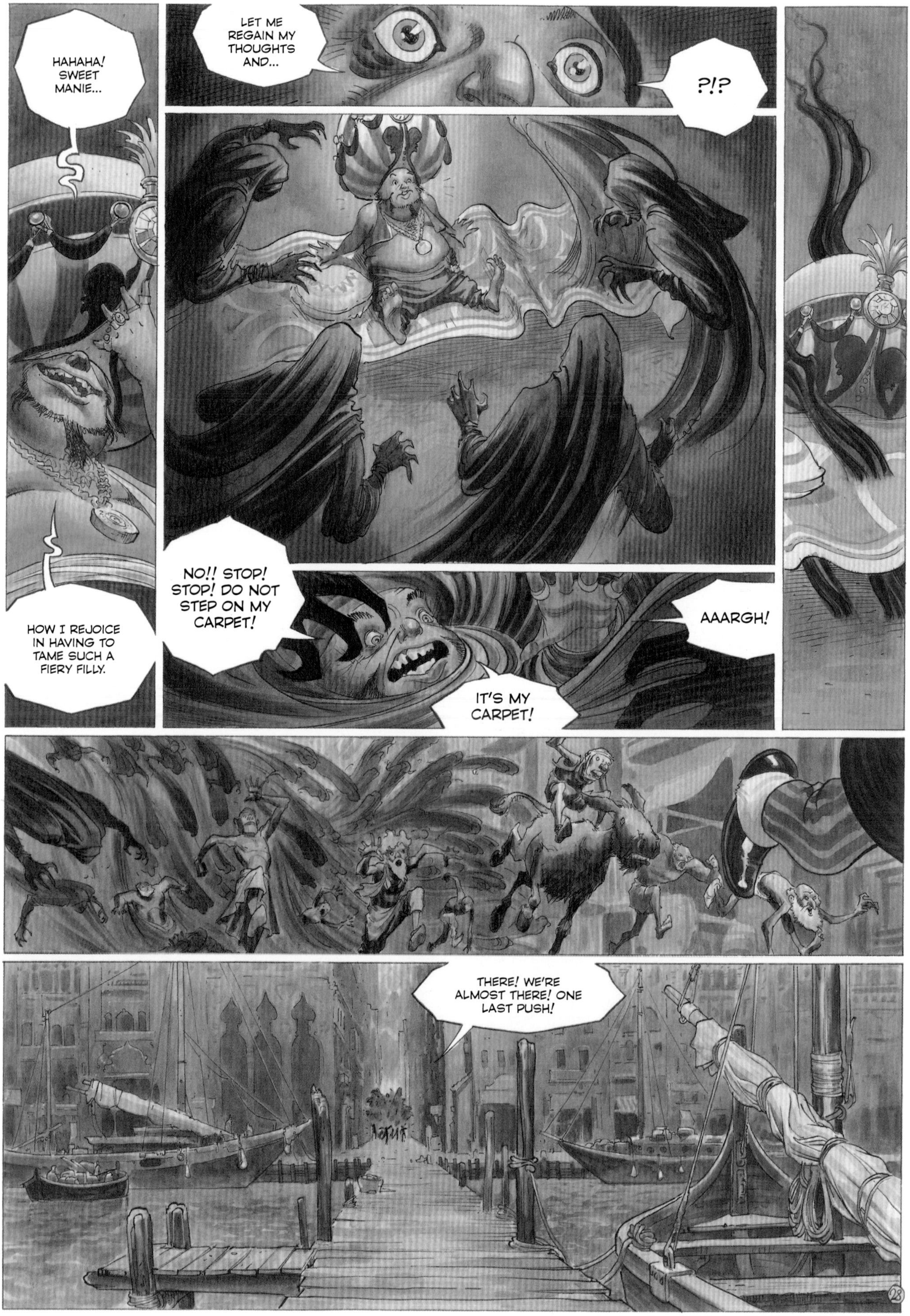
HAHAHA! SWEET MANIE...
LET ME REGAIN MY THOUGHTS AND...
?!?
HOW I REJOICE IN HAVING TO TAME SUCH A FIERY FILLY.
NO!! STOP! STOP! DO NOT STEP ON MY CARPET!
AAARGH!
IT'S MY CARPET!
THERE! WE'RE ALMOST THERE! ONE LAST PUSH!
28

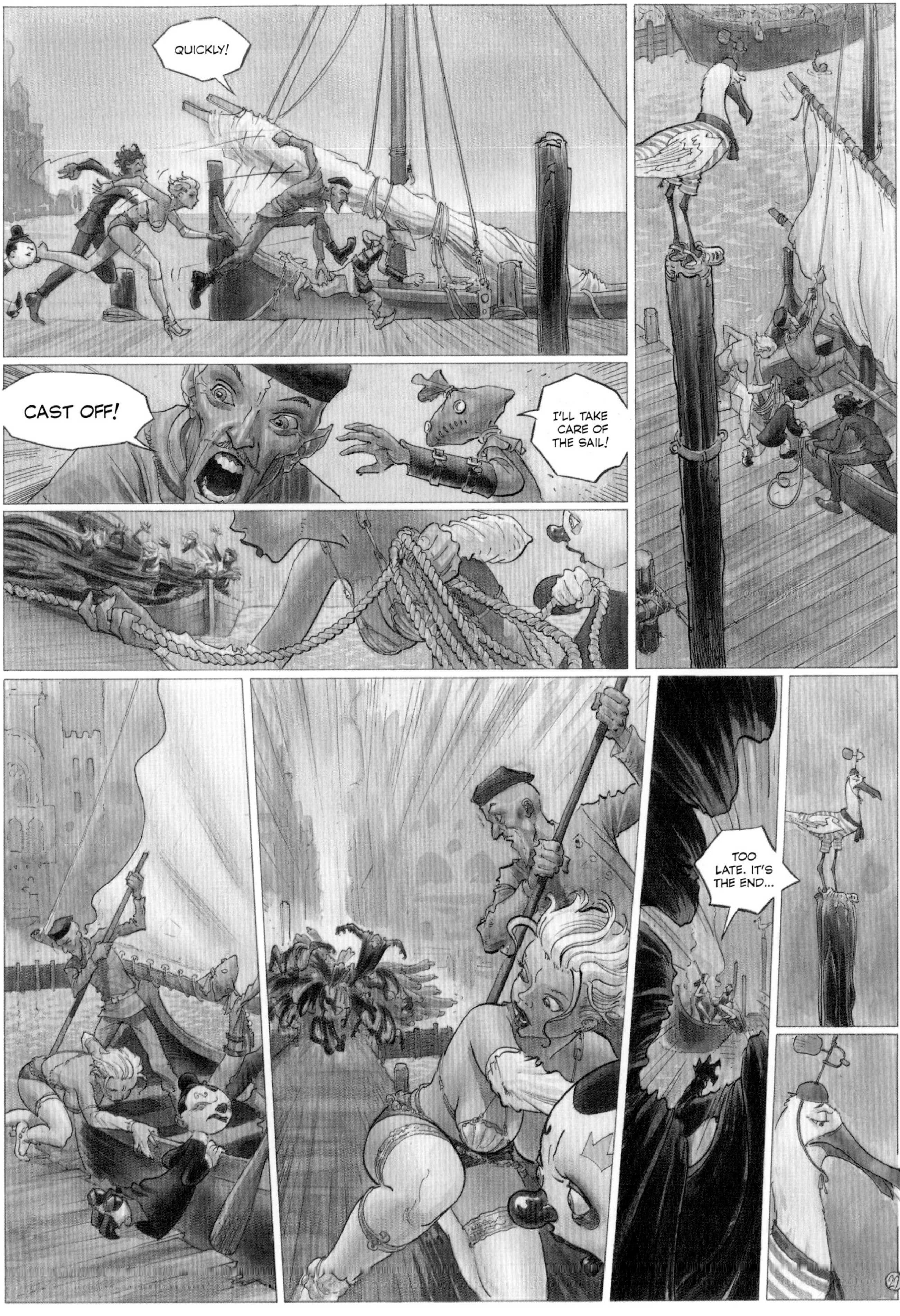
QUICKLY!
CAST OFF!
I'LL TAKE CARE OF THE SAIL!
TOO LATE. IT'S THE END...
PFF

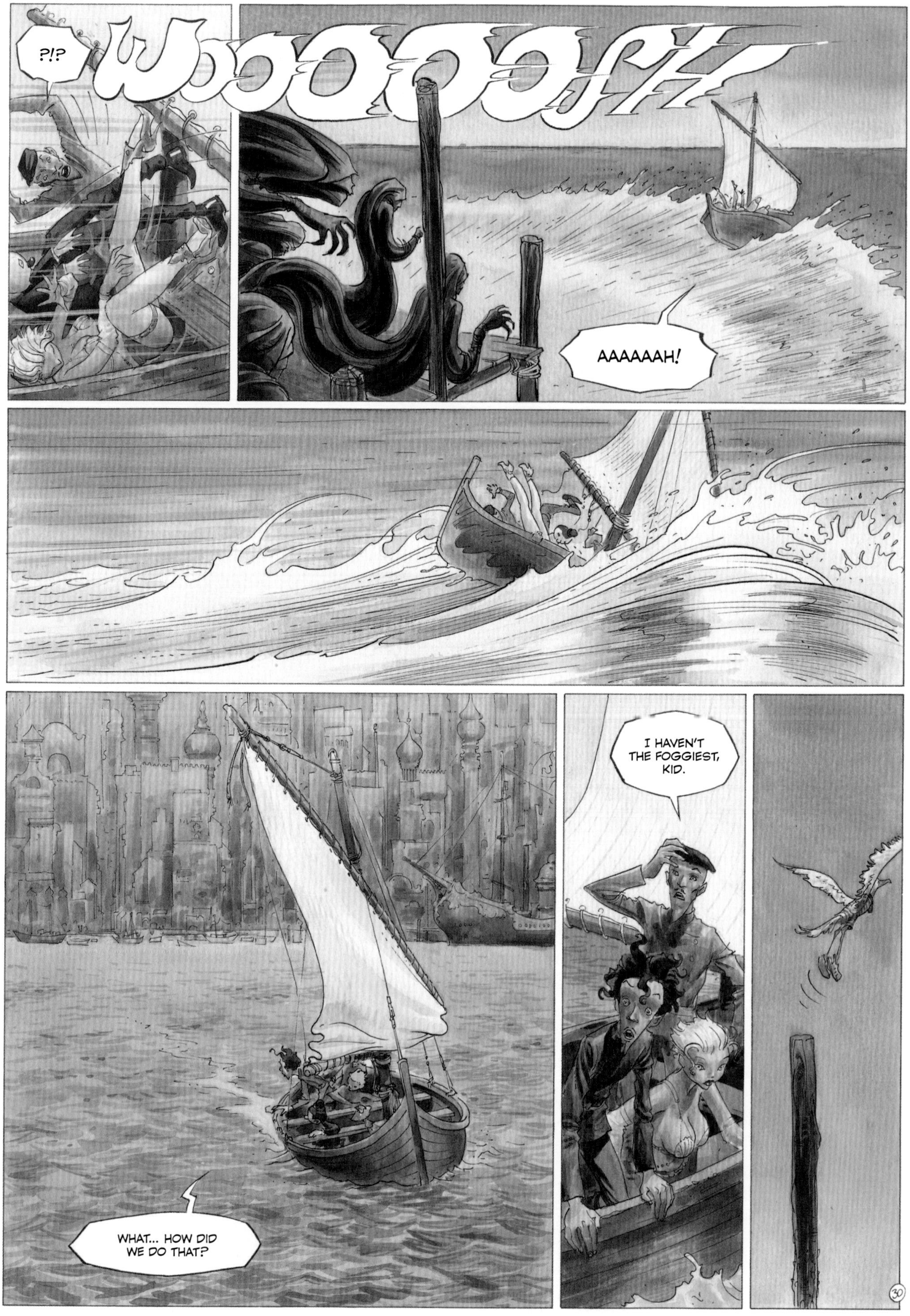
?!?
WOOOOOSH
AAAAAAH!
WHAT... HOW DID WE DO THAT?
I HAVEN'T THE FOGGIEST, KID.
30

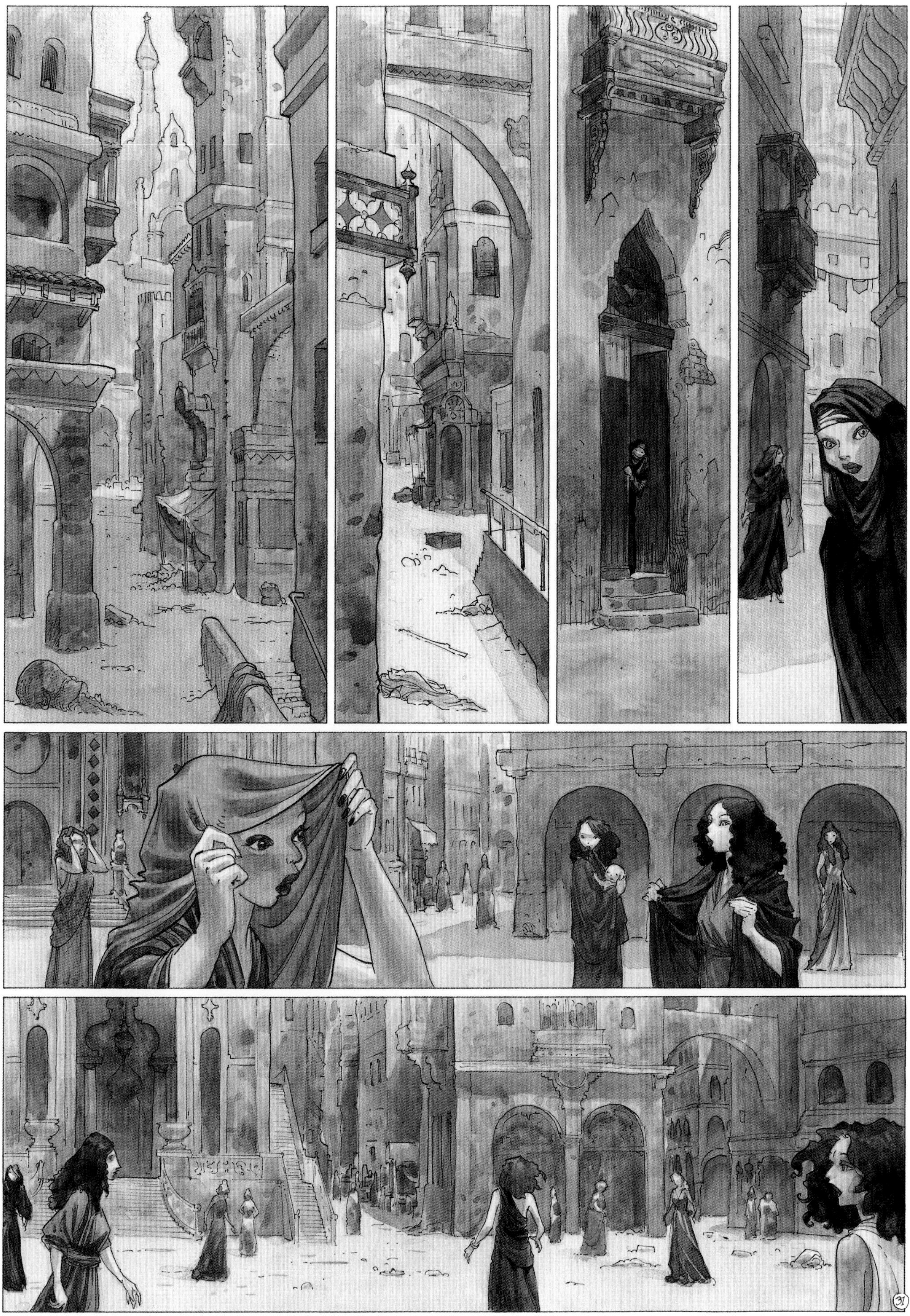

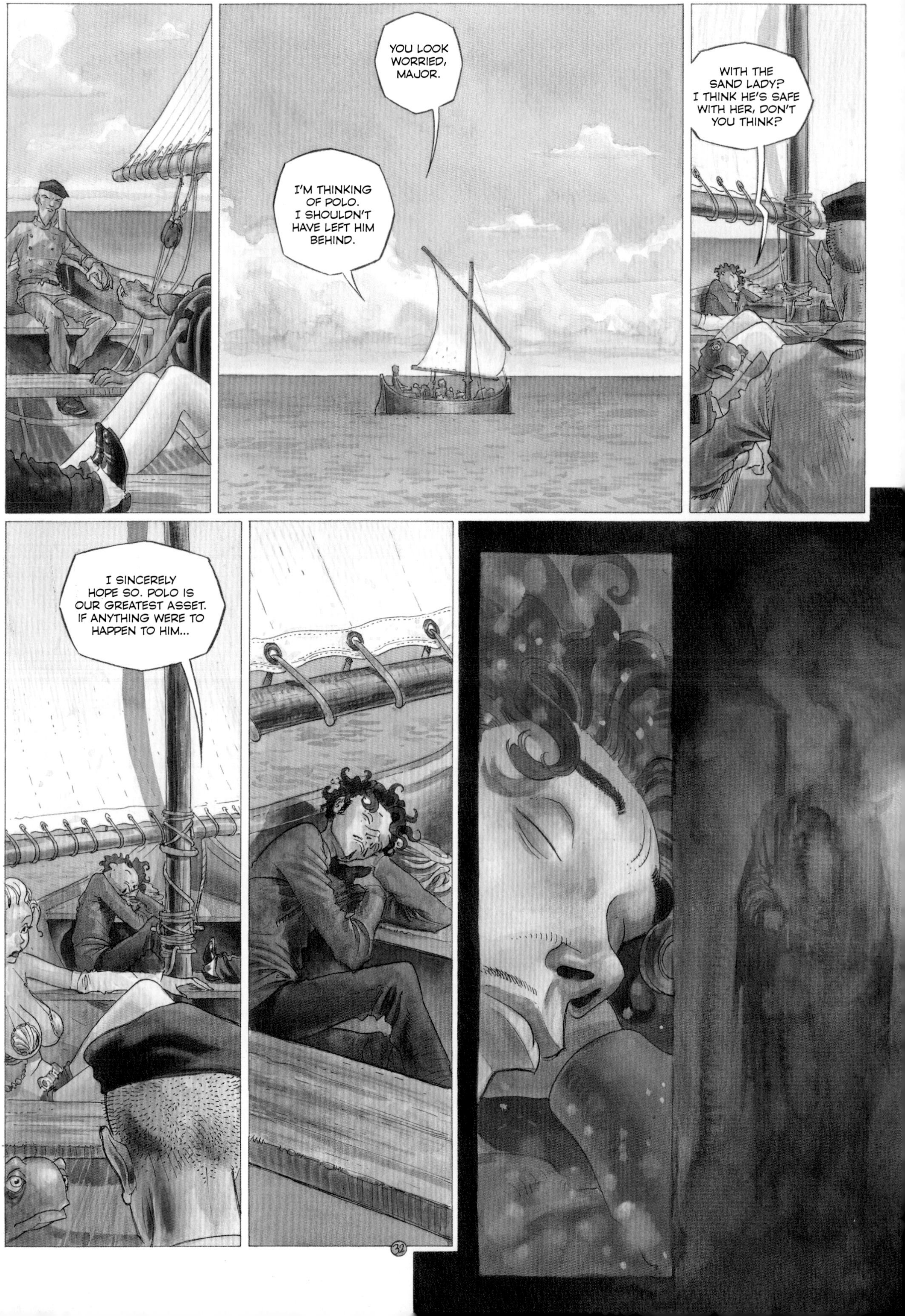
YOU LOOK WORRIED, MAJOR.
I'M THINKING OF POLO. I SHOULDN'T HAVE LEFT HIM BEHIND.
WITH THE SAND LADY? I THINK HE'S SAFE WITH HER, DON'T YOU THINK?
I SINCERELY HOPE SO. POLO IS OUR GREATEST ASSET. IF ANYTHING WERE TO HAPPEN TO HIM...

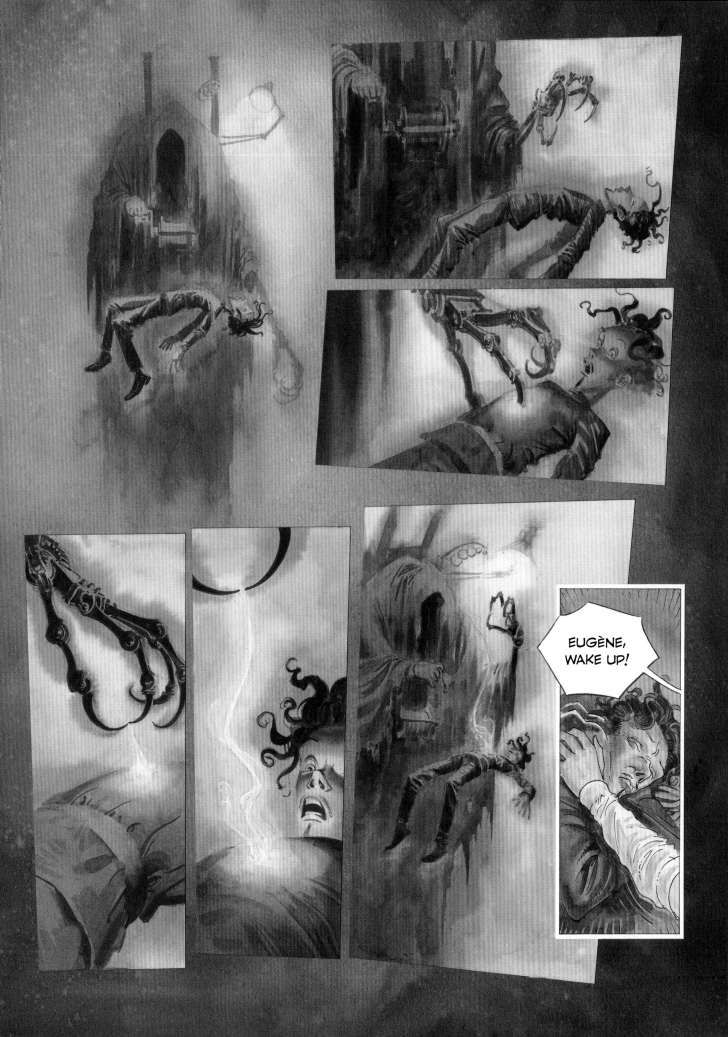

EUGÈNE, WAKE UP!

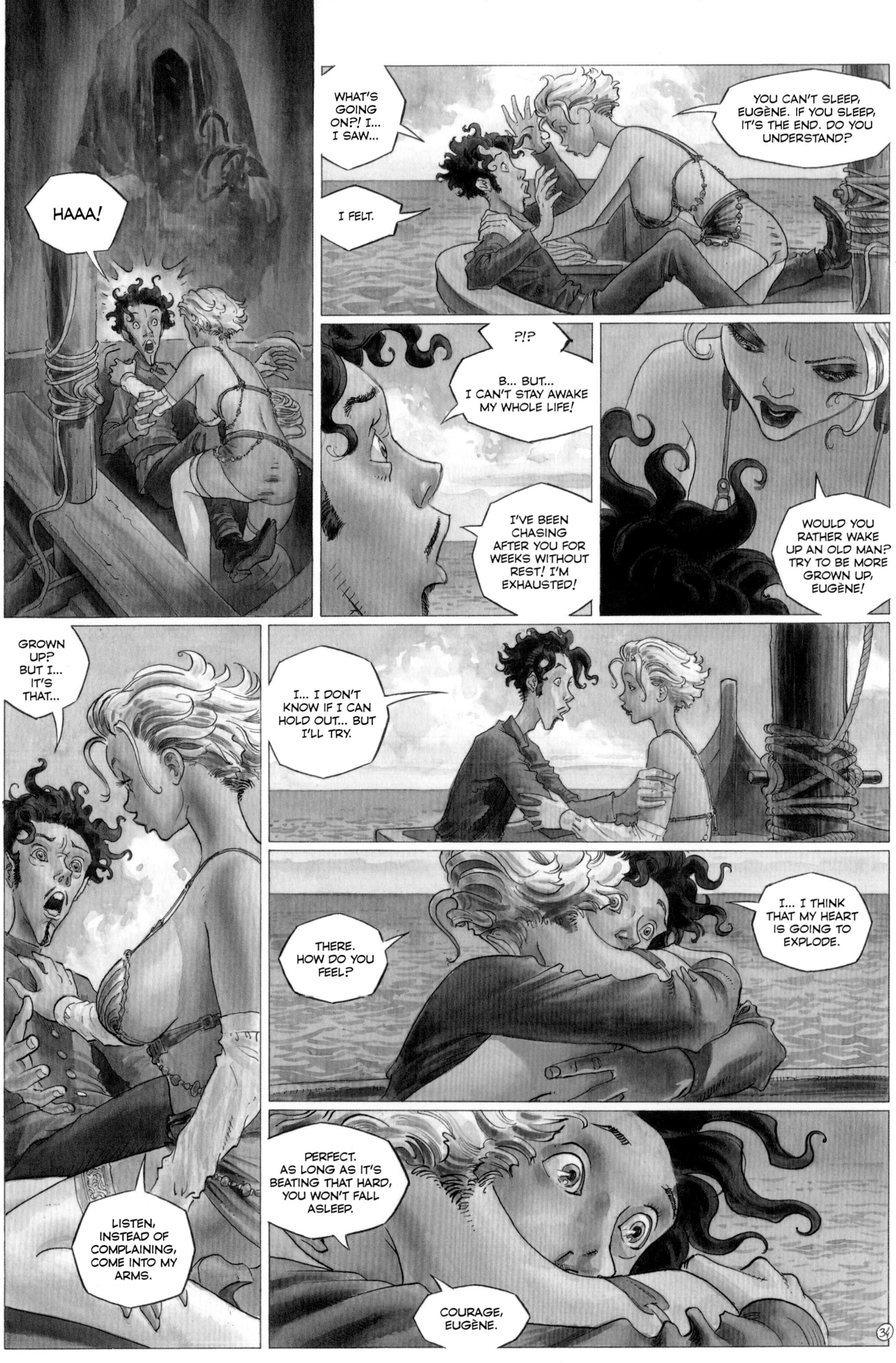
HAAA!
WHAT'S GOING ON?! I... I SAW...
I FELT.
YOU CAN'T SLEEP, EUGÈNE. IF YOU SLEEP, IT'S THE END. DO YOU UNDERSTAND?
?!?
B... BUT... I CAN'T STAY AWAKE MY WHOLE LIFE!
I'VE BEEN CHASING AFTER YOU FOR WEEKS WITHOUT REST! I'M EXHAUSTED!
WOULD YOU RATHER WAKE UP AN OLD MAN? TRY TO BE MORE GROWN UP, EUGÈNE!
GROWN UP? BUT I... IT'S THAT...
LISTEN, INSTEAD OF COMPLAINING, COME INTO MY ARMS.
I... I DON'T KNOW IF I CAN HOLD OUT... BUT I'LL TRY.
THERE. HOW DO YOU FEEL?
I... I THINK THAT MY HEART IS GOING TO EXPLODE.
PERFECT. AS LONG AS IT'S BEATING THAT HARD, YOU WON'T FALL ASLEEP.
COURAGE, EUGÈNE.

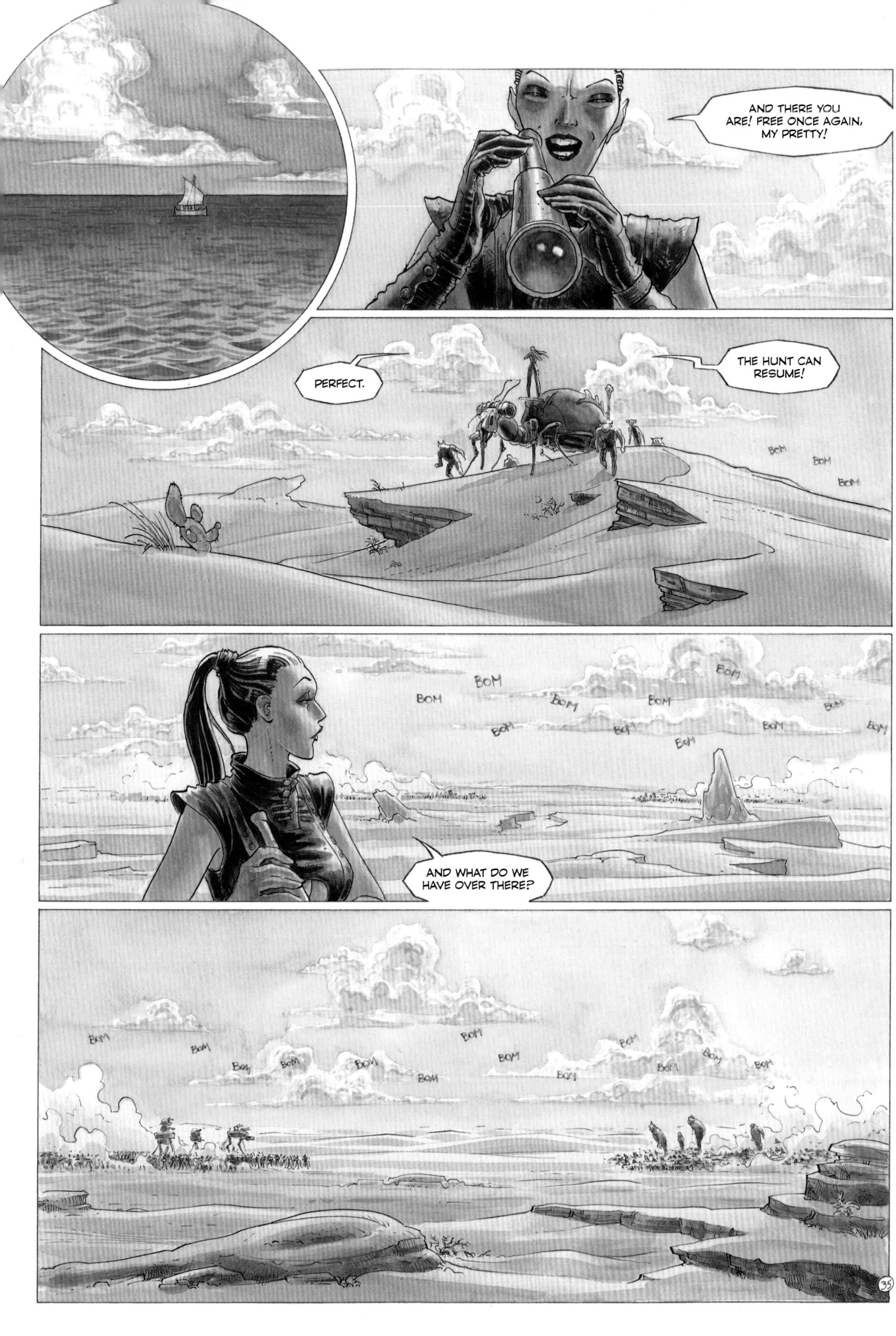
AND THERE YOU ARE! FREE ONCE AGAIN, MY PRETTY!
PERFECT.
THE HUNT CAN RESUME!
BOM BOM BOM
AND WHAT DO WE HAVE OVER THERE?

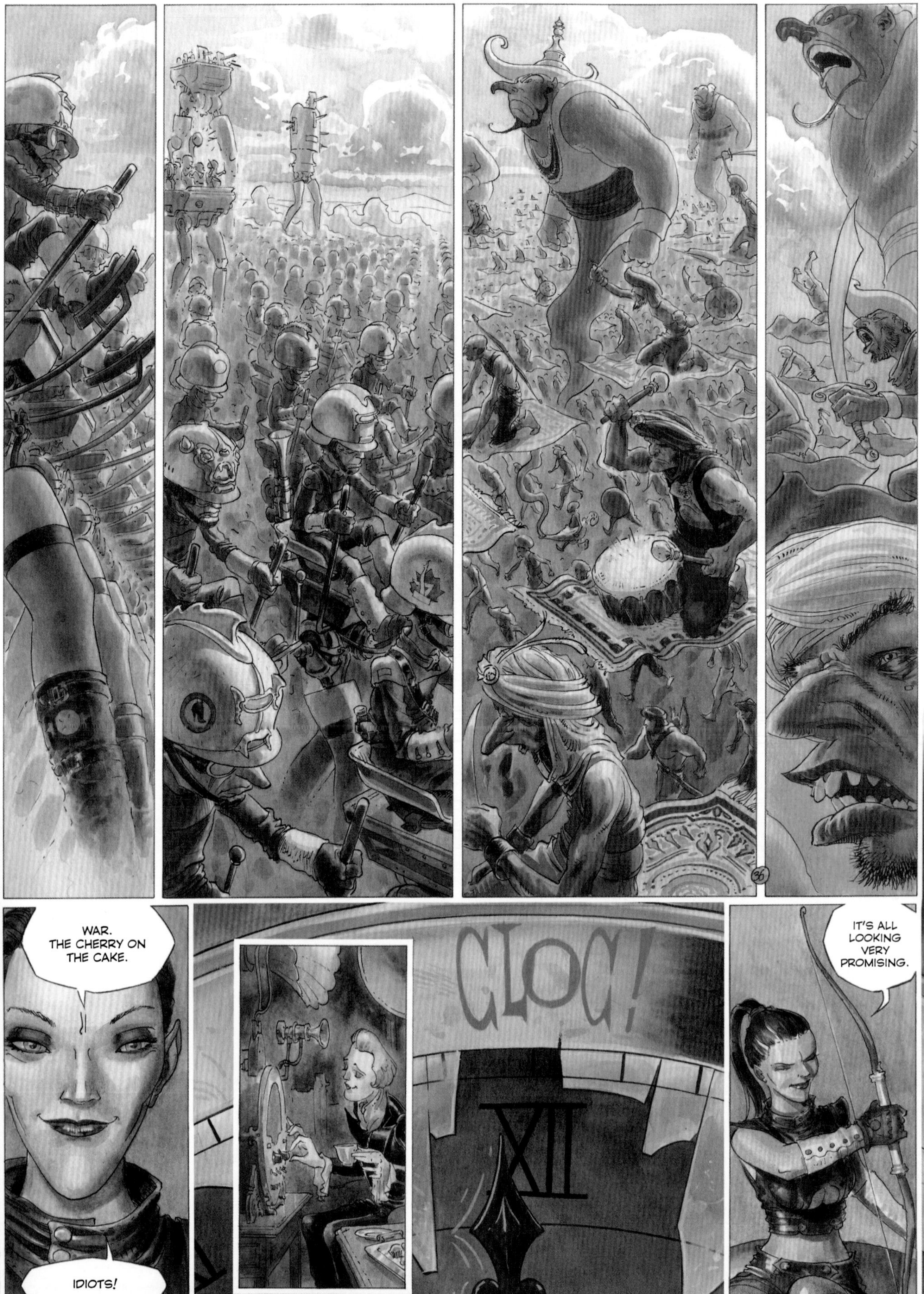
WAR. THE CHERRY ON THE CAKE.
IDIOTS!
CLOC!
IT'S ALL LOOKING VERY PROMISING.

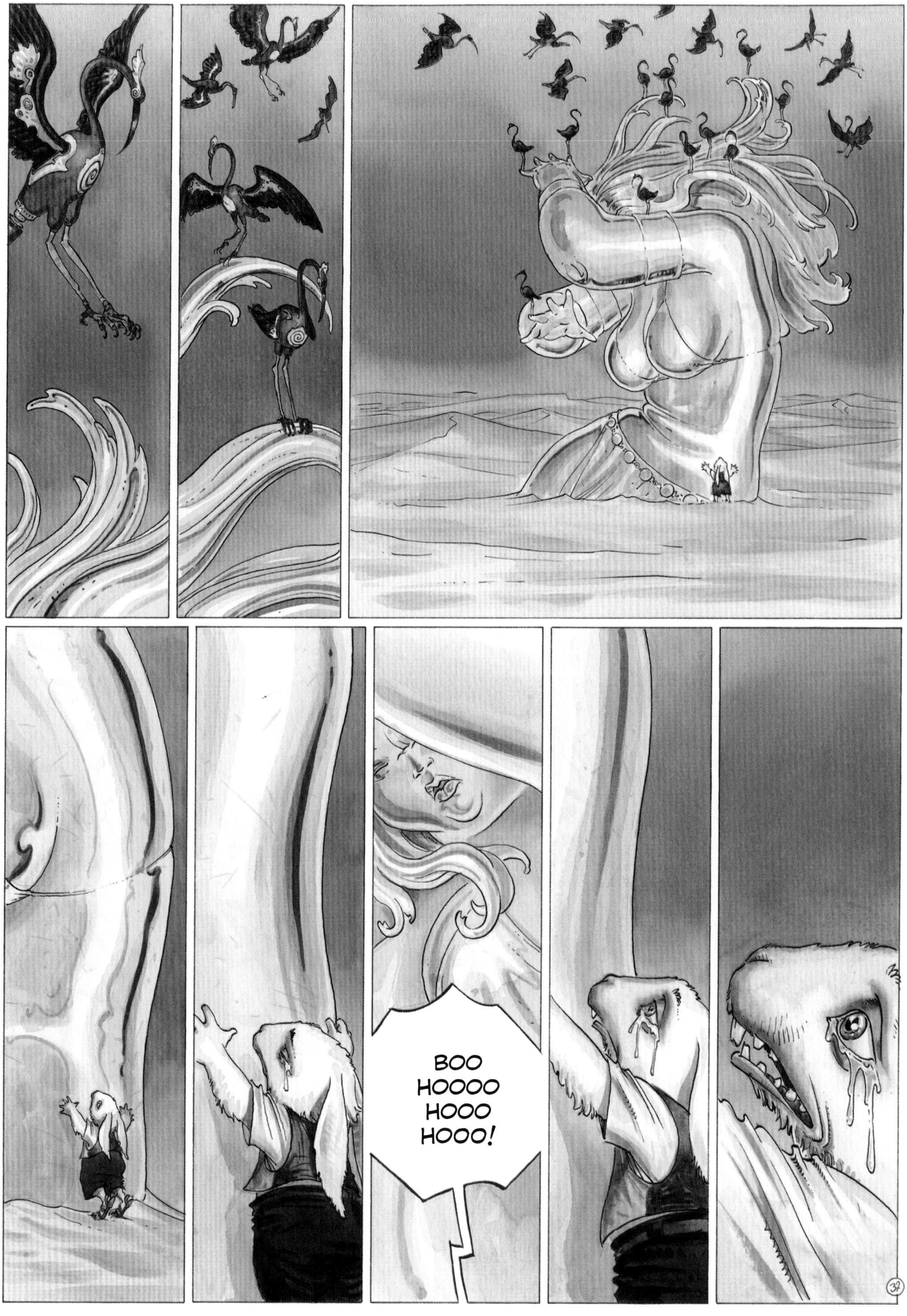
BOO HOOOO HOOO HOOO!

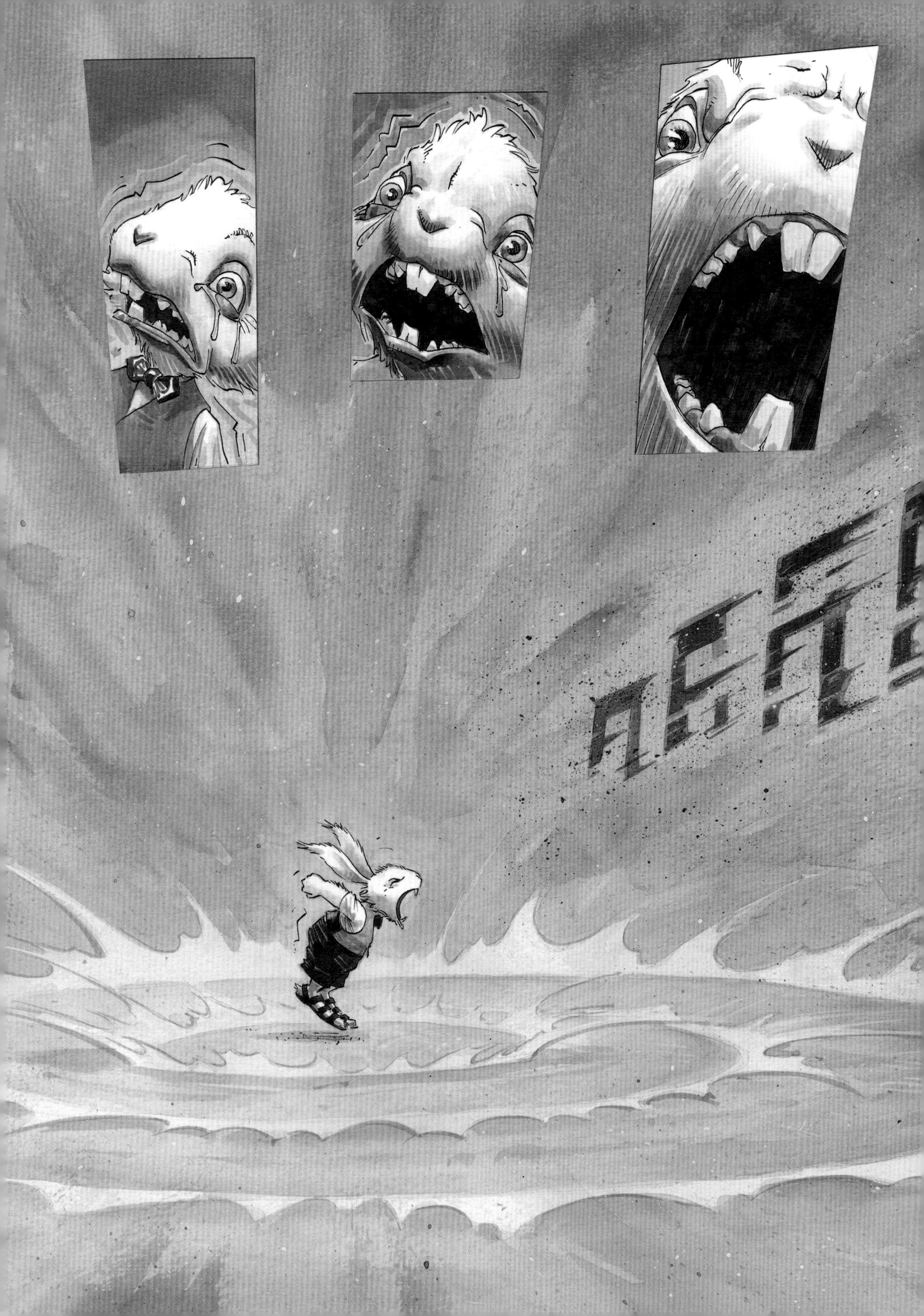
AAA

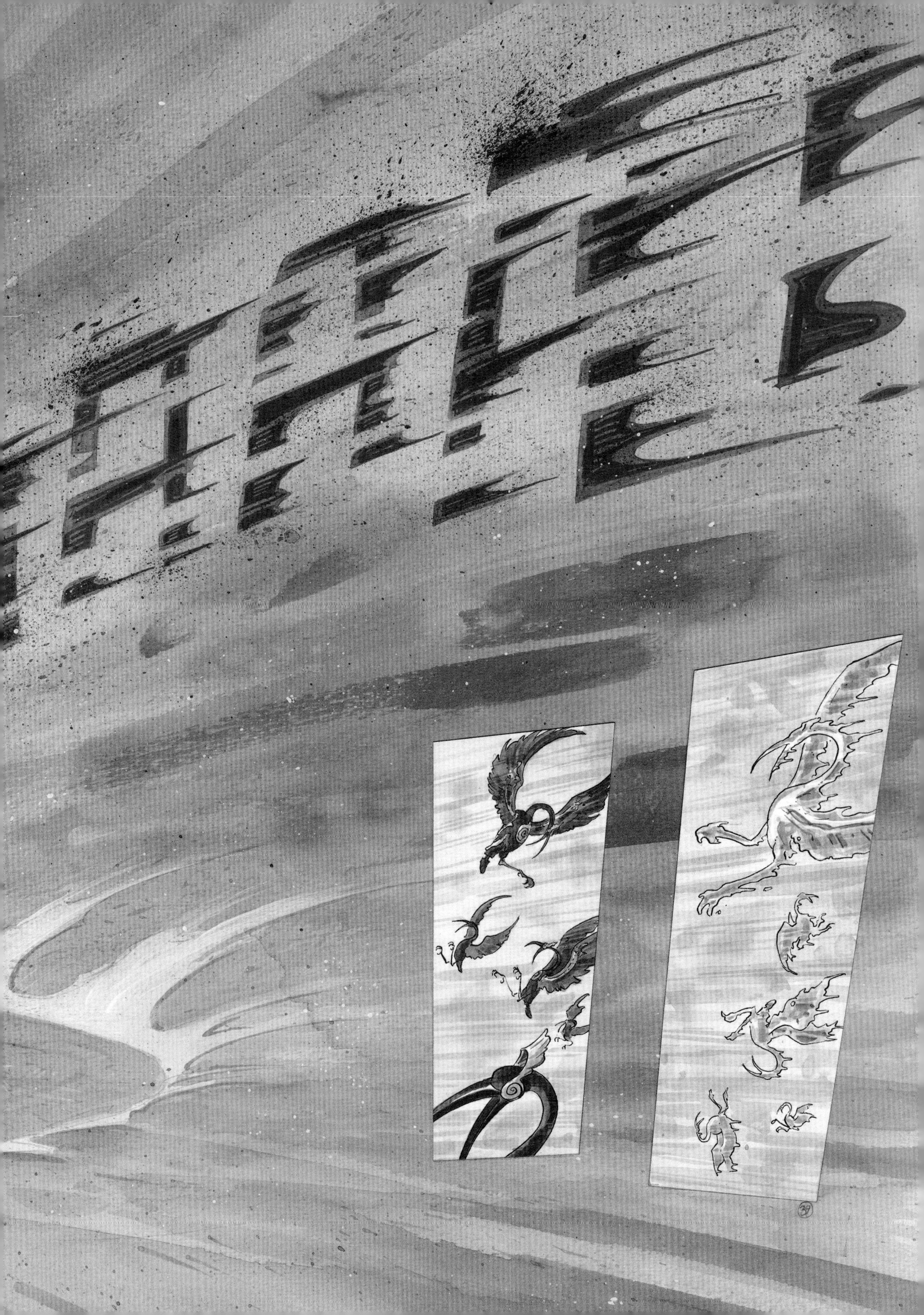

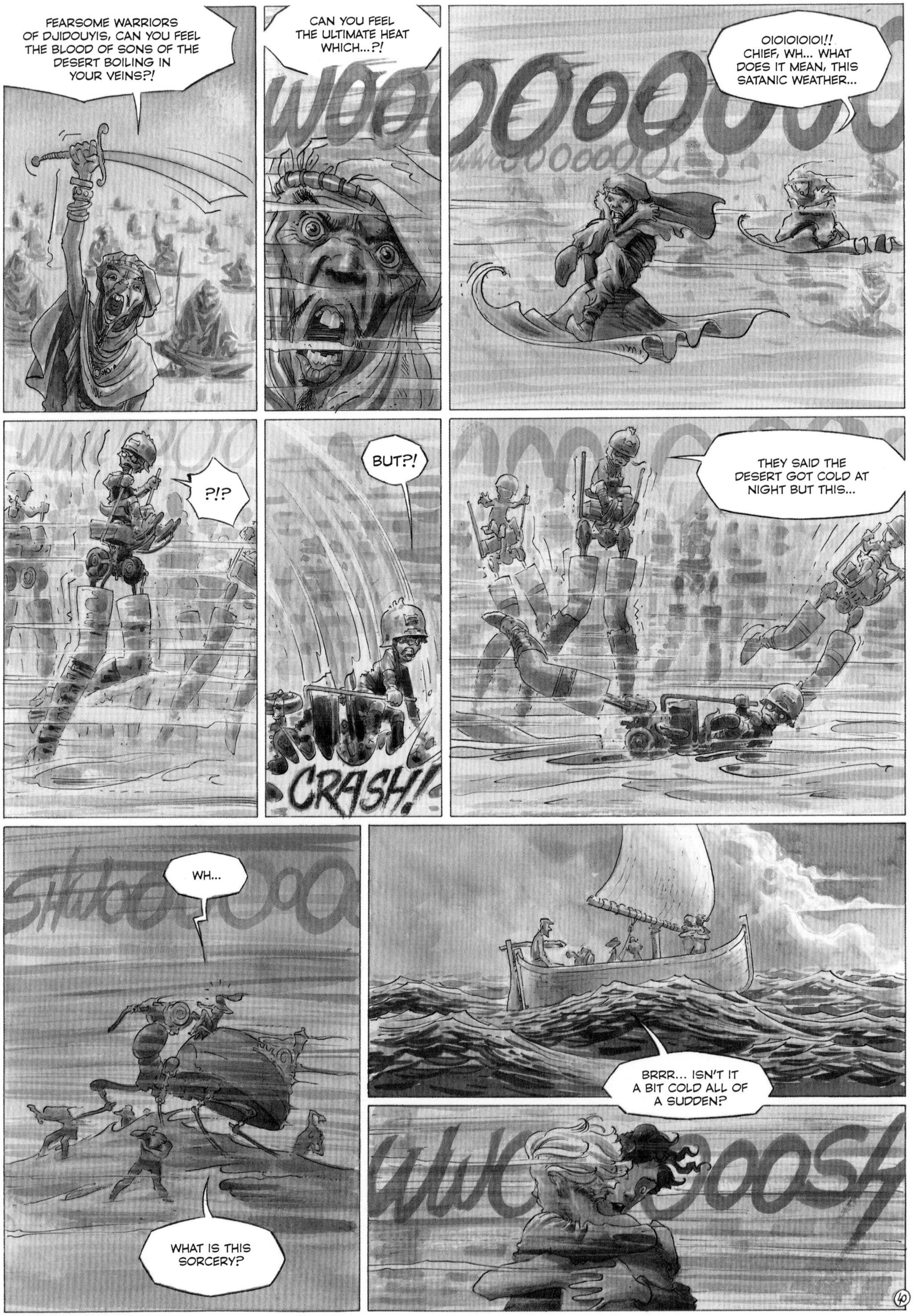
FEARSOME WARRIORS OF DJIDOUYIS, CAN YOU FEEL THE BLOOD OF SONS OF THE DESERT BOILING IN YOUR VEINS?!
CAN YOU FEEL THE ULTIMATE HEAT WHICH...?!
WOOOOOOOOOO
OIOIOIOIOI!! CHIEF, WH... WHAT DOES IT MEAN, THIS SATANIC WEATHER...
?!?
BUT?!
CRASH!
THEY SAID THE DESERT GOT COLD AT NIGHT BUT THIS...
SHWOOOOOO
WH...
WHAT IS THIS SORCERY?
BRRR... ISN'T IT A BIT COLD ALL OF A SUDDEN?
WWOOOOOSH

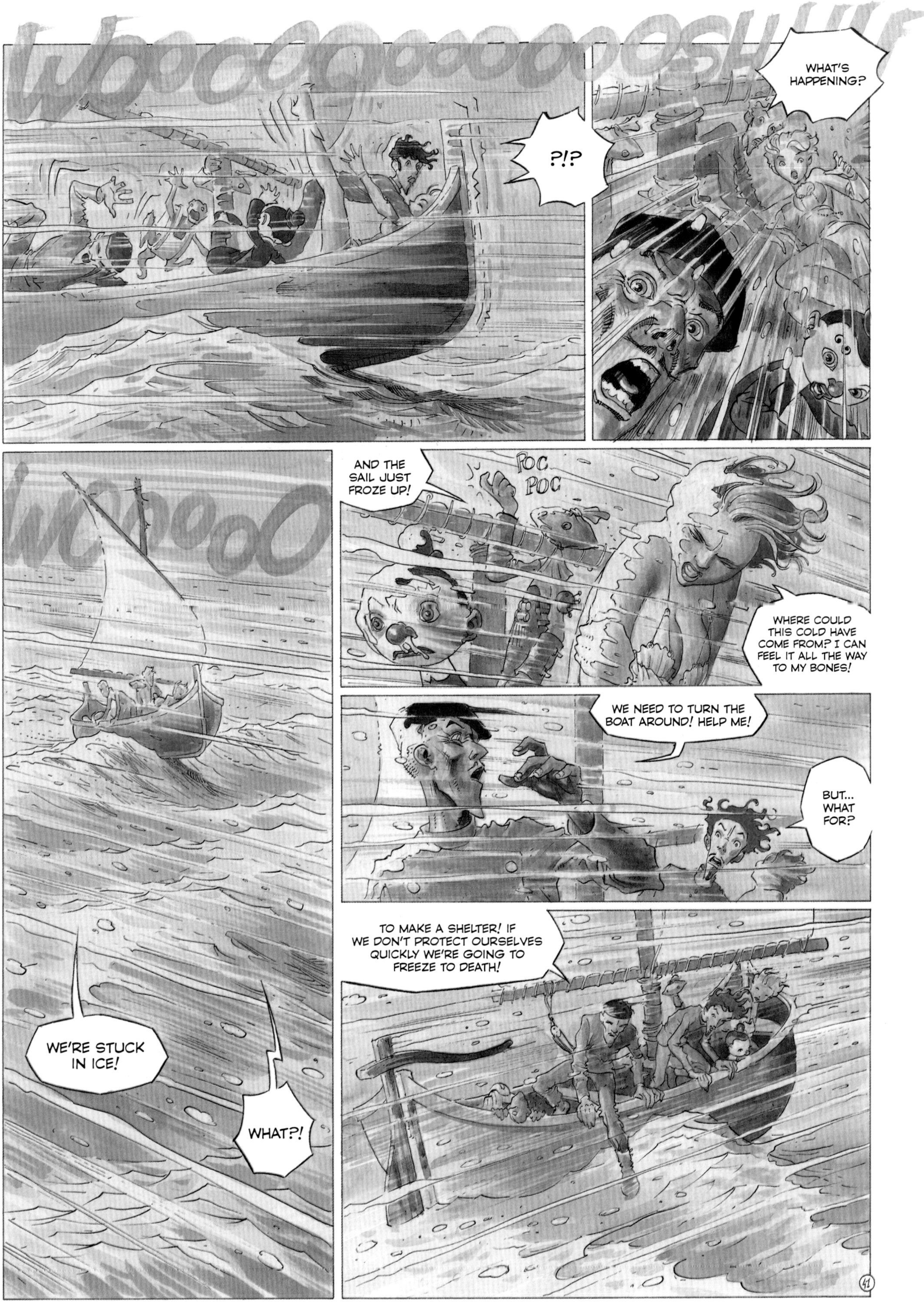
?!?
WHAT'S HAPPENING?
WE'RE STUCK IN ICE!
WHAT?!
AND THE SAIL JUST FROZE UP!
POC POC
WHERE COULD THIS COLD HAVE COME FROM? I CAN FEEL IT ALL THE WAY TO MY BONES!
WE NEED TO TURN THE BOAT AROUND! HELP ME!
BUT... WHAT FOR?
TO MAKE A SHELTER! IF WE DON'T PROTECT OURSELVES QUICKLY WE'RE GOING TO FREEZE TO DEATH!

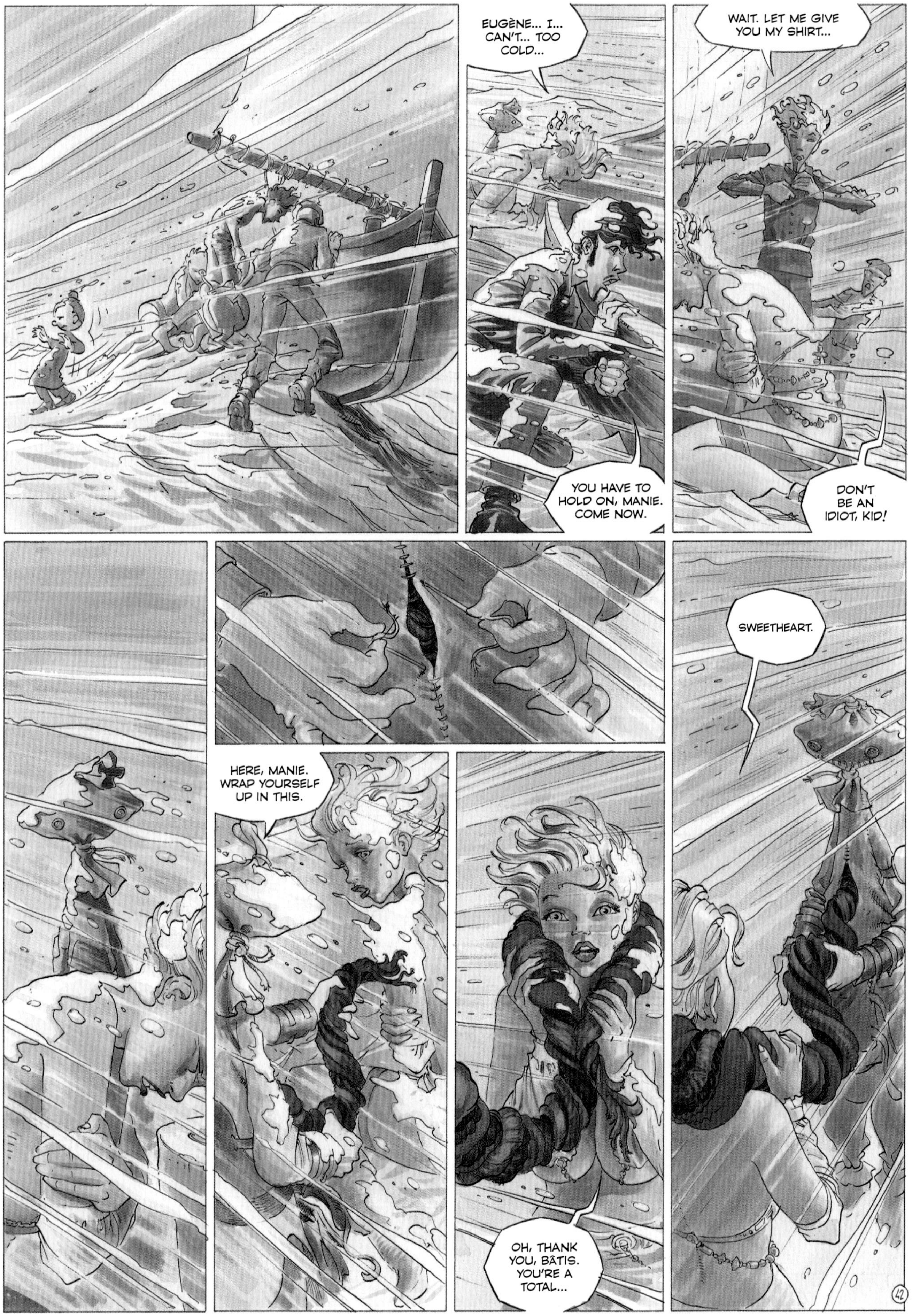
EUGÈNE... I... CAN'T... TOO COLD...
YOU HAVE TO HOLD ON, MANIE. COME NOW.
WAIT. LET ME GIVE YOU MY SHIRT...
DON'T BE AN IDIOT, KID!
HERE, MANIE. WRAP YOURSELF UP IN THIS.
OH, THANK YOU, BÂTIS. YOU'RE A TOTAL...
SWEETHEART.

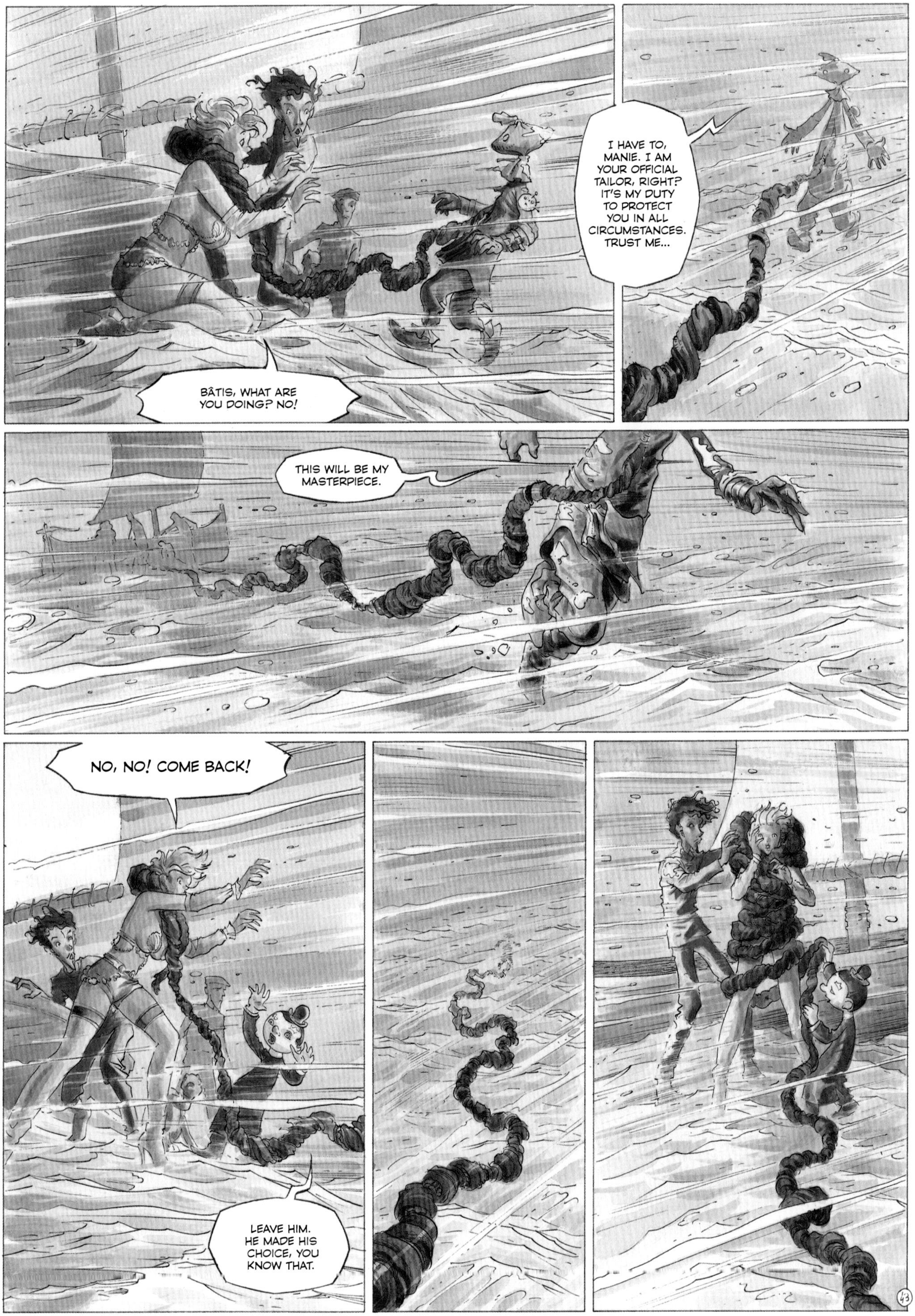
BÂTIS, WHAT ARE YOU DOING? NO!
I HAVE TO, MANIE. I AM YOUR OFFICIAL TAILOR, RIGHT? IT'S MY DUTY TO PROTECT YOU IN ALL CIRCUMSTANCES. TRUST ME...
THIS WILL BE MY MASTERPIECE.
NO, NO! COME BACK!
LEAVE HIM. HE MADE HIS CHOICE, YOU KNOW THAT.

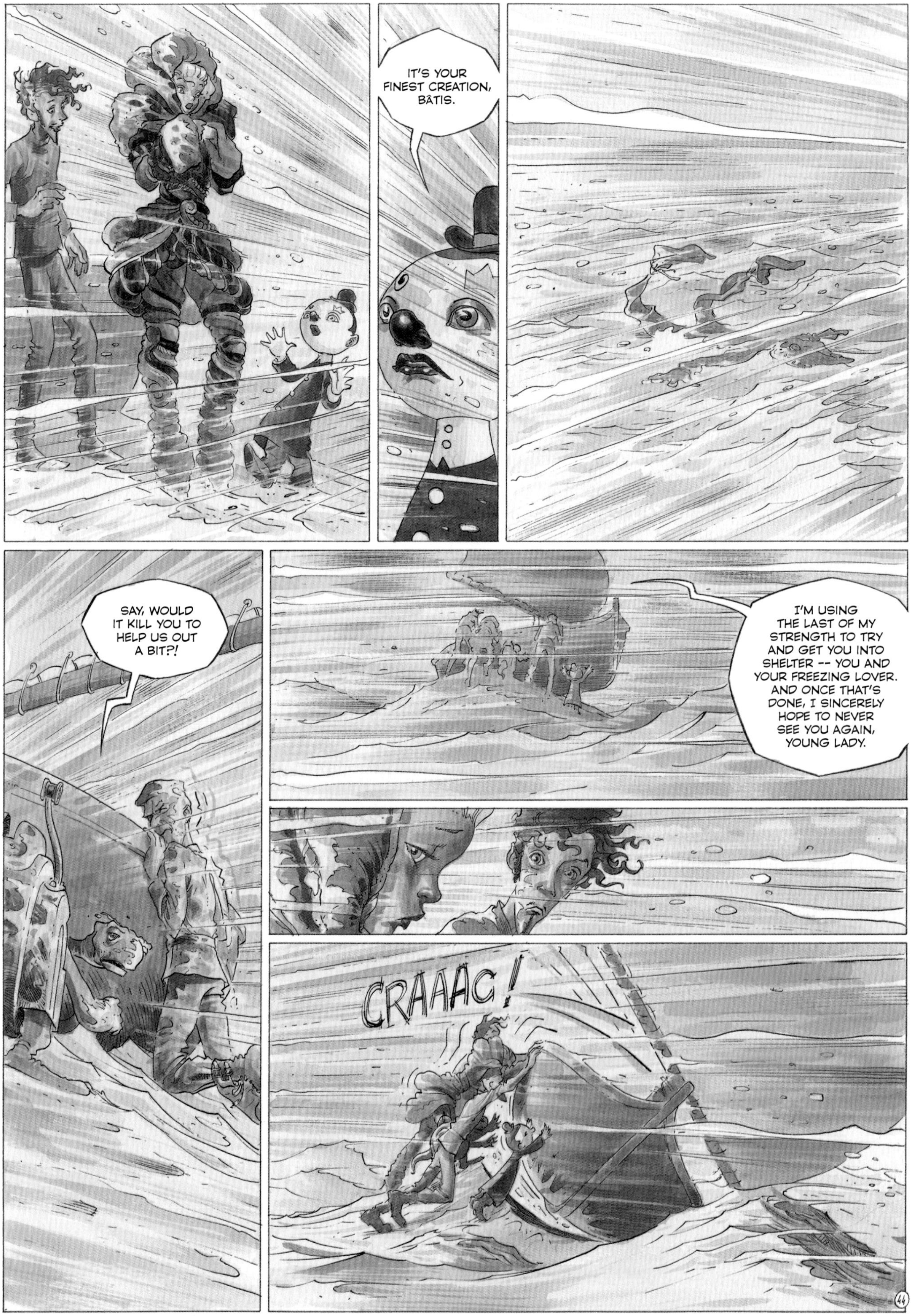
IT'S YOUR FINEST CREATION, BÂTIS.
SAY, WOULD IT KILL YOU TO HELP US OUT A BIT?!
I'M USING THE LAST OF MY STRENGTH TO TRY AND GET YOU INTO SHELTER -- YOU AND YOUR FREEZING LOVER. AND ONCE THAT'S DONE, I SINCERELY HOPE TO NEVER SEE YOU AGAIN, YOUNG LADY.
CRAAAC!

KBORF

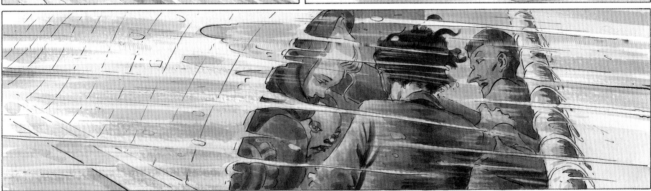

AUGUR, DO YOU RECKON THAT WE...

SOME OF US, YES.

HOW CAN YOU ANSWER BEFORE SHE'S EVEN FINISHED ASKING THE QUESTION?

WHAT DOES IT CHANGE?

IF WE HAVE TO DIE, MY LOVE, IT WILL BE ONE AGAINST THE OTHER. WITH A BIT OF LUCK, WE'LL FREEZE TOGETHER FOR ALL ETERNITY.

WONDERFUL.

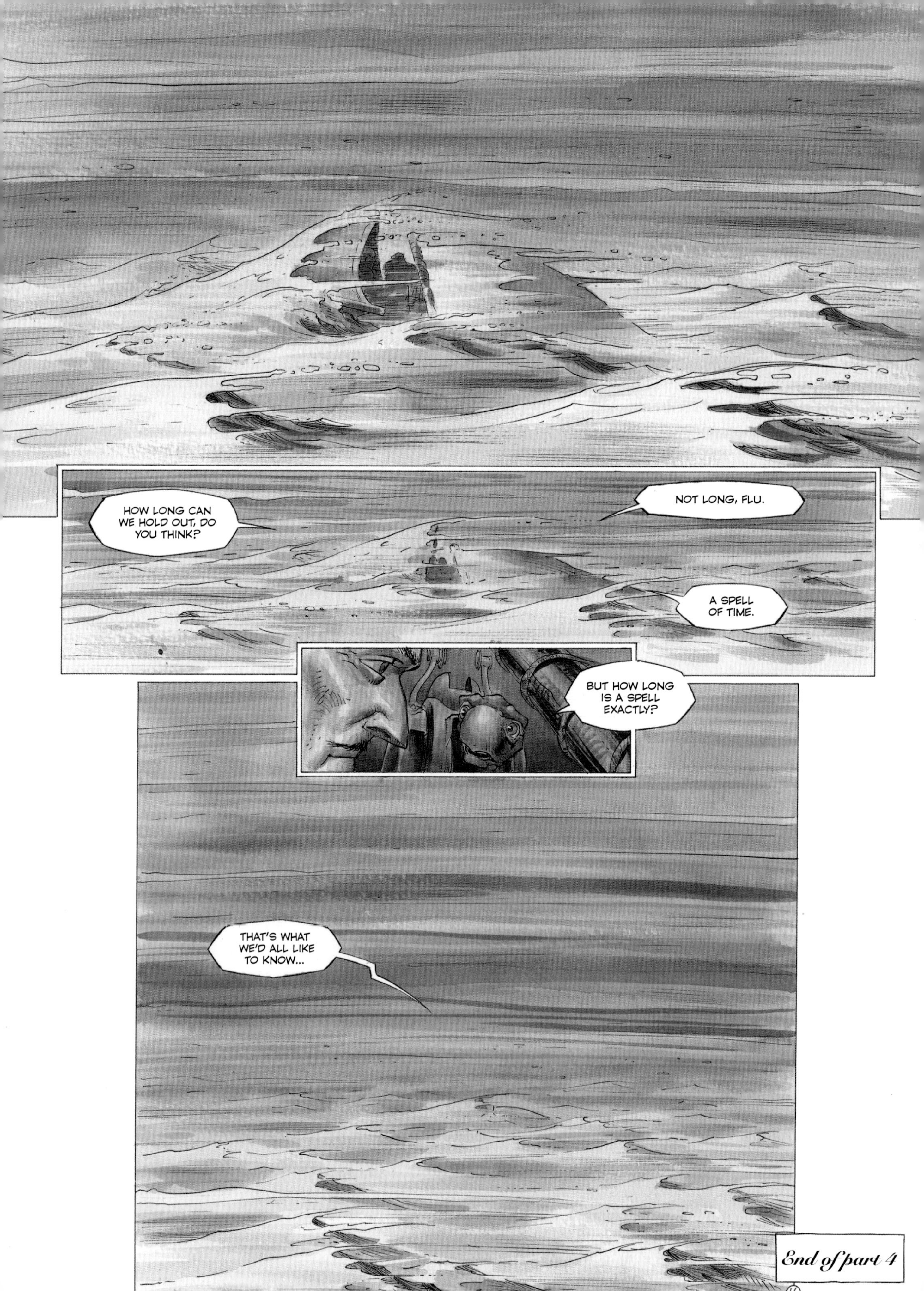
HOW LONG CAN WE HOLD OUT, DO YOU THINK?
NOT LONG, FLU.
A SPELL OF TIME.
BUT HOW LONG IS A SPELL EXACTLY?
THAT'S WHAT WE'D ALL LIKE TO KNOW...
End of part 4

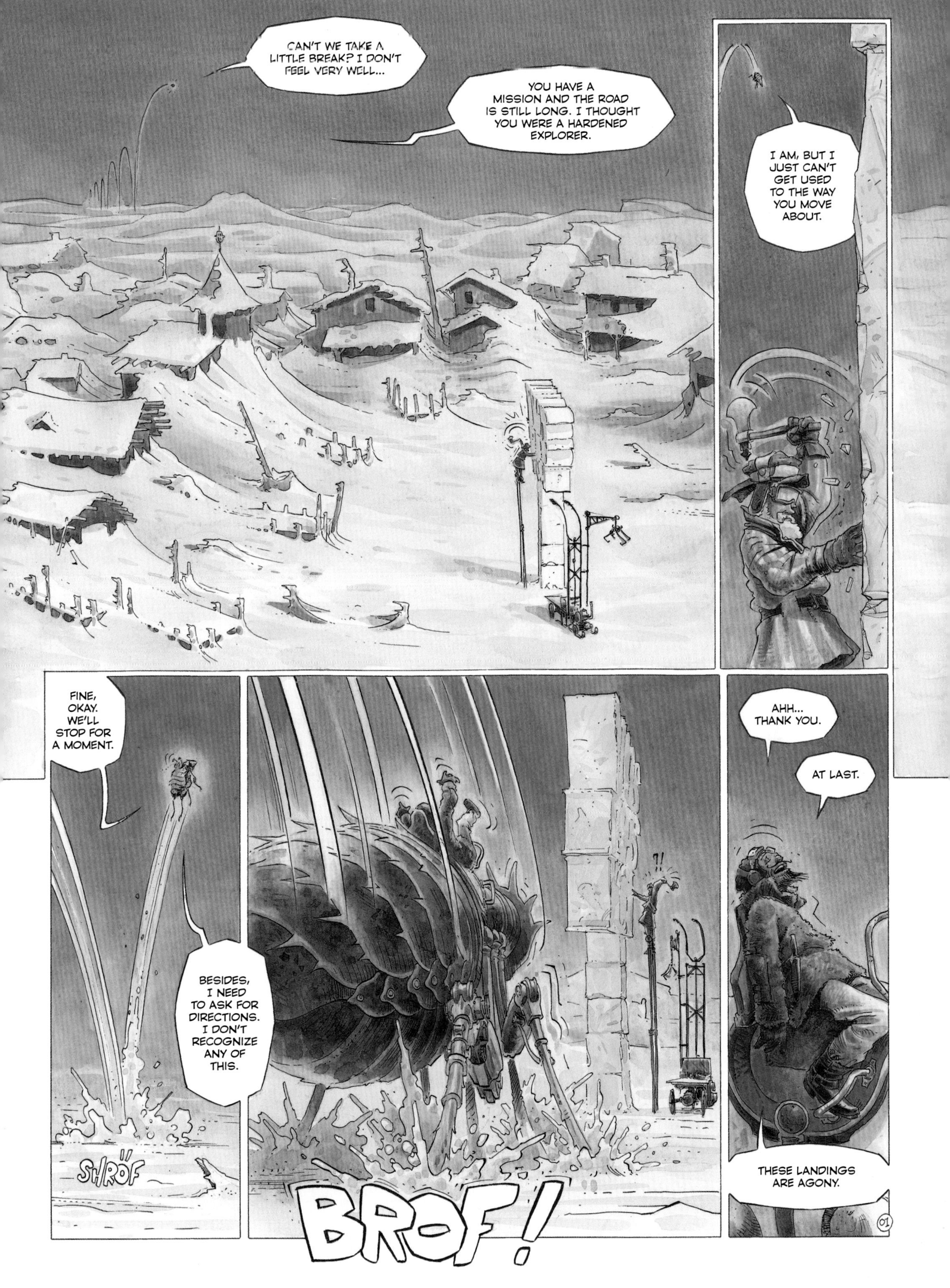
CAN'T WE TAKE A LITTLE BREAK? I DON'T FEEL VERY WELL...
YOU HAVE A MISSION AND THE ROAD IS STILL LONG. I THOUGHT YOU WERE A HARDENED EXPLORER.
I AM, BUT I JUST CAN'T GET USED TO THE WAY YOU MOVE ABOUT.
FINE, OKAY. WE'LL STOP FOR A MOMENT.
BESIDES, I NEED TO ASK FOR DIRECTIONS. I DON'T RECOGNIZE ANY OF THIS.
SHRÖF
BROF!
?!
AHH... THANK YOU.
AT LAST.
THESE LANDINGS ARE AGONY.

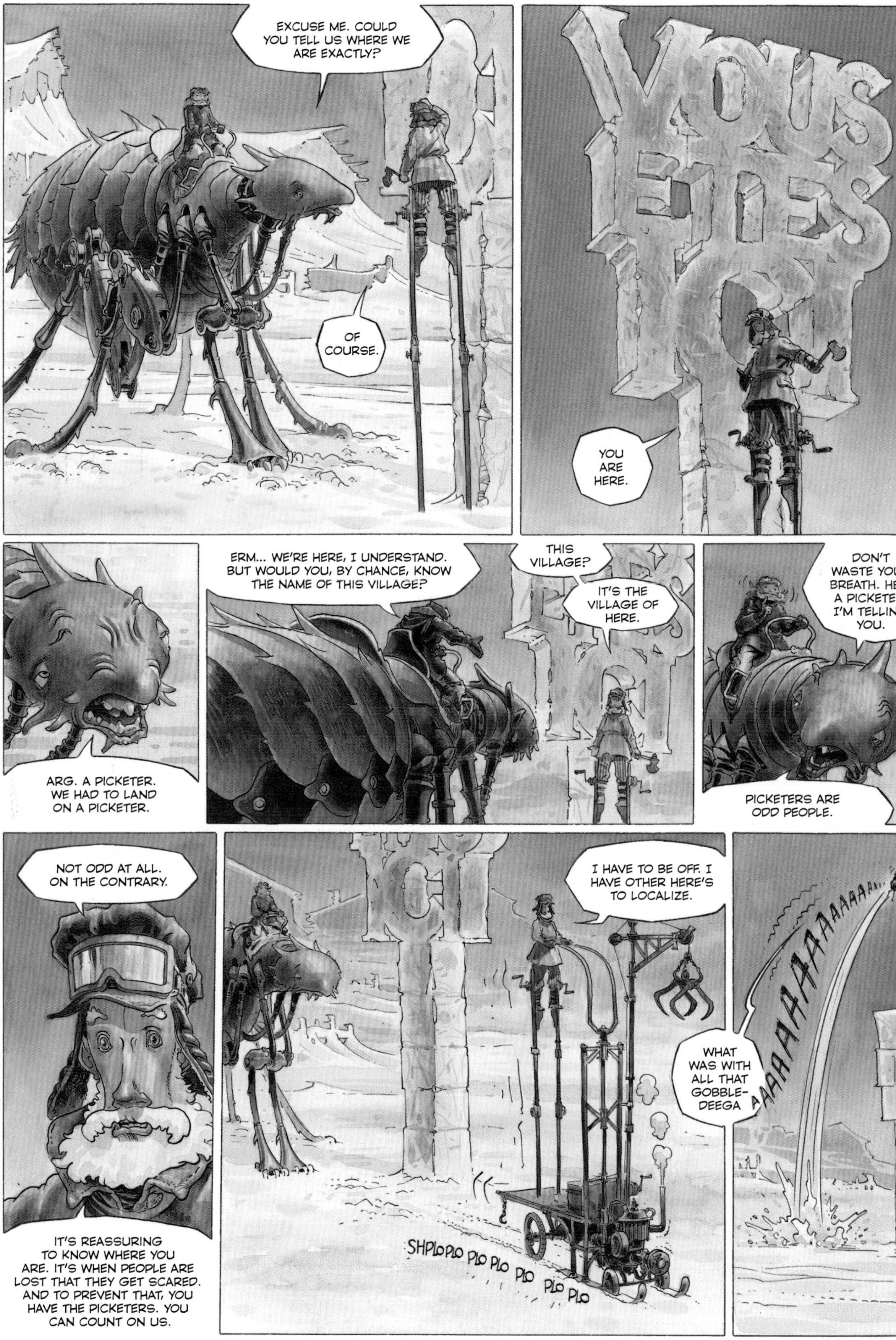
EXCUSE ME. COULD YOU TELL US WHERE WE ARE EXACTLY?
OF COURSE.
YOU ARE HERE.
ARG. A PICKETER. WE HAD TO LAND ON A PICKETER.
ERM... WE'RE HERE, I UNDERSTAND. BUT WOULD YOU, BY CHANCE, KNOW THE NAME OF THIS VILLAGE?
THIS VILLAGE?
IT'S THE VILLAGE OF HERE.
DON'T WASTE YOUR BREATH. HE'S A PICKETER, I'M TELLING YOU.
PICKETERS ARE ODD PEOPLE.
NOT ODD AT ALL. ON THE CONTRARY.
IT'S REASSURING TO KNOW WHERE YOU ARE. IT'S WHEN PEOPLE ARE LOST THAT THEY GET SCARED. AND TO PREVENT THAT, YOU HAVE THE PICKETERS. YOU CAN COUNT ON US.
I HAVE TO BE OFF. I HAVE OTHER HERE'S TO LOCALIZE.
SHPLOPLO PLO PLO PLO PLO PLO PLO
AAAAAAAAAAAAAAAAAAAAAAAAAAAAAAA...
WHAT WAS WITH ALL THAT GOBBLE-DEEGA
02

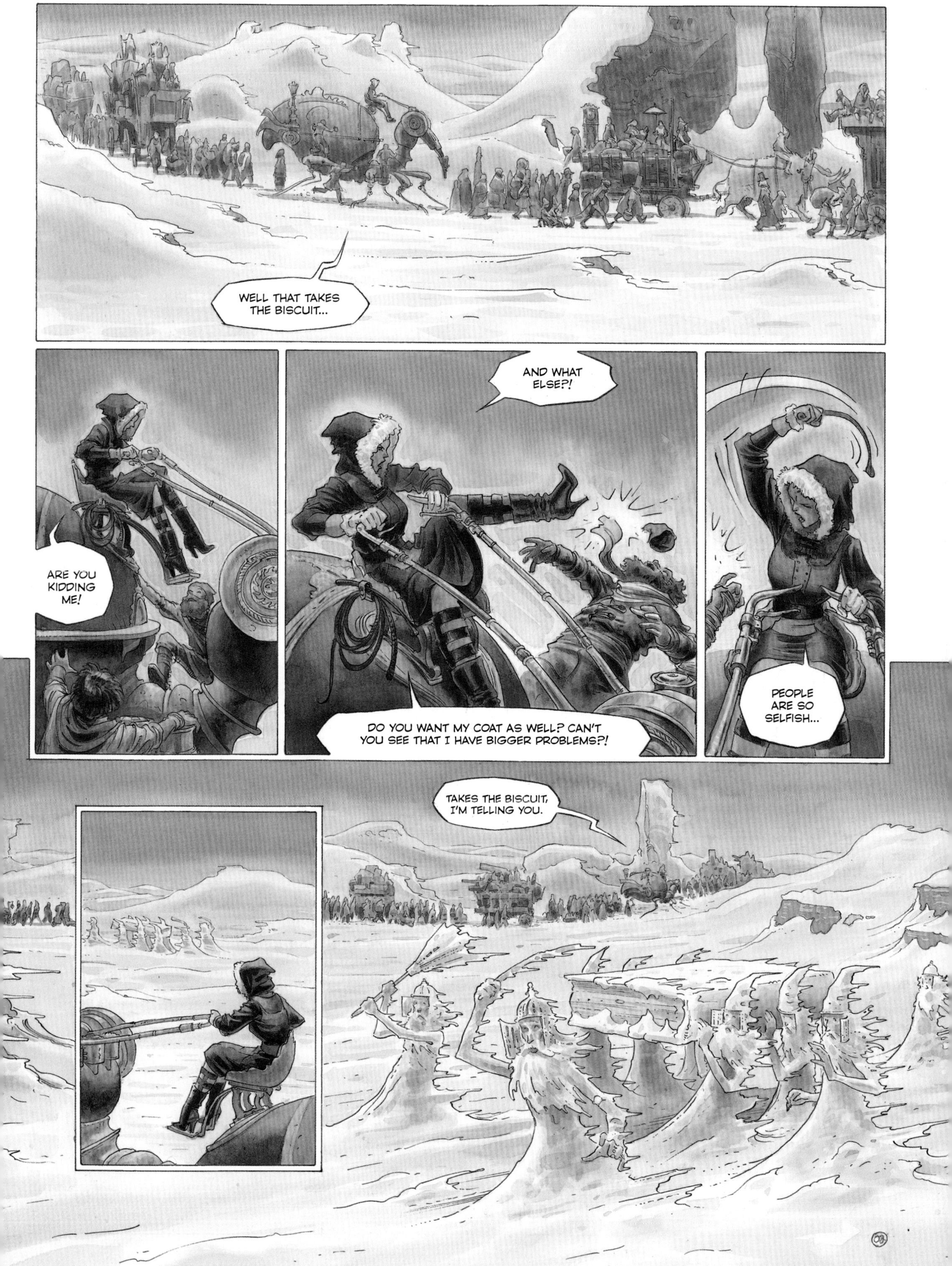
WELL THAT TAKES THE BISCUIT...
ARE YOU KIDDING ME!
AND WHAT ELSE?!
DO YOU WANT MY COAT AS WELL? CAN'T YOU SEE THAT I HAVE BIGGER PROBLEMS?!
PEOPLE ARE SO SELFISH...
TAKES THE BISCUIT, I'M TELLING YOU.

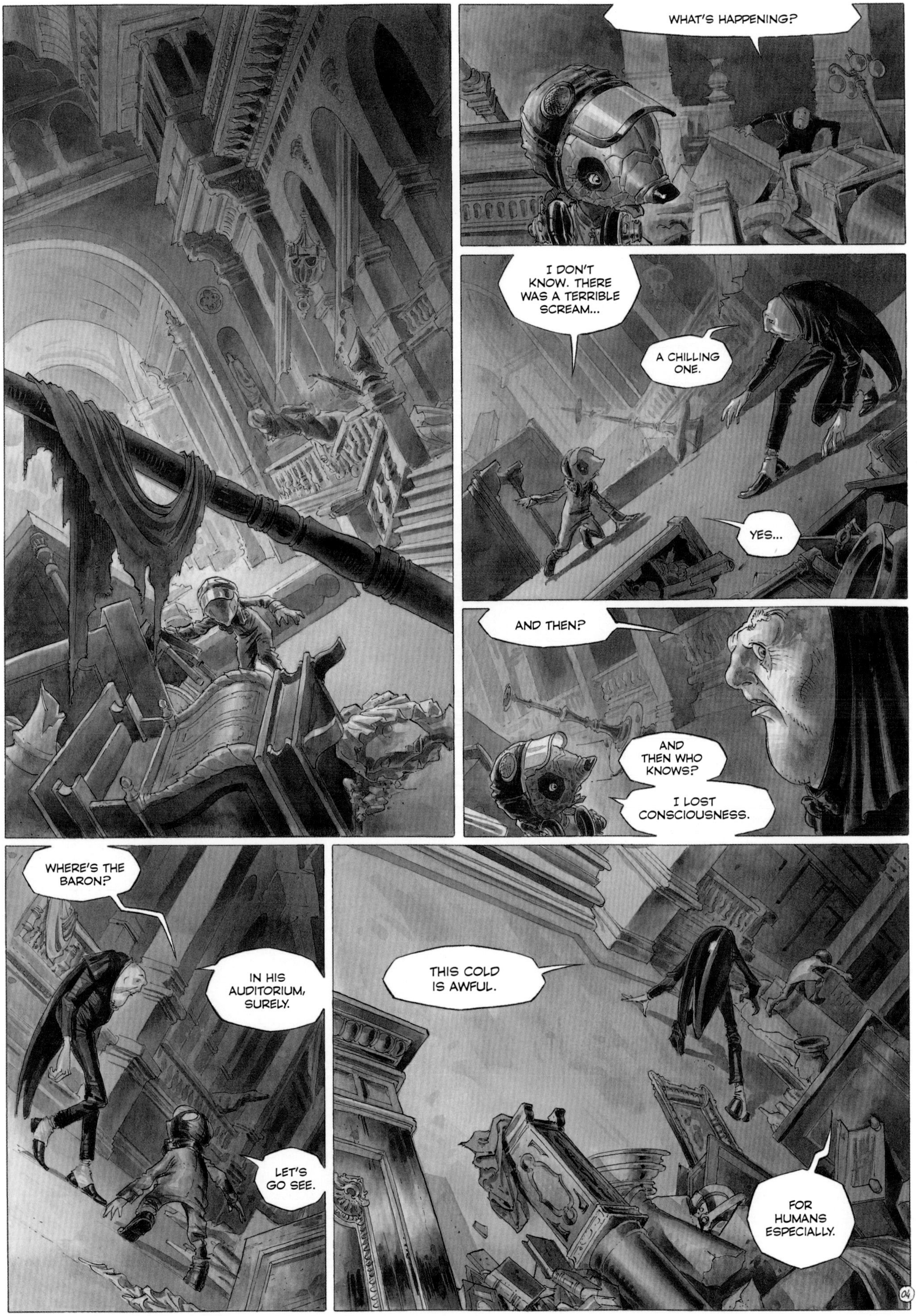
WHAT'S HAPPENING?
I DON'T KNOW. THERE WAS A TERRIBLE SCREAM...
A CHILLING ONE.
YES...
AND THEN?
AND THEN WHO KNOWS?
I LOST CONSCIOUSNESS.
WHERE'S THE BARON?
IN HIS AUDITORIUM, SURELY.
LET'S GO SEE.
THIS COLD IS AWFUL.
FOR HUMANS ESPECIALLY.
04

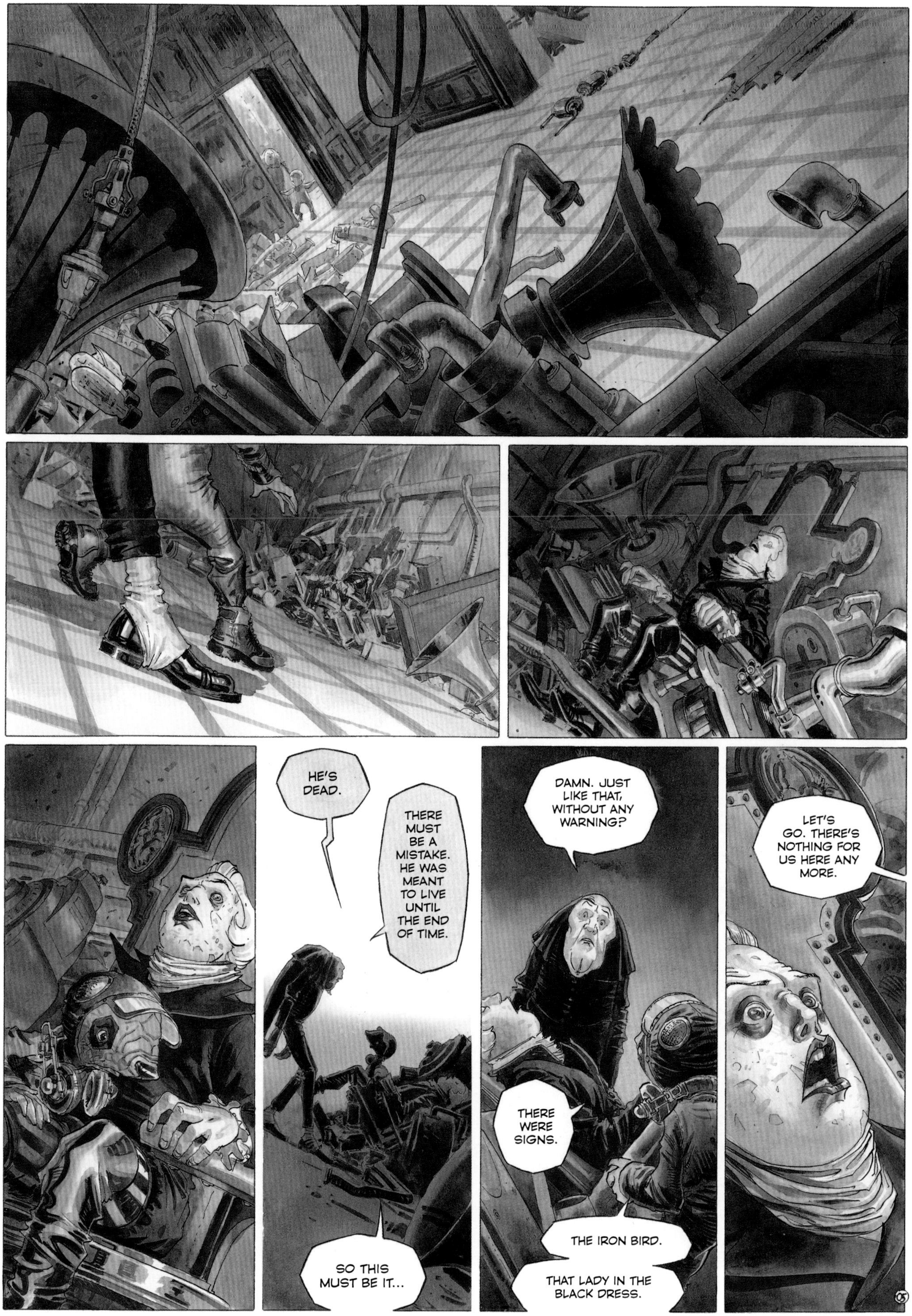
HE'S DEAD.
THERE MUST BE A MISTAKE. HE WAS MEANT TO LIVE UNTIL THE END OF TIME.
SO THIS MUST BE IT...
DAMN. JUST LIKE THAT, WITHOUT ANY WARNING?
THERE WERE SIGNS.
THE IRON BIRD.
THAT LADY IN THE BLACK DRESS.
LET'S GO. THERE'S NOTHING FOR US HERE ANY MORE.

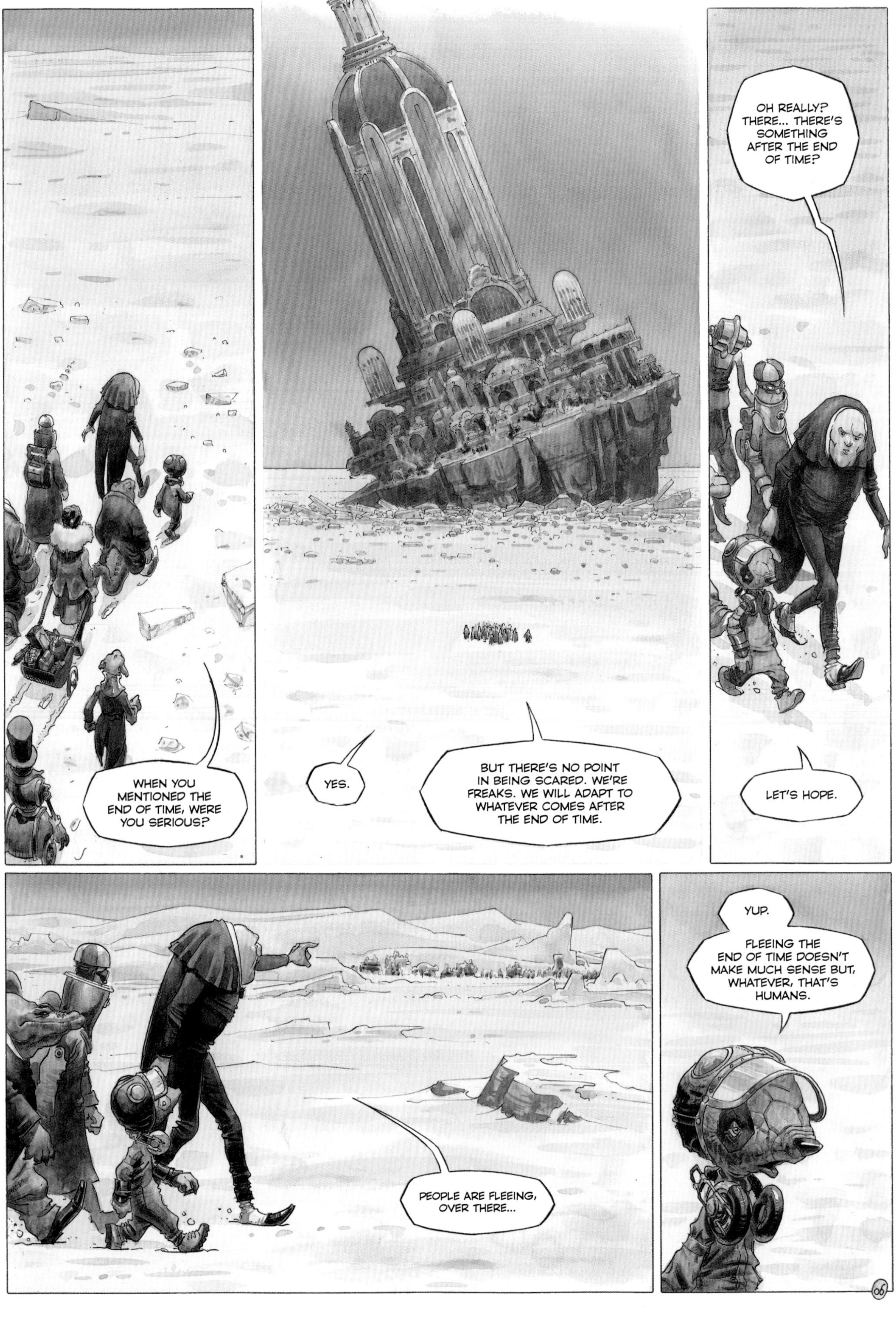
WHEN YOU MENTIONED THE END OF TIME, WERE YOU SERIOUS?
YES.
BUT THERE'S NO POINT IN BEING SCARED. WE'RE FREAKS. WE WILL ADAPT TO WHATEVER COMES AFTER THE END OF TIME.
OH REALLY? THERE... THERE'S SOMETHING AFTER THE END OF TIME?
LET'S HOPE.
PEOPLE ARE FLEEING, OVER THERE...
YUP.
FLEEING THE END OF TIME DOESN'T MAKE MUCH SENSE BUT, WHATEVER, THAT'S HUMANS.

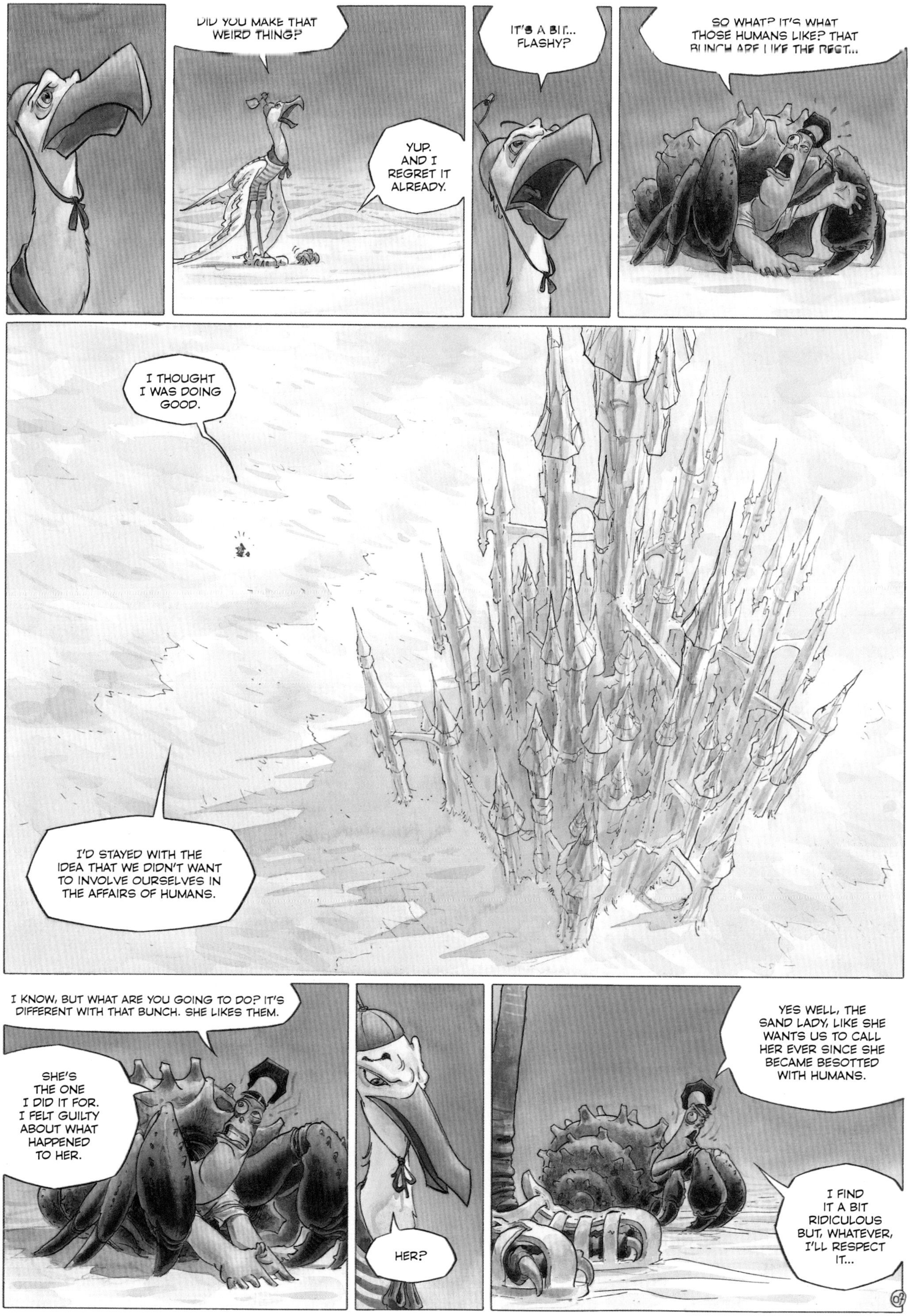
DID YOU MAKE THAT WEIRD THING?
YUP. AND I REGRET IT ALREADY.
IT'S A BIT... FLASHY?
SO WHAT? IT'S WHAT THOSE HUMANS LIKE? THAT BUNCH ARE LIKE THE REST...
I THOUGHT I WAS DOING GOOD.
I'D STAYED WITH THE IDEA THAT WE DIDN'T WANT TO INVOLVE OURSELVES IN THE AFFAIRS OF HUMANS.
I KNOW, BUT WHAT ARE YOU GOING TO DO? IT'S DIFFERENT WITH THAT BUNCH. SHE LIKES THEM.
SHE'S THE ONE I DID IT FOR. I FELT GUILTY ABOUT WHAT HAPPENED TO HER.
HER?
YES WELL, THE SAND LADY, LIKE SHE WANTS US TO CALL HER EVER SINCE SHE BECAME BESOTTED WITH HUMANS.
I FIND IT A BIT RIDICULOUS BUT, WHATEVER, I'LL RESPECT IT...

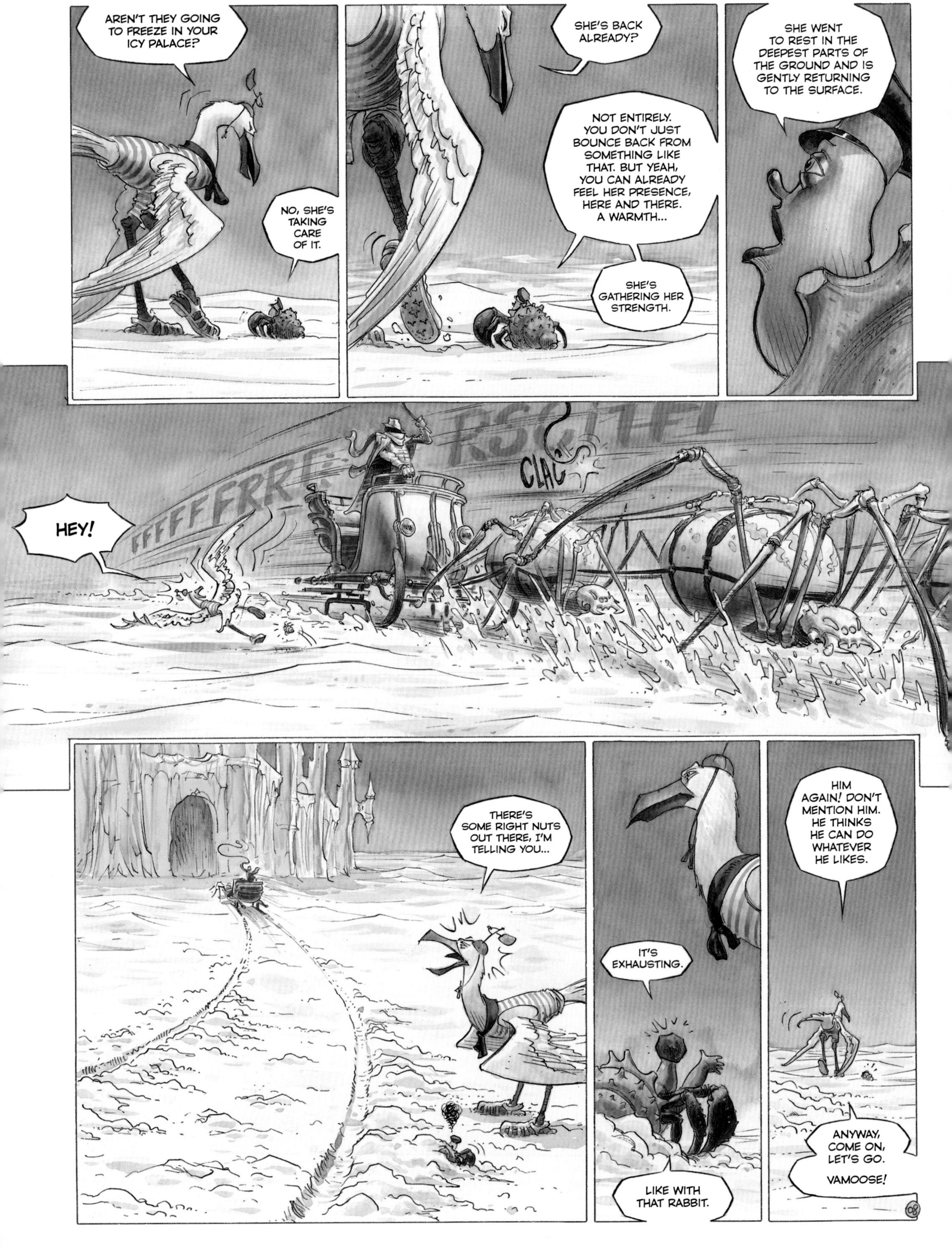

AREN'T THEY GOING TO FREEZE IN YOUR ICY PALACE?
NO, SHE'S TAKING CARE OF IT.
SHE'S BACK ALREADY?
NOT ENTIRELY. YOU DON'T JUST BOUNCE BACK FROM SOMETHING LIKE THAT. BUT YEAH, YOU CAN ALREADY FEEL HER PRESENCE, HERE AND THERE. A WARMTH...
SHE'S GATHERING HER STRENGTH.
SHE WENT TO REST IN THE DEEPEST PARTS OF THE GROUND AND IS GENTLY RETURNING TO THE SURFACE.
FFFFFFRRRC
RSCHHH
CLAC
HEY!
THERE'S SOME RIGHT NUTS OUT THERE, I'M TELLING YOU...
IT'S EXHAUSTING.
LIKE WITH THAT RABBIT.
HIM AGAIN! DON'T MENTION HIM. HE THINKS HE CAN DO WHATEVER HE LIKES.
ANYWAY, COME ON, LET'S GO.
VAMOOSE!

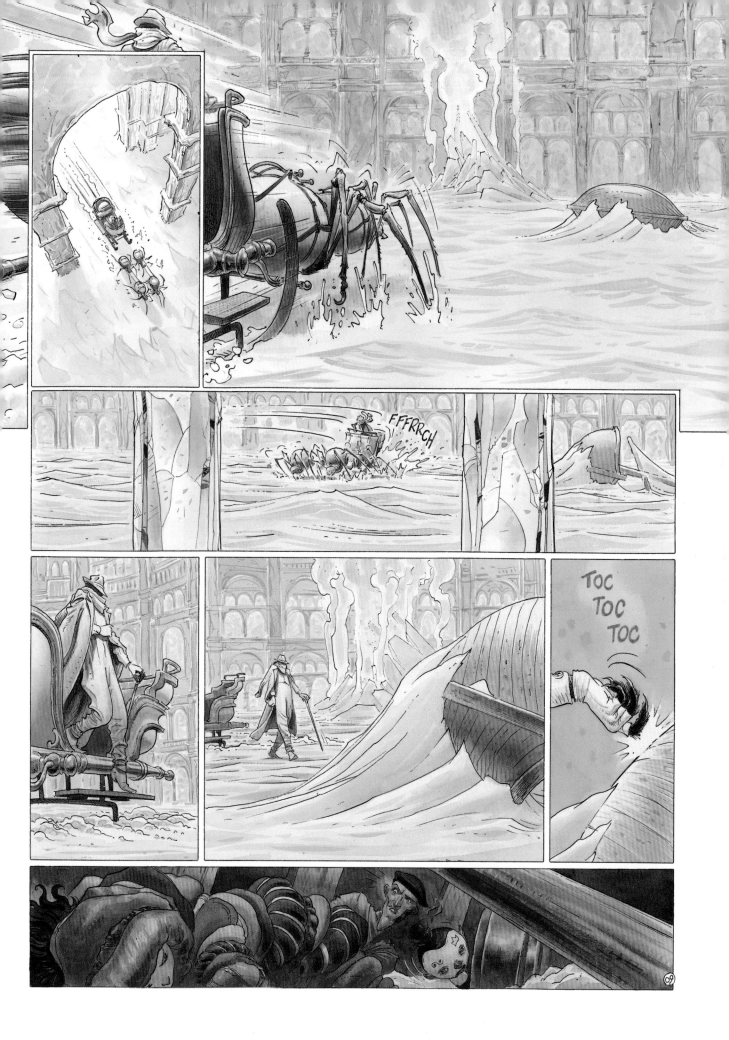

FFFRRCH

TOC
TOC
TOC

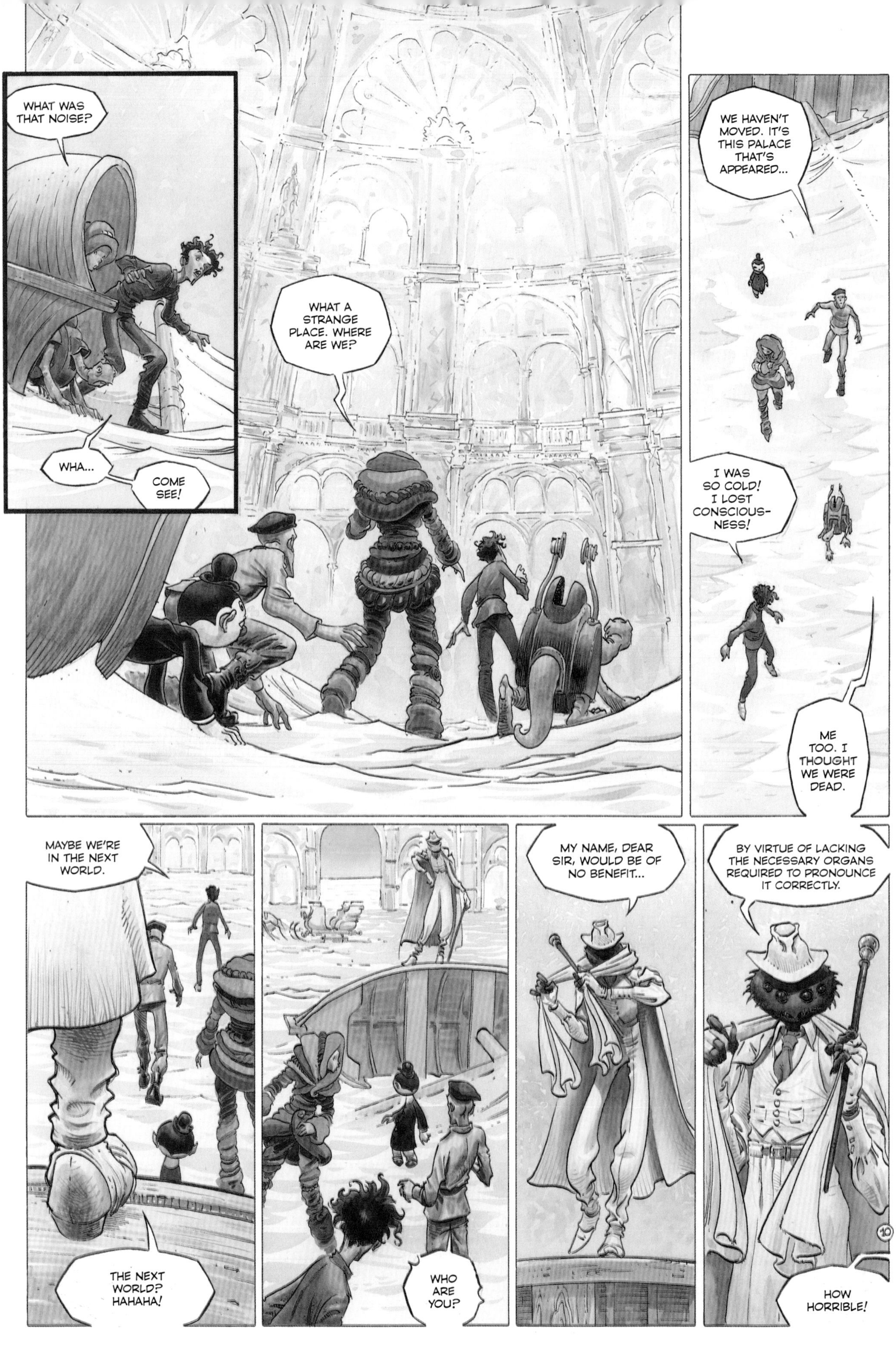
WHAT WAS THAT NOISE?
WHA...
COME SEE!
WHAT A STRANGE PLACE. WHERE ARE WE?
WE HAVEN'T MOVED. IT'S THIS PALACE THAT'S APPEARED...
I WAS SO COLD! I LOST CONSCIOUS-NESS!
ME TOO. I THOUGHT WE WERE DEAD.
MAYBE WE'RE IN THE NEXT WORLD.
THE NEXT WORLD? HAHAHA!
WHO ARE YOU?
MY NAME, DEAR SIR, WOULD BE OF NO BENEFIT...
BY VIRTUE OF LACKING THE NECESSARY ORGANS REQUIRED TO PRONOUNCE IT CORRECTLY.
HOW HORRIBLE!
10

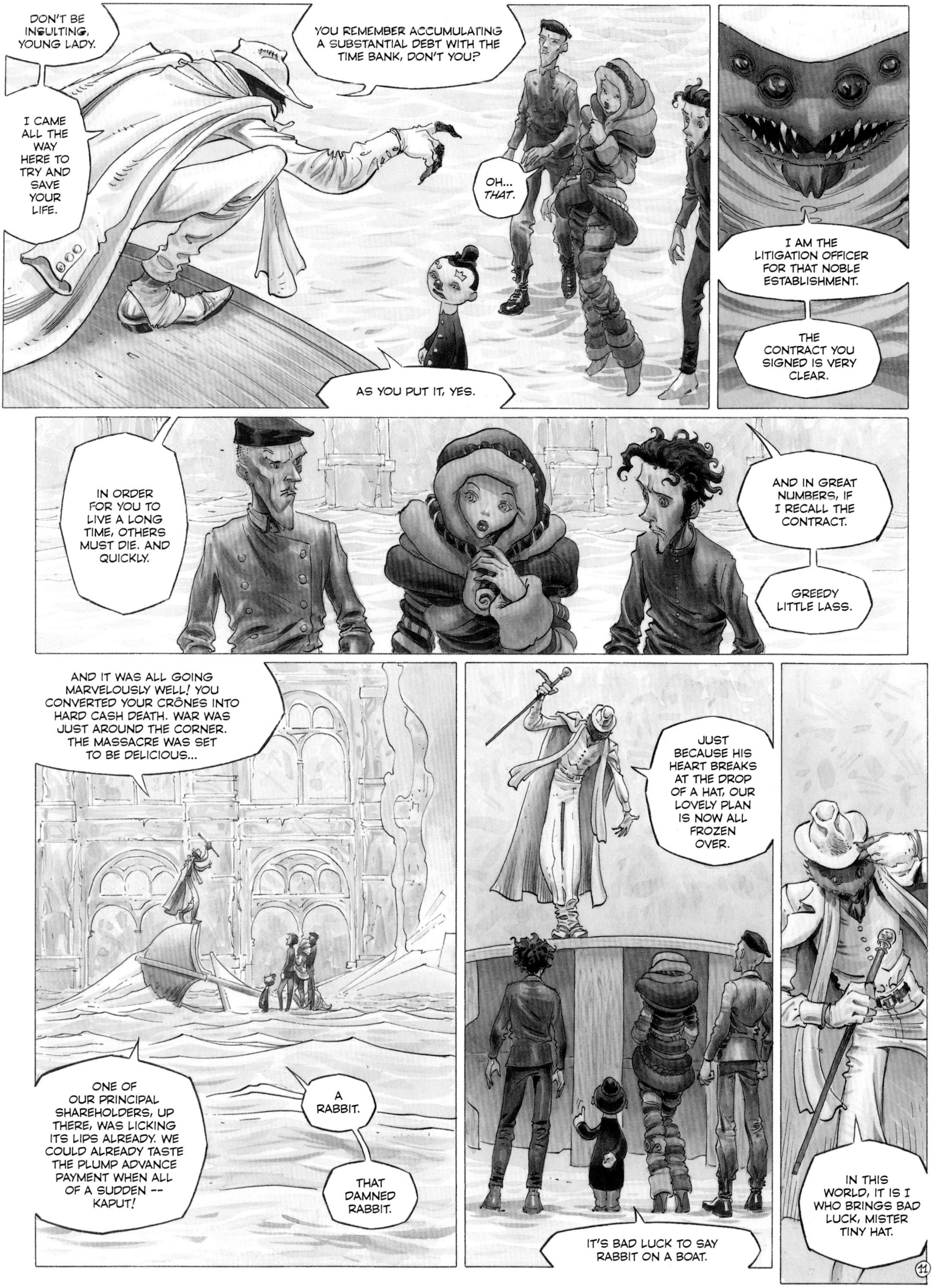

DON'T BE INSULTING, YOUNG LADY.
I CAME ALL THE WAY HERE TO TRY AND SAVE YOUR LIFE.
YOU REMEMBER ACCUMULATING A SUBSTANTIAL DEBT WITH THE TIME BANK, DON'T YOU?
OH... *THAT*.
AS YOU PUT IT, YES.
I AM THE LITIGATION OFFICER FOR THAT NOBLE ESTABLISHMENT.
THE CONTRACT YOU SIGNED IS VERY CLEAR.
IN ORDER FOR YOU TO LIVE A LONG TIME, OTHERS MUST DIE. AND QUICKLY.
AND IN GREAT NUMBERS, IF I RECALL THE CONTRACT.
GREEDY LITTLE LASS.
AND IT WAS ALL GOING MARVELOUSLY WELL! YOU CONVERTED YOUR CRÔNES INTO HARD CASH DEATH. WAR WAS JUST AROUND THE CORNER. THE MASSACRE WAS SET TO BE DELICIOUS...
ONE OF OUR PRINCIPAL SHAREHOLDERS, UP THERE, WAS LICKING ITS LIPS ALREADY. WE COULD ALREADY TASTE THE PLUMP ADVANCE PAYMENT WHEN ALL OF A SUDDEN -- KAPUT!
A RABBIT.
THAT DAMNED RABBIT.
JUST BECAUSE HIS HEART BREAKS AT THE DROP OF A HAT, OUR LOVELY PLAN IS NOW ALL FROZEN OVER.
IT'S BAD LUCK TO SAY RABBIT ON A BOAT.
IN THIS WORLD, IT IS I WHO BRINGS BAD LUCK, MISTER TINY HAT.

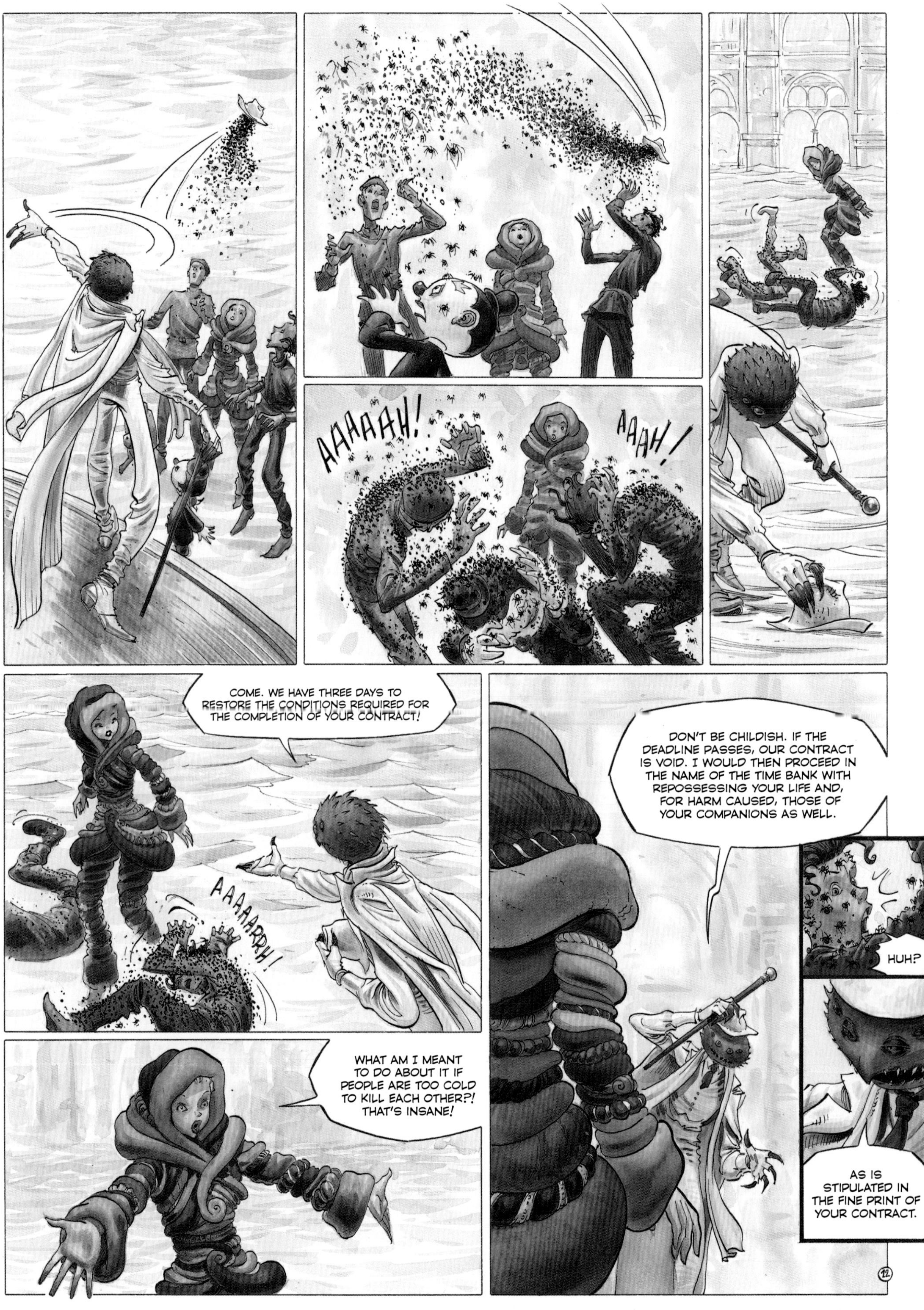
AAAAAH!
AAAH!
COME. WE HAVE THREE DAYS TO RESTORE THE CONDITIONS REQUIRED FOR THE COMPLETION OF YOUR CONTRACT!
AAAAAARRH!
WHAT AM I MEANT TO DO ABOUT IT IF PEOPLE ARE TOO COLD TO KILL EACH OTHER?! THAT'S INSANE!
DON'T BE CHILDISH. IF THE DEADLINE PASSES, OUR CONTRACT IS VOID. I WOULD THEN PROCEED IN THE NAME OF THE TIME BANK WITH REPOSSESSING YOUR LIFE AND, FOR HARM CAUSED, THOSE OF YOUR COMPANIONS AS WELL.
HUH?
AS IS STIPULATED IN THE FINE PRINT OF YOUR CONTRACT.

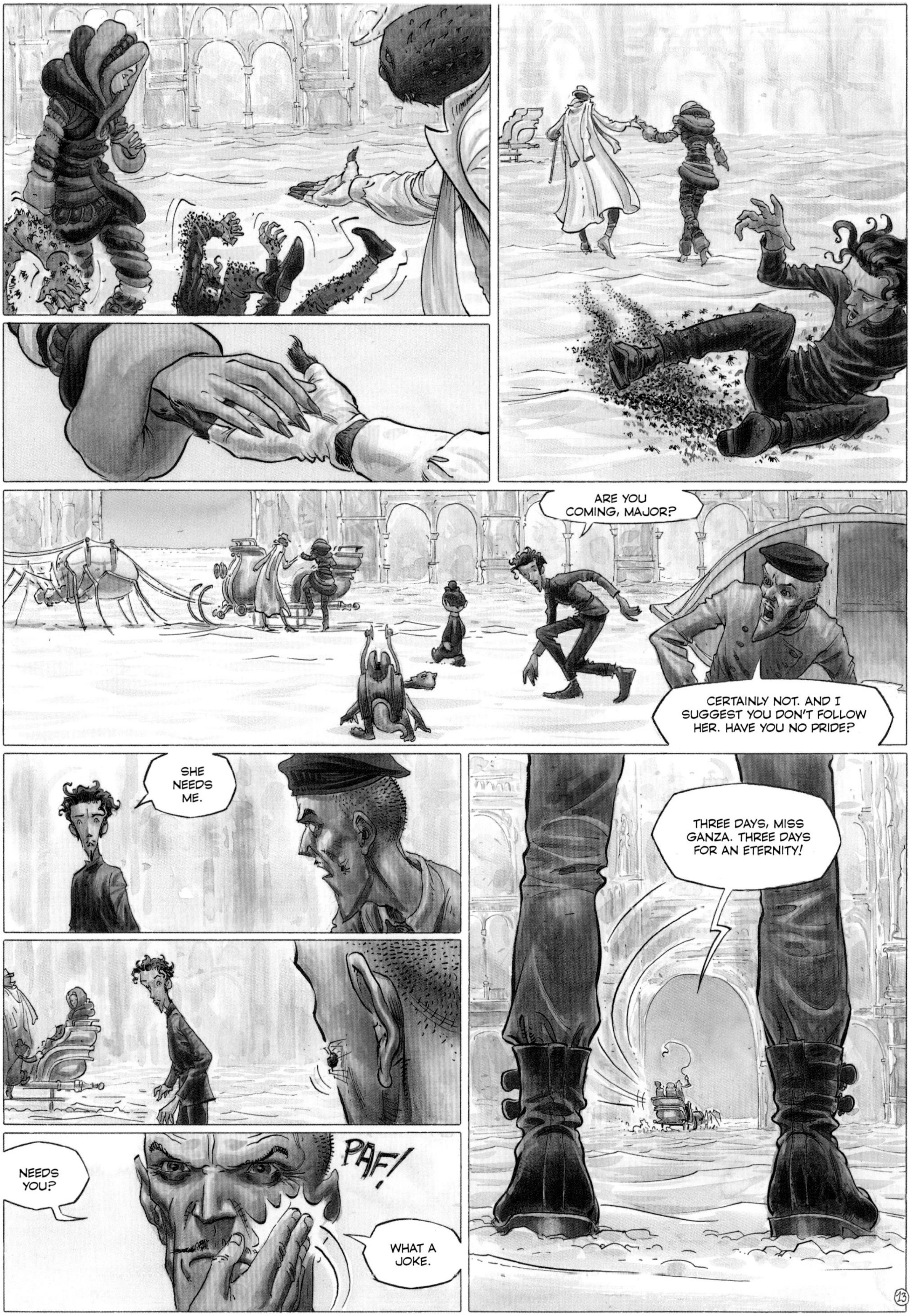
ARE YOU COMING, MAJOR?
CERTAINLY NOT. AND I SUGGEST YOU DON'T FOLLOW HER. HAVE YOU NO PRIDE?
SHE NEEDS ME.
NEEDS YOU?
PAF!
WHAT A JOKE.
THREE DAYS, MISS GANZA. THREE DAYS FOR AN ETERNITY!

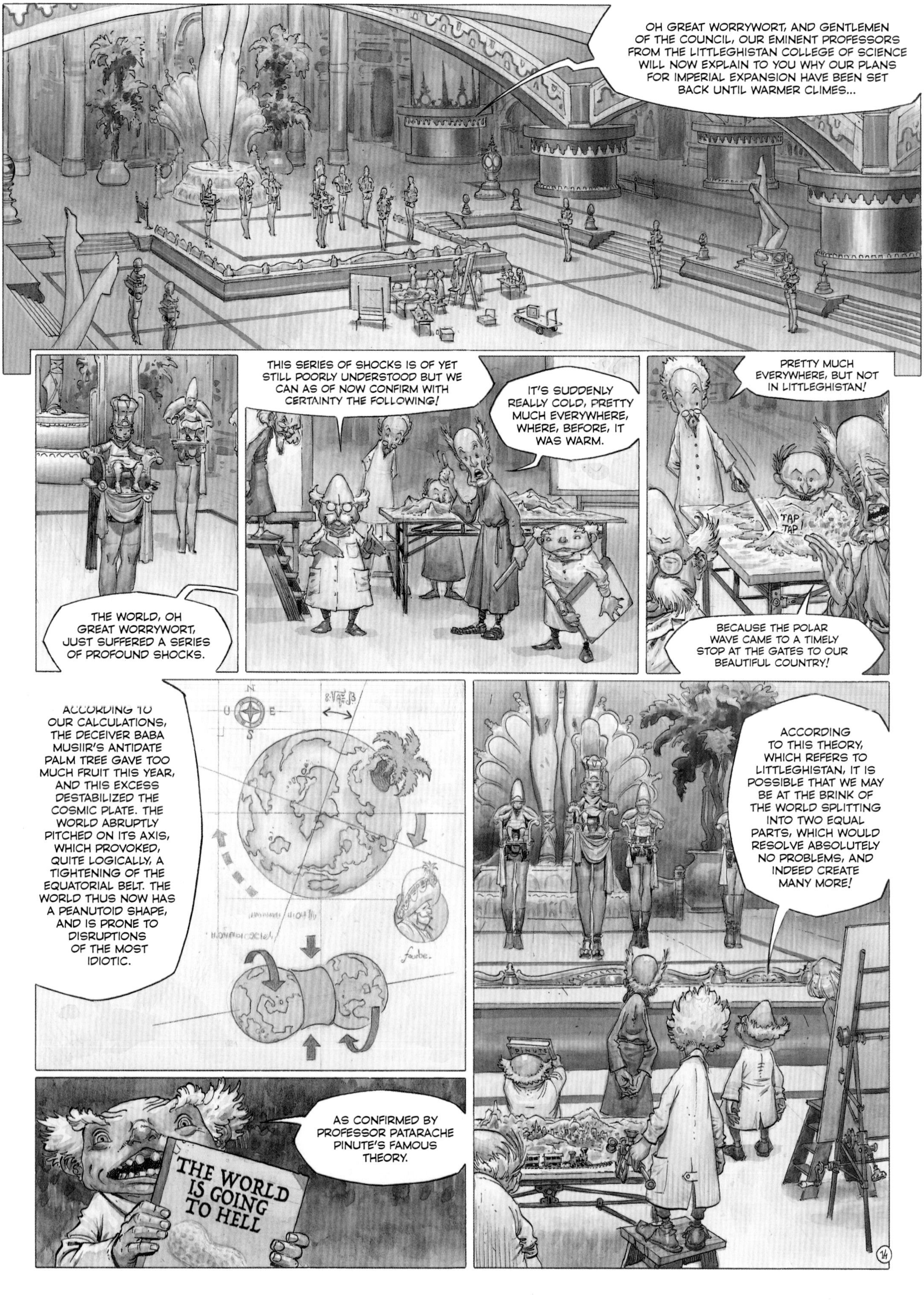
OH GREAT WORRYWORT, AND GENTLEMEN OF THE COUNCIL, OUR EMINENT PROFESSORS FROM THE LITTLEGHISTAN COLLEGE OF SCIENCE WILL NOW EXPLAIN TO YOU WHY OUR PLANS FOR IMPERIAL EXPANSION HAVE BEEN SET BACK UNTIL WARMER CLIMES...
THE WORLD, OH GREAT WORRYWORT, JUST SUFFERED A SERIES OF PROFOUND SHOCKS.
THIS SERIES OF SHOCKS IS OF YET STILL POORLY UNDERSTOOD BUT WE CAN AS OF NOW CONFIRM WITH CERTAINTY THE FOLLOWING!
IT'S SUDDENLY REALLY COLD, PRETTY MUCH EVERYWHERE, WHERE, BEFORE, IT WAS WARM.
PRETTY MUCH EVERYWHERE, BUT NOT IN LITTLEGHISTAN!
TAP TAP
BECAUSE THE POLAR WAVE CAME TO A TIMELY STOP AT THE GATES TO OUR BEAUTIFUL COUNTRY!
ACCORDING TO OUR CALCULATIONS, THE DECEIVER BABA MUSIIR'S ANTIDATE PALM TREE GAVE TOO MUCH FRUIT THIS YEAR, AND THIS EXCESS DESTABILIZED THE COSMIC PLATE. THE WORLD ABRUPTLY PITCHED ON ITS AXIS, WHICH PROVOKED, QUITE LOGICALLY, A TIGHTENING OF THE EQUATORIAL BELT. THE WORLD THUS NOW HAS A PEANUTOID SHAPE, AND IS PRONE TO DISRUPTIONS OF THE MOST IDIOTIC.
N
E
S
fourbe.
ACCORDING TO THIS THEORY, WHICH REFERS TO LITTLEGHISTAN, IT IS POSSIBLE THAT WE MAY BE AT THE BRINK OF THE WORLD SPLITTING INTO TWO EQUAL PARTS, WHICH WOULD RESOLVE ABSOLUTELY NO PROBLEMS, AND INDEED CREATE MANY MORE!
PINUTE
AS CONFIRMED BY PROFESSOR PATARACHE PINUTE'S FAMOUS THEORY.
THE WORLD IS GOING TO HELL
14

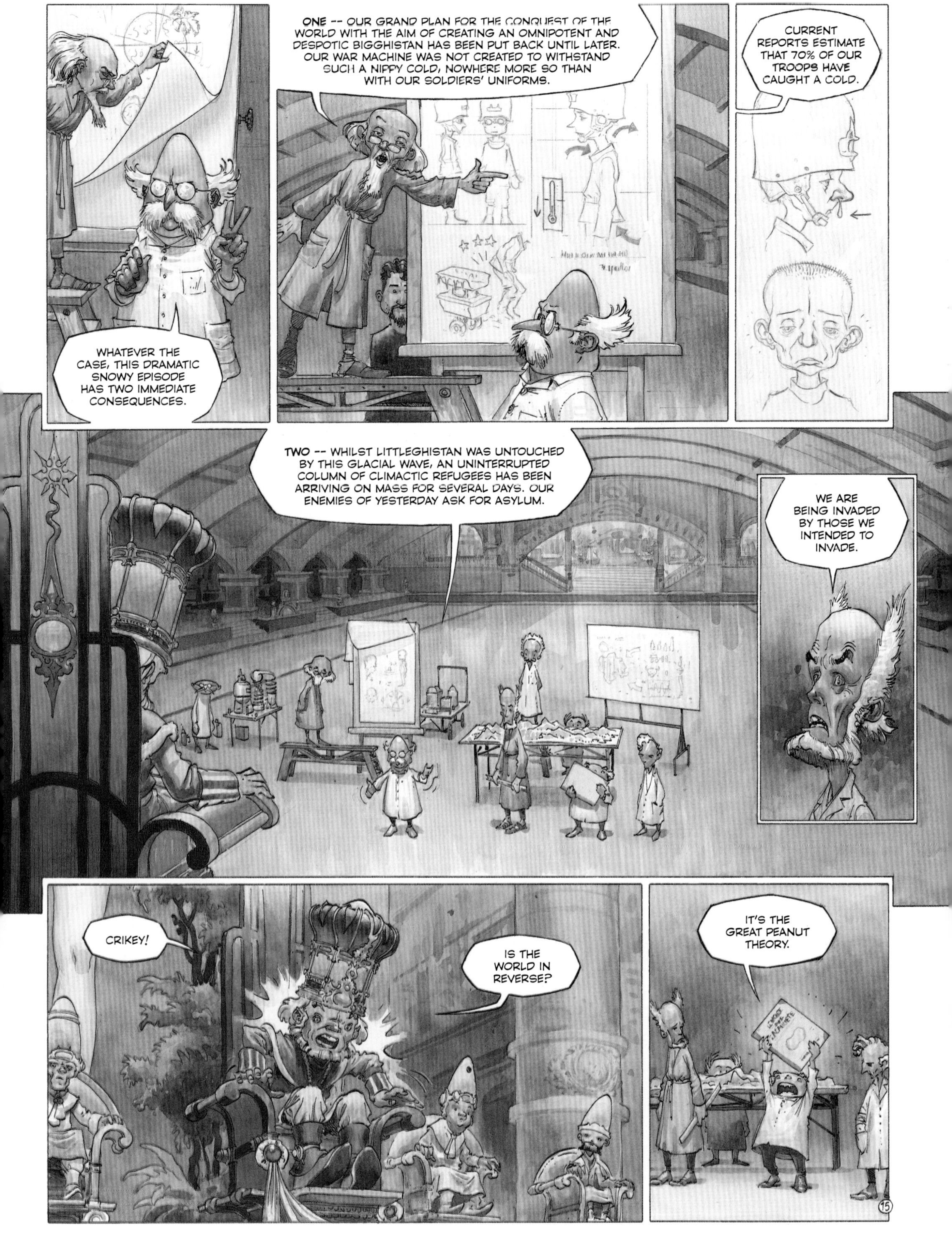
WHATEVER THE CASE, THIS DRAMATIC SNOWY EPISODE HAS TWO IMMEDIATE CONSEQUENCES.
ONE -- OUR GRAND PLAN FOR THE CONQUEST OF THE WORLD WITH THE AIM OF CREATING AN OMNIPOTENT AND DESPOTIC BIGGHISTAN HAS BEEN PUT BACK UNTIL LATER. OUR WAR MACHINE WAS NOT CREATED TO WITHSTAND SUCH A NIPPY COLD, NOWHERE MORE SO THAN WITH OUR SOLDIERS' UNIFORMS.
CURRENT REPORTS ESTIMATE THAT 70% OF OUR TROOPS HAVE CAUGHT A COLD.
TWO -- WHILST LITTLEGHISTAN WAS UNTOUCHED BY THIS GLACIAL WAVE, AN UNINTERRUPTED COLUMN OF CLIMACTIC REFUGEES HAS BEEN ARRIVING ON MASS FOR SEVERAL DAYS. OUR ENEMIES OF YESTERDAY ASK FOR ASYLUM.
WE ARE BEING INVADED BY THOSE WE INTENDED TO INVADE.
CRIKEY!
IS THE WORLD IN REVERSE?
IT'S THE GREAT PEANUT THEORY.
15

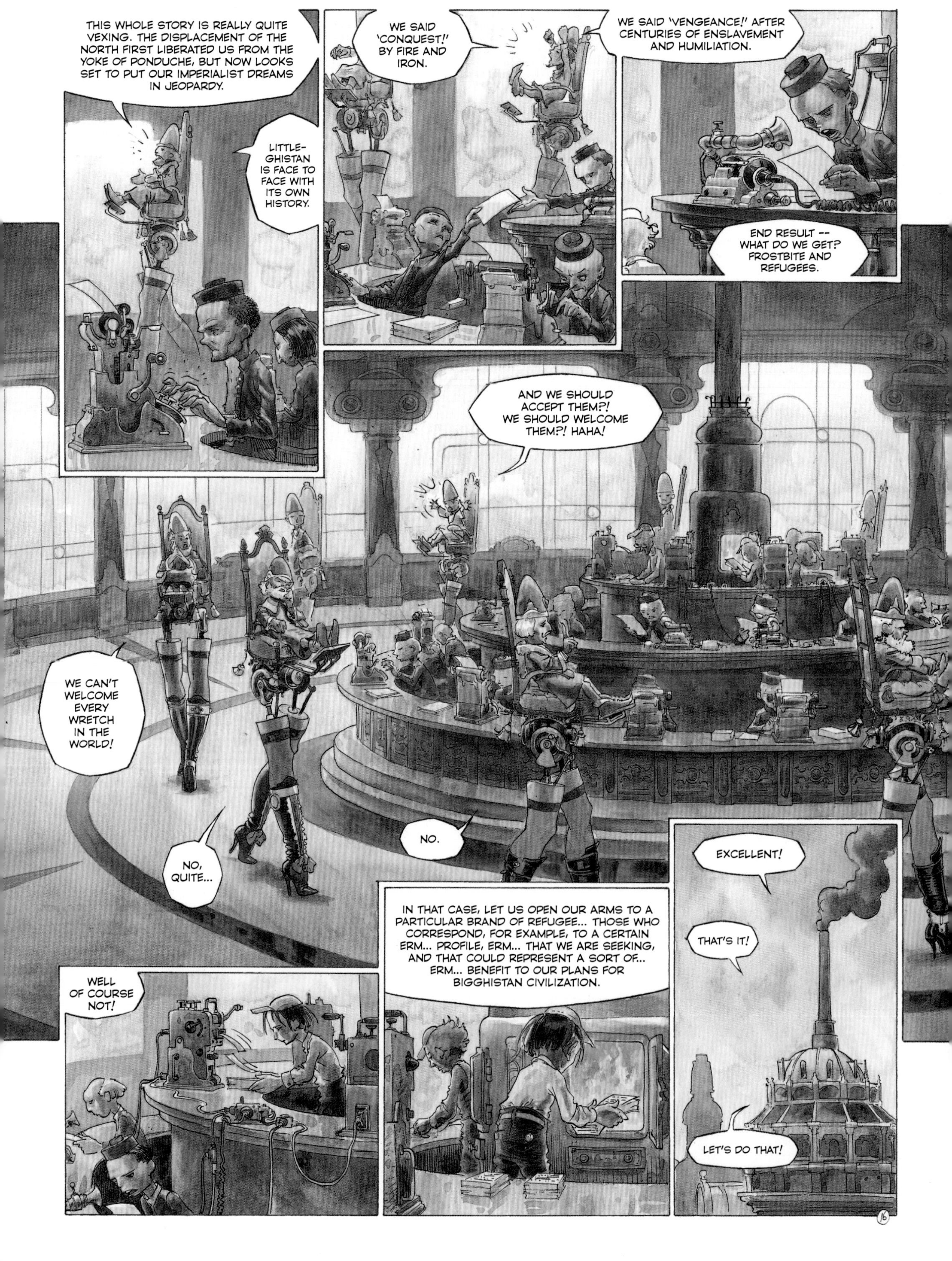
THIS WHOLE STORY IS REALLY QUITE VEXING. THE DISPLACEMENT OF THE NORTH FIRST LIBERATED US FROM THE YOKE OF PONDUCHE, BUT NOW LOOKS SET TO PUT OUR IMPERIALIST DREAMS IN JEOPARDY.
LITTLE-GHISTAN IS FACE TO FACE WITH ITS OWN HISTORY.
WE SAID 'CONQUEST!' BY FIRE AND IRON.
WE SAID 'VENGEANCE!' AFTER CENTURIES OF ENSLAVEMENT AND HUMILIATION.
END RESULT -- WHAT DO WE GET? FROSTBITE AND REFUGEES.
AND WE SHOULD ACCEPT THEM?! WE SHOULD WELCOME THEM?! HAHA!
WE CAN'T WELCOME EVERY WRETCH IN THE WORLD!
NO, QUITE...
NO.
EXCELLENT!
WELL OF COURSE NOT!
IN THAT CASE, LET US OPEN OUR ARMS TO A PARTICULAR BRAND OF REFUGEE... THOSE WHO CORRESPOND, FOR EXAMPLE, TO A CERTAIN ERM... PROFILE, ERM... THAT WE ARE SEEKING, AND THAT COULD REPRESENT A SORT OF... ERM... BENEFIT TO OUR PLANS FOR BIGGHISTAN CIVILIZATION.
THAT'S IT!
LET'S DO THAT!

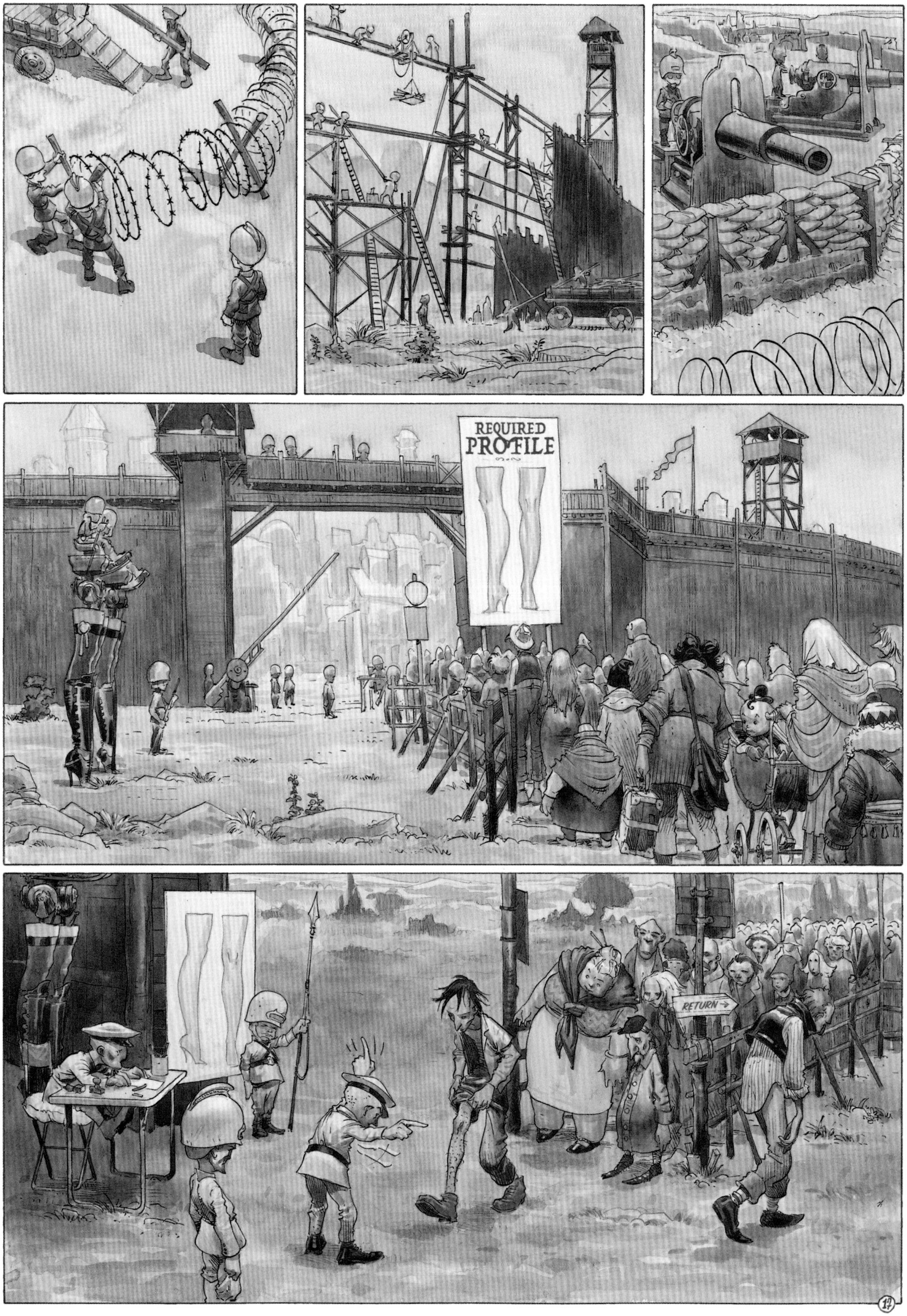
REQUIRED
PROFILE
RETURN

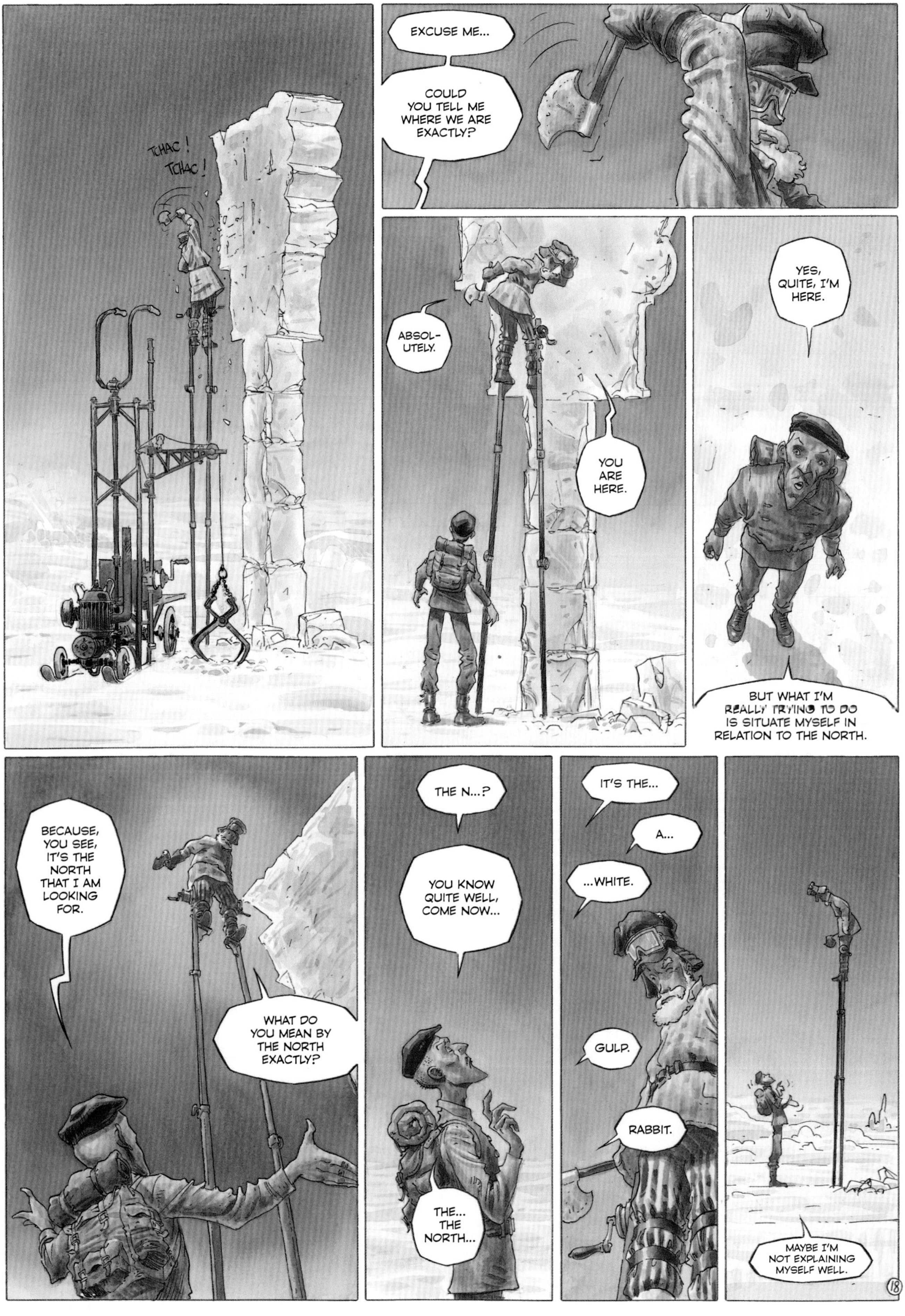
TCHAC !
TCHAC !
EXCUSE ME...
COULD YOU TELL ME WHERE WE ARE EXACTLY?
ABSOL-UTELY.
YOU ARE HERE.
YES, QUITE, I'M HERE.
BUT WHAT I'M REALLY TRYING TO DO IS SITUATE MYSELF IN RELATION TO THE NORTH.
BECAUSE, YOU SEE, IT'S THE NORTH THAT I AM LOOKING FOR.
WHAT DO YOU MEAN BY THE NORTH EXACTLY?
THE N...?
YOU KNOW QUITE WELL, COME NOW...
THE... THE NORTH...
IT'S THE...
A...
...WHITE.
GULP.
RABBIT.
MAYBE I'M NOT EXPLAINING MYSELF WELL.

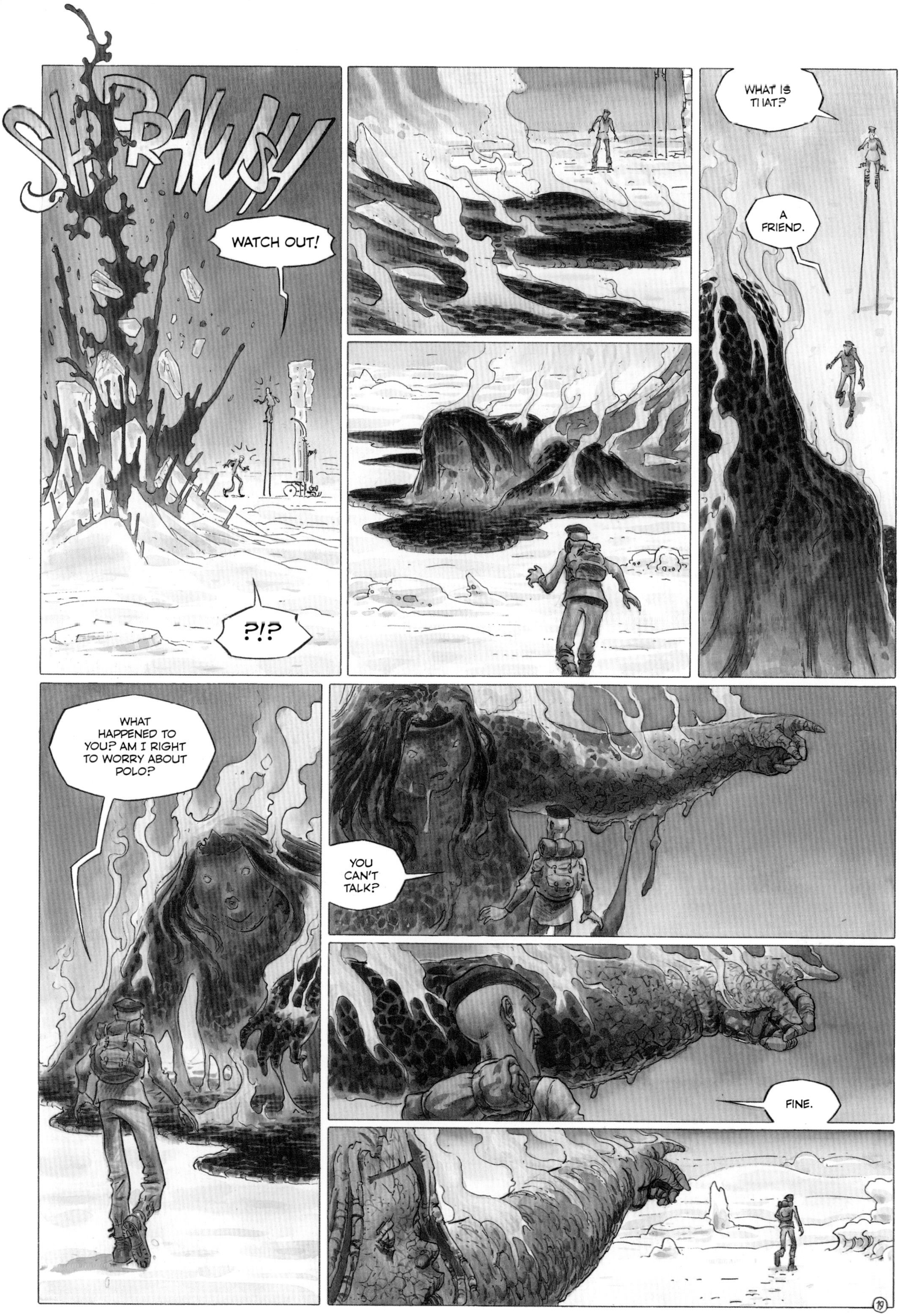
SHPRAWSH
WATCH OUT!
?!?
WHAT IS THAT?
A FRIEND.
WHAT HAPPENED TO YOU? AM I RIGHT TO WORRY ABOUT POLO?
YOU CAN'T TALK?
FINE.

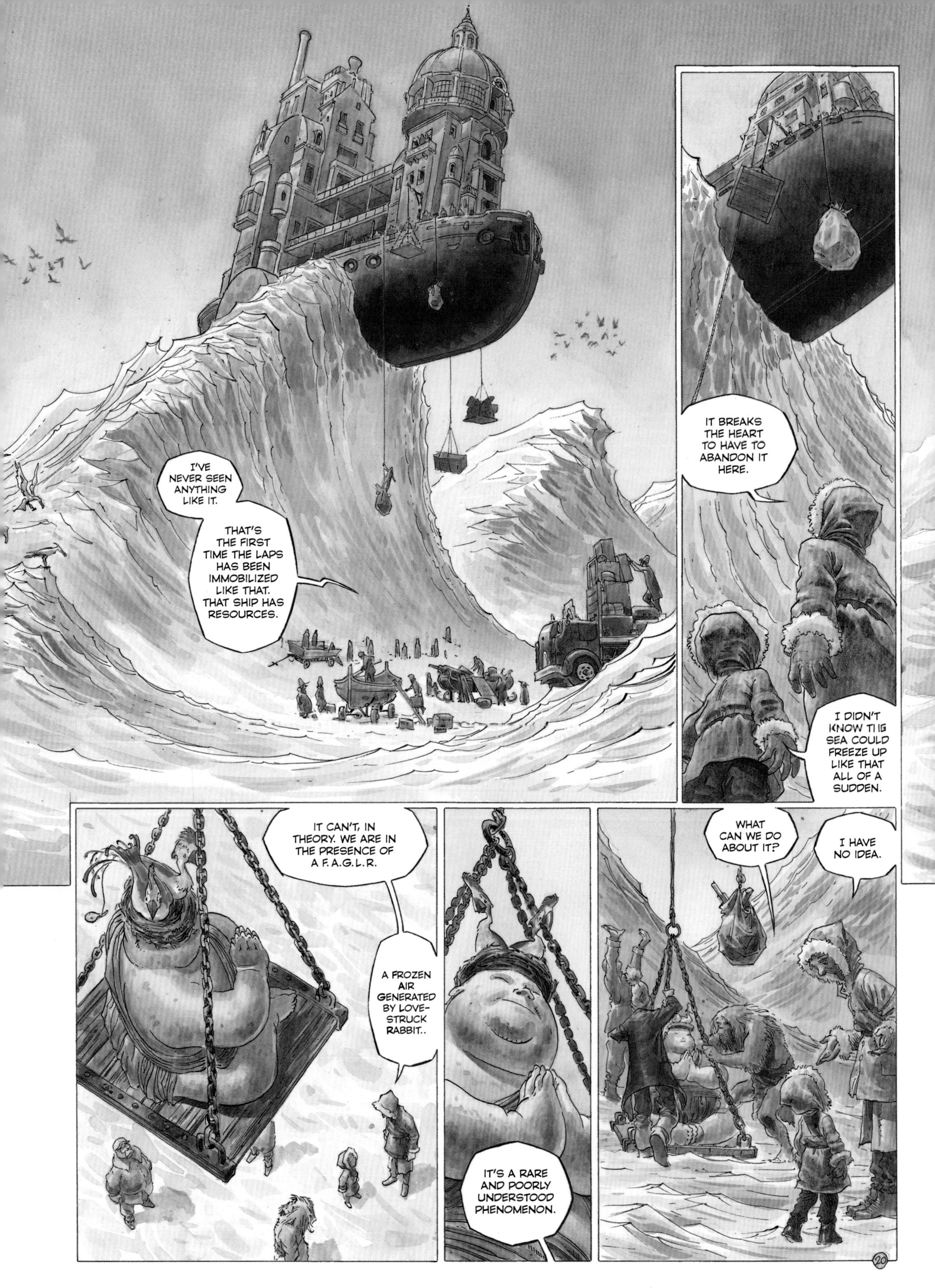
I'VE NEVER SEEN ANYTHING LIKE IT.
THAT'S THE FIRST TIME THE LAPS HAS BEEN IMMOBILIZED LIKE THAT. THAT SHIP HAS RESOURCES.
IT BREAKS THE HEART TO HAVE TO ABANDON IT HERE.
I DIDN'T KNOW THE SEA COULD FREEZE UP LIKE THAT ALL OF A SUDDEN.
IT CAN'T, IN THEORY. WE ARE IN THE PRESENCE OF A F.A.G.L.R.
A FROZEN AIR GENERATED BY LOVE-STRUCK RABBIT..
IT'S A RARE AND POORLY UNDERSTOOD PHENOMENON.
WHAT CAN WE DO ABOUT IT?
I HAVE NO IDEA.

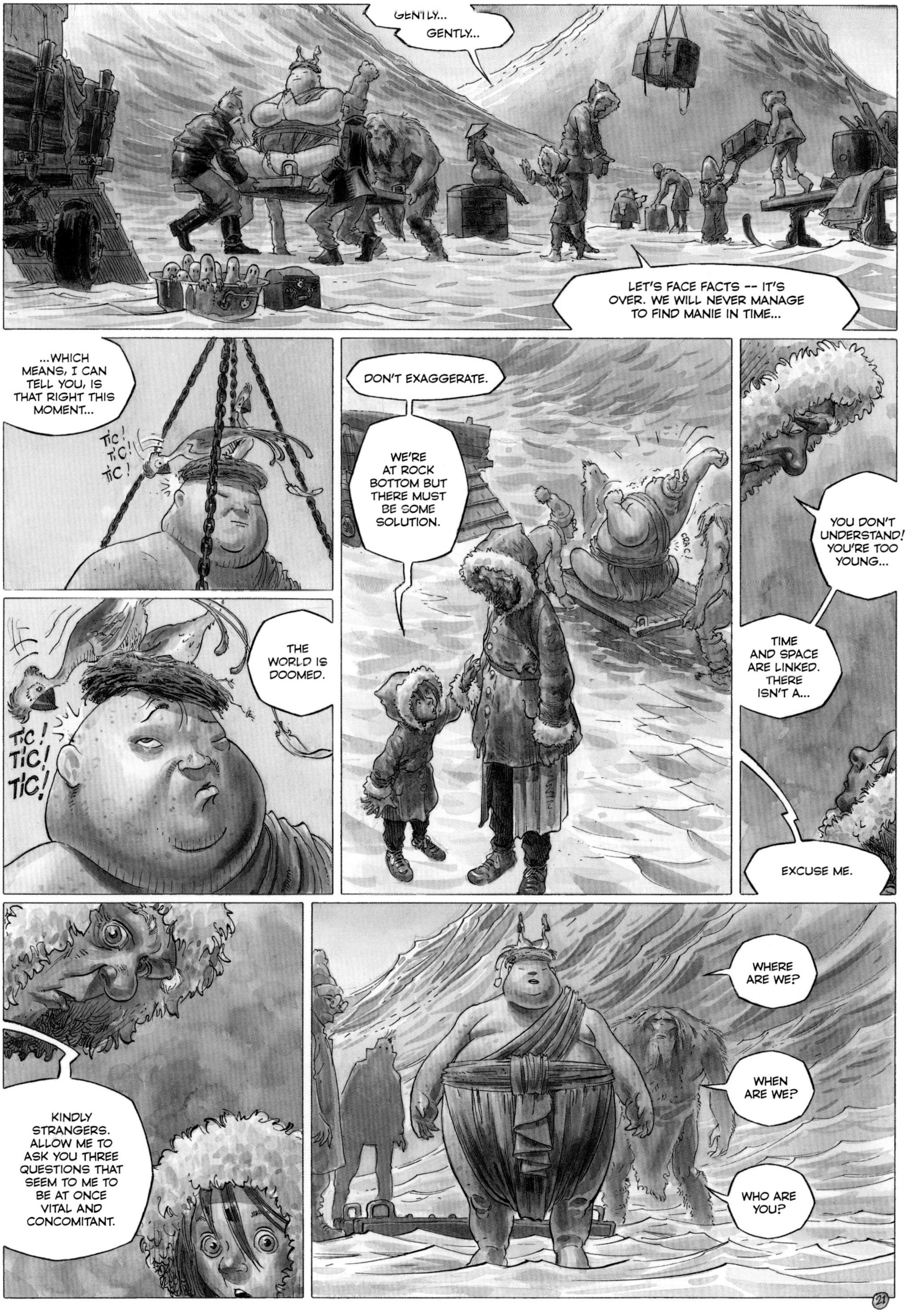
GENTLY...
GENTLY...
LET'S FACE FACTS -- IT'S OVER. WE WILL NEVER MANAGE TO FIND MANIE IN TIME...
...WHICH MEANS, I CAN TELL YOU, IS THAT RIGHT THIS MOMENT...
TIC! TIC! TIC!
THE WORLD IS DOOMED.
TIC! TIC! TIC!
DON'T EXAGGERATE.
WE'RE AT ROCK BOTTOM BUT THERE MUST BE SOME SOLUTION.
CRAC!
YOU DON'T UNDERSTAND! YOU'RE TOO YOUNG...
TIME AND SPACE ARE LINKED. THERE ISN'T A...
EXCUSE ME.
KINDLY STRANGERS. ALLOW ME TO ASK YOU THREE QUESTIONS THAT SEEM TO ME TO BE AT ONCE VITAL AND CONCOMITANT.
WHERE ARE WE?
WHEN ARE WE?
WHO ARE YOU?

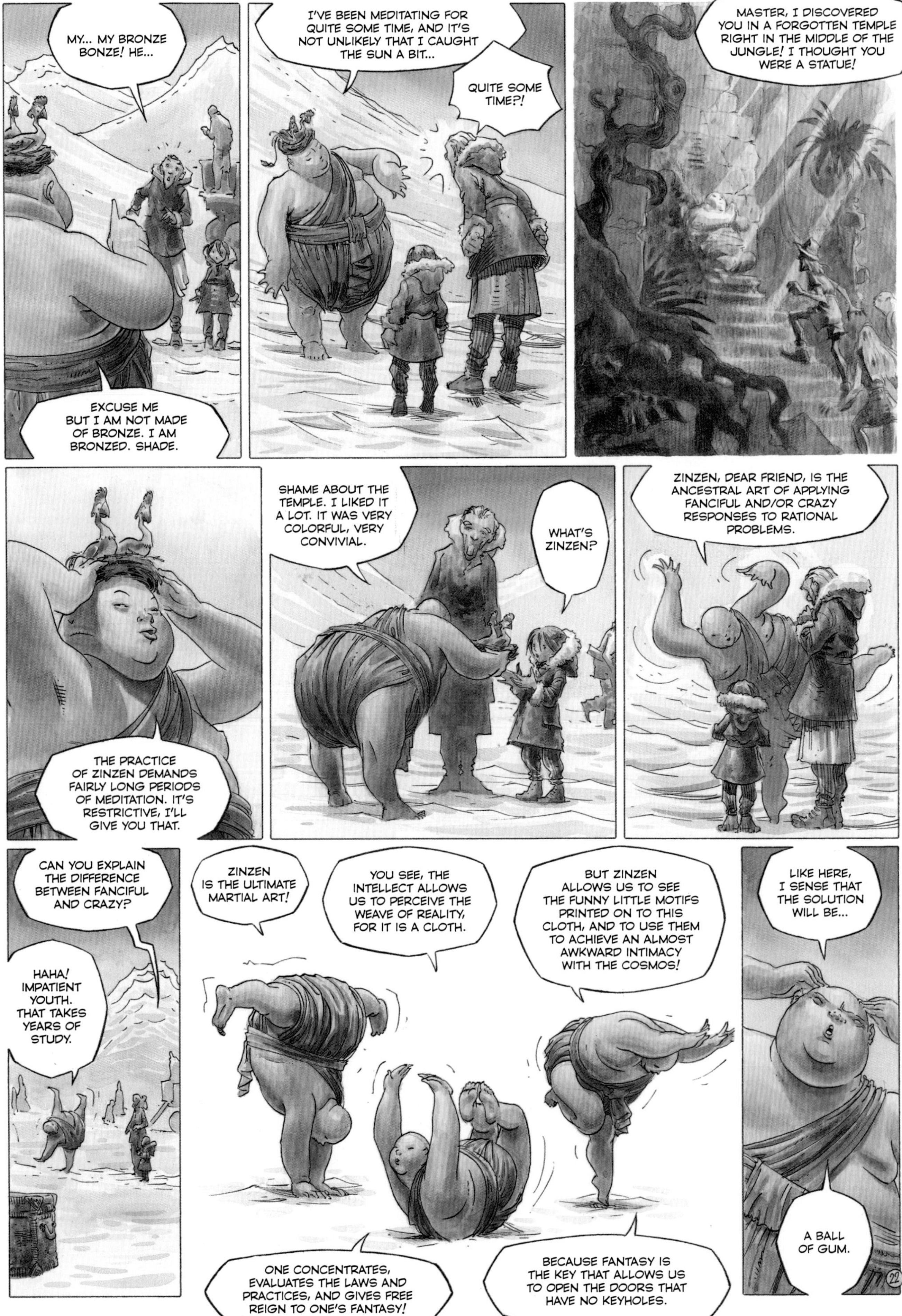
MY... MY BRONZE BONZE! HE...
EXCUSE ME BUT I AM NOT MADE OF BRONZE. I AM BRONZED. SHADE.
I'VE BEEN MEDITATING FOR QUITE SOME TIME, AND IT'S NOT UNLIKELY THAT I CAUGHT THE SUN A BIT...
QUITE SOME TIME?!
MASTER, I DISCOVERED YOU IN A FORGOTTEN TEMPLE RIGHT IN THE MIDDLE OF THE JUNGLE! I THOUGHT YOU WERE A STATUE!
THE PRACTICE OF ZINZEN DEMANDS FAIRLY LONG PERIODS OF MEDITATION. IT'S RESTRICTIVE, I'LL GIVE YOU THAT.
SHAME ABOUT THE TEMPLE. I LIKED IT A LOT. IT WAS VERY COLORFUL, VERY CONVIVIAL.
WHAT'S ZINZEN?
ZINZEN, DEAR FRIEND, IS THE ANCESTRAL ART OF APPLYING FANCIFUL AND/OR CRAZY RESPONSES TO RATIONAL PROBLEMS.
CAN YOU EXPLAIN THE DIFFERENCE BETWEEN FANCIFUL AND CRAZY?
HAHA! IMPATIENT YOUTH. THAT TAKES YEARS OF STUDY.
ZINZEN IS THE ULTIMATE MARTIAL ART!
YOU SEE, THE INTELLECT ALLOWS US TO PERCEIVE THE WEAVE OF REALITY, FOR IT IS A CLOTH.
ONE CONCENTRATES, EVALUATES THE LAWS AND PRACTICES, AND GIVES FREE REIGN TO ONE'S FANTASY!
BUT ZINZEN ALLOWS US TO SEE THE FUNNY LITTLE MOTIFS PRINTED ON TO THIS CLOTH, AND TO USE THEM TO ACHIEVE AN ALMOST AWKWARD INTIMACY WITH THE COSMOS!
BECAUSE FANTASY IS THE KEY THAT ALLOWS US TO OPEN THE DOORS THAT HAVE NO KEYHOLES.
LIKE HERE, I SENSE THAT THE SOLUTION WILL BE...
A BALL OF GUM.

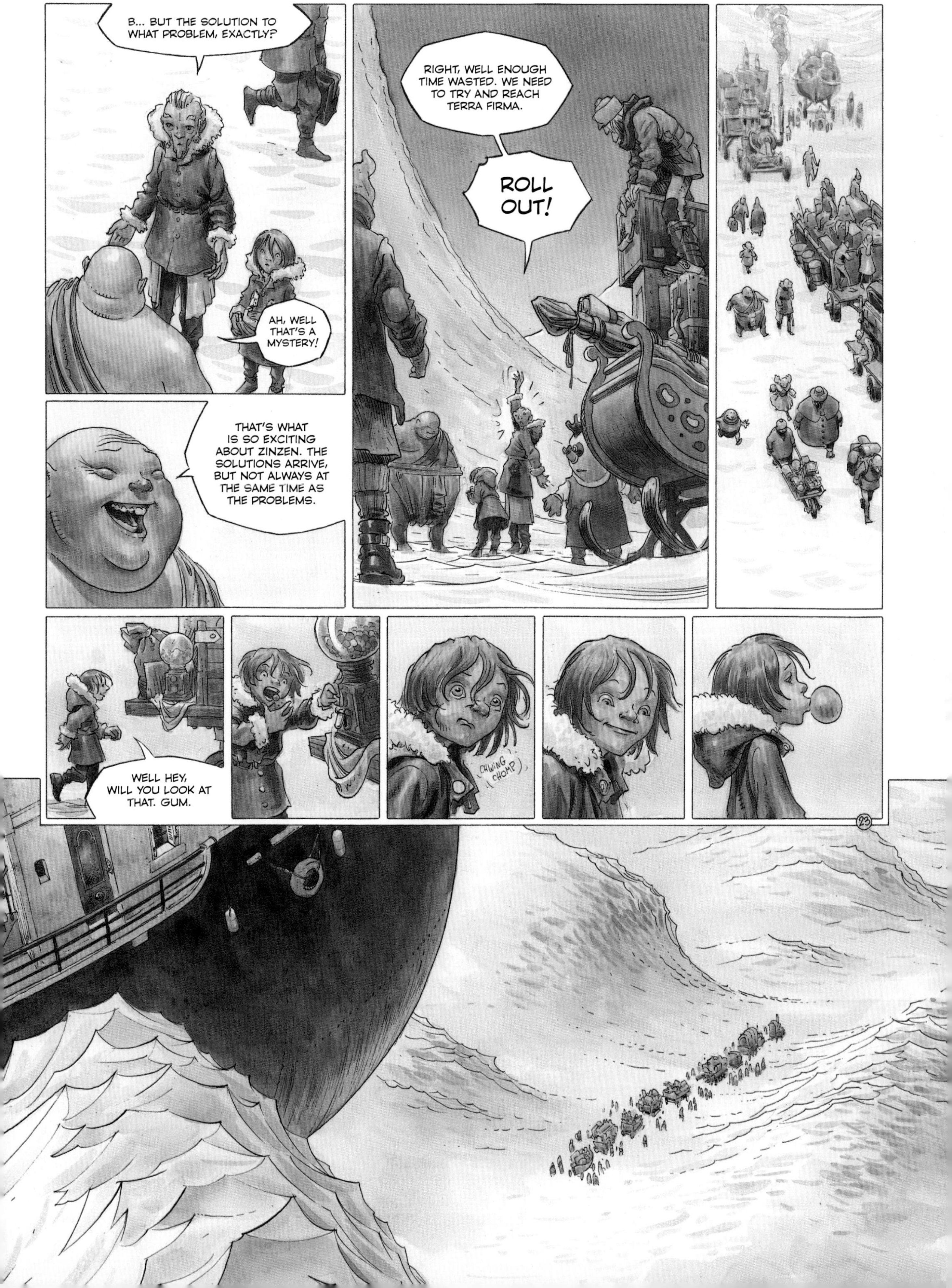
B... BUT THE SOLUTION TO WHAT PROBLEM, EXACTLY?
AH, WELL THAT'S A MYSTERY!
THAT'S WHAT IS SO EXCITING ABOUT ZINZEN. THE SOLUTIONS ARRIVE, BUT NOT ALWAYS AT THE SAME TIME AS THE PROBLEMS.
RIGHT, WELL ENOUGH TIME WASTED. WE NEED TO TRY AND REACH TERRA FIRMA.
ROLL OUT!
WELL HEY, WILL YOU LOOK AT THAT. GUM.
CHWING CHOMP
23

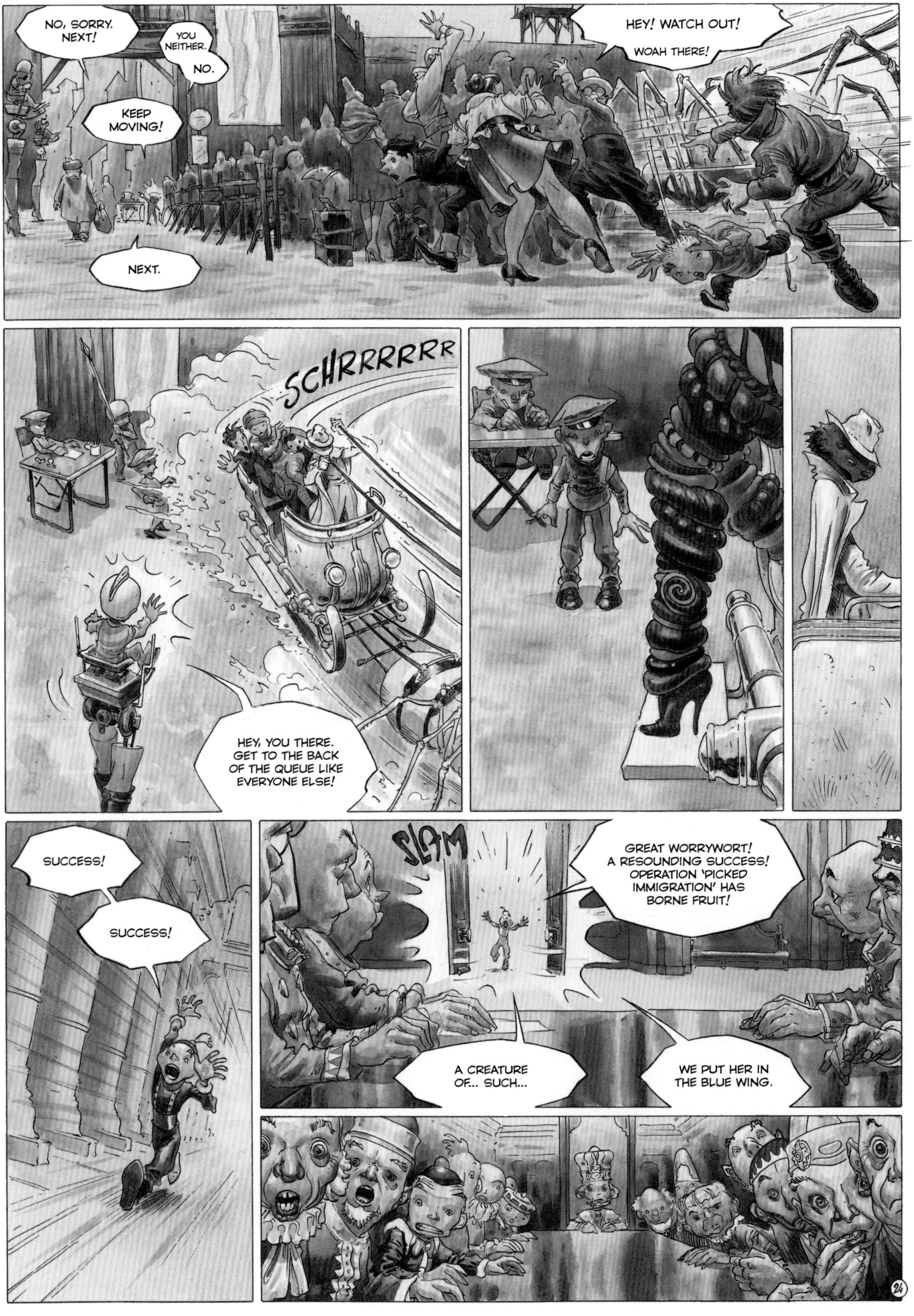

NO, SORRY. NEXT!
YOU NEITHER.
NO.
KEEP MOVING!
NEXT.
HEY! WATCH OUT!
WOAH THERE!
SCHRRRRRR
HEY, YOU THERE. GET TO THE BACK OF THE QUEUE LIKE EVERYONE ELSE!
SUCCESS!
SUCCESS!
SLAM
GREAT WORRYWORT! A RESOUNDING SUCCESS! OPERATION 'PICKED IMMIGRATION' HAS BORNE FRUIT!
A CREATURE OF... SUCH...
WE PUT HER IN THE BLUE WING.

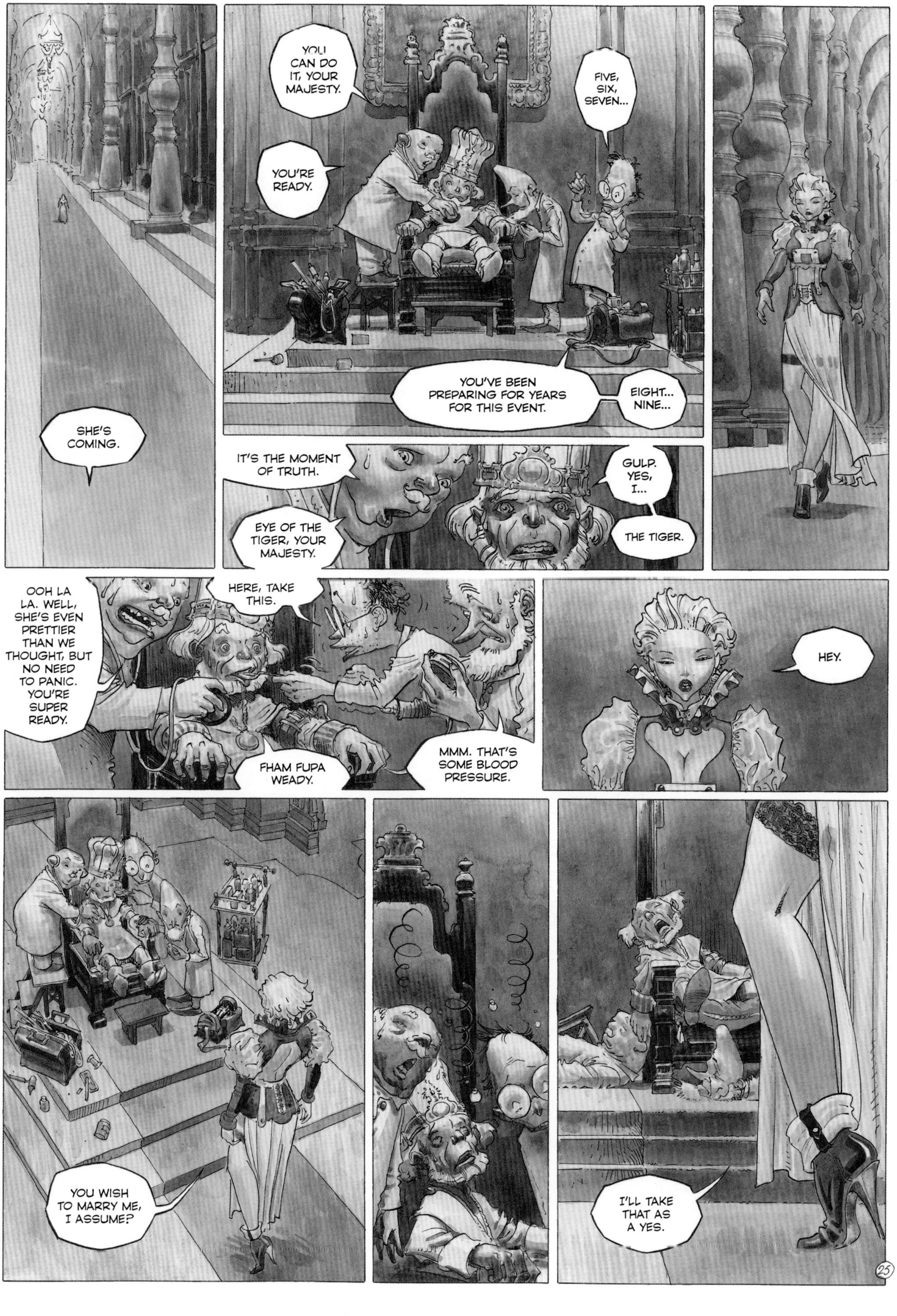

SHE'S COMING.
YOU CAN DO IT, YOUR MAJESTY.
YOU'RE READY.
FIVE, SIX, SEVEN...
YOU'VE BEEN PREPARING FOR YEARS FOR THIS EVENT.
EIGHT... NINE...
IT'S THE MOMENT OF TRUTH.
EYE OF THE TIGER, YOUR MAJESTY.
GULP. YES, I...
THE TIGER.
OOH LA LA. WELL, SHE'S EVEN PRETTIER THAN WE THOUGHT, BUT NO NEED TO PANIC. YOU'RE SUPER READY.
HERE, TAKE THIS.
FHAM FUPA WEADY.
MMM. THAT'S SOME BLOOD PRESSURE.
HEY.
YOU WISH TO MARRY ME, I ASSUME?
I'LL TAKE THAT AS A YES.

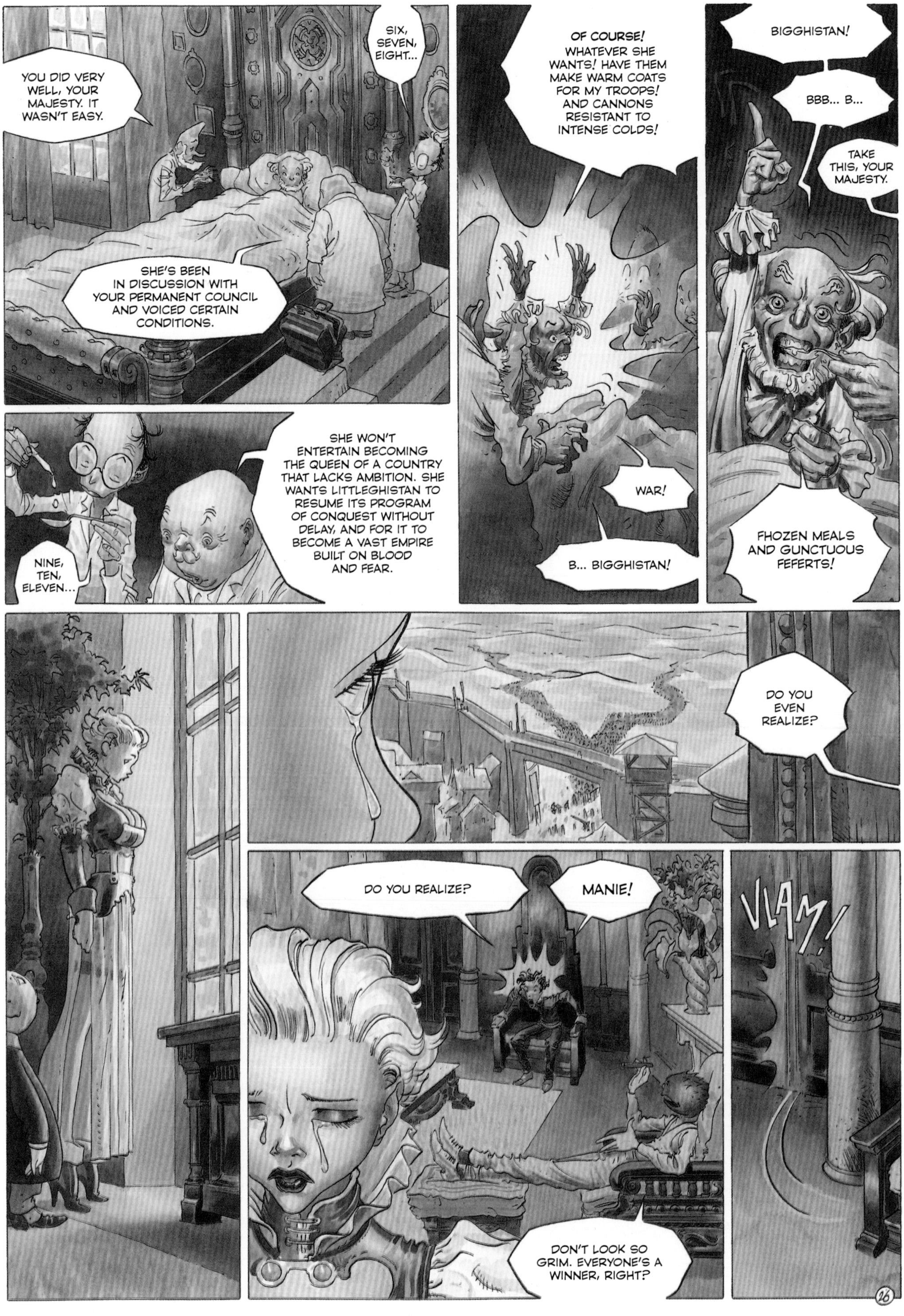
SIX, SEVEN, EIGHT...
YOU DID VERY WELL, YOUR MAJESTY. IT WASN'T EASY.
SHE'S BEEN IN DISCUSSION WITH YOUR PERMANENT COUNCIL AND VOICED CERTAIN CONDITIONS.
SHE WON'T ENTERTAIN BECOMING THE QUEEN OF A COUNTRY THAT LACKS AMBITION. SHE WANTS LITTLEGHISTAN TO RESUME ITS PROGRAM OF CONQUEST WITHOUT DELAY, AND FOR IT TO BECOME A VAST EMPIRE BUILT ON BLOOD AND FEAR.
NINE, TEN, ELEVEN...
OF COURSE! WHATEVER SHE WANTS! HAVE THEM MAKE WARM COATS FOR MY TROOPS! AND CANNONS RESISTANT TO INTENSE COLDS!
WAR!
B... BIGGHISTAN!
BIGGHISTAN!
BBB... B...
TAKE THIS, YOUR MAJESTY.
FHOZEN MEALS AND GUNCTUOUS FEFERTS!
DO YOU EVEN REALIZE?
DO YOU REALIZE?
MANIE!
DON'T LOOK SO GRIM. EVERYONE'S A WINNER, RIGHT?
VLAM!

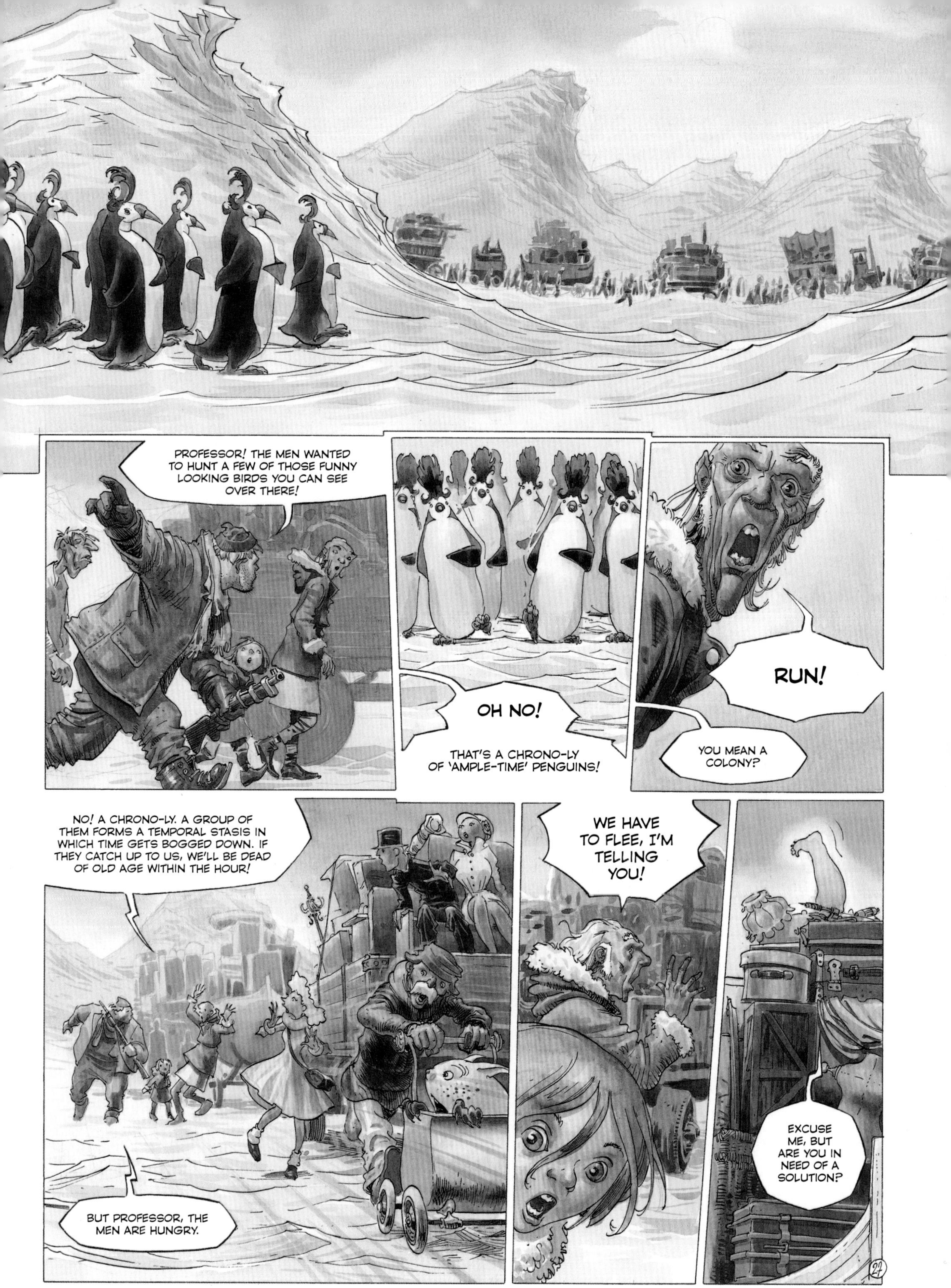
PROFESSOR! THE MEN WANTED TO HUNT A FEW OF THOSE FUNNY LOOKING BIRDS YOU CAN SEE OVER THERE!
OH NO!
THAT'S A CHRONO-LY OF 'AMPLE-TIME' PENGUINS!
RUN!
YOU MEAN A COLONY?
NO! A CHRONO-LY. A GROUP OF THEM FORMS A TEMPORAL STASIS IN WHICH TIME GETS BOGGED DOWN. IF THEY CATCH UP TO US, WE'LL BE DEAD OF OLD AGE WITHIN THE HOUR!
BUT PROFESSOR, THE MEN ARE HUNGRY.
WE HAVE TO FLEE, I'M TELLING YOU!
EXCUSE ME, BUT ARE YOU IN NEED OF A SOLUTION?
27

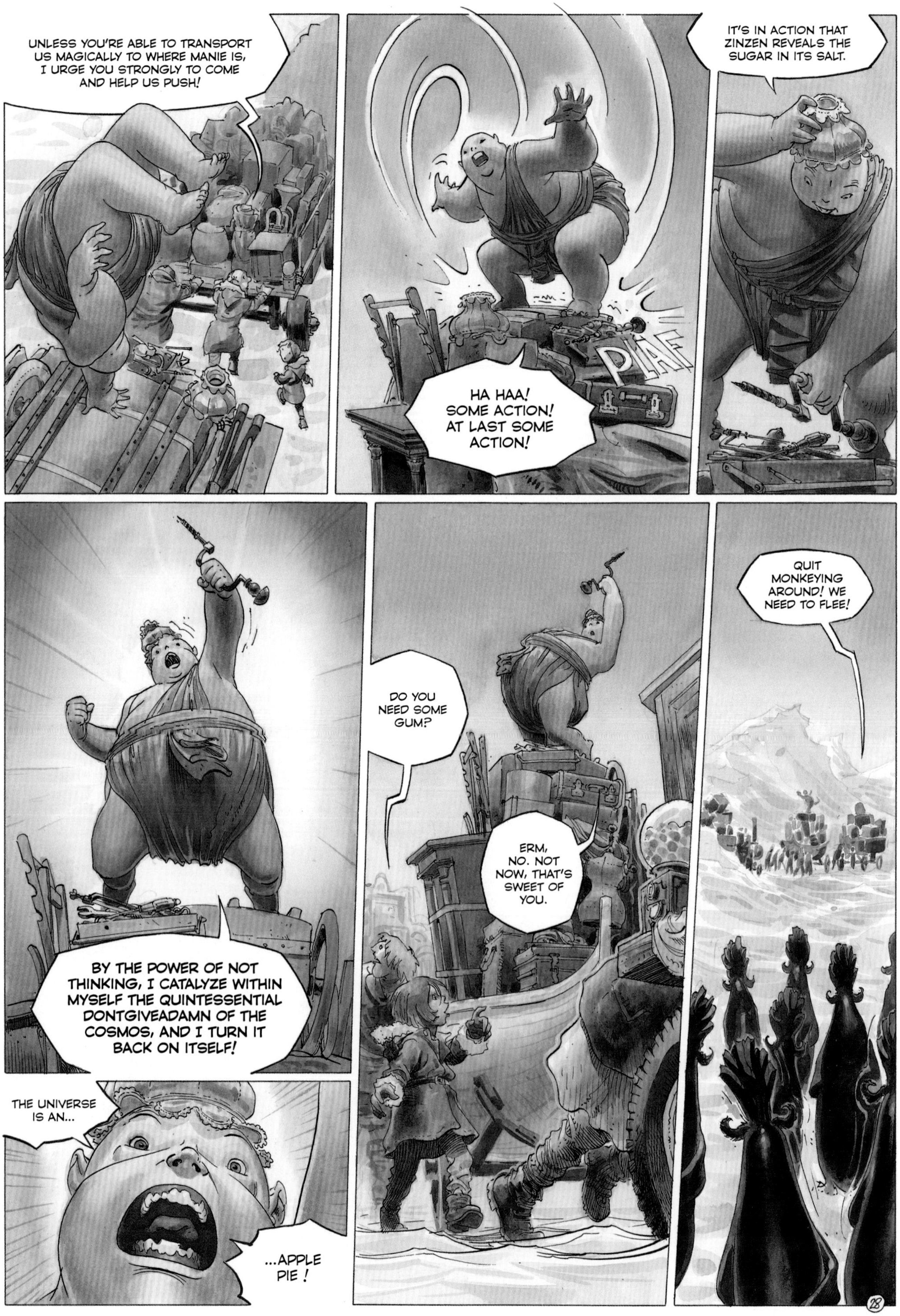
UNLESS YOU'RE ABLE TO TRANSPORT US MAGICALLY TO WHERE MANIE IS, I URGE YOU STRONGLY TO COME AND HELP US PUSH!
HA HAA! SOME ACTION! AT LAST SOME ACTION!
PLAF
IT'S IN ACTION THAT ZINZEN REVEALS THE SUGAR IN ITS SALT.
BY THE POWER OF NOT THINKING, I CATALYZE WITHIN MYSELF THE QUINTESSENTIAL DONTGIVEADAMN OF THE COSMOS, AND I TURN IT BACK ON ITSELF!
THE UNIVERSE IS AN...
...APPLE PIE !
DO YOU NEED SOME GUM?
ERM, NO. NOT NOW, THAT'S SWEET OF YOU.
QUIT MONKEYING AROUND! WE NEED TO FLEE!

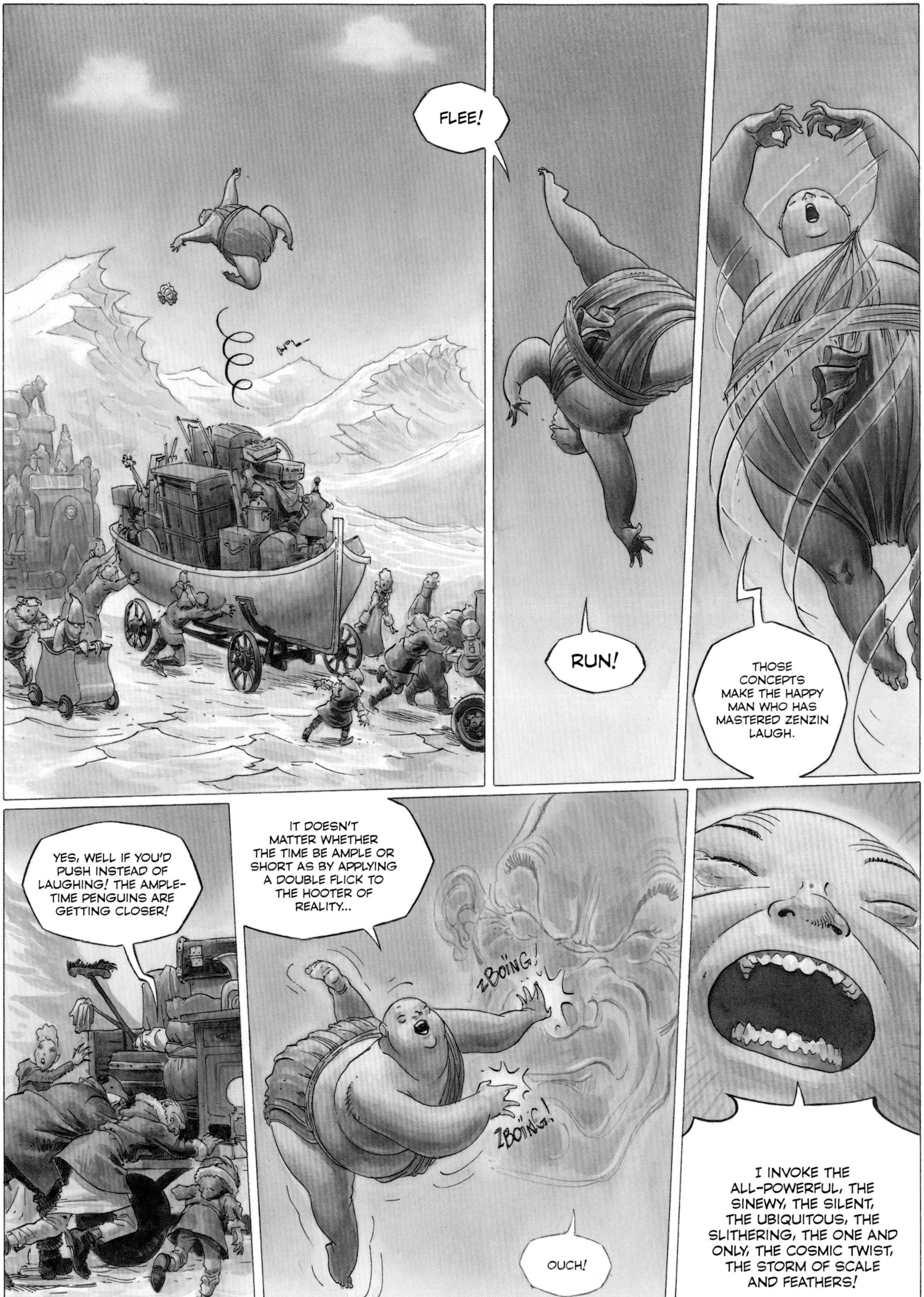
FLEE!
RUN!
THOSE CONCEPTS MAKE THE HAPPY MAN WHO HAS MASTERED ZENZIN LAUGH.
YES, WELL IF YOU'D PUSH INSTEAD OF LAUGHING! THE AMPLE-TIME PENGUINS ARE GETTING CLOSER!
IT DOESN'T MATTER WHETHER THE TIME BE AMPLE OR SHORT AS BY APPLYING A DOUBLE FLICK TO THE HOOTER OF REALITY...
ZBOÏNG!
ZBOÏNG!
OUCH!
I INVOKE THE ALL-POWERFUL, THE SINEWY, THE SILENT, THE UBIQUITOUS, THE SLITHERING, THE ONE AND ONLY, THE COSMIC TWIST, THE STORM OF SCALE AND FEATHERS!

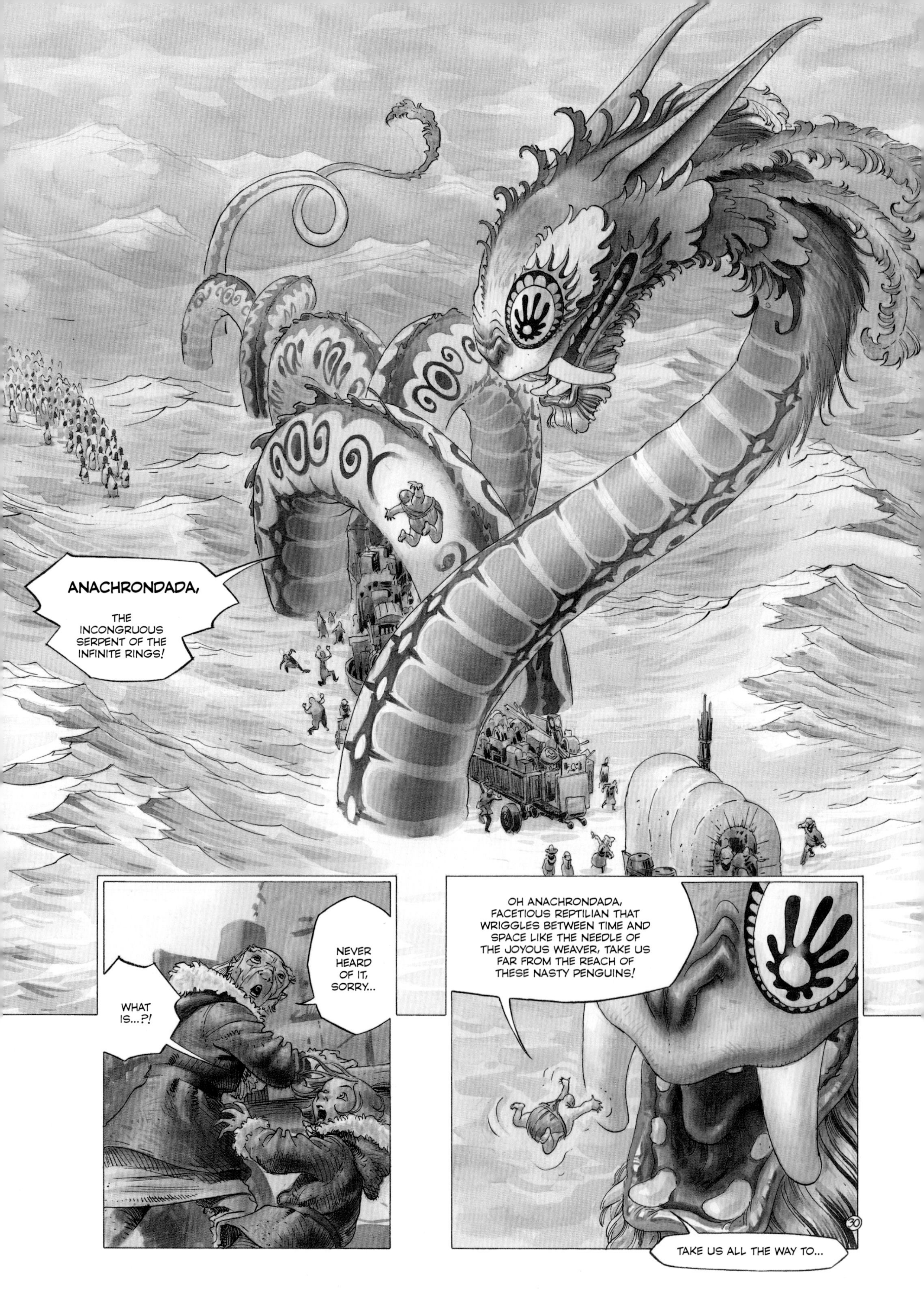
ANACHRONDADA,
THE INCONGRUOUS SERPENT OF THE INFINITE RINGS!
NEVER HEARD OF IT, SORRY...
WHAT IS...?!
OH ANACHRONDADA, FACETIOUS REPTILIAN THAT WRIGGLES BETWEEN TIME AND SPACE LIKE THE NEEDLE OF THE JOYOUS WEAVER, TAKE US FAR FROM THE REACH OF THESE NASTY PENGUINS!
TAKE US ALL THE WAY TO...

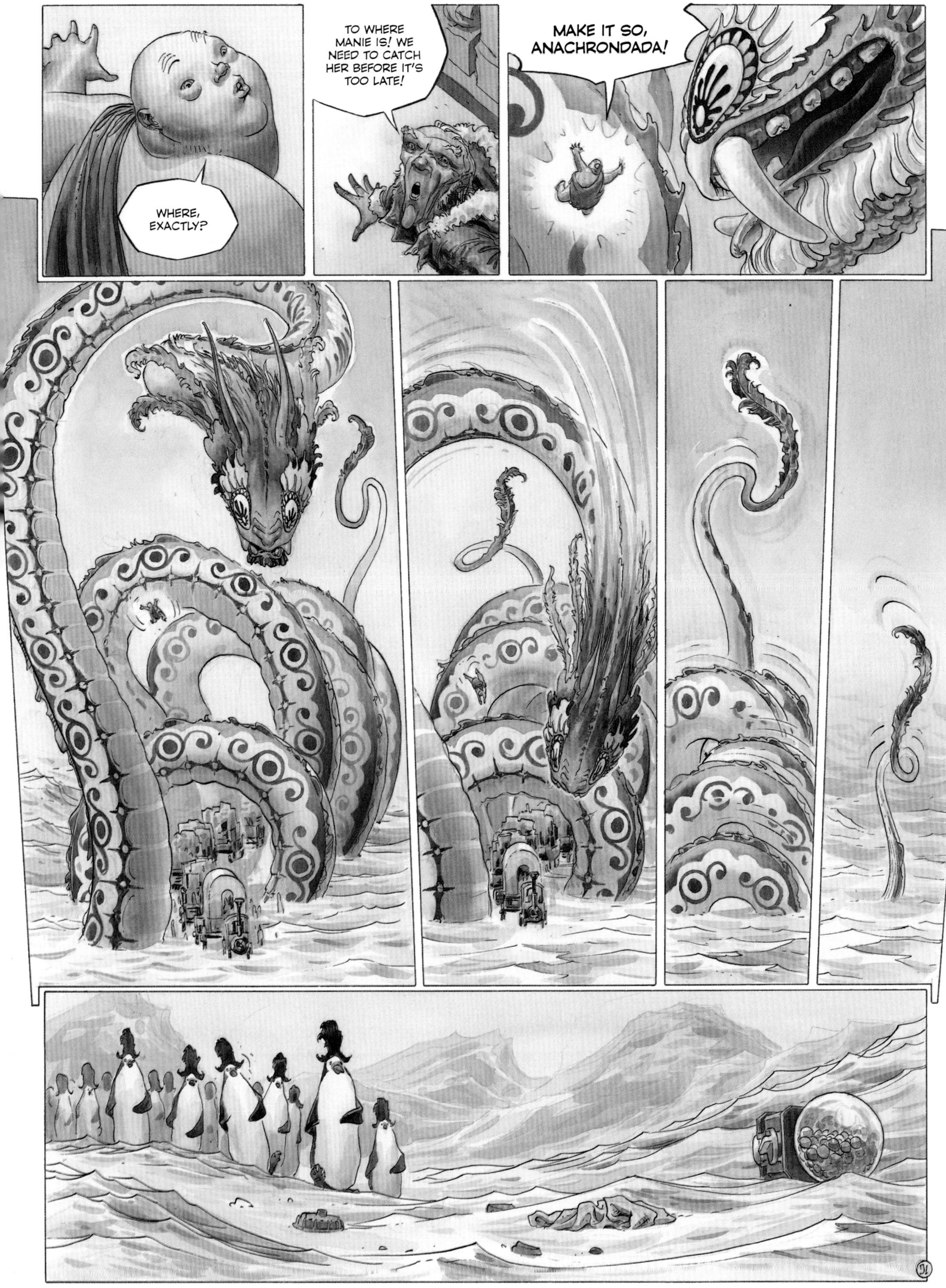
WHERE, EXACTLY?
TO WHERE MANIE IS! WE NEED TO CATCH HER BEFORE IT'S TOO LATE!
MAKE IT SO, ANACHRONDADA!

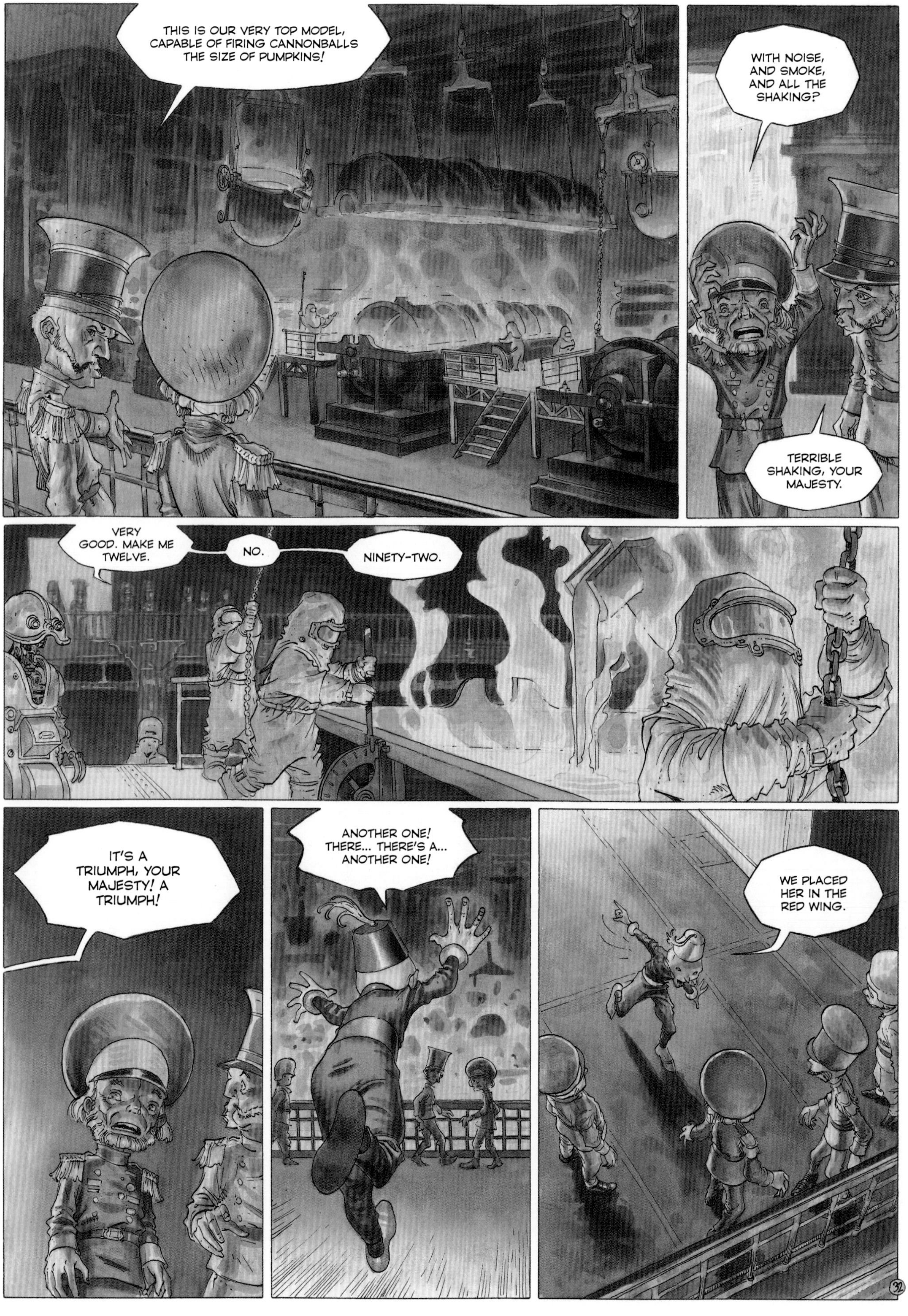

THIS IS OUR VERY TOP MODEL, CAPABLE OF FIRING CANNONBALLS THE SIZE OF PUMPKINS!
WITH NOISE, AND SMOKE, AND ALL THE SHAKING?
TERRIBLE SHAKING, YOUR MAJESTY.
VERY GOOD. MAKE ME TWELVE.
NO.
NINETY-TWO.
IT'S A TRIUMPH, YOUR MAJESTY! A TRIUMPH!
ANOTHER ONE! THERE... THERE'S A... ANOTHER ONE!
WE PLACED HER IN THE RED WING.

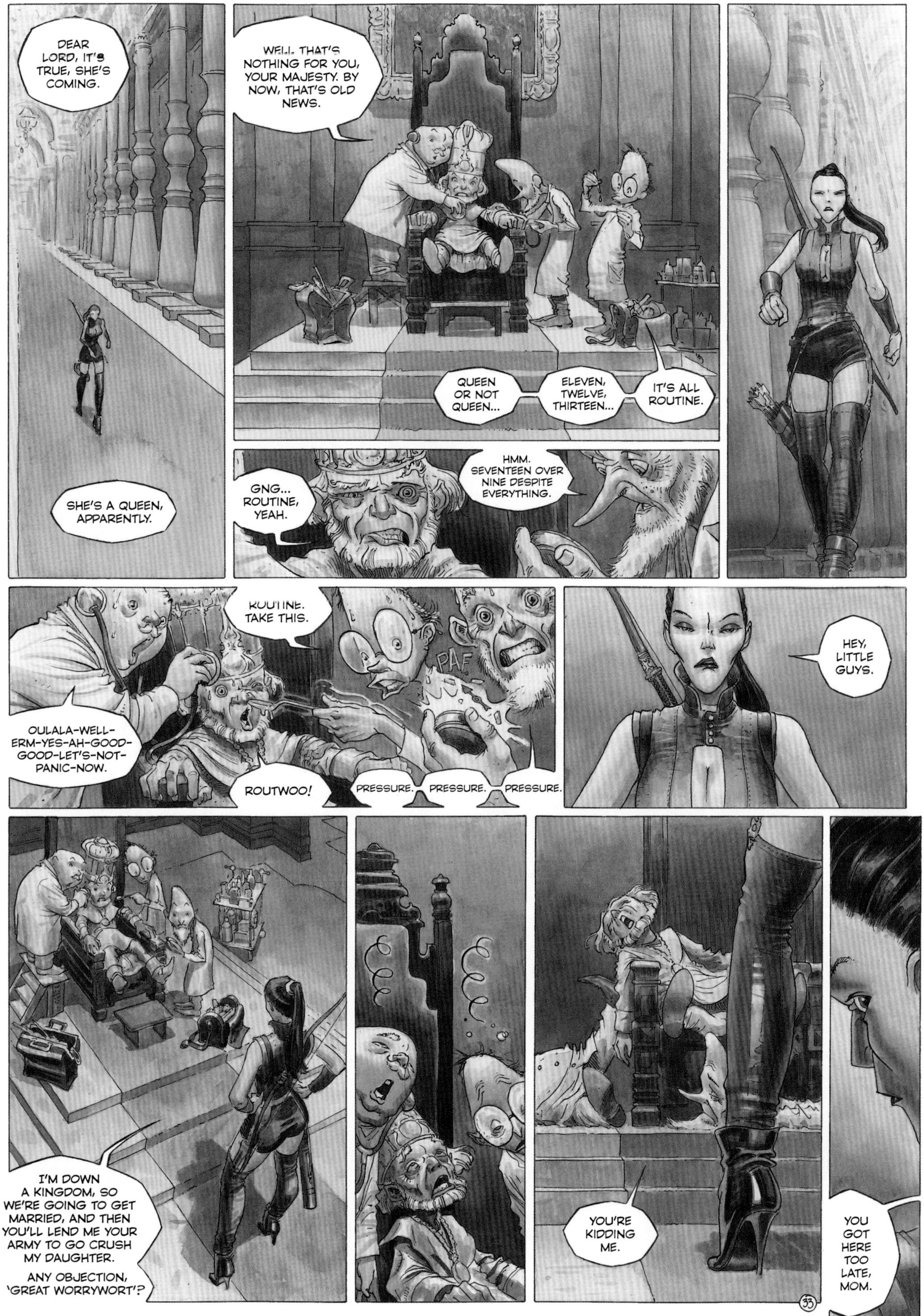

DEAR LORD, IT'S TRUE, SHE'S COMING.
SHE'S A QUEEN, APPARENTLY.
WELL THAT'S NOTHING FOR YOU, YOUR MAJESTY. BY NOW, THAT'S OLD NEWS.
QUEEN OR NOT QUEEN...
ELEVEN, TWELVE, THIRTEEN...
IT'S ALL ROUTINE.
GNG... ROUTINE, YEAH.
HMM. SEVENTEEN OVER NINE DESPITE EVERYTHING.
OULALA-WELL-ERM-YES-AH-GOOD-GOOD-LET'S-NOT-PANIC-NOW.
ROUTINE. TAKE THIS.
PAF
ROUTWOO!
PRESSURE.
PRESSURE.
PRESSURE.
HEY, LITTLE GUYS.
I'M DOWN A KINGDOM, SO WE'RE GOING TO GET MARRIED, AND THEN YOU'LL LEND ME YOUR ARMY TO GO CRUSH MY DAUGHTER.
ANY OBJECTION, 'GREAT WORRYWORT'?
YOU'RE KIDDING ME.
YOU GOT HERE TOO LATE, MOM.

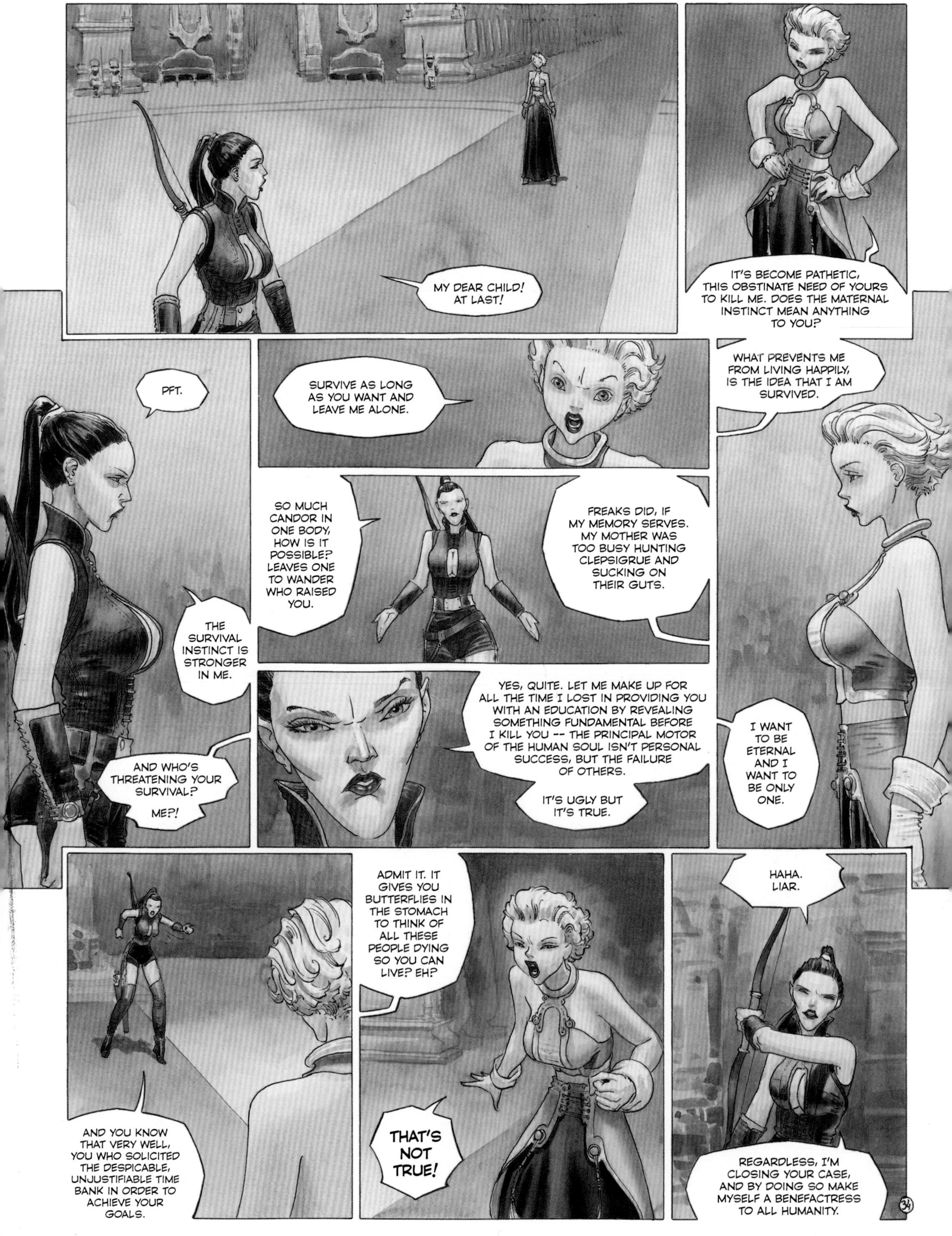
MY DEAR CHILD! AT LAST!
IT'S BECOME PATHETIC, THIS OBSTINATE NEED OF YOURS TO KILL ME. DOES THE MATERNAL INSTINCT MEAN ANYTHING TO YOU?
PFT.
SURVIVE AS LONG AS YOU WANT AND LEAVE ME ALONE.
WHAT PREVENTS ME FROM LIVING HAPPILY, IS THE IDEA THAT I AM SURVIVED.
SO MUCH CANDOR IN ONE BODY, HOW IS IT POSSIBLE? LEAVES ONE TO WANDER WHO RAISED YOU.
FREAKS DID, IF MY MEMORY SERVES. MY MOTHER WAS TOO BUSY HUNTING CLEPSIGRUE AND SUCKING ON THEIR GUTS.
THE SURVIVAL INSTINCT IS STRONGER IN ME.
AND WHO'S THREATENING YOUR SURVIVAL?
ME?!
YES, QUITE. LET ME MAKE UP FOR ALL THE TIME I LOST IN PROVIDING YOU WITH AN EDUCATION BY REVEALING SOMETHING FUNDAMENTAL BEFORE I KILL YOU -- THE PRINCIPAL MOTOR OF THE HUMAN SOUL ISN'T PERSONAL SUCCESS, BUT THE FAILURE OF OTHERS.
IT'S UGLY BUT IT'S TRUE.
I WANT TO BE ETERNAL AND I WANT TO BE ONLY ONE.
AND YOU KNOW THAT VERY WELL, YOU WHO SOLICITED THE DESPICABLE, UNJUSTIFIABLE TIME BANK IN ORDER TO ACHIEVE YOUR GOALS.
ADMIT IT. IT GIVES YOU BUTTERFLIES IN THE STOMACH TO THINK OF ALL THESE PEOPLE DYING SO YOU CAN LIVE? EH?
THAT'S NOT TRUE!
HAHA. LIAR.
REGARDLESS, I'M CLOSING YOUR CASE, AND BY DOING SO MAKE MYSELF A BENEFACTRESS TO ALL HUMANITY.
34

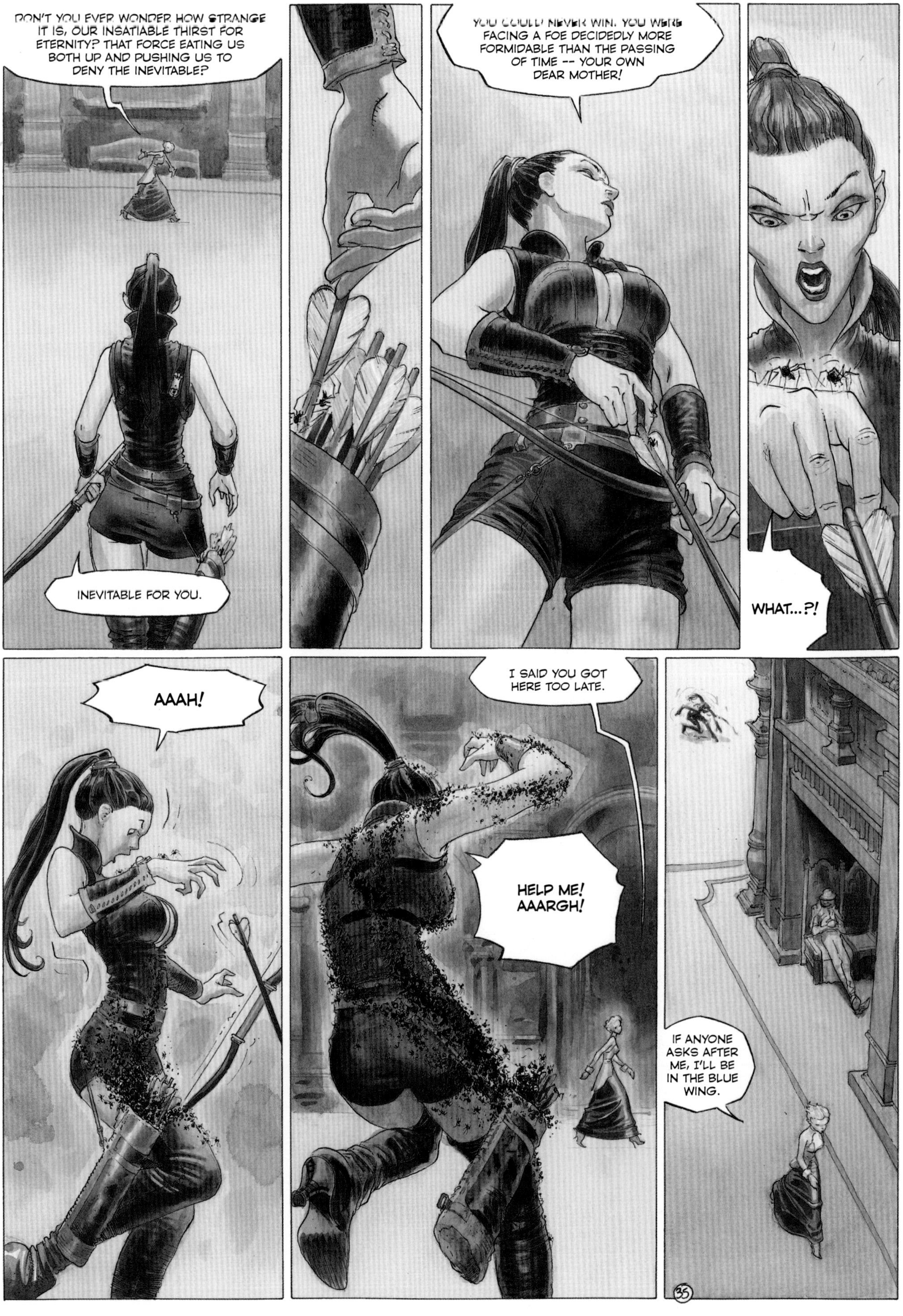
DON'T YOU EVER WONDER HOW STRANGE IT IS, OUR INSATIABLE THIRST FOR ETERNITY? THAT FORCE EATING US BOTH UP AND PUSHING US TO DENY THE INEVITABLE?
INEVITABLE FOR YOU.
YOU COULD NEVER WIN. YOU WERE FACING A FOE DECIDEDLY MORE FORMIDABLE THAN THE PASSING OF TIME -- YOUR OWN DEAR MOTHER!
WHAT...?!
AAAH!
I SAID YOU GOT HERE TOO LATE.
HELP ME! AAARGH!
IF ANYONE ASKS AFTER ME, I'LL BE IN THE BLUE WING.

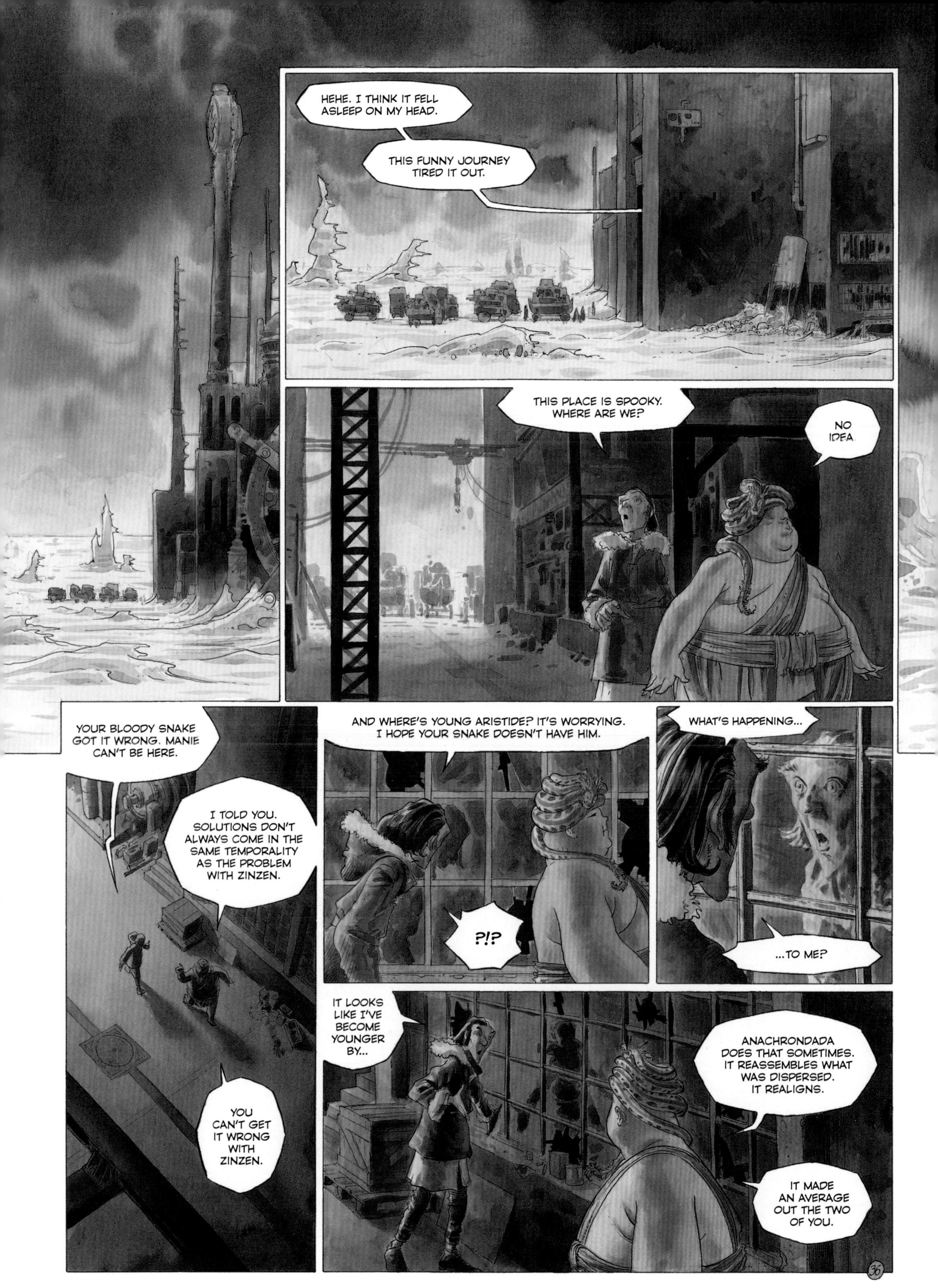
HEHE. I THINK IT FELL ASLEEP ON MY HEAD.
THIS FUNNY JOURNEY TIRED IT OUT.
THIS PLACE IS SPOOKY. WHERE ARE WE?
NO IDEA
YOUR BLOODY SNAKE GOT IT WRONG. MANIE CAN'T BE HERE.
I TOLD YOU. SOLUTIONS DON'T ALWAYS COME IN THE SAME TEMPORALITY AS THE PROBLEM WITH ZINZEN.
YOU CAN'T GET IT WRONG WITH ZINZEN.
AND WHERE'S YOUNG ARISTIDE? IT'S WORRYING. I HOPE YOUR SNAKE DOESN'T HAVE HIM.
?!?
WHAT'S HAPPENING...
...TO ME?
IT LOOKS LIKE I'VE BECOME YOUNGER BY...
ANACHRONDADA DOES THAT SOMETIMES. IT REASSEMBLES WHAT WAS DISPERSED. IT REALIGNS.
IT MADE AN AVERAGE OUT THE TWO OF YOU.

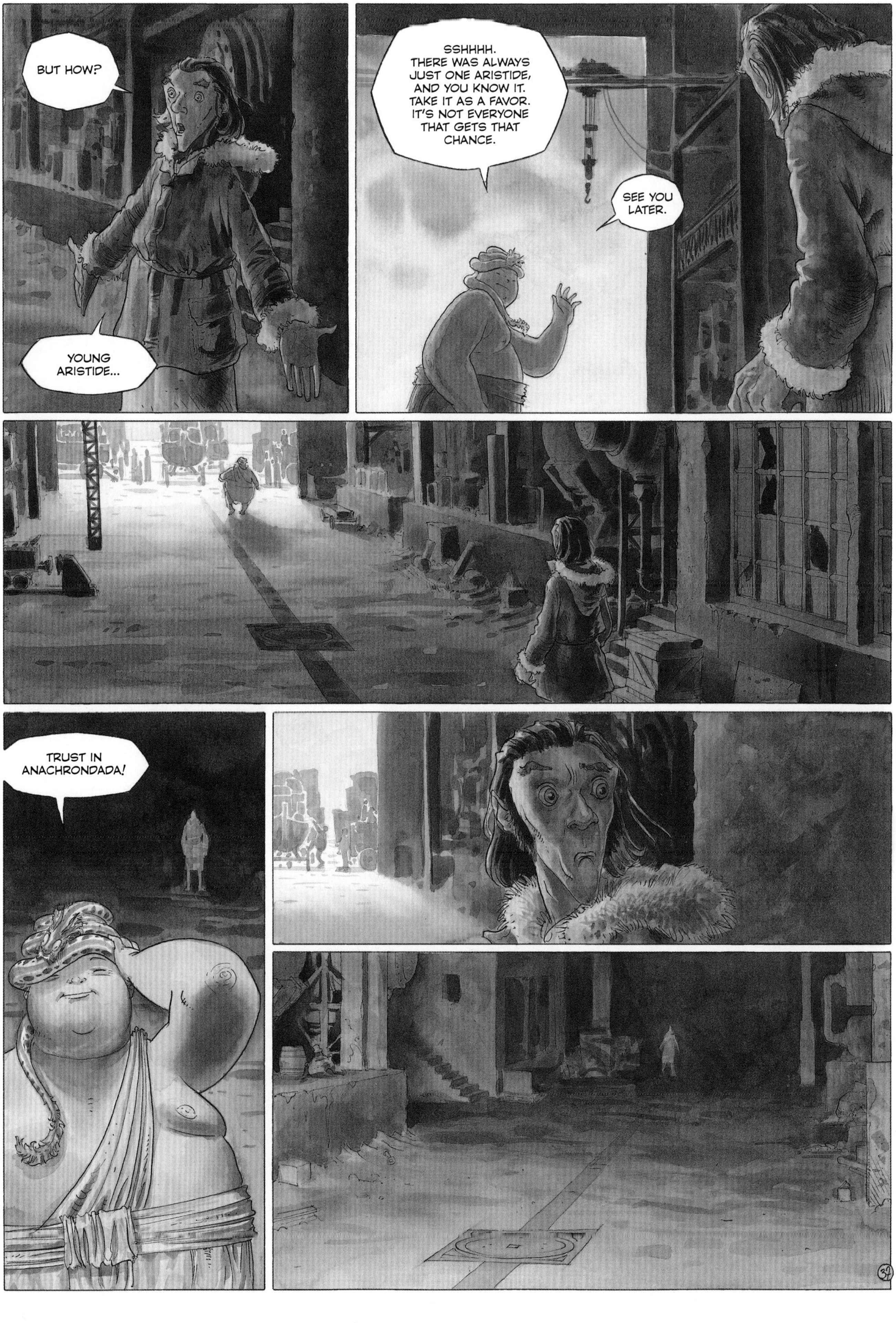
BUT HOW?
YOUNG ARISTIDE...
SSHHHH. THERE WAS ALWAYS JUST ONE ARISTIDE, AND YOU KNOW IT. TAKE IT AS A FAVOR. IT'S NOT EVERYONE THAT GETS THAT CHANCE.
SEE YOU LATER.
TRUST IN ANACHRONDADA!

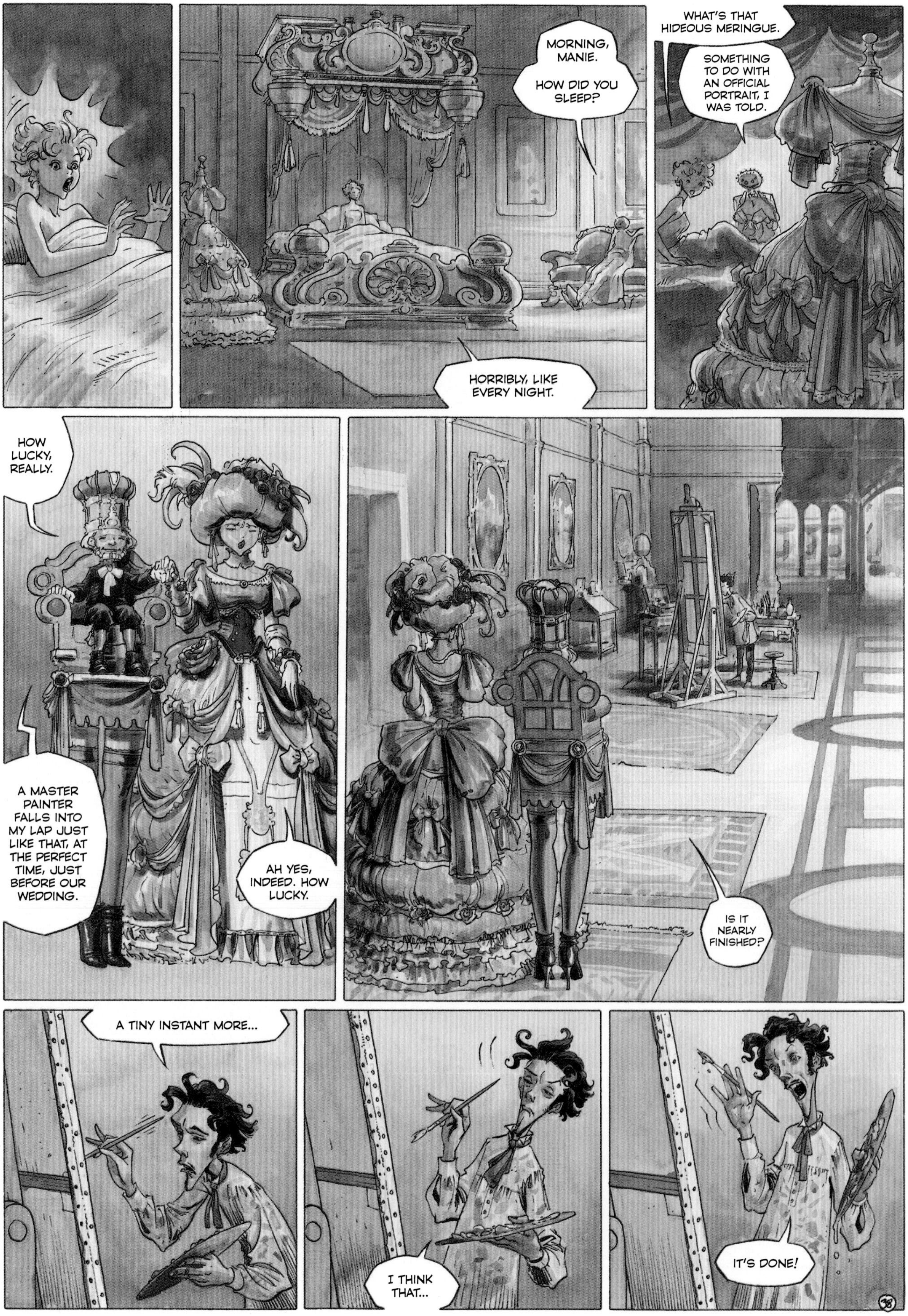
MORNING, MANIE.
HOW DID YOU SLEEP?
HORRIBLY, LIKE EVERY NIGHT.
WHAT'S THAT HIDEOUS MERINGUE.
SOMETHING TO DO WITH AN OFFICIAL PORTRAIT, I WAS TOLD.
HOW LUCKY, REALLY.
A MASTER PAINTER FALLS INTO MY LAP JUST LIKE THAT, AT THE PERFECT TIME, JUST BEFORE OUR WEDDING.
AH YES, INDEED. HOW LUCKY.
IS IT NEARLY FINISHED?
A TINY INSTANT MORE...
I THINK THAT...
IT'S DONE!

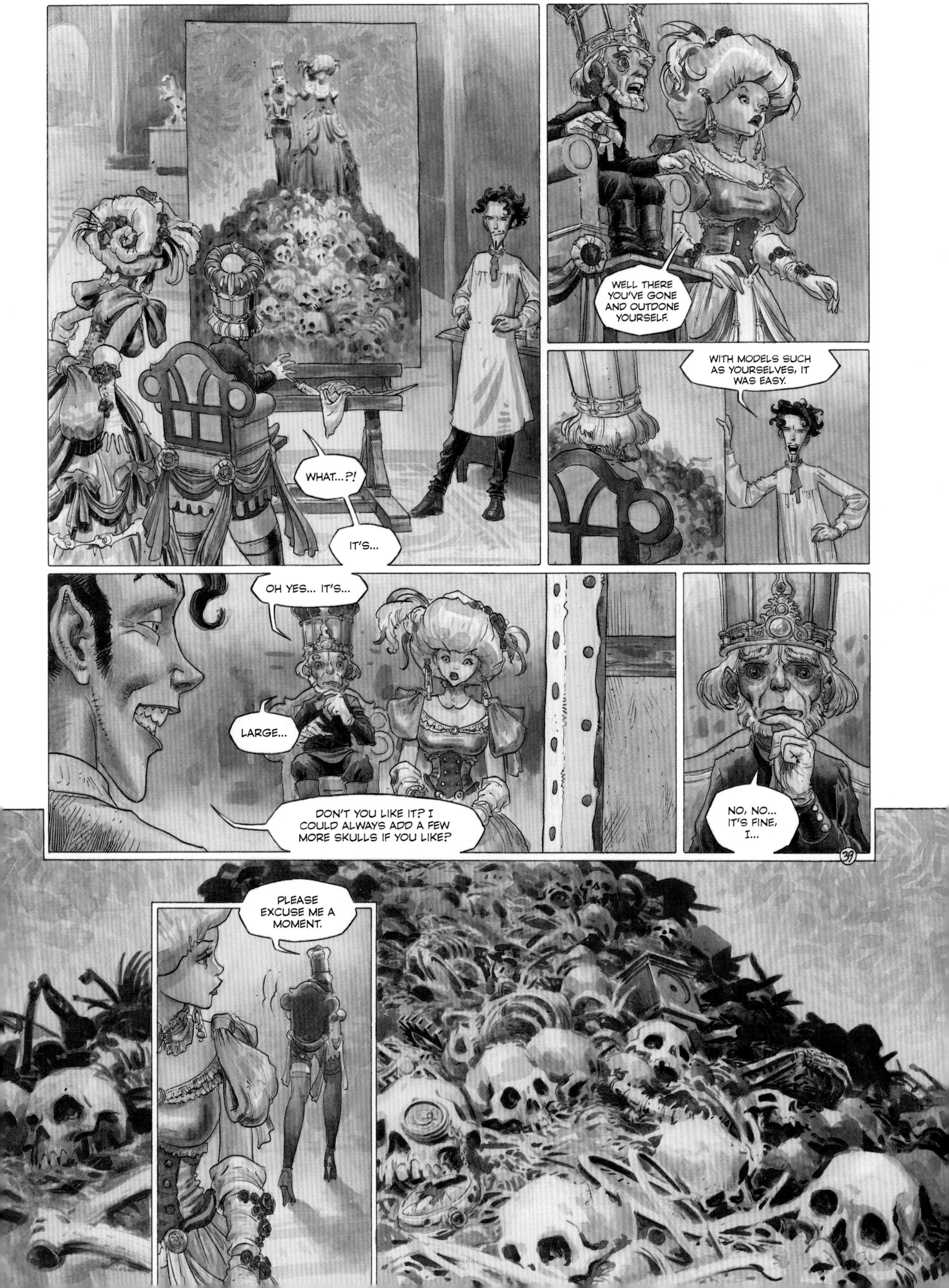
WHAT...?!
IT'S...
WELL THERE YOU'VE GONE AND OUTDONE YOURSELF.
WITH MODELS SUCH AS YOURSELVES, IT WAS EASY.
OH YES... IT'S...
LARGE...
DON'T YOU LIKE IT? I COULD ALWAYS ADD A FEW MORE SKULLS IF YOU LIKE?
NO, NO... IT'S FINE, I...
39
PLEASE EXCUSE ME A MOMENT.

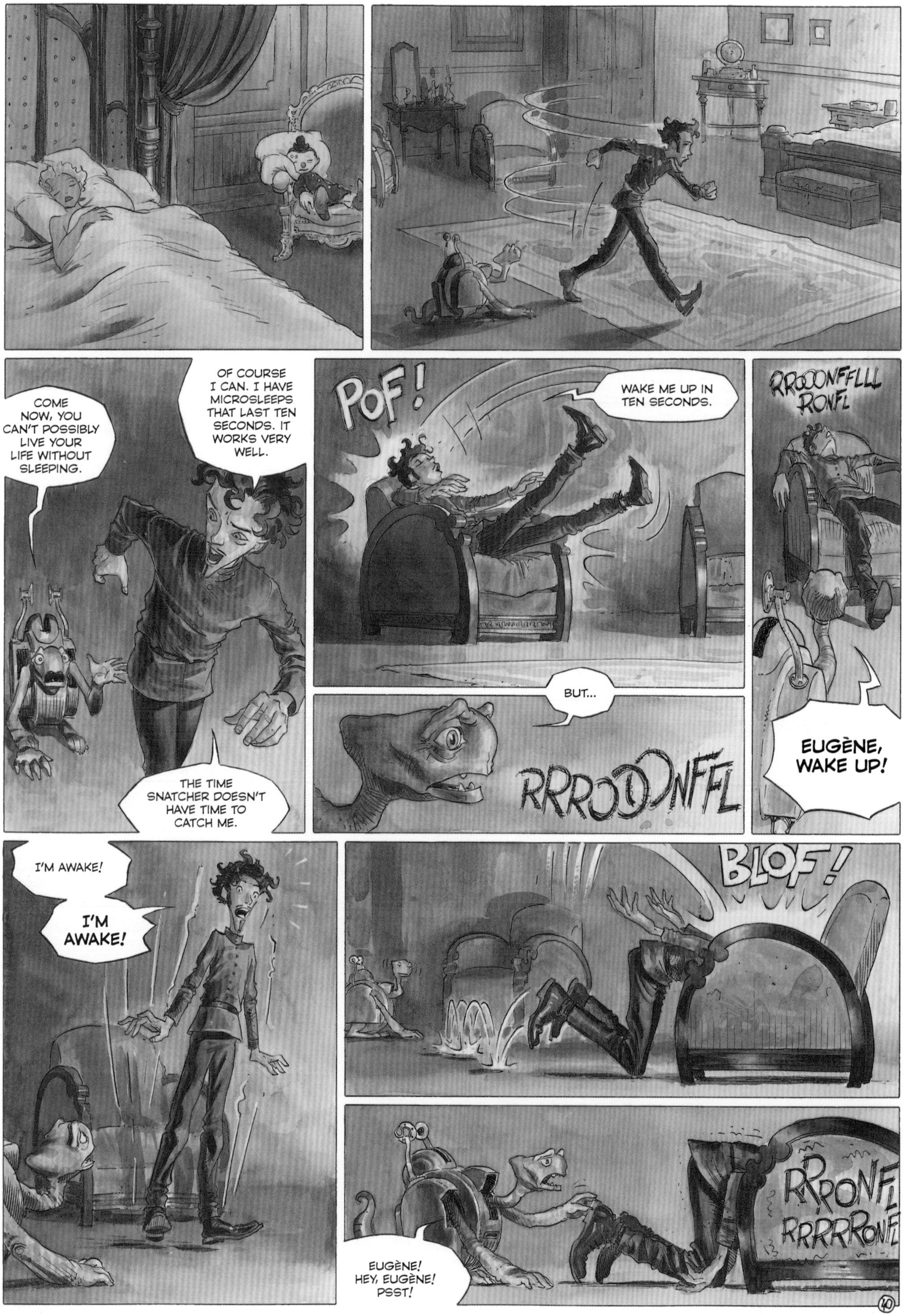
COME NOW, YOU CAN'T POSSIBLY LIVE YOUR LIFE WITHOUT SLEEPING.
OF COURSE I CAN. I HAVE MICROSLEEPS THAT LAST TEN SECONDS. IT WORKS VERY WELL.
THE TIME SNATCHER DOESN'T HAVE TIME TO CATCH ME.
POF!
WAKE ME UP IN TEN SECONDS.
BUT...
RRROOONFFL
RROOONFFLLL RONFL
EUGÈNE, WAKE UP!
I'M AWAKE!
I'M AWAKE!
BLOF!
RRRONFL RRRRRONFL
EUGÈNE! HEY, EUGÈNE! PSST!

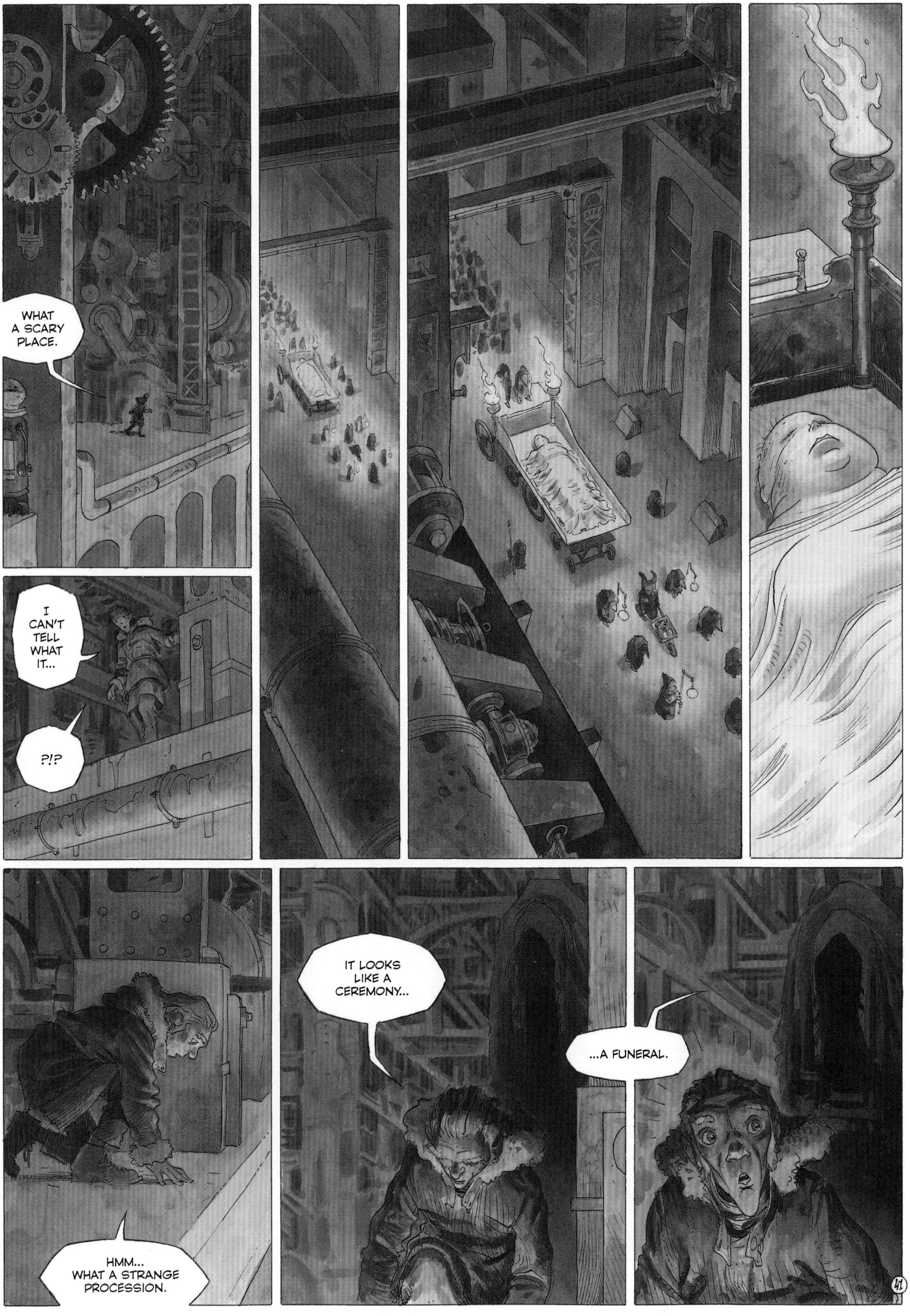
WHAT A SCARY PLACE.
I CAN'T TELL WHAT IT...
?!?
HMM... WHAT A STRANGE PROCESSION.
IT LOOKS LIKE A CEREMONY...
...A FUNERAL.

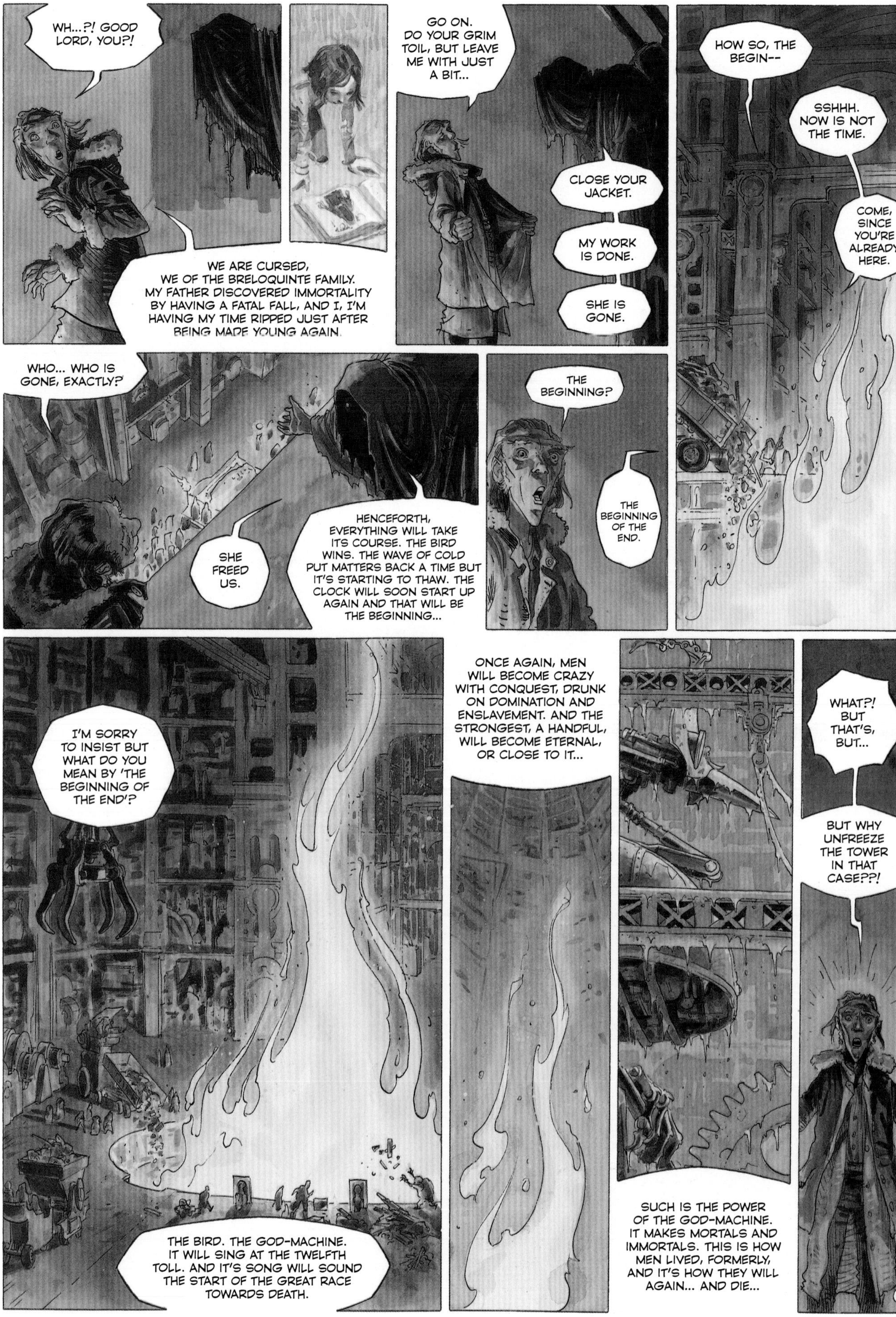
WH...?! GOOD LORD, YOU?!
WE ARE CURSED, WE OF THE BRELOQUINTE FAMILY. MY FATHER DISCOVERED IMMORTALITY BY HAVING A FATAL FALL, AND I, I'M HAVING MY TIME RIPPED JUST AFTER BEING MADE YOUNG AGAIN.
GO ON. DO YOUR GRIM TOIL, BUT LEAVE ME WITH JUST A BIT...
CLOSE YOUR JACKET.
MY WORK IS DONE.
SHE IS GONE.
HOW SO, THE BEGIN--
SSHHH. NOW IS NOT THE TIME.
COME, SINCE YOU'RE ALREADY HERE.
WHO... WHO IS GONE, EXACTLY?
SHE FREED US.
HENCEFORTH, EVERYTHING WILL TAKE ITS COURSE. THE BIRD WINS. THE WAVE OF COLD PUT MATTERS BACK A TIME BUT IT'S STARTING TO THAW. THE CLOCK WILL SOON START UP AGAIN AND THAT WILL BE THE BEGINNING...
THE BEGINNING?
THE BEGINNING OF THE END.
I'M SORRY TO INSIST BUT WHAT DO YOU MEAN BY 'THE BEGINNING OF THE END'?
THE BIRD. THE GOD-MACHINE. IT WILL SING AT THE TWELFTH TOLL. AND IT'S SONG WILL SOUND THE START OF THE GREAT RACE TOWARDS DEATH.
ONCE AGAIN, MEN WILL BECOME CRAZY WITH CONQUEST, DRUNK ON DOMINATION AND ENSLAVEMENT. AND THE STRONGEST, A HANDFUL, WILL BECOME ETERNAL, OR CLOSE TO IT...
SUCH IS THE POWER OF THE GOD-MACHINE. IT MAKES MORTALS AND IMMORTALS. THIS IS HOW MEN LIVED, FORMERLY, AND IT'S HOW THEY WILL AGAIN... AND DIE...
WHAT?! BUT THAT'S, BUT...
BUT WHY UNFREEZE THE TOWER IN THAT CASE??!
42

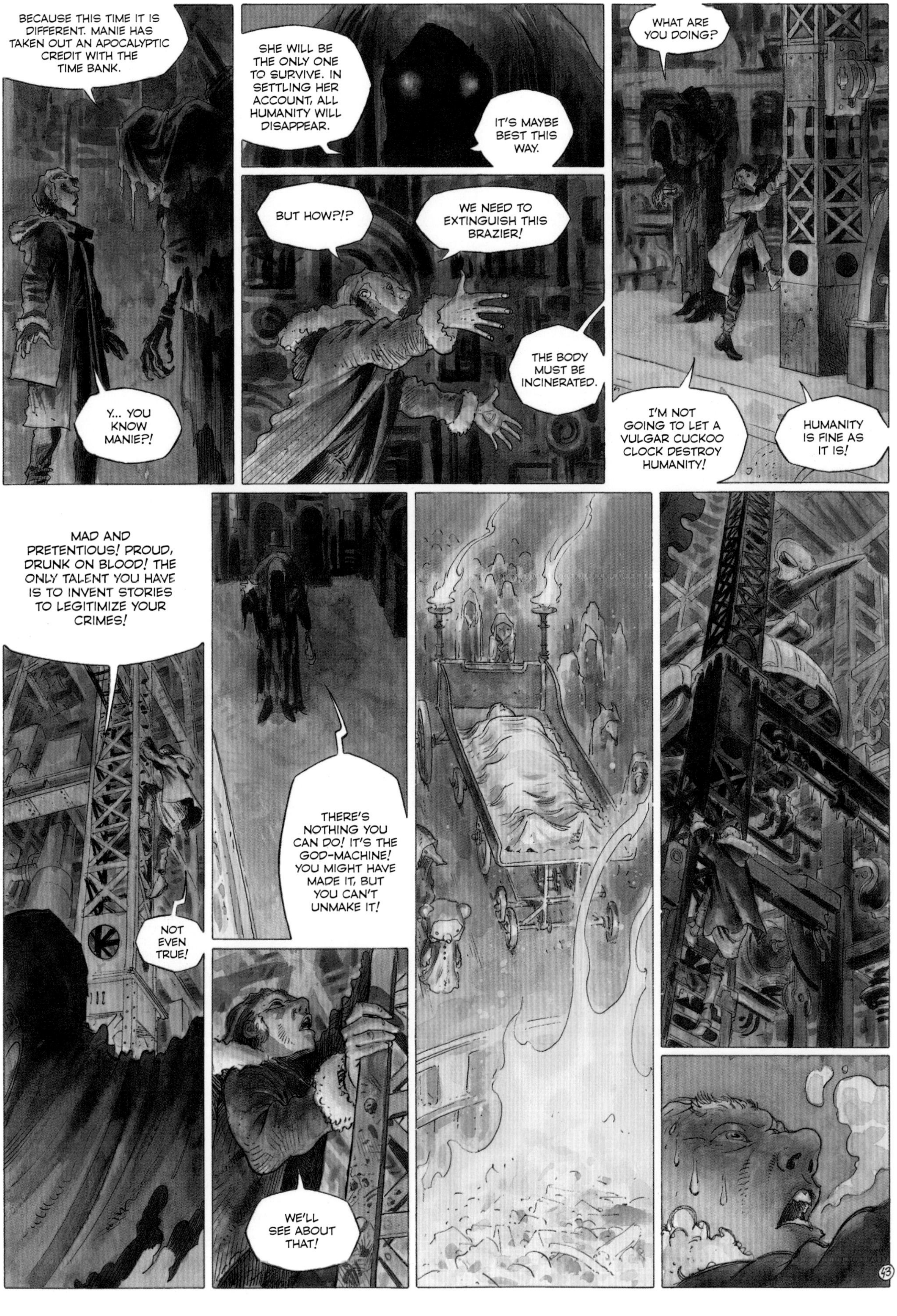
BECAUSE THIS TIME IT IS DIFFERENT. MANIE HAS TAKEN OUT AN APOCALYPTIC CREDIT WITH THE TIME BANK.
Y... YOU KNOW MANIE?!
SHE WILL BE THE ONLY ONE TO SURVIVE. IN SETTLING HER ACCOUNT, ALL HUMANITY WILL DISAPPEAR.
IT'S MAYBE BEST THIS WAY.
BUT HOW?!?
WE NEED TO EXTINGUISH THIS BRAZIER!
THE BODY MUST BE INCINERATED.
WHAT ARE YOU DOING?
I'M NOT GOING TO LET A VULGAR CUCKOO CLOCK DESTROY HUMANITY!
HUMANITY IS FINE AS IT IS!
MAD AND PRETENTIOUS! PROUD, DRUNK ON BLOOD! THE ONLY TALENT YOU HAVE IS TO INVENT STORIES TO LEGITIMIZE YOUR CRIMES!
NOT EVEN TRUE!
THERE'S NOTHING YOU CAN DO! IT'S THE GOD-MACHINE! YOU MIGHT HAVE MADE IT, BUT YOU CAN'T UNMAKE IT!
WE'LL SEE ABOUT THAT!

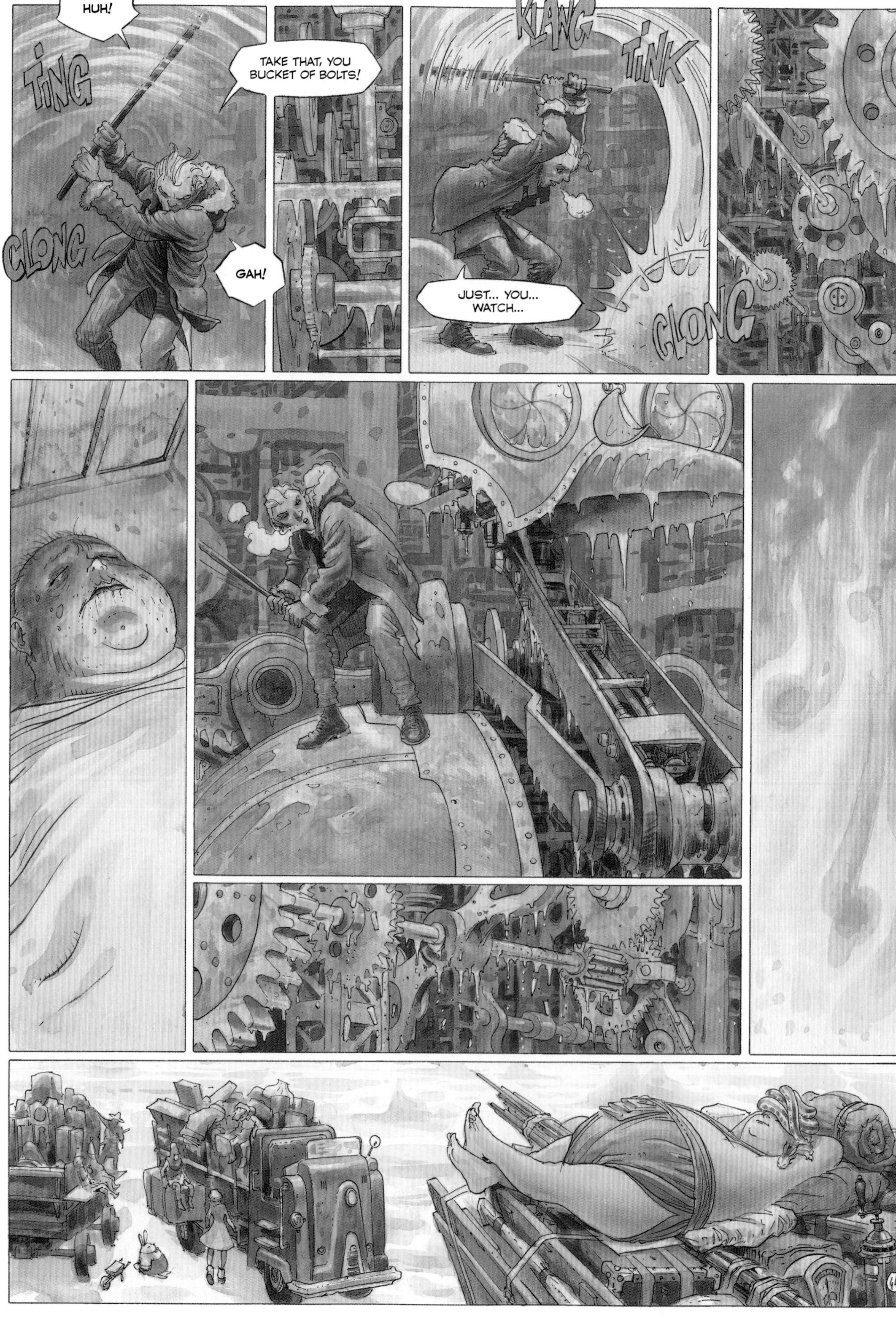
HUH!
TING
CLONG
GAH!
TAKE THAT, YOU BUCKET OF BOLTS!
KLANG
TINK
JUST... YOU... WATCH...
CLONG
44

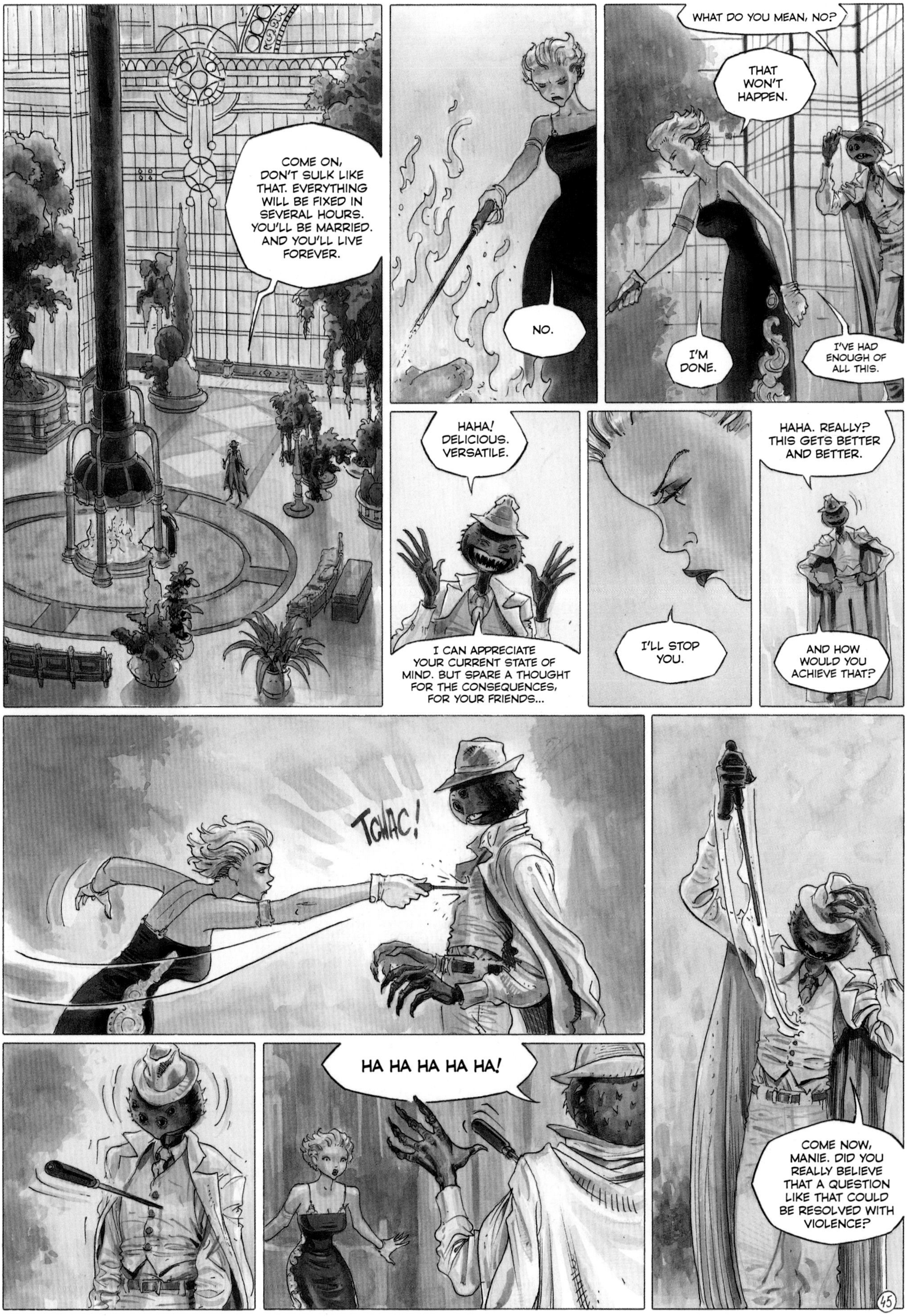
COME ON, DON'T SULK LIKE THAT. EVERYTHING WILL BE FIXED IN SEVERAL HOURS. YOU'LL BE MARRIED. AND YOU'LL LIVE FOREVER.
NO.
WHAT DO YOU MEAN, NO?
THAT WON'T HAPPEN.
I'M DONE.
I'VE HAD ENOUGH OF ALL THIS.
HAHA! DELICIOUS. VERSATILE.
I CAN APPRECIATE YOUR CURRENT STATE OF MIND. BUT SPARE A THOUGHT FOR THE CONSEQUENCES, FOR YOUR FRIENDS...
I'LL STOP YOU.
HAHA. REALLY? THIS GETS BETTER AND BETTER.
AND HOW WOULD YOU ACHIEVE THAT?
TCHAC!
HA HA HA HA HA!
COME NOW, MANIE. DID YOU REALLY BELIEVE THAT A QUESTION LIKE THAT COULD BE RESOLVED WITH VIOLENCE?
45

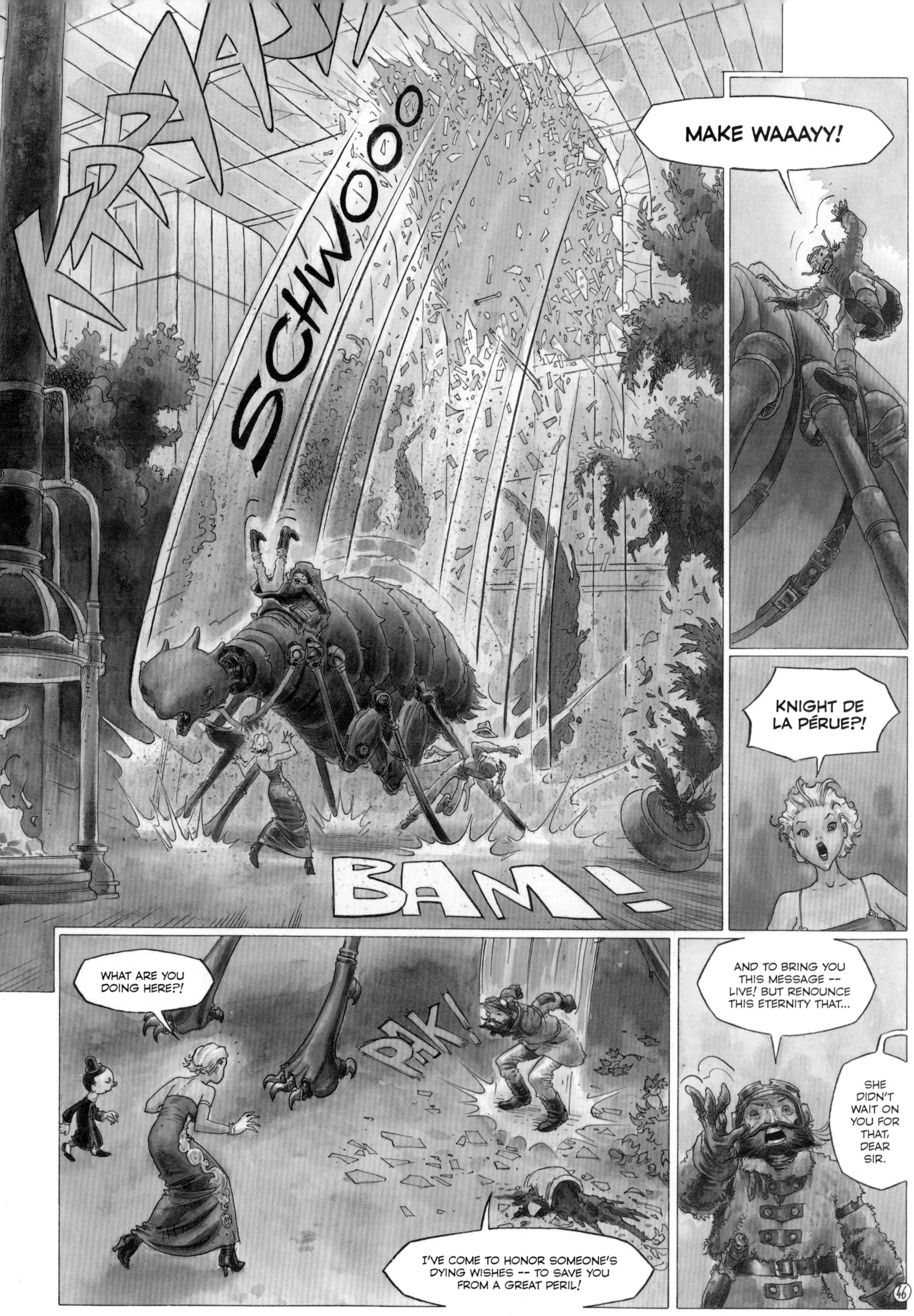
KRAAAAK!
SCHWOOO
BAM!
MAKE WAAAYY!
KNIGHT DE LA PÉRUE?!
WHAT ARE YOU DOING HERE?!
PAK!
I'VE COME TO HONOR SOMEONE'S DYING WISHES -- TO SAVE YOU FROM A GREAT PERIL!
AND TO BRING YOU THIS MESSAGE -- LIVE! BUT RENOUNCE THIS ETERNITY THAT...
SHE DIDN'T WAIT ON YOU FOR THAT, DEAR SIR.

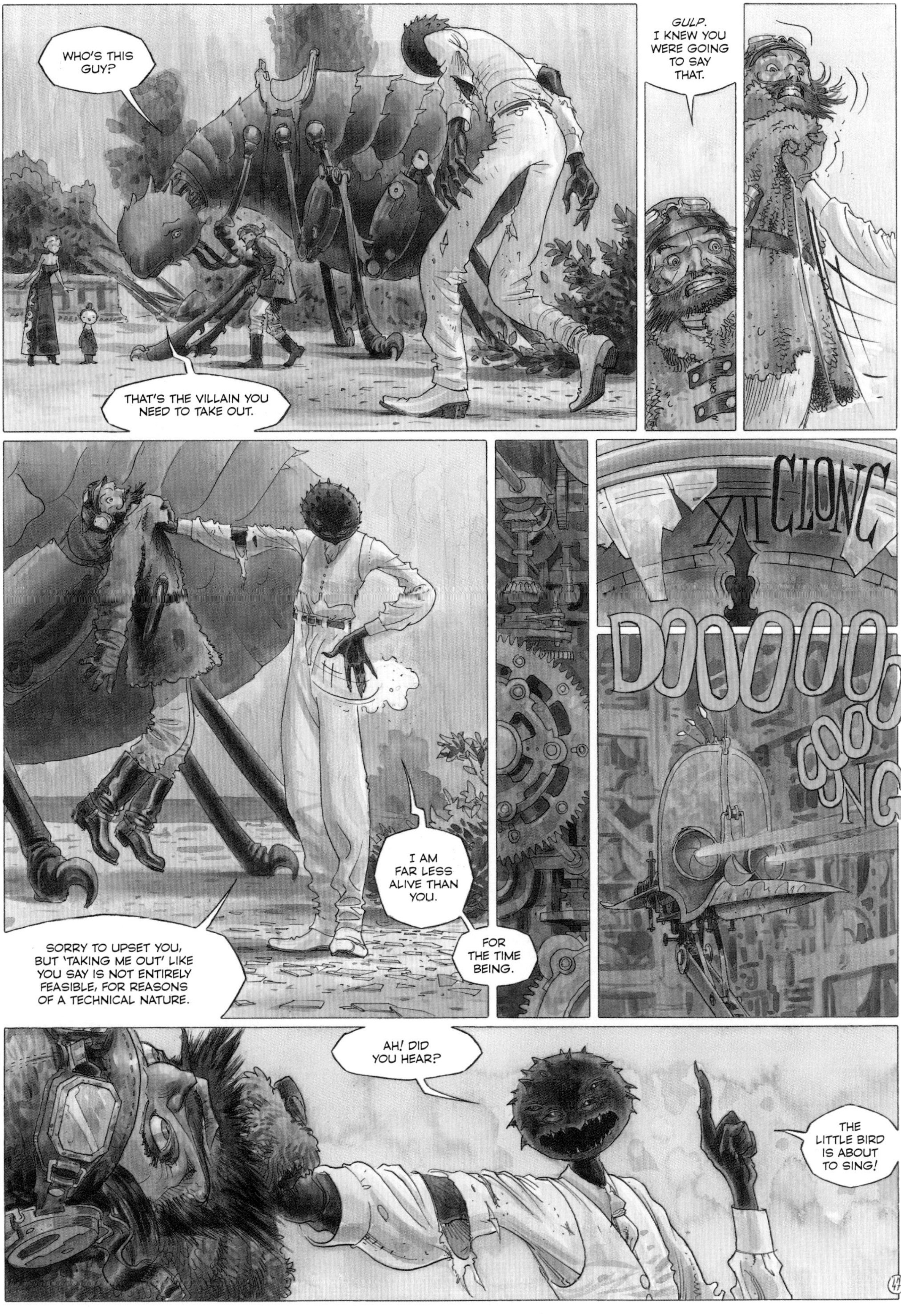
WHO'S THIS GUY?
THAT'S THE VILLAIN YOU NEED TO TAKE OUT.
GULP. I KNEW YOU WERE GOING TO SAY THAT.
I AM FAR LESS ALIVE THAN YOU.
FOR THE TIME BEING.
SORRY TO UPSET YOU, BUT 'TAKING ME OUT' LIKE YOU SAY IS NOT ENTIRELY FEASIBLE, FOR REASONS OF A TECHNICAL NATURE.
XII
CLONG
DOOOOOOOOOOONG
AH! DID YOU HEAR?
THE LITTLE BIRD IS ABOUT TO SING!
47

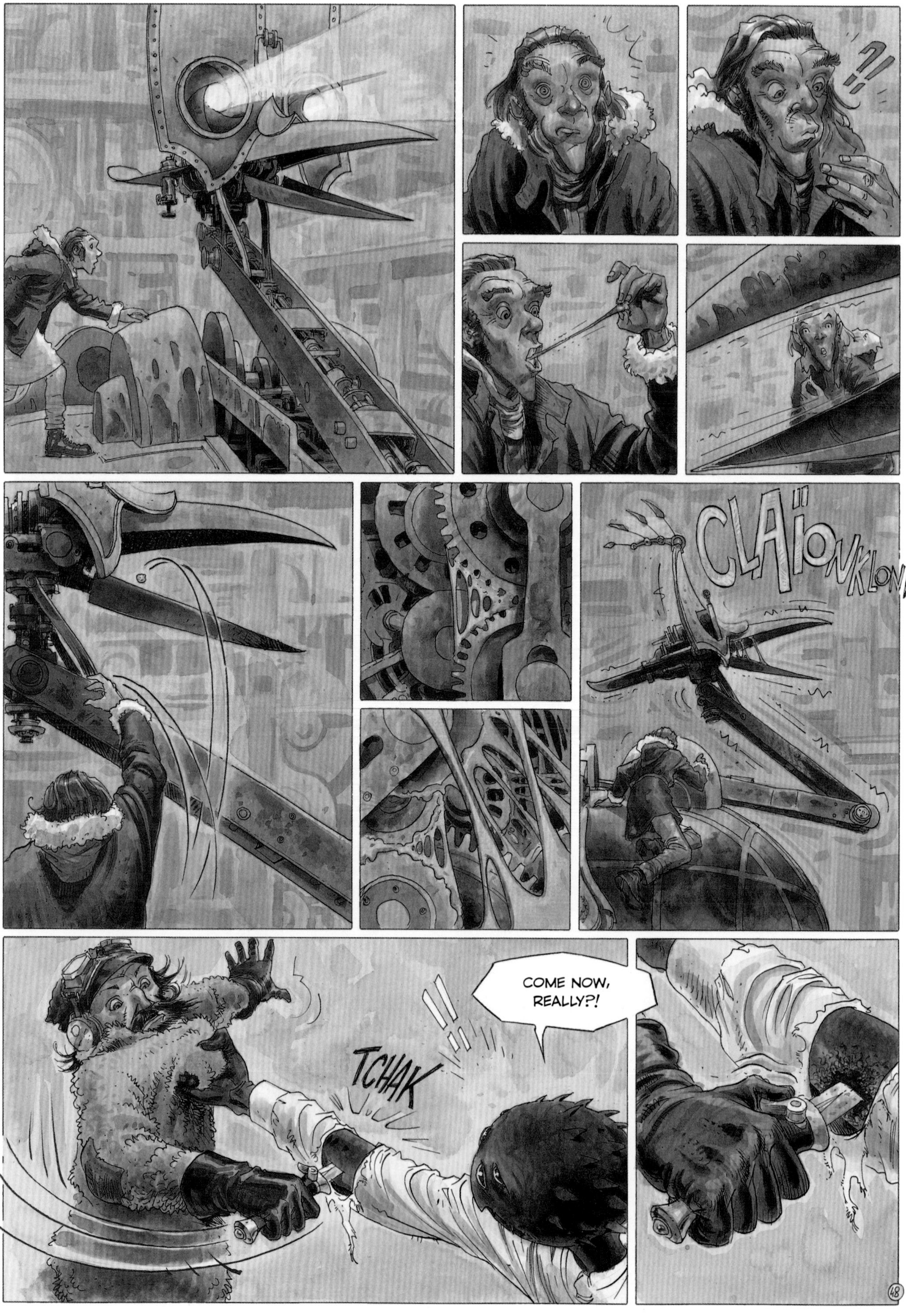
?!
CLAÏONKKLONK
COME NOW, REALLY?!
!!
TCHAK

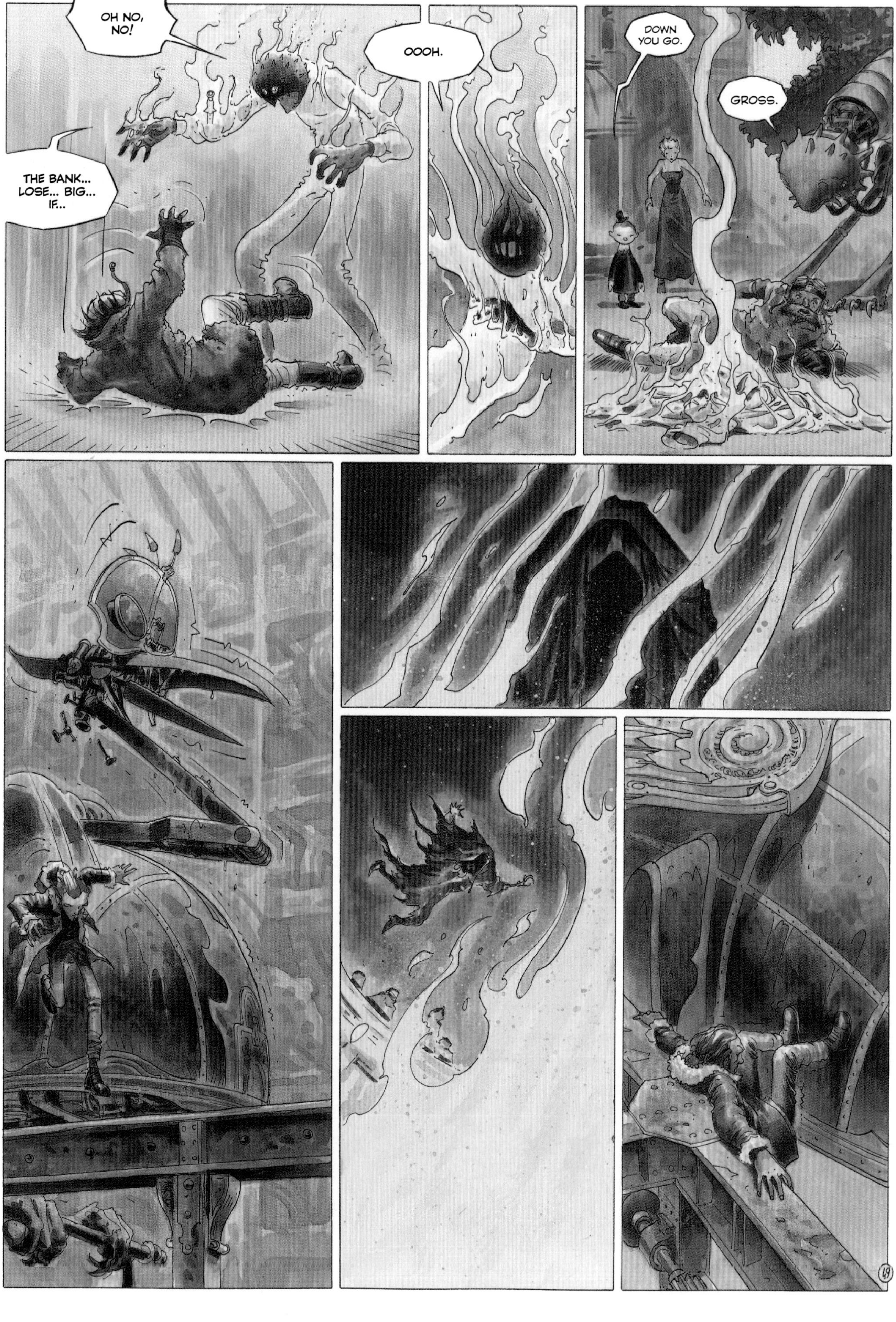
OH NO, NO!
THE BANK... LOSE... BIG... IF...
OOOH.
DOWN YOU GO.
GROSS.

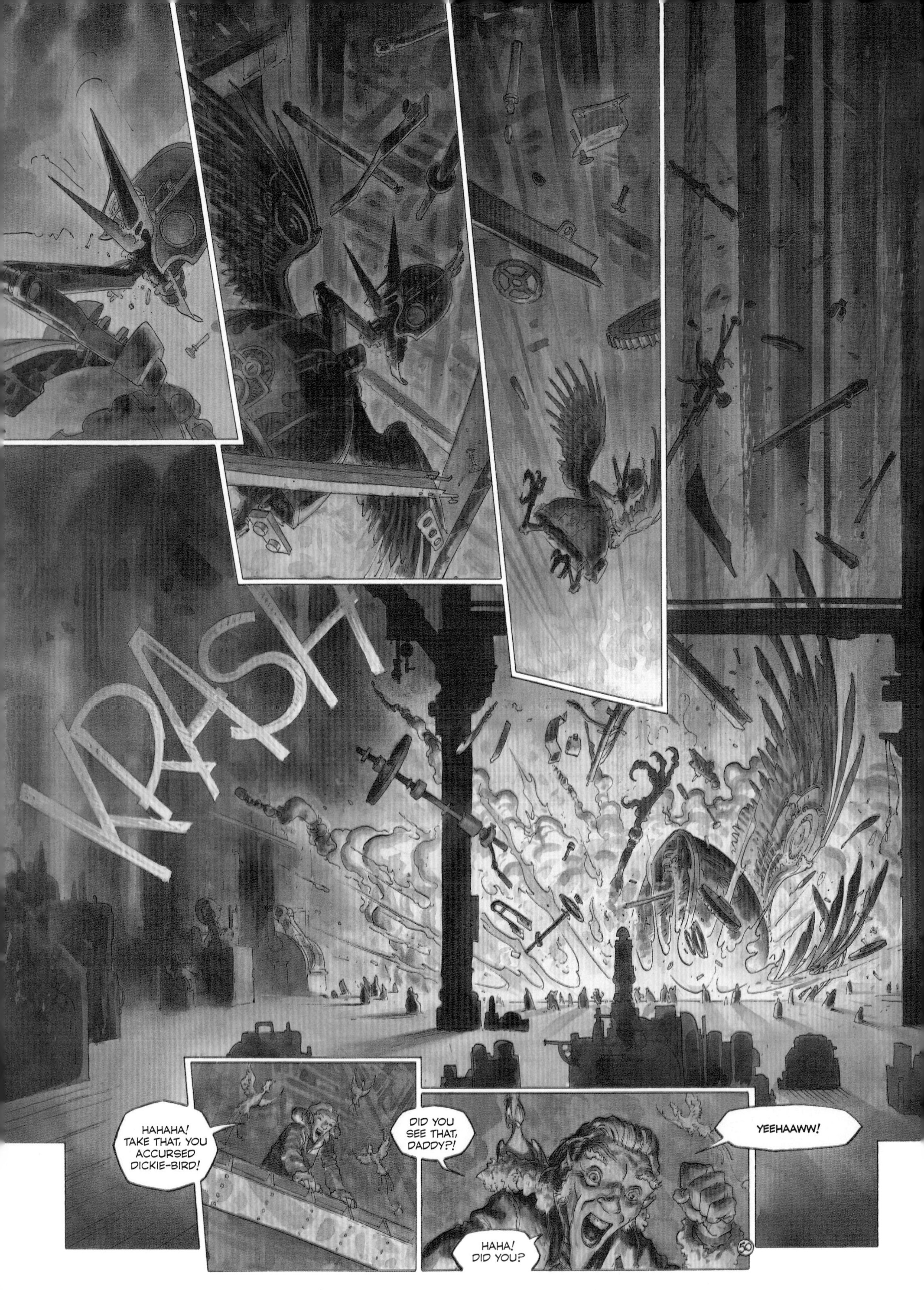
KRASH
HAHAHA! TAKE THAT, YOU ACCURSED DICKIE-BIRD!
DID YOU SEE THAT, DADDY?!
YEEHAAWW!
HAHA! DID YOU?

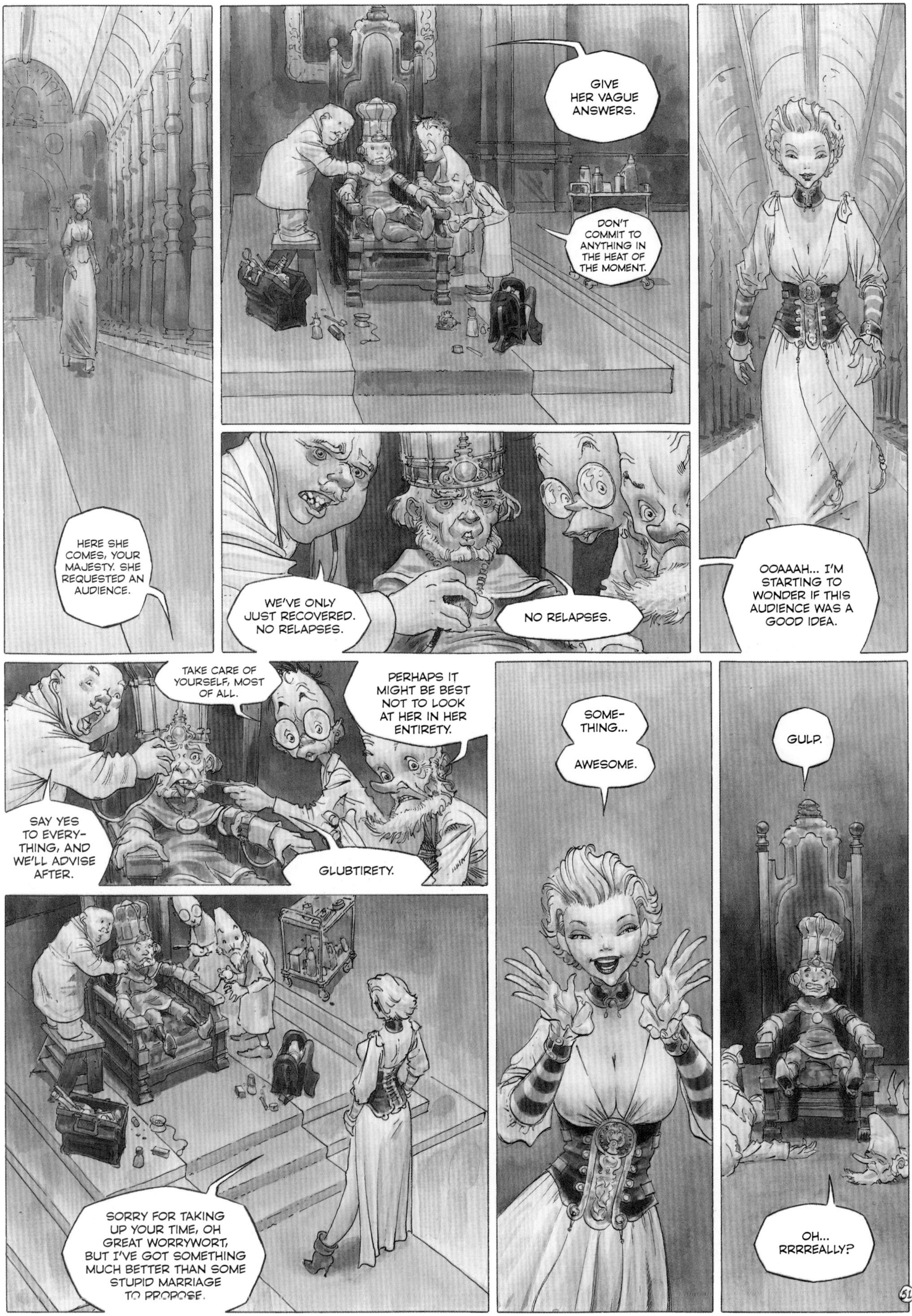
GIVE HER VAGUE ANSWERS.
DON'T COMMIT TO ANYTHING IN THE HEAT OF THE MOMENT.
HERE SHE COMES, YOUR MAJESTY. SHE REQUESTED AN AUDIENCE.
WE'VE ONLY JUST RECOVERED. NO RELAPSES.
NO RELAPSES.
OOAAAH... I'M STARTING TO WONDER IF THIS AUDIENCE WAS A GOOD IDEA.
TAKE CARE OF YOURSELF, MOST OF ALL.
PERHAPS IT MIGHT BE BEST NOT TO LOOK AT HER IN HER ENTIRETY.
SAY YES TO EVERY-THING, AND WE'LL ADVISE AFTER.
GLUBTIRETY.
SOME-THING...
AWESOME.
GULP.
SORRY FOR TAKING UP YOUR TIME, OH GREAT WORRYWORT, BUT I'VE GOT SOMETHING MUCH BETTER THAN SOME STUPID MARRIAGE TO PROPOSE.
OH... RRRREALLY?

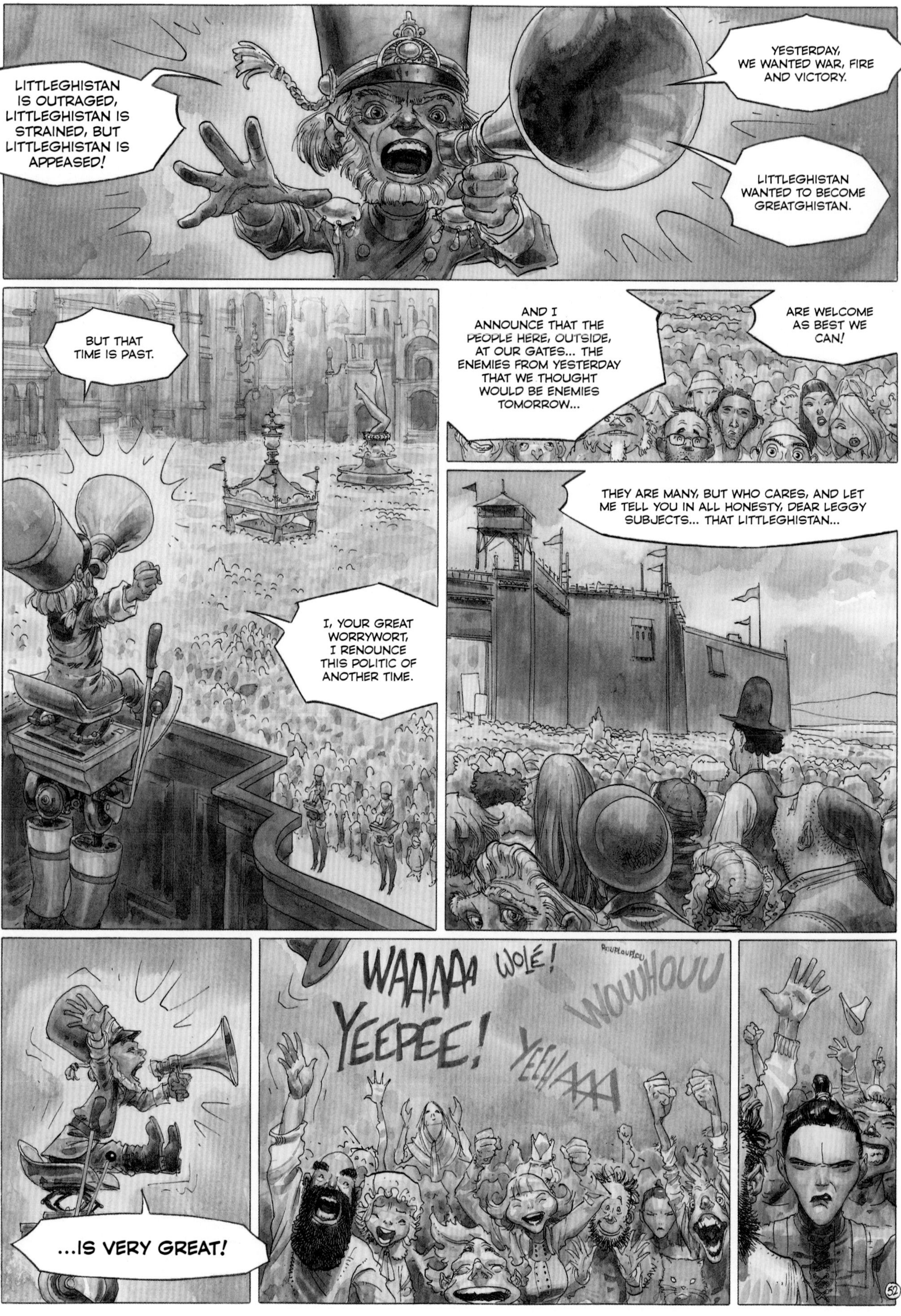
LITTLEGHISTAN IS OUTRAGED, LITTLEGHISTAN IS STRAINED, BUT LITTLEGHISTAN IS APPEASED!
YESTERDAY, WE WANTED WAR, FIRE AND VICTORY.
LITTLEGHISTAN WANTED TO BECOME GREATGHISTAN.
BUT THAT TIME IS PAST.
I, YOUR GREAT WORRYWORT, I RENOUNCE THIS POLITIC OF ANOTHER TIME.
AND I ANNOUNCE THAT THE PEOPLE HERE, OUTSIDE, AT OUR GATES... THE ENEMIES FROM YESTERDAY THAT WE THOUGHT WOULD BE ENEMIES TOMORROW...
ARE WELCOME AS BEST WE CAN!
THEY ARE MANY, BUT WHO CARES, AND LET ME TELL YOU IN ALL HONESTY, DEAR LEGGY SUBJECTS... THAT LITTLEGHISTAN...
...IS VERY GREAT!
WAAAAA
WOLÉ!
WOUHOUU
YEEPEE!
YEEHAAA

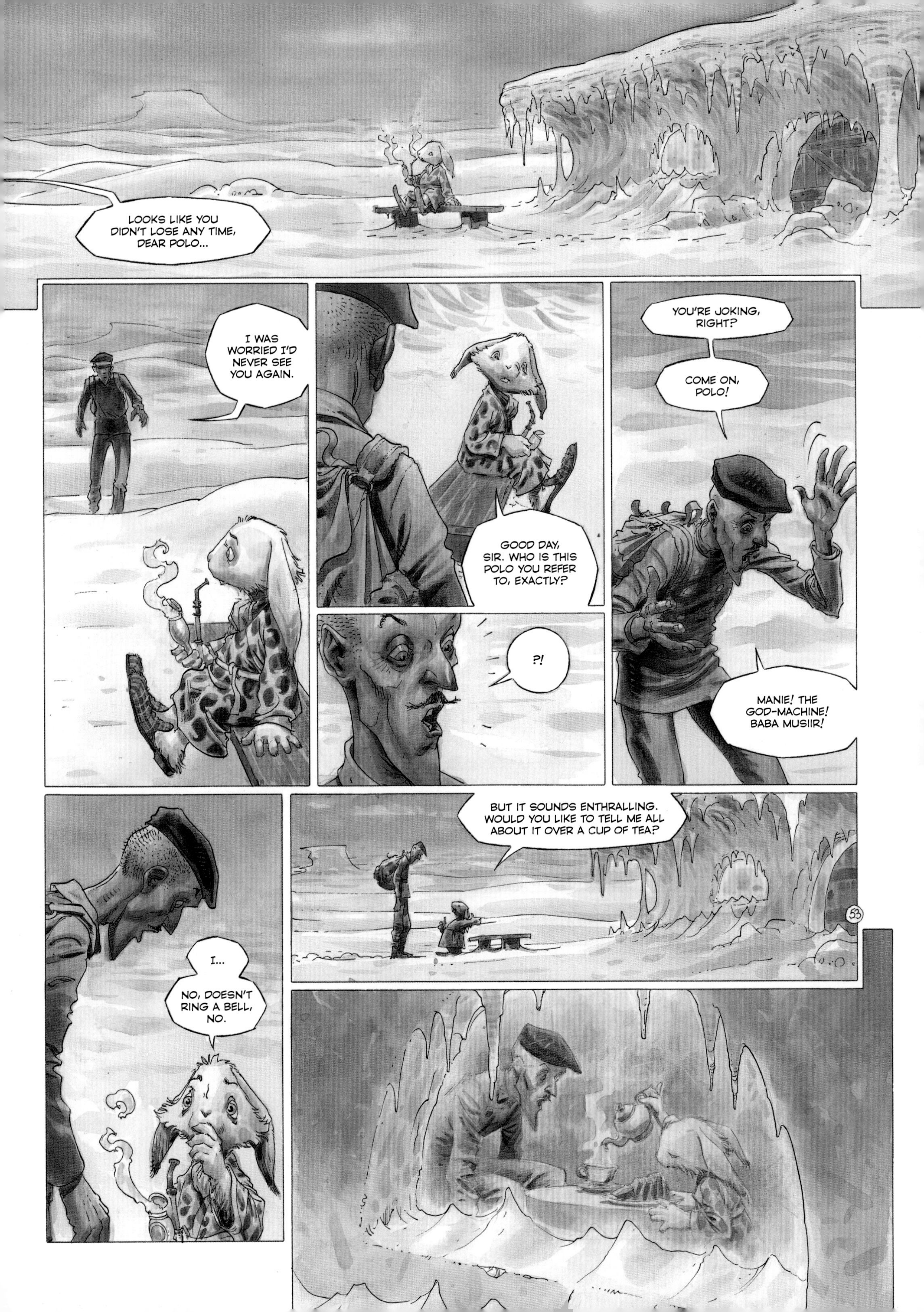
LOOKS LIKE YOU DIDN'T LOSE ANY TIME, DEAR POLO...
I WAS WORRIED I'D NEVER SEE YOU AGAIN.
GOOD DAY, SIR. WHO IS THIS POLO YOU REFER TO, EXACTLY?
?!
YOU'RE JOKING, RIGHT?
COME ON, POLO!
MANIE! THE GOD-MACHINE! BABA MUSIIR!
I...
NO, DOESN'T RING A BELL, NO.
BUT IT SOUNDS ENTHRALLING. WOULD YOU LIKE TO TELL ME ALL ABOUT IT OVER A CUP OF TEA?
53

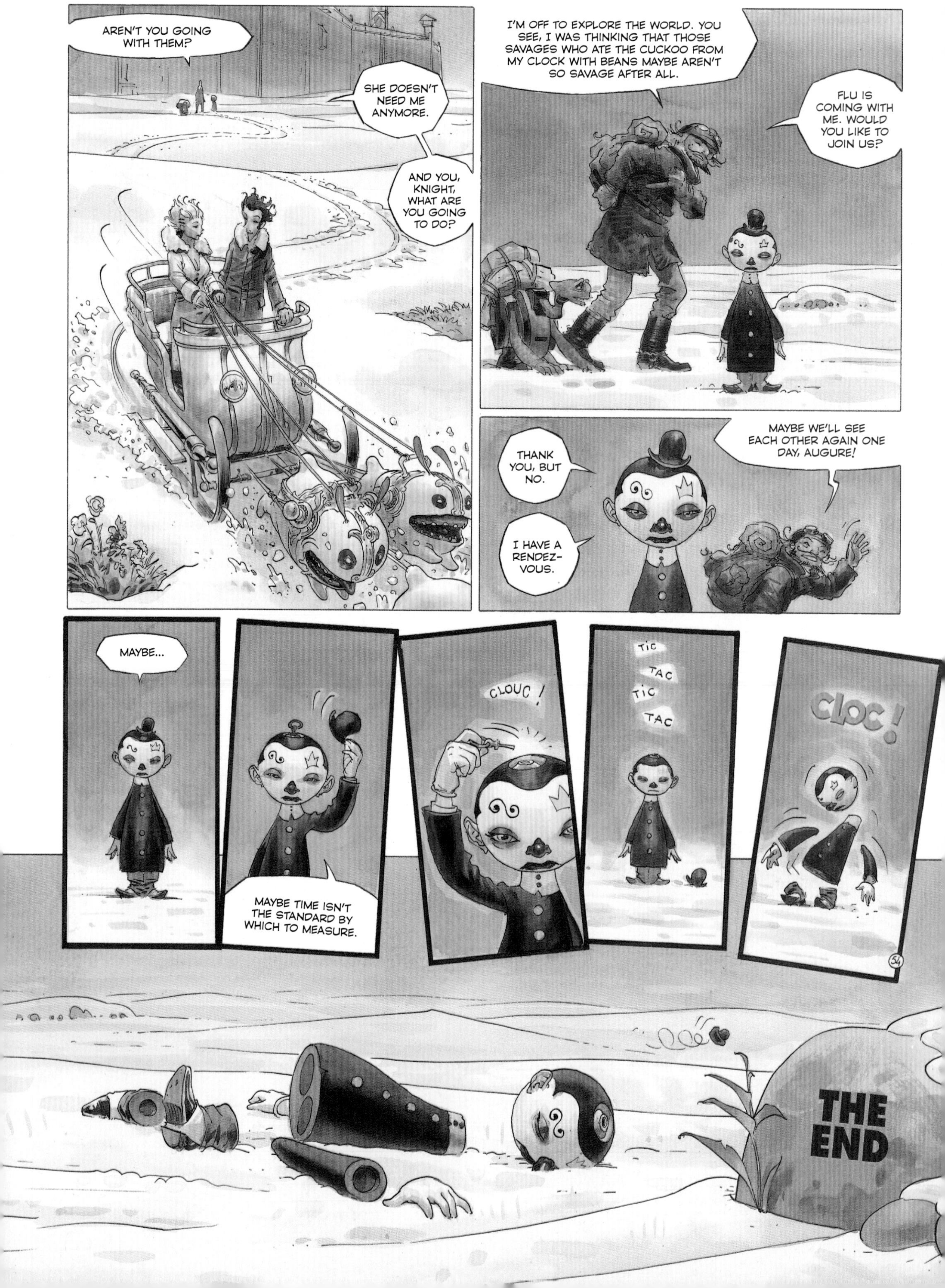
AREN'T YOU GOING WITH THEM?
SHE DOESN'T NEED ME ANYMORE.
AND YOU, KNIGHT, WHAT ARE YOU GOING TO DO?
I'M OFF TO EXPLORE THE WORLD. YOU SEE, I WAS THINKING THAT THOSE SAVAGES WHO ATE THE CUCKOO FROM MY CLOCK WITH BEANS MAYBE AREN'T SO SAVAGE AFTER ALL.
FLU IS COMING WITH ME. WOULD YOU LIKE TO JOIN US?
THANK YOU, BUT NO.
I HAVE A RENDEZ-VOUS.
MAYBE WE'LL SEE EACH OTHER AGAIN ONE DAY, AUGURE!
MAYBE...
MAYBE TIME ISN'T THE STANDARD BY WHICH TO MEASURE.
CLOUC !
TIC
TAC
TIC
TAC
CLOC !
54
THE END

Covers Gallery

AZIMUT

BOOK ONE

ART BY JEAN-BAPTISTE ANDREAE

Covers

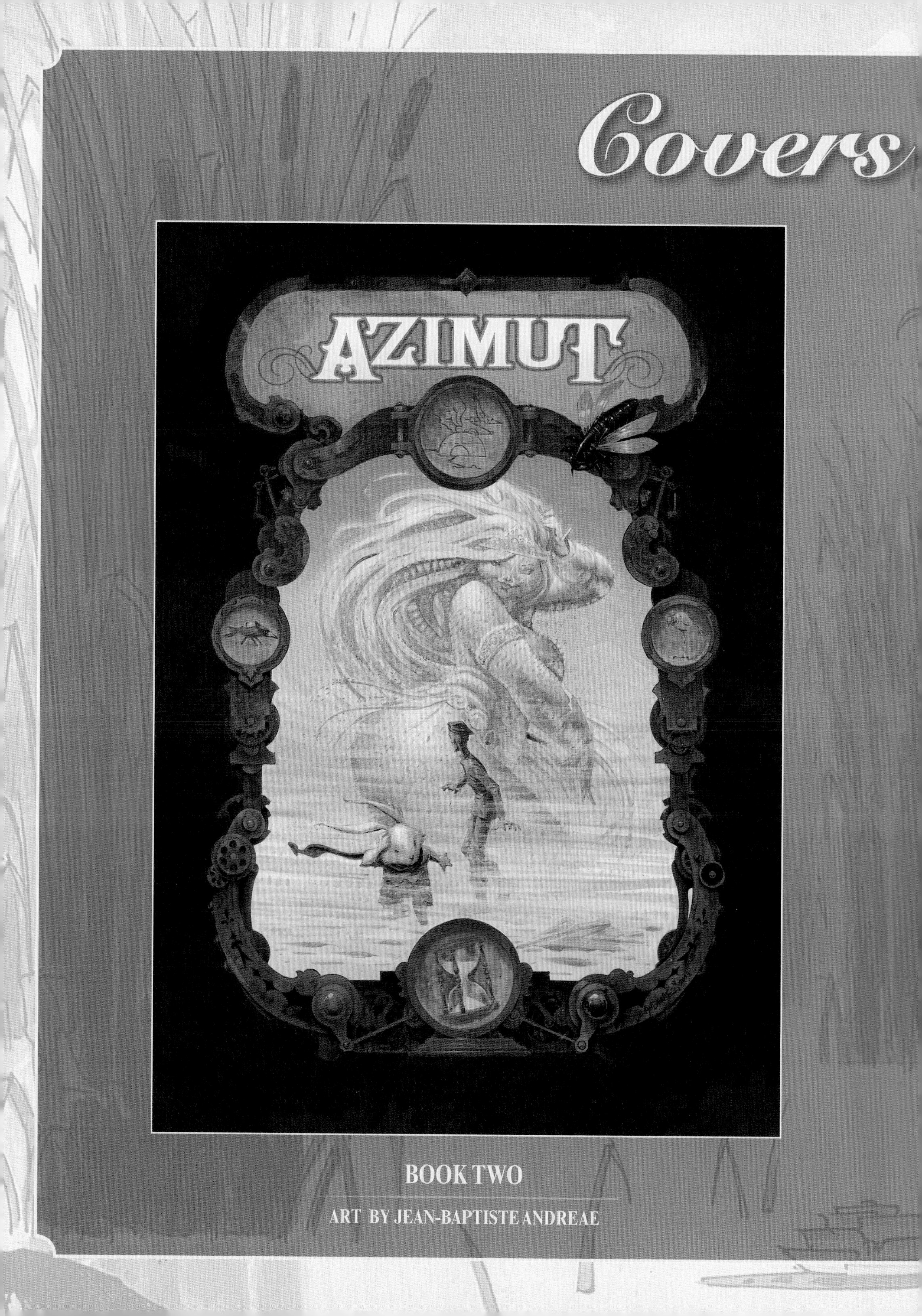
AZIMUT

BOOK TWO

ART BY JEAN-BAPTISTE ANDREAE

Gallery

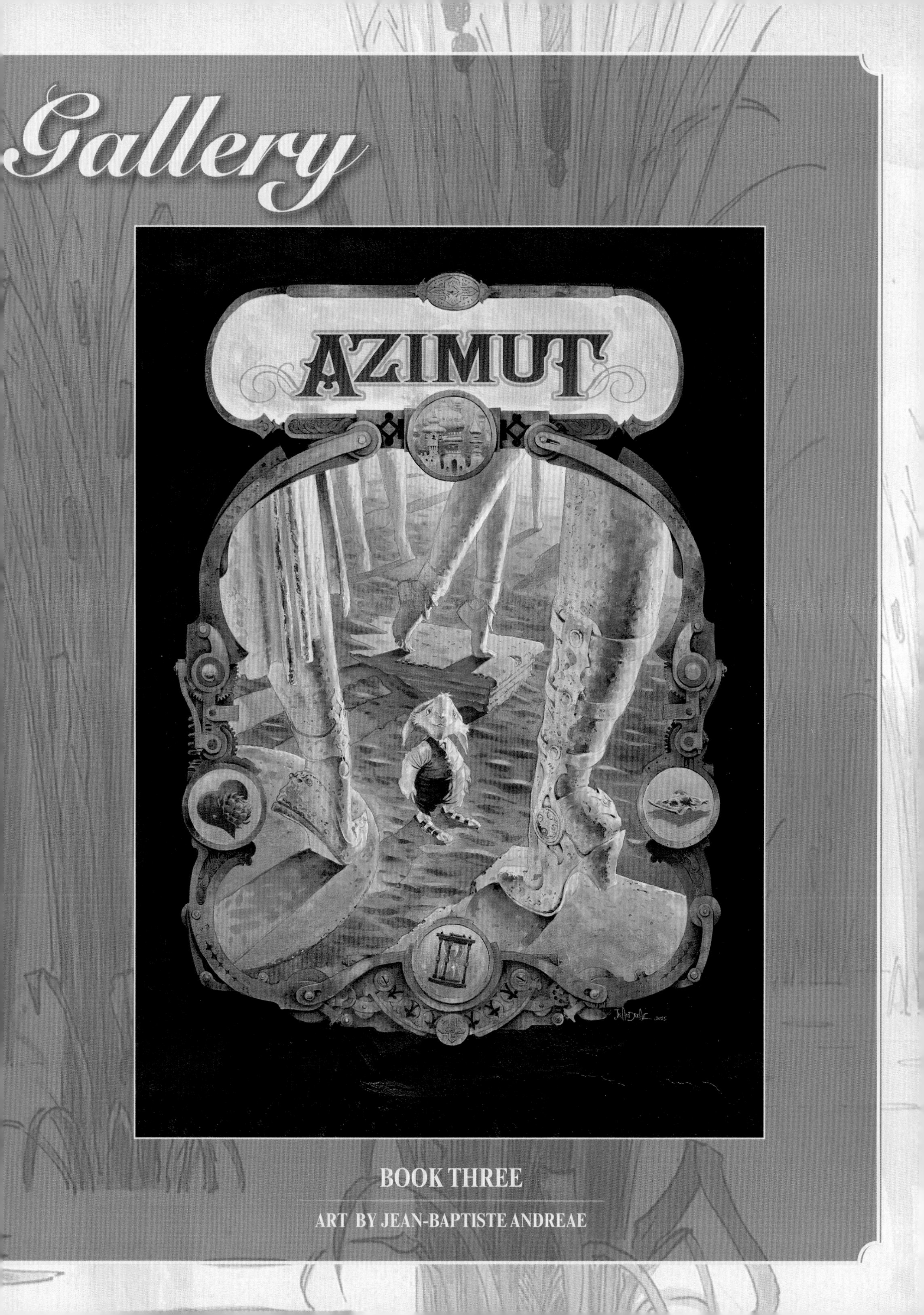
AZIMUT

BOOK THREE

ART BY JEAN-BAPTISTE ANDREAE

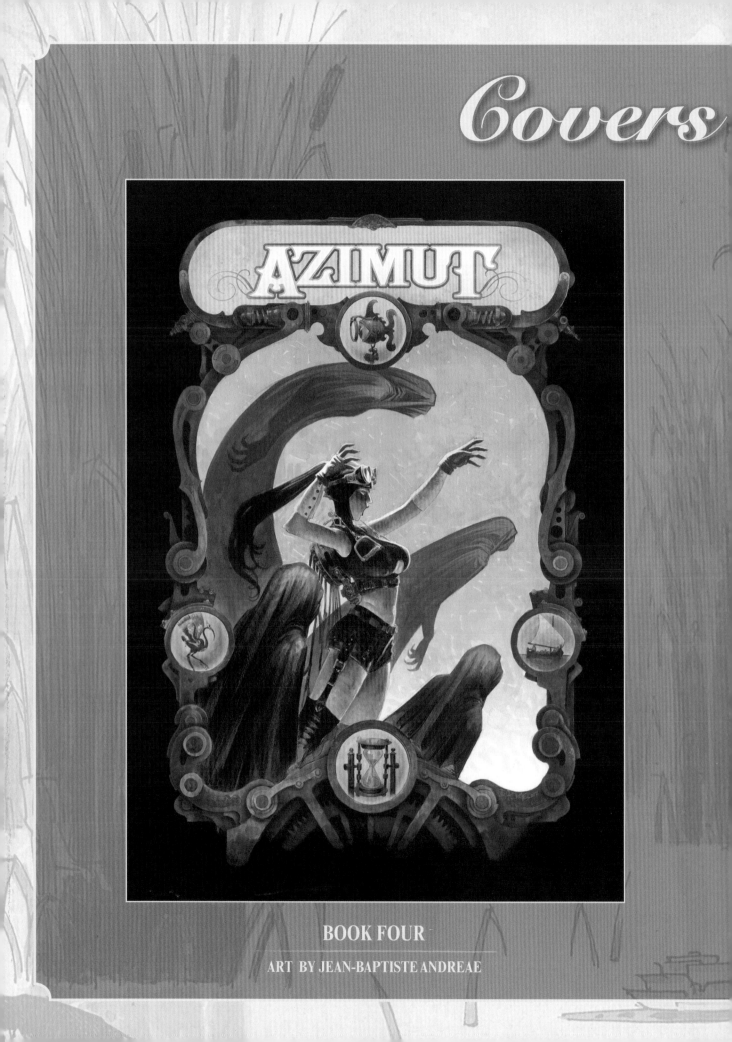

BOOK FOUR

ART BY JEAN-BAPTISTE ANDREAE

Gallery

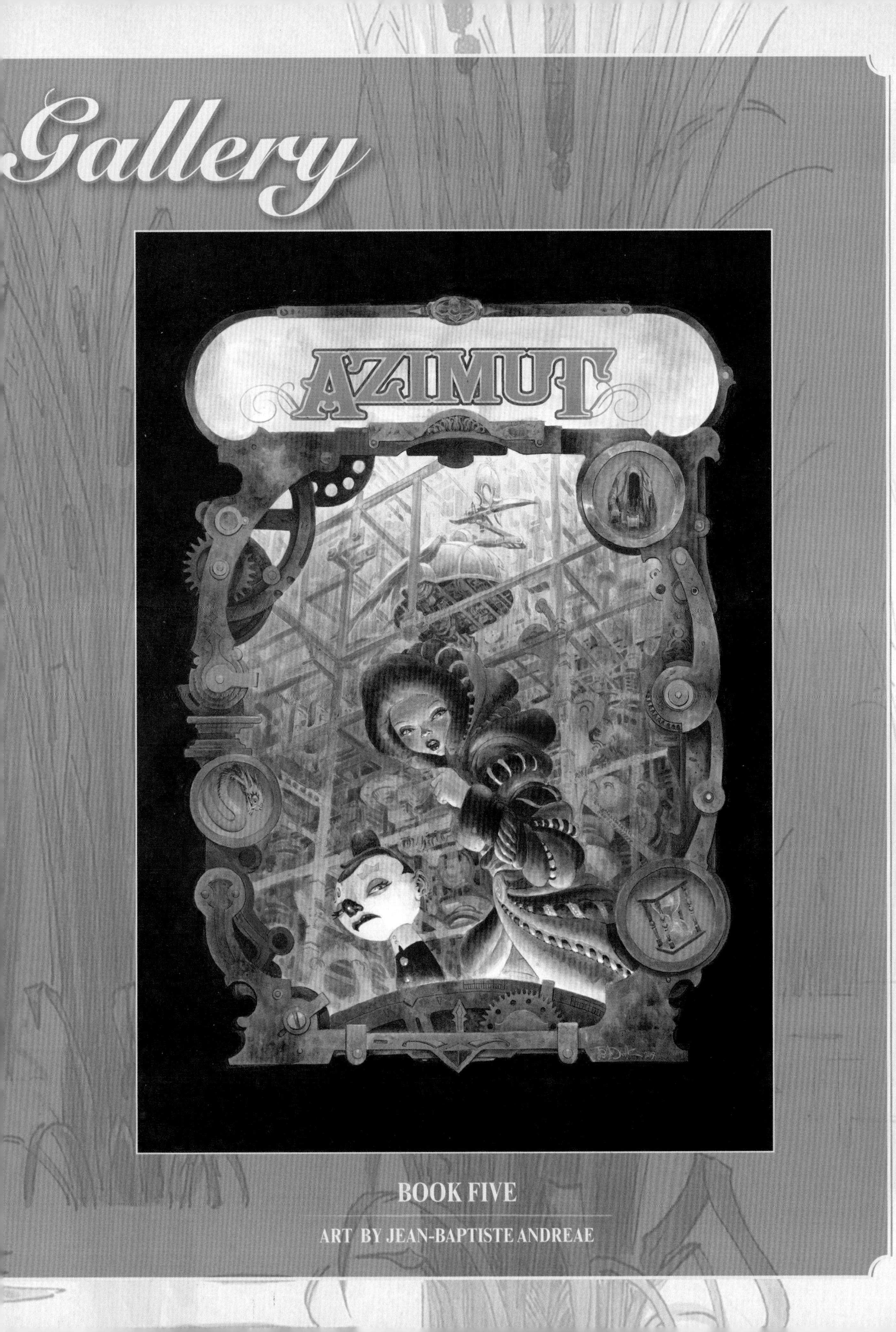
AZIMUT

BOOK FIVE

ART BY JEAN-BAPTISTE ANDREAE

Author Bios

Lupano

Spending the majority of his childhood in Pau, Wilfrid Lupano's passion for comics was ignited by his parents' collection and his love of roleplaying games. While working as a waiter to finance his study of philosophy and English, Lupano met his first creative partners, Roland Pignault and Fred Campoy. Together they collaborated to create the Old West comedy *Little Big Joe* (2001). After penning countless titles, including *The Old Geezers* (2017) he then worked on the legendary Valerian franchise, penning the *Shingouzlooz INC.* (2018) spin-off with artist Mathieu Lauffray. His most recent work includes the historical drama *White All Around* (2020).

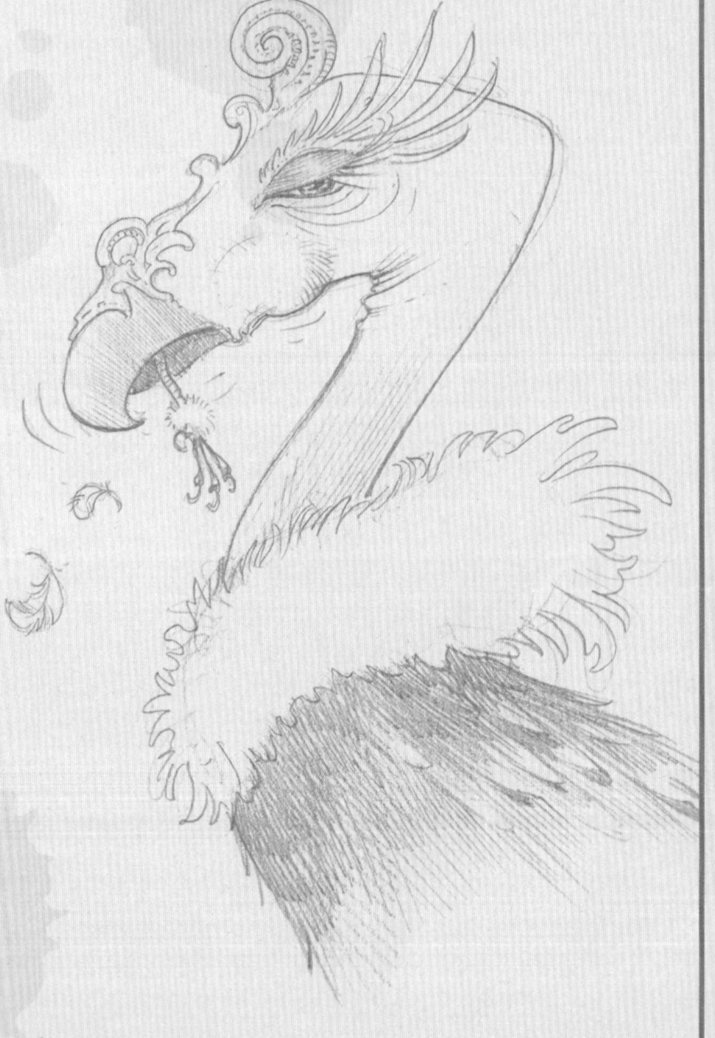

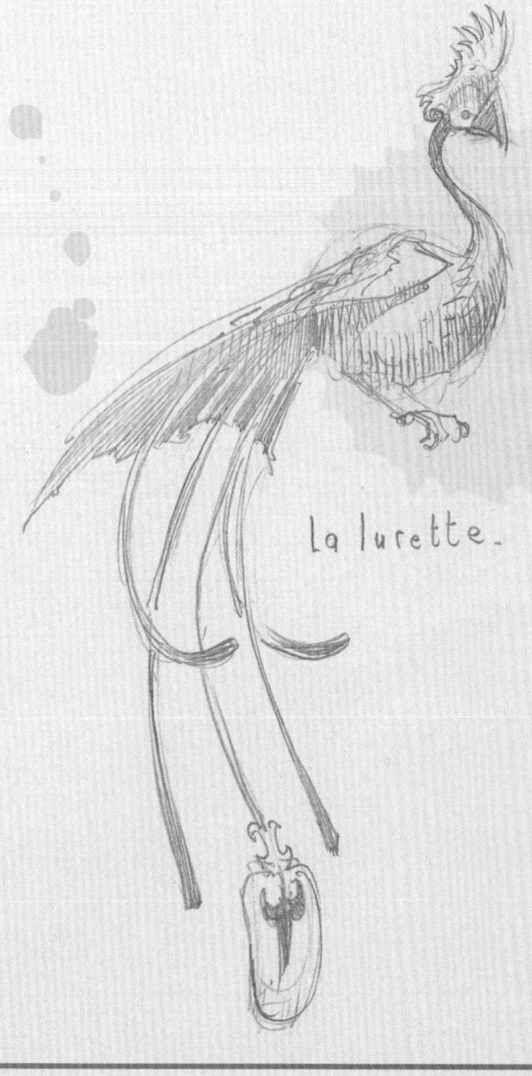
La lurette.

Andréae

After studying art at Lycée Michel Montaigne, Jean-Baptiste Andréae went on to study Plastic Arts at the University of Bordeaux. After a stint in advertising he taught himself digital painting and went on to collaborate with Mathieu Gallié on the series *Mangecour*. The series ran from 1993 to 1996, winning the Youth Prize at the Angoulême International Festival and by 1999 had sold 15,000 copies. The team collaborated again in 1998 on *Wendigo*, inspired by the works of Jack London. Between 2002 and 2009 he illustrated the series *Terre Mécanique*. The art from the series was then exhibited in the Chamber of Commerce and Industry of Pau in 2010. This was followed by a 2014 exhibition of his work at the Maison des Consuls at Saint Junien. In 2015 he was awarded the Crayon d'Or for his work on *Azimut*.